LEARNING ABOUT LEARNING DISABILITIES

THIRD EDITION

Edited by

Bernice Y. L. Wong

Faculty of Education
Simon Fraser University
Burnaby, British Columbia, Canada

ELSEVIER
ACADEMIC
PRESS

Amsterdam • Boston • Heidelberg • London
New York • Oxford • Paris • San Diego
San Francisco • Singapore • Sydney • Tokyo

Elsevier Academic Press
525 B Street, Suite 1900, San Diego, California 92101-4495, USA
84 Theobald's Road, London WC1X 8RR, UK

This book is printed on acid-free paper. ∞

Library of Congress Cataloging-in-Publication Data
Learning about learning disabilities / edited by Bernice Y. L. Wong.–3rd ed.
    p. cm.
  Includes bibliographical references and index.
  ISBN 0–12–762533–X
 1.   Learning disabilities. 2.   Learning disabled children–Education.
 3.   Learning disabled youth–Education. 4.   Learning disabled–Education.
 I.   Wong, Bernice Y. L.

  LC4704.L376 2004
  371.9–dc22

                                                                    200400886

British Library Cataloguing in Publication Data
A catalogue record for this book is available from the British Library

ISBN: 0-12-762533-X

For all information on all Academic Press publications
visit our Web site at www.academicpress.com

Printed in the United States of America
03   04   05   06   07   08   9   8   7   6   5   4   3   2   1

This book is dedicated to my husband Rod, and daughter, Kristi
And to
Nancy Hutchinson, Lorraine Graham, Deb Butler and
John McNamara

Contents

4. Peer Relationships and Learning Disabilities
Ruth Pearl and Mavis L. Donahue

5. Self-Regulation among Students with LD and ADHD
Karen R. Harris, Robert R. Reid, and Steve Graham

6. The Reading Brain in Children and Youth: A Systems Approach
Virginia W. Berninger

SECTION II

Instructional Aspects of Learning Disabilities

7. Difficulties in Reading Comprehension for Students with Learning Disabilities
Lorraine Graham and Anne Bellert

8. Writing Instruction
Steve Graham, Karen R. Harris, and Charles MacArthur

SECTION III

A Lifespan Approach to Understanding Learning Disabilities

Contributors

Anne Bellert (251)
School of Educational Studies
University of New England
Armidale, New South Wales
2351 Australia

Derek H. Berg (415)
Faculty of Education
Queen's University
Kingston, Ontario
Canada K7L 3N6

Virginia W. Berninger (197)
Department of Educational Psychology
University of Washington
Seattle, Washington 98195

Deborah L. Butler (565)
Faculty of Education
University of British Columbia
Vancouver, British Columbia
Canada V6T 1Z4

John B. Cooney (41)
Department of Educational
  Psychology
University of Northern Colorado
Greeley, Colorado 80639

Jean Crockett (449)
Department of Educational
  Leadership & Policy Studies
Virginia Polytechnic Institute &
  State University
Blacksburg, Virginia 24061

Jane N. Cutter (485)
Learning Resources Coordinator

University Prep School
Seattle, Washington 98195

Tracy Davidson (315)
Graduate School of Education
George Mason University
Fairfax, Virginia 22030

Don Deschler (535)
Center for Research on Learning
University of Kansas
Lawrence, Kansas 66045

Mavis L. Donahue (133)
School of Education
University of Illinois at Chicago
Chicago, Illinois 60607

Edwin S. Ellis (375)
Department of Special
  Education
University of Alabama
Tuscaloosa, Alabama 35487

John G. Freeman (415)
Faculty of Education
Queen's University
Kingston, Ontario
Canada K7L 3N6

Lorraine Graham (251)
School of Educational Studies
University of New England
Armidale, New South Wales
2351 Australia

Steve Graham (167, 281)
Department of Special Education

University of Maryland
College Park, MD 20740

Karen R. Harris (167, 281)
Department of Special Education
University of Maryland
College Park, MD 20740

Maureen Hoskyn (93)
Faculty of Education
Simon Fraser University
Burnaby, British Columbia
Canada V5A 1S6

Nancy L. Hutchinson (415)
Faculty of Education
Queen's University
Kingston, Ontario
Canada K7L 3N6

Ae-Hwa Kim (341)
Department of Special Education
Dankook University
Seoul, Korea 140-714

Martha J. Larkin (375)
Department of Special Education &
   Speech Language Pathology
State University of West Georgia
Carrollton, Georgia 30118

Keith Lenz (535)
Center for Research on Learning
University of Kansas
Lawrence, Kansas 66045

Charles MacArthur (281)
School of Education
University of Delaware
Newark, Delaware 19716

Shirley J. Magnusson (485)
School of Education
University of Michigan
Ann Arbor, Michigan 48109

J. D. Mashburn (599)
3122 Gracefield Road
Silver Springs, Maryland 20904

Margo A. Mastropieri (315)
Graduate School of Education
George Mason University
Fairfax, Virginia 22030

John K. McNamara (41)
College of Education
University of Saskatchewan
Saskatoon, Saskatchewan
Canada 37N 0X1

Annemarie Sullivan Palincsar (485)
School of Education
University of Michigan
Ann Arbor, Michigan 48109

Ruth Pearl (133)
School of Education
University of Illinois at Chicago
Chicago, Illinois 60607

Ritu K. Rana (315)
Graduate School of Education
George Mason University
Fairfax, Virginia 22030

D. Kim Reid (513)
Department of Curriculum & Teaching
Teachers College
Columbia University
New York, New York 10027

Robert R. Reid (167)
Department of Special Education
University of Nebraska-Lincoln
Lincoln, Nebraska 68583

Thomas E. Scruggs (315)
Graduate School of Education
George Mason University
Fairfax, Virginia 22030

Jane Sinagub (341)
School of Education
University of Miami
Coral Gables, Florida 33146

H. Lee Swanson (41)
School of Education
University of California
Riverside, California 92521

Joseph K. Torgesen (3)
Department of Psychology
Florida State University
Tallahassee, Florida 32306

Jan Weatherly Valle (513)
Department of Curriculum & Teaching
Teachers College
Columbia University
New York, New York 10027

Sharon Vaughn (341)
Department of Special Education
University of Texas at Austin
Austin, Texas 78712

Preface

When I first began producing a text in learning disabilities in 1991 for advanced undergraduate and graduate students, I had two goals. The first was to provide students with a rock-solid unassailable knowledge base. I want them to have the most current information about the learning disabilities field. To meet this goal, I turned to my esteemed colleagues and friends for help. And they have **never** disappointed me.

My second goal was to get students to wrestle with the issues and implications arising from the given information. Most of our advanced and graduate students come from the teaching corps. Instructional, curricular, and behavior management demands tend to reinforce a more concrete mindset in teachers. In turn, this mindset makes wrestling with conceptual and research implications a rough ride for our students. But professors' gentle prompts and more pointed questions on important issues can effectively scaffold the mental shift necessary for successful learning and performance. Individual and assigned questions for collaborative group work in initial seminars usually effect a smooth cognitive transition to the desired mental frame necessary for lively seminars. Once set on track, like a train off from inertia, the students will take off and generate thought-provoking questions on the chapters read!

My two goals have been constant across the revised editions of my text. As evident from the table of contents, there is a balanced coverage of materials. We begin in section I with chapters covering conceptual and research areas, including new entries on language processes, self-regulation, and brain structures. I choose to include self-regulation because I foresee its promise as an area for future research. Research on self-regulated learning has been a major dominating force in educational psychology in recent years and interest in it will spill over to learning disabilities because the concept of self-regulated learner dovetails with the conceptual and intervention needs of students with learning disabilities.

In the second section, intervention research is the theme and updates in all the major areas are given. Early reading instruction does not appear here because Dale Willows had been ill and regrettably could not complete the chapter. Readers should not be too disheartened. With early intervention research well underway in several research centers in U.S., it may be more useful for someone to await the data and then summarize the findings so that we learn about effective ways of teaching all children to read. At any rate, Lorraine Graham and Anne Bellert's chapter on reading comprehension more than compensates the absence of a chapter on early intervention. With the intervention focus **steadily** shifting to intermediate grades, their chapter couldn't have been more timely! In this second section, the new topic entry is the chapter on community of practice by Annemarie Palincsar and Shirley Magnusson. I asked them to contribute on this particular topic because their conceptual frame has much promise for research on effective inclusion.

In the last section of the book, I focus on researchers/scholars' thoughts about issues in areas of children, adolescents, and adults with learning disabilities. The book wraps up with a short but poignant piece by a father of an individual with learning disabilities. I believe it is through a father's eyes that we best understand the need for a life-span perspective in understanding and learning about learning disabilities.

Bernice Wong

Acknowledgments

To the contributors of this third edition of my graduate text, *Learning about Learning Disabilities*, I want to say thank you from the bottom of my heart! Anyone who has friends who generously donate their time and cognitive energy to focus on writing these well-researched, insightful, and stimulating chapters, is indeed blessed. And I have never stopped counting my blessings!

I also want to thank Nikki Levy, Publisher, for her receptiveness to my suggestion for another revised edition of this book; and to Barbara Makinster for all her coordinations among the various departments to insure this book appears in print! Last but not least, I want to thank the copy-editor and the production department staff for their contributions to this book.

With gratitude,

Bernice Wong

To the student,

Someone posed a naïve question to me. She asked why do I want to revise my text? I revised this text for the third time because learning disabilities is a vibrant field with much new information that needs to be shared and the implications arising from it thoroughly considered! The nature of this new information comes in diverse forms. There are new research findings, revamping of old information in light of new, and new areas of research. These chapters provide exciting readings that will get you to cogitate and produce some probing questions for your seminars and theses research. Already, as this book is going to print, new discussions are being held on issues that will impact on the learning disabilities field, for example, the issue of resistance to instruction as a way of identifying learning disabilities in students. You see how dynamic the field is, always bubbling with conceptual issues and empirical directions, the implications of which need to be debated and sorted out. Consequently, there is always the need to revise what we know and what we think in learning disabilities!

Cheers!

Bernice Wong

Conceptual, Historical, and Research Aspects of Learning Disabilities

CHAPTER 1

Learning Disabilities: An Historical and Conceptual Overview

Joseph K. Torgesen
Florida State University

I. CURRENT STATUS OF THE FIELD

The importance of learning disabilities (LD) as a field of professional practice and scientific inquiry can be appreciated by considering its achievements in four areas. First, more children are currently being served in LD programs than in any other area of special education. According to data currently available from the United States Department of Education, Office of Special Education Programs, 50.5% of all children identified for special services in the schools are classified as LD. During the 1999–2000 school year, approximately 2.9 million students were identified as LD in the United States.

In addition to being the largest field of special education, LD also continues to grow at a rapid rate. Although it has not continued to grow as fast as it did during its early years, it remains the fastest-growing category for all high-incidence disabilities. The most rapid period of growth in the numbers of students identified as LD occurred in the six years following the passage of legislation requiring schools to provide services to students with learning disabilities. From 1976 to 1982, numbers of children with LD served by schools in the United States grew by 130%, for an annual growth rate of almost 20%! In contrast, during the period between 1983 and 1988, a period

Learning about Learning Disabilities, Third Edition

of consolidation occurred in which the annual growth rate slowed to a little under 2%. The most recent figures indicate that the growth rate between 1990–91 and 1999–2000 was 3.4% per year, while during the same period, total school enrollment increased at a rate of about 1.4% a year. It is not clear why the last 10 years have seen a slight rise in growth rates for students identified as learning disabled in the United States. The rise may reflect the influence of a number of different factors, such as increases in the diversity of the student population or rising pressure on schools to increase student performance, driven by new accountability standards.

Overall, approximately 5.7% of all children in public schools in the United States are being served in programs for the learning disabled. However, a continuing problem is that prevalence rates vary considerably from state to state, with a range from about 3% in Kentucky and Georgia to close to 9.0 and 9.6% in Massachusetts and Rhode Island, respectively. Of course, the differing criteria used by various states can create problems for children and their families when they move across state boundaries. While these figures from the U.S. amply document the importance of learning disabilities as a field within special education, formal programs for children with LD are not restricted to the United States. Canada has an extensive system of services for children with LD, as do most of the countries of Western Europe.

A. Legal Status within the Law

The extensive services to children and youth with learning disabilities in the United States are the result of the field's firm status within the law. Beginning with P.L. 94-142 (The Education of the Handicapped Act of 1975), all school districts are required to provide free and appropriate education to children identified as learning disabled. The law, and federal regulations developed to implement it, specified a wide range of practices that were to be followed in delivering services to children with LD. The essential provisions of PL 94-142 were reaffirmed in P.L. 98-199 (The Education of the Handicapped Act of 1983), which also contained some provision for expansion of services at preschool, secondary, and postsecondary levels. Finally, this legislation, now known as the Individuals with Disabilities Education Act (IDEA) was reauthorized in 1997, with provisions to assist with discipline, assessment and accountability, and development of individualized educational programs for children with disabilities. IDEA will be considered for reauthorization by the U.S. Congress in 2003.

B. Professional Associations

A third indication of the current status of the LD field is found in the number of associations that have been formed to advocate on behalf of children with

LD, support professional development, and provide a forum for discussion of research. Currently, seven major organizations focus exclusively on the interests of children with LD and professionals who work in the field. The largest of these organizations is the Learning Disabilities Association of America (LDA), formerly known as the Association for Children and Adults with Learning Disabilities. Formed in 1964, this organization has over 40,000 members, with nearly 300 local affiliates in 50 states, Washington, D.C., and Puerto Rico. It has been concerned primarily with advocacy for learning disabled children at the state and federal levels, parental issues, and the communication of information about educational programs and practices. The Learning Disabilities Association of Canada was incorporated in 1971, has an additional 10,000 members, and has goals very similar to those of its sister organization in the United States.

The Division for Learning Disabilities (DLD) is the largest division within the Council for Exceptional Children. With about 10,000 members, it is focused on enhancement of professional practices in the field. The Council for Learning Disabilities (CLD) is an independent organization of 5000 members with goals similar to those of DLD. The oldest professional organization in the field is the Orton Dyslexia Society, which changed its name to the International Dyslexia Association (IDA) in 1998. The organization was formed in 1949 and currently numbers about 13,000 members. IDA contributes primarily to professional development and communication of research about children with specific reading disabilities.

Two smaller organizations focus primarily on discussion of issues and dissemination of information about learning disabilities. The National Joint Committee on Learning Disabilities (NJCLD) is a small organization composed of appointed representatives from the other major LD associations and other groups that have an interest in learning disabilities. Its purpose is to provide a forum for communication among associations and interdisciplinary consideration of many of the issues confronting the field. This organization periodically issues position statements on many of these issues. The NJCLD is in a position to be uniquely influential because its member organizations represent such a large portion of the entire LD community. Another relatively small organization whose mission is to disseminate information about LD is the National Center for Learning Disabilities (NCLD).

Finally, the only organization devoted exclusively to promoting and disseminating research about learning disabilities is the International Academy for Research in Learning Disabilities (IARLD). Membership in this group is by invitation and consists mainly of active researchers. Its purpose is to provide a means for international communication about research on learning disabilities.

These organizations play a very important role in contributing to the development and continuing visibility of the field. Most of them hold at least annual meetings at the national level, and several of them publish professional journals on a monthly or quarterly basis. Their large and growing membership attests to the high level of concern for children with learning disabilities manifested by parents, educators, and researchers.

C. Active Area of Research

A final indicator of the current status of the LD field is the level of interest in the topic among researchers. It is a very active area of research. Research on LD within the United States received a major impetus with the passage of the Health Research Extension Act of 1985, which mandated the formation of an Interagency Committee on Learning Disabilities. This committee was charged to examine the current state of knowledge in the field of LD and then make a report to congress with recommendations for a research initiative in the area. This report was submitted in 1987, and a year later, its major content was published as the Proceedings of the National Conference on Learning Disabilities (Kavanagh & Truss, 1988). The report recommended that the National Institute of Child Health and Human Development, a unit within the National Institutes of Health, take the lead in establishing a comprehensive, multidisciplinary program of research on learning disabilities. In the words of the report, "A major goal of this research should be the development of a classification system that more clearly defines and diagnoses LD, conduct disorders, and attention deficit disorders, and their interrelationships. Such information is prerequisite to the delineation of homogeneous subgroups and the delineation of more precise and reliable strategies for treatment, remediation, and prevention that will increase the effectiveness of both research and therapy." (Interagency Committee on Learning Disabilities, (1987), p. 224).

Based on these recommendations, the NICHD began a very active and programmatic series of studies that focused primarily on children with reading disabilities. This research has borne considerable fruit, with one indirect result being the largest national initiative to prevent reading difficulties ever undertaken in the United States. This initiative, called "Reading First," was part of a larger education bill called "The No Child Left Behind Act," which was signed into law by President George W. Bush in January, 2002. The initiative has been both energized and directed by findings from the research on reading, reading growth, and reading disabilities that has been supported by NICHD and the U.S. Office of Education over the past 15 years. Another effect of the additional support for research in LD has been to attract professionals from fields other than those traditionally associated with learning disabilities (i.e., special education) to research in this area. In particular, well-trained researchers from the fields of psychology, medicine, and linguistics promise to make important new contributions to knowledge about learning disabilities.

Communication about research and professional issues in learning disabilities is aided by the publication of six journals devoted exclusively to the topic. The most widely circulated of these is the *Journal of Learning Disabilities* (published by PRO-ED, Inc.). Others include *Learning Disabilities Quarterly* (published by CLD), *Learning Disabilities Research and Practice* (published by DLD), *Learning Disabilities: A Multidisciplinary Journal* (published by LDA), and *Annals of Dyslexia* (published by the International Dyslexia Association). IARLD publishes two or three monographs a year on topics related to learning disabilities as well as a periodical called *Thalamus*. In addition to these outlets devoted exclusively to topics of learning disabilities, research related to learning disabilities is also frequently published in journals such as *Journal of Educational Psychology, Reading Research Quarterly, Journal of Experimental Child Psychology, Brain and Behavior, Developmental Medicine and Child Neurology, Scientific Studies of Reading*, and the *Journal of Applied Behavior Analysis*, which accept articles on a variety of topics.

II. A HISTORICAL PERSPECTIVE

When considering the history of the field of learning disabilities, it is helpful from the outset to make a distinction between learning disabilities as an applied field of special education and learning disabilities as an area of research on individual differences in learning and performance. In the former sense, the field shares many attributes with other political/social movements, while in the latter sense, it is a loosely joined, interdisciplinary area of scientific inquiry. It will be a central point of this chapter that confusion and occasional conflict between these two aspects of the field have created many problems over the course of its history, and continues to be a source of many challenges for the field. It is also true that, although both aspects have some elements of history in common, the primary impetus for learning disabilities as a social/political movement has a narrower historical base than for the field as a whole. This discussion will outline the broad history of ideas about individuals with specific learning difficulty, but will also point out the special historical antecedents of the field as a movement. This discussion will be brief, but more detailed information about many historical points is available in other sources (Coles, 1987; Doris, 1986; Hallahan & Cruickshank, 1973; Hallahan *et al.*, 1985; Hallahan & Mercer, 2002; Kavale & Forness, 1985; Myers & Hammill, 1990; Wiederholt, 1974).

A. Early Developments

Interest in the possible causes and consequences of individual differences in mental functioning extends back at least as far as early Greek civilization (Mann, 1979). However, the beginning of scientific work of immediate relevance to learning disabilities was probably that of Joseph Gall at the beginning of the nineteenth century (Wiederholt, 1974). Gall described a number of cases in which specific loss of mental function in adults occurred as a result of brain damage. His description of one of his patients is interesting because it shows his concern with establishing that the patient's loss of functioning was isolated to one particular ability:

> In consequence of an attack of apoplexy a soldier found it impossible to express in spoken language his feelings and ideas. His face bore no signs of a deranged intellect. His mind (espirit) found the answer to questions addressed to him and he carried out all he was told to do; shown an armchair and asked if he knew what it was, he answered by seating himself in it. He could not articulate on the spot a word pronounced for him to repeat; but a few moments later the word escaped from his lips as if involuntarily.... It was not his tongue which was embarrassed; for he moved it with great agility and could pronounce quite well a large number of isolated words. His memory was not at fault, for he signified his anger at being unable to express himself concerning many things which he wished to communicate. It was the faculty of speech alone which was abolished (Head, 1926, p. ll).

Over the next century, many clinical studies of speech and language disorders were reported; among the best known are those of Bouillaud, Broca, Jackson, Wernicke, and Head (Wiederholt, 1974). The major goals of this work were to document the specific loss of various speech and language functions in adults who had previously shown these abilities, and to identify the types of brain damage associated with the different kinds of functional disturbance. Of relevance to the study of learning disabilities, this work did establish the fact that very specific types of mental impairment can occur as a result of damage to isolated regions of the brain.

The first systematic clinical studies of specific reading disability were reported in 1917 by James Hinshelwood, a Scottish ophthalmologist. Hinshelwood had examined a number of cases in which adults suddenly lost the ability to read while other areas of mental functioning remained intact. As with cases of sudden loss of oral language facility, the loss of reading ability was attributed to damage to specific areas of the brain. Hinshelwood tried to support this hypothesis by citing evidence from the patient's history or postmortem examination.

In addition to his work on loss of function with adults, Hinshelwood also saw cases of children who had extreme difficulties acquiring reading skills. In his descriptions of these cases, Hinshelwood was careful to document that their reading difficulties occurred alongside quite normal abilities in other intellectual skills. For example, in his description of one ten year old boy with severe reading problems, he states:

> The boy had been at school three years, and had got on well with every subject except reading. He was apparently a bright and, in every respect, intelligent boy. He had been learning music for a year, and had made good progress in it . . . In all departments of his studies where the instruction was oral he had made good progress, showing that his auditory memory was good . . . He performs simple sums quite correctly, and his progress in arithmetic has been regarded as quite satisfactory. He has no difficulty in learning to write. His visual acuity is good, (pp. 46–47).

Hinshelwood attributed the boy's problems to a condition which he called "congenital word blindness," resulting from damage to a specific area of the brain that stored visual memories for words and letters. Given the similarities in symptoms between his cases of developmental reading problems and those of the adults he had observed, as well as his medical orientation, it is easy to see how Hinshelwood arrived at his explanation for specific reading disability in children. However, recent analysis of several of his cases suggests that he may have overlooked a number of environmental influences that could also have explained the reading problems of children he studied (Coles, 1987). Whatever the ultimate cause of the reading problems he studied, Hinshelwood clearly showed that severe reading problems could exist in children with average or superior intellectual abilities in other areas. He also believed that cases of true "word blindness" were very rare, with an incidence of less than one in a thousand.

Following Hinshelwood, the next major figure to report clinical studies of children with reading disabilities was Samuel Orton, an American child neurologist. Based on his clinical examinations of children over a 10-year period, Orton (1937) developed an explanation for reading disability that was quite different from Hinshelwood's. Rather than proposing that children with specific reading disabilities had actual damage to a localized area of their brains, he proposed that the difficulty was caused by delay, or failure, in establishing dominance for language in the left hemisphere of the brain. He used the term "strephosymbolia," or twisted symbols, to refer to the fact that reading disabled children, as he observed them, frequently had special difficulties reading reversible words (saw–was, not–ton) or letters (b–d, p–q) correctly. His theory explained reversals as resulting from confusions between the visual images of these stimuli projected on the two different brain hemispheres. Since, according to his theory, these projections were mirror images of one another, and since neither hemispheric image was consistently dominant, sometimes the child saw the stimulus as "b" and sometimes as "d."

Neither Orton's particular neurological theories of dyslexia (reading disability) nor his ideas that reversals are especially symptomatic of the disorder have stood the test of subsequent research (Liberman *et al.*, 1971). However, his broad emphasis on dysfunction in the language-related areas of the brain as a cause of specific developmental dyslexia is consistent with important current theories in the field (Torgesen, 1999; Shankweiler & Liberman, 1989).

Orton's work did have a broader contemporary impact than Hinshelwood's, principally in the stimulation of research and the founding of several special schools and clinics to serve children with reading disabilities. The special educational techniques he developed for helping reading disabled children were particularly influential, and in 1949, the Orton Dyslexia Society was formed in partial recognition of his contributions. It is interesting that the educational programs developed by Orton and Hinshelwood were similar: they both recommended systematic and explicit instruction combined with intensive skill-building practice in using letter–sound relationships (phonics) to recognize words. In their emphasis on direct instruction and practice in skills required for reading, these educational programs were quite different from the "process training" approaches that were advocated 30 years later by many educators once the field of learning disabilities was officially established.

Although Orton's work did have an impact on the treatment of reading disorders in a number of isolated special schools and clinics, neither his nor Hinshelwood's theories about the neurological basis for reading disorders was widely assimilated in scientific and educational circles as an explanation for individual differences in reading ability (Doris, 1986). Educators and psychologists who dealt with the vast majority of reading disability cases in the public schools attributed reading problems to a variety of environmental, attitudinal, and educational problems. Texts on the diagnosis and remediation of reading problems published during the 1940s (Durrell, 1940) and 1950s (Vernon, 1957) generally discredited these theories and suggested that, at best, inherent brain dysfunction accounted for only a very small proportion of reading failure.

B. Immediate Precursors to the Field of Learning Disabilities

The work described thus far is part of the overall history of ideas concerning specific learning disabilities in children. However, the research and clinical activity that led most directly to the initial establishment of a formally organized field of learning disabilities was conducted by Heinz Werner and Alfred Strauss at the Wayne County Training School in Northville, Michigan. In fact, the historical threads between the work of Hinshelwood and Orton and the development of the learning disabilities movement in special education are quite tenuous. In retrospect, it seems that their work has assumed greater historical importance with the developing recognition that the vast majority of children with LD have reading as their primary academic problem (Lyon, 1985), and as scientific interest in specific reading disabilities has increased over the last 15 to 20 years (Raynor *et al.*, 2001).

The work of Werner and Strauss was fundamentally different from that of Hinshelwood and Orton, in that they sought to describe deficient general learning processes rather than seeking to describe and explain failure on a specific academic task. Their work was interpreted as establishing the existence of a subgroup of children who, presumably because of mild brain damage, experienced specific limitations in their ability to process certain kinds of information. Werner and Strauss's work placed much more emphasis on deficient learning processes themselves (which were presumed to powerfully affect learning in many different situations) than on the specific academic tasks that were affected.

What were these deficient learning processes? They centered mostly on what would be called today distractibility, hyperactivity, visual perceptual, and perceptual/motor problems. Werner and Strauss were influenced heavily by the work of Kurt Goldstein, who had studied the behavior of soldiers with head wounds during World War I. Goldstein observed that a number of behavioral characteristics were reliably found in many of his patients: inability to inhibit responding to certain external stimuli, figure–background confusions, hyperactivity, meticulosity, and extreme emotional lability.

Werner and Strauss sought to document the presence of similar behavioral/cognitive difficulties in a subgroup of children at their school. These children were presumed to have brain damage because of their medical histories and other aspects of their behavior. They compared the behavior of these "brain-damaged" children with that of other mentally retarded children who were presumed not to be brain-damaged. Their general conclusions were that the brain-damaged children showed specific difficulties in attention (distractibility) and perception. These findings were coupled with other observations (Kephart & Strauss, 1940) that the subgroup identified as brain damaged did not profit from the educational curriculum at the Wayne County School as much as other children. Specifically, while the IQs of the non-brain-damaged children tended to increase over several years at the school, the IQs of the brain-damaged children declined.

From these observations, Werner and Strauss concluded that the brain-damaged children needed special educational interventions designed to overcome the weaknesses their research had identified (Strauss, 1943). In Strauss's words (Strauss & Lehtinen, 1947), "the erratic behavior of brain-injured children in perceptual tasks might be explained by a figure–ground deficiency, and an approach to remedy such deficiency should be directed toward strengthening the figure–ground perception" (p. 50). Strauss's educational orientation was toward interventions that focused on either remediation of deficient learning processes (primarily perceptual in nature) or educational adjustments (eliminating distracting stimuli in the classroom) that sought to minimize the impact of these deficient processes. In the classic volumes, *Psychopatholoqy and Education of the Brain-Injured Child* (Strauss & Lehtinen, 1947) and *Psychopathology and Education of the Brain-Injured Child: Progress in Theory and Clinic* (Vol. 2) (Strauss & Kephart, 1955), he and his colleagues developed an extensive set of educational recommendations that became very influential in the education of mentally retarded and brain-injured children.

As Hallahan and Cruickshank (1973) have pointed out, Werner and Strauss's influence on the future learning disabilities field was profound. Not only did they develop specific educational recommendations that focused on a special set of deficient learning abilities, but they also provided a general orientation to the education of exceptional children that became very influential. The elements of this general orientation were that (1) individual differences in learning should be understood by examining the different ways that children approach learning tasks (the processes that aid or interfere with learning); (2) educational procedures should be tailored to patterns of processing strengths and weaknesses in the individual child; and (3) children with deficient learning processes might be helped to learn normally if those processes are strengthened, or if teaching methods which did not stress weak areas could be developed. As the learning disabilities movement began to gather strength after its inception in 1963, these three concepts were repeatedly used to provide a rationale for its development as an entity separate from other fields of education. They provided the core of what was unique about educational programming for learning disabled children.

In retrospect, it is interesting to note that the scientific support for Werner and Strauss's ideas about unique processing disabilities in brain-damaged children was exceedingly weak. As far back as 1949, Sarason attacked their work because of the way they formed their groups of children with and without brain damage. Werner and Strauss sometimes assigned children to the brain-damaged group based on behavior alone, even in the absence of direct evidence from neurological tests or medical history. Unfortunately, some of the behaviors that led to selection of children as brain-damaged were very similar to those that were studied in the experiments. The circular reasoning involved in attributing experimental differences between groups to brain damage is obvious.

Apart from the problems of interpretation caused by weaknesses in their experimental design, it also turns out that the actual differences between groups in distractibility and perceptual/motor problems were not very large. For example, Kavale and Forness (1985) report a meta-analysis of 26 studies conducted by Werner, Strauss, and their colleagues comparing "brain-damaged" and non-brain-damaged children. When all measures are combined, the overall difference between groups was 0.104 standard deviations! When the results were examined for different dependent variables (perceptual–motor, cognition, language, behavior, and intelligence), none of the estimates of effect size was statistically significant. Kavale and Forness concluded, "this meta-analytic synthesis offered little empirical support for the alleged behavioral differences between exogenous (brain injured) and endogenous (non-brain injured) mentally retarded children." (p. 57).

Although the scientific work of Werner and Strauss on learning deficiencies resulting from brain damage does not stand up well to close scrutiny, their ideas strongly influenced a number of colleagues who carried their work forward. William Cruickshank, for example, showed that cerebral palsied children of normal intelligence exhibited some of the same intellectual characteristics as the "brain-damaged" retardates in earlier studies (Cruickshank *et al.*, 1957). Cruickshank also extended the teaching methods advocated by Werner and Strauss to children of normal intelligence, and his extensive evaluation of these techniques is reported in *A Teaching Method for Brain Injured and Hyperactive Children* (Cruickshank *et al.*, 1961).

About this same time, another former staff member at the Wayne County Training School, Newell Kephart, wrote *Slow Learner in the Classroom* (1960). In this work, he embellished a theory first proposed by Werner and Strauss, that perceptual–motor development is the basis for all higher mental development, such as conceptual learning. A suggestion derived from this theory was that training in perceptual–motor skills should be helpful to many children experiencing learning difficulties in school. In his book, which was to be very helpful in providing "unique" educational procedures for learning disabilities classrooms, he detailed a number of procedures that teachers could use to enhance the perceptual–motor development of their students.

It should be emphasized that all during the 1940s and 1950s, and into the early 1960s, there was no field of learning disabilities per se. Rather, researchers and clinicians were observing a variety of problems in children of normal intelligence that seemed to interfere with learning. Children manifesting these difficulties went by a variety of labels including minimally brain-damaged, perceptually impaired, aphasic, or neurologically impaired. In addition to perceptual motor processing difficulties, a variety of disorders with auditory and language processes were also being studied. Helmer Mykelbust, who had extensive experience working with the deaf, became interested in children who had more subtle problems in auditory and linguistic processing. In his words (Johnson & Mykelbust, 1967):

> children who have auditory verbal comprehension disabilities resulting from central nervous system dysfunction hear but do not understand what is said... Language disabilities of this type have been described in both children and adults and have been designated as receptive aphasia, sensory aphasia, auditory verbal agnosia, or word deafness.... [T]hese disabilities should be differentiated from the language deficits resulting from deafness or mental retardation. Frequently such a distinction is not easy to make in those who have serious impairments, but it is essential in planning an adequate educational program (p. 74).

Language disabilities were also emphasized in the work of Samual Kirk, who had served for a brief time as a staff member at the Wayne County Training School with Werner and Strauss. In 1961, he published the experimental version of the *Illinois Test of Psycho-linguistic abilities* (McCarthy & Kirk). The purpose of this instrument was to allow an examination of a child's strengths and weaknesses in the area of language processing. It stimulated the development of a number of educational programs that specified unique interventions for children with different patterns of disabilities (Bush & Giles, 1969; Kirk & Kirk, 1971), and thus was used in a way consistent with the original educational ideas of Werner and Strauss. Although there were many other important researchers and teachers concerned with specific learning disorders during this time, the major themes of the period are represented in the work already described. Concern was focused on children who appeared normal in many intellectual skills, but who also displayed a variety of cognitive limitations that seemed to interfere with their ability to learn in the regular classroom. Not only were educational and mental health professionals concerned about these children, but the concerns of parent's groups were also becoming more focused and mobilized.

C. Formal Beginnings of the LD Movement

In 1963, at the Conference on Exploration into Problems of the Perceptually Handicapped Child, which was sponsored by the Fund for Perceptually Handicapped Children, Inc., Samual Kirk proposed the term "learning disabilities" as a descriptive title for the kind of children being generally discussed at the conference. In his words:

> I have used the term "learning disabilities" to describe a group of children who have disorders in development in language, speech,

reading, and associated communication skills needed for social interaction. In this group I do not include children who have sensory handicaps such as blindness or deafness, because we have methods of managing and training the deaf and the blind, I also exclude from this group children who have generalized mental retardation" (Kirk, 1963, p. 2–3).

This speech served as a catalyst to focus the concern of many of those in attendance, and that evening they voted to form the Association for Children with Learning Disabilities. The establishment of ACLD represents the formal beginnings of the learning disabilities field as a social/political/ educational movement. It was primarily an organization for parents. Its professional advisory board was formed from many of the leading professionals of the day (i.e., Kirk, Cruickshank, Kephart, Frostig, Lehtinen, Mykelbust), but its board of directors was composed of parents and leaders from other segments of society. As the leader of a movement, its goal was to mobilize social and political concern for the plight of children with learning disabilities and to create public sector services for them. The material presented in the beginning of this chapter attests to the enormous influence that ACLD and associated organizations have had on education over the past 40 years.

At its inception, the movement faced three major challenges. First, it had to establish a clear sense of its identity as a field separate from special and remedial education areas that already existed. Second, it had to develop a broad base of support for publicly funded educational programs for children with LD. Third, it had to encourage training efforts to prepare a large group of professionals for service in the field.

The LD movement approached the first challenge by selecting and promoting ideas about children with LD that emphasized their differences from other children currently receiving services in the schools. The centerpiece of the distinction between LD and other children having trouble in school was that their learning problems were the result of inherent and specific difficulties in performing some of the psychological processes, or mental operations, required for learning. This was a powerful idea, in that it implied these children were genuinely handicapped through no fault of their own, their parents, or their teachers. The idea was also appealing because it was optimistic; if the right remediation for deficient processes were prescribed, these children's achievement in school might become consistent with their generally "normal" abilities in other areas.

The research and theories of Werner and Strauss were instrumental in providing support for these foundational assumptions about learning disabilities. For example, the focus of the new field on remediation of disabilities in fundamental learning processes separated it from the fields of remedial reading and remedial math both by making it more general and by giving the impression that it was attacking educational difficulties in a more basic and powerful way (Hartman & Hartman, 1973). Professional fields are characterized by the "special" knowledge and expertise they possess. Claims about special knowledge in the diagnosis and treatment of specific processing disorders were instrumental in helping the learning disabilities movement to establish an identity of its own.

It was also important for the young field to establish that its clients, and the services to be provided them, were distinct from the existing fields of mental retardation and emotional/behavior disorders. Here, an emphasis on the generally "normal" academic potential of children with LD, and on the specific, and probably short-term, interventions they would require, were helpful in distinguishing between children with LD and mental retardation. In differentiating LD children from children with behavior disorders, the idea that the learning problems of children with LD are inherent (caused by brain dysfunction), and not the result of environmental influences, was also important.

Some of the ideas that helped support the formation of the new field of LD were soon questioned by professionals within the field itself (Mann & Phillips, 1967; Hammill, 1972). Further, many of the basic assumptions about learning disabilities that were so strongly advocated in the early days have been seriously challenged in later research that will be considered in another section of this chapter (Coles, 1987; Fletcher *et al.*, 1994; Francis *et al.*, 1996; Stanovich, 1993; Siegel, 1989; Torgesen, 1979). Original support for these ideas had come primarily from the clinical experience of the field's founders with a broad variety of unusual children. These clinically unique children thus provided the basis for what became a very broad social movement. At least part of the power of this movement came from the strength and certainty with which it generalized its assumptions about learning disabilities to relatively larger groups of children in the public schools. As Gerald Senf has pointed out (1986), the young field had strong motives to include as many children under the LD umbrella as possible.

Although one certainly cannot blame those who provided impetus for the original movement (they were attempting to develop public support for their clients and their children), their very success in publicizing the concept of LD has created problems for the science of learning disabilities. Research attempting to verify foundational assumptions about learning disabilities using samples of children with LD being served in the public schools frequently obtained negative results (Ysseldyke, 1983). However, as Stanovich has shown in his model of reading disabilities (1990), these negative results are the likely product of overgeneralization of the LD label in current practice. Thus, the political success of the LD movement in generating funds for services to very large numbers of children created inevitable ambiguities in the LD concept. The resolution of these ambiguities can only come through a more carefully disciplined use of the LD label in research and practice.

Historical developments with regard to public programs for children with LD and training of LD professionals are closely intertwined and shall be reported together. Involvement of the U.S. government in activities that supported development of the field began as a series of Task Force reports between 1966 and 1969. These reports reviewed a variety of topics including characteristics of children with LD, extent of current services, methods of treatment, and estimates of prevalence. The report of Task Force III (Chalfant & Sheffelin, 1969) described how little was actually known about assessing and remediating psychological processing disorders.

The first major legislative success came in 1969 with the passage of the Children with Learning Disabilities Act, which authorized the U.S. Office of Education to establish programs for students with LD. The government also sponsored an institute in which plans for the training of LD professionals were discussed (Kass, 1970). In 1971, the Bureau of Education of the Handicapped initiated a program to fund Child Service Demonstration Projects to be conducted in the different states. These demonstration projects were to directly serve children with learning disabilities as well as to provide a means for developing professional expertise in the area. Further support for professional development came through the Leadership Training Institute in Learning Disabilities at the University of Arizona that was funded for two years beginning in 1971. In 1975, the learning disabilities field achieved a firm basis in law with the passage of PL 94-142, which required all states to provide an appropriate public education for children with learning disabilities. It was this law that stimulated the enormous growth in the field that has occurred since the mid-1970s.

D. The Role of Psychological Processes in Learning Disabilities

As has been mentioned, at least part of the LD field's claims for a unique professional identity came from its focus on identifying and remediating the specific psychological processing difficulties of children with LD. A number of tests to identify specific processing disorders were developed, among them the *Developmental Test of Visual Perception* (Frostig *et al.*, 1964) and the *Illinois Test of Psycho-linguistic abilities* (McCarthy & Kirk, 1961), and various programs to remediate specific deficits in these processes were published. Popular activities in many learning disabilities classrooms during the 1960s and 1970s included practice in various visual/motor, auditory sequencing, visual/perceptual, or crossmodality training exercises. The rationale for these exercises was that improvement in deficient underlying learning processes would allow children to achieve their full potential in learning academic skills such as reading and math. Since many of the leading professionals at the time placed an emphasis on visual/perceptual and visual/motor processing difficulties as a fundamental cause of learning disabilities, many of the training activities had a decided emphasis on visual perceptual processes (Hallahan & Cruickshank, 1973).

The first published attacks on this approach to the education of children with LD came from Lester Mann (Mann & Phillips, 1967; Mann, 1971), who criticized the approach on theoretical and philosophical grounds. Shortly thereafter, a number of empirical investigations of the efficacy of perceptual/ motor process training began to appear, and many of these were summarized and commented on by Donald Hammill and his colleagues (Hammill, 1972; Hammill et al., 1974; Wiederholt & Hammill, 1971). Criticism of process training soon spread to psycholinguistic processes (Hammill & Larsen, 1974; Newcomer & Hammill, 1975), with the research reviews generally demonstrating that process training did not generalize to improvements in learning academic skills.

These initial reviews sparked a period of intense controversy within the learning disabilities movement for almost a decade. The scientific questions at issue became politicized and polarized, with discussions sometimes containing more personal acrimony than reasoned debate (Hammill, 1990). This is not too surprising, for these criticisms were directed at one of the foundational pillars of the LD movement. It seems natural that the learning disabilities movement, with its political/social aims, would strongly resist a weakening of any aspect of its raison d'etre. When further evidence (Arter & Jenkins, 1979; Vellutino et al., 1977; Ysseldyke, 1973) effectively closed the case against process training as a means for treating learning disabilities, the field turned to direct instruction of academic skills as its dominant mode of intervention. In Hammill's (1990) words: "Learning disabilities needed an approach with a better data base for its foundation; at the time, the principles of direct instruction satisfied this purpose" (p. 11).

By 1977, dissatisfaction with the processing orientation to diagnosis and remediation of learning disabilities had become widespread. In fact, the federal regulations implementing PL 94-142 did not require assessment of psychological processes as part of the procedures to identify children with LD for public school programs. Although learning disabilities were still defined as resulting from deficiencies in the basic psychological processes required for learning, children with LD were to be diagnosed primarily in terms of a discrepancy between general measures of intelligence and measures of achievement in specific areas of learning.

Both the lack of positive criteria for the identification of LD (it was identified as underachievement not explicable in terms of physical, cultural, or environmental handicap) and the adoption of direct instruction as the treatment of choice undermine the rationale for establishing learning disabilities as a distinct field within remedial and special education. Although direct instruction in academic skills may be effective with children who have LD, these procedures do not provide a foundation for learning disabilities as a distinct field of professional expertise in education. Rather, as Hallahan *et al.*, (1985) suggest, the striking similarities in educational procedures across various remedial and special education programs seriously undermine the educational placement of children with LD in programs separate from those of other children experiencing academic problems.

There are at least two possible explanations for the failure of the LD movement to document the utility of process-oriented approaches to identification and treatment of children with LD. The first is to concede that the fundamental assumptions are simply wrong. Coles (1987), for example, maintains that there is insufficient evidence that children with LD actually have inherent limitations in the ability to process specific kinds of information. Others (Hammill, 1990; Mann, 1979) suggest that there is no evidence to suggest training in "hypothetical processes" can be more effective than direct instruction in academic skills as an intervention for children with LD.

In contrast to these views, Torgesen (1979, 1986, 1993, 2002) has suggested that the LD field's problems with psychological processes arose because it was an idea ahead of its time. That is, approaches to identifying and training deficient processes in children with LD were pressed into service when our understanding of mental processing operations, and their relationships to learning and performing academic tasks, were at only a rudimentary stage of development. Since the 1960s and 1970s, we have learned an enormous amount about how to measure mental processing operations, and many of our fundamental conceptualizations about them have changed (Butterfield & Ferretti, 1987; Brown & Campione, 1986; Lyon, 1994; Siegler, 1998). For example, we now recognize that processing operations are much more context sensitive than previously supposed, which makes the problem of generalization of training particularly important. Further, we have a much better understanding of how differences in domain-specific knowledge can influence performance on tasks supposedly measuring processing differences (Ceci & Baker, 1990). Finally, we have come to appreciate the enormous influence that differences in cognitive strategies can play on many different kinds of tasks (Meltzer, 1993). All of these improvements in understanding suggest that future developments in cognitively oriented training of psychological processes as an aid to academic improvement will look very different from techniques used in the past. In fact, there are some strong indications that cognitively oriented training programs in reading comprehension strategies (Mastropieri & Scruggs, 1997; Palincsar *et al.*, 1993), writing strategies (Harris & Graham, 1996) phonological awareness (Ehri *et al.*, 2001), and general study strategies (Ellis *et al.*, 1987) can be quite effective in raising academic achievement in school. However, whether any of these interventions will prove uniquely useful to children with LD, as opposed to other types of poor learners, remains to be demonstrated.

Although the strategy training and phonological awareness training mentioned in the preceding paragraph has some superficial similarities to the kind of process training advocated earlier in the history of the LD field, it is fundamentally different in two ways. First, this training is closely tied to specific academic outcomes. Educators do not train phonemic awareness or writing strategies expecting to obtain general improvements in children's "learning abilities." Rather, this training is provided because it provides knowledge and skill in executing the processes required for good performance on specific academic tasks. Second, current training in these areas is not conceptualized as remediating a "basic processing disorder" that is the direct result of brain dysfunction. Instead, limitations in phonemic awareness are thought to reflect either a lack of learning opportunities or limitations in some more fundamental processing capability (Torgesen, 2002). Children's phonemic awareness can be improved through careful and systematic instruction, even when their ability to process the phonological features of speech is limited by some more basic, and as yet unidentified, processing weakness. Inefficiencies in using strategic behaviors on academic tasks can also result either from a lack of opportunity to learn the strategies or from a more fundamental learning difficulty of an unspecified type (Siegler, 1998).

There is, however, one line of current research that does purport to remediate a basic and generalized processing disorder that affects the growth of both language comprehension and reading abilities. Paula Tallal and her colleagues (Tallal, 1980; Tallal et al., 1996) have developed a theory to explain language disabilities by suggesting that some children have special difficulties processing rapidly changing or rapidly sequential auditory stimuli. This difficulty arises because these children's brains do not sample acoustic signals sufficiently rapidly to note changes of short temporal duration. Thus, the children perceive some speech contrasts, or other rapid temporal events, inaccurately. When listening to speech, these children often confuse words, or parts of words, because they do not notice the very rapid changes in the acoustic pattern of speech that signals the presence of different phonemes (sounds) in words. Thus, they might sometimes confuse "bat" with "pat" because the difference between the beginning phonemes of these two words is signaled by a very brief difference in voice onset time.

These investigators have reported success in directly modifying children's ability to process these rapidly changing or rapidly successive features of auditory signals (Merzenich et al., 1996). In effect, they claim to have a technique, using a series of computer programs, called *Fast ForWord Language*, that can change the way the brain processes acoustic stimuli, so that perception and understanding of speech and language is improved. These effects have been documented primarily for language comprehension in children with severe language disabilities, but some evidence has also been reported that the method can lead directly to improvements in phonemic awareness (Habib *et al.*, 1999). A very recent study (Temple *et al.*, 2003) has also reported substantial improvements in both word level and reading comprehension skills in a sample of 10-year-old children with reading disabilities following intensive work with the *Fast ForWord* program over a period of 8 weeks.

These latter findings are consistent with the idea that the method may have some use in treating the core information-processing deficits of children with specific reading disabilities that are caused by difficulties processing spoken phonological information. Because negative results for this method and its theory are also being reported (cf. Hook *et al.*, 2001; Nittrouer, 1999, McAnally *et al.*, 1997; Mody *et al.*, 1997), its applicability as a widely useful intervention technique for children with reading disabilities is still uncertain. Although the field of learning disabilities is rightfully wary of instructional methods that claim to affect basic processing capabilities and thus to improve academic learning outcomes (Hallahan & Cruickshank, 1973; Hammill & Larson, 1974; Torgesen, 1979), we must remain open to genuine scientific achievements that may be powerfully beneficial to many children.

III. CURRENT AND FUTURE ISSUES

This section contains very brief discussions of several issues that are of current importance to the field of LD. Some of these issues, such as those of definition, have the potential to alter drastically the identity of the field, while others have more to do with practical issues of identification and service delivery. Since each of the issues to be discussed is very complex, I cannot hope to represent them fully in the brief space allotted. Rather, I will state the essential questions in each area, suggest why they are important to the field, and provide a very limited exposure to current work in the area.

A. The Problem of Definition

Definitions, such as those proposed for learning disabilities, are offered to specify a particular type of condition or individual. They are valid as long as there is at least one individual to whom they apply. Definitions of learning disabilities are frequently critiqued because they almost universally state that neurological impairment is the presumed cause of the problem. However, even the most severe critics of the LD concept (cf. Coles, 1987) agree that at least a few children may have specific neurological impairment that interferes with school learning. The important question for these critics is how many of the 5% of school children currently identified as LD are adequately described by current definitions? Answers to this question may affect the numbers of children legitimately served under current law, but they do not threaten the validity of the concept.

The definition of learning disabilities accepted by the majority of persons in the field has changed in subtle ways since it was first formalized in 1967 by the National Advisory Committee on Handicapped Children (the definition later incorporated in PL 94-142). Most of the changes reflect additions to our knowledge about learning disabilities derived from research and practice. That first formal definition stated:

> Specific learning disability means a disorder in one or more of the basic psychological processes involved in understanding or in using language, spoken or written, which may manifest itself in an imperfect ability to listen, think, speak, read, write, spell, or to do mathematical calculations. The term includes such conditions as perceptual handicaps, brain injury, minimal brain dysfunction, dyslexia, and developmental aphasia. The term does not include children who have learning problems which are primarily the result of visual, hearing, or motor handicaps, of mental retardation, of emotional disturbance, or of environmental, cultural, or economic disadvantage.

The interagency report to the U.S. Congress (1987) identified at least four problems with this definition: (1) it does not indicate clearly enough that learning disabilities are a heterogeneous group of disorders; (2) it fails to recognize that learning disabilities frequently persist and are manifest in adults as well as children; (3) it does not clearly specify that, whatever the cause of LD, the "final common path" is inherent alterations in the way information is processed; and (4) it does not adequately recognize that persons with other handicapping or environmental limitations may have a learning disability concurrently with these conditions. Newer definitions, such as those proposed by the National Joint Committee on Learning Disabilities in 1981 and revised in 1988, or that proposed by ACLD in 1986, attempted to incorporate this new information in their definitions.

An interesting controversy was stimulated by the definition proposed in the Interagency Committee's report to Congress (1987). Recognizing research findings on the problems children with LD show in many social interactions, this definition added deficits in social skills as a type of learning disability. This proposal was explicitly rejected by the U.S. Department of Education. NJCLD's new definition, given in the following text, also specifically excludes problems in social interaction as a defining characteristic of children with learning disabilities:

> Learning disabilities is a general term that refers to a heterogeneous group of disorders manifested by significant difficulties in the acquisition and use of listening, speaking, reading, writing, reasoning, or mathematical abilities. These disorders are intrinsic to the individual, presumed to be due to central nervous system dysfunction, and may occur across the life span. Problems in self-regulatory behaviors, social perception, and social interaction may exist with learning disabilities but do not by themselves constitute a learning disability. Although learning disabilities may occur concomitantly with other handicapping conditions (for example, sensory impairment, mental retardation, serious emotional disturbance) or with extrinsic influences (such as cultural differences, insufficient or inappropriate instruction), they are not the result of those conditions or influences (NJCLD memorandum, 1988, p. 1).

In an article in the *Journal of Learning Disabilities*, Hammill (1990) argued strongly that the NJCLD definition represents the broadest current consensus in the field, and that remains the case in 2003. For example, the U.S. Department of Education convened a study group of research scientists in the LD field in November, 2001, to formulate statements about learning disabilities on which there was current consensus. The study group was part of a larger Learning Disabilities Initiative that extended over 2 years to identify issues and build consensus in the field prior to the reauthorization of the Individuals with Disabilities Education Act. With regard to the concept of learning disabilities, the study group agreed to the following statement:

> Strong converging evidence supports the validity of the concept of specific learning disabilities (SLD). This evidence is particularly impressive because it converges across different indicators and methodologies. The central concept of SLD involves disorders of learning and cognition that are intrinsic to the individual. SLD are specific in the sense that these disorders each significantly affects a relatively narrow range of academic and performance outcomes. SLD may occur in combination with other disabling conditions, but they are not due primarily to other conditions, such as mental retardation, behavioral disturbance, lack of opportunities to learn, or primary sensory deficits. (Danielson & Bradley, 2002, p. 792).

It is important for the field of learning disabilities as an educational/political movement to obtain relatively wide acceptance of a single broad definition of LD. However, this type of definition also has some serious drawbacks. The most important of these limitations may be that such definitions are not helpful in guiding research because they allow study of too great a variety of children under the same definition (Wong, 1986). When researchers attempt to compare findings across studies that have used broad definitions as a guide to sample selection, they often find, not surprisingly, that they have obtained different results. Many scholars now feel that it may be time for a moratorium on the development of such broad definitions. For example, Stanovich (1993) argues:

> Scientific investigations of some generically defined entity called "learning disability" simply make little sense given what we already know about heterogeneity across various learning domains. Research investigations must define groups specifically in terms of the domain of deficit (reading disability, arithmetic disability). (p. 273)

An example of such a domain-specific definition of a type of learning disability is found in the definition of reading disabilities that was recently proposed by the research committee of the International Dyslexia Association in collaboration with the National Center for Learning Disabilities and scientists from the National Institute of Child Health and Human Development. This definition incorporates what has been learned about reading disabilities as a result of recent research initiatives in this area. The definition states:

> Dyslexia is one of several distinct learning disabilities. It is a specific language-based disorder of constitutional origin characterized by difficulties in single word decoding, usually reflecting insufficient phonological processing. These difficulties in single word decoding are often unexpected in relation to age and other cognitive and academic abilities; they are not the result of generalized developmental disability or sensory impairment. Dyslexia is manifest by variable difficulty with different forms of language, often including, in addition to problems with reading, a conspicuous problem with acquiring proficiency in writing and spelling" (Lyon, 1995, p. 9)

It is beyond the scope of this chapter to detail the enormous amount of research knowledge about reading disabilities that is reflected in this definition (cf. Raynor et al., 2001; Share & Stanovich, 1995; Torgesen, 1999). It is important to recognize that this definition does not cover all possible forms of reading disability, only the most common one (Fletcher et al., 2002). Although the definition will undoubtedly change as more knowledge about reading disabilities is acquired, it may serve as a model for the development of other domain-specific definitions of learning disabilities as we acquire more understanding of the specific factors that are responsible for difficulties learning in other academic areas.

B. Etiology

As I mentioned earlier, the concept of learning disabilities is not threatened by our inability to show that every child being served in special education programs for children with learning disabilities has a processing disability resulting from neurological impairment. However, if only a minuscule percentage of children being served as LD actually fit the definition, this would clearly create problems for the learning disabilities movement. The fundamental assumption about LD at present is that they result from neurological impairment affecting specific brain functions. This is why they are given special status as a handicapping condition.

The area of learning disabilities, as a movement, has not been strongly concerned with questions of etiology (preferring to focus instead on problem description and intervention). However, its ultimate integrity as a separate field of education depends upon finding answers to questions about the extent of brain pathology in the population it serves.

At present, the best evidence that learning disabilities are a genuinely handicapping condition arising from differences in brain function comes from studies of the genetic transmission of reading disabilities. These studies (Olson, 1997; Wadsworth et al., 2000) indicate that approximately 50 to 70% (depending on level of general IQ) of all variability in the phonological processes that cause specific reading disability can be attributed to genetic factors. This genetic research has demonstrated that the risk in the offspring of a parent with a reading disability is eight times higher than in the general population.

These genetic studies are being supplemented by very active research programs to identify the specific locus of brain dysfunction responsible for difficulties learning to read. We now have substantial evidence indicating that poor readers exhibit disruption primarily, but not exclusively, in the left hemisphere serving language. Thus, neurobiological investigations using postmortem brain specimens, (Galaburda et al., 1994), brain morphometry (Filipek, 1996), and diffusion tensor MRI imaging (Klingberg et al., 2000) suggest that there are subtle structural differences in several regions of the brain between children who are learning to read normally and children with reading disabilities. There is also emerging evidence from a number of laboratories using functional brain imaging that indicates an atypical pattern of brain organization in children with reading disabilities. These studies show reductions in brain activity while performing reading tasks usually, but not always, in the left hemisphere (Shaywitz et al., 2000). In a recent summary of the evidence concerning the neurobiological substrate for specific reading disabilities, Zeffiro and Eden (2000) conclude that, "the combined evidence demonstrating macroscopic, morphologic, microscopic neuronal, and microstructural white matter abnormalities in dyslexia is consistent with a localization of the principal pathophysiological process to perisylvian structures predominantly in the left hemisphere." (p. 23) However, these authors also hint at the possible need to enlarge our conceptualization of the biological differences between dyslexic and typical children by pointing out that there is emerging evidence for brain abnormalities in these children extending beyond the classically defined language areas.

Although these findings do provide strong support for the concept of constitutionally based reading disabilities, they do not answer questions about the proportion of students identified as LD who actually have these kinds of disabilities. The findings from the genetic studies suggest that biologically based reading disabilities may be relatively common among school-identified samples of children with LD. Certainly, studies of the cognitive abilities of reading-disabled children indicate that difficulties processing phonological information are the most common cause of this disorder (Fletcher et al., 1994). However, at least half of the variability in phonological processing "talent" is the result of environmental influences, and phonological abilities themselves are influenced by how well children acquire reading skills (Wagner et al., 1997). Thus, it would be difficult to defend the proposition that all, or even most, children currently being served as reading disabled in public schools have reading disabilities of constitutional origin.

Compared to our knowledge about reading disabilities, we have very little information about potential biological bases for other types of learning disabilities. Byron Rourke (1995) has proposed a theory of nonverbal learning disabilities that identifies a clear biological basis for difficulties acquiring certain types of skills in mathematics. However, by Rourke's own estimate, this type of disability is very rare, and it thus may not provide an adequate description of the factors that are most commonly responsible for academic disabilities in the area of math.

C. Differentiation of LD from Other Conditions

The issue of etiology is important to the field of learning disabilities because it provides a basis for establishing that the learning problems of children with LD are fundamentally different from those experienced by other types of poor learners. Another way to address the question of differences between children with LD and other poor learners is in terms of their cognitive or behavioral characteristics. Differences at this level are important to our ability to differentiate reliably between those with LD and other poor learners during the assessment/diagnostic process.

This issue was forcibly raised relatively early in the history of LD as a formal discipline through the research of James Ysseldyke and his colleagues at the Minnesota Institute for the Study of Learning Disabilities. For example, Ysseldyke summarized over 5 years of research on assessment issues by stating that it was not possible, using current procedures, to reliably differentiate LD from other low achievers (Ysseldyke, 1983). In support of this contention, his group reported data in several studies showing a large degree of overlap in test scores, and test score patterns, between groups of school-identified children with LD and nonidentified slow learners (Ysseldyke *et al.*, 1982; Shinn *et al.*, 1982). Further, they also showed that a sample of school psychologists and resource room teachers could not reliably classify children as LD or slow learners using clinical judgment applied to test data (Epps *et al.*, 1981). Other investigators have found similarly high degrees of communality on cognitive, affective, and demographic variables between samples of LD, educable mentally retarded, and behaviorally disturbed children in the public schools (Gajar, 1980; Webster & Schenck, 1978).

Although these findings are potentially troublesome to the LD movement because they suggest that public monies are being selectively channeled to support a group of children (LD) who are not being reliably differentiated from other poor learners, they are irrelevant to basic scientific and conceptual issues. They say more about the social/political process of identification in the public schools than they do about the scientific validity of the concept of learning disabilities (Senf, 1986). While these findings may suggest that the concept has been overextended in practice, or that factors other than data about the child's psychological characteristics are important to placement decisions (Ysseldyke, 1983), they do not address basic scientific questions about the uniqueness of Children with LD.

However, other work on reading disabilities has addressed this question directly. The preponderance of this work directly challenges the validity of traditional operational definitions of reading disability that have utilized a discrepancy between general intelligence and reading ability as part of the diagnostic process. Traditional diagnostic practices have assumed that specific reading disability (reading ability discrepant from intelligence) was fundamentally different from reading problems in children whose level of general ability was consistent with their poor reading skills. There are now four major kinds of evidence against this assumption (Fletcher *et al.*, 2002).

First, early reports (Rutter & Yule, 1975) that reading disabilities were distributed bi-modally (implying that there were two different underlying populations of poor readers) have not been replicated in later, well-designed epidemiological studies (Shaywitz *et al.*, 1992; Silva *et al.*, 1985; Stevenson, 1988). Second, careful investigations of the cognitive profiles of discrepant and nondiscrepant poor readers indicate that they do not differ in the cognitive abilities most related to word-level reading difficulties (Fletcher *et al.*, 1994; Stanovich & Siegel, 1994). Third, discrepant and nondiscrepant groups show a similar rate of growth in word-level reading skill, both during early elementary school (Foorman *et al.*, 1995) and into early adolescence (Francis *et al.*, 1995). Finally, studies of the genetics of reading disabilities have shown that discrepant and nondiscrepant word-level reading disabilities are both heritable (Wadsworth *et al.*, 2000).

The fundamental conceptual error involved in using a discrepancy between broad intelligence and reading ability to differentiate between children with a "true reading disability" and children who struggle in reading because they are "generally slow learners" arises from the fact that both of these groups of children experience difficulties acquiring basic reading skills for the same reason. It was the discovery that the majority of children who experience difficulties learning to read printed words do so because they have weaknesses in the phonological domain of language (Torgesen & Wagner, 1998) that made this point clear. Early reading difficulties are not predicted well by general intelligence because phonological language abilities are only weakly correlated with IQ (Wagner *et al.*, 1994). Thus, some children with above average intelligence can experience reading disabilities because of specific weaknesses in the phonological domain, and other children with phonological weaknesses, who also happen to have limitations in a broader range of cognitive and language skills, experience reading difficulties for the same reason. Both groups of children need the same kind of instruction to acquire proficient word-reading skills, but one of the groups will also require additional interventions that address their broader range of language and cognitive impairment (Foorman & Torgesen, 2001).

Although movement away from discrepancy-based definitions of reading disability toward more inclusive definitions will create many difficult issues in practice (i.e., how to serve the expanded numbers of children with genuine disabilities in reading), it will assist in the early identification of children at risk for reading failure. At present, identification must wait for a discrepancy between IQ and reading ability to develop. However, a more valid approach would be to identify children who show the specific linguistic/phonological characteristics of reading-disabled children (without regard to general ability level) and provide special services to them.

D. Issues in Identification and Service Delivery

As was mentioned earlier, there is currently no convincing evidence that children with LD require qualitatively different kinds of instructional interventions than other types of poor learners in the area of their disability. What we do know is that they must be provided with a different kind of instruction than is typically available in the regular classroom. After all, it is their inability to profit from regular classroom instruction that usually leads to a diagnosis of learning disability! In the case of reading disabilities, which is the most common form of learning disability and the one we know the most about, it appears that these children require instruction which is more explicit, more intensive, and more supportive than is typically provided in the classroom (Foorman & Torgesen, 2001).

Instruction must be more explicit in the sense that it makes fewer assumptions about pre-existing skills or children's abilities to make inferences about language regularities that are useful in reading. In other words, children with reading disabilities must be directly taught almost everything they need to know in order to be good readers (Gaskins *et al.*, 1997).

In addition to being more explicit, reading instruction for children with disabilities in this area must be more intense. Greater intensity can be achieved either by lengthening instruction time or by reducing teacher-pupil ratios. Greater intensity of instruction is required not only because reading-disabled children learn these skills more slowly, but also because increased explicitness of instruction requires that more things be taught directly by the teacher. Unless beginning reading instruction for children with reading disabilities is more intensive (or lasts significantly longer) than normal instruction, these children will necessarily lag significantly behind their peers in reading growth. Substantially increased intensity of instruction seems especially critical in remedial settings, where children *begin* the instruction already significantly behind their peers (Torgesen, 2004).

A third way in which instruction for children with reading disabilities must be modified in order to be successful involves the quality of support that is provided. At least two kinds of special support are required. First, because acquiring reading skills is more difficult for children with reading disabilities than others, they will require more *emotional* support in the form of encouragement, positive feedback, and enthusiasm from the teacher in order to maintain their motivation to learn. Second, instructional interactions must be more supportive in the sense that they involve carefully scaffolded interactions with the child. In a recent investigation of the characteristics of effective reading tutors, Juel (1996) identified the number of *scaffolded* interactions during each teaching session as one of the critical variables predicting differences in effectiveness across tutors. A scaffolded interaction is one in which the teacher enables the student to complete a task (i.e., read a word) by directing the student's attention to a key piece of information or by breaking the task up into smaller, easier-to-manage ones. The goal of these interactions is to provide just enough support so the child can go through the processing steps necessary to find the right answer. With enough practice, the child becomes able to go through the steps independently. Juel's finding about the importance of carefully scaffolded instructional interactions is consistent with the emphasis on these types of interactions in the teacher's manuals that accompany two instructional programs shown to be effective with children who have severe reading disabilities (Lindamood & Lindamood, 1984; Wilson, 1988).

Although these instructional needs seem well established from research and theory, there is, at present, little consensus about how they can be met within typical school settings. The traditional approach to educating learning disabled children has been in pullout programs, in which one teacher works with relatively small groups (5–15) of children in a special classroom setting. This approach has been criticized because it typically does not lead to "normalization" of academic skills for most children with LD (Hanushek et al., 1998). However, the model that has emerged as its replacement, variously labeled the regular education initiative, mainstreaming, or the inclusion movement, is also problematic. For example, Vaughn and her colleagues (Vaughn & Schumm, 1996), after extensive studies of regular classroom teachers' responses to LD students, indicate "general education teachers find many more accommodations desirable than feasible, and are unlikely to make extensive, time-consuming adaptations to meet the individual needs of students" (p. 109). Further, "practices that require an inordinate amount of teacher effort for an individual child or subgroup of children are not likely to be adopted" (p. 122). In a series of studies of academic outcomes for Children with LD being educated with inclusionary practices, Zigmond (1996) reported very discouraging outcomes for the majority of LD students in these settings.

The problem with current intervention and service delivery methods appears to be that they are not delivered with sufficient intensity, and they may not be delivered with sufficient skill. The most convincing evidence for this point is found in recent intervention research that has delivered significant amounts of instruction (60–100 hours) with reasonable intensity (either 1:1 or in very small groups of 3 to 5 children), over relatively short periods of time (2 to 6 months). This research has focused on children with serious to moderate reading difficulties in late elementary school (Torgesen et al., 2003), and it has demonstrated that the reading accuracy and reading comprehension skills of the large majority of these children can be brought into the normal range. Although reading fluency can be improved, it is much more difficult to "close the gap" in reading fluency than it is for other reading skills (Torgesen et al., 2001).

Can learning disabilities by prevented? One obvious consequence of moving toward more inclusive definitions of learning disabilities (that do not require aptitude–achievement discrepancies) is that children at risk for learning disabilities may be identified very early in their school experience. If special preventive instruction could be provided at the appropriate time, will this eliminate the need for further special instruction for children with LD? At present, there are two different ways to answer this question, and both indicate that we do not yet have viable preventive solutions for reading disabilities. First, several early intervention studies have been conducted using a range of service delivery methods from one-on-one instruction, to small group instruction, to whole class instruction (Brown & Felton, 1990; Foorman *et al.*, 1998; Torgesen *et al.*, 1999; Vellutino *et al.*, 1996). After total instructional times varying from 88 to 340 hours, these interventions proved to be ineffective with from 2 to 6% of the total population (Torgesen, 2000). While the preventive interventions substantially reduced the number of children potentially "at risk" for reading disabilities, they were not sufficient to help all children acquire basic beginning reading skills. Further, there is some beginning evidence that even children who respond positively to early interventions may require additional intervention at a later point to maintain normal growth in reading skill (Torgesen, 2004). For example, follow-up studies of children who successfully complete the popular Reading Recovery program as first graders indicate that a very substantial portion of them either fall behind in reading development or require special reading interventions at some point later in elementary school (Shanahan & Barr, 1995).

   In summary, the most critical issue for service delivery is one that has been with the field since its inception. How can we deliver high-quality, effective instruction to all children with learning disabilities? At present, the zeitgeist suggests that the regular classroom is the place where all learning disabled children should be educated. However, the needs of children with LD for instruction that is more explicit, more intensive, and more supportive than normal are going to be very difficult to meet in most regular classroom settings. In addition to the time constraints involved, in the case of reading, added explicitness of instruction implies that teachers need much more knowledge about language and reading processes than they currently possess (Moats, 1995). Much of our current research on reading disabilities suggests that we have seriously underestimated the amount and quality of instruction these children will require in order to acquire useful reading skills. One of the great challenges for our field in the next decade will be to learn the conditions that need to be in place, and then to accomplish the political work to put them in place, for all children with learning disabilities to acquire a full range of useful academic skills.

IV. CONCLUDING COMMENTS

When I wrote the first version of this chapter about 12 years ago, I predicted that the coming decade would be a time of great change for the field of learning disabilities. I was right in one sense and wrong in another. The sense in which I was wrong is that there has been little change in the status of the field as a social/political/educational movement over the past 12 years. The study of learning disabilities continues as a strong and vital force within the larger special and regular education communities. Its services, which are mandated by law in many countries, are offered to vast numbers of children with a variety of very difficult and unusual educational problems. Professionals in the field continue to organize themselves into strong associations which provide adequate means for communication about research and professional issues. Additionally, the interests of children and adults with LD are served by a number of strong associations which have as a primary aim the protection of their rights to a free and appropriate education as well as appropriate accommodations in the workplace. Finally, research in the area has continued to grow and become more diverse, and many new research initiatives have been supported by governmental agencies.

The sense in which I was right is that there has been a substantial improvement in our knowledge about learning disabilities, particularly for the most common disability that affects acquisition of reading skills. We know, for example, that reading disability most frequently involves difficulties in learning to identify words rapidly and accurately, and that the primary cause of this problem is deficiencies in the ability to process the phonological features of language. Further, we know that substantial proportions of individual differences in phonological abilities are transmitted genetically, and we are beginning to form relatively clear ideas of the specific locations in the brain that are affected. All these facts support traditional definitions of learning disabilities that suggest they arise from intrinsic processing disabilities that are constitutionally based. However, the consistent finding that reading problems arise from essentially the same handicapping conditions in children whose reading levels are discrepant and nondiscrepant from their IQ invalidates commonly used aptitude–achievement discrepancy formulae to identify children with LD. In order to bring practice in line with the best scientific information currently available, the field should adopt a more inclusive definition of reading disabilities. Children should not be denied LD services because their aptitude–achievement discrepancy is not large enough; rather, all children who show the primary symptoms of phonologically based reading disabilities should receive appropriate instructional interventions.

At this point in time, the field of learning disabilities is on an exciting path. It is solidly supported in law, it has an enormous number of well-informed advocates and professionals working on its behalf, and it is the subject of challenging and programmatic research. Let us hope that the next decade brings continued new knowledge and appropriate expansion of services to all children and adults with learning disabilities.

References

Arter, J. A., & Jenkins, J. R. (1979). Differential diagnostic prescriptive teaching: A critical appraisal. *Review of Educational Research, 49,* 517–555.

Brown, A. L., & Campione, J. C. (1986). Psychological theory and the study of learning disabilities. *American Psychologist, 14,* 1059–1068.

Brown, I. S., & Felton, R. H. (1990). Effects of instruction on beginning reading skills in children at risk for reading disability. *Reading and Writing: An Interdisciplinary Journal, 2,* 223–241.

Bush, W. J., & Giles, M. T. (1969). *Aids to psycholinguistics teaching.* Columbus, Ohio: Merrill.

Butterfield, E. D., & Ferretti, R. P. (1987) Toward a theoretical integration of cognitive hypotheses about intellectual differences among children. In L. Borkowski & L. D. Day (Eds.), *Cognition in special children: Comparative approaches to retardation, learning disabilities, and giftedness* (pp. 195–234) New York: Ablex.

Ceci, S. J., & Baker, J. G. (1990). On learning . . . more or less: A knowledge × process × context view of learning disabilities. In J. K. Torgesen (Ed.), *Cognitive and behavioral characteristics of children with learning disabilities.* Austin, TX: PRO-ED.

Chalfant, J. C., & Scheffelin, M. A. (1969). Central processing dysfunctions in children: A review of research. *NINDS Monographs,* Bethesda, MD. U.S. Department of Health, Education, and Welfare.

Coles, G. S. (1987). *The learning mystique: A critical look at "learning disabilities."* New York: Pantheon.

Cruickshank, W. M., Bentzen, F. A., Ratzeburg, F. H., & Tannhauser, M. T. (1961). *A teaching method for brain-injured and hyperactive children.* Syracuse, NY: Syracuse University Press.

Cruickshank, W. M., Bice, H. V., & Wallen, N. E. (1957). Perception and cerebral palsy. Syracuse, NY: Syracuse University Press.

Danielson, L., & Bradley, R. (2002). Specific learning disabilities: Building consensus for identification and classification. In R. Bradley, L. Danielson, & D. P. Hallahan (Eds.) *Identification of learning disabilities: Research into practice* (pp. 791–804). Mahwah, NJ: Lawrence Erlbaum Associates.

Doris, J. (1986). Learning disabilities. In S. J. Ceci (Ed.), Handbook of cognitive, social, and neuropsychological aspects of learning disabilities (pp. 3–53) Hillsdale, NJ: Erlbaum Assoc.

Durrell, D. D. (1940). Improvement of basic reading abilities. New York, NY: World Book Company.

Ehri, L. C., Nunes, S. R., Willows, D. M., Schuster, B. V., Yaghoub-Zadeh, Z., & Shanahan, T. (2001). Phonemic awareness instruction helps children learn to read: Evidence from the National Reading Panel's meta-analysis. *Reading Research Quarterly, 36,* 250–287.

Ellis, E. S., Lenz, B. K., & Sabornie, E. J. (1987). Generalization and adaptation of learning strategies to natural environments: Part 2: Research into practice. *Remedial and Special Education, 8,* 6–23.

Epps, S., Ysseldyke, J. E., & McGue, M. (1981). Differentiating LD and non-LD students: "I know one when I see one." Minneapolis, MN: Institute for Research on Learning Disabilities.

Filipek, P. (1996). Structural variations in measures in the developmental disorders. In R. Thatcher, G. Lyon, J. Rumsey, & N. Krasnegor (Eds.), *Developmental neuroimaging: Mapping the development of brain and behavior* (pp. 169–186). San Diego, CA: Academic Press.

Fletcher, J. M., Lyon, G. R., Barnes, M., Stuebing, K. K., Francis, D. J., Olson, R. K., Shaywitz, S. E., & Shaywitz, B. A. (2002). Classification of learning disabilities: An evidence-based evaluation. In R. Bradley, L. Danielson, & D. Hallahan (Eds.) *Identification of Learning disabilities: Research to practice* (pp. 185–250). Mahwah, NJ: Lawrence Erlbaum Associates.

Fletcher, J. M., Shaywitz, S. E., Shankweiler, D. P., Katz, L., Liberman, I. Y., Stuebing, K. K., Francis, D. J., Fowler, A. E., & Shaywitz, B. A. (1994). Cognitive profiles of reading disability: Comparisons of discrepancy and low achievement definitions. *Journal of Educational Psychology*, **86**, 6–23.

Foorman, B. R., Francis, D. J., & Fletcher, J. M. (1995). Growth of phonological processing skills in beginning reading: The lag versus deficit model revisited. Paper presented at the Society for Research on Child Development, Indianapolis, IN, March 31, 1995.

Foorman, B. R., Francis, D. J., Fletcher, J. M., Schatschneider, C., & Mehta, P. (1998). The role of instruction in learning to read: Preventing reading failure in at-risk children. *Journal of Educational Psychology*, **90**, 37–55.

Foorman, B., & Torgesen, J. K. (2001). Critical elements of classroom and small-group instruction to promote reading success in all children. *Learning Disabilities Research and Practice*, **16**, 203–212.

Francis, D. J., Shaywitz, S. E., Stuebing, K. K., Shaywitz, B. A., & Fletcher, J. M. (1996). Developmental lag versus deficit models of reading disability: A longitudinal, individual growth curves analysis. *Journal of Educational Psychology*, **88**, 3–17.

Frostig, M., Lefever, D. W., & Whittlesey, J. R. B. (1964). The Marianne Frostig developmental test of visual perception. Palo Alto: Consulting Psychology Press.

Gajar, A. H. (1980). Characteristics across exceptional categories: EMR, LD, and ED. *Journal of Special Education*, **14**, 165–173.

Galaburda, A. M., Menard, M., & Rosen, G. (1994). Evidence for aberrant auditory anatomy in developmental dyslexia. *Proceedings of the National Academy of Science*, **91**, 8010–8013.

Gaskins, I. W., Ehri, L. C., Cress, C., O'Hara, C., & Donnelly, K. (1997). Procedures for word learning: Making discoveries about words. *The Reading Teacher* **50**, 312–327.

Habib, M., Espresser, R., Rey, V., Giraud, K., Braus, P., & Gres, C. (1999). Training dyslexics with acoustically modified speech: Evidence of improved phonological performance. *Brain & Cognition*, **40**(1), 143–146.

Hallahan, D. P., & Cruickshank, W. M. (1973). *Psycho-educational foundations of learning disabilities*. Englewood Cliffs, NJ: Prentice-Hall.

Hallahan, D. P., Kauffman, J. M., & Lloyd, J. W. (1985). Introduction to learning disabilities. Englewood Cliffs, NJ: Prentice-Hall.

Hallahan, D. P., & Mercer, C. D. (2002) Learning disabilities: Historical perspectives. In R. Bradley, L. Danielson, & D. Hallahan (Eds.) *Identification of learning disabilities: Research to practice* (pp. 1–67). Mahwah, NJ: Lawrence Erlbaum Associates.

Hammill, D. D. (1972). Training visual perceptual processes. *Journal of Learning Disabilities*, **5**, 552–559.

Hammill, D. D. (1990). On defining learning disabilities: An emerging consensus. *Journal of Learning Disabilities*, **23**, 74–84.

Hammill, D. D., Goodman, L., & Wiederholt, J. L. (1974). Visual motor processes: What success have we had in training them? *The Reading Teacher*, **27**, 469–478.

Hammill, D. D., & Larson, S. C. (1974). The efficacy of psycholinguistic training. *Exceptional Children*, **4I**, 5–14.

Hanushek, E. A., Kain, J. F., & and Rivkin, S. G. (1998). *Does special education raise academic achievement for students with disabilities?* National Bureau of Economic Research, Working Paper No. 6690, Cambridge, MA.

Harris, K., & Graham, S. (1996). *Making the writing process work: Strategies for composition and self-regulation* (2nd Ed.). Cambridge: Brookline Books.

Hartman, N. C., & Hartman, R. K. (1973). Perceptual handicap or reading disability? *The Reading Teacher*, **26**, 684–695.

Head, H. (1926). Aphasia and kindred disorders of speech. Vol. I. London, UK: Cambridge University Press.

Hinshelwood, J. (1917). Congenital word blindness. London, UK: H. K. Lewis.

Hook, P. E., Macaruso, P., & Jones, S. (2001). Efficacy of Fast ForWord training on facilitating acquisition of reading skills by children with reading difficulties—A longitudinal study. *Annals of Dyslexia*, **51**, 75–96.

Interagency Committee on Learning Disabilities. (1987). Learning disabilities: A report to the U.S. Congress. Bethesda, MD: National Institutes of Health.

Johnson, D. J., & Mykelbust, H. R. (1967). Learning disabilities: Educational principles and practices. New York: Grune & Stratton.

Juel, C. (1996). What makes literacy tutoring effective? *Reading Research Quarterly*, **31**, 268–289.

Kass, C. E. (1970). Final report: Advanced institute for leadership personnel in learning disabilities. Contract No. OEG-09-121013-3021-031, U.S. Office of Education, Department of Special Education, University of Arizona, Tucson, Arizona.

Kavale, K., & Forness, S. (1985). *The science of learning disabilities*. San Diego, CA: College-Hill Press.

Kavanagh, J. F., & Truss, T. J. (1988). Learning disabilities: Proceedings of the national conference. Parkton, MD: York Press.

Kephart, N. C. (1960). *The slow learner in the classroom*. Columbus, OH: Charles E. Merrill.

Kephart, N. C., & Strauss, A. A. (1940). A clinical factor influencing variations in IQ. *American Journal of Orthopsychiatry*, **10**, 345–350.

Kirk, S. A. (1963). Behavioral diagnosis and remediation of learning disabilities. *Proceedings of the Annual Meeting of the Conference on Exploration into the Problems of the Perceptually Handicapped Child. Vol. 1.*

Kirk, S. A., & Kirk, W. D. (1971). *Psycholinguistic learning disabilities: Diagnosis and remediation.* Chicago, IL: University of Illinois Press.

Klingberg, T., Hedehus, M., Temple, E., Salz, T., Gabrieli, J., Moseley, M., & Poldrack, R. (2000). Microstructure of temporo-parietal white matter as a basis for reading ability: Evidence from diffusion tensor magnetic resonance imaging. *Neuron, 25,* 493–500.

Liberman, L. Y., Shankweiler, D., Orlando, C., Harris, K. S., & Berti, F. B. (1971). Letter confusions and reversals of sequence in the beginning reader: Implications for Orton's theory of developmental dyslexia. *Cortex, 7,* 127–142.

Lindamood, C. H., & Lindamood, P. C. (1984). *Auditory discrimination in depth.* Austin, TX: PRO-ED, Inc.

Lyon, G. R. (1985). Identification and remediation of learning disability subtypes: Preliminary findings. *Learning Disabilities Focus, 1,* 21–35.

Lyon, G. R. (1994). *Frames of reference for the assessment of learning disabilities: New views on measurement issues.* Baltimore, MD: Brooks Publishing.

Lyon, G. R. (1995). Toward a definition of dyslexia. *Annals of Dyslexia, 45,* 3–27.

Mann, L. (1971). Psychometric phenology and the new faculty psychology: The case against ability assessment and training. *Journal of Special Education, 5,* 3–14.

Mann, L. (1979). *On the trail of process.* New York: Grune & Stratton.

Mann, L., & Phillips, W. A. (1967). Fractional practices in special education: A critique. *Exceptional Children, 33,* 311–317.

Mastropieri, M. A., & Scruggs, T. E. (1997). Best practices in promoting reading comprehension in students with learning disabilities: 1976–1996. *Remedial and Special Education, 18,* 197–213.

McAnally, D. I., Hansen, P. C., Cornelissen, P. L., & Stein, J. F. (1997). Effect of time and frequency manipulation on syllable perception in developmental dyslexics. *Journal of Speech, Language, and Hearing Research, 40,* 912–924.

McCarthy, J. J., & Kirk, S. A. (1961). Illinois Test of Psycholinguistic Abilities: Experimental version. Urbana, IL: University of Illinois Press.

Meltzer, L. J. (1993). Strategy assessment and instruction for students with learning disabilities. Austin, TX: PRO-ED, Inc.

Merzenich, M. M., Jenkins, W. M., Johnston, P., Schreiner, C., Miller, S. L., & Tallal, P. (1996). Temporal processing deficits of language-learning impaired children ameliorated by training. *Science, 271,* 77–81.

Moats, L. C. (1995). The missing foundation in teacher education. *American Educator, 19,* 9–51.

Mody, M., Studdert-Kennedy, M., & Brady, S. (1997). Speech perception deficits in poor readers: Adutory processing or phonological coding? *Journal of Experimental Child Psychology, 64,* 199–231.

Myers, P., & Hammill, D. D. (1990). *Learning disabilities: Basic concepts, assessment practices, and instructional strategies.* Austin, TX.: PRO-ED.

National Joint Committee on Learning Disabilities. (1988). Letter to NJCLD organizations.

Newcomer, P. L., & Hammill, D. D. (1975). ITPA and academic achievement. *The Reading Teacher*, **28**, 731–741.

Nittrouer, S. (1999). Do temporal processing deficits cause phonological processing problems? *Journal of Speech, Language, and Hearing Research*, **42**, 925–942.

Olson, R. (1997). The genetics of LD: Twin studies. Address presented at conference titled "Progress and promise in research and education for individuals with learning disabilities." Washington, DC, May.

Orton, S. T. (1937). *Reading, writing, and speech problems in children*. New York: Norton.

Palincsaar, A. S., Winn, J., David, Y., Snyder, B., & Stevens, D. (1993). Approaches to strategic reading instruction reflecting different assumptions regarding teaching and learning. In L. J. Meltzer, (Ed.), *Strategy assessment and instruction for students with learning disabilities*. Austin, TX.: PRO-ED, Inc.

Raynor, K., Foorman, B. R., Perfetti, C. A., Pesetsky, D., & Seidenberg, M. S. (2001). How psychological science informs the teaching of reading. *Psychological Science in the Public Interest*, **2**, 31–73.

Rourke, B. P. (1995). *Syndrome of nonverbal learning disabilities: Neurodevelopmental manifestiations*. New York: Guilford Press.

Rutter, M., & Yule, W. (1975). The concept of specific reading retardation. *Journal of Child Psychology and Psychiatry*, **16**, 181–197.

Sarason, S. B. (1949). Psychological problems in mental deficiency. New York: Harper.

Senf, G. M. (1986). LD research in sociological and scientific perspective. In J. K. Torgesen & B. Y. L. Wong (Eds.), *Psychological and educational perspectives on learning disabilities*. New York: Academic Press.

Shanahan, T., & Barr, R. (1995). Reading recovery: An independent evaluation of the effects of an early instructional intervention for at-risk learners. *Reading Research Quarterly*, **30**, 958–996.

Shankweiler, D., & Liberman, I. Y. (1989). *Phonology and reading disability*. Ann Arbor: University of Michigan Press.

Share, D. L., & Stanovich, K. E. (1995). Cognitive processes in early reading development: A model of acquisition and individual differences. *Issues in Education: Contributions from Educational Psychology*, **1**, 1–35.

Shaywitz, S. E. (1996). Dyslexia. *Scientific American*, **97**, 98–104.

Shaywitz, S. E., Escobar, M. D., Shaywitz, B. A., Fletcher, J. M., & Makuch, R. (1992). Evidence that dyslexia may represent the lower tail of a normal distribution of reading ability. *The New England Journal of Medicine*, **326**, 145–150.

Shaywitz, S. E., Pugh, K. R., Jenner, A. R., Fulbright, R. K., Fletcher, J. M., Gore, J. C., & Shaywitz, B. A. (2000). The neurobiology of reading and reading disability (dyslexia). In M. L. Kamil, P. B. Mosenthal, P. D. Pearson, & R. Barr (Eds.), *Handbook of reading research*, Vol. III (pp. 229–249). Mahway, NJ: Lawrence Erlbaum.

Shinn, M. R., Ysseldyke, J., Deno, S., & Tindal, G. (1982). Comparison of psychometric and functional differences between students labeled learning disabled and low achieving. Research report no. 71, Institute for Research on Learning Disabilities, University of Minnesota.

Siegel, L. S. (1989). IQ is irrelevant to the definition of learning disabilities. *Journal of Learning Disabilities*, **22**, 469–479.

Siegler, R. S. (1998). *Children's thinking: Third edition*. Upper Saddle River, NJ: Prentice-Hall, Inc.

Silva, P. A., McGee, R., & Williams, S. (1985). Some characteristics of 9-year-old boys with general reading backwardness or specific reading retardation. *Journal of Child Psychology and Psychiatry*, **26**, 407–421.

Stanovich, K. E. (1990). Explaining the differences between the dyslexic and the garden-variety poor reader: The phonological-core variable-difference model. In J. Torgesen (Ed.), *Cognitive and behavioral characteristics of children with learning disabilities*. Austin, TX: PRO-ED.

Stanovich, K. E. (1993). The construct validity of discrepancy definitions of reading disability. In G. R. Lyon, D. Gray, J. Kavanagh, & N. Krasnegor (Eds.), *Better understanding learning disabilities: New views on research and their implications for public policies*. Baltimore: Paul H. Brookes Publishing.

Stanovich, K. E., & Siegel, L. S. (1994). The phenotypic performance profile of reading-disabled children: A regression-based test of the phonological-core variable-difference model. *Journal of Educational Psychology*, **86**, 24–53.

Stevenson, J. (1988). Which aspects of reading disability show a "hump" in their distribution? *Applied Cognitive psychology*, **2**, 77–85.

Strauss, A. A. (1943). Diagnosis and education of the cripplebrained, deficient child. *Journal of Exceptional Children*, **9**, 163–168.

Strauss, A. A., & Kephart, N. C. (1955). *Psychopathology and education of the brain-injured child: Progress in theory and clinic* (Vol. 2). New York: Grune and Stratton.

Strauss, A. A., & Lehtinen, L. E. (1947). *Psychopathology and education of the brain-injured child*. New York: Grune & Stratton.

Tallal, P. (1980). Auditory temporal perception, phonics, and reading disabilities in children. *Brain and Language*, **9**, 182–198.

Tallal, P., Miller, S. L., Bedi, G., Byma, G., Wang, X., Nagarajan, S. S., Schreiner, C., Jenkins, W. M., & Merzenich, M. M. (1996). Language comprehension in language-learning impaired children improved with acoustically modified speech. *Science*, **271**, 81–84.

Temple, E., Deutsch, G. K., Poldrack, R. A., Miller, S. L., Tallal, P., Merzenich, M. M., & Gabrieli, J. D. (2003). Neural deficits in children with dyslexia ameliorated by behavioral intervention: Evidence from functional MRI. *Proceedings of the National Academy of Sciences*, **100**, 2860–2865.

Torgesen, J. K. (1979). What shall we do with psychological processes? *Journal of Learning Disabilities*, **12**, 514–521.

Torgesen, J. K. (1986). Learning disabilities theory: Its current state and future prospects. *Journal of Learning Disabilities*, **19**, 399–407.

Torgesen, J. K. (1993). Variations on theory in learning disabilities. In R. Lyon, D. Gray, N. Krasnegor, and J. Kavenagh (Eds.), *Better understanding learning disabilities: Perspectives on classification, identification, and assessment and their implications for education and policy*. Baltimore: Brookes Publishing.

Torgesen, J. K. (1999). Phonologically based reading disabilities: Toward a coherent theory of one kind of learning disability. In R. J. Sternberg & L. Spear-Swerling (Eds.), *Perspectives on learning disabilities* (pp. 231–262). New Haven: Westview Press.

Torgesen, J. K. (2000). Individual differences in response to early interventions in reading: The lingering problem of treatment resisters. *Learning Disabilities Research and Practice*, **15**, 55–64.

Torgesen, J. K. (2002). Empirical and theoretical support for direct diagnosis of learning disabilities by assessment of intrinsic processing weaknesses. In R. Bradley, L. Danielson, & D. Hallahan (Eds.), *Identification of learning disabilities: Research to practice* (pp. 565–613). Mahwah, NJ: Lawrence Erlbaum Associates.

Torgesen, J. K. (2004). Lessons learned from the last 20 years of research on interventions for students who experience difficulty learning to read. In McCardle, P. & Chhabra, V. (Eds.), *The voice of evidence in reading research* (pp. 225–229). Baltimore: Brookes Publishing.

Torgesen, J. K., Rashotte, C. A., & Alexander, A. (2001). Principles of fluency instruction in reading: Relationships with established empirical outcomes. In M. Wolf (Ed.), *Dyslexia, fluency, and the brain*. Parkton, MD: York Press.

Torgesen, J. K., Rashotte, C. A., Alexander, A., & MacPhee, K. (2003). Progress towards understanding the instructional conditions necessary for remediating reading difficulties in older children. In B. Foorman (Ed.), *Preventing and Remediating Reading Difficulties: Bringing Science to Scale* (pp. 275–298). Parkton, MD: York Press.

Torgesen, J. K., & Wagner, R. K. (1998). Alternative diagnostic approaches for specific developmental reading disabilities. *Learning Disabilities Research and Practice* **13**, 220–232.

Torgesen, J. K., Wagner, R. K., Rashotte, C. A., Rose, E., Lindamood, P., Conway, T., & Garvin, C. (1999). Preventing reading failure in young children with phonological processing disabilities: Group and individual responses to instruction. *Journal of Educational Psychology*, **91**, 579–593.

Vaughn, S., & Schumm, J. S. (1996). Classroom ecologies: Classroom interactions and implications for inclusion of students with learning disabilities (pp. 107–124). In D. L. Speece & B. K. Keogh (Eds.), *Research on classroom ecologies*. Mahwah, NJ: Lawrence Erlbaum Associates.

Vellutino, F. R., Scanlon, D. M., Sipay, E. R., Small, S. G., Pratt, A., Chen, R., & Denckla, M. B. (1996). Cognitive profiles of difficult-to-remediate and readily remediated poor readers: Early intervention as a vehicle for distinguishing between cognitive and experiential deficits as basic causes of specific reading disability. *Journal of Educational Psychology*, **88**, 601–638.

Vellutino, F. R., Steger, B. M., Moyer, S. C., Hardin, C. J., & Niles, J. A. (1977). Has the perceptual deficit hypothesis led us astray? *Journal of Learning Disabilities*, **10**, 375–385.

Vernon, M. D. (1957). Backwardness in reading. London, UK: Cambridge University Press.

Wadsworth, S. J., Olson, R. K., Pennington, B. F., & DeFries, J. C. (2000). Differential genetic etiology of reading disability as a function of IQ. *Journal of Learning Disabilities*, **33**, 192–199.

Wagner, R. K., Torgesen, J. K., & Rashotte, C. A. (1994). The development of reading-related phonological processing abilities: New evidence of bi-directional causality from a latent variable longitudinal study. *Developmental Psychology*, **30**, 73–87.

Wagner, R. K., Torgesen, J. K., Rashotte, C. A., Hecht, S. A., Barker, T. A., Burgess, S. R., Donahue, J., & Garon, T. (1997). Changing causal relations between phonological processing abilities and word-level reading as children develop from beginning to fluent readers: A five-year longitudinal study. *Developmental Psychology*, **33**, 468–479.

Webster, R. E., & Schenck, S. J. (1978). Diagnostic test pattern differences among LD, ED, EMH, and multi-handicapped students. *Journal of Educational Research*, **72**, 75–80.

Wiederholt, J. L. (1974). Historical perspectives on the education of the learning disabled. In L. Mann & D. A. Sabatino (Eds.), *The second review of special education* (pp. 103–152). Austin, TX: PRO-ED.

Wiederholt, J. L., & Hammill, D. D. (1971). Use of the FrostigHorne Visual Perceptual Program in the urban school. *Psychology in the Schools*, **8**, 268–274.

Wilson, B. A. (1988). *Instructor manual*. Millbury, MA: Wilson Language Training.

Wong, B. Y. L. (1986). Problems and issues in the definition of learning disabilities. In J. K. Torgesen & B. Y. L. Wong (Eds.), *Psychological and educational perspectives on learning disabilities* (pp. 1–25). San Diego: Academic Press.

Ysseldyke, J. E. (1973). Diagnostic–prescriptive teaching: The search for aptitude–treatment interactions. In L. Mann & D. Sabatino (Eds.), *The first review of special education*. Austin, TX: PRO-ED.

Ysseldyke, J. E. (1983). Current practices in making psychoeducational decisions about learning disabled students. *Journal of Learning Disabilities*, **16**, 209–219.

Ysseldyke, J. E., Algozzine, B., Shinn, M., & McGue, M. (1982). Similarities and differences between students labeled underachievers and learning disabled. *Journal of Special Education*, **16**, 73–85.

Zeffiro, T. J., & Eden, G. (2000). The neural basis of developmental dyslexia. *Annals of Dyslexia*, **50**, 1–30.

Zigmond, N. (1996). Organization and management of general education classrooms. In D. L. Speece & B. K. Keogh (Eds.), *Research on classroom ecologies* (pp. 163–190). Mahwah, NJ: Lawrence Erlbaum Associates.

CHAPTER 2

Learning Disabilities and Memory

H. Lee Swanson,* John B. Cooney,[†] and John K. McNamara

University of California*, University of Northern Colorado[†], University of Saskatchewan

I. INTRODUCTION

Memory is the ability to encode, process, and retrieve information that one has been exposed to. As a skill, it is inseparable from intellectual functioning and learning. Individuals deficient in memory skills, such as children and adults with learning disabilities (LD), would be expected to have difficulty on a number of academic and cognitive tasks. Although memory is linked to performance in several academic (e.g., reading) and cognitive areas (e.g., problem-solving), it is a critical area of focus in the field of LD for three reasons. First, it reflects applied cognition; that is, memory functioning reflects all aspects of learning. Second, several studies suggest that the memory skills used by students with LD do not appear to exhaust or even tap their ability, and therefore we need to discover instructional procedures that capitalize on their potential. Finally, several intervention programs that attempt to enhance the overall cognition of children and adults with LD rely on principles derived from memory research. This chapter characterizes and selectively reviews past and current research on memory skills, describes the components and stages of processing that influence memory performance, and discusses current trends and the implications of memory research for the instruction of children and adults with LD.

Learning about Learning Disabilities, Third Edition

41

II. A HISTORICAL PERSPECTIVE

The earliest link between LD and memory was established in the literature on reading disabilities by Kussmaul. In 1877, Kussmaul called attention to a disorder he labeled "word blindness," which was characterized as an inability to read, although vision, intellect, and speech were normal. Following Kussmaul's contribution, several cases of reading difficulties acquired by adults due to cerebral lesions, mostly involving the angular gyri of the left hemisphere, were reported (see Hinshelwood, 1917, for a review). In one important case study published by Morgan (1896), a 14-year-old boy of normal intelligence had difficulty recalling letters of the alphabet. He also had difficulty recalling written words, which seemed to convey "no impression to this mind." Interestingly, the child appeared to have good memory for oral information. This case study was important because word blindness did not appear to occur as a result of a cerebral lesion. After Morgan's description of this condition, designated as a specific reading disability, research on memory was expanded to include children of normal intelligence who exhibited difficulties in reading. Hinshelwood's (1917) classic monograph presents a number of case studies describing reading disabilities in children of normal intelligence with memory problems. On the basis of these observations, Hinshelwood inferred that reading problems of these children were related to a "pathological condition of the visual memory center" (p. 21).

At the same time Hinshelwood's monograph appeared, a little-known text by Bronner (1917) reviewed case studies linking memory difficulties to children of normal intelligence. For example, consider Case 21:

> Henry J., 16 years old, was seen after he had been in court on several occasions. The mental examination showed that the boy was quite intelligent and in general capable, but had a very specialized defect. The striking feature of all the test work with this boy was the finding that he was far below his age in the matter of rote memory. When a series of numerals was presented to him auditorially, he could remember no more than four. His memory span for numerals presented visually was not much better...he succeeded here with five. Memory span for syllables was likewise poor...On the other hand when ideas were to be recalled, that is, where memory dealt with logical material, the results were good. (p. 120)

A majority of case studies reviewed in Bronner's text suggested that immediate (short-term) memory of children with reading disabilities was deficient and that remote (long-term) memory was intact. Bronner also noted that little about memory and its application to complex learning activities was known. For example, the author stated, "very many practic-ally important laws of memory have not yet been determined; those most firmly established concern themselves mainly with nonsense or other type of material quite unlike the activities of everyday life. In a common sense way we are aware that both immediate and remote memory are essential, that we need to remember what we see and hear . . . that to remember an idea is probably more useful in general, than to have a good memory for rote material, but a defect for the latter may be of great significance in some kinds of school work." (p. 110)

Researchers from the 1920s to the 1950s generally viewed reading difficul-ties as being associated with structural damage to portions of the brain that support visual memory (e.g., see Geschwind, 1962, for a review; also see Monroe, 1932). A contrasting position was provided by Orton (1925, 1937), who suggested that reading disorders were reflective of a neurological mat-urational lag resulting from a delayed lateral cerebral dominance for lan-guage. Orton described the phenomenon of a selective loss or diminished capacity to remember words as strephosymbolia (twisted symbols). Orton (1937) noted that "although these children show many more errors of a wide variety of kinds it is clear that their difficulty is not in hearing and not in speech mechanism . . . but in recalling words previously heard again or used in speech, and that one of the outstanding obstacles to such recall is *remem-bering* (emphasis added) all of the sounds in their proper order." (p. 147) In cases of visual memory, Orton stated that such children with reading dis-abilities have major difficulties in "recalling the printed word in terms of its spatial sequence of proper order in space." (p. 148) Thus, for Orton, reading disabled children's memory difficulties were seen as reflecting spatial se-quences in visual memory or temporal sequences in auditory memory. Although the conceptual foundation of much of Orton's research was chal-lenged in the 1970s (see Vellutino, 1979, for a review), much of the evidence for linking LD and memory processes was established from the earlier clinical studies of Morgan, Hinshelwood, and Orton. Today, reading diffi-culties are viewed primarily as language problems (e.g., Siegel, 2003), and memory difficulties are popularly conceptualized in terms of language pro-cesses (Siegel, 2003; Swanson & Siegel, 2001a).

It was not until the late 1960s and early 1970s that experimental (non-clinical) studies appeared comparing children with LD and nondisabled (NLD) children's performance on memory tasks. The majority of these studies focused on modality-specific memory processes (i.e., auditory vs visual memory) and cross-modality (e.g., visual recognition of auditorially presented information) instructional conditions, but they provided conflict-ing evidence. For example, in the area of visual memory, Conners *et al.*, (1969) compared children with LD and normally achieving children on their abilities to remember numbers presented to them on a dichotic listening task.

The results of their study were that children with LD did not differ from their NLD peers in short-term recall. In contrast, Bryan (1972) compared learning disabled and normally achieving children on a task that required them to recall a list of words presented by tape recorder and words presented by slide projector. Learning disabled and comparison samples performed better with the visual than with the auditory stimuli, but children with LD performed more poorly than the NLD children under both conditions.

Conflicting results were also found among studies investigating visual memory information-processing abilities of children with reading disabilities. Goyen and Lyle (1971, 1973) investigated young reading disabled students' (children under 8.5 years) recall of critical details of visual stimuli presented tachistoscopically for various exposure duration intervals. Their results showed that the students with reading disabilities did not recall as well as younger and older normal readers. In another study, Guthrie and Goldberg (1972) compared disabled and skilled readers on several tests designed to measure visual short-term memory (STM). In contrast to Goyen and Lyle, they found that the performance of children on visual memory subtests did not clearly differentiate the ability groups.

Conflicts in findings also emerged in cross-modality research. For example, Senf and Feshbach (1970) found differences between good and poor readers' memory on cross-modality presentation conditions. That is, students were compared on their recall of digits presented auditorially, visually, and audio-visually and retrieval responses were verbal or written. Samples included culturally deprived learning disabled and normal control readers of elementary and junior high school age. The sample with LD exhibited poor recall of stimuli organized into audiovisual pairs, which was attributed to problems of cross-modality matching. Older culturally deprived and normal children recalled the digits in audiovisual pairs more accurately than their younger counterparts, whereas older children with LD recalled no better than younger children with LD. The sample with LD also exhibited a higher prevalence of visual memory errors. The implication of this research was that some prerequisite skills of pairing visual and auditory stimuli had not developed in the children with LD, and the possession of these skills was essential for reading. In contrast to this study, Denckla and Rudel (1974) found that poor recall of children with LD was not related to visual encoding errors, but rather to temporal sequencing. Their results suggested that children who had difficulties in temporal sequencing would have difficulty recalling information from spatial tasks or tasks that required matching of serial and spatial stimuli (as in the Senf & Feshbach, 1970, study).

To summarize, the studies in the late 1960s and early 1970s, although contradictory, did establish a foundation for the study of LD in the context of memory. Children with LD experienced memory difficulties on laboratory tasks that required the sequencing of information presented visually and auditorially. Differences in results were most likely due to variations in how the ability groups were defined and selected. We now turn to a discussion of the more recent conceptualizations related to memory problems of children and adults with LD.

III. CONTEMPORARY RESEARCH

A. Overview

For the last 25 years, the study of memory in the area of LD has been strongly influenced by the hypothesis that variations in memory performance are rooted in the children's acquisition of mnemonic strategies. Strategies are deliberate, consciously applied procedures that aid in the storage and subsequent retrieval of information. Most strategy-training studies that include children with LD can trace their research framework back to earlier research on metacognition (to be discussed; Flavell, 1979) and/or research on production deficiencies (Flavell *et al.*, 1966). In this research, a distinction is made between the concepts of production and mediational deficiencies. Mediational deficiencies refer to the fact that children are unable to utilize a strategy efficiently. For example, young children may not spontaneously produce a potential mediator to process task requirements, but even if they did, they would fail to use it efficiently to direct their performance. On the other hand, production deficiencies suggest that children can be taught efficient strategies that they fail to produce spontaneously and that these taught strategies will direct and improve their performance. The assumption when applied to LD was that the more strategic information needed for effective memory performance, the more likely the task will be affected by the cognitive growth in the child.

The preeminence of this strategy hypothesis (various names have been used, e.g., passive learner) has been virtually synonymous with the study of memory in children with LD up to the late 1980s. Studies that focused on memory activities such as clustering, elaboration, and rehearsal were studies that were primarily motivated by this hypothesis. The emphasis in these studies was on teaching children with LD under various conditions or with different types of memory strategies how to remember presented material (e.g., see Scruggs & Mastroperi, 2000, for a review). In general, earlier studies showed that children with LD can be taught through direct instructions (e.g., Gelzheiser, 1984), modeling (e.g., Dawson *et al.*, 1980), and reinforcement (e.g., Bauer & Peller-Porth, 1990) to use some simple strategies that they do not produce spontaneously (e.g., Dallego & Moely, 1980). Further, the strategy hypothesis has been generalized into other areas besides memory, such as reading comprehension (e.g., Borkowski *et al.*, 1988; Wong & Jones, 1982), writing (e.g., Graham & Harris, 2003), mathematics (e.g., Geary, 2003, for a review; Montague, 1992), and problem solving (e.g., Borkowski *et al.*, 1989).

In the last few years, memory research has been moving in a different direction, toward an analysis of nonstrategic processes that are not necessarily consciously applied. Many of these studies are framed within Baddeley's multiple component model (to be discussed; Baddeley & Logie, 1999). The major motivation behind this movement has been that important aspects of memory performance are often disassociated with changes in mnemonic strategies. The most striking evidence has come from research that shows differences between children with and without LD after using an optimal strategy (a strategy shown advantageous in the majority of studies). Prior to reviewing the current focus of memory research, however, an understanding of research conducted in the late 1970s to the early 1990s is necessary. This review will be divided into two parts: (1) studies that parallel normal child development in memory and (2) studies that identify memory components in which children or adults with LD are deficient.

IV. PARALLELS TO NORMAL MEMORY DEVELOPMENT

There is some agreement among researchers that what we know about the memory of children with LD is somewhat paralleled by what we know about the differences between older and younger children's memory (e.g., Gathercole, 1998; Siegel & Ryan, 1989; Swanson, 1999a, b). Such parallels in performance do not mean that learning disabled children experience a lag in all memory processes or that faulty memory performance is primarily related to immature development. Rather, faulty memory performance reflects overt performance in some memory areas that is comparable to that of young children. Therefore, in most studies, memory performance of children with LD has been likened to that of younger NLD children even though the mechanisms that underlie learning disabled children's poor performance may not be the same as those that underlie the performance of younger children (De Jong, 1998; Swanson & Sachse-Lee, 2001a, b). The parallels between learning disabled vs NLD chronologically age-matched children and research on younger vs older NLD children are apparent in that performance differences: (1) emerge on tasks that require the use of cognitive strategies (e.g., rehearsal and organization); (2) emerge on effortful memory tasks, but not on tasks requiring automatic processing; (3) are influenced by the individual's knowledge base; and (4) are influenced by the individuals' awareness of their own memory processes (metacognition). We briefly review each of these parallels.

A large body of research suggests that remembering becomes easier in children with age because control processes become more automatic through repeated use (e.g., Gathercole, 1998; Pressley, 1994, for a review). Control processes in memory reflect choices as to which information to scan as well as choices of what and how to rehearse and/or organize information. Rehearsal refers to the conscious repetition of information, either vocally or subvocally, to enhance recall at a later time. Learning a telephone number or a street address illustrates the primary purpose of rehearsal. Other control processes include organization, such as ordering, classifying, or tagging information to facilitate retrieval, and mediation, such as comparing new items with information already in memory. Various organizational strategies studied (e.g., Borkowski *et al.*, 1988; Dallego & Moely, 1980; Krupski *et al.*, 1993; Lee & Obrzut, 1994) that have been linked to children with LD include:

1. Chunking: Grouping items so that each one brings to mind a complete series of items (e.g., grouping words into a sentence).
2. Clustering: Organizing items into categories (e.g., animals, furniture).
3. Mnemonics: Idiosyncratic methods for organizing information.
4. Coding: Varying the qualitative form of information (e.g., substituting pictures for words).

Studies (e.g., Scruggs & Mastropieri, 2000; Swanson, 1989) have also been directed to procedures to help children with LD mediate information such as:

1. Making use of preexisting associations, thereby eliminating the need for new ones.
2. Utilizing instructions: asking the student to mediate information verbally or through imagery, to aid in organization and retrieval.
3. Employing cuing: using verbal and imaginary cues to facilitate recall.

An excellent example of a study to enhance mediation of information in a learning-disabled student is provided by Mastropieri *et al.* (1985). Mastropieri *et al.* conducted two experiments in which adolescents with LD recalled the definitions of 14 vocabulary words according to either a pictorial mnemonic strategy (the "keyword" method) or a traditional instructional approach. The keyword method involved constructing an interactive visual image of the to-be-associated items. For example, to remember that the English word *carlin* means "old woman" via the keyword method, the learner is directed to the fact that the first part of carlin sounds like the familiar word *car*. Then the learner constructs an interactive image that relates a car and an old woman, such as an elderly woman driving an old car. The results of the first experiment (experimenter-generated mnemonic illustrations) and the second experiment (student-generated mnemonic images) indicated that the keyword strategy was substantially more effective than the traditional approach.

Perhaps one of the most significant studies in terms of bringing research in memory with learning disabled students into a developmental perspective was conducted by Tarver *et al.* (1976). In their first study, they compared learning disabled children of approximately 8 years of age to normal-achieving boys on a serial recall task of pictures that included central and incidental information. They found that the serial position curve of normals revealed the common primacy–recency effect (remembering the first and last presented items better than the middle items), whereas the performance of learning disabled children revealed a recency effect only. In the second study, they compared learning-disabled boys 10 and 13 years of age on the same tasks. They found that the 10- and 13-year-old learning disabled children exhibited both a primacy and recency effect for nonrehearsal and rehearsal conditions. For both studies, an analysis of central recall (children attend to specific items based on experimenter instructions) in the three age groups revealed a constant age-related increase in overall recall and in primacy (recalling the first few items presented) performance. The normal achievers recalled more information that was central to the task when compared to learning disabled children, whereas learning disabled children recalled more incidental information than did normal achievers. Thus, although learning disabled children were deficient in selective attention, their selective attention improved with age. These results were interpreted as reflecting a developmental lag. Learning disabled students were viewed as delayed in their utilization of the strategies for serial recall (verbal rehearsal) and selective attention.

Earlier studies that covered some of the same developmental themes as the Tarver et al. (1976) study were Torgesen and Goldman (1977), in which they investigated the role of rehearsal on serial and free recall performance; Swanson (1977), in which he investigated the role of primacy performance on the nonverbal serial recall of visual information; Bauer (1977), in which he investigated the role of rehearsal and serial recall; and Wong (1978), in which she investigated the effect of cued recall and organization on children with LD. For example, in the Bauer (1977) study, learning disabled and NLD children were required to free-recall as many words as possible from lists of monosyllabic nouns. Recall for each serial position showed that children with LD were deficient in the recall of items early in the list (primacy), but not recency performance. Primacy performance at that time was associated with rehearsal (Ornstein & Naus, 1978), as well as elaborative encoding (e.g., Bauer & Emhert, 1984). In contrast to research on primacy performance, studies that examined the recency effect have found that learning disabled are not unlike NLD youngsters, and that younger and older children are comparable in performance (e.g., Bauer, 1977; Swanson, 1977; Tarver et al., 1976). It is assumed that recall of the most recently presented items represents the encoding of information in an automatic (non-effortful) fashion (i.e., without the benefit of using deliberate mnemonic strategies; Swanson, 1983a).

The trend found with free-recall tasks in the majority of studies published in the late 1970s and early 1980s was that ability-group and age-related differences tend to be limited to items that occur at the beginning and middle serial positions and thus reflect strategy deficits, such as rehearsal. For example, when Torgesen and Goldman (1977) studied lip movements of children during a memorization task, children with LD were found to exhibit fewer lip movements than did the NLD students. To the extent that these lip movements reflect the quantity of rehearsal, these data support a rehearsal-deficiency hypothesis. Haines and Torgesen (1979) and others (e.g., Dawson et al., 1980; Koorland & Wolking, 1982) also reported that incentives could be used to increase the amount of rehearsal. Bauer and Emhert (1984) found that the difference between LD and NLD students is in the quality of the rehearsal rather than the quantity of rehearsal, per se.

In addition to the ability-group and age-related differences in the use of rehearsal, differences in the use of organizational strategies were also investigated. Ability-group and age-related differences have suggested that learning disabled and younger children are less likely to organize or take advantage of the organizational structure of items (Swanson & Rathgeber, 1986). Intervention strategies (i.e., directing children to sort or cluster items prior to recall) have in many cases lessened or eliminated ability-group differences (e.g., Dallego & Moley, 1980; however, see Gelzheiser et al., 1987; Krupski et al., 1993). Although learning disabled and younger children tend to make less use of semantic relationships inherent in the free-recall material (Swanson, 1986; Swanson & Rathgeber, 1986), when organizational instructions are provided, both learning disabled and younger children are capable of using a semantic organizational strategy with some degree of effectiveness (e.g., Lee & Obrzut, 1994).

Difficulties in categorization that children with LD experience during their attempts to memorize difficult material were highlighted in an earlier study by Gelzheiser et al. (1983). These authors recorded a brief statement made by a student with LD following an attempt to retain a passage containing four paragraphs about diamonds. The student reported that she could identify major themes of the story, but could not categorize the various pieces of information under major topics. She was able to abstract the essence of the story, but was unable to use her knowledge as a framework to organize the retention of the specific passage. This research suggests that students with

LD may be capable of abstracting categories of words from serially pre-sented lists of words, but they may not be able to chunk (i.e., categorize together) these words for use at later retrieval.

Cermak (1983) presented evidence to support this thesis in a study in which learning disabled and NLD children were asked to learn a list of 20 common nouns in five trials. The children were told to rehearse the words aloud during each trial. At the conclusion of each trial, they were asked to recall as many of the words as they could. Three types of word lists were used: a random list of unrelated words, a list containing five words from each of four categories randomly distributed within the list, and a list containing five words from each of four categories with the words presented in category blocks. The students with LD recalled fewer words than did NLD students following all types of presentation.

Swanson (1983b) arrived at a similar conclusion when he found that children with LD rarely reported the use of an organizational strategy when they were required to rehearse several items. He reasoned that because these children were capable of rehearsal, the problem was not an inability to rehearse, but instead a failure to perform elaborative processing of each word. Elaborative processing was defined as the processing that goes beyond the initial level of analysis to include more sophisticated features of the words and ultimately the comparison of these features with others in the list.

The research of the early 1970s to the late 1980s also suggested that a distinction can be made between the development of memory processes that are dependent upon overt conscious "effort" and those that are not (e.g., Ceci, 1984; Swanson, 1984a). Memory that results only after some conscious intent to remember is said to be effortful; that which occurs without intent or effort is considered to be automatic (e.g., Guttentag, 1984; Miller *et al.*, 1991). Effortful memory is assumed to be dependent upon the development of an available store of "cognitive resources." Thus, differences in memory performance between ability groups (learning disabled vs NLD) and age groups are presumed to be dependent upon effortful memory, or memory that is due to individual differences in the amount of cognitive resources available (e.g., Howe *et al.*, 1989; Swanson *et al.*, 1996). In contrast, auto-matic memory is assumed to be comparable between ability groups (e.g., Ceci, 1984). The empirical evidence for this effortful–automatic dis-tinction has emerged with respect to the presence or absence of individual differences across ages in measures of memory functioning (e.g., Harnishfe-ger & Bjorklund, 1994; Miller & Seier, 1994). The research on memory of children with LD directly parallels memory development in the area of effortful processing. For example, it has been shown that normally achieving children below the age of 9 years and children with LD perform quite poorly relative to older children or age-related counterparts on tasks such as free recall (e.g., Guttentag, 1984). Older children and NLD age-related counterparts have been found to utilize deliberate mnemonic strategies to remember information (e.g., see Pressley, 1994, for a review). An example of studies that suggest high-effort demands underlie ability group differences can be found when comparing LD and NLD children on verbal tasks (Swanson, 1984a). Swanson (1984a) conducted three experiments related to performance of students with LD on a word recall task, and found that recall is related to the amount of cognitive effort or the mental input that a limited-capacity system expends to produce a response. He found that readers with LD were inferior to NLD readers in their recall of materials that made high-effort demands. Furthermore, skilled readers accessed more usable information from semantic memory for enhancing recall than did learning disabled readers. In a subsequent study, Swanson (1986) found that disabled children were inferior in the quantity and internal coherence of information stored in semantic memory, as well as in the means by which it is accessed.

Another important parallel between LD research and age-related normal memory development comes from studies that focus on children's knowledge about the world (see Bjorklund *et al.*, 1992; Kee, 1994, for reviews). For example, familiarity with words, objects, and events permits people to integrate new information with what they already know (e.g., see Ericsson & Delaney, 1999; Ericsson & Kintsch, 1995, for a review). One way in which a knowledge base may affect memory performance is through its influence on the efficiency of mental operations performed upon the to-be-memorized items. Several authors (e.g., Bjorklund *et al.*, 1994) have suggested that, in some situations, an individual's knowledge base may mediate strategy use; that is, organizational and rehearsal strategies may be executed more spontaneously and efficiently contingent upon an individual's knowledge base. Indirect support for this view was provided by Torgesen and Houch (1980). Learning disabled students with severe STM problems, learning disabled youngsters with normal STM, and normal children were compared for their recall of material scaled for familiarity. Their results indicate that children who learn normally and children with LD who have no STM problems gained an advantage in recall as their familiarity with the items increased; that is, recall differences were reduced with less familiar material. This finding suggests that an individual's knowledge base (i.e., an individual's familiarity with material) influences the development or utilization of memory processes (also see Torgesen *et al.*, 1991, for an update on these findings).

Another important link between LD memory research and age-related research is the focus on children's thinking about cognitive strategies. Earlier, Brown (1975), summarized this development as "knowing how to know" and "knowing about knowing." Developmental improvement in remembering and the advantage accrued by NLD children is associated with the use of rehearsal, organization, and elaboration strategies to facilitate encoding and retrieval. Research (e.g., see Borkowski *et al.*, 1990; Borkowski & Muthukrishna, 1992; Hasselhorn, 1992) has focused on how and to what degree the effective use of effortful processes (e.g., cognitive strategies) relates to metacognition. Metacognition refers to knowledge of general cognitive strategies (e.g., rehearsal); awareness of one's own cognitive processes; the monitoring, evaluating, and regulating of those processes; and beliefs about factors that affect cognitive activities (see Pressley, 1994; Wong *et al.*, 2003). Differences in metacognition have been proposed as one source of individual differences in intelligence and memory (Brown & Campione, 1981; Borkowski & Muthukrishna, 1992). Comparisons of various groups of children (e.g., normal, mentally retarded, disabled) have revealed substantial differences in metacognitive knowledge, at least about memory and the memorial processes (see Campione *et al.*, 1982; Male, 1996, for a review). At present, what we know from the literature is that children between 4 and 12 years of age become progressively more aware of the person, task, and strategy variables that influence remembering (e.g., Pressley, 1994). Wong (1982) compared children with LD, normally achieving, and gifted children in their recall of prose. Her results indicated that when compared with the normal and gifted children, children with LD lacked self-checking skills and were less exhaustive in their selective search of retrieval cues. These results suggest that learning disabled children were less aware of efficient strategies related to prose recall.

As reviewed, there are some parallels between the performance of younger children and those of older children with LD. The performance of children with LD may reflect deficits and/or immature development. We will next turn our attention to the components and stages of processing that may underlie some of the memory problems of children with LD.

V. COMPONENTS AND STAGES OF INFORMATION PROCESSING

The majority of memory research, whether of developmental and/or instructional interest, draws from the information-processing literature, because this is the most influential model in cognitive psychology to date (see Anderson, 1990; Baddeley & Logie, 1999; Miyake, 2001; for a review). The central assumptions of the information-processing model are: (1) a number of operations and processing stages occur between a stimulus and a response, (2) the stimulus presentation initiates a sequence of stages, (3) each stage operates on the information available to it, (4) these operations transform the information in some manner, and (5) this new information is the input to the succeeding stage. In sum, the information-processing approach focuses on how input is transformed, reduced, elaborated, stored, retrieved, and used.

One popular means of explaining learning disabled students' cognitive performance is by drawing upon fundamental constructs that are inherent in most models of information processing. Three constructs are fundamental: (1) a constraint or structural component, akin to the hardware of a computer, which defines the parameters within which information can be processed at a particular stage (e.g., sensory storage, STM, working memory, long-term memory); (2) a strategy component, akin to the software of a computer system, which describes the operations of the various stages; and (3) an executive component, by which learners' activities (e.g., strategies) are overseen and monitored.

This multistore model views information as flowing through component stores in a well-regulated fashion, progressing from the *sensory register*, to *STM*, and finally to *long-term memory*. These stores can be differentiated in children's functioning by realizing that (1) STM has a limited capacity, and thus makes use of rehearsal and organizing mechanisms; (2) storage in long-term memory is mostly semantic; and (3) two critical determinants of forgetting in long-term memory are item displacement and interference, possibly as a result of a lack of retrieval strategy.

Briefly, the structural components are sensory, short-term, working, and long-term memory. Sensory memory refers to the initial representation of information that is available for processing for a maximum of 3 to 5 seconds; STM processes information between 3 and 7 seconds and is primarily concerned with storage, via rehearsal processes. Working memory also focuses on the storage of information as well as the active interpretation of newly presented information plus information from long-term memory, whereas long-term memory is a permanent storage with unlimited capacity. The executive component monitors and coordinates the functioning of the entire system. Some of this monitoring may be automatic, with little awareness on the individual's part, whereas other types of monitoring require effortful and conscious processing. These components will become clearer later when we discuss current research findings.

A. Sensory Register

Basic structural environmental information (e.g., visual auditory) is assumed first to enter the appropriate sensory register. Information in this initial store is thought to be a relatively complete copy of the physical stimulus that is available for further processing for a maximum of 3 to 5 seconds. An example of sensory registration for the visual modality is an image or icon. In a reading task, if an array of letters is presented on a computer screen and the child is then asked to press the appropriate key of the letters after a 30-sec delay between instructions, the child can correctly reproduce about six or seven letters. Incoming information from other modalities (auditory, kinesthetic) receives sensory registration, but less is known about their representation. For example, students who are presented a letter of the alphabet may produce a photographic trace that decays quickly, or they may physically scan the letter and transfer the information into an auditory (e.g., echo of sound) visual–linguistic (meaning) representation. In other words, information presented visually may be recorded into other modalities (e.g., the transfer of a visual image to the auditory–visual–linguistic store). In the reading process, each letter or word is scanned against information in long-term memory and the verbal name. This representation will facilitate transfer of information from the sensory register to a higher level of information processing. A common paradigm used to assess the processing of sensory information is recognition. The participant is asked to determine whether information that was presented briefly (i.e., millisecond) had occurred. The task may be simply "yes" or "no" to individual items, or may require selecting among a set of items. Common dependent measures are correct detection and response time (Rt's).

In general, research on the sensory register of children with LD suggests it is somewhat intact (see Aaron, 1993; Eden *et al.*, 1995; Lorsbach *et al.*, 1992; Santiago & Matos, 1994, for review). For example, Elbert (1984) has provided evidence that LD and non-learning disabled (NLD) students are comparable at the encoding stage of word recognition, but that children with LD require more time to conduct a memory search (see also Manis, 1985; Mazer *et al.*, 1983). Additional evidence that LD and NLD children are comparable at the recognition stage of information processing was provided by Lehman and Brady (1982). Using a release from proactive inhibition procedure (see Dempster & Cooney, 1982), Lehman and Brady found that reading-disabled and normal readers were comparable in their ability to encode word information (e.g., indicating whether a word was heard or seen and information concerning a word's category). However, reading-disabled children relied on smaller subword components in the decoding process than did normal readers.

Many accounts of poor recognition of quickly presented information by LD students has been attributed to attention deficits (see Hallahan & Reeve, 1980, for review)—although this conclusion has been questioned (see Samuels, 1987). For example, using a psychological technique free of memory confounds, McIntyre *et al.* (1978) reported a lower-than-normal span of attention in students identified as LD. Mazer *et al.* (1983) attributed the lower span of attention to a slower rate of information pickup from the sensory store. Despite the common assumption of differences between LD and NLD children in attention to visual and auditory stimulus, an earlier study by Bauer (1979a) argued that the attentional resources of the children with LD are adequate for performance on a variety of memory tasks. In other words, the residual differences are not great enough to account for the differences in memory performance. For example, LD and NLD children are comparable in their ability to recall orally presented sets of three letters or three words within 4 sec after presentation (Bauer, 1979a). Similarly, LD and NLD students are comparable in their ability to recognize letters and geometric shapes after a brief visual presentation when recognition is less than 300 msec after stimulus offset (Morrison *et al.*, 1977). In view of these findings, the retrieval of information from sensory storage is an important, although not a major, factor in the memory deficits exhibited in LD students (see Willows *et al.*, 1993, for a review).

B. Short-Term Memory

From the sensory register, information is transferred into the limited capacity STM. Short-term memories are retained as auditory–verbal linguistic representations (Atkinson & Shiffrin, 1968; Baddeley, 1986). Information lost in this memory is assumed to decay or disappear, but actual time of decay is longer than in the sensory register. Exact rate of decay of information cannot be estimated, because this component of memory is controlled by the subject. Using the example of a child recalling letters, the child may rehearse the letters by subvocally repeating them over and over. This is a control process that helps keep the letters in STM until either they are transferred to long-term memory or the information decays.

The primary measures used to assess STM are recall tasks that measure free recall or serial recall of items such as numbers, shapes, or words. Free recall tasks are those in which the subject recalls stimuli without regard to order immediately after auditory or visual presentation. In contrast, serial recall tasks require the subject to recall stimuli in the exact order in which they are presented. Variations of these tasks include probe recall and cued recall. In probe recall, the subject must recall particular elements within a sequence of stimuli; whereas, in cued recall, the subject is given a portion of previously presented stimuli asked to reproduce the remainder of the items. This measure has been employed to determine the extent to which recall may be prompted by appropriate cues, thus highlighting the difference between item accessibility (i.e., processing efficiency) and item availability (i.e., storage).

One major source of difficulty related to STM processing has been attributed to LD children's lack or inefficient use of a phonological code (sound representation within the child's mind). Hulme (1992) has reviewed several studies of subjects who performed in the retarded range of verbatim recall on sequences of verbal information. His analysis of the literature on LD students' memory performance deficits suggests that they represent the phonological features of language (also see Siegel, 2003). He suggests that LD children's memory problems relate to the acquisition of fluent word identification and word analysis skills.

Support for the notion of phonological coding errors comes from studies suggesting that good and poor readers differ in the extent to which they recall similar- and dissimilar-sounding names (Stanovich & Siegel, 1994). Several researchers have found that good and poor readers differ in the way they access phonological information in memory (see Siegel, 2003, for a review). An earlier seminal study by Shankweiler *et al.* (1979) compared the ability of superior, marginal, and poor second grade readers to recall rhyming and nonrhyming letter strings. The superior readers were found to have a greater deal of difficulty recalling the rhyming letter strings than the nonrhyming strings. Poor readers, however, appeared to perform comparably on rhyming and nonrhyming tasks. The authors suggested that the phonological confuseability created by the rhyming letters interfered with good readers' recall because these readers relied on phonological information to a greater degree than did poor readers.

Thus, an interaction is usually found in which poor readers perform better on "rhyming-word and similar letter-sounding tasks" because they have poor access to a phonological code (e.g., Shankweiler *et al.*, 1979; Siegel & Linder, 1984). That is, good readers recall more information for words or letters that have distinct sounds (e.g., mat vs book, A vs F) than words or letters that sound alike (mat vs cat, b vs d). In contrast, poor readers are more comparable in their recall of similar and dissimilar words or sounds than skilled readers. This finding suggests that good readers are disrupted when words or sounds are alike because they process information in terms of sound (phonological) units. In contrast, poor readers are not efficient in processing information into sound units (phonological codes) and, therefore, are not disrupted in performance if words or letters sound alike.

In a study by Johnson *et al.* (1987), 8- and 11-year-old good and poor readers of average and below-average intelligence were compared on their ability to recall strings of similar and dissimilar sounding letters. When a control was made of differences in memory span between ability groups, high- and low-IQ poor readers were comparable with their chronological age (CA) and reading-level matched controls in similarity effects; i.e., the study did not directly support the contention that difficulties in immediate memory are primarily due to difficulty with phonological coding. Some other contrasting studies (e.g., Sipe & Engle, 1986) have suggested that poor readers may be adequate in phonological coding, but show a fast decline in their ability to recall as the retention interval (time between item presentation and recall) is increased. Hall *et al.* (1983) also did not find consistent differences between good and poor readers on serial letter recall task. The author suggested that this task was more difficult for poor readers because it obscured phonological similarity effects, suggesting that the actual differences in access or use of phonological information in memory may be comparable between ability groups. Unfortunately, small sample sizes, differing degrees of task difficulty, and sampling differences make comparisons difficult across these studies.

Although information in STM can be represented in sound (phonological) units, it can also be represented semantically (Shulman, 1971). Research in the area of semantic coding (attaching meaning to information) appears more mixed than in the area of phonological processing. Waller (1976) suggested that both reading disabled and NLD children rely on semantic information for retention, but the disabled children appeared to rely on this type of memory to an even greater degree than do NLD subjects (also see Siegel, 1993). However, other studies have found semantic coding deficits in learning disabled children (e.g., Ceci *et al.*, 1980; Swanson, 1984a; Vellutino *et al.*, 1995). Dallego and Moely (1980) found that poor readers performed similarly to their peers on a free recall task when items were semantically cued. Dallego and Moely concluded that reading disabled subjects could use semantic cues in recalling information, but they had difficulty in the deliberate use of such strategies. In other words, learning disabled children were able to make use of semantic information, but did not take advantage of the semantic properties of information initially.

Perhaps the issue regarding whether phonological and semantic coding underlies STM deficits in learning-disabled children has to do with when and where the deficit in the memory system occurs. Some researchers embraced the notion that there are dual storages of memory and they have suggested that storage differs with regard to type of information coded (Conrad, 1964; Baddeley, 1976), with the phonological code utilized in short-term memory and a semantic code in long-term memory. Evidence of a phonological code use in long-term memory (Gruneberg & Sykes, 1969) and semantic information use in short-term memory (Shulman, 1971), however, suggests that simplistic views of short-term memory are unlikely. Some researchers argued for a connectionist model of information processing, whereby learning and memory occur over repeated associations (i.e., strength of activations) rather than in stages or storage compartments (Seidenberg, 1989). Such an activation model suggests that the focus on STM or long-term memory (LTM) storage is not as important as a memory system based on the strength of associations, whereby associations are built on phonetically, semantically, and/or visual–spatial information. Unfortunately, research on the interaction of phonological and semantic processes with reading disabled individuals is scarce (Swanson, 1984b; Waterman & Lewandowski, 1993).

Meta-Analysis.   Because STM is clearly the most widely researched area related to the cognitive processing problems of students with LD, a comprehensive meta-analysis (quantitative synthesis) was conducted comparing the performance of LD and NLD students on STM tasks (O'Shaughnessy & Swanson, 1998). The analysis covered articles published during a 20-year period. To be included in the analysis, each study must meet the following criteria: (1) It must directly compare learning disabled readers with average readers, as identified on a standardized reading measure, on at least one short-term measure; (2) it must report standardized reading scores which indicate that learning disabled students are at least 1 year below grade level; and (3) it must report intelligence scores for learning disabled students which are in the average range (85 to 115). Although the search resulted in approximately 155 articles on immediate memory and LD, only 38 studies met the criteria for inclusion (24.5%). Effect sizes (ESs) were computed for each experiment; effect size (ES) was defined as the mean memory score of the learning disabled group minus the mean memory score of the NLD group divided by the pooled standard deviation of both groups and then corrected for sample size. Negative values for ES represent poorer immediate memory performance in the learning disabled group. The interpretation of ES is similar to a z-score if one assumes the data are normally distributed. For comparisons, an ES magnitude of 0.20, in absolute value, is considered small, 0.50 is moderate, and 0.80 is considered a large ES (Cohen, 1988).

Based on a review of the studies included in this analysis, two broad categories were developed to organize the results: studies that use (1) verbal stimuli and/or (2) nonverbal stimuli. In addition, the following subcategories were developed to organize each of the broad categories: free recall and serial recall memory tasks, with and without instruction in mnemonic strategies, auditory and visual presentation, and age (7–8 years, 9–11 years, 12–13 years, 14–17 years, and 18 years and older). The analysis of each category/subcategory was performed separately, but in each case the same analytic method was used. The average sample size per study was 36 (range 8 to 66; *n* = 1354) for students with LD, and 42 (range 8 to 88; *n* = 1600) for average students. Within the learning disabled group of subjects, the average age was 11 years with 240 females and 894 males. Within the NLD group, the average age was 11 with 382 females and 949 males. The majority of studies involved 4th, 5th, and 6th grade students.

The important findings of the synthesis were as follows:

1. The learning disabled group performed poorly on tasks requiring memorization of verbal information in comparison to the NLD group. More specifically, verbal memory tasks yielded an overall mean ES of −0.68, which indicates that 75.17% of students in the average reading group performed above the mean of the reading disabled group.
2. Memory tasks that employed stimuli that could not easily be named, such as abstract shapes, did not produce large differences between good and poor readers (ES = −0.15). In this case, only 55.96% of the NLD group performed above the mean of the learning disabled group.

3. Memory tasks requiring learning disabled readers to recall exact sequences of verbal stimuli, such as words or digits, immediately after a series was presented yielded a much greater overall mean ES (ES = −0.80) than nonverbal serial recall tasks (ES = −0.17). Thus, reading-disabled students' serial recall performance with verbal material was over three-quarters of a standard deviation below that of average readers compared to their memory performance with nonverbal stimuli, which was less than one-quarter of a standard deviation below that of average readers.

4. The overall mean ES for studies which provided instructions in mnemonic strategies (e.g., rehearsal and sorting items into groups) prior to recall and used verbal stimuli is −0.54; whereas, the overall mean ES for studies using verbal stimuli, but not providing instructions to students about how to use mnemonic strategies, is −0.71. This indicates that although the memory performance of students who are reading disabled improved with training in mnemonic strategies, the memory performance of 70.5% of average readers is still above the mean of the reading disabled group.

5. Memory tasks that involved the auditory presentation of verbal stimuli resulted in an overall mean ES of −0.70, while those that involved a visual presentation of verbal stimuli resulted in an overall mean ES of −0.66. In terms of percentiles, 75.8 and 74.5% of normally achieving students scored above the mean of the reading disabled group, respectively. Thus, the inferior verbal memory performance of reading disabled students appears unrelated to the modality in which a stimulus is received.

6. Memory tasks that involved the visual presentation of nonverbal stimuli, such as abstract shapes, resulted in an overall mean ES of −0.15. This can be interpreted as a small difference between the average and learning disabled reading groups.

In summary, this quantitative analysis of the literature indicates that children and adults with LD are inferior to their counterparts on measures of STM. Most critically, students with LD are at a distinct disadvantage compared to their normal-achieving peers when they are required to memorize verbal information. Students with LD have difficulty remembering familiar items such as letters, words, and numbers, and unfamiliar items such as abstract shapes that can be named. A brief description of two of the individual studies supporting this conclusion follows.

Bauer and Peller-Porth (1990) investigated the effects of incentive on verbal free recall performance. Children with and without LD were matched on age, gender, IQ, and race. The mean age of participants was 9.87 years. Children were classified as learning disabled based on a discrepancy between expected and actual academic achievement (i.e., in spite of normal IQs, children with LD were 2 to 3 years behind their expected reading grade level). The stimuli and procedure used were similar to those already described in Bauer (1979b); however, 4 to 5 days after participating in a first free recall session, the same children were tested again on immediate free recall with incentives. Although incentives improved the recall of both groups to a similar degree, overall recall was significantly higher by students without LD than by students with LD (ES = −1.01). In addition, the learning disabled group displayed lower recall of the first few words which, again, suggests deficient memorization strategies, such as rehearsal. In contrast, recall of the last few words was similar between disabled and NLD children, indicating that attention and immediate memory are comparable.

Siegel and Linder (1984) compared the STM performance of 45 children with a learning disability in reading and 89 children who were normally achieving in school. The children, aged 7 to 13 years, were administered several verbal serial recall tasks involving visual or auditory presentation of rhyming and nonrhyming letters. In this study, reading disability was defined as a Wide Range Achievement Test reading score below the 21st percentile. The mean reading percentile for the normally achieving children was 74.9, that is, in the average range. In addition, to be included in the study, a child had to achieve a Peabody Picture Vocabulary Test (PPVT) score of at least 80. The results of this study indicated that the youngest children (7 to 8 years) with a reading disability did not show any difference between recall of nonrhyming letters (e.g., H, K, L, Q) and rhyming letters (e.g., B, C, D, G), whereas, the normally achieving children of the same age found the rhyming items more difficult to remember than the nonrhyming ones. It was postulated that the poorer performance by normally achieving children is due to their use of a speech-based coding system in STM that presents greater difficulty with similar than nonsimilar sounds. In contrast, the older reading disabled children (9 to 13 years), similar to their normally achieving peers, exhibited significantly poorer recall of rhyming than nonrhyming letters. The authors concluded that a deficiency in phonological coding may characterize younger children with LD; whereas older children with LD appear to be using a speech-based coding system but have a more general deficit in STM. The ESs for this study were collapsed across age groups because data were not available to calculate separate ESs for each group. The overall mean ES for this study was −1.50 (range −1.22 to −1.84), indicating that overall the children with LD displayed inferior memory performances on verbal serial recall tasks compared to their normally achieving counterparts.

Summary.   The most important conclusion to be drawn from the literature review on STM is that learning disabled readers, as a group, are distinctly disadvantaged compared to their peers who are average readers when they are required to memorize verbal information. Students who are learning disabled in reading have difficulty remembering familiar items such as letters, words, and numbers and unfamiliar items that can easily be named and stored phonetically in memory. Moreover, when a task demands that verbal information be recalled in sequential order, the memory performance of students with LD declines even further. Because skillful reading involves processing ordered information (i.e., words are written from left to right and composed of specific sequences of letters), it seems likely that memory deficits could play a role in reading disabilities. For example, beginning readers must obtain the sounds of words from their written representations. These print-to-sound codes must be stored in memory in order and then blended together, while simultaneously searching LTM for a word that matches the string of sounds. Because low verbal materials (e.g., geometric shapes) produce small differences between skilled and learning-disabled readers in recall, the memory deficits of LD readers do not appear to involve general memory ability.

C. Long-Term Memory

The amount of information as well as the form of information transferred to LTM is primarily a function of control processes (e.g., rehearsal). LTM is a permanent storage of information of unlimited capacity. How information is stored is determined by the uses of links, associations, and general organizational plans. Information stored in LTM is primarily semantic. Forgetting occurs because of item decay (loss of information) or interference.

In comparison to the volume of research on STM processes, research on LD children's LTM is meager; however, the available research provides considerable support for the assertion that storage and retrieval problems are primary sources of individual differences in LTM performance (e.g., Swanson & Sachse-Lee, 2001b). Concerning retrieving information from LTM, children with LD can use organized strategies for selecting retrieval cues (Wong, 1982) and different word attributes (e.g., graphophonic, syntactic, semantic) to guide retrieval (Blumenthal, 1980); however, they appear to select less efficient strategies, conduct a less exhaustive search for retrieval cues, and lack self-checking skills in the selection of retrieval cues (Wong, 1982). Swanson (1984b, 1987) also provided evidence suggesting that LTM deficits may arise from failure to integrate visual and verbal memory traces of visually presented stimuli at the time of storage or retrieval. His findings suggested that semantic memory limitations underlie LD children's failure to integrate verbal and visual codes. Ceci *et al.* (1980) presented data that suggested separate pathways for auditory and visual inputs to the semantic memory system and that children with LD may have impairment in one or both of these pathways. For children with visual and auditory impairments, the recall deficit arises in both storage and retrieval. When only one modality is impaired, the LTM deficit is hypothesized to arise at the time of storage. Furthermore, semantic orienting tasks were found to ameliorate the recall deficits of the children with single modality impairments but not those with impairments in both visual and verbal modalities (Ceci *et al.*, 1980; Experiment 2).

Some earlier reviews (e.g., see Worden, 1986) have suggested that LD children's LTM is intact, but the strategies necessary to gain access to this information are impaired. This notion has been challenged, and evidence suggests that LD children's LTM for tasks that require semantic processing is clearly deficient when compared with that of NLD peers (Howe *et al.*, 1989; Swanson *et al.*, 1996). For example, Brainerd and his colleagues undertook a series of analyses to investigate the development of LTM processes in children with LD and normally achieving children (see Brainerd & Reyna, 1991, for a review). For example, Howe *et al.* (1989) reported that NLD children exhibited better recall when the to-be-remembered items belonged to taxonomic categories than when the to-be-remembered items are unrelated. However, recall by children with LD was not greatly enhanced when the to-be-remembered items are taxonomically related. Both learning-disabled and NLD children exhibit better cued recall relative to free recall. Although children with LD appear to derive some benefit from cued recall procedures, it is not nearly as great as that exhibited by NLD children. Additional experiments reported in Brainerd *et al.* (1990) indicate that children with LD exhibit higher rates of storage failure than do NLD children, regardless of whether the to-be-learned information is taxonomically related or not.

In a review of several studies, Brainerd and Reyna (1991) suggest that children with LD (1) may have generalized cognitive difficulties and (2) that cognitive difficulties are larger on the acquisition side of the learning process than on the forgetting side. That is, children with LD have more difficulty establishing new memory traces relative to retaining memory traces once they have been acquired. An important implication of this work is that although much of the difference between children with LD and NLD children in learning declarative information can be ameliorated, children with LD exhibit slightly higher rates of forgetting (via storage failure). Procedures for mitigating storage failure remain the subject of future research (see Swanson, 2000, for a study on this issue).

Taken as a whole, the results reviewed here suggest that the processes involved in entering a memory trace into the long-term store are important sources of ability group differences in children's long-term recall. Research to discover methods for remediating these deficits is certainly warranted. More direct research linking deficits in memory performance to mechanism in LTM is provided in the section on research on working memory (WM). Working memory is considered an active component of LTM (Baddeley & Logie, 1999).

D. Working Memory

Current perspectives on the study of memory in learning disabled samples focus on WM (e.g., Bull et al., 1999; Chiappe et al., 2000; De Beni et al., 1998; Swanson, 1999b). Before this research is reviewed, a brief overview of the most popular model is in order. The tripartite model by Baddeley (Baddeley, 1986; Baddeley & Logie, 1999) views WM as comprising a central executive controlling system that interacts with a set of two subsidiary storage systems: the speech-based phonological loop and the visual–spatial sketch pad. The phonological loop is responsible for the temporary storage of verbal information; items are held within a phonological store of limited duration, maintained through the process of subvocal articulation. The visual–spatial sketchpad is responsible for the storage of visual–spatial information over brief periods and plays a key role in the generation and manipulation of mental images. The central executive is involved in the control and regulation of the WM system. According to Baddeley and Logie (1999), it coordinates the two subordinate systems, focusing and switching attention, in addition to activating representations within LTM. Correlates in the neuropsychological literature complement the tripartite structure, showing functional independence among the three systems (e.g., Joindes, 2000).

How does this WM formulation help us understand LD better than the concept of STM? First, it suggests that strategies play a smaller role in learning and memory than previously thought. This is an important point because some studies do show that performance deficits of children with LD are not related to rehearsal, per se (e.g., Swanson, 1983a,b). Second, the idea of a WM system is useful because it is viewed as an active memory system directed by a central executive. This is important because the central executive can become a focus of instruction and influence on academic performance. Finally, and most importantly, WM processes are strongly related to achievement (e.g., Daneman & Merikle, 1996) and less strongly to STM (Daneman & Carpenter, 1980; Engle et al., 1992).

We will briefly review the psychological evidence on those components of WM that underlie LD.

Executive System

There are several cognitive activities that have been assigned to the central executive (see Miyake et al., 2000, for a review). These include controlling verbal and visual–spatial memory systems, control of encoding and retrieval strategies, attention-switching during manipulation of material held in the verbal and visual–spatial systems, suppressing irrelevant information, LTM knowledge retrieval, and so on (e.g., Baddeley, 1996). Several of these activities have been reduced to three functions: (1) updating and monitoring of working memory representations, (2) inhibition of irrelevant responses, and (3) shifting between mental sets (Miyake et al., 2000). The research appears to support the notion that children with LD suffer from deficient skills in two processes of the executive system: the suppression of irrelevant information and updating.

Suppression of irrelevant information. One activity related to the central executive that has been implicated as deficient in children with LD is their ability to suppress irrelevant information under high processing demand conditions (Chiappe *et al.*, 2000; De Beni *et al.*, 1998; Swanson &Cochran, 1991). These studies have investigated whether children with LD had greater trade-offs and weaker inhibition strategies than did average achievers on divided attention tasks. For example, Swanson designed three experiments to reflect attentional demands on both the verbal and visual–spatial systems. In one of the experiments (Swanson, 1993b, Exp. 1), a concurrent memory task, adapted from Baddeley (Baddeley *et al.*, 1984), was administered to LD and skilled readers. The task required subjects to remember digit strings (e.g., 9, 4, 1, 7, 5, 2) while they concurrently sorted blank cards, cards with pictures of nonverbal shapes, and cards with pictures of items that fit into semantic categories (e.g., vehicles—car, bus, truck; clothing—dress, socks, belt). Demands on the central executive capacity system were manipulated through the level of difficulty (three- vs six-digit strings) and type of sorting required (nonverbal shapes, semantic categories, blank cards). The results showed that LD readers could perform comparably to chronological age (CA)-matched peers on verbal and visual–spatial sorting conditions that involved low demands (i.e., three-digit strings), and that only when the coordination of tasks became more difficult (e.g., six digit strings) did ability-group differences emerge. More important, the results for the high memory load condition indicated less recall for LD readers than CA-matched (and achievement-matched) peers during both verbal and non-verbal sorting. Because recall performance was not restricted to a particular storage system (i.e., verbal storage), one can infer that processes other than a language-specific system accounted for the results.

LD children's selective attention to word features within and across the cerebral hemispheres has also been explored. For example, Swanson and Cochran (1991) compared 10-year-old average achieving children and same-aged peers with LD on a dichotic-listening task. Participants were asked to recall words organized by semantic (e.g., red, black, green, orange), phono-logical (e.g., sit, pit, hit), and orthographic (e.g., sun, same, seal, soft) features presented to either the left or right ear. The study included two experiments. Experiment 1 compared free recall with different orienting instructions to word lists. For example, in the orienting condition, children were told about the organizational structure of the words to be presented, such as to remember all of the words heard, "but to specifically remember words that go with _____" (e.g., colors—semantic feature orientation) or "words that rhyme with _____" (e.g., it—phonological feature orientation) or "words that start with the letter _____" (e.g., s—orthographic feature orientation). For the nonorienting condition, children were told to remember all words, but no mention was made of the distinctive organizational features of the words. Experiment 2 extended Exp. 1 by implementing a cued recall condition. In both experiments, children were told they would hear someone talking through a set of earphones, but that they should only pay attention to what was said in one of the ears (i.e., the targeted ear). The children were told that when they stopped hearing the information in both ears, they were to tell the experimenter all the words they could remember.

In both experiments, NLD children had higher levels of targeted and nontargeted recall compared to children with LD. More important, ability-group differences emerged in how specific word features were selectively attended to. The selective attention index focused on the targeted words in comparison to the background words (targeted word recall minus background word recall from other lists *within* the targeted ear), as well as background items in the contra-lateral ear. Regardless of word features, whether competing word features were presented (within-ear or across-ear conditions), or whether retrieval conditions were cued or noncued, LD readers' selective attention scores were smaller (the difference score between targeted items and nontargeted items was closer to zero) than those of NLD readers. Thus, when compared with LD children, NLD children were more likely to ignore irrelevant information in the competing conditions. Taken together, the results of this study, as well as those of three earlier dichotic listening studies (Swanson, 1986), suggest that children with LD have difficulties in inhibiting irrelevant information, regardless of the type of word features, retrieval conditions, or ear presentation.

Updating. Several studies (e.g., Swanson, 1994; Swanson & Ashbaker, 2000; Swanson et al., 1996; Swanson & Sachse-Lee, 2001b) on executive processing have included tasks that follow the format of Daneman and Carpenter's Sentence Span measure, a task strongly related to student achievement (see Daneman & Merikle, 1996, for a review). The format of the tasks requires simultaneous juggling of storage and processing requirements. For example, in the reading span task by Daneman and Carpenter (1980), participants are required to read sentences and verify their truthfulness (processing requirement) while trying to remember the last word of each sentence (storage requirement). These studies have consistently found LD readers to be more deficient than skilled readers in WM performance using this task format, which taps central executive processes related to "updating" (Miyake *et al.*, 2000). Updating requires monitoring and coding of information for relevance to the task at hand, and then appropriately revising items held in WM.

A cross-sectional study (Swanson, 2003) compared skilled readers and LD readers across four age groups (7, 10, 13, 20) on phonological, semantic, and visual–spatial WM measures administered under conditions referred to in Swanson *et al.* (1996): initial (no probes or cues), gain (cues that bring performance to an asymptotic level), and maintenance conditions (asymptotic conditions without cues). The results clearly showed that the LD readers had less WM recall than skilled readers for all task conditions, tasks that involved the processing of phonological, visual–spatial, and semantic information. Further, the study provided no evidence that LD readers' WM skills "catch up" with those of skilled readers as they age, suggesting that a deficit model rather than a developmental lag model best captures such readers' age-related performance. Further studies (Swanson, 1992; Swanson *et al.*, 1996) have found evidence of domain general processing deficits in children and adults with LD, suggestive of executive system involvement.

In summary, a number of studies show that some participants with LD matched to NLD participants on IQ are deficient on tasks that measure specific components of executive processing. Those components of the executive system deficient in individuals with LD are related to updating (Siegel & Ryan, 1989; Swanson *et al.*, 1996) and the inhibition of irrelevant responses (Chiappe *et al.*, 2000). Some alternative explanations to these findings on executive processing [(Swanson & Siegel, 2001), e.g., deficits are due to ADHD, domain specific knowledge, and/or low-order processes (such as phonological coding)] have been addressed elsewhere (see Swanson & Siegel, 2001a, for a review of studies). For example, it has been argued that WM deficits are secondary to problems in achievement or phonological memory (verbal STM). However, participants with LD have significantly lower WM when compared to NLD participants when the influence of reading and verbal STM skills have been statistically controlled in the analysis (Swanson, 1999b; Swanson *et al.*, 1996).

Phonological Loop

In Baddeley's model (1986), the phonological loop is specialized for the retention of verbal information over short periods of time. It is composed of both a phonological store, which holds information in phonological form, and a rehearsal process, which serves to maintain representations in the phonological store (see Baddeley *et al.*, Gathercole, & 1998, for an extensive review). A substantial number of studies support the notion that children with LD experience memory deficits in processes related to the phonological loop (see Siegel, 1993, for a review of studies showing deficits in LD readers related to phonological representations). This difficulty in forming and accessing phonological representations impairs the ability to retrieve verbal information. Before reviewing the evidence on verbal memory, the overlap and distinctions between verbal STM and verbal WM must be addressed.

Are verbal STM deficits found in children with LD synonymous with deficits in verbal WM? We tested whether the operations related to STM and WM operated independently of one another. A study by Swanson and Ashbaker (2000) compared LD and skilled readers and younger achievement-matched children on a battery of WM and STM tests to assess executive and phonological processing. Measures of the executive system were modeled after Daneman and Carpenter's (1980) WM tasks (tasks demanding the coordination of both processing and storage), whereas measures of the phonological system included those that related to articulation speed, digit span, and word span. The Swanson and Ashbaker (2000) study yielded two important results. First, although the LD reading group was inferior to skilled readers in WM, verbal STM, and articulation speed, the differences in verbal STM and WM revealed little relation with articulation speed. That is, reading-related differences on WM and STM measures remained when articulation speed was partialed from the analysis. These reading-group differences were pervasive across verbal and visual–spatial WM tasks, even when the influence of verbal STM was removed, suggesting that reading-group differences are domain general. Second, WM tasks and verbal STM tasks contributed unique, or independent, variance to word recognition and reading comprehension beyond articulation speed. These results are consistent with those of Daneman and Carpenter (1980) and others (e.g., Engle *et al.*, 1999), who have argued that verbal STM tasks and WM tasks are inherently different, and while phonological coding might be important to recall in STM, it may not be a critical factor in WM tasks.

The findings from Swanson and Ashbaker's study are consistent with early work on LD samples (Swanson, 1994; Swanson & Berninger, 1995). In a 1994 study, Swanson tested whether STM and WM contributed unique variance to academic achievement in children and adults with LD. Swanson found that STM and WM tasks loaded on different factors. Further, these two factors both contributed unique variance to reading and mathematics performance. A study by Swanson and Berninger (1995) also examined potential differences between STM and WM by testing whether STM and WM accounted for different cognitive profiles in LD readers. Swanson and Berninger used a double dissociation design to compare children deficient in reading comprehension (based on scores from the Passage Comprehension subtest of the Woodcock Reading Mastery Test, and/or word recognition (based on scores from the Word Identification subtest of the Woodcock Reading Mastery Test) on WM and phonological STM measures. Participants were divided into four ability groups: High Comprehension/High Word Recognition, Low Comprehension/High Word Recognition, High Comprehension/Low Word Recognition, and Low Comprehension/Low Word Recognition. The results were straightforward: WM measures were related primarily to reading comprehension, whereas phonological STM measures were related primarily to reading recognition. Most critically, because no significant interaction emerged, the results further indicated that the co-morbid group (children low in both comprehension and word recognition) had combined memory deficits. That is, WM deficits were reflective of the poor comprehension-only group and STM deficits were reflective of the poor recognition-only group.

What is the distinction between STM and WM? WM tasks require the active monitoring of events. Monitoring of events within memory is distinguishable from simple attention to stimuli held in STM. There are many mnemonic situations in which a stimulus in memory is attended to and the other stimuli exist as a background—that is, they are not the center of current awareness. These situations, in our opinion, do not challenge monitoring. Monitoring within WM implies attention to the stimulus that is currently under consideration together with active consideration (i.e., attention) of several other stimuli whose current status is essential for the decision to be made. Results from our lab have suggested that the tasks differ in subtle ways. Simply stated, some children with LD perform poorly on tasks that require accurate and/or speedy recognition/recall of letter and number strings or real words and pseudowords. Tasks, such as these, which have a "read in and read out" quality to them (i.e., place few demands on LTM to infer or transform the information) reflect STM. One common link among these tasks is the ability to store and/or access the sound structure of language (phonological processing). However, some children with LD also do poorly on tasks that place demands on attentional capacity, a characteristic of WM tasks.

In summary, there is abundant evidence that participants with LD suffer deficits in STM, a substrate of the phonological system. A substrate of this system may also contribute to problems in verbal WM that are independent of problems in verbal STM. In addition, these problems in verbal WM are not removed by partialing out the influence of verbal articulation speed, reading comprehension, verbal STM, or IQ scores (see Swanson & Siegel, 2001b, for a review).

Visual–Spatial Sketchpad

In Baddeley's model (1986; Baddeley & Logie, 1999), the visual–spatial sketchpad is specialized for the processing and storage of visual material, spatial material, or both, and for linguistic information that can be recoded into imaginable forms. The literature linking LD to visual–spatial memory deficits is mixed. For example, several studies in the STM literature suggest that learning-disabled children's visual STM is intact (see O'Shaughnessy & Swanson, 1998, for a comprehensive review). Some studies have found that visual–spatial WM in students with LD is intact when compared with their same-age counterparts (e.g., Swanson *et al.*, 1996, Exp. 1), whereas others suggest problems in various visual–spatial tasks (Swanson *et al.*, 1996, Exp. 2). Most studies indicate, however, greater problems in performance are more likely to occur on verbal than visual–spatial WM tasks. For example, Swanson *et al.* (1999) found by partialing out the influence of verbal IQ via regression analysis that students with reading disabilities were inferior in performance to slow learners (i.e., garden variety poor readers) on visual–spatial and verbal WM measures. That is, although children with a specific reading disability demonstrated a greater deficit on the verbal WM task than on the visual–spatial WM task, performance on both types of tasks was inferior to other poor learning groups when verbal IQ was statistically controlled.

In summary, the evidence for whether children with LD have any particular advantage on visual–spatial WM tasks, when compared to their normal-achieving counterparts, appears to fluctuate with processing demands. If relatively low-capacity demands are placed on processing, then a clear advantage in visual–spatial WM performance when compared to verbal WM performance emerges for children with LD. On the other hand, when high demands (maximal performance) are placed on processing, no verbal vs visual–spatial WM advantage emerges. The reader is referred to Swanson (2000), who proposed a model that may account for these mixed findings.

Swanson and Siegel (2001a, b) completed a review of the literature on the relationship between WM and LD. Three main conclusions are drawn from this review:

1. Individuals with LD have smaller general working-memory capacity than their normal achieving counterparts and this capacity deficit is *not* entirely specific to their academic disability (i.e., reading or math) or intelligence. This is because problems in WM capacity remained for individuals with LD when compared to their counterparts after achievement and psychometric IQ were partialed out or controlled in the statistical analysis.
2. Individuals with LD suffer WM deficits related to isolated components of the phonological and executive system. Difficulties related to the phonological loop are related to the sequential recall of letters, numbers, real words, and pseudo words whereas problems in executive processing relate to monitoring resources (decisions related to the allocation of attention to

the stimulus under consideration together with the active consideration of several other stimuli whose current status is essential for successfully completing the task) and interference (a competing memory trace that draws away from the targeted memory trace).

3. In general, both the executive system and the phonological loop predict performance for complex academic tasks (e.g., reading comprehension) and basic skills (e.g., calculation).

The review by Swanson and Siegel concludes by suggesting that constraints in specific components of working-memory underlie LD. It is further suggested that individuals with LD perform well in some academic domains or on specific cognitive tasks because (a) those domains or tasks do *not* place heavy demands on WM operations, and/or (b) they compensate for WM limitations by increasing domain-specific knowledge and/or their reliance on environmental support.

E. Everyday Memory

Although a consistent finding in the literature is that children with LD suffer deficiencies on verbal memory tasks as well as complex tasks that exceed the processing capacity of WM, conclusions are open to question because most of the findings are related to laboratory tasks. Thus, we have little understanding of how the memory of children and adults with LD operates in everyday life. Only two studies were identified in the memory literature that linked laboratory measures of memory to everyday cognition in children with LD.

Swanson, Reffel, and Trahan (1990) assessed naturalistic memory of children with LD in three experiments. In Experiment 1, 10-year-old readers with and without LD were compared on their recall of common objects and events, such as recall name of their kindergarten teacher, items on a telephone and a penny, as well as information related to the 1986 space shuttle disaster. (These children had watched the Space Shuttle Disaster 2 years earlier on television in a classroom setting.) Also studied, via questionnaire, was the relationship between the children's memory and their strategies for recalling activities of their daily life.

There were three important findings when the ability groups were compared. First, recall differences on the coin task (recalling information on a penny) indicated that children with LD are poorer than are skilled readers in their recall of common visual and verbal information. Second, children with LD are less likely to remember facts about a consequential event (e.g., date of the space shuttle disaster) or facts that include their earlier experiences in school (e.g., name of their kindergarten teacher). Finally, the results from the questionnaire suggest that LD readers are less likely to report using an external memory aid (e.g., write a note to themselves) so they will remember information than are skilled readers.

Experiment 2 sought to better understand the relationship between everyday memory and reading ability with a group of adolescents (15- and 16-year-olds). Researchers substituted a number of tasks from Experiment 1. The array of questions about the 1986 space shuttle disaster was expanded to better assess the scope of adolescents' recall for consequential events. Further, in Experiment 2, these adolescents were asked to recall the presidents of the United States in their correct ordinal position according to their term of office.

In this study, adolescents with LD were poorer in recall across the majority of tasks than readers without LD. But what was unclear was whether poor recall performance in adolescents with LD was related to *memory storage* (item availability) or difficulty *accessing* certain types of information. This issue was addressed in Experiment 3. Cuing procedures were implemented for the coin, presidential, and space shuttle tasks. The results of Experiment 3 indicated that learning disabled readers were comparable to CA controls in the recall of common objects (coins) and consequential events (shuttle task), and the serial recall of some LTM information (presidents). When the results of Experiment 3 are combined with those of Experiment 2, they indicate that storage of everyday information in adolescents with LD is comparable to CA-matched skill readers on some tasks, suggesting that memory difficulties were related to access.

A study by McNamara and Wong (2003) compared 11-year-old children with and without LD on their recall of complex academic information and information encountered in children's everyday lives. As the researchers were interested in WM, children with LD were screened to include those with poor verbal WM skills. The academic recall measures included a sentence listening span test, a rhyming words WM test, and a visual matrix WM task. The everyday WM tasks included recall of an experienced event (a dance workshop), recall of an everyday procedure (checking a book out of the school library), and recall of common objects (information on the face of a coin, the components of a telephone, and the features of a McDonald's sign). Additionally, children's cued recall of all the tasks was measured. Compared to children without LD, those children with LD performed poorly on both the academic recall tasks and the everyday recall tasks. Results support the notion that some students with LD may have WM problems that affect their performance on tasks beyond reading. Further, results of the cued recall condition showed that the availability of cues decreased significantly the ability-group differences on many of the academic and everyday tasks. This result suggests further that students with LD do not use retrieval strategies effectively and that some students with LD may have a production deficiency that affects retrieval of previously encoded information.

Taken together, the results of this type of research suggest that memory deficits in children with LD are pervasive across everyday and laboratory measures. Also, results of research by Swanson *et al.* (1990) suggest that these memory difficulties for everyday tasks may be more pervasive at a younger age but may diminish for adolescents.

VI. MEMORY RESEARCH IN PERSPECTIVE

As can be surmised from a cursory review of the historical and contemporary literature, there are a number of hypotheses that have occurred in memory research linked to learning disabled samples. Several hypothesized mediators of memory problems could be metacognitive ability, strategy effectiveness, strategy utilization, strategy awareness, knowledge (quantity or quality), efficacy of a specific component (encoding, retrieving, storage), WM capacity (executive function, phonological system, visual–spatial system), and attentional capacity, as well as other areas that were not discussed (e.g., self-efficacy beliefs and motivation). We have attempted to capture some of the findings during early and contemporary time periods. We now attempt to place the memory research in theoretical perspective by reviewing the major hypothesis that has directed research on LD, summarize the assumption, and point out a major limitation.

An early hypothesis, the perceptual (visual) and cross-modality hypothesis, suggested that memory difficulties in children with LD is related to their inability to perceive visual–spatial information and remember visual–spatial relationships and/or integrate information across modalities (visual to writing). This theory was popularized in the early development of the field as related to reading problems. It was displaced in the early 1970s, primarily by research which showed that learning disabled and nondisabled children were statistically comparable in their recall of visual–spatial and nonverbal information, suggesting that memory problems reside primarily in the language domain.

A hypothesis that emerged during the 1970s and 1980s was the assumption that improvements in memory performance for children with LD were strongly related to the acquisition of learning and recall strategies. Although recall strategies were found to play a primary role in improvements related to memory performance, the strategy hypothesis did not provide the whole picture about differences between children and adults with and without LD. Some studies indicated that when rehearsal was controlled, or organization was provided to the learning disabled sample, ability-group differences still emerged. That is, rehearsal or organization did not account for enough of the significant variation between the groups to remain a viable hypothesis by itself.

Another hypothesis that was popular in the late 1980s was the assumption that children with LD suffered metacognitive deficits (i.e., one's knowledge about appropriate and effective strategies in a particular situation). Thus, the development of metamemory was seen as an important variable in accounting for problems found in memories of the learning disabled child. However, the mnemonic model or the metamemory model has not always been shown to find differences between children with and without LD (McBride-Chang *et al.*, 1993). In addition, some of the metacognitive questionnaires are imbedded in language, and therefore the evidence on actual metacognitive differences apart from language competence in children and adults with and without LD is equivocal.

Two additional hypotheses that are certainly popular in the developmental child literature, but which have not been adequately tested in the learning disabled literature, were the knowledge hypothesis and the capacity hypothesis. The knowledge hypothesis is based upon an assumption that changes in memory performance depend upon the quality and quantity of domain-specific knowledge. As a consequence, memory development is determined by increased general world knowledge and the acquisition of content-specific knowledge in many domains. While the knowledge hypothesis is important in child development, there are no studies that we came across that actually tested this hypothesis with learning disabled samples. No published study manipulated relevant knowledge about a domain to see if in fact the learning disabled sample's memory performance matches the NLD sample with comparable knowledge base. Indirectly, there have been studies that measure clustering that do not necessarily reflect a deliberate strategic expression of organizing information (Lee & Obrzut, 1994; Krupski *et al.*, 1993). That is, clustering is a byproduct of general learning ability, and the differences you find between children with and without LD are probably related to this general knowledge.

Another theory that has not been thoroughly tested in the learning disabled research is the capacity hypothesis. The assumption of this model is that differences in memory are somehow related to the maturational growth of WM capacity (Swanson, 2003). Some researchers suggest that the relationship between LD and memory might be partially attributable to processing capacity or a limitation of resources (e.g., Swanson, 1984a). However, these speculations are controversial because a concept of capacity or resource is not usually defined explicitly. Explanations related to the LD student's inability to hold, receive, store, or accommodate information suggest that there is a sort of basic processing inefficiency, whereas explanations about their inability to apply a strategy refers to pertain more to their mental capability. The fundamental assumption, however, is that a learning disability is somehow reflective of a quantitative and/or qualitative restraint in processing. In addition to its restrictions on strategy application, capacity is associated with the quantity or quality of effective application of different types of knowledge. The relative importance of these structural or capacity factors will vary across task, but the basic assumption is that processing capacity is attributable to some of the variation we find between LD and NLD children.

In summary, there are a number of gaps in the research on memory that need to be tended to if we are to make progress in understanding the cognitive dimensions of memory dysfunctions in children and adults with LD. Although this chapter has reviewed some of the empirical evidence regarding mechanisms that are different between children and adults with and without LD on many memory phenomena, there are no descriptive models about the interrelationship between the acquisition, the availability, and the accessibility of content-specific knowledge, general strategies, and metacognitive skills on memory performance in samples with LD (e.g., Borkowski *et al.*, 1989). There are discussions about the theoretical frameworks and processes that are suggested as accounting for the reason why we find memory deficits in learning disabled samples; however, there has not been a comprehensive model linking low-order processing (e.g., phonological coding) and high-order processing (executive processing), strategy use, knowledge, metacognition, capacity constraints, and so on. Research in WM may play a major role in helping this movement (Siegel, 2003; Swanson & Siegel, 2001a, b).

VII. TRENDS IN MEMORY RESEARCH

Within the last 10 years, memory research on learning disabled samples has indicated some cycles not considered in earlier research. First, the main line of inquiry on memory in children with LD no longer concentrates on just an empirical description of general changes of memory performance and memory processes, but rather on how the memory performance does or does not change under certain situational conditions. For example, Swanson *et al.*'s (1996) study mentioned previously looked at WM performance under initial conditions, under conditions in which memory can be influenced, and under conditions in which memory can be retained after help has been provided. Second, a general lesson seems to be that there is a great deal of variability in samples with LD, and only by attempting to explain this variability can we advance our understanding of why children with LD have memory difficulties. Studies that subtype learning disabled children by achievement suggest that different components of memory may underlie performance. Different subgroups as a function of reading and mathematics problems reflect executive and/or phonological and/or visual–spatial memory deficits (Siegel & Ryan, 1989; Swanson, 1991, 1993b). A third trend is that there seems to be some fusion between memory performance and research on reading. The literature goes back and forth on whether reading influences memory performance or memory performance is independent of reading. For the time being, the research interests concentrate on both the interdependence of different cognitive processes, understanding memory, and on the development of the cognitive processes that are employed.

Fourth, another trend is that researchers in LD are seeking and finding associations between cognitive hypotheses and neurological and genetic indices (e.g., Wadsworth *et al.*, 1995). This applies to research in reading as well as WM. Fifth, LD is no longer studied as exclusively a childhood disability. Increasing numbers of investigations have looked at adults with LD (Bruck, 1992; Ransby & Swanson, 2003).

Finally, there are indications emerging for looking at memory under laboratory conditions, and extending those findings to everyday conditions in an environmental context (McNamara & Wong, 2003). This involves also looking at the motivational influences of memory performance. The question of how research results can be applied to memory instruction in schools or performance of the LD student in an everyday community context is only beginning to be investigated (however, see Scruggs & Mastropieri, 2000, for an earlier review).

VIII. IMPLICATIONS FROM CONTEMPORARY MEMORY RESEARCH FOR INSTRUCTION

Good memory performance as indicated by Pressley (1994) is a product of a number of factors: strategies, knowledge, metacognitive processing and understanding, motivation, and capacity. None of these factors operates in isolation but rather effective cognition is a product of these components and interactions. Sometimes strategic processing will be prominent in cognition more than other factors, sometimes relating content to prior knowledge will be the most salient mechanism, and on still other occasions, there will be obvious reflections by a child on the task demands (on what he/she knows how to do in this particular situation, or in situations similar to it that have been encountered in the past). On some occasions, metacognition is more salient than other components in task performance and then there will be situations when the child's motivation will be especially apparent. All of these processes depend heavily on consciousness, knowledge, memory, attributions, and motivation.

Based on this extensive literature, some very practical concepts and principles from memory research can serve as guidelines for the instruction of students with LD. We can assume that effective instruction must entail information (1) about a number of strategies, (2) about how to control and implement those strategies, and (3) about the importance of effort and personal causality in producing successful performance. Furthermore, any of these components taught in isolation is likely to have diminished value in the classroom context. The following section describes eight major principles that must be considered if strategy instruction is to be successful (also see Montague, 1993, for further application of these principles).

A. Memory Strategies Serve Different Purposes

One analysis of the memory strategy research suggests there is no single best strategy for LD students. A number of studies, for example, have looked at enhancing LD children's performance by using advanced organizers, skimming, questioning, taking notes, summarizing, and so on. But apart from the fact that LD students have been exposed to various types of strategies, which strategies are the most effective is not known. We know in some situations, such as remembering facts, the keyword approach appears to be more effective than direct instruction models (Scruggs & Mastropieri, 2000), but, of course, the rank ordering of different strategies changes in reference to the different types of learning outcomes expected. For example, certain strategies are better suited to enhancing students' understanding of what they have previously read, whereas other strategies are better suited to enhancing students' memory of words or facts. The point is that different strategies can effect different cognitive outcomes in a number of ways.

B. Good Memory Strategies for NLD Students Are Not Necessarily Good Strategies for LD Students and Vice Versa

Strategies that enhance access to knowledge for normally developing students will not be well-suited for all children with LD. For example, Wong and Jones (1982) trained LD and NLD adolescents in a self-questioning strategy to monitor reading comprehension. Results indicated that although the strategy training benefited the adolescents with LD, it actually lowered the performance of NLD adolescents. To illustrate this point further, Swanson (1989) presented students with LD, mental retardation, giftedness, and average development a series of tasks that involved base and elaborative sentences. Their task was to recall words embedded in a sentence. The results of the first experiment suggested that children with LD differ from the other groups in their ability to benefit from elaboration. That is, while the other groups clearly benefited from the elaborative when compared to the base sentence condition, there was no clear advantage for either type of sentence for participants with LD. In another study (Swanson *et al.*, 1988), college students with LD were asked to recall words in a sentence under semantic and imagery instructional conditions. The results suggested, contrary to the extant literature, that readers with disabilities were better able to remember words in a sentence during instructional conditions that induced semantic processing. In contrast,

NLD readers favored imagery processing over semantic processing conditions. In sum, these results suggest that strategies that are effective for NLD students may be less effective for students with LD.

C. Effective Memory Strategies Do Not Necessarily Eliminate Processing Differences

It appears logical that if children with LD use a strategy that allows them to process information efficiently, then improvement in performance is due to the strategies' affecting the same processes that they do in NLD students. This assumption has emanated primarily from studies that have imposed organization on seemingly unorganized material. For example, considerable evidence indicates that readers with LD do not initially take advantage of the organizational features of material (Dallego & Moely, 1980; Lee & Obrzut, 1994). However, the notion that readers with disabilities process the organizational features of information in the same manner as NLD students do is questionable (Swanson, 1986). For example, Swanson and Rathgerber (1986) found in categorization tasks that readers with disabilities can retrieve information without interrelating superordinate, subordinate, and coordinate classes of information, as the NLD children do. Thus, children with LD can learn to process information in an organizational sense without knowing the meaning of the material. The point is that simply because children with LD are sensitized to internal structure of material via some strategy (e.g., by cognitive strategies that require the sorting of material), it does not mean they will make use of the material in a manner consistent with what was intended from the instructional strategy.

D. The Strategies Taught Are Not Necessarily The Ones Used

The previous principle suggests that, during intervention, different processes may be activated that are not necessarily the intent of the instructional intervention. It is also likely that students with disabilities use different strategies on tasks in which they seem to have little difficulty, and these tasks will likely be overlooked by the teacher for possible intervention. It is commonly assumed that although students with LD may have isolated memory deficits (verbal domain) and require general learning strategies to compensate for these processing deficits, their processing of information is comparable with that of their normal counterparts on tasks with which they have little trouble. Several authors suggest, however, that there are a number of alternative ways for achieving successful performance (Pressley, 1994), and some indirect evidence indicates that the learning disabled may use qualitatively different mental operations (Shankweiler et al., 1979) and processing routes (e.g., Swanson, 1988) from those used by their NLD counterparts.

E. Memory Strategies in Relation to a Student's Knowledge Base and Capacity

One important variable that has been overlooked in the LD intervention literature is the notion of processing constraints (Swanson *et al.*, 1996). Memory capacity seems to increase with development, with a number of factors potentially contributing to the overall effect. STM capacity increases with age (Case *et al.*, 1982). The number of component processes increases the speed with development, with faster processes generally consuming less effort than slow processes, and thus the same amount of capacity can seem greater (i.e., there is a functional increase of capacity with increasing efficiency of processing). The older children are likely to have more organized prior knowledge which can reduce total number of chunks of information that are processed and decrease the amount of effort to retrieve information from LTM. These developmental relationships may play a role in strategy effectiveness. To test this possibility, Pressley *et al.* (1987) studied children's ability to execute a capacity-demanding imagery representation strategy for the learning of sentences. Children in the experimental condition of these experiments were presented a series of highly concrete sentences (e.g., The angry bird shouted at the white dog, The turkey pecked the coat). They were asked to imagine the meanings of these sentences. Control-condition participants were given no instruction. Children benefited from imagery instruction. However, performance depended on the child's functional STM capacity, as reflected by individual differences in performance on a classic memory span task. That is, the imagery vs control difference in performance was only detected when functional STM was relatively high.

F. Comparable Memory Strategy May Not Eliminate Performance Differences

Several studies have indicated that residual differences remain between ability groups even when ability groups are instructed and/or prevented from strategy use (Gelzheiser *et al.*, 1987). For example, in a study by Gelzheiser *et al.* (1987), discussed earlier, LD and NLD children were compared on their ability to use organizational strategies. After instruction in organizational strategies, the LD and NLD children were compared on their abilities to recall information on a posttest. The results indicated that children with LD were comparable in strategy use to NLD children, but were deficient in overall performance. In another study, Swanson (1983b) found that the recall of a group with LD did not improve from baseline level when trained with rehearsal strategies. They recalled less than normally achieving peers, although the groups were comparable in the various types of strategy used. The results support the notion that groups of children with different learning histories may continue to learn differently, even when the groups are equated in terms of strategy use.

G. Memory Strategies Taught Do Not Necessarily Become Transformed into Expert Strategies

Children who become experts at certain tasks often have learned simple strategies and, through practice, have discovered ways to modify them into more efficient and powerful procedures (Schneider, 1993). In particular, the proficient learner uses higher-order rules to eliminate unnecessary or redundant steps to hold increasing amounts of information. The LD child, in contrast, may learn most of the skills related to performing an academic task and perform appropriately on that task by carefully and systematically following prescribed rules or strategies. Although children with LD can be taught strategies, some studies suggest that the difference between NLD (experts in this case) and children with LD is that the former have modified such strategies to become more efficient (Swanson & Cooney, 1985). It is plausible that the LD child remains a novice in learning new information because he or she fails to transform memory strategies into more efficient forms (see Swanson & Rhine, 1985).

H. Strategy Instruction Must Operate on the Law of Parsimony

A number of multiple-component packages of strategy instruction have been suggested for improving LD children's functioning. These components have usually encompassed some of the following: skimming, imagining, drawing, elaborating, paraphrasing, using mnemonics, accessing prior knowledge, reviewing, orienting to critical features, and so on. No doubt there are some positive aspects to these strategy packages in that:

1. These programs are an advance over some of the strategies seen in LD literature to be rather simple or "quick-fix" strategies (e.g., rehearsal or categorization to improve performances).
2. These programs promote a domain skill and have a certain metacognitive embellishment about them.
3. The best of these programs involve (a) teaching a few strategies well rather than superficially, (b) teaching students to monitor their performance, (c) teaching students when and where to use the strategy to enhance generalization, (d) teaching strategies as an integrated part of an existing curriculum, and (e) teaching that includes a great deal of supervised student practice and feedback.

The difficulty of such strategy packages, however, at least in terms of theory, is that little is known about which components best predict student performance, nor do they readily permit one to determine why the strategy worked. The multiple-component approaches that are typically found in a number of strategy intervention studies must be carefully contrasted with a component analysis approach that involves the systematic combination of instructional components known to have an additive effect on performance. As stated by Pressley (1986, p. 140), "Good strategies are composed of the sufficient and necessary processes for accomplishing their intended goal, consuming as few intellectual processes as necessary to do so."

IX. SUMMARY AND CONCLUSION

In summary, we have briefly characterized research on memory and LD. Our knowledge of LD individuals' memory somewhat parallels our knowledge about the differences between older and younger children's memory. The parallel relies in effortful processing, the focus on cognitive strategies, the development of a knowledge base, and the awareness of one's own memory processes. Most memory research emanates from an information-processing framework. Earlier research tends to emphasize the integration of information across modalities (visual–auditory) and perception (visual memory), whereas more recent studies tend to focus on the representation, control, and executive process (e.g., strategies) of memory. Current research on memory is beginning to examine the interaction of structures and processes on performance. Most of the current research is occurring in the area of WM. The limitations of previous models are highlighted as well as recent trends in memory research on students with LD. A number of principles related to memory strategy instruction have emerged that have direct application to the instruction of children and adults with LD. Some of these principles are related to (1) the purposes of strategies, (2) parsimony with regard to the number of processes, (3) individual differences in strategy use and performance, (4) learner constraints, and (5) the transfer of strategies into more efficient processes.

References

Aaron, P. G. (1993). Is there a visual dyslexia? *Annals of Dyslexia,* **43**, 110–124.
Anderson, J. (1990). *Cognitive psychology and its implications.* New York: Freeman.
Atkinson, R., & Shiffrin, R. (1968). Human memory, a proposed system and its control processes. In K. Spence & J. Spence (Eds.), *The psychology of learning and motivation: Advances in research and theory, Vol. 2* (pp. 85–195). New York: Academic Press.
Baddeley, A. D. (1986). *Working memory.* London, UK: Oxford University Press.

Baddeley, A. D. (1996). Exploring the central executive. *Quarterly Journal of Experimental Psychology: Human Experimental Psychology*, **49**(1), 5–28.

Baddeley, A. D., Gathercole, S. E., & Papagno, C. (1998). The phonological loop as a language learning device. *Psychological Review*, **105**(1), 158–173.

Baddeley, A. D., & Logie, R. H. (1999). Working memory: The multiple component model. In A. Miyake & P. Shah (Eds.) *Models of working memory: Mechanisms of active maintenance and executive control* (pp. 28–61). New York: Cambridge University Press.

Baddeley, A. D., Lewis, V., Eldridge, M., & Thomson, N. (1984). Attention and retrieval from long-term memory. *Journal of Experimental Psychology: General*, **113**(4), 518–540.

Bauer, R. H. (1977). Memory processes in children with learning disabilities: Evidence for deficient rehearsal. *Journal of Experimental Child Psychology*, **24**, 415–430.

Bauer, R. H. (1979a). Memory processes in children with learning disabilities: Evidence for deficient rehearsal. *Journal of Experimental Child Psychology*, **24**, 415–430.

Bauer, R. H. (1979b). Memory, acquisition, and category clustering in learning disabled children. *Journal of Experimental Child Psychology*, **27**, 365–383.

Bauer, R. H., & Emhert, J. (1984). Information processing in reading-disabled and nondisabled children. *Journal of Experimental Child Psychology*, **37**, 271–281.

Bauer, R. H., & Peller-Porth, V. (1990). The effect of increased incentive on free recall by learning-disabled and nondisabled children. *The Journal of General Psychology*, **117**, 447–462.

Bjorklund, D. F. (1985). The role of conceptual knowledge in the development of organization in children's memory. In C. J. Brainerd (Ed.), *Basic processes in memory development* (pp. 103–134). New York: Springer-Verlag.

Bjorklund, D. F., Coyle, T. R., & Gaultney, J. F. (1992). Developmental differences in the acquisition and maintenance of an organizational strategy: Evidence for the utilization deficiency hypothesis. *Journal of Experimental Child Psychology*, **54**, 434–448.

Bjorklund, D. F., Schneider, W., Cassel, W. S., & Ashley, E. (1994). Training and extension of a memory strategy: Evidence for utilization deficiencies in the acquisition of an organizational strategy in high- and low-IQ children. *Child Development*, **65**, 951–965.

Blumenthal, S. H. (1980). A study of the relationship between speed of retrieval of verbal information and patterns of oral reading errors. *Journal of Learning Disabilities*, **3**, 568–570.

Borkowski, J. G., Carr, M., Rellinger, E. A., & Pressley, M. (1990). Self-regulated strategy use: Interdependence of metacognition, attributions, and self-esteem. In B. F. Jones (Ed.), *Dimensions of thinking: Review of research* (pp. 53–92). Hillsdale, NJ: Erlbaum.

Borkowski, J. G., Estrada, M., Milstead, M., & Hale, C. A. (1989). General problem-solving skills: Relations between metacognition and strategic processing. *Learning Disability Quarterly*, **12**, 57–70.

Borkowski, J. G., & Muthukrishna, N. (1992). Moving metacognition into the classroom: "Working models" and effective strategy teaching. In M. Pressley, K. R. Harris, & J. T. Guthrie (Eds.), *Promoting academic competence and literacy in school* (pp. 477–501). Toronto, Canada: Academic Press.

Borkowski, J. G., Weyhing, R. S., & Carr, M. (1988). Effects of attributional retraining on strategy-based reading comprehension in learning-disabled students. *Journal of Educational Psychology*, **80**, 46–53.

Brainerd, C. J., Kingma, J., & Howe, M. L. (1986). Long-term memory development and learning disability: Storage and retrieval loci of disabled/nondisabled differences. In S. J. Ceci (Ed.), *Handbook of cognitive, social, and neuropsychological aspects of learning disabilities* (Vol. 1, pp. 161–184). Hillsdale, NJ: Lawrence Erlbaum.

Brainerd, C. J., & Reyna, V. F. (1991). Acquisition and forgetting processes in normal and learning-disabled children: A disintegration/reintegration theory. In J. Obrzut & G. W. Hynd (Eds.), *Neuropsychological foundations of learning disabilities* (pp. 147–175). New York: Academic Press.

Brainerd, C. J., Reyna, V. F., Howe, M. L., & Kingma, J. (1990). The development of forgetting and reminiscence. *Monographs of the Society for Research in Child Development*, **53**(3–4, Whole No. 222).

Bronner, A. F. (1917). *The psychology of special abilities and disabilities*. Boston, MA: Little, Brown.

Brown, A. L. (1975). The development of memory: Knowing, knowing about knowing, and knowing how to know. In H. Reese (Ed.), *Advances in child development and behavior* (Vol. 10). New York: Academic Press.

Brown, A. L., & Campione, J. C. (1981). Inducing flexible thinking: The problem of access. In M. Friedman, J. P. Das, & N. O'Connor (Eds.), *Intelligence and learning* (pp. 515–530). New York: Plenum Press.

Brown, A. L., & Palincsar, A. S. (1988). Reciprocal teaching of comprehension strategies: A natural history of one program for enhancing learning. In J. Borkowski & J. P. Das (Eds.), *Intelligence and cognition in special children: Comparative studies of giftedness, mental retardation, and learning disabilities*. New York: Ablex.

Brown, K. F. (1988). Development of long-term memory retention processes among learning disabled and nondisabled children. Unpublished doctoral dissertation. University of Arizona, Tucson.

Brown, R., Pressley, M., Van Meter, P., & Schuder, T. (1996). A quasi-experimental validation of transactional strategies instruction with low-achieving second-grade readers. *Journal of Educational Psychology*, **88**, 18–37.

Bruck, M. (1992). Persistence of dyslexics' phonological awareness deficits. *Developmental Psychology*, **28**, 874–886.

Bryan, T. (1972). The effect of forced mediation upon short-term memory of children with learning disabilities. *Journal of Learning Disabilities*, **5**, 605–609.

Bull, R., Johnston, R. S., & Roy, J. A. (1999). Exploring the roles of the visual-spatial sketch pad and central executive in children's arithmetical skills: Views from cognition and developmental neuropsychology. *Developmental Neuropsychology*, **15**(3), 421–442.

Campione, J. C., Brown, A. L., & Ferrara, F. A. (1982). Mental retardation and intelligence. In R. I. Sternberg (Ed.), *Handbook of human intelligence* (pp. 392–490). New York: Cambridge.

Cantor, J., & Engle, R. W. (1993). Working memory capacity as long-term memory activation: An individual differences approach. *Journal of Experimental Psychology: Learning, Memory, and Cognition*, **18**, 972–992.

Case, R., Kurland, D. M., & Goldberg, J. (1982). Operational efficiency and the growth of short-term memory span. *Journal of Experimental Child Psychology*, **33**, 386–404.

Ceci, S. J. (1984). Developmental study of learning disabilities and memory. *Journal of Experimental Child Psychology*, **38**, 352–371.

Ceci, S. J., Ringstrom, M. D., &, Lea, S. E. G. (1980). Coding characteristics of normal and learning-disabled 10-year-olds: Evidence for dual pathways to the cognitive system. *Journal of Experimental Psychology: Human Learning, & Memory*, **6**, 785–797.

Cermak, L. (1983). Information processing deficits in learning disabled children. *Journal of Learning Disabilities*, **16**, 599–605.

Chiappe, P., Hasher, L., & Siegel, L. S. (2000). Working memory, inhibitory control, and reading disability. *Memory & Cognition*, **28**(1), 8–17.

Cohen, J. (1988). *Statistical power analysis for the behavioral sciences*. San Diego, CA: Academic Press.

Conners, C. K., Kramer, K., & Guerra, F. (1969). Auditory synthesis and dichotic listening in children with learning disabilities. *Journal of Special Education*, **3**, 163–170.

Conrad, R. (1964). Acoustic confusion in immediate memory. *British Journal of Psychology*, **55**, 75–84.

Cooper, H., & Hedges, L. C. (1994). *Handbook on research synthesis*. New York: Russell Sage.

Dallego, M. L., & Moely, B. E. (1980). Free recall in boys of normal and poor reading levels as a function of task manipulation. *Journal of Experimental Child Psychology*, **30**, 62–78.

Daneman, M., &, Carpenter, P. A. (1980). Individual differences in working memory and reading. *Journal of Verbal Learning Behavior*, **19**, 450–466.

Daneman, M., & Merikle, P. M. (1996). Working memory and language comprehension: A meta-analysis. *Psychonomic Bulletin & Review*, **3**(4), 442–463.

Dawson, M. H., Hallahan, D. P., Reeves, R. E., & Ball, D. W. (1980). The effect of reinforcement and verbal rehearsal on selective attention in learning disabled children. *Journal of Abnormal Child Psychology*, **8**, 133–144.

De Beni, R., Palladino, P., Pazzaglia, F., & Cornoldi, C. (1998). Increases in intrusion errors and working memory deficit of poor comprehenders. *Quarterly Journal of Experimental Psychology: Human Experimental Psychology*, **51**(2), 305–320.

De Jong, P. (1998). Working memory deficits of reading disabled children. *Journal of Experimental Child Psychology*, **70**(2), 75–95.

Dempster, F. N., & Cooney, J. B. (1982). Individual differences in digit span, susceptibility to proactive interference, and aptitude/achievement test scores. *Intelligence*, **6**, 399–416.

Denckla, M. B., & Rudel, R. G. (1974). Rapid "automatized" naming of pictured objects, colors, letters, and numbers by normal children. *Cortex*, **10**, 186–202.

Eden, G. F., Stein, J. F., Wood, H. M., & Wood, F. B. (1995). Temporal and spatial processing in reading disabled and normal children. *Cortex*, **31**, 451–468.

Elbert, J. C. (1984). Short-term memory encoding and memory search in the word recognition of learning-disabled children. *Journal of Learning Disabilities*, **17**, 342–345.

Engle, R. W., Cantor, J., & Carullo, J. J. (1992). Individual differences in working memory and comprehension: A test of four hypotheses. *Journal of Experimental Psychology: Learning, Memory and Cognition*, **18**, 972–992.

Engle, R. W., Tuholski, S. W., Laughlin, J. E., & Conway, A. R. (1999). Working memory, short-term memory, and general fluid intelligence: A latent-variable approach. *Journal of Experimental Psychology: General*, **128**(3), 309–331.

Ericsson, K., & Kintsch, W. (1995). Long-term working memory. *Psychological Review*, **102**, 211–245.

Ericsson, K., & Delaney, P. F. (1999). Long-term memory as an alternative to capacity models of working memory in everyday skilled performance. In A. Miyake & P. Shah (Eds.) *Models of working memory: Mechanisms of active maintenance and executive control* (pp. 257–297). New York: Cambridge University Press.

Flavell, J. H. (1970). Developmental studies of mediated memory. In H. W. Reese & L. P. Lipsitt (Eds.), *Advances in child development and child behavior, Vol. 5* (pp. 181–211). New York: Academic Press.

Flavell, J. (1979). Metacognition and cognitive monitoring. *American Psychologist*, **34**, 906–911.

Flavell, J. H., Beach, D. R., & Chinsky, J. M. (1966). Spontaneous verbal rehearsal in a memory task as a function of age. *Child Development*, **37**, 283–299.

Gathercole, S. E. (1998). The development of memory. *Journal of Child Psychology and Psychiatry*, **39**, 3–27.

Gathercole, S. E., & Baddeley, A. D. (1993). *Working memory and language*, Hove, UK: Erlbaum.

Geary, C. (2003). Learning disabilities in arithmetic: Problem-solving differences and cognitive deficits. Swanson, K. Harris, & S. Graham (Eds.) *Handbook on learning disabilities* (pp. 199–213) New York: Guilford.

Gelzheiser, L. M. (1984). Generalization from categorical memory tasks to prose by learning disabled adolescents. *Journal of Educational Psychology*, **76**, 1128–1138.

Gelzheiser, L. M., Cort, R., & Shephard, M. J. (1987). Is minimal strategy instruction sufficient for LD children? Testing the production deficiency hypothesis. *Learning Disability Quarterly*, **10**, 267–276.

Gelzheiser, L. M., Solar, R. A., Shepherd, M. J., &, Wozniak, R. H. (1983). Teaching learning disabled children to memorize: Rationale for plans and practice. *Journal of Learning Disabilities*, **16**, 421–425.

Geschwind, N. (1962). The anatomy of acquired disorders of reading. In J. Money (Ed.), *Reading disability: Progress and research needs in dyslexia* (pp. 115–129). Baltimore: Johns Hopkins Press.

Goyen, J. D., & Lyle, J. (1971). Effect of incentives upon retarded and normal readers on a visual-associate learning task. *Journal of Experimental Child Psychology*, **11**, 274–280.

Goyen, J. D., & Lyle, J. (1973). Short-term memory and visual discrimination in retarded readers. *Perceptual and Motor Skills*, **36**, 403–408.

Graham, S., & Harris, K. (2003). Students with learning diabilities and the process of writing: A meta-analysis of the SRSD studies. In Swanson, K. Harris, & S. Graham (Eds.) *Handbook on learning disabilities*. (pp. 323–344) New York: Guilford.

Gruneberg, M. M., & Sykes, R. (1969). Acoustic confusion in long-term memory. *Acta Psychologica*, **29**, 293–296.

Guthrie, J. T., & Goldberg, H. K. (1972). Visual sequential memory in reading disability. *Journal of Learning Disabilities*, **5**, 41–46.

Guttentag, R. E. (1984). The mental effort requirement of cumulative rehearsal: A developmental study. *Journal of Experimental Child Psychology*, **37**, 92–106.

Haines, D. J., & Torgesen, J. K. (1979). The effects of incentives on rehearsal and short-term memory in children with reading problems. *Learning Disability Quarterly*, **2**, 48–55.

Hall, J., Wilson, K., Humphreys, M., Tinzmann, M., & Bowyer, P. (1983). Phonemic-similarity effects in good vs poor readers. *Memory & Cognition*, **11**, 520–527.

Hallahan, D. P., & Reeve, R. (1980). Selective attention and distractibility. In B. Keogh (Ed.), *Advances in special education* (pp. 141–182). Greenwich, CT: JAI Press.

Harnishfeger, K. K., & Bjorklund, D. F. (1994). A developmental perspective on individual differences in inhibition. *Learning & Individual Differences*, **6**, 331–357.

Harris, K. R., Graham, S., & Pressley, M. (1992). Cognitive behavioral approaches in reading and written language: Developing self-regulated learners. In N. N. Singh & I. L. Beale (Eds.), *Current perspectives in learning disabilities: Nature, theory, and treatment* (pp. 415–451). New York: Springer-Verlag.

Hasselhorn, M. (1992). Task dependency and the role of category typicality and metamemory in the development of an organizational strategy. *Child Development*, **63**, 202–214.

Hinshelwood, J. (1917). *Congenital word blindness*. London, UK: Lewis.

Howe, M. L., & Brainerd, C. J. (1989). Development of children's long-term retention. *Developmental Review*, **9**, 301–340.

Howe, M. L., Brainerd, C. J., & Kingma, J. (1985). Storage-retrieval processes of normal and learning disabled children: A stages-of-learning analysis of picture–word effects. *Child Development*, **56**, 1120–1133.

Howe, M. L., Brainerd, C. J., & Kingma, J. (1989). Localizing the development of ability differences in organized memory. *Contemporary Educational Psychology*, **14**, 336–356.

Howe, M. L., O'Sullivan, J. T., Brainerd, C. J., & Kingma, J. (1989). Localizing the development of ability differences in organized memory. *Contemporary Educational Psychology*, **14**, 336–356.

Hulme, C. (1992). *Working memory and severe learning difficulties—Essays in cognitive psychology.* East Sussex, UK: Lawrence Erlbaum Associates.

Johnson, R. S., Rugg, M., & Scott, T. (1987). Phonological similarity effects, memory span, and developmental reading disorders. *British Journal of Psychology,* **78,** 205–211.

Jonides, J. (2000). Mechanism of verbal working memory revealed by neuroimaging studies. In B. Landau *et al.* (Eds.) *Perception, cognition, and language: Essays in honor of Henry and Lila Gleitman* (pp. 87–104). Cambridge, MA: MIT Press.

Just, M. A., & Carpenter, P. A. (1992). A capacity theory of comprehension: Individual differences in working memory. *Psychological Review,* **99,** 122–149.

Kee, D. W. (1994). Development differences in associative memory: Strategy use, mental effort, and knowledge-access interaction. In H. W. Reese (Ed.), *Advances in child development and behavior,* (Vol. 25). New York: Academic Press.

Koorland, M. A., & Wolking, W. D. (1982). Effect of reinforcement on modality of stimulus control in learning. *Learning Disabilities Quarterly,* **5,** 264–273.

Krupski, A., Gaultney, J. F., Malcolm, G., & Bjorklund, D. F. (1993). Learning disabled and nondisabled children's performance on serial recall tasks: The facilitating effect of knowledge. *Learning & Individual Differences,* **5,** 199–210.

Kussmaul, A. (1877). Disturbances of speech. *Cyclopedia of Practical Medicine,* **14,** 581–875.

Lee, C. P., & Obrzut, J. E. (1994). Taxonomic clustering and frequency associations as features of semantic memory development in children with learning disabilities. *Journal of Learning Disabilities,* **27,** 454–462.

Lehman, E. B., & Brady, K. M. (1982). Presentation modality and taxonomic category as encoding dimensions from good and poor readers. *Journal of Learning Disabilities,* **15,** 103–105.

Lorsbach, T. C., Sodoro, J., & Brown, J. S. (1992). The dissociation of repetition priming and recognition memory in language/learning-disabled children. *Journal of Experimental Child Psychology,* **54,** 121–146.

Lucangeli, D., Galderisi, D., & Cornoldi, C. (1995). Specific and general transfer effects following metamemory training. *Learning Disabilities Research & Practice,* **10,** 11–21.

Male, D. R. (1996). Metamemorial functioning of children with moderate learning difficulties. *British Journal of Educational Psychology,* **66,** 145–157.

Manis, F. R. (1985). Acquisition of word identification skills in normal and disabled readers. *Journal of Educational Psychology,* **27,** 28–90.

Mastropieri, M. A., Scruggs, T. E., Levin, J. R., Gaffney, J., & McLoone, B. (1985). Mnemonic vocabulary instruction for learning disabled students. *Learning Disability Quarterly,* **8,** 57–63.

Mazer, S. R., McIntyre, C. W., Murray, M. E., Till, R. E., & Blackwell, S. L. (1983). Visual persistence and information pick-up in learning disabled children. *Journal of Learning Disabilities,* **16,** 221–225.

McBride-Chang, C., Manis, F. R., Seidenberg, M. S. Custodio, R., & Doi, L. M. (1993). Print exposure as a predictor of word reading and reading comprehension in disabled and nondisabled readers. *Journal of Educational Psychology,* **85,** 230–238.

McIntyre, C. W., Murray, M. E., Coronin, C. M., &, Blackwell, S. L. (1978). Span of apprehension in learning disabled boys. *Journal of Learning Disabilities*, **11**, 13–20.

McNamara, J. K., & Wong, B. Y. L. (2003). Memory for everyday information in students with learning disabilities. *Journal of Learning Disabilities*, **36**, 394–406.

Miller, P. H., & Seier, W. L. (1994). Strategy utilization deficiencies in children: When, where, and why. In H. W. Reese (Ed.), *Advances in child development and behavior, Vol. 25* (pp. 107–156). New York: Academic Press.

Miller, P. H., Woody-Ramsey, J., & Aloise, P. A. (1991). The role of strategy effortfulness in strategy effectiveness. *Developmental Psychology*, **27**, 738–745.

Miyake, A., Carpenter, P. A., & Just, M. A. (1994). A capacity approach to syntactic comprehension disorders: Making normal adults perform like aphasic patients. *Cognitive Neuropsychology*, **11**, 671–717.

Miyake, A. Just, M., & Carpenter, P. (1994). Working memory constraints on the resolution of lexical ambiguity. *Cognitive Neuropsychology*, **33**, 175–202.

Miyake, A., Friedman, N. P., Emerson, M. J., Witzki, A. H., & Howerter, A. (2000). The unity and diversity of executive functions and their contributions to complex "frontal lobe" tasks: A latent variable analysis. *Cognitive Psychology*, **41**(1), 49–100.

Monroe, M. (1932). *Children who cannot read*. Chicago: University of Chicago Press.

Montague, M. (1992). The effects of cognitive and metacognitive strategy instruction on the mathematical problem solving of middle school students with learning disabilities. *Journal of Learning Disabilities*, **25**, 230–248.

Montague, M. (1993). Student-centered or strategy-centered instruction: What is our purpose? *Journal of Learning Disabilities*, **26**, 433–437.

Morgan, W. P. (1896). A case of congenital word blindness. *British Medical Journal*, **2**, 1378–1379.

Morrison, F. J., Giordani, B., &, Nagy, J. (1977). Reading disability: An information processing analysis. *Science*, **196**, 77–79.

Miyake, A. (2001). Individual differences in working memory: Introduction to the special section. *Journal of Experimental Psychology*, **130**, 163–168.

Ornstein, P. A., & Naus, M. J. (1978). Rehearsal processes in children's memory. In P. A. Ornstein (Ed.), *Memory development in children*. Hillsdale, NJ: Erlbaum.

Orton, S. T. (1925). "Word-blindness" in school children. *Archives of Neurology and Psychiatry*, **14**, 581–615.

Orton, S. T. (1937). *Reading, writing, and speech problems in children*. New York: Norton.

O'Shaughnessy, T., & Swanson, H. L. (1998). Do immediate memory deficits in students with learning disabilities in reading reflect a developmental lag or deficit? A selective meta-analysis of the literature. *Learning Disability Quarterly*, **21**(2), 123–148.

Passolunghi, M. C., Cornoldi, C., & De Liberto, S. (1999). Working memory and intrusions of irrelevant information in a group of specific poor problem solvers. *Memory & Cognition*, **27**(5), 779–790.

Pennington, B. F., Van Orden, G. C., Kirson, D., & Haith, M. M. (1991). What is the causal relation between verbal STM problems and dyslexia? In S. A. Brady & D. P. Shankweiler (Eds.), *Phonological processes in literacy* (pp. 173–186). Hillsdale, NJ: Erlbaum.

Pressley, M. (1986). The relevance of the good strategy user model to the teaching of mathematics. *Educational Psychology*, **21**, 139–161.

Pressley, M. (1991). Can learning disabled children become good information processors? How can we find out? In L. Feagans, E. Short, & L. Meltzer (Eds.), *Subtypes of learning disabilities* (pp. 137–162). Hillsdale, NJ: Erlbaum.

Pressley, M. (1994). Embracing the complexity of individual differences in cognition: Studying good information processing and how it might develop. *Learning & Individual Differences*, **6**, 259–284.

Pressley, M., Borkowski, J. G., & Schneider, W. (1987). Cognitive strategies: Good strategy users coordinate metacognition and knowledge. *Annals of Child Development*, **4**, 89–129.

Pressley, M., Cariglia-Bull, S. D., & Schneider, W. (1987). Short-term memory, verbal competence, and age as predictors of an imaginary structural effectiveness. *Journal of Experimental Child Psychology*, **43**, 194–211.

Ransby, M., & Swanson, H. L. (2003). Reading comprehension skills of young adults with childhood diagnosis of dyslexia. *Journal of Learning Disabilities*, **36**, 538–555.

Samuels, S. J. (1987). Information processing and reading. *Journal of Learning Disabilities*, **20**, 18–22.

Santiago, H. C., & Matos, I. (1994). Visual recognition memory in specific learning-disabled children. *Journal of the American Optometric Association*, **65**, 690–700.

Schneider, W. (1993). Acquiring expertise: Determinants of exceptional performance. In K. A. Heller, F. J. Monks, & A. H. Passow (Eds.), *Research and development of giftedness and talent*. New York: Pergamon.

Scruggs, T. E., &, Mastropieri, M. A. (1989). Mnemonic instruction of LD students: A field-based evaluation. *Learning Disability Quarterly*, **12**, 119–125.

Scruggs, T. E., & Mastropieri, M. (2000). The effectiveness of mnemonic instruction for students with learning and behavior problems: An update and research synthesis. *Journal of Behavioral Education*, **10**, 163–173.

Seidenberg, M. S. (1989). Reading complex words. In G. N. Carlson and M. Tanenhaus (Eds.), *Linguistic structure in language processing* (pp. 53–105). New York: Kluver Academic Publishers.

Senf, G. M., & Feshbach, S. (1970). Development of bisensory memory in culturally deprived, dyslexic, and normal readers. *Journal of Educational Psychology*, **61**, 461–470.

Shankweiler, D., Liberman, I. Y., Mark, S. L., Fowler, L. A., & Fischer, F. W. (1979). The speech code and learning to read. *Journal of Experimental Psychology: Human, Learning, & Memory*, **5**, 531–545.

Shulman, H. G. (1971). Similarity effects in short-term memory. *Psychological Bulletin*, **75**, 389–415.

Siegel, L. S. (1993). Phonological processing deficits as the basis of a reading disability. Special issue: Phonological processes and learning disability. *Developmental Review*, **13**, 246–257.

Siegel, L. S. (1993). The cognitive basis of dyslexia. In M. Howe & R. Pasnak (Eds.), *Emerging themes in cognitive development* (pp. 33–52). New York: Springer-Verlag.

Siegel, L. S. (2003). Basic cognitive processes and reading disabilities. In H. L. Swanson, K. Harris, & S. Graham (Eds.), *Handbook on learning disabilities* (pp. 158–198). New York: Guilford.

Siegel, L. S., & Linder, B. A. (1984). Short-term memory processing in children with reading and arithmetic learning disabilities. *Developmental Psychology, 20,* 200–207.

Siegel, L. S., & Ryan, E. B. (1988). Development of grammatical sensitivity, phonological, and short-term memory skills in normally achieving and learning disabled children. *Developmental Psychology, 24,* 28–37.

Siegel, L. S., & Ryan, E. B. (1989). The development of working memory in normally achieving and subtypes of learning disabled children. *Child Development, 60,* 973–980.

Sipe, S., and Engle, R. (1986). Echoic memory processes in good and poor readers. *Journal of Experimental Psychology: Learning, Memory, and Cognition, 12,* 402–412.

Stanovich, K. E. (1990). Concepts in developmental theories of reading skill: Cognitive resources, automaticity, and modularity. *Developmental Review, 10,* 72–100.

Stanovich, K. E., & Siegel, L. S. (1994). Phenotypic performance profile of children with reading disabilities: A regression-based test of the phonological-core difference model. *Journal of Educational Psychology, 86,* 24–53.

Swanson, H. L. (1977). Nonverbal visual short-term memory as a function of age and dimensionality in learning disabled children. *Child Development, 45,* 51–55.

Swanson, H. L. (1978). Verbal coding effects on the visual short-term memory of learning disabled and normal readers. *Journal of Educational Psychology, 70,* 539–544.

Swanson, H. L. (1983a). A study of nonstrategic linguistic coding on visual recall of learning disabled and normal readers. *Journal of Learning Disabilities, 16,* 209–216.

Swanson, H. L. (1983b). Relations among metamemory, rehearsal activity, and word recall in learning disabled and nondisabled readers. *British Journal of Educational Psychology, 53,* 186–194.

Swanson, H. L. (1984a). Effects of cognitive effort and word distinctiveness on learning disabled and nondisabled readers' recall. *Journal of Educational Psychology, 76,* 894–908.

Swanson, H. L. (1984b). Semantic and visual memory codes in learning disabled readers. *Journal of Experimental Child Psychology, 37,* 124–140.

Swanson, H. L. (1986). Do semantic memory deficiencies underlie disabled readers' encoding processes? *Journal of Experimental Child Psychology, 41,* 461–488.

Swanson, H. L. (1987). Verbal-coding deficits in the recall of pictorial information by learning disabled readers: The influence of a lexical system. *American Educational Research Journal, 24,* 143–170.

Swanson, H. L. (1988). Learning disabled children's problem solving: Identifying mental processes underlying intelligent performance. *Intelligence, 12,* 261–278.

Swanson, H. L. (1989). The effects of central processing strategies on learning disabled, mildly retarded, average, and gifted children's elaborative encoding abilities. *Journal of Experimental Child Psychology*, **47**, 370–397.

Swanson, H. L. (1991). A subgroup analysis of learning-disabled and skilled readers' working memory: In search of a model of reading comprehension. In L. Feagans, E. Short, & L. Meltzer (Eds.), *Subtypes of learning disabilities: Theoretical perspectives and research* (pp. 209–228). Hillsdale, NJ: Erlbaum.

Swanson, H. L. (1992). Generality and modifiability of working memory among skilled and less skilled readers. *Journal of Educational Psychology*, **64**, 473–488.

Swanson, H. L. (1993a). Executive processing in learning-disabled readers. *Intelligence*, **17**, 117–149.

Swanson, H. L. (1993b). Working memory in learning disability subgroups. *Journal of Experimental Child Psychology*, **56**, 87–114.

Swanson, H. L. (1994). Short-term memory and working memory. Do both contribute to our understanding of academic achievement in children and adults with learning disabilities? *Journal of Learning Disabilities*, **27**, 34–50.

Swanson, H. L. (1999a). What develops in working memory? A life span perspective. *Developmental Psychology*, **35**, 986–1000.

Swanson, H. L. (1999b). Reading comprehension and working memory in skilled readers: Is the phonological loop more important than the executive system? *Journal of Experimental Child Psychology*, **72**, 1–31.

Swanson, H. L. (2000). Are working memory deficits in readers with learning disabilities hard to change? *Journal of Learning Disabilities*, **33**, 551–566.

Swanson, H. L., & Ashbaker, M. (2000). Working memory, short-term memory, articulation speed, word recognition, and reading comprehension in learning disabled readers: Executive and/or articulatory system? *Intelligence*, **28**(1), 1–30.

Swanson, H. L., Ashbaker, M., & Lee, C. (1996). The effects of processing demands on the working memory of learning disabled readers. *Journal of Experimental Child Psychology*, **61**, 242–275.

Swanson, H. L., & Berninger, V. (1995). The role of working memory in skilled and less skilled readers' comprehension. *Intelligence*, **21**, 83–108.

Swanson, H. L., Cochran, K., & Ewers, C. (1989). Working memory and reading disabilities. *Journal of Abnormal Child Psychology*, **17**, 745–756.

Swanson, H. L., & Cochran, K. (1991). Learning disabilities, distinctive encoding, and hemispheric resources. *Brain and Language*, **40**(2), 202–230.

Swanson, H. L., Cochran, K. F., & Ewers, C. A. (1990). Can learning disabilities be determined from working memory performance. *Journal of Learning Disabilities*, **23**, 59–67.

Swanson, H. L., & Cooney, J. (1985). Strategy transformations in learning disabled children. *Learning Disability Quarterly*, **8**, 221–231.

Swanson, H. L., Cooney, J. D., & Overholser, J. D. (1988). The effects of self-generated visual mnemonics on adult learning disabled readers' word recall. *Learning Disabilities Research*, **4**, 26–35.

Swanson, H. L., Mink, J., & Bocian, K. M. (1999). Cognitive processing deficits in poor readers with symptoms of reading disabilities and ADHD: More alike than different? *Journal of Educational Psychology*, **91**(2), 321–333.

Swanson, H. L., & Rathgenber, A. J. (1986). The effects of organizational dimension on memory for words in learning-disabled and nondisabled readers. *Journal of Educational Research*, **79**, 155–162.

Swanson, H. L., Reffel, J., & Trahan, M. (1990). Naturalistic memory in learning disabled and skilled readers. *Journal of Abnormal Child Psychology*, **19**, 117–148.

Swanson, H. L., & Rhine, B. (1985). Strategy transformations in learning disabled children's math performance: Clues to the development of expertise. *Journal of Learning Disabilities*, **18**, 596–603.

Swanson, H. L., & Siegel, L. (2001a). Elaborating on working memory and learning disabilities: A reply to commentators. *Issues in Education: Contributions from Educational Psychology*, **7**(1), 107–129.

Swanson, H. L., & Siegel, L. (2001b). Learning disabilities as a working memory deficit. *Issues in Education: Contributions from Educational Psychology*, **7**(1), 1–48.

Swanson, H. L., & Sachse-Lee, C. (2001a). A subgroup analysis of working memory in children with reading disabilities: Domain-general or domain-specific deficiency? *Journal of Learning Disabilities*, **34**, 249–263.

Swanson, H. L., & Sachse-Lee, C. (2001b). Mathematical problem solving and working memory in children with learning disabilities: Both executive and phonological processes are important. *Journal of Experimental Child Psychology*, **79**, 294–321.

Swanson, H. L. (2003). Age-related differences in learning disabled and skilled readers working memory. *Journal of Experimental Child Psychology*, **85**, 1–31.

Tarver, S. G., Hallahan, D. P., Kauffman, J. M., & Ball, D. W. (1976). Verbal rehearsal and selective attention in children with learning disabilities: A developmental lag. *Journal of Experimental Child Psychology*, **22**, 375–385.

Torgesen, J. K., & Goldman, T. (1977). Rehearsal and short-term memory in second-grade reading disabled children. *Child Development*, **48**, 56–61.

Torgesen, J. K., & Houck, D. G. (1980). Processing deficiencies of learning disabled children who perform poorly on the digit span subtest. *Journal of Educational Psychology*, **72**, 141–160.

Torgesen, J. K., Rashotte, C. A., Greenstein, J., & Portes, P. (1991). Further studies of learning disabled children with severe performance problems on the Digit Span Test. *Learning Disabilities Research & Practice*, **6**, 134–144.

Vellutino, F. R. (1979). *Dyslexia: Theory and research*. Cambridge, MA: MIT Press.

Vellutino, F., Scanlon, D. M., & Spearing, D. (1995). Semantic and phonological coding in poor and normal readers. *Journal of Experimental Child Psychology*, **59**, 76–123.

Wadsworth, S. J., DeFries, J. C., Fulker, D. W., Olson, R. K., *et al.* (1995). Reading performance and verbal short-term memory: A twin study of reciprocal causation. *Intelligence*, **20**, 145–167.

Waller, T. G. (1976). Children's recognition memory for written sentences: A comparison of good and poor readers. *Child Development*, **47**, 90–95.

Waterman, B., & Lewandowski, L. (1993). Phonological and semantic processing in reading disabled and nondisabled males at two age-levels. *Journal of Experimental Child Psychology*, **55**, 87–103.

Wilhardt, L., & Sandman, C. A. (1988). Performance of nondisabled adults and adults with learning disabilities on a computerized multiphasic cognitive memory battery. *Journal of Learning Disabilities*, **21**, 179–185.

Willows, D. M., Corcos, E., & Kershner, J. R. (1993). Perceptual and cognitive factors in disabled and normal readers' perception and memory of unfamiliar visual symbols. In S. F. Wright & R. Groner (Eds.), *Facts of dyslexia and its remediation. Studies in visual information processing, Vol. 3* (pp. 163–177). Amsterdam, Netherlands: North-Holland/Elsevier Science Publishers.

Wong, B. Y. L. (1978). The effects of directive cues on the organization of memory and recall in good and poor readers. *Journal of Educational Research*, **72**, 32–38.

Wong, B. Y. L. (1982). Strategic behaviors in selecting retrieval cues in gifted, normal achieving, and learning disabled children. *Journal of Learning Disabilities*, **15**, 33–37.

Wong, B. Y. L. (1991). Assessment of metacognitive research in learning disabilities: Theory, research, and practice. In H. L. Swanson (Ed.), *Handbook on the assessment of learning disabilities* (pp. 265–284). Austin, TX: PRO-ED.

Wong, B. Y. L., & Jones, W. (1982). Increasing metacomprehension of learning disabled and normal achieving students through self-questioning training. *Learning Disability Quarterly*, **5**, 228–240.

Wong, B. Y. L., Harris, K., Graham, S., & Butler, D. (2003) Cognitive strategies instruction in learning disabilities. Swanson, K. Harris, & S. Graham (Eds.) *Handbook on learning disabilities*. (pp. 383–402) New York: Guilford.

Worden, P. E. (1986). Comprehension and memory for prose in the learning disabled. In S. J. Ceci (Ed.), *Handbook of cognitive social and neuropsychological aspects of learning disabilities*, Vol. 1 (pp. 241–262). Hillsdale, NJ: Erlbaum.

CHAPTER 3

Language Processes and Reading Disabilities

Maureen Hoskyn
Simon Fraser University

I. INTRODUCTION

The primary outcome of over 40 years of research on the language basis of reading is a general acceptance that children who are poor readers have an impairment specific to phonological processing (Adams, 1990). Increasingly, however, researchers have started to question whether language processes beyond the phonological core also contribute to individual variation in reading development. Recent studies show that attempts to classify large samples of children with reading disabilities into subtypes based only on phonological deficits fail to capture all children with reading difficulties (Castles & Coltheart, 1993; Manis *et al.*, 1996). Some poor readers have limited vocabularies (Nation & Snowling, 1998), other children have difficulty comprehending syntactic structures (Bashir & Scavuzzo, 1992) or are unable to make accurate inferences (Cain & Oakhill, 1999; Oakhill, 1984). Moreover, there is a growing body of evidence that suggests young children with weak language skills are at greater risk for developing reading disabilities than are young children whose language abilities are strong in relation to their age peers (Storch & Whitehurst, 2002). For example, Scarborough (1990) charted the development of spoken language and reading abilities of 32 toddlers in families where either one or both parents had a history of reading problems and found that children with depressed syntactical *and* phonological abilities at the age of $2\frac{1}{2}$ years experienced word recognition problems in grade two. Catts *et al.* (2002) also report that performance on language-related (letter identification, sentence imitation, rapid naming) as well as specific speech processing tasks predict the probability that young children will be diagnosed with reading disabilities when they are in second grade. Other sources show that the language-related reading difficulties of children identified in the primary grades are pervasive over time and influence children's academic performance well beyond the elementary school years into adolescence and adulthood (Snowling *et al.*, 2000; Wilson & Lesaux, 2001; Young *et al.*, 2002). In addtion to research that demonstrates weak language skills are predictive of reading problems, studies also show that proficiency in oral language skills can act as a protective buffer against the formulation of reading disabilities for some children. In a longitudinal study of 56 children with a familial risk of acquiring dyslexia, Snowling *et al.* (2003) observed that 6 year-old children who had adequate vocabulary development, good expressive language and grammatical skills were more likely to compensate for phonological processing deficits and become normal readers at the age of 8 years than were children who had poor language abilities.

In sum, investigators have accumulated extensive knowledge about the relations between language and reading development for children with reading disabilities; however, little is known about the origins of these language difficulties, the influences that maintain them, and whether they change in form or severity over time. A frequently overlooked, but important, consideration for theorists and researchers interested in the emergence and maintenance of language-related reading disabilities is that young children who are learning to read are at the same time acquiring proficiency in their native language. Language difficulties observed among poor readers in the primary grades may therefore, at least initially, present as an arrest or delay in the acquisition of language rather than a specific language deficit. Moreover, the language of older disabled readers may in some ways, correspond to the emerging language abilities of younger, typically developing readers. Clarifying language-reading relations for young children at risk of reading failure as well as for older children who have established reading problems therefore begins, as does this chapter, with a discussion of child language acquisition. Using these theories of language acquisition as a conceptual backdrop, the second part of the chapter outlines three conceptualizations of the reading process that have implications for understanding relations between language and reading disabilities: single route, dual route, and developmental models. Finally, the chapter concludes by describing possible origins of language problems for children with reading disabilities and future challenges for researchers in the field.

II. THEORETICAL APPROACHES TO LANGUAGE ACQUISITION

One problem facing researchers interested in emerging language–reading relations is that few theorists agree on what children are doing when they hear or speak a language (Gleason, 2001; Ritchie & Bhatia, 1999). Speculation about the nature of language and language acquisition is historically controversial and is rooted in very different philosophical traditions that attempt to understand the mind. A complete discussion and critique of these competing strands of philosophical thought is well beyond the scope of this chapter; therefore, our review is limited to outlining theories that contribute to the understanding of reading disabilities: linguistic, cognitive constructivist, social constructionist, and connectionist approaches.

A. A Linguistic Perspective

Linguistic approaches to language acquisition have their origins in the ideas of such philosophers as Plato, Leibniz, and Descartes and are based on rationalist theory: the idea that intelligent thought arises from the manipulation of arbitrary symbols by an abstract system of rules. When symbols stand for concepts, logic becomes the system of rules that allows inference to occur. When symbols stand for linguistic units (e.g., phonemes, morphemes, words), phonology is the rule system that specifies legal combinations and pronunciations of phonemes, morphology governs the pairing of morphemes with meaning, syntax defines the relations of words to each other, semantics describes the truth-conditions under which words refer to the objects they represent, and pragmatics regulates the use of speech forms in interpersonal situations (Pinker, 1999). To have linguistic competence in a language, children are required to know about the component rule systems that govern language form and content. To have communicative competence, children must also know how to make language function or work for them during social interaction (Ninio *et al.*, 1994). Distinguishing language form and content from language function is central to all theories of language acquisition; however, linguistic approaches emphasize the importance of children's implicit knowledge of linguistic structure over language use in social contexts.

The study of formal linguistics is closely tied to the ideas of Davidson, who proposes a truth-conditional theory of meaning in which the truth of a sentence is a relation between a sentence, a person, and a time, all of which are observable and verifiable through experience in an external world (Glock, 2003). Linguistic meaningfulness or the sense of a sentence, therefore, is determined by the structural conditions under which the sentence has truth. For instance, consider the following sentences:

Brittany cried when Sally hurt herself.
Brittany cried when Sally hurt her.

According to English grammar rules, reflexive pronouns are bound to referents within the same clause, whereas anaphoric pronouns link to referents that are not in the same clause. In the first sentence, the reflexive pronoun *herself* is bound to *Sally*, the referent located within the same clause. Thus, for the first sentence to be true, Sally is the person hurt. In the second sentence, the anaphoric pronoun, *her*, is bound to *Brittany*, a referent that occurs previously in the text and not within the same clause. In this case, for the sentence to have truth, Brittany is hurt. Grammatical rules such as the two illustrated here can be evaluated, first on whether they represent the external world and second, whether the symbolic correspondence can be verified as true in the external world. Pinker (1999) suggests that children who are acquiring a language are accumulating an inventory of known words, along with knowledge of the universal, steady-state system of principles and rules that specifies the truth conditions under which specific combinations of these words have meaning.

While linguists agree that meaningful language is bound by a system of structural rules, there is no consensus among investigators on how children acquire knowledge of this regulatory system. Much of the theoretical debate within the field of linguistics has been in response to positions first articulated by Chomsky and his colleagues (Chomsky, 1980, 1999) about the universality and generative nature of language grammar. Chomsky (1999) argues that natural principles and parameters, common to all children, cultures, and languages, guide language organization and acquisition. These universal linguistic parameters, conceptualized by Chomsky as a combination of "switches" that signal relations between words, are biologically available and set internally in children's minds when they hear a language. Input data that the child hears consists of ambient evidence grounded in the grammar spoken by the adults around them. Although this primary linguistic data must be available to children, the quantity or quality of input involved is not a significant factor in explaining children's language acquisition. Chomsky argues that language grammars are far too complex and are acquired too quickly to be learned through known learning methods such as imitation or making associations from external input. Therefore, some sort of cognitive processing ability, specific to language, must be available to very young children as a consequence of human genetic endowment (Chomsky, 1968). This language faculty is assumed to be a physiological component of the brain that is prewired with knowledge of the formal principles and rules of phonology, morphology, syntax, and semantics that link language the child hears to the underlying mental linguistic representations (i.e., the structural aspect of language) held in the child's mind. Rules that guide the use of linguistic forms in social contexts (i.e., pragmatics, or the functional aspect of language) are not included in the language faculty (Chomsky, 1980).

Botanical metaphors, such as "a flower blooming under optimal light conditions," are frequently used by linguists to characterize the unfolding of language in a predetermined way from the language faculty when children have exposure to a linguistic environment. Two competing hypotheses explicate the nature of this acquisition process. Continuity theories posit that the language faculty available to infants at birth is representative of a single grammar that is continuous with the adult system (Chomsky, 1999; Pinker, 1994). Alternatively, maturation theories propose that the language faculty is a sequence of grammar modules, and the grammar that infants and young children have biologically available to them might look very different from those of adults (Wexler, 1999).

A common feature of both continuity and maturation theories is that switch-setting occurs during critical periods of brain development and, after a specific point in time, acquiring a first language becomes more difficult, if not impossible. The point in time when the critical period for language acquisition ends is not well defined. Some researchers suggest the window of opportunity for language acquisition closes when children reach the age of 6 or 7 years (Berninger & Richards, 2002), whereas other investigators suggest that the optimal time for language acquisition continues until children reach puberty (Nelson & Bloom, 1997; Newport, 1990). Critical periods are thought to result from a loss of neural plasticity or as a consequence of increased lateralization in the brain. However, findings from recent studies of brain function and neural activity after cerebral damage suggest that brain operations are more flexible than initially thought and brains continue to adjust and adapt to change throughout development. Therefore, to counter the rigidity of constraints implicit in the term "critical period," researchers have increasingly used the term "sensitive periods" to refer to times during which children become progressively less efficient in acquiring new language concepts.

Direct evidence of critical or sensitive periods for language acquisition is limited primarily to fMRI studies of brain activation among groups of hearing, English-speaking adults who have learned American Sign Language (ASL) either before or after puberty (see Newman *et al.*, 2002). ASL is a language that is similar in structure to spoken English. When hearing adults who have learned both English and ASL from birth (because they were born to deaf parents whose primary language is ASL) read English text, extensive left hemisphere (LH) activation is found, whereas viewing ASL activates similar regions in the LH as well as specific areas in the right hemisphere (RH) (i.e., the superior temporal sulcus, the angular gyrus, and the posterior area of the precentral sulcus). When hearing English-speaking adults who acquired ASL after puberty read English, the LH is activated, however when this group processes ASL, the RH angular gyrus does not activate. Taken together, these findings suggest that a "critical" period exists during which RH activation contributes to the learning of ASL (and possibly other languages that involve activation of a RH structure).

Indirect evidence of critical or sensitive periods comes from case studies of congenitally deaf or feral children who have been deprived of any linguistic input until late adolescence (i.e., well after the critical language acquisition period ends). Syntactical abilities of these children typically do not improve, even with intensive intervention (Goldin-Meadow et al., 1994; Kenneally et al., 1998). Case studies of children in Romanian orphanages, whose language fails to develop in part, because they receive minimal attention and language input due to limited interaction with their caregivers—also provide inferential evidence that critical periods for language acquisition exist (Ames & Chisholm, 2001). The difficulty with this research, however, is that determining the effect of minimal linguistic input on language acquisition, independent of that attributable to the effect of living in a socially barren environment, is difficult to assess.

Limited support for the concept of critical periods is also available from studies that chart the language acquisition of children with mental impairments (i.e., associated with Down's syndrome or Fragile-X syndrome) or with specific language impairments (SLI). Children with mental impairments acquire linguistic rules in the same way, but at a slower rate than age peers until the critical time frame for language acquisition comes to a close and the rate of growth in language skills becomes highly irregular (Fowler et al., 1994). Among children with SLI, when the acquisition of inflectional morphology (i.e., grammatical morphemes and function words such as articles and auxiliaries) is stalled at an early age, acquisition of this rule system is difficult and occurs only with intensive intervention (Clahsen, 1999).

The notion of critical periods for language acquisition has historically provided social policymakers with the theoretical rationale for the implementation of early intervention programs. In this view, openings in critical "windows of opportunity" for acquiring language occur during the first three years of children's lives, long before children enter school and formalized reading instruction begins. Bailey (2002) argues, however, that early childhood initiatives can be justified without relying on a critical periods argument and he challenges the idea that experiences must be provided during the general age parameters of 0 to 3 years to ensure child language development proceeds normally (also see Bailey et al., 2001, for an edited collection of papers presented at the National Centre for Learning and Development conference on "Critical Thinking about Critical Periods" 1999). Support for this position is bolstered by recent research that shows that the time frame for learning language skills is longer than initially expected and the skills that children continue to acquire in adolescence differ from skills acquired earlier in development (Nippold, 2000). Furthermore, language acquisition among children with mental impairments after the age of puberty may be more similar to that of typically developing children than initially thought. Using a research design in which adolescents and young adults with Down's Syndrome were matched with younger typically developing children (aged 2.1 to 4 years) on mean length of utterance, Thordardottir *et al.* (2002) found that both groups showed similar patterns of syntax acquisition. The authors conclude that the acquisition of syntax for older children and adults with Down's Syndrome occurs much in the same way as syntax is acquired among younger, typically developing children, however, development for the children with Down's Syndrome occurs at a monotonic pace.

Whether biological events determine optimal times for acquiring language skills that are essential for learning to read is not well understood. Using fMRI methods, Shaywitz and her colleagues (Shaywitz *et al.*, 2003) compared the neural functioning of two groups of young adults who were poor readers as children with a control group of adult readers who had learned to read without difficulty. One of the adult comparison groups met criteria for poor reading in the second or fourth grade, but not in grade 9 or 10 (i.e., relatively compensated group (RC)), suggesting that adults in this group became literate in late childhood or adolescence. Adults in the second group met the criteria for poor reading in the second or fourth grade and again in grade 9 or 10, and were remarkable for having reading difficulties that were pervasive over time (PRD). Performance, on measures of reading of adults in the nonimpaired, control group, on average, was significantly better than in the RC group, whose performance, in turn, was significantly better than that of adults in the PRD group. Moreover, when performing a reading task, a greater number of ancillary systems were active among the RC group compared to the PRD group. Specifically, compared to the PRD group, adults in the RC group had more activation in the right superior frontal and right middle temporal gyri, as well as the left anterior cingulate gyrus. This increased activation was additional to the greater level of activity in the right inferior frontal gyrus, (relative to nonimpaired controls) that was also found in the PRD group. Shaywitz *et al.* speculate that these differences may represent the neural correlates of compensation that are associated with superior language and reasoning abilities as well as better quality school experiences of the RC group relative to the PRD group (however, see

Shaywitz *et al.*, 2003, for a complete analysis and discussion of these findings). Whether compensation occurs only during optimal times in reading development however, remains unclear because the quality of educational experiences among children in the RC group was superior to that available to the PRD group. To address this issue, further research is needed that investigates whether neural activity among adult, poor readers increases to levels found among compensated readers once the poor readers are provided with high quality reading instruction.

Other features of a biologically constrained language apparatus are important to theories of language-related reading disabilities. First, language is viewed as a modular system that is supported by specialized brain systems that operate specific to the verbal domain and are not shared by other cognitive systems (Caplan & Waters, 1999; Chomsky, 1999). Second, the principles and rules which underlie phonology, syntax, and semantics are autonomous subcomponents of this encapsulated verbal system (Crain & Wexler, 1999) that are not affected by general cognitive mechanisms or real-world knowledge (Fodor, 2000). Third, subcomponent processes do not interact during language production; rather, structural representations of language are first computed at lower levels and the results of these operations are transferred to higher levels for further processing (Crain & Shankweiler, 1991; Shankweiler *et al.*, 1999). This means that deficits in the phonological rule system act as a bottleneck that constrains higher-level language operations (i.e., syntax, semantics, discourse processes); however, the reverse does not occur (Brown & Felton, 1990). Capacity limitations in executive processes (e.g., working memory, attention) may exist concomitantly with language deficits and may constrain children's performance on language comprehension and/or reading comprehension tasks; however, these independent cognitive processes do not explain the origin of deficiencies at lower levels in the language system.

Many core assumptions of a linguistic approach have been debated in the literature. Perhaps the premise disputed most frequently is the position that language is biologically innate and unfolds according to a predetermined, genetic blueprint; therefore, the quantity or quality of adult linguistic input has minimal bearing on the success of children's language acquisition. As previously discussed, some research in neuroscience suggests that neural circuitry in the brain is fine-tuned as a result of social and cultural experience (also see Berninger & Richards, 2002, for a complete review). Clearly, brain maturation both influences language acquisition and is moderated by experiences in a linguistic environment. We return to a discussion of the role of experience on language acquisition later in the chapter. First, however, we review a second approach that is foundational to understanding relations between children's cognition and language acquisition processes: a cognitive constructivist perspective.

B. A Cognitive Constructivist Perspective

As in formal linguistic approaches, cognitive constructivist theories of language and language development have their roots in rationalist philosophical traditions. Moreover, language acquisition is conceptualized in both perspectives as universally sequential and invariant: rules that guide the structure of language (i.e., syntax, semantics) are acquired prior to, and remain separate from, rules that specify use of linguistic structures in social situations (i.e., pragmatics). Differences between the two theoretical perspectives reside in how each explains the mechanisms that underlie the emergence language structure. Whereas traditional linguistic theories assume language form and content emerges from a universal language faculty, developmental approaches posit language structure develops secondary to changes in cognition that occur through interaction in a physical environment.

Piaget (1954) suggests that language is not entirely innate or learned. Rather, the biological origins of language reside in the universal tendency of children to seek equilibration between their internal cognitive processes and events they encounter in the physical environment. According to this viewpoint, children construct mental representations of external events (e.g., interactions with objects, activities in the environment) within cognitive frameworks that organize and guide thinking about the environment. Emergent language structure, therefore, is the solution constructed by children to the problem they face when mapping nonlinguistic cognitive meanings to the language they hear about them. As children learn new concepts, they reestablish equilibration by reorganizing their thinking. This is accomplished through revising current cognitive schemas to accommodate new vocabulary or by adjusting the meanings of previous words to assimilate new knowledge within existing mental models. The symbolic structure of language, therefore, is only one of several symbolic functions that are internally constructed from the ongoing interaction between children's current level of cognitive functioning and their linguistic and nonlinguistic environment. Moreover, linguistic meaning resides in the minds of children as the result of an interaction between children's logical reasoning and their changing perception of reality in an external world.

According to a constructivist viewpoint, even very young children and infants are active problem-solvers who pay attention to the linguistic meanings of things and to the significance of events that occur around them. In a study of oral language comprehension among infants aged 15, 18, and 24 months, Meints and her colleagues (Meints et al., 2002) found that children as young as 15 months are able to discriminate the meanings of the spatial prepositions "on" and "under" in environments previously rated as "typical" by parents (e.g., a picture of a cat located either on the surface or under the center of a table), and by the age of 18 months, their understanding was generalized to situations that were parent-rated as "atypical" (e.g., a picture of a cat located either on the surface or under the edge of a table).

As children grow older, they reason better. Developmental change in children's language abilities, in this view, is assumed to be linear and results from quantitative and qualitative advances in cognition (i.e., such as developing concepts of number, causality, reciprocity, space, quality, and class). By the time children enter school, they usually have a sound understanding of the basic grammar of their native language. However, with increases in children's world knowledge come improved language abilities. For instance, estimates of children's root vocabulary show increases in the lexicon of approximately 3000 words each year in school (Just & Carpenter, 1987). Moreover, school-aged children continue to improve in their ability to formulate complex knowledge structures that are qualitatively different from the ones they produced at younger ages. Kamhi and Catts (2002) describe four types of knowledge structures children construct as cognitive demands of their physical and linguistic environment increase: lexical knowledge, structural knowledge, propositional knowledge, and situational knowledge. Children also develop metalinguistic awareness: an ability to know about, regulate, and voluntarily control their own use of language forms.

Developmental theories acknowledge that not all children learn language at the same rate or with the same ease. Even typically developing children are expected to have errors in language comprehension or production, as a natural outcome of trying to perform on tasks for which they are not developmentally ready. However, for some young children, maturational lags in language development and language production errors are more pervasive. Within this group, some children have global language delays that are concomitant with delays in general cognitive development (e.g., as occurs for children with general intellectual disabilities) and some children have maturational delays in language that occur despite normal cognitive development (e.g., as in the case of children with specific language impairments). Numerous studies report that the prevalence of reading disabilities among children with severe language impairments is higher than found in the general population. For instance, McArthur *et al.* (2000) studied the reading abilities of children with severe language impairment and found that 51% of the 102 children in the sample (6.1 to 9.9 years of age) had concomitant reading disabilities. The investigators also studied the performance of 110 children (aged 6.9 to 13.9 years) with reading disabilities on language tasks and found that 55% of the sample also had problems with oral language.

The co-occurrence of reading disability and severe language impairment is not surprising when similar assumptions underlie the criteria that define both groups. For instance, children in both groups are assumed to have a specific cognitive/language deficit that is not attributable to a delay in cognitive development. Alternatively, children whose poor reading performance can be traced to a general cognitive delay are described in the literature as "slow learners", "developmentally delayed", "reading retarded", and "low achievers". The label "reading disabled" is reserved exclusively for children whose reading performance is not commensurate with "expected" levels, based on their general cognitive ability (Gough & Tunmer, 1986). The statistical and conceptual problems associated with using a cognitive reference point such as the intelligence quotient (IQ) to identify children with language and/or reading disabilities has been well documented (for an edited review of literature on this topic, see Siegel, 2003). Cognitive referencing assumes, first, that cognition and language develop continuously and in tandem with each other and, second, that cognition is a necessary prerequisite for language learning. Research suggests, however, that relations between cognition and language development are not linear or continuous once children have moved beyond the early language-learning period. Moreover, the assumption that cognition is a necessary prerequisite or even sufficient for language learning is debatable, given that children's cognitive achievements do not always precede their attainment of linguistic milestones (see Bohannon & Bonvillan, 2001, for a review of this literature).

Numerous studies have shown that irrespective of cognitive development, children with language delays have problems learning to read once they enter school (Catts et al., 2002; Roth et al., 2002; Scarborough, 1990) and that young children who respond best to intervention are those individuals with more fully developed language systems (Berninger & Richards, 2002; Berninger et al., 2002). A considerable body of research has documented that children who are "late talkers" are at greater risk for acquiring reading disabilities than children whose spoken language production develops normally. Late talkers are children, who at the age of 24 months, have very little expressive vocabulary (i.e., fewer than 50 words) and have not produced more than single-word utterances in spontaneous conversation (Rescorla et al., 2001; Scarborough & Dobrich, 1990). Compared to normally developing peers, late talkers vocalize less often and have less knowledge of the phonetic structure of their language (Rescorla & Ratner, 1996). While some researchers report that children with small expressive vocabularies at the age of 2 years tend to "recover" by the age of 5 years (Whitehurst & Fischel, 2000), other investigators propose that this is simply a plateau or an "illusionary recovery" period and that by the age of 6 to 7 years, children once again fall behind their age peers in language (Scarborough & Dobrich, 1990), which, in turn, affects reading development (Catts, 1993).

An important feature of the cognitive constructivist or developmental approach is that it provides a rationale for researchers and curriculum developers to investigate the cognitive strategies that facilitate and/or constrain children's ability to comprehend and produce oral and written language at different times in development. Moreover, reading problems experienced by children as they progress through school is attributed to a mismatch between the cognitive resources available to a child at a specific time in development and the language requirements of an academic curriculum. Both linguistic and cognitive constructivist approaches view language acquisition as an outcome experiences children have during optimal points in brain maturation or cognitive development. In the following section, we review an approach that emphasizes the role of experience on the acquisition of language: the social interactionist approach.

C. A Social Interactionist Perspective

In contrast to cognitive constructivism, which assumes children's cognitive development precedes and directs formulation of language, a social interactionist view proposes the relations between cognition and language are bidirectional. Moreover, a social interactionist approach assumes that child language acquisition is moderated by social and cultural experience. This viewpoint is mutually reinforcing of action-oriented approaches to language, identified with such authors as Wittgenstein (Wittgenstein & Waismann, 2003), Austin (1962), and Searle (1998). In this view, people accomplish things with their words as they speak: they describe, question, state a position, criticize, and so on, and the structure of the language is a function of the relations between words and the conditions of their use. Whereas according to the traditional truth-conditional view of language, sentences are intended as statements of truth by their speakers, this is not the case for use-conditional approaches (Austin, 1962). An utterance, dismissed as nonsense because its truth cannot be verified, may have a communicative function, such as influencing people or drawing the listener's attention to some important feature of the situation in which the utterance is made. Austin (1962) contrasts "performative" utterances that are used to perform an act that changes the world in some way for the speaker (e.g., "I promise that I will finish my degree") from "constative" utterances that are used to report on acts for which a truth value can be determined (i.e., "I promised that I will finish my degree"). The distinction between performative and constative utterances, and the idea that meaning resides in both the function and form of language has led many researchers to consider the influence of pragmatic or social factors, such as the quantity and quality of communicative intents present in parent–child, sibling–child, and peer–child interaction, on language acquisition (see Blum-Kulka & Snow, 2002).

Even in infancy, mother–child experiences can facilitate language growth and development. For example, Kitamura and Burnaham (2003) measured pitch and communicative intent in the speech of mothers as they spoke to their infants at 3, 6, 9, and 12 months of age and found that speech patterns varied according to age and gender of the infants. In a study of eleven mother–child dyads, Rollins (2003) also found that the type of early maternal input an infant receives at the age of 9 months affects language production abilities at 30 months of age. Young infants whose mothers discussed objects of joint focus of attention and narrated ongoing activities with them were more likely to use a variety of syntactic and morphological forms later in development than infants whose mothers' communication was less contingent on a joint focus of attention (e.g., child-centered social routines such as "peek-a-boo," feeling state exchanges such as "do you like that?," directives such as "put the blue one on," "look at this". Studies also show that young children whose mothers frequently engage in conversation and ensure that their child's attention is drawn to whatever is being talked about tend to label items/events more frequently than children of mothers who interact less often and offer less guidance (Tomasello & Farrar, 1986). As children grow older, they have experiences in a social environment beyond those provided by their mothers or immediate caregivers and these interactions also influence language acquisition, including the development of referential and/or expressive speech, word learning, and grammar (see Goldfield & Snow, 2001; Tomasello & Bates, 2001, for reviews of related literature). What is unique to this point of view is the idea that the quality and frequency of social interactions that children encounter either facilitate or constrain the child's learning of language structure or form.

Other investigators have adopted a more extreme stance and suggest that the structural end-state of language itself is use-conditional (Tomasello, 2003; see Ninio & Snow, 1999, for a review). In this view, language is a "ready-made product of sociohistorical development" and is used as a tool by children to analyze, generalize, and encode experience (Luria, 1982). In the process of language acquisition, children name things, and assign meanings to social events and activities using linguistic tools that have historical and cultural significance. Thus, mentally active children construct language in dynamic, active environments using tools that have value in a specific sociocultural context.

Vygotsky (1962) argues that the early social speech of infants and toddlers is multifunctional and is used solely for social contact and influencing others (children and adults influence each other). As children interact with adults in their social community, this social speech becomes more directed to the purpose of controlling social acts. Preschool-aged children's egocentric speech (e.g., talking aloud during play activities) serves as a running record of this directed activity. This view contrasts that of Piaget, who describes the egocentric speech of young preschool-aged children as a monologue, in which the child speaks about him/herself, without trying to take the perspective of a listener. Piaget argues that social speech (i.e., when a child exchanges ideas and thoughts with others) occurs only after significant changes in cognition and symbolic knowledge have occurred. Alternatively, Vygotsky (1978) describes the self-talk of children as their internal use of language structure to plan and control activity within their social community. As children become more proficient in their use of language to self-regulate their social environment, egocentric speech "goes underground" and formulates inner speech (Wertsch, 1998). Inner speech, in turn, is responsible for governing or directing thought. Thus, language mediates child perception and words carry not only meaning but are also the fundamental units of thinking to control an external world. Communicative exchanges and the interpretation of communicative intents are, in Vygotsky's view, foundational to language learning and thought development over the lifespan.

According to a use-conditional perspective, meanings reside in the social activity of the speech communities that surround children and for children to attach meaning to linguistic structures they hear, they must also attend to the communicative intents of the speakers that are addressing them. This activity is complex because social phenomena can be represented in different ways, depending upon the perspective and motivation of the speaker. For instance, Christiansen (1999) argues that the term "learning disability" (or "reading disability") reflects a form of social practice in which diversity in student achievement is transformed into individual pathology. Moreover, the communicative act of labeling children "learning disabled" functions to legitimize school failure for children whose learning difficulties are "unexpected." In this view, language is a powerful tool that can be used to shape our views and thought processes, and as such, it lies not within the psychology of the individual but is created through political, cultural, and social agency.

Exploring causal links between children's experiences and language acquisition holds promise as one of the more fruitful lines of future research. Much needs to be determined about the experiences that are essential to facilitate language acquisition and the times during which these critical experiences will have the most impact on children's language and literacy development. At the same time, it is important that future research also investigates the effects of different cultural and social experiences on the reading of children-who struggle in school.

D. Connectionist Models of Language Learning

Another alternative to rationalist, rule-governed views of language acquisition is to consider language as a connection of ideas governed by principles of resemblance, contiguity in time or place, and cause and effect. Originating with the ideas of Hume and Locke, these principles underlie the theory of associationism, which is a major tenet of the philosophical tradition called "empiricism." According to this viewpoint, the mind connects things that are experienced together and generalizes to new objects and events according to their similarity to known ones with comparable sensible qualities. This theoretical perspective is foundational to conceptualizing stimulus–response bonds in traditional behaviorist learning theory and, more recently, to interpreting the nature of connections that underlie network models that simulate the operation of neural networks in the brain (e.g., McClelland & Rummelhart, 1981). Assuming a one-to-one correspondence between neurons in a neural net and the mental representations that they encode is clearly an oversimplification of the workings of the brain (Berninger & Richards, 2002; Bishop, 2000). Nevertheless, connectionist models are helpful because they explain the changing way input is reduced, encoded, stored, and retrieved in a general language system. In the following discussion, we review the competition model, a connectionist account of language acquisition proposed by MacWhinney (1999, 1987).

The competition model (MacWhinney, 1999, 1987) draws on the notion of parallel distributed processors (PDP; McClelland & Rummelhart, 1981) to explain how children learn to communicate. PDPs are multilayered networks of processing units that operate simultaneously together to interpret linguistic input and produce speech. This distributed system of processing units functions in the same way that neural networks operate in the brain to solve information-processing problems (Christiansen & Chater, 2001). Each unit or "activation node" (i.e., neuron) receives information from the environment and sends excitatory or inhibitory messages to other nodes by pathways (i.e., the dendrites and axons that make up the neural pathways that connect neurons in the brain). Nodes, like neurons, receive input from other activated nodes across pathways of varying strength. These connection weights are stored and continuously readjusted based on experience. All known phonological patterns, words, and syntactic forms are the activated units that compete simultaneously to represent a particular meaning or communicative function. In the process of acquiring language, the linguistic forms that match a communicative function become strengthened with repeated use, and linguistic forms that are functionally marginal, rare, or have errors, disappear. This process begins prior to formal speech production, when infants perform communicative acts (e.g., requesting by gestures) that are essentially similar to substitutions of verbalizations for nonverbal behaviors. As they grow older, children learn to use cues (i.e., form–function relationships) to generate linguistic forms that match functional adult speech. Thus, language is learned by experience rather than by design. Moreover, the rate that children learn language is determined by the validity and strength of cues in their language, the frequency with which cues are presented, and the ability of children to successfully perceive and integrate cues to meet their social needs.

Common to all connectionist models is the idea that critical information becomes encoded economically. Thus, the process of language learning is not simply additive, but includes processes of subtraction and reorganization. Distinctions between the formal structural systems of phonology, syntax, semantics, and pragmatics become blurred as the interactions among components in a connectionist model are probabilistic and contextual. Levels of language are less modular and more integrated with other cognitive systems. Moreover, there is some indication that the integrated language systems of young children are continuous with the corresponding language systems of adults. In contrast to linguistic and developmental theories that describe hierarchal language system, connectionist models assume that cognitive and language processes interact at all levels of language. Executive capacity is conceptualized here as the total amount of activation available on the language net. When deficiencies or breaks in the system occur, the total amount of activation remains stable; however, resources may be reallocated to different areas to compensate for the breakage in the system. Whether the influence of executive processes (e.g., working memory, attentional capacity) on the language system of poor readers can be generalized to other cognitive domains, or whether the relations between executive functions and reading are isolated to a domain-specific language system has not been resolved and is an issue of much debate in the current literature (see Swanson & Cooney, this volume, for a complete discussion). Distributed connectionist frameworks have been used to produce computer simulations of word reading and word reading difficulties (Plaut *et al.*, 1996; Seidenberg & MeClelland, 1989). Modeling the complexities of spoken conversational discourse and/or comprehension of extended reading texts (i.e., beyond words or single sentences) with computers, however, is beyond the scope of most current connectionist models.

E. Implications

Language acquisition is likely not a unitary phenomenon that is fully explained by one theoretical approach. A large body of research evidence exists both to support and to refute the central tenets of each position, suggesting that language acquisition is a complex, multidimensional construct that can be viewed from diverse perspectives. One issue, however, is whether research findings from these diverse perspectives converge in ways that further our understanding of the emergence reading disabilities. One point of general agreement that has implications for investigators and professionals interested in language-related reading disabilities is that a child's capacity for language acquisition is a function of genetic predisposition, brain maturation, cognition, and experiences in the physical and culturally defined social environment. Theoretical perspectives differ only to the extent that each dimension is emphasized in the explanation of the emergence of language. Thus, individual differences in language acquisition for children with language-based reading disabilities may arise from diverse, but complementary origins and include genetic, biological, cognitive, environmental, and cultural factors. Arguments about whether language-based reading disabilities are best approached from one or more of these levels of analysis are moot if research findings complement each other. Moreover, studies from diverse theoretical perspectives have the potential to inform theorists as well as practitioners on complex issues concerning the heterogeneity and changing nature of reading disabilities over the lifespan. In the following sections, we discuss what is currently known about language–reading relations for typically developing readers and about the language origins of reading disabilities. Themes highlighted in our previous review of theories of language acquisition filter through this body of research. One challenge for the reader is to tease out the ways in which these themes compliment and support each other to further our understanding of language-reading relations for children with reading disabilities.

III. LANGUAGE AND READING

The difficulty confronting investigators interested in linking children's language acquisition with reading development is that although the general language system that guides listening and speaking is assumed to be continuous with the language system that underlies the reading development, each modality (listening, speaking, reading, writing) draws on specialized functional components within this general language system. Listening and speaking, therefore, do not correspond exactly to reading and writing. When in conversation, a speaker and listener communicate in an interactive, social context that is face-to-face, immediate, and shared. In comparison, a writer and reader communicate from contexts that are distal from each other and through a code of abstract, written symbols. In contrast to a speaker who addresses a listener directly, an author may not have a specific reader or audience in mind when writing. Whereas the unit of analysis in oral communication is the utterance, the unit of analysis in written communication can be either the utterance (i.e., in written dialogue) or the sentence (i.e., in formal written discourse).

Learning to read is a decontextualized activity that clearly presents linguistic and cognitive challenges for children that are somewhat separate from those presented during highly contextualized, spoken communication. This may account for the finding that some children have word reading difficulties despite normal language comprehension/production abilities. Kamhi and Catts (2002) refer to this group of poor readers as children with *dyslexia*. The authors also identify two other subgroups of children who have reading disabilities. One group, referred to as *language learning disabled*, have poor word recognition difficulties as well as poor language comprehension. Another group of poor readers have normal or above word identification skills; however, they may not understand the language they are able to decode. The authors refer to this group of children as *hyperlexic* (Aaron *et al.*, 1999; Catts & Kamhi, 1999). All three groups of children have reading comprehension difficulties (Kamhi, 1997). The source of reading comprehension failure for children with dyslexia is inaccurate and/or slow decoding. For children with hyperlexia, problems with reading comprehension are the result of language and cognitive deficits. Children with language learning disabilities have difficulties in both word recognition and listening comprehension. The challenge for investigators interested in emerging language–reading relations for children with reading disabilities, therefore, is first, to identify the linguistic origins of two overlapping but, to some extent, independent facets of reading: word recognition and text comprehension (Hoover & Gough, 1990; Gough & Tunmer, 1986) once the association of language to word recognition and textcomprehension is understood, attention is directed to determining whether deficiencies in language processes affect the emergence and maintenance of reading disabilities over time.

IV. LANGUAGE, WORD RECOGNITION, AND READING DISABILITIES

A. Dual-Route and Single-Route Models

In the Dual-Route Cascaded (DRC) model proposed by Castles and Coltheart (1993), there are two discrete, nonsemantic routes that lead to effective word recognition: "a phonological route" and a "lexical route." In the phonological route, children utilize the linguistic rules of phonology to recognize phonetically regular words (e.g., cat, dog) or nonwords (e.g., wup, mag). In the lexical route, children draw on their knowledge of the orthographic code and semantics to store and retrieve phonetically irregular or exceptional words (e.g., yacht, because) from their lexicon with a specific pronunciation. Phonetically regular words can be identified using either route. Irregular or exception words are identified solely by the lexical route because their phonological representation cannot be derived using phonetic rules. Nonwords (e.g., wep, pud) are identified solely by the phonological route because these words are not part of the child's lexicon. Two main types of reading impairment, based on whether the child relies primarily on the phonological or lexical route during word recognition, are proposed. "Surface dyslexics" are children who have damage to the whole word pathway and rely extensively on phonological strategies in word reading. "Phonological dyslexics" are children who have damage to the phonological rule pathway and who rely primarily on orthographic coding skill to recognize printed words. In support of their theory, Castles and Coltheart report that 55% of a referred sample of children with reading disabilities had phonological dyslexia and 30% had surface dyslexia. A small portion of the reading-disabled children (10%) had a combination of both subtypes. Phonological and surface dyslexic subtypes have been validated in numerous studies of poor readers (Murphy & Pollatsek, 1994; Manis *et al.*, 1996; Stanovich *et al.*, 1997).

Alternatively, single-route or distributed connectionist models of word reading propose that uniformity exists in the way that regular and exception words are represented in a multilayered network of processing units. That is, phonological, orthographic, and semantic processing units become simultaneously activated and interact both cooperatively and competitively with each other during word reading. The values assigned to connections within the system oscillate with repeated experiences until a stable pattern of connection weights is established. In this view, skilled word reading involves the simultaneous activation of *both* phonological and semantic pathways and *all* parts of the system participate in processing, although different parts of the network may be more important, depending on whether the input is an exception word or a regular word or nonword (Plaut, 2001). Reading exception words, for instance, requires additional support from the semantic pathway. When the contribution of the semantic pathway is removed from the system, or when the division of labor between the semantic and phonological pathways is unbalanced, the system manifests itself as *surface dyslexia*. On the other hand, when the orthographic–phonological pathway is damaged and when the semantic pathway cannot compensate for this damage, such as in the case where children have difficulty reading phonetically regular words or nonwords, the system reflects *phonological dyslexia*.

B. Developmental Models

Another way to conceptualize word recognition difficulties of reading-disabled children is from a developmental perspective. Several authors have proposed schemes that describe the phases through which developing readers pass to become fluent readers (e.g., Chall, 1996; Fitzgerald & Shanahan, 2000; Goswami, 1986; Juel, 1988, 1991). Ehri and McCormick (1998) propose a comprehensive cognitive framework that describes five continuous phases of word learning among beginning readers; each phase is distinguished by critical differences in the developing reader's understanding of the alphabetic writing system to read words. Visual and memory processes explain variance in individual differences in children's printed word learning independently of that attributed to language factors; however, in the following discussion, we emphasize the relations between language and visual or memory processes that are necessary to progress through each phase (see Ehri & McCormick, 1998, for a complete overview of the model).

Children who are reading at the pre-alphabetic phase in Ehri and McCormick's (1998) model have a very limited knowledge of the structure of their writing system. Although they may understand that logos or signs in their environment have meaning (e.g. stop, MacDonald's, Coke), children at this phase have little structural knowledge of letter names and are unaware that graphemes map to phonemes. Pre-alphabetic readers attend to selective, nonphonetic, visual cues to remember words, such as the shape or the length of the word (Juel, 1991) or the picture that illustrates the word. Readers at the partial-alphabetic phase begin to distinguish the graphemes in words and are able to match phonemes with letter names: [b], [d], [f], [j], [k], [l], [m], [n], [p], [r], [s], [t], [v], and [z]. Ehri and her colleagues claim that children at this phase read words using memory of the word's visual form and structure and by using partial graphophonetic cues. At the full-alphabetic phase, children form accurate phonological representations from grapheme–phoneme relationships they see in words because they have phoneme awareness together with their knowledge of grapheme–phoneme relations. This allows children to simultaneously decode unfamiliar words, store in memory the results of their phonetic analyses, and read unfamiliar words by comparing the obtained structure to familiar words they have previously stored in memory. The consolidated-alphabetic phase overlaps considerably with the full-alphabetic phase and describes a time when children acquire knowledge about inflectional morphemes. The final phase is the automatic phase, when children develop automaticity and speed in identifying both familiar and unfamiliar words. Automatic, fluent word identification frees the reader's attention to focus on constructing meaning from a sentence being read or from extended text in which the sentence is embedded.

Ehri's developmental phases of reading provide important indicators of how language demands of reading change over time. Each phase, therefore, has potential to act as a language marker of reading difficulties. Whether these language markers are specific to reading or extend across other academic (i.e., writing, math) domains may help to explain the pervasive effect of reading disabilities on learning in school. Developmental models, such as Ehri's, also offer researchers a starting point to link individual differences in children's language acquisition with reading development. In the following section, we review the literature on individual differences in language among children with reading disabilities, while keeping in mind the importance of embedding this knowledge within a developmental framework.

V. SOURCES OF INDIVIDUAL DIFFERENCES

A. Phonological Processing

A large body of research has identified deficient phonological processing, an important component of the partial- and full-alphabetic phases of reading development, as a primary cause of reading disabilities. Literally hundreds of studies have shown that poor readers tend to form less stable phonological (Snowling, 2000; Stanovich & Siegel, 1994; Torgesen et al., 1994) or morphophonological representations in memory than normally developing readers, and, without intervention, difficulties in phonological processing that emerge either in the primary or upper elementary grades (Leach et al., 2003) pervade well into adulthood (Berninger, 2000; Bruck, 1992; Naucler & Magnusson, 2002). Moreover, research findings that link phonological processing with individual differences in reading performance are robust across languages and orthographies (Chiappe & Siegel, 1999; Goswami, 2002; Goswami et al., 1998; Naucler & Magnusson, 2000); however, the degree to which phonological processing predicts word recognition is a function of the shallowness of orthography of the language (Goswami et al., 2003). Readers of alphabetic languages in which graphemes correspond directly to phonemes (e.g., Swedish) tend to be highly sensitive to the phonemic level during reading words (Magnusson & Nauclér, 1990) compared to readers of languages in which the grapheme–phoneme correspondence is not high. Phonological awareness–reading relations are also mediated by general spoken language ability (Cooper et al., 2002) and by semantic knowledge (Snowling et al., 2000).

There are three ways that theorists have conceptualized the origins of phonological processing difficulty. According to one position, children's awareness of the phonemes in their language emerges as a result of increases in vocabulary growth. With increases in word knowledge, children are required to discriminate similar-sounding words to allow for efficient storage in their mental lexicons (for a complete discussion, see the lexical restructuring model first proposed by Metsala & Walley, 1998, as well as Metsala, 1999; Walley et al., 2003). For instance, toddler-aged English-speaking children who hear the word *cat* likely perceive a holistic sound pattern (i.e.,/kæt/). When speaking the word *cat*, very young children attempt to produce the sound representation of the word that is stored as a whole in their memory. They are not required, and are likely not able, to consciously segment the word into its constituent sounds (i.e., /k/, /æ/, /t/) (Chiat, 2001; Jusczyk et al., 1998). With a growth in vocabulary, however, children are faced with the problem of storing similar-sounding words that have different meanings (e.g., cat, catch, catcher, bobcat). At this point, spoken word recognition strategies shift from whole to part processing and children begin to construct phonological and morphophonological representations from the speech code. This ability to form accurate phonological and/or morphophonological representations from the speech code is necessary for a young child to identify and manipulate phonemes, which are the smallest sound units of language onto which map graphemes, the written symbols of an alphabetic script (e.g. /k/ /æ/ /t/ c-a-t; Perfetti, 1985). Without the ability to form precise phonological or morphophonological representations from spoken words, children have difficulty learning the phonic skills (e.g., that the consonant and vowel sounds of a word can be represented by letters) that are prerequisite skills to single word reading. Moreover, they are less likely to develop an explicit awareness of phonemes and/or benefit from print-related activities that operate in reverse to improve phonological skills.

In contrast to the view that phonemes become identifiable as units to children with increases in children's vocabulary, a second account holds that phoneme segments available to infants for speech perception and production are functionally identical to units accessed by older children for reading or writing. However, it is not until children are faced with the task of learning to read or write and are presented with an alphabetic orthography that they develop a conscious awareness of phonemic units (Bowers & Newby-Clark, 2002). At the same time, to become consciously aware of phonemes, children must be able to decenter from the meaning of a whole word to attend to individual phonemic units in speech. Learning to read is thought to support this developmental process because children's experiences with an alphabetic orthography make the segmental structure of spoken syllables (i.e., consonants and vowels) more transparent (Dale *et al.*, 1995; Ehri, 1997). This view is supported by the finding that when early intervention procedures for children with low levels of literacy target the orthography of the language, phonemic awareness improves (e.g., Juel & Minden-Cup, 2000). Children's problems with phonological processing, therefore, are thought to originate from two possible sources: underdeveloped metacognitive skills and/or a lack of experience reading texts.

Another group of researchers argue that speech perception deficits are a source of phonological processing difficulty for some children, given that the acoustic signal corresponding to a phoneme may sound different depending on the sounds that are adjacent to it (Liberman, 1997). Although discriminating the speech signal is not a straightforward task, most children's phonological sensitivity to speech sounds seems to stabilize once they enter school and reading instruction begins (Burgess, 2002). On the other hand, some children's sensitivity to different speech sounds may not be firmly established at school entry, placing them at risk for reading problems. Lyytinen and his colleagues (Lyytinen *et al.*, 2001) suggest that these speech perception differences of poor readers may be identifiable during infancy. They compared the developmental pathways of infants with and without familial risk for dyslexia and found that group differences in speech perception (as measured by event-related potential responses to speech sounds and in head-turn responses) could be found as early as a few days and 6 months of age.

B. Morphological Awareness

Some researchers suggest that morphological awareness may be a source of individual differences in word recognition for children in the mid- to late-elementary grades (Singson *et al.*, 2000) as well as in the high school years (Carlisle, 2000). Derivational morphemes such as suffixes that alter the syntactic category of the attached base (e.g., *function* is a noun, *functional* is an adjective; *familiar* is an adjective, *familiarize* is a verb) and awareness of the semantic, syntactic, phonological, and relational properties of morphemes have been shown to contribute to the prediction of both word recognition and reading comprehension (Mahoney *et al.*, 2000). What is not clear from these studies, however, and a topic for future research, is whether the deficient morphological awareness of some poor readers stems from a basic insensitivity to the grammatical rules that govern morpheme structures or whether it evolves as an outcome of early deficits in phonological processing. In this view, constraints in phonological processing slow reading development and limit the experiences of readers that are critical to facilitate development of an awareness of morphological distinctions (Bryant *et al.*, 1998).

C. The Timing Hypothesis

According to the timing hypothesis, children become poor readers as a result of the slow rate at which they process information or by a deficit in their ability to process information temporally (Chiappe *et al.*, 2002; Share *et al.*, 2002). Temporal processing refers here to the duration, sequencing, and rhythm of events. Tallal and her colleagues (Tallal, 1980, 1984, 1988; Tallal *et al.*, 1997; Tallal & Piercy 1975) propose that children with reading disabilities are unable to discriminate speech sounds because of the rapid, temporal dimensions of incoming auditory signals (Tallal & Piercy, 1975; Farmer & Klein, 1995).

Temporal processing, however, also takes place in the visual system. It is now well established that children's performance on naming tasks, such as naming serially presented letter, colors, numbers, and objects, contributes to the variance in the prediction of word recognition, beyond that attributable to phonological awareness (Bowers, 1995, Wolf & Bowers, 1999; Wolf *et al.*, 2002, 2000) and that this prediction is significant both for young, elementary school-aged children as well as for children in the middle school grades (Scarborough, 1998). What remains controversial is whether the relation between rapid naming and word recognition for children with reading difficulty is mediated by a timing deficit, as previously discussed (Wolf, 1991, 1997; Wolf *et al.*, 2002) or a language-specific, phonological processing difficulty (Chiappe *et al.*, 2002; Wagner & Torgesen, 1987), a global processing inefficiency (Catts *et al.*, 2002; Kail *et al.*, 1999), or attentional constraints (Neuhaus *et al.*, 2001).

D. Implications

The picture that emerges from the foregoing discussion suggests that much of the heterogeneity associated with the construct of reading disabilities may be attributed to diversity in the way that children process and use language to recognize printed words. As a result, one may hypothesize that subgroups of poor readers can be identified based on constraints in phonological processing, morphological awareness, or temporal processing. Moreover, it also seems reasonable to assume that instructional strategies can be mapped to children's processing needs, which, in turn, suggests that when poor readers do not benefit from instruction that is based on sound teaching principles, the underlying cause is a mismatch between children's constraints in language processing and the actual instructional objectives set. Further research is needed, however, to substantiate these assumptions.

VI. LANGUAGE, READING COMPREHENSION AND READING DISABILITIES

Developing fluency in word identification is necessary, but not sufficient, for a young reader to understand the message communicated by an author through a writing system (deJong & van der Leij, 2002). Meanings of individual words in text must be integrated with meanings of other words stored in a child's mental lexicon. Moreover, meaning is also constructed through syntactic parsing and semantic integration to develop local coherence at the sentence level, and by monitoring comprehension to formulate a cohesive, global representation of the text as a whole (Ehrilick *et al.*, 1999). It follows, therefore, that children with language-related reading disabilities may have constraints in vocabulary acquisition and/or difficulties manipulating the syntactic and semantic structure of language. Moreover, these language comprehension difficulties may be evident early on, possibly before a child has developed fluent word recognition processes.

A. Vocabulary

Individual differences in children's vocabulary size predicts variability in word recognition (Dickinson & Snow, 1987) and reading comprehension performance (Bast & Reitsma, 1998; Bashir & Scavuzzo, 1992). In a longitudinal study of reading development of English-speaking, school-aged children, Torgesen and his colleagues (Torgesen *et al.*, 1997) found that after statistically controlling for an autoregressive effect, vocabulary knowledge predicted reading comprehension from the second to the fifth grade. These findings have been replicated in several other languages. For example, in a five-year longitudinal study of Dutch children's early home and literacy experiences and later reading abilities, Senechal and LeFavre (2002) found that preschool-aged children's early experiences listening to stories in books predicted vocabulary development, which, in turn, was a predictor of reading comprehension ability in grade 3. A similar finding is reported by Dufva and her colleagues (Dufva *et al.*, 2001), who studied the listening comprehension and phonological awareness of Finnish children in preschool and found that children's listening comprehension significantly predicted independent variance in reading performance in second grade.

Increases in children's vocabulary size at least partially explain reading development and limitations in vocabulary knowledge are associated with reading comprehension failure (Catts, 1999; Nation & Snowling, 1998; Stanovich & Siegel, 1994). However, having a large inventory of known vocabulary words in a mental lexicon is not sufficient for children to become good readers. Good readers also know how vocabulary is integrated into complex semantic, syntactic, and discourse structures and they utilize these structures to monitor and integrate meaning across words, sentences, and throughout the text. Children's ability to perform this complex juggling act is further mediated by working memory capacity, executive function, and metacognition, all of which can be sources of reading difficulty for children with reading disabilities (Swanson & Alexander, 1997; Swanson & Ashbaker, 2000; Swanson & Trahan, 1996).

B. Semantic/Syntactic/Discourse Abilities

Growth in semantics and syntactical abilities undergoes subtle and gradual change that begins in childhood and extends well into the adolescent and adult years (Nippold 1999, 2000). In a longitudinal study of the language and reading abilities of 39 children in kindergarten, Roth *et al.*, (2002) found that phonological awareness predicted word recognition, whereas semantic skills (i.e., oral word definitions and word retrieval) predicted independent variance in reading comprehension in second grade. The authors argue that the nature of language–reading relations appears to change over time and whether language skills are associated with later reading ability is a function of the reading measure that is predicted, the language domain sampled, and the point in development when the measure of language is taken. Support for this idea is also provided by Nation and Snowling (1998), who compared a group of 9-year-old children with reading comprehension difficulties with good readers, matched on age and decoding ability, and found that poor comprehenders were less able to read irregular and low-frequency words that require knowledge of semantics as well as phonological skills. As children mature as readers, it appears that they draw on semantic skills that interact with low-level phonological processing to decode unfamiliar words.

A second source of reading comprehension difficulty for developing readers is associated with a limited knowledge of syntactic structure (Craig *et al.*, 2003; Vos & Friederici, 2003). In a study of good and poor readers matched on age, nonverbal ability, and decoding ability, Nation and Snowling (2000) asked participants to first listen to a sentence with a jumbled word order and, second, to put the words in the correct order. Children with poor reading comprehension were less able than good readers to correct active and passive sentences. Passive sentences were the most difficult for all children; however, for children with reading comprehension problems, the difficulty was greater. The authors conclude that poor readers have weak syntactic awareness skills relative to good readers; however, because the good readers were also influenced by experimental manipulations (i.e., active, passive sentences), this weakness in syntactic awareness is viewed as an arrest in language development, not a deficit.

As children mature linguistically, they develop the ability to comprehend texts that have been written in more complex genres (e.g., persuasion) and for a variety of audiences. Moreover, children also develop a sophisticated understanding of figurative language (e.g., metaphors, idioms, proverbs) that is interpretable only through knowledge of language structure and use in a social and/or cultural context. For example, a statement such as "The early bird catches the worm" has both a literal and a culturally determined, metaphorical meaning. One theory postulates that when children encounter metaphorical expressions in text, they must inhibit acceptance of the literal meaning in favor of a metaphorical interpretation, based on previous cues in the text (Glucksberg *et al.*, 2001). Difficulty understanding metaphors in text could theoretically be a result of a child's inability to recognize or interpret cues, an attention deficit (related to inhibition), or possibly a combination of both factors.

Language effects on reading comprehension are mediated by a number of cognitive influences including world knowledge, working memory, the ability to generate inferences, and story structure knowledge (Cain *et al.*, 2000). Moreover, there is some evidence to suggest that language mediates the role of cognitive processes on reading comprehension (Nation *et al.*, 1999). Future research is required to determine how language processes influence the components of a complex reading system and the ways that these relations change over time; however, it seems unlikely that any one route will explain reading comprehension failure for all children.

C. Implications

Reading–language relations become increasingly complex as children's reading development progresses beyond word recognition to comprehension of connected text; therefore, a constraint in a single language process is probably insufficient to explain all children's reading problems. Moreover, no one instructional approach will likely remediate the underlying language problems of all children who have difficulty understanding connected text. A better approach that has emerged from meta-analytic reviews of effective interventions for children with reading comprehension difficulties is to adhere to principles of instruction that lead to positive outcomes. Although these principles may operate differently for children with different language problems, several instructional principles have been identified in the research that contribute to effective instruction (see Swanson & Deschler, 2003). Case studies of children who are nonresponsive to interventions based on these instructional principles may provide valuable information about the complex language system that underlies reading comprehension for children with reading disabilities.

VII. FUTURE CHALLENGES

One may think that given the diverse perspectives outlined in this chapter, there is little hope for consensus among researchers and theorists about the nature of language origins of reading disabilities. However, current research findings converge on three important points that have implications for future research and for educators:

1. *When children experience difficulty learning to read, this problem is best viewed as a complex interplay among linguistic, cognitive, social–interactionist, connectionist, and sociocultural phenomena.*

   Children are born with a genetic predisposition to learn language and the language they learn is predetermined by the cultural and social contexts in which they live. Learning to understand and speak a language is complex and draws on a child's perceptual, cognitive, social communicative, and linguistic skills and is facilitated by years of experience actively interacting with competent speakers in a linguistic community. This linguistic community is itself a product of centuries of socio-historical development. Learning to read is also a multifaceted, cognitively demanding activity that draws on a child's knowledge of language form, content, and function within a sociocultural context. Singular, pathological explanations of reading failure (i.e., phonological processing "deficit") are simplistic and probably inaccurate, considering the complexity of the processes involved. Learning language and learning to read are dynamic processes, subject to developmental and/or cultural change, and static or specific explanations are likely to be unreliable causes of reading failure as children mature, even though these language processes may have considerable impact on reading at specific points in time. There are many reasons intrinsic to the child that explain why not every child learns to read at the same rate or to the same level of proficiency. Children may have difficulty processing language at one or more levels, and this processing has an effect on and is influenced by the timing and nature of children's experiences in a highly contextualized, social world. Viewing children's language-related reading difficulties from a single perspective is clearly an ineffective approach, and one of the undeniable challenges faced by future researchers in the area of reading disabilities is to integrate findings that arise from diverse theoretical accounts. Research on reading disabilities is best conceptualized as an interdisciplinary endeavor that requires a broad spectrum of ideas and solutions to the problem of why some children find learning to read a daunting process.

2. *Learning to read an alphabetic language draws on children's knowledge of language form, content, and use within the cultural context in which they live.*

Children from diverse cultural backgrounds who are learning to read an alphabetic script draw on similar language skills (Mann & Wimmer, 2002; McBride-Chang & Kail, 2002). Therefore, studies that compare the difficulties of poor readers who speak alphabetic languages with transparent orthographies with the problems faced by poor readers of languages that are less regular or opaque may provide further understanding of the more subtle language problems children face when learning to read an alphabetic script as well as the difficulties that are universal across orthographies.

At the same time, studies of children's poor reading in languages with similar orthographies may provide important information about the influences of children's social environment on language and reading acquisition. This examination can occur at different levels of analysis. For example, on one level, studies that investigate the efficacy of broadbased government initiatives that aim to improve overall literacy and close achievement gaps between poor and good readers (e.g., the "Leave No Child Behind" legislation in the United States and the "National Literacy Strategy" in England) are helpful to compare and contrast the sociocultural contexts that are most effective at promoting literacy acquisition for children who lag behind in reading development. At another level, longitudinal case studies of the communicative interactions of children who have a familial risk for reading problems within a specific cultural context are helpful to determine whether some early experiences with language are essential to protect against the formation of reading problems. Regardless of the approach taken, there is a general consensus among researchers that children's language experiences and the quality of language input they receive has much potential for understanding the emergence of reading disabilities.

3. *Although sensitive periods for language acquisition exist, there is little evidence to support the notion that language and/or literacy intervention should be limited to the early childhood and/or early school years.*

Relying on a "critical period" argument as theoretical justification for early intervention programs that provide experiences to facilitate language acquisition during early childhood (0 to 3 years of age) and to encourage reading acquisition during the primary school years (kindergarten to grade 3) is not necessary, nor is it entirely justifiable, given current research findings. The time frame for language learning extends into late adolescence and reading skills continue to develop well beyond the elementary school years into middle and high school years. Bailey (2002) argues that timing is best conceptualized as the match between experiences of the child, the child's development, and the child's need or readiness to learn a novel concept. Future research endeavors that focus on the quality of experiences that are critical for language and reading growth throughout childhood and adolescence are crucial for typically developing readers as well as for children with reading disabilities.

Of course, having diverse theoretical perspectives also means that debates will continue in the field. However, these issues have considerable potential to inform us about the nature of reading disabilities. For example, whether components in the language system that underlies reading for children with reading disabilities are best viewed as modular and encapsulated within a domain specific to language or whether these processes are integrated and overlap across several domains needs resolution. Whether a language system is modular or connected has several implications for instruction. For example, in a modular system, intervention to improve performance on a language-related reading task will not affect performance tasks with similar language requirements in other academic domains because a different hierarchy of skill acquisition defines each domain. In an integrated system, however, language-based activities that improve reading task performance will likely improve performance in other academic domains. A second issue concerns whether discrete subtypes of reading disabilities can be identified, based on children's specific language deficits or whether language-related reading difficulties are best viewed. Third, it is of interest to determine whether reading disabilities are a function of an arrest in the acquisition of formal structural rules or a result of limitations in the quality or amount of input a child receives throughout language development. Studies that utilize alternate hypotheses to test opposing theoretical positions such as these are clearly more informative to the field than investigations that rely solely on a null hypothesis.

The processes of language acquisition and reading development constitutes a complex phenomenon; therefore, the study of reading disabilities can also be expected to be multifaceted. Instead of trying to describe reading disabilities through a single lens, future researchers in the field must be prepared to consider several perspectives to fully capture the meaning and multidimensionality of the construct. How language influences the emergence of reading disabilities is not a unitary explanation, but a composite of diverse strands of thought.

References

Aaron, P. G., Joshi, M., & Williams, K. A. (1999). Not all reading disabilities are alike. *Journal of Learning Disabilities*, **32**, 120–137.

Adams, M. (1990). *Beginning to read. Thinking and learning about print*. Cambridge, MA: MIT Press.

Ames, E. W., & Chisholm, K. (2001). Social and emotional development in children adopted from institutions. In D. Bailey, Jr., T. Bruer, F. J. Symons, & J. W. Lichtman (Eds.), *Critical thinking about critical periods* (pp. 129–148). Baltimore, MD: Paul H. Brookes Pub.

Austin, J. L. (1962). *How to do things with words*. Oxford: Clarendon Press.

Bailey, D. (2002). Are critical periods critical for early childhood education? The role of timing in early childhood pedagogy. *Childhood Research Quarterly*, **17**, 281–294.

Bailey, D., Bruer, J. T., Symons, F. J., & Lichtman, J. W. (2001). *Critical thinking about critical periods*. Baltimore, MD: Paul H. Brookes Pub.

Bashir, A. S., & Scavuzzo, A. (1992). Children with language disorders: Natural history and academic success. *Journal of Learning Disabilities*, **25**, 53–65.

Bast, J., & Reitsma, P. (1998). Analyzing the development of individual differences in terms of Matthew effects in reading: Results from a Dutch longitudinal study. *Developmental Psychology*, **34**, 1373–1399.

Berninger, V. (2000). Dyslexia: The invisible, treatable disorder. The story of Einstein's Ninja turtles. *Learning Disability Quarterly*, **23**, 175–195.

Berninger, V., Abbott, R., Abbott, S., Graham, S., & Richards, T. (2002). Writing and reading: Connections between language by hand and language by eye. *Journal of Learning Disabilities*, **35**, 39–56.

Berninger, V., & Richards, T. (2002). *Brain literacy for educators and psychologists.* Amsterdam: Academic Press.

Bishop, D. V. M. (2000). How does the brain learn language? Insights from the study of children with and without language impairment. *Developmental Medicine and Child Neurology*, **42**, 133–142.

Blum-Kulka, S., & Snow, C. (2002). *Talking to adults: The contribution of multiparty discourse to language acquisition.* Mahwah, NJ: Erlbaum.

Bohannon, J. N., & Bonvillian, J. D. (2001) Theoretical approaches to language acquisition. In J. B. Gleason (Ed.), *Development of language* (5th ed., pp. 254–315). Boston: Allyn & Bacon.

Bowers, P. G. (1995). Tracing symbol naming speed's unique contributions to reading disability over time. *Reading and Writing: An Interdisciplinary Journal*, **7**, 189–216.

Bowers, P. G., & Newby-Clark, E. (2002). The role of naming speed within a model of reading acquisition. *Reading and Writing: An Interdisciplinary Journal*, **15**, 109–126.

Brown, I. S., & Felton, R. H. (1990). Effects of instruction on beginning reading skills in children at-risk for reading disability. *Reading and Writing: An Interdisciplinary Journal*, **2**, 223–241.

Bruck, M. (1992). Persistence of dyslexics' phonological awareness deficits. *Developmental Psychology*, **28**, 874–887.

Burgess, S. R. (2002). The influence of speech perception, oral language ability, the home literacy environment, and pre-reading knowledge on the growth of phonological sensitivity: A one-year longitudinal investigation. *Reading and Writing: An Interdisciplinary Journal*, **15**, 709–737.

Bryant, P., Nunes, T., & Bindman, M. (1998). Awareness of language in children who have reading difficulties: Historical comparisons in a longitudinal study. *Journal of Child Psychology and Psychiatry and Allied Disciplines*, **39**, 501–510.

Cain, K., & Oakhill, J. V. (1999). Inference-making ability and its relation to comprehension failure in young children. *Reading and Writing: An Interdisciplinary Journal*, **11**, 489–503.

Cain, K., Oakhill, J. V., & Bryant, P. (2000). Phonological processing skills and comprehension failure: A test of the phonological processing deficit hypothesis. *Reading and Writing: An Interdisciplinary Journal*, **13**, 31–56

Caplan, D., & Waters, G. S. (1999). Issues regarding general and domain-specific resources. *Behavioral and Brain Sciences*, **22**, 114–126.

Carlisle, J. F. (2000). Awareness of the structure and meaning of morphologically complex words: Impact on reading. *Reading and Writing: An Interdisciplinary Journal*, **12**, 169–190.

Castles, A., & Coltheart, M. C. (1993). Varieties of developmental dyslexia. *Cognition*, **47**, 149–180.

Catts, H. W. (1993). The relationship between speech–language impairments and reading disabilities. *Journal of Speech and Hearing Research*, **36**, 948–958.

Catts, H. W. (1999). Phonological awareness: Putting research into practice. *Language Learning and Education*, **6**, 17–19.

Catts, H. W., Fey, M. E., Tomblin, J. B. (2002). A longitudinal analysis of reading outcomes in children with language impairments. *Journal of Speech, Language, & Hearing Research*, **45**, 1142–1157.

Catts, H. W., Gillespie, M., Leonard, L., Kail, R., & Miller, C. (2002). The role of processing, rapid naming, and phonological awareness in reading achievement. *Journal of Learning Disabilities*, **35**, 510–535.

Catts, H. W., & Kamhi, A. (1999). Classification of reading disabilities. In H. Catts & A. Kamhi (Eds.), *Language and reading disabilities* (pp. 73–94). Needham, MA: Allyn & Bacon.

Chall, J. S. (1996). *Stages of reading development*. Fort Worth, TX: Harcourt Brace.

Chiappe, P., & Siegel, L. (1999). Phonological awareness and reading acquisition in English and Punjabi-speaking Canadian children. *Journal of Educational Psychology*, **91**, 20–28.

Chiappe, P., Stringer, R., Siegel, L., & Stanovich, K. E. (2002). Why the timing deficit hypothesis does not explain reading disability in adults. *Reading and Writing: An Interdisciplinary Journal*, **5**, 73–107.

Chiat, S. (2001). Mapping theories of developmental language impairment: Premises, predictions, and evidence. *Language and Cognitive Processes*, **16**, 113–142.

Chomsky, N. (1968). *Language and mind*. New York: Harcourt, Brace & World.

Chomsky, N. (1980). On cognitive structures and their development: A reply to Piaget. In M. Piattelli-Palmarini (Ed.), *Language and learning: The debate between Jean Piaget and Noam Chomsky* (pp. 35–52). Cambridge, MA: Harvard University Press.

Chomsky, N. (1999). On the nature, use and acquisition of language. In W. Ritchie & T. Bhatia (Eds.), *Handbook of child language acquisition* (pp. 13–39). New York: Academic Press.

Christiansen, M. H., & Chater, N. (2001). Connectionist psycholinguistics: Capturing the empirical data. *Trends in Cognitive Sciences*, **5**, 82–88.

Christensen, C. (1999). Learning disability: Issues of representation, power, and the medicalization of school failure. In R. J. Sternberg & L. Spear-Swerling (Eds.), *Perspectives on learning disabilities* (pp. 227–249). Oxford: Westview Press.

Clahsen, H. (1999). Linguistic perspectives in specific language impairment. In W. Ritchie & T. Bhatia (Eds.), *Handbook of child language acquisition* (pp. 675–704). New York: Academic Press.

Cooper, D. H., Roth, F. P., Speece, D. L., & Schatschneider, C. (2002). The contribution of oral language skills to the development of phonological awareness. *Applied Psycholinguistics*, **23**, 399–416.

Craig, H. K., Connor, C. M., & Washington, J. A. (2003). Early positive predictors of later reading comprehension for African American students: A preliminary investigation. *Language, Speech and Hearing Services in Schools*, **34**, 31–43.

Crain, S., & Shankweiler, D. (1991). Modularity and learning to read. In I. G. Mattingly & M. Studdert-Kennedy (Eds.), *Modularity and the motor theory of speech perception* (pp. 375–392). New Haven, CT: Haskins Laboratory.

Crain, S., & Wexler, K. (1999). Methodology in the study of language acquisition: A modular approach. In W. Ritchie & T. Bhatia (Eds.), *Handbook of child language acquisition* (pp. 387–425). New York: Academic Press.

Dale, P. S., Crain-Thoreson, C., & Robinson, M. (1995). Linguistic precocity and the development of reading: The role of extralinguistic factors. *Applied Psycholinguistics*, **16**, 173–187.

deJong, P., & van der Leij, A. (2002). Effects of phonological abilities and listening comprehension on the development of reading. *Scientific Studies of Reading*, **6**, 51–77.

Dickinson, D. K., & Snow, C. (1987). Interrelationships among pre-reading and oral language skills in kindergartners from two social classes. *Early Childhood Research Quarterly*, **2**, 1–25.

Dufva, M., Niemi, P., & Voeten, M. (2001). The role of phonological memory, word recognition, and comprehension skills in reading development: From preschool to grade 2. *Reading & Writing: An Interdisciplinary Journal*, **14**, 91–117.

Ehri, L. C. (1997). Learning to read and learning to spell are one and the same, almost. In C. Perfetti, L. Rieben, & M. Fayol (Eds.), *Learning to spell: Research, theory and practice across languages* (pp. 237–269). Mahwah, NJ: Erlbaum.

Ehri, L. C., & McCormick, S. (1998). Phases of word learning: Implications for instruction with delayed and disabled readers. *Reading and Writing Quarterly*, **14**, 35–164.

Ehrilick, M., Remond, M., & Tardieu, H. (1999). Processing of anaphoric devices in young skilled and less skilled comprehenders: Differences in metacognitive monitoring. *Reading and Writing: An Interdisciplinary Journal*, **11**, 29–63.

Farmer, M. E., & Klein, R. M. (1995). The evidence for a temporal processing deficit linked to dyslexia: A review. *Psychonomic Society*, **2**, 460–493.

Fitzgerald, J., & Shanahan, T. (2000). Reading and writing relations and their development. *Educational Psychologist*, **35**, 39–50.

Fodor, J. (2000). *The mind doesn't work that way: The scopes and limits of computational psychology*. Cambridge, MA: MIT Press.

Fowler, A., Gelman, R., & Gleitman, L. R. (1994). The course of language learning in children with Down syndrome. In H. Tager-Flusberg (Ed.), *Constraints on language acquisition* (pp. 91–140). Hillsdale, NJ: Erlbaum.

Fowler, J. (2003, April 24). US Bridles as UN's Kofi Annan Calls It "Occupying Power," *Associated Press*, Retrieved April 24, 2003, from http://www.ap.org.

Gleason, J. B. (2001). *The development of language*. Boston: Allyn and Bacon.

Glock, H. (2003). Quinn and Davidson on language, thought, and reality. Cambridge: Cambridge University Press.

Glucksberg, S., Newsome, M., & Goldvarg, Y. (2001). Inhibition of the literal: Filtering metaphor-irrelevant information during metaphor comprehension. *Metaphor & Symbol*, **16**, 277–293.

Goldfield, B. A., & Snow, C. E. (2001). Individual differences: Implications for the study of language acquisition. In J. B. Gleason (Ed.), *Development of language* (5th edition, pp. 315–346). Boston: Allyn & Bacon.

Goldin-Meadow, S., Butcher, C., & Mylander, C. (1994). Nouns and verbs in a self-styled gesture system: What's in a name? *Cognitive Psychology*, **27**, 259–319.

Goswami, U. (2002). Phonology, reading, and dyslexia: A cross linguistic perspective. *Annals of Dyslexia*, **52**, 141–163.

Goswami, U. (1986). Children's use of analogy in learning to read: A developmental study. *Journal of Experimental Child Psychology*, **42**, 73–83.

Goswami, U., Ziegler, J. C., Dalton, D., & Schneider, W. (2003). Nonword reading across orthographies: How flexible is the choice of reading units? *Applied Psycholinguistics*, **24**, 235–247.

Goswami, U., Gombert, J. E., & de Barrera, L. F. (1998). Children's orthographic representations and linguistic transparency: Nonsense word reading in English, French, and Spanish. *Applied Psycholinguistics*, **19**, 19–52.

Gough, P. L., & Tunmer, W. (1986). Decoding, reading, and reading disability. *Remedial and Special Education*, **7**, 6–10.

Hoover, W. A., & Gough, P. B. (1990). The simple view of reading. *Reading and Writing: An Interdisciplinary Journal*, **2**, 127–160.

Juel, C. (1988). Learning to read and write: A longitudinal study of 54 children from the first through fourth grades. *Journal of Educational Psychology*, **91**, 44–49.

Juel, C. (1991). Beginning reading. In R. Barr, M. Kamil, P. Mosenthal, & P. Pearson (Eds.), *Handbook of reading research* (Vol. 2, pp. 759–788). New York: Longman.

Juel, C., & Minden-Cupp, C. (2000). Learning to read words: Linguistic units and instructional strategies. *Reading Research Quarterly*, **35**, 458–492.

Just, M., & Carpenter, P. (1987). *The psychology of reading and language comprehension*. Boston: Allyn & Bacon.

Jusczyk, P. W., Hohne, E. A., & Bauman, A. (1998). Infants' sensitivity to allophonic cues for word segmentation. *Perception & Psychophysics*, **61**, 1465–1476.

Kail, R., Hall, L., & Caskey, B. J. (1999). Processing speed, exposure to print, and naming speed. *Applied Psycholinguistics*, **20**, 303–314.

Kamhi (1997). Three perspectives on comprehension: Implications for assessing and treating comprehension problems. *Topics in Language Disorders*, **17**, 62–74.

Kamhi, A. G., & Catts, H. W. (2002). The language basis of reading: Implications for classification and treatment of children with reading disabilities. In K. G. Butler & E. R. Silliman (Eds.), *Speaking, reading, and writing in children with language learning disabilities: New paradigms in research and practice* (pp. 45–72). Mahwah, NJ: Lawrence Erlbaum Assoc.

Kenneally, S. M., Bruck, G. E., Frank, E. M., & Nalty, L. (1998). Language intervention after thirty years of isolation: A case study of a feral child. *Education and Training in Mental Retardation and Developmental Disabilities*, **33**, 13–23.

Kitamura, C., & Burnham, D. (2003). Pitch and communicative intent in mother's speech: Adjustments for age and sex in the first year. *Infancy*, **4**, 85–110.

Leach, J. M., Scarborough, H., & Rescorla, L. (2003). Late emerging reading disabilities. *Journal of Educational Psychology*, **95**, 211–224.

Liberman, A. M. (1997). How theories of speech affect research in reading and writing. In Benita A. Blachman (Ed.), *Foundations of reading acquisition and dyslexia: Implications for early intervention* (pp. 3–19). Mahwah, NJ: Lawrence Erlbaum Assoc.

Luria, A. R. (1982). *Language and cognition*. James V. Wertsch (Ed.), Washington: V H Winston.

Lyytinen, H., Ahonen, T., Eklund, K., Guttorm, T. K., Laakso, M., Leinonen, S., Leppanen, P., Lyytinen, P., Poikkeus, A., Puolakanaho, A., Richardson, U., &

Viholainen, H. (2001). Developmental pathways of children with and without familial risk for dyslexia during the first years of life. *Developmental Neuropsychology*, **20**, 535–554.

McArthur, G. M., Hogben, J. H., Edwards, V. T., Heath, S. M., & Mengler, E. D. (2000). On the "specifics" of specific reading disability and specific language impairment. *Journal of Child Psychology and Psychiatry*, **41**, 869–874.

Mann, V., & Wimmer, H. (2002). Phoneme awareness and pathways into literacy: A comparison of German and American children. *Reading & Writing*, **5**, 653–682.

McBride-Chang, C., & Kail, R. V. (2002). Cross-cultural similarities in the predictors of reading acquisition. *Child Development*, **73**, 1392–1407.

McClelland, J. L., & Rummelhart, D. E. (1981). An interactive activation model of context effects in letter perception: An account of basic findings. *Psychological Review*, **88**, 375–407.

MacWhinney, B. (1987). The competition model. In B. MacWhinney (Ed.), *Mechanisms of language acquisition* (pp. 249–308). Hillsdale, NJ: Lawrence Erlbaum Assoc.

MacWhinney, B. (1999). The emergence of language from embodiment. In B. MacWhinney (Ed.), *The emergence of language* (pp. 213–256). Pittsburgh, PA: Carnegie Mellon.

Magnusson, E., & Nauclér, K. (1990). Can preschool data predict language-disordered children's reading and spelling at school? *Folia Phoniatrica*, **42**, 277–282.

Mahoney, D., Singson, M., & Mann, V. (2000). Reading ability and sensitivity to morphological relations *Reading and Writing: An Interdisciplinary Journal*, **12**, 191–218.

Manis, F. R., Seidenberg, M. S., Doi, L. M., McBride-Chang, C., & Peterson, A. (1996). On the bases of two subtypes of developmental dyslexia. *Cognition*, **58**, 157–195.

Meints, K., Plunkett, K., Harris, P., & Dimmock, D. (2002). What is "on" and "under" for 15-, 18-, and 24-month-olds? Typicality effects in early comprehension of spatial prepositions. *British Journal of Developmental Psychology*, **20**, 113–130.

Metsala, J. L. (1999). Young children's phonological awareness and nonword repetition as a function of vocabulary development. *Journal of Educational Psychology*, **81**, 3–19.

Metsala, J. L., & Walley, A. C. (1998). Spoken vocabulary growth and the segmental restructuring of lexical representations: Precursors to phonemic awareness and early reading ability. In J. L. Metsala and L. C. Ehri (Eds.), *Word recognition in beginning literacy* (pp. 89–120). Mahwah, NJ: Lawrence Erlbaum Assoc.

Murphy, L., & Pollatsek, A. (1994). Developmental dyslexia: Heterogeneity without discrete subgroups. *Annals of Dyslexia*, **44**, 120–146.

Nation, K., Adams, J. W., Bowyer-Crane, C. A., & Snowling, M. J. (1999). Working memory deficits in poor comprehenders reflect underlying language impairments. *Journal of Experimental Child Psychology*, **73**, 139–158.

Nation, K., & Snowling, M. E. (2000). Factors influencing syntactic awareness skills in normal readers and poor comprehenders. *Applied Psycholinguistics*, **21**, 229–241.

Nation, K., & Snowling, M. E. (1998). Semantic processing and the development of word-recognition skills: Evidence from children with reading comprehension difficulties. *Journal of Memory and Language*, **39**, 85–101.

Naucler, K., & Magnusson, E. (2000). Language problems in poor readers. *Logopedics, Phoniatrics, Vocology*, **25**, 12–21.

Naucler, K., & Magnusson, E. (2002). How do preschool language problems affect language problems in adolescence? In F. Windsor & M. L. Kelly (Eds.), *Investigations in clinical phonetics and linguistics* (pp. 99–114). Mahwah, NJ: Lawrence Erlbaum Assoc.

Neuhaus, G., Foorman, B., Francis, D. J., & Carlson, C. D. (2001). Measures of information processing in rapid automatized naming (RAN) and their relation to reading. *Journal of Experimental Child Psychology*, **78**, 359–373.

Nelson, C. A., & Bloom, F. E. (1997). Child development and neuroscience. *Child Development*, **68**, 770–987.

Newman, A. J., Bavelier, D., Corina, D., Jezzard, P., & Neville, H. J. (2002). A critical period for right hemisphere recruitment in American Sign Language processing. *Nature Neuroscience*, **5**, 76–80.

Newport, E. I. (1990). Maturational constraints of language learning. *Cognitive Science*, **14**, 11–28.

Ninio, A., & Snow, C. (1999). The development of pragmatics: Learning to use language appropriately. In W. Ritchie & T. Bhatia (Eds.), *Handbook of child language acquisition* (pp. 347–386). New York: Academic Press.

Ninio, A., Snow, C., & Pan, B. A. (1994). Classifying communicative acts in children's interactions. *Journal of Communication Disorders*, **27**, 157–187.

Nippold, M. A. (1999). Word definition in adolescents as a function of reading proficiency: A research note. *Child Language Teaching & Therapy*, **15**, 171–176.

Nippold, M. A. (2000). Language development during the adolescent years: Aspects of pragmatics, syntax, and semantics. *Topics in Language Disorders*, **20**, 15–28.

Oakhill, J. V. (1984). Inferential and memory skills in children's comprehension of stories. *British Journal of Educational Psychology*, **54**, 31–39.

Perfetti, C. A. (1985). *Reading ability*. New York: Oxford University Press.

Piaget, J. (1954). *The construction of reality in the child*. New York: Basic Books.

Pinker, S. (1994). *The language instinct: How the mind creates language*. New York: Morrow.

Pinker, S. (1999). *Words and rules*. New York: Morrow.

Plaut, D. (2001). A connectionist approach to word reading and acquired dyslexia: Extension to sequential processing. In M. H. Christiansen & N. Chater (Eds.), *Connectionist psycholinguistics* (pp. 244–278). Westport, CT: Ablex Pub.

Plaut, D., McClelland, J. L., Seidenberg, M., & Patterson, K. (1996). Understanding normal and impaired word reading: Computational principles in quasi-regular domains. *Psychological Review*, **103**, 56–115.

Rescorla, L., Bascome, A., Lampard, J., & Feeny, N. (2001). Conversational patterns in late talkers at age 3. *Applied Psycholinguistics*, **22**, 235–251.

Rescorla, L., & Ratner, N. (1996). Phonetic profiles of toddlers with specific expressive language impairment (SLI-E). *Journal of Speech and Hearing Research*, **39**, 153–165.

Ritchie, W., & Bhatia, T. (1999). *Handbook of language acquisition*. New York: Academic Press.

Rollins, P. (2003). Caregivers' contingent comments to 9-month-old infants: Relationships with later language. *Applied Psycholinguistics*, **24**, 221–234.

Roth, F., Speece, D., & Cooper, D. (2002). A longitudinal analysis of the connection between oral language and early reading. *Journal of Educational Research*, **95**, 259–272.

Scarborough, H. S. (1990). Very early language deficits in dyslexic children. *Child Development*, **61**, 1728–1743.

Scarborough, H. S. (1998). Predicting the future achievement of second graders with reading disabilities: Contributions of phonemic awareness, verbal memory, rapid naming, and IQ. *Annals of Dyslexia*, **48**, 115–136.

Scarborough, H. S., & Dobrich, W. (1990). Development of children with early language delay. *Journal of Speech and Hearing Research*, **33**, 70–83.

Searle J. (1998). *Mind, language, and society: Philosophy in the real world*. New York: Basic Books.

Seidenberg, M., & McClelland, J. (1989). A distributed developmental model of word recognition and naming. *Psychological Review*, **96**, 523–568.

Senechal, M., & LeFavre, J. (2002). Parental involvement in the development of children's reading skill: A five-year longitudinal study. *Child Development*, **73**, 445–460.

Shankweiler, D., Lundquist, E., Katz, L., Stuebing, K., Fletcher, J., Brady, S., Fowler, A., Dreyer, L., Marchione, K., Shaywitz, S., & Shaywitz, B. (1999). Comprehension and decoding: Patterns of association in children with reading difficulties. *Scientific Studies of Reading*, **3**, 69–94.

Share, D. L., Jorm, A. F., MacLean, R., & Matthews, R. (2002). Temporal processing and reading disability. *Reading and Writing: An Interdisciplinary Journal*, **15**, 151–178.

Shaywitz, S., Shaywitz, B., Fulbright, R., Skudlarski, P., Einar Mencl, W., Constable, R. T., Pugh, K. R., Holahan, J. M., Marchione, K. E., Fletcher, J. M., Lyon, G. R., & Gore, J. (2003). Neural systems for compensation and persistence: Young adult outcome of childhood reading disability. *Biological Psychiatry*, **54**, 25–33.

Siegel, L. (2003). IQ-discrepancy definitions and the diagnosis of LD: Introduction to the special issue. *Journal of Learning Disabilities*, **36**, 2–3.

Singson, M., Mahoney, D., & Mann, V. (2000). The relation between reading ability and morphological skills: Evidence from derivation suffixes. *Reading and Writing: An Interdisciplinary Journal*, **12**, 219–252.

Snowling, M. J. (2000). Language and literacy skills: Who is at risk and why. In D. Bishop & L. B. Leonard (Eds.), *Speech and language impairments in children: Causes, characteristics, intervention, and outcome* (pp. 245–259). Philadelphia, PA: Psychology Press.

Snowling, M. J., Gallagher, A., & Frith, U. (2003). Family risk of dyslexia is continuous: Individual differences in the precursors of reading skill. *Child Development*, **74**, 358–373.

Snowling, M. J., Bishop, D. M. V., & Stothard, S. E. (2000). Is preschool language impairment a risk factor for dyslexia in adolescence? *Journal of Child Psychology and Psychiatry and Allied Disciplines*, **41**, 587–600.

Stanovich, K., Siegel, L., & Gottardo, A. (1997). Converging evidence for phonological and surface subtypes of reading disability. *Journal of Educational Psychology*, **89**, 114–127.

Stanovich, K. E., & Siegel, L. S. (1994). Phenotypic performance profile of children with reading disabilities: A regression-based test of the phonological-core variable difference model. *Journal of Educational Psychology*, **86**, 24–53.

Storch, S., & Whitehurst, G. J. (2002). Oral language and code-related precursors to reading: Evidence from a longitudinal structural model. *Developmental Psychology*, **38**, 934–947.

Swanson, H. L., & Alexander, J. E. (1997). Cognitive processes as predictors of word recognition and reading comprehension in learning-disabled and skilled readers: Revisiting the specificity hypothesis. *Journal of Educational Psychology*, **89**, 128–158.

Swanson, H. L., & Ashbaker, M. (2000). Working memory, short-term memory, speech rate, word recognition, and reading comprehension in learning disabled readers: Does the executive system have a role? *Intelligence*, **28**, 1–30.

Swanson, H. L., & Deshler, D. (2003). Instructing adolescents with learning disabilities: Converting a meta-analysis to practice. *Journal of Learning Disabilities*, **36**, 124–135.

Swanson, H. L., & Trahan, M. (1996). Learning disabled and average readers' working memory and comprehension: Does metacognition play a role? *British Journal of Educational Psychology*, **66**, 333–355.

Tallal, P. (1980). Auditory temporal perception, phonics, and reading disabilities in children. *Brain and Language*, **9**, 182–198.

Tallal, P. (1984). Temporal or phonetic processing deficit in dyslexia? That is the question. *Applied Psycholinguistics*, **5**, 167–169.

Tallal, P. (1988). Developmental language disorders, Part 1: Definition. *Human Communication Canada*. **12**, 7–22.

Tallal, P., Miller, S. L., Jenkins, W. M., & Merzenich, M. M. (1997). The role of temporal processing in developmental language-based learning disorders: Research and clinical implications. In B. Blachman (Ed.), *Cognitive and linguistic foundations of reading acquisition* (pp. 49–66). Hillsdale, NJ: Erlbaum.

Tallal, P., & Piercy, M. (1975). Developmental aphasia: The perception of brief vowels and extended stop consonants. *Neuropsychologia*, **13**, 69–74.

Thordardottir, E., Chapman, R., and Wagner, L. (2002). Complex sentence production by adolescents with Down syndrome. *Applied Psychololinguistics*, **23**, 163–183.

Tomasello, M. (2003). *Constructing a language*. Cambridge, MA: Harvard University Press.

Tomasello, M., & Bates, E. (2001). *Language development: The essential readings*. Malden, MA: Blackwell.

Tomasello, M., & Farrar, M. J. (1986). Joint attention and early language. *Child Development*, **57**, 1454–1463.

Torgesen, J. K., Wagner, R. K., & Rashotte, C. A. (1994). Longitudinal studies of phonological processing and reading. *Journal of Learning Disabilities*, **27**, 276–286.

Torgesen, J. K., Wagner, R. K., Rashotte, C. A., Burgess, S., & Hecht, S. (1997). Contributions of phonological awareness and rapid automatic naming ability to the growth of word-reading skills in second- to fifth-grade children. *Scientific Studies of Reading*, 1, 161–185.

Vos, S., & Friederici, H. (2003). Intersentential syntactic context effects on comprehension: The role of working memory. *Cognitive Brain Research*, 16, 111–122.

Vygotsky, L. (1962). *Thought and language*. Cambridge, MA: MIT Press.

Vygotsky, L. (1978). *Mind in society: The development of higher psychological processes*. M. Cole (Ed.), Cambridge: Harvard University Press.

Wagner, R. K., & Torgesen, J. K. (1987). The nature of phonological processing and its causal role in the acquisition of reading skills. *Psychological Bulletin*, 101, 192–212.

Walley, A. C., Metsala, J. L., & Garlock, V. M. (2003). Spoken vocabulary growth: Its role in the development of phoneme awareness and early reading ability. *Reading and Writing: An Interdisciplinary Journal*, 16, 5–20.

Wertsch, J. V. (1998). *Mind as action*. New York: Oxford University Press.

Wexler, K. (1999). Maturation and growth of grammar. In W. Ritchie & T. Bhatia (Eds.), *Handbook of child language acquisition* (pp. 55–109). New York: Academic Press.

Whitehurst, G. J., & Fischel, J. E. (2000). A developmental model of reading and language impairments arising in conditions of economic poverty. In D. Bishop & L. Leonard (Eds.), *Speech and language impairments in children: Causes, characteristics, intervention, and outcome* (pp. 53–71). Philadelphia, PA: Psychology Press.

Wilson, A. M., & Lesaux, L. (2001). Persistence of phonological processing deficits in college students with dyslexia who have age-appropriate reading skills. *Journal of Learning Disabilities*, 34, 394–400.

Wittgenstein, L., & Waismann, F. (2003). *The voices of Wittgenstein*. England: Routledge.

Wolf, M. (1991). Naming speed and reading: The contribution of the cognitive neurosciences. *Reading Research Quarterly*, 26, 125–141.

Wolf, M. (1997). A provisional integrative account of phonological and naming-speed deficits in dyslexia: Implications for diagnosis and intervention. In B. Blachman (Ed.), *Foundations of reading acquisition* (pp. 67–92). Mahwah, NJ: Lawrence Erlbaum Assoc.

Wolf, M., & Bowers, P. (1999). The question of naming-speed deficits in developmental reading disabilities: An introduction to the double-deficit hypothesis. *Journal of Educational Psychology*, 19, 1–24.

Wolf, M., Bowers, P., & Biddle, K. (2000). Naming-speed processes, timing, and reading: A conceptual review. *Journal of Learning Disabilities*, 33, 387–407.

Wolf, M., Goldberg O'Rourke, A., Gidney, C., Lovett, M., Cirino, P., & Morris, R. (2002). The second deficit: An investigation of the independence of phonological and naming-speed deficits in developmental dyslexia. *Reading and Writing: An Interdisciplinary Journal*, 15, 43–72.

Young, A., Beitchman, J. H., Johnson, C., Douglas, L., Atkinson, L., Escobar, M., & Wilson, B. (2002). Young adult academic outcomes in a longitudinal sample of early identified language impaired and control children. *Journal of Child Psychology and Psychiatry*, 43, 635–645.

CHAPTER 4

Peer Relationships and Learning Disabilities

Ruth Pearl and Mavis L. Donahue
University of Illinois at Chicago

I. INTRODUCTION

Every day in every classroom students face the social tasks of initiating and maintaining interaction with their peers, resolving conflicts, building friendships, and achieving shared interpersonal goals. A major sign of progress in our field is that there is no longer a need to justify the importance of a chapter on peer social relationships in a book on learning disabilities. In the past three decades, a number of disparate theoretical models, research findings, and educational practices have converged on the inherently social nature of learning. Validating the awareness of generations of teachers and parents that children's academic and peer difficulties are intertwined, the research base now indicates that three out of four students with learning disabilities differ from their typical peers in some aspect of social competence (Kavale & Forness, 1996). Tanis Bryan's radical claim in 1976 that "social status should be considered part of the child's learning disability" (p. 311) is now a guiding principle of assessment and intervention models for these students.

Yet understanding the complex interactions among peer relationships and academic learning remains a daunting task (Wong & Donahue, 2002). In addition to the attentional, perceptual, memory, and language disabilities that a child may bring to a social encounter, he or she may face a more difficult task than other students in making friends because of some peers'

Learning about Learning Disabilities, Third Edition

intolerance. These social challenges can, in turn, deny children the very experiences needed to hone their social skills and to learn what peers expect from a social partner. If negative self-concepts, loneliness, and depression ensue, these may further contribute to the students' difficulties with peers, both by making the students reticent to assert themselves in interactions with peers and, possibly, by making them less appealing as friends. Also, their marginal social status may encourage them to associate with peers who are somewhat accepting, but not particularly supportive, or who model less than desirable behaviors. Coming full circle, fewer opportunities to interact positively with achieving peers may result in even less access to the general education curriculum for students with learning disabilities, as academic content is increasingly embedded in cooperative and other social learning activities.

Despite this potential for spiraling negative outcomes, there is reason for optimism. First, the sources of peer relationship problems of children with learning disabilities are multifaceted and complicated, and, indeed, vary for different children. Perhaps because this complexity offers multiple points where interventions may make a difference, many researchers have been intrigued by the challenge of understanding this phenomenon. Fortunately, we know much more today about the nature of peer relationships of students with learning disabilities, and about specific factors that might be related to how these children fare in their social world. This information is critical not only for providing an understanding of these children's day-to-day experiences, but also because relationships with peers can influence both classroom engagement and long-term adjustment (e.g., Bagwell *et al.*, 2001; Erdley *et al.*, 2001).

This chapter begins with a description of what is known about the nature of peer relationships of students with learning disabilities, with an emphasis on research conducted during the past several years. A variety of factors that have been linked to or that might be related to the quality of these children's social lives will be described in the following section. Finally, directions for future research on peer relationships will be suggested.

II. WHAT ARE THE CHARACTERISTICS OF PEER RELATIONSHIPS OF STUDENTS WITH LEARNING DISABILITIES?

A. Research Using Sociometric Methods of Assessing Peer Relationships

Systematic research on the peer relationships of children with learning disabilities began in 1974 with the publication of a now classic study entitled simply "Peer Popularity of Learning-Disabled Children." The study, conducted by Tanis Bryan, asked elementary school children to name classmates who were and were not desired as friends, classmate neighbors, and guests at a party. In addition, they were asked to answer questions like, "Who is handsome or pretty?" and "Who finds it hard to sit still in class?" Comparisons of the nominations revealed that the children with learning disabilities were not faring so well in the social world of their classrooms: compared to their classmates, they received fewer positive nominations and more negative nominations. Concern was heightened as a result of a follow-up study conducted with these children the next school year (Bryan, 1976). Although now in new classrooms and, for the most part, with different classmates, the children with learning disabilities again received fewer positive and more negative nominations.

These two studies, not surprisingly, generated great interest, and were soon followed by over 200 research efforts that confirmed and extended the findings. Studies using both nomination and rating scale measures found that a disproportionate number of students with learning disabilities were less well-accepted, more rejected, or more neglected than their peers without learning disabilities. Several meta-analyses, which combine the results of many studies in a single analysis, have examined the sociometric studies as a group. These meta-analyses, like the individual studies, confirm the consistent and enduring pattern that students with learning disabilities across the age range are often not held in high regard by classmates (Kavale & Forness, 1996; Ochoa & Olivarez, 1995; Swanson & Malone, 1992).

Do these findings hold true for the peer relationships of other students with low academic achievement? A number of investigations have compared the peer acceptance of children with learning disabilities to that of children who were low achievers but who had not been identified as having learning disabilities. Although some studies found the status of children with learning disabilities to be no worse than that of other low-achievers (e.g., Bursuck, 1983; Coleman et al., 1992; Haager & Vaughn, 1995; Sater & French, 1989; Vaughn et al., 1992, 1993), other studies have found the children with learning disabilities to have even lower sociometric status (e.g., Bursuck, 1989; La Greca & Stone, 1990; Ochoa & Palmer, 1995; Perlmutter et al., 1983).

The consistency of this pattern is remarkable, especially given the well-known heterogeneity of study samples of students with learning disabilities. Yet it is important to note that the percentage of children with learning disabilities found to be of low status differs somewhat in different investigations. Although several meta-analyses suggest that approximately 80% of the students with learning disabilities have lower status than their peers (Kavale & Forness, 1996; Swanson & Malone, 1992), individual studies report varying percentages. One study found that more than half of the students with learning disabilities had low status compared to their classmates, with about half of these low-status children rejected by their peers and half neglected (Stone & LaGreca, 1990). Other studies have found half or more of the students with learning disabilities to have at least average status (e.g., Conderman, 1995; Kistner & Gatlin, 1989b; Wiener *et al.*, 1990), and a few studies have found no differences in the social acceptance of students with learning disabilities (e.g., Prilliman, 1981; Sabornie & Kauffman, 1986; Sainato *et al.*, 1983).

This variation across study findings highlights two key points. First, although this research shows that many students with learning disabilities have low social status, it also indicates that not all do. This means that it is necessary for teachers and parents to be sensitive to possible problems with peers, but it would not be correct to simply assume that every child with learning disabilities will have this problem. Second, the heterogeneity in social status may help to solve the mystery of why some students with learning disabilities are accepted by peers while others are not. For example, examinations of whether different child characteristics are related to acceptance, or whether certain types of classroom placements are likely to bring about more positive peer relationships for children, can provide important clues about which children are at risk and about what might be done to lessen this risk. Section III in this chapter explores these issues in more detail.

B. Research on Additional Dimensions of Peer Relationships

Sociometric research brought attention to the peer relationships of students with learning disabilities by showing that these children often were generally less liked or accepted by their classmates than other children. Although this is certainly an important aspect of peer relationships, there are dimensions of relationships not captured by sociometric assessments. For example, regardless of the degree of their general peer acceptance, children may or may not have a friend. And regardless of whether or not children are generally accepted or have a friend, they may tend to associate with particular other children. Recent research has begun to extend the research on peer relationships of students with learning disabilities to include these topics.

1. Friendships

a. Number of friendships.   Friendship has been defined as the relationship between a pair of individuals who have positive feelings toward each other (Bukowski & Hoza, 1989). Some researchers suggest that having even a single friend can buffer the negative impact of rejection or neglect by the larger peer group (e.g., Howes, 1988). Although reciprocity is a defining feature of friendships, one issue is whether students with learning disabilities feel they have friends, even if the person identified as a friend does not feel the same way. Most students with learning disabilities seem to feel that they have at least one friend. In one study (Vaughn & Elbaum, 1999), 96% of students with learning disabilities listed at least one person as a best friend, with about two-thirds of the children indicating that they had six or more friends (Vaughn et al., 2001). Another study of children in middle school found no difference between students with learning disabilities and typical classmates in the number of close friends they felt they had; each group reported having about four good friends. Interestingly, the students with learning disabilities reported having more friends who were at least a year older (Fleming et al., 2002). In contrast, a study of elementary school children found that, although most of the friends named by students with learning disabilities were similar to them in age, these students named younger children as friends more often than did students without learning disabilities (Wiener, 2002).

Reciprocal friendships have been identified by examining whether children actually name each other when asked for either "best friend" or "liked most" nominations. Several studies have found similar numbers of reciprocal friendships in elementary school children with and without learning disabilities (Bear et al., 1993; Juvonen & Bear, 1992; Vaughn & Haager, 1994; Vaughn et al., 1993). However, not all reports are so positive. For example, in one study, only 26% of elementary school students with learning disabilities had reciprocal friendships in the fall, compared to 71% of non-disabled low achievers and 63% of average/high-achieving students. Although the percentage of students with learning disabilities with reciprocal friendships more than doubled in the spring, these students were still less likely to have a reciprocal friendship than the average/high-achievers (53 compared to 72%; Vaughn et al., 1996).

Another study suggests that friendships of elementary school students with learning disabilities may actually deteriorate over the school year (Tur-Kaspa et al., 1999). Compared to classmates, more students with learning disabilities had no reciprocal friends at the beginning of the school year (31% of students with learning disabilities compared to 20% of non-disabled students). By spring, this difference had only increased; the proportion of children with learning disabilities who had no reciprocal friendships rose to 39%, while the number of such nondisabled children decreased to 17%. Even more troubling, by the end of the year, more children with learning disabilities had developed a mutual animosity with a classmate. When asked, "Which of the boys and girls in your class would you least like to have as your friend," 56% of children with learning disabilities named someone who also named them, compared to 27% of the nondisabled classmates.

b. Friendship quality. Overall, the results suggest that the majority of children with learning disabilities have at least one reciprocal friend, at least by the end of the school year. But what is the nature of these friendships? The quality of children's friendships has been found to vary in such features as closeness, security, and conflict (e.g., Bukowski *et al.*, 1994; Parker & Asher, 1993); not all friendships are characterized by high levels of intimacy and support. An important issue, then, is whether the quality of friendships experienced by students with learning disabilities is similar to that experienced by other children.

The few studies on this topic suggest that these students may, in fact, experience friendships of lower quality. For example, Vaughn *et al.* (2001) reported that elementary school children with learning disabilities perceived somewhat lower quality friendships than nondisabled children, and while the quality of the friendships of the nondisabled children increased through high school, that of children with learning disabilities did not. Specifically, students without learning disabilities perceived higher levels of intimacy and support for self-esteem in their friendships than did the students with learning disabilities (Vaughn & Elbaum, 1999). In another study, students with learning disabilities indicated having fewer friends from whom they would seek support if dealing with a stressful event (Geisthardt & Munsch, 1996). Further, in comparison to the perceptions of nondisabled students about their friendships, students with learning disabilities indicated that they felt less validated by their friends and that their friendships were more fraught with conflict (Wiener, 2002).

To obtain more information about the friendships of children with learning disabilities, Wiener and Sunohara (1998) interviewed the parents of children who were receiving services from a mental health center. According to the parents' reports, almost half of the children had relationships that were unstable and characterized by little companionship and sharing. As the authors point out, this was not a representative sample of children with learning disabilities, but the study confirms other findings that "having a friend" does not necessarily provide children with learning disabilities with unequivocal acceptance and support.

2. Social Networks

In classrooms, children commonly interact more frequently with some classmates than with others. These classroom social groups are identified by research on children's social networks. In this methodology, students are asked, "Are there some kids in your classroom who hang around together a lot? Who are they?" By examining the groups identified by the students, one can get a sense not only whether students with learning disabilities belong to a group, but if they do, the characteristics of their groups' members.

The social networks in 59 classrooms were examined by Pearl *et al.* (1998). Each classroom had at least two students with mild disabilities who were in the classroom for the majority of the school day. The group of students with mild disabilities consisted primarily of children with learning disabilities. According to the students' reports, the majority of the students with mild disabilities were part of a group. Nevertheless, compared to the nondisabled peers, more of them were not; 19% of the children with mild disabilities were not named as belonging to a group, compared to 7% of the nondisabled children. Further analyses examined the types of groups that included students with mild disabilities. Were they in groups with classmates average in prosocial behavior and misconduct? Or were they in groups consisting of children high in prosocial characteristics, or that were characterized by misconduct?

To address these questions, groups were identified in which the mean score of the nondisabled students in the group was at or above the 80th percentile in peer-assessed prosocial behavior or misconduct. Findings indicated that 49% of the children with mild disabilities were in groups that were about average in prosocial and problem behavior. But, disturbingly, students with mild disabilities were underrepresented in the high prosocial groups (which contained 11% of the students with mild disabilities) and overrepresented in the groups high in problem behavior (which contained 21% of the children with mild disabilities). An analysis that assessed the percentage of group members who had learning disabilities found the largest proportions to be in groups highest in problem behavior (Farmer et al., 1999).

To get an idea of the role the students with mild disabilities played in the problem groups, the number of times the children with mild disabilities were named to the group was examined. The assumption was that if many classmates named them as members of the group, then they were salient, central group members. If fewer classmates mentioned them, then they were probably more secondary or marginal members. When looking at the position of students with mild disabilities in all the groups high in problem behavior, the students with mild disabilities tended to have lower centrality scores than the general education students, but the difference was not quite significant. However, when looking just at the groups that were most prominent in the classroom, that most of the students mentioned, the difference was significant. Hence, it appears that most children with learning disabilities play a secondary or marginal role in these groups rather than being their groups' "ringleaders" (Farmer et al., 1999).

In summary, a disproportionate number of children with mild disabilities were not a part of a classroom group, and of those who were, a disproportionate number were in groups high in problem behaviors. Similar results were found in a study in which middle school students with learning disabilities reported higher levels of involvement with peers engaged in negative behaviors than were reported by nondisabled students (Fleming et al., 2002). Ironically, these findings suggest that for some students with learning disabilities, making connections with peers may not necessarily be the positive development that it is often assumed to be. That is, the peers with whom they interact may not be likely to promote positive, prosocial behavior and, of even more concern, may actually encourage misconduct. Adding weight to this concern, compared to nondisabled students, junior high school students with learning disabilities reported more willingness to acquiesce to the urging of peers to join them in misconduct (Bryan *et al.*, 1989, 1982). Nevertheless, it is important not to overstate these findings, given that the majority of children with mild disabilities were not in high-problem groups, and the majority of children in high-problem groups did not have mild disabilities.

III. WHAT FACTORS MIGHT BE LINKED TO THE PEER RELATIONSHIPS OF STUDENTS WITH LEARNING DISABILITIES?

Regardless of the measures used to assess peer relationships, there is remarkable consistency in the research evidence that students with learning disabilities are vulnerable to social difficulties. Yet the mystery of what child and contextual factors are linked to these often problematic relationships remains largely unsolved, and we know even less about why some students with learning disabilities are skilled at forming positive peer relationships. As suggested in the introduction of this chapter, a variety of factors may be contributors to children's social difficulties or successes. Surprisingly, there has been relatively little research that has investigated what factors are actually correlates of sociometric, friendship, or social network status in students with learning disabilities. Nevertheless, using developmental research models, many studies have examined whether students with learning disabilities differ from their peers on various characteristics that have been hypothesized to contribute to the quality of social relationships.

These group comparison studies are valuable for providing insights into possible causes of social relationship problems, but they, and, in fact, the studies that actually identify specific correlates of social relationship indices as well, often present the classic chicken-and-egg question. Namely, it is often impossible to determine whether these factors are the cause of the children's social problems or the result of them. For instance, feelings of inadequacy might make children act passively or withdraw from social interaction, and thus might contribute to their being overlooked by classmates. On the other hand, one can easily imagine that being overlooked by classmates would cause a child to develop feelings of inadequacy. Most likely, both of these possibilities are true to some degree.

Keeping in mind the difficulty of establishing cause vs. effect, the next sections examine factors that may relate to the peer relationships of students with learning disabilities. First, we consider whether children with specific attributes—for instance, who are male vs female or who have certain types of disability—might be more or less vulnerable to problems. Because individuals' interpretation of the meaning of a social interaction can affect their behavior, in the second section we examine whether children with learning disabilities differ from others in the way they process social information. Research on self-perceptions that may contribute to (or result from) peer difficulties is described in the third section. Since classroom conduct can provoke either the admiration or the ire of classmates, the fourth section examines whether the behavior of children with learning disabilities differentiates them from their peers. Fifth, emotional concomitants—loneliness and depression, for example—are examined. Finally, contextual variables that may relate to the degree of acceptance of children with learning disabilities are considered.

A. Characteristics of Students with Learning Disabilities

Several studies have found gender to be related to the sociometric status of children with learning disabilities. Girls appear to be at particular risk for low status (e.g., Conderman, 1995, Juvonen & Bear, 1992; LaGreca & Stone, 1990; Stiliadis & Wiener, 1989; Stone & LaGreca, 1990). However, studies using friendship measures found that boys with learning disabilities had fewer reciprocal friendships (Wiener, 2002) and friendships of lower quality (Tur-Kaspa *et al.*, 1999) than did nondisabled children or girls with learning disabilities. Gender did not affect the likelihood that children with learning disabilities were members of classroom social groups (Pearl *et al.*, 1998).

Other studies have found influences of race, and even interactions between race and gender, on children's sociometric status. For example, one study found greater rejection for European American but not for African American girls with learning disabilities (Kistner & Gatlin, 1989a). Two other studies also suggest that African American children with learning disabilities may experience higher sociometric status than European American children (Bryan, 1974; Gresham & Reschly, 1987). However, because the ethnicity of the children doing the sociometric ratings was not reported, the interpretation of this pattern of findings is somewhat equivocal. It could mean that African American children are more accepting of differences (or at least of the kind of differences found in children with learning disabilities) or it could reflect different expectations for children of varying backgrounds. More research on ethnicity differences is needed to clarify the role cultural values may play in the degree to which a learning disability affects social relationships.

The severity of a learning disability may also be related to peer acceptance. In a study conducted in a camp for children with learning disabilities, children who had discrepancies of more than 2 years between their age and achievement level received more negative and fewer positive nominations from other campers than did those with lesser discrepancies (Wiener, 1980). Comorbidity with attention deficit–hyperactivity disorder (ADHD) may also increase the likelihood of social problems (e.g., Flicek & Landau, 1985; Wiener, 2002). On the other hand, having valued attributes like being athletic or good-looking seems to bolster the sociometric status of students with learning disabilities (e.g., Conderman, 1995; Siperstein & Goding, 1983; Siperstein et al., 1978).

Whether specific types of learning disabilities are more likely to lead to the development of social problems has been the focus of some research. One study suggests that boys with stronger oral language skills may not receive the same degree of rejection as other boys with learning disabilities. Boys who performed better on the verbal than on the performance scales of the Wechsler Intelligence Scale for Children–Revised (WISC–R), while considered less likeable by peers than were nondisabled boys, nevertheless did not receive the degree of rejection indicated for the boys who had higher performance than verbal scores or boys who performed equally on the two scales (Landau et al., 1987). The role played by language disabilities in peer rejection is confirmed by research on students identified as having specific language impairments despite typical cognitive development, a population whose diagnostic criteria overlap a great deal with those of learning disability samples. Children with oral language disabilities were viewed as less desirable playmates than typical children even on the preschool level (e.g., Gertner et al., 1994; Rice, 1993). Nevertheless, the finding that peer preference in an elementary school sample of students with learning disabilities was negatively correlated with reading subtest scores (Wiener et al., 1990) indicates that research is still needed to clarify how different types of learning disabilities affect social functioning (e.g., Rourke & Fuerst, 1996).

B. Social Information Processing of Students with Learning Disabilities

Processing social information is a complex task. One prominent model of this process posits that children approach any social situation with a database of memories of past social experiences, as well as acquired social rules and schemas, and then receive a particular set of social cues as input that they process through a number of steps (Crick & Dodge, 1994). Children's behavioral responses (Step 6) are an outcome of the ways in which these cues are processed through the first five steps: (1) encoding, through attending to and perceiving social cues; (2) representing and interpreting the cues; (3) selecting a goal; (4) retrieving possible responses from long-term memory; and (5) evaluating and choosing a response. Feedback loops connect all previous steps, filtered through the database of stored social experiences and knowledge. Using this model as an organizational device, we describe here research on the social information processing skills of students with learning disabilities.

1. Steps 1 and 2: Social Perception and Interpretation

Given that early characterizations of learning disabilities focused on problems in perceptual processing, it is no surprise that one of the first and most common hypotheses for these students' negative peer relations points to difficulties or differences in the perception and interpretation of interpersonal cues. In fact, across an age range from elementary school through college, and using a variety of social perception measures, many studies have confirmed that, compared to nondisabled peers, students with learning disabilities are less skillful in interpreting social displays (see Tur-Kaspa, 2002a, for a review). A recent meta-analysis found that interpretation of nonverbal behavior was less accurate in 80% of students with learning disabilities (Kavale & Forness, 1996).

For example, in a study that looked at students' skill in detecting emotion communicated through facial expressions, gestures, and posture, students with learning disabilities were found to be less proficient than nondisabled students in identifying feelings conveyed in all of three of these domains (Nabuzoka & Smith, 1995). Certain emotions were easier to detect than others; even the youngest students with learning disabilities had little trouble detecting happiness. For most other emotions, older children with learning disabilities (approximately 11 years old) were more accurate than younger children with learning disabilities (approximately $6\frac{1}{2}$ old), suggesting that the social perception skills of children with learning disabilities may improve with age.

Several studies have found that disregarding their own perspective when making an inference about another person's experience may be more difficult for students with learning disabilities (e.g., Kravetz et al., 1999; Wong & Wong, 1980). Examples of how inadequate perspective-taking may lead to less skilled social behavior can be found in several studies which required for competent performance an understanding of another person's viewpoint. In one study, although students with learning disabilities recognized deceptive statements as being untrue, they were not able to detect that the speaker was deliberately lying (Pearl et al., 1991). In another, students with learning disabilities were less likely than peers to be tactful when role-playing how they would give disappointing news to another child (Pearl et al., 1985). Similarly, students with learning disabilities have been found to be less likely to accommodate the feelings and thoughts of others on tasks in which they attempted to persuade listeners to change their opinions (Bryan et al., 1981a; Donahue, 1981).

2. Step 3: Goal Selection

One potential explanation for the social difficulties of students with learning disabilities is that these emerge because the children are simply less interested in developing relationships with their peers. This, however, does not appear to be the case. In studies that measured amount of peer interaction, students with learning disabilities often did not differ from other children; in studies that assessed willingness to join in activities with peers, they reported being at least as willing as other students to participate (Pearl, 1992).

Nevertheless, the specific objectives the children have for their interaction with peers may differ from those of nondisabled students. Two studies that presented boys with hypothetical situations involving the establishment or maintenance of peer relationships found that the goals of boys with learning disabilities may, in fact, differ from those of other boys. One study found that, in response to conflict, nondisabled boys were more likely to have the goal of compromise, while the boys with learning disabilities were more likely to have as their goal accommodation, avoidance, or following rules (Carlson, 1987). In the second study, boys' goals in different situations were scored according to their degree of sophistication and specificity (Oliva & LaGreca, 1988). For instance, on the first day at a new school, joining other children at recess for the purpose of making friends was considered a more sophisticated and specific response than joining them because others did or because it was boring to stay inside. Analyses indicated that although the boys with learning disabilities indicated they would be as friendly as nondisabled boys, the goals of boys with learning disabilities were less specific and sophisticated. Thus, these two studies suggest that, although likely to be equally interested in peers, the goals of boys with learning disabilities may differ from those of nondisabled boys in both their aims and specificity. To our knowledge, the social goals of girls with learning disabilities have not been studied.

3. Steps 4 and 5: Retrieval and Selection of Responses

How students generate and select responses to social dilemmas has also been examined. For example, when asked about how a child might join in an activity with others or resolve a situation involving conflict, students with learning disabilities have been found to generate fewer alternative responses (Carlson, 1987; Hartas & Donahue, 1997; Toro *et al.*, 1990; Tur-Kaspa & Bryan, 1994) and to prefer less competent strategies (Bryan *et al.*, 1981; Carlson, 1987; Tur-Kaspa & Bryan, 1994) than their classmates. In addition, even when students with learning disabilities choose to use the same strategy as nondisabled students, they may use it less skillfully (Stone & La Greca, 1984; Tur-Kaspa & Bryan, 1994).

4. Comprehensive Assessment of Social Information Processing

Most studies have looked at isolated components of information processing. However, one study conducted a comprehensive assessment of all the steps in an earlier version (Dodge, 1986) of the Crick and Dodge (1994) model with one sample of participants. The findings indicated that students with learning disabilities were less skillful than average-achieving students on all social information-processing steps. Further, these students were less skillful than low-achieving classmates (who had not been identified as having learning disabilities) on two of the steps, encoding social information and choosing a response (Tur-Kaspa and Bryan, 1994).

5. Social Database

Overall, then, the research indicates that for many students with learning disabilities, processing social information (or processing it in conventional ways) may pose a challenge. As the Crick and Dodge (1994) model suggests, their interpretations may also be influenced by the fact that every step of the processing of social information is filtered through the lens of their own social memories and knowledge. Although a number of studies have not found students with learning disabilities to differ from others in their social knowledge (Bryan & Sonnefeld, 1981; Bursuck, 1983; McLeod *et al.*, 1994; Stone & La Greca, 1984), there is evidence that, for certain situations at least, their expectations may differ. For instance, adolescents with learning disabilities were less likely than others to expect that teens would use persuasive ploys if they were trying to influence a peer to join in misconduct, a finding that may, in part, reflect deficiencies in perspective-taking (Pearl & Bryan, 1992; Pearl *et al.*, 1990). Students with learning disabilities were also less likely than others to expect that a teenager caught in misconduct by authorities would accept the consequences, while being more likely than others to think the teenager would try to escape (Pearl & Bryan, 1994). In cases where students with learning disabilities lack social knowledge shared by others, it may well put them at a disadvantage; they may be less equipped to anticipate and deal with these situations if they actually occur.

Children's own particular history with their peers also contributes to their view of appropriate behavior. For instance, while considering responding in a particular way in a particular situation (e.g., entering a peer group, dealing with a conflict), a child evaluates his or her own self-efficacy in successfully enacting this verbal bid, based on previous peer experiences as well as knowledge of appropriate social schemas. Thus, one's own social experiences, as well as more general social knowledge, make up the social database. This database, then, is both an influence on and an outcome of social behavior.

In the next section, the self-perceptions of students with learning disabilities about their social status and skills are examined to evaluate whether these may shed some light on the quality of their peer interactions and relationships. In particular, findings that students with learning disabilities are aware of their lower social status may help to explain the apparent "disconnect" between some children's social knowledge and actual social behavior. For example, some children with learning disabilities may know what behaviors are appropriate for a typical peer to use in a particular situation, but may believe that their marginal social status calls for different social strategies in order to be accepted (e.g., giving in to a peer's request rather than being assertive).

C. Self-Perceptions of Students with Learning Disabilities

1. Self-Assessments of Social Competence

How do students with learning disabilities view themselves and their experiences in the social domain? Several studies have found that compared to nondisabled students, they gave lower ratings to their own social competence and behavior (e.g., Bear et al., 1991; Dalley et al., 1992; Montgomery, 1994; Raviv & Stone, 1991), level of peer acceptance (Halmhuber & Paris, 1993; Harter et al., 1998; Kistner & Osborne, 1987; Smith & Nagle, 1995), and chance of future social success (Sobol et al., 1983).

In contrast, other studies have not found differences in nonacademic self-perceptions (e.g., Vaughn et al., 1990; Vaughn et al., 1992, 1996), perhaps because having a few close friends mitigates any negative self-perceptions that result from lower levels of peer acceptance in general (Bear et al., 1993). Students' social self-perceptions may, in part, depend as well on the specific type of behavior being assessed; self-assessments in one study were lower for cooperation, but not for assertion, responsibility, or self-control (Haager & Vaughn, 1995). Findings that lower social self-perceptions are not consistently found may also reflect the heterogeneity of these children's social adjustment. Consistent with this possibility, one study found that self-perceptions of social acceptance and feelings of self-worth in fifth grade boys were negatively correlated with the number of negative sociometric nominations they received (Bear et al., 1993). This relationship was not found among third graders, however, suggesting that as children with learning disabilities get older, they may become more sensitive to and/or accord more importance to their relationships with peers.

Another study addressing this heterogeneity also found that students with mild disabilities vary in their self-perceptions. This study identified groups of students with mild disabilities (mainly, learning disabilities) who had different configurations of characteristics, based on a teacher questionnaire, and then compared the groups' self-perceptions (Farmer *et al.*, 1999). A number of differences were found, but differences between two configurations that consisted of boys rated by teachers above average in aggression illustrate why self-perceptions may be important to consider. One group was also rated as above average in popularity, sports ability, and looks; these boys had higher self-perceptions of both their level of aggression and their level of popularity than did most other groups of boys with mild disabilities. The other group was also rated as above average in internalizing (that is, sad and worried) and academics; these boys tended to underestimate their aggression while overestimating their popularity and friendliness, compared to the ratings given to them by teachers and peers. The differences in the self-perceptions between these two groups suggest that efforts to improve social behavior may need to attend closely to the particular self-perceptions that students hold. In some cases, students may be unmotivated to change negative behavior if they believe it to be working for them; in other cases, students may even be unaware of or unwilling to admit their negative behavior.

2. Self-Perceptions and Interactions with Peers

The influence of self-perceptions on children's interactions with peers was demonstrated in an interesting study by Settle and Milich (1999). The fourth and fifth grade participants were first asked to rate different possible causes of several examples of social rejection. Although both students with learning disabilities and nondisabled students chose "misunderstanding" as being the most likely reason, there was one telling difference. Students with learning disabilities were not as able as others to dismiss these incidents as due to something for which they were not responsible. While they did not directly indicate that they would be the cause of a rejection, they were less likely than nondisabled children to think that such rejections would be due to a trait of the other child (e.g., meanness).

In the next part of the study, the students were introduced to a same-sex child who had been trained to act unfriendly and unresponsive. Following a 5-minute interaction, they were introduced to a second same-sex child who, in contrast, had been trained to be friendly and moderately responsive. Questionnaires given after each interaction asked the participants to rate their own and the other child's performance in the interaction (e.g., "How much did he/she like you?" "How well do you think he/she got to know you?").

Responses to the questionnaires indicated that the students with learning disabilities viewed the unfriendly interaction more negatively and the friendly interaction more positively than did nondisabled children. Looking just at the question about how much the other child liked them, the girls with learning disabilities felt less well-liked than nondisabled girls after the inter-action with the unfriendly child and, compared to nondisabled children, both boys and girls with learning disabilities felt more liked after the inter-action with the friendly child. Consistent with these findings, observers rating the interactions found the students with learning disabilities to be less positive than nondisabled students when they were with the unfriendly child, but more friendly than nondisabled students when they were with the friendly child.

These findings, then, indicated that compared to nondisabled children, "children with learning disabilities seemed more responsive to both social rejection and subsequent acceptance" (p. 208). The implication is that these students may be likely to withdraw prematurely from interactions with peers who are perceived to be less than friendly, while being especially welcoming of seemingly friendly overtures from others.

D. Behavior of Children with Learning Disabilities

1. Classroom Behavior

Because the classroom is the arena in which peer relationship problems usually first emerge, researchers have examined classroom behavior in stu-dents with learning disabilities to see whether it differs from that of class-mates. The results of a meta-analysis combining the results of 25 studies of classroom conduct found that, according to both observations and teacher reports, students with learning disabilities showed deficits in a number of behaviors. Compared to nondisabled students, the students with learning disabilities were more off-task, less on-task, more distractible, more shy and withdrawn, and exhibited more conduct disorders (Bender & Smith, 1990). Other studies indicate that teachers view students with learning disabilities as possessing more negative and fewer adaptive social skills than nondisabled classmates (e.g., Dalley et al., 1992; Halmhuber & Paris, 1993; Touliatos & Lindholm, 1980; Tur-Kaspa, 2002b; Vallance et al., 1998). Although in several studies these problems did not distinguish them from other low achievers (Coleman et al., 1992; Haager & Vaughn, 1995; Tur-Kaspa & Bryan, 1995; Vaughn et al., 1993), it appears that the behavior of many students with learning disabilities does differ, in some respects, from that of the majority of their classmates.

2. Use of Language in Social Contexts

Given the integration of social information processing and oral language abilities needed for effective communication with peers, children's know-ledge of the use of language in social contexts—called "pragmatics"—has been a valuable research site. Methods for assessing peer communicative interactions can be organized along a continuum of "how natural/authentic is the interaction?" These methods range from "scripted" tasks in which children enact a discourse genre with a real peer, to role-playing tasks with tight constraints on topic and no listener feedback (Donahue, 2002).

In general, the pattern of findings echoes the dilemmas that were raised earlier in the chapter. In some contexts, students with learning disabilities participate in peer discourse as if they are *newcomers* or *immigrants* to the peer culture. These styles may be due not only to their social information processing and language deficits, but also to the likelihood that they are receiving quantitatively and qualitatively different data from peers for deriving social norms (Donahue, 1994). In other words, students who are neglected or disliked by peers are likely to have fewer opportunities to observe and model the conversational rules and scripts that other students follow. In addition, peers may offer different kinds of feedback to the conversational contributions of students with learning disabilities than to those of typical classmates, e.g., showing less tolerance for topic changes or efforts to tell a personal narrative. Other studies suggest that students with learning disabilities communicate like *imposters*, that is, they are well aware of the appropriate rules for peer discourse but are selecting compensatory strategies that accommodate their self-perceptions as marginal members of the peer group.

One example of the "newcomer" or "immigrant" communicative profile is provided by studies of children's ability to enter ongoing peer interactions. In order to control for peer reputation and history, unacquainted pairs of children are introduced and invited to play a game together. After about 10 minutes, a target child (also unacquainted) is brought into the room. Craig and Washington (1993) compared the peer access abilities of 7-year-old children with specific language impairments with two comparison groups with typical language development: younger children matched on expressive language ability and age-matched children. Startling group differences were found. All of the typical children gained peer access quickly and easily. Most of the children with language disabilities were never successful in joining the interactions; a few gained access using only nonverbal means (i.e., without speaking). In a replication of this study with older children (between 8 and 12 years old), Brinton et al. (1997) showed that even the children with language disabilities who managed to gain peer access were not equal partners in the subsequent discourse.

Studies using group decision-making tasks illustrate the "imposter" style of communicating, in which students' primary goals are camouflaging their social–cognitive and communication limitations while appearing to be equal partners in the discourse. Triads of children were asked to reach a consensus on the ranking of possible gifts or snacks (Brinton et al., 1998; Bryan et al., 1981a; Donahue & Prescott, 1988; Fujiki et al., 1997). In general, students with language or learning disabilities talked as much as their partners, and were more eager to agree with their classmates' opinions and to respond to requests for information. However, they avoided those strategies that may have demanded linguistic fluency or conflict-resolution skills. For example, they were less likely to disagree, to attempt to negate their partners' opinions, to bid for the conversational floor, to make comments that kept the group on task (Bryan *et al.*, 1981), or to use sophisticated persuasive tactics (Brinton *et al.*, 1998). Not surprisingly, students with language or learning disabilities had less impact on their groups' final decisions. Interestingly, this strategically passive conversational style was found even in young poor readers who had not yet been identified as having reading disabilities (Donahue & Prescott, 1988).

What happens when students with language-learning disabilities are given a script that compels them to take an unaccustomed social role, such as the dominant conversational partner? When students with learning disabilities (grades 2 and 4) played the role of a "talk show host" interviewing nondisabled classmates, they had difficulty maintaining the flow of the dialogue. In particular, they asked fewer open-ended questions and their "guests" produced fewer elaborated responses (Bryan *et al.*, 1981b). In a second study with a brief modeling intervention, boys with learning disabilities were induced to increase their use of open-ended questions and topic-extending comments to the level of their nondisabled comparison group (Donahue & Bryan, 1983). However, these changes in conversational behavior actually led to fewer elaborated responses and more requests for clarification from the classmates being interviewed. Even more unexpectedly, boys with learning disabilities who had changed their conversation style showed greater awareness of their own communication skills and of the verbal and nonverbal responses of their peer interviewees than did the comparison group. These findings suggest that the boys recognized the social "cost" of changing one's interactional style, illustrating that even subtle conversational norms are enacted in delicately balanced social relationships.

3. Behavior and Peer Relations

Do these differences in social behavior affect the peer status of students with learning disabilities? The few studies that actually test the correlations among these measures illustrate the challenge of understanding the complex factors underlying peer acceptance. It should be noted, too, that most of these studies measured teachers', parents', or peers' perceptions of the children's behavior rather than directly observing the children's conduct.

Students whose teachers detected fewer behaviors presumed to be caused by social perception deficits (Stiliadis & Wiener, 1989) and who had higher rates of positive interactions with peers (Coleman & Minnett, 1992) were found to have higher sociometric status. According to parent and teacher reports, rejected students with learning disabilities had lower social competence and more behavior problems than did accepted students with learning disabilities (Sater & French, 1989), while teacher ratings of inattention/overactivity and aggression were associated with negative sociometric nominations (Kistner & Gatlin, 1989b).

Students rated by peers as higher in aggression and withdrawal received both more negative nominations and fewer positive nominations than students who received lower ratings; peer ratings of dependence, unassertiveness, and passivity were positively related to the number of negative nominations received (Kistner & Gatlin, 1989b). Similarly, peer preference (liked-most minus liked-least nominations) correlated negatively with peer nominations for the descriptors of disruptive, dependent, and fights, and correlated positively with nominations for being cooperative (Wiener et al., 1990). Popular adolescents with learning disabilities were considered by peers to be independent and withdrawn (Perlmutter et al., 1983).

Not surprisingly, these findings seem to indicate that perceived negative behaviors are related to lower status, but data on classroom social networks suggest that the role played by negative behaviors may, in fact, be more complex. Although girls with learning disabilities were more likely to be a member of a classroom group and less likely to be isolated if they were considered by peers to be leaders and prosocial (that is, "studious" and "cooperative"), boys with learning disabilities were more apt to be in groups if they were thought to be leaders, athletic, and antisocial (composed of nominations for "disruptive," "starts fights, and "gets in trouble"; Pearl et al., 1998). This last finding suggests the troubling possibility that being perceived to be antisocial may be, in some respects, an asset for boys wishing to be part of the social world of their peers. Recall the two groups of aggressive boys with mild disabilities described in an earlier section of this chapter. One of these groups had been described by teachers as high in aggression, popularity, sports ability, and looks (and consisted of approximately 14% of the boys with mild disabilities). These boys, in particular, seemed to receive peer support for their behavior: they were nominated as "cool" by 20% of their classmates. The aggressiveness of this group of boys, then, did not keep them from receiving the esteem of their peers. As mentioned earlier, not only were these students aware of their aggressiveness, they also perceived themselves to be popular. Boys with this configuration of characteristics, then, may have little incentive for changing their aggressive behavior.

However, not all boys with mild disabilities who were perceived to be aggressive were considered cool and, as mentioned earlier, in some studies, being viewed as aggressive was related to lower sociometric status in students with learning disabilities. The secondary role that children with mild disabilities appear to play in aggressive groups (Farmer et al., 1999) also indicates that for some boys, aggressiveness may be the result of, not a reason for, association with aggressive classmates. In other words, similarities among children who affiliate with each other can result from socialization by fellow group members as well as an attraction to others with similar characteristics (e.g., Farmer *et al.*, 1996).

Although aggressive behavior is typical of only a small group of socially "successful" boys with learning disabilities, the type of peer support that appears to sustain or promote this type of negative behavior may operate similarly with other behaviors. For instance, consider the lack of assertiveness shown by many students with learning disabilities. It might be the case that inducing these students to be as assertive as nondisabled classmates will improve their level of acceptance. On the other hand, making these students more assertive might not improve their social lot if deferential behavior is considered by peers to be appropriate for these children; assertive responses by students with learning disabilities may not be particularly well-received. Or, as in the findings regarding aggressive boys, assertive behavior may be considered differently, depending on the children's other characteristics. That is, assertive behavior may be welcomed from some students with learning disabilities but not from others.

Research efforts need to continue to confront the complexity of the classroom social systems in which behaviors are embedded. That is, in addition to identifying behavioral differences between children with and without learning disabilities, and behavioral correlates of peer acceptance in the general population of students with learning disabilities, it will be important to look more closely at the processes by which the responses of peers serve to promote or maintain behaviors—both negative and positive—of students with learning disabilities with different configurations of characteristics.

E. Emotional Concomitants of Learning Disabilities

Perhaps because of their experiences of unsatisfying and unstable peer relationships, students with learning disabilities appear to be at some risk for developing emotional problems. For example, students with learning disabilities—even those attending college (Hoy *et al.*, 1997; Reiff *et al.*, 2001)—have been found to have higher levels of anxiety or stress (Fisher *et al.*, 1996; Margalit & Shulman, 1986; Margalit & Zak, 1984). Loneliness is also sometimes experienced by children with learning disabilities (e.g., Margalit & Ben-Dov, 1992, reported in Margalit & Levin-Alyagon, 1994; Pavri & Monda-Amaya, 2000; Sabornie, 1994; Tur-Kaspa *et al.*, 1998; Tur-Kaspa *et al.*, 1999), as is depression (e.g., Stanley *et al.*, 1997). One study found that, among elementary school students with learning disabilities, loneliness was related to perceptions of friendship quality. Additionally, loneliness at the beginning of the school year was related to the children's number of reciprocal rejections, while at the end, loneliness was related to the number of reciprocal friendships (Tur-Kaspa *et al.*, 1999). In students with learning disabilities in early to mid-adolescence, loneliness was found to be related to peer acceptance, peer rejection, and number of reciprocal friendships (Tur-Kaspa *et al.*, 1999). In students with learning disabilities in early to mid-adolescence, loneliness was found to be related to peer acceptance, peer rejection, and number of reciprocal friendships (Tur-Kaspa, 2002b).

The prevalence of serious depression in elementary school students with learning disabilities has been estimated to range from 14 to more than 35% (Stevenson & Romney, 1984; Wright-Strawderman & Watson, 1992). Elevated rates have also been found in adolescents with learning disabilities (Dalley *et al.*, 1992; Maag & Behrens, 1989), with approximately 32% of the participants in one study indicating moderate to severe symptoms of depression. Guidance counselors in this study believed that 43% actually had levels of depression within the clinically significant range (Howard & Tryon, 2002). Students with negative perceptions of their social acceptance were found in one study to be particularly vulnerable to depression (Heath & Wiener, 1996). Even more alarming is the evidence that a disproportionate number of students who committed suicide have been reported to have had learning disabilities (e.g., Huntington & Bender, 1993). Clearly, the frequent co-occurrence of learning disabilities and serious psychological problems requires more attention (Rock *et al.*, 1997; San Miguel *et al.*, 1996).

One study suggests that the affect or mood states of students with learning disabilities can, in turn, influence their social information processing (Bryan *et al.*, 1998). Positive affect was induced by, for one minute, having students either close their eyes and recall the happiest time of their lives or listen to "happy" music. Students were then given a social problem-solving task (i.e., how to join an ongoing game). Compared to students in a neutral condition, who had simply closed their eyes for one minute and counted, those who had thought of a happy memory generated more solutions, while those who had listened to happy music interpreted the situation as more positive but made more embellishments in their descriptions of it. These findings were the same for children with and without learning disabilities. Thus, although the music condition was not entirely beneficial, the positive affect conditions did produce some improvements in information-processing. This suggests that the lack of positive feelings or moods experienced by some students with learning disabilities may contribute to their social difficulties.

F. Contextual Influences

The "playing field" of the classroom is not necessarily an even one; the social lot of students with learning disabilities is a function not only of their own social skills and behavior, but also of the tolerance and understanding of classmates. Therefore, it seems reasonable to assume that in settings that minimize or counteract possible negative biases, students with learning disabilities will have less difficulty with their peers.

In recent years, inclusion has been advocated as a means of promoting better social acceptance. It has been hypothesized that if students with learning disabilities receive special education services while being full-time members of the general education classroom, their social acceptance and functioning will improve. This assumption stems, in part, from a belief that having a different classroom assignment or frequently leaving the classroom for special services stigmatizes students, leading to lower regard by their classmates. Additionally, it has been argued that more consistent exposure to typical students will provide students with learning disabilities with better models for successful classroom behavior.

However, there is unfortunately little evidence that inclusive settings will automatically result in the hoped-for positive outcomes (Sale & Carey, 1995; Vaughn et al., 1998, 1996). For example, although compared to children with learning disabilities in inclusion programs, children in self-contained special education placements reported more conflict in their relationships and less companionship with their best school friends, comparisons of children in inclusion, in-class support, and resource room support placements revealed no differences in number of friends, friendship quality, social skills, self-concept, loneliness, and depression. Thus, leaving the classroom to attend a resource room for up to 90 minutes a day did not influence children's classroom social functioning (Wiener, 2002). Further, a meta-analysis found no differences in the social and personal/emotional self-concepts (or, for that matter, the general, academic, and physical self-concepts) of students with learning disabilities included in general classrooms vs. those who attended resource rooms or who were in self-contained classrooms (Elbaum, 2002).

What seems to be important is not simply whether a student is in an inclusive classroom, but whether the particular setting provides the support required for meeting the child's social and academic needs. Social outcomes appear to be better, for instance, when teachers have positive attitudes toward their students with learning disabilities (Vaughn et al., 1993), have special education certification (Madge et al., 1990), or have considerable support in the classroom from special education teachers (e.g., Juvonen & Bear, 1992; Vaughn et al., 1998).

Even more important, however, may be the degree to which a concerted effort is made to promote positive interaction among classmates. Promising methods for improving peer relationships include cooperative learning groups (e.g., Anderson, 1985; Putnam et al., 1996), and peer tutoring, in which the student with learning disabilities works with a partner as both the tutor and tutee (Fuchs *et al.*, 2002). These, too, are not simple panaceas; students with and without learning disabilities may first need instruction on how to work with other children in groups (Bryan *et al.*, 1982). In a study of students' science learning in inclusive classrooms, Palincsar *et al.*, (2000) discussed how students with learning disabilities were often marginalized by peers during small-group work. Fortunately, teachers engaged in case-based professional development conversations about these students' negative small-group experiences were found to change their thinking and practices about selecting group members and preparing them to support each other, a change accompanied by increased science learning for the students with learning disabilities.

IV. FUTURE RESEARCH DIRECTIONS

As we described in this chapter, a disproportionate number of children with learning disabilities experience problematic peer relationships, but, at the same time, some children are as socially successful as their typical peers. Although progress has been made in understanding why this may be the case, many questions remain. For instance, how can we identify in early childhood those students who may be most vulnerable to later peer relationship problems? Children with oral language problems are rejected even as preschoolers—are these the children most at risk? Identifying early precursors of peer relationship problems might allow us to intervene in more comprehensive ways and at a point before these problems take hold.

Further, surprisingly little research has directly addressed the question of what concurrent factors relate to obtaining positive regard from classmates. The answers are not likely to be simple. For instance, we know that having desirable characteristics may relate to the acceptance of children with learning disabilities, but also that for boys, being aggressive is associated with being included in a classroom group. These findings raise a series of issues, some of which have been mentioned earlier in the chapter. What is the relative importance of different attributes, skills, and behaviors? Do these differ for different relationship measures? Does their significance to peers differ depending on the configuration of characteristics possessed by particular children with learning disabilities? How does the behavior of peers foster or discourage the development of skills and behaviors that influence these children's attractiveness as companions? And how do gender and culture impact these issues?

Widening the lens beyond the peer setting would provide a deeper understanding of the contributions of others in the child's life. What role do parents and teachers play in nurturing skills and behaviors that enhance the children's social acceptance? What role do they play in structuring situations that support positive relationships? When do teachers' attitudes and behaviors toward their students with disabilities influence the reactions of other children? What specific classroom practices offer the best chance at encouraging good relationships among all class members? How can mutual interests and hobbies be recruited to create opportunities for students to participate fully in peer groups? The impact of promising school-wide programs that view fostering positive peer relationships as essential for promoting motivation and achievement (e.g., the Child Development Project; Solomon *et al.*, 1996) also needs study. Moreover, we need to know whether relationships with children outside school settings—for example, with neighborhood playmates, with cousins, at Scouts, at church—can buffer some of the effects of social difficulties in school.

Many of these findings raise fundamental questions about the scope and methods of intervention models. For example, do intervention goals of enhancing group acceptance have a bigger "pay-off" than helping children develop a few good friends? Are relationships with other children with learning disabilities any less beneficial than those with nondisabled children? As we have noted, some children with learning disabilities associate with classmates who exhibit less than desirable behavior, and sometimes their friendships do not provide them with much validation and support. In such cases, could encouraging these relationships cause more harm than good? And, most importantly, how do we know when social discomfort turns into something more dangerous that requires immediate attention, like a risk for suicide?

After 30 years of research, educators and parents of students with learning disabilities are now well aware of the critical importance of peer relationships. However, the voices of students with learning disabilities remain curiously absent in this body of research. How can we be alert to and support the successful strategies that some students have constructed to find their own social niches (e.g., Donahue *et al.*, 1999)? For example, some students with strong out-of-school interests and hobbies may focus their social lives on others who share their enthusiasm. Our efforts to create opportunities for students with learning disabilities to develop positive peer relationships will be incomplete without a clear understanding of individual students' own social goals and beliefs.

References

Anderson, M. A. (1985). Cooperative group tasks and their relationship to peer acceptance and cooperation. *Journal of Learning Disabilities*, **18**, 83–86.

Bagwell, C. L., Schmidt, M. E., Newcomb, A. F., & Bukowski, W. M. (2001). Friendship and peer rejection as predictors of adult adjustment. *New Directions for Child and Adolescent Development*, **91**, 25–49.

Bear, G. G., Clever, A., & Proctor, W. A. (1991). Self-perceptions of nonhandi-capped children with learning disabilities in integrated classes. *Journal of Special Education*, **24**, 409–426.

Bear, G. G., Juvonen, J., & McInerney, F. (1993). Self-perceptions and peer relations of boys with and boys without learning disabilities in an integrated setting: A longitudinal study. *Learning Disability Quarterly*, **16**, 127–136.

Bender, W. N., & Smith, J. K. (1990). Classroom behavior of children and adolescents with learning disabilities: A meta-analysis. *Journal of Learning Disabilities*, **23**, 298–305.

Brinton, B., Fujiki, M., & Mckee, L. (1998). Negotiation skills of children with specific language impairment. *Journal of Speech, Language, and Hearing Research*, **41**, 927–940.

Brinton, B., Fujiki, M., Spencer, J., & Robinson, L. (1997). The ability of children with specific language impairment to access and participate in an ongoing inter-action. *Journal of Speech, Language, and Hearing Research*, **40**, 1011–1025.

Bryan, J. H., & Sonnefeld, L. J. (1981). Children's social desirability ratings of ingratiation tactics. *Learning Disability Quarterly*, **4**, 287–293.

Bryan, J. H., Sonnefeld, L. J. & Greenberg, F. Z. (1981). Ingratiation preferences of learning disabled children. *Learning Disability Quarterly*, **4**, 170–179.

Bryan, T. H. (1974). Peer popularity of learning disabled children. *Journal of Learning Disabilities*, **7**, 621–625.

Bryan, T. H. (1976). Peer popularity of learning disabled children: A replication. *Journal of Learning Disabilities*, **9**, 307–311.

Bryan, T., Cosden, M., & Pearl, R. (1982). The effects of cooperative goal structures and cooperative models on learning disabled and nondisabled students. *Learning Disability Quarterly*, **5**, 415–421.

Bryan, T., Donahue, M., & Pearl, R. (1981a). Learning disabled children's peer interactions during a small-group problem-solving task. *Learning Disability Quarterly*, **4**, 13–22.

Bryan, T., Donahue, M., Pearl, R., & Sturm, C. (1981b). Learning disabled children's conversational skills: The television talk show. *Learning Disability Quarterly*, **4**, 250–259.

Bryan, T., Pearl, R., & Fallon, P. (1989). Conformity to peer pressure by students with learning disabilities: A replication. *Journal of Learning Disabilities*, **22**, 458–459.

Bryan, T., Sullivan-Burstein, K., & Mathur, S. (1998). The influence of affect on social-information processing. *Journal of Learning Disabilities*, **31**, 418–426.

Bryan, T., Werner, M., & Pearl, R. (1982). Learning disabled students' conformity responses to prosocial and antisocial situations. *Learning Disability Quarterly*, **5**, 344–352.

Bukowski, W. M., & Hoza, B. (1989). Popularity and friendship. Issues in theory, measurement, and outcome. In T. J. Berndt & G. W. Ladd (Eds.), *Peer relationships in child development* (pp. 15–45). New York: Wiley.

Bukowski, W. M., Hoza, B., & Boivin, M. (1994). Measuring friendship quality during pre- and early adolescence: The development and psychometric properties of the Friendship Qualities Scale. *Journal of Social and Personal Relationships*, **11**, 471–484.

Bursuck, W. (1983). Sociometric status, behavior ratings, and social knowledge of learning disabled and low-achieving students. *Learning Disability Quarterly*, **6**, 329–338.

Bursuck, W. (1989). A comparison of students with learning disabilities to low achieving and higher achieving students on three dimensions of social competence. *Journal of Learning Disabilities*, **22**, 188–194.

Carlson, C. I. (1987). Social interaction goals and strategies of children with learning disabilities. *Journal of Learning Disabilities*, **20**, 306–311.

Coleman, J. M., McHam, L. A., & Minnett, A. M. (1992). Similarities in the social competencies of learning disabled and low achieving elementary school children. *Journal of Learning Disabilities*, **25**, 671–677.

Coleman, J. M., & Minnett, A. M. (1992). Learning disabilities and social competence: A social Ecological perspective. *Exceptional Children*, **59**, 234–246.

Conderman, G. (1995). Social status of sixth- and seventh-grade students with learning disabilities. *Learning Disability Quarterly*, **18**, 13–24.

Craig, H., & Washington, J. (1993). Access behaviors of children with specific language impairment. *Journal of Speech and Hearing Research*, **36**, 322–337.

Crick, N. R., & Dodge, K. A. (1994). A review and reformulation of social information-processing mechanisms in children's social adjustment. *Psychological Bulletin*, **115**, 74–101.

Cutter, J., Palincsar, A. S., & Magnusson, S. J. (2002). Supporting inclusion though case-based vignette conversations. *Learning Disabilities Research and Practice*, **17**(3), 186–200.

Dalley, M. B., Bolocofsky, D. N., Alcorn, M. B., & Baker, C. (1992). Depressive symptomatology, attributional style, dysfunctional attitude, and social competency in adolescents with and without learning disabilities. *School Psychology Review*, **21**, 444–458.

Dodge, K. A. (1986). A social information processing model of social competence in children. In M. Perlmutter (Ed.), The Minnesota Symposium on Child Psychology (Vol. 18, pp. 77–125). Hillsdale, NJ: Lawrence Erlbaum.

Donahue, M. (1981). Requesting strategies of learning disabled children. *Applied Psycholinguistics*, **2**, 213–234.

Donahue, M. (1994). Differences in classroom discourse styles of students with learning disabilities. In D. Ripich and N. Creaghead (Eds.), *School discourse* (pp. 229–261). San Diego, CA: Singular Press.

Donahue, M. (2002). "Hanging with friends": Making sense of research on peer discourse in children with language and learning disabilities. In K. Butler & E. Silliman (Eds.), *Speaking, reading, and writing in students with language learning disabilities* (pp. 239–258). Mahwah, NJ: Lawrence Erlbaum.

Donahue, M., & Bryan, T. (1983). Conversational skills and modeling in learning disabled boys. *Applied Psycholinguistics*, **44**, 251–278.

Donahue, M., & Prescott, B. (1988). Reading disabled children's conversational participation in dispute episodes with peers. *First Language*, **8**, 247–258.

Donahue, M., Szymanski, C., & Flores, C. (1999). "When Emily Dickinson met Steven Spielberg": Assessing social information processing in literacy contexts. *Language, Speech, and Hearing Services in Schools*, **30**, 274–284.

Donahue, M., & Wong, B. Y. L. (2002). How to start a revolution. In B. Y. L. Wong and M. Donahue (Eds.), *Social dimensions of learning disabilities: Essays in honor of Tanis Bryan*. Mahwah, NJ: Lawrence Erlbaum.

Elbaum, B. (2002). The self-concept of students with learning disabilities: A meta-analysis of comparisons across different placements. *Learning Disabilities & Practice*, **17**, 216–226.

Erdley, C. A., Nangle, D. W., Newman, J. E., & Carpenter, E. M. (2001). Children's friendship experiences and psychological adjustment: Theory and research. *New Directions for Child and Adolescent Development*, **91**, 5–24.

Farmer, T. W., Pearl, R, & Van Acker, R. (1996). Expanding the social skills framework: A developmental synthesis perspective, classroom social networks, and implications for the social growth of students with disabilities. *Journal of Special Education*, **30**, 232–256.

Farmer, T. W., Rodkin, P. C., Pearl, R., & Van Acker, R. (1999). Teacher-assessed behavioral configurations, peer-assessments, and self-concepts of elementary students with mild disabilities. *Journal of Special Education*, **33**, 66–80.

Farmer, T. W., Van Acker, R. M., Pearl, R., & Rodkin, P. C. (1999). Social networks and peer-assessed problem behavior in elementary classrooms. *Remedial and Special Education*, **20**, 244–256.

Fisher, B. L., Allen, R., & Kose, G. (1996). The relationship between anxiety and problem-solving skills in children with and without learning disabilities. *Journal of Learning Disabilities*, **29**, 439–446.

Fleming, J. E., Cook, T. D., & Stone, C. A. (2002). Interactive influences of perceived social contexts on reading achievement of urban middle schoolers with learning disabilities. *Learning Disabilities Research & Practice*, **17**, 47–64.

Flicek, M., & Landau, S. (1985). Social status problems of learning disabled and hyperactive/learning disabled boys. *Journal of Clinical Child Psychology*, **14**, 340–344.

Fuchs, D., Fuchs, L. S., Mathes, P. G., & Martinez, E. A. (2002). Preliminary evidence on the social standing of students with learning disabilities in PALS and No-PALS classrooms. *Learning Disabilities Research & Practice*, **17**, 205–215.

Fujiki, M., Brinton, B., Robinson, L., & Watson, V. (1997). The ability of children with specific language impairment to participate in a group decision task. *Journal of Children's Communication Development*, **18**(2), 1–10.

Geisthardt, C., & Munsch, J. (1996). Coping with school stress: A comparison of adolescents with and without learning disabilities. *Journal of Learning Disabilities*, **29**, 287–296.

Gertner, B., Rice, M., & Hadley, P. (1994). Influence of communicative competence on peer preferences in a preschool classroom. *Journal of Speech and Hearing Research*, **37**, 913–923.

Gresham, F., & Reschly, D. (1987). Sociometric differences between mildly handicapped and nonhandicapped Black and White students. *Journal of Educational Psychology*, **79**, 195–197.

Haager, D., & Vaughn, S. (1995). Parent, teacher, peer, and self-reports of the social competence of students with learning disabilities. *Journal of Learning Disabilities*, **28**, 205–215.

Halmhuber, N. L., & Paris, S. G. (1993). Perceptions of competence and control and the use of coping strategies by children with disabilities. *Learning Disability Quarterly*, **16**, 93–111.

Hartas, D., & Donahue, M. (1997). Conversational and social problem-solving skills in adolescents with learning disabilities. *Learning Disabilities Research and Practice*, **12**, 213–220.

Harter, S., Whitesell, N. R., & Junkin, L. J. (1998). Similarities and differences in domain-specific and global self-evaluations of learning-disabled, behaviorally disordered, and normally achieving adolescents. *American Educational Research Journal*, **35**, 653–680.

Heath, N. L., & Wiener, J. (1996). Depression and nonacademic self-perceptions in children with and without learning disabilities. *Learning Disability Quarterly*, **19**, 34–44.

Howard, K. A., & Tryon, G. S. (2002). Depressive symptoms in and type of classroom placement for adolescents with LD. *Journal of Learning Disabilities*, **35**, 185–190.

Howes, C. (1988). Peer interactions of young children. *Monographs of the Society for Research in Child Development*, **53**, (1, Serial No. 217).

Hoy, C., Gregg, N., Wisenbaker, J., Manglitz, E., King, M., & Moreland, C. (1997). Depression and anxiety in two groups of adults with learning disabilities. *Learning Disability Quarterly*, **20**, 280–291.

Huntington, D. D., & Bender, W. N. (1993). Adolescents with learning disabilities at risk? Emotional well-being, depression, suicide. *Journal of Learning Disabilities*, **26**, 159–166.

Juvonen, J., & Bear, G. (1992). Social adjustment of children with and without learning disabilities in integrated classrooms. *Journal of Educational Psychology*, **84**, 322–330.

Kavale, K. A., & Forness, S. R. (1996). Social skill deficits and learning disabilities: A meta-analysis. *Journal of Learning Disabilities*, **29**, 226–237.

Kistner, J. A., & Gatlin, D. F. (1989a). Sociometric differences between learning-disabled and nonhandicapped students: Effects of sex and race. *Journal of Educational Psychology*, **81**, 118–120.

Kistner, J. A., & Gatlin, D. (1989b). Correlates of peer rejection among children with learning disabilities. *Learning Disability Quarterly*, **12**, 133–140.

Kistner, J., & Osborne, M. (1987). A longitudinal study of LD children's self-evaluations. *Learning Disability Quarterly*, **10**, 258–266.

Kravetz, S., Faust, M., Lipshitz, S., & Shalhav, S. (1999). LD, interpersonal understanding, and social behavior in the classroom. *Journal of Learning Disabilities*, **32**, 248–255.

La Greca, A. M., & Stone, W. L. (1990). LD status and achievement: Confounding variables in the study of children's social status, self-esteem, and behavioral functioning. *Journal of Learning Disabilities*, **23**, 483–490.

Landau, S., Milich, R., & McFarland, M. (1987). Social status differences among subgroups of LD boys. *Learning Disability Quarterly*, **10**, 277–282.

Maag, J. W., & Behrens, J. T. (1989). Depression and cognitive self-statements of learning disabled and seriously emotionally disturbed adolescents. *Journal of Special Education*, **23**, 17–27.

Madge, S., Affleck, J., & Lowenbraun, S. (1990). Social effects of integrated classrooms and resource room/regular class placements on elementary students with learning disabilities. *Journal of Learning Disabilities*, **23**, 439–445.

Margalit, M., & Ben-Dov, I. (1992). *Kibbutz versus city comparisons of social competence and loneliness among students with and without learning disabilities.* Paper presented at the annual IARLD Conference, Amsterdam, Netherlands.

Margalit, M., & Levin-Alyagon, M. (1994). Learning disability, subtyping, loneliness, and classroom adjustment. *Learning Disability Quarterly*, **17**, 297–310.

Margalit, M., & Shulman, S. (1986). Autonomy perceptions and anxiety expressions of learning disabled adolescents. *Journal of Learning Disabilities*, **19**, 291–293.

Margalit, M., & Zak, I. (1984). Anxiety and self-concept of learning disabled children. *Journal of Learning Disabilities*, **17**, 537–539.

McLeod, T. M., Kolb, T. L., & Lister, M. O. (1994). Social skills, school skills, and success in the high school: A comparison of teachers' and students' perceptions. *Learning Disabilities Research & Practice*, **9**, 142–147.

Montgomery, M. S. (1994). Self-concept and children with learning disabilities: Observer–child concordance across six context-dependent domains. *Journal of Learning Disabilities*, **27**, 254–262.

Nabuzoka, D., & Smith, P. K. (1995). Identification of expressions of emotions by children with and without learning disabilities. *Learning Disabilities Research & Practice*, **10**, 91–101.

Ochoa, S. H., & Olivarez, Jr., A. (1995). A meta-analysis of peer rating sociometric studies of pupils with learning disabilities. *Journal of Special Education*, **29**, 1–19.

Ochoa, S. H., & Palmer, D. J. (1995). Comparison of the peer status of Mexican-American students with learning disabilities and non-disabled low-achieving students. *Learning Disability Quarterly*, **18**, 57–63.

Oliva, A. H., & La Greca, A. M. (1988). Children with learning disabilities: Social goals and strategies. *Journal of Learning Disabilities*, **21**, 301–306.

Palincsar, A., Magnusson, S., Collins, K., & Cutter, J. (2000). Investigating the engagement and learning of students with learning disabilities in guided inquiry science. *Language, Speech, and Hearing Services in Schools*, **31**, 240–251.

Parker, J. G., & Asher, S. R. (1993). Friendship and friendship quality in middle childhood: Links with peer group acceptance and feelings of loneliness and social dissatisfaction. *Developmental Psychology*, **29**, 611–621.

Pavri, S., & Monda-Amaya, L. (2000). Loneliness and students with learning disabilities in inclusive classrooms: Self-perceptions, coping strategies, and preferred interventions. *Learning Disabilities Research & Practice*, **15**, 22–33.

Pearl, R. (1992). Psychosocial characteristics of learning disabled students. In N. N. Singh and I. L. Beale (Eds.), *Current perspectives in learning disabilities: Nature, theory, and treatment.* New York: Springer-Verlag.

Pearl, R., & Bryan, T. (1994). Getting caught in misconduct: Conceptions of adolescents with and without learning disabilities. *Journal of Learning Disabilities*, **27**, 193–197.

Pearl, R., & Bryan, T. (1992). Students' expectations about peer pressure to engage in misconduct. *Journal of Learning Disabilities*, **25**, 582–585, 597.

Pearl, R., Bryan, T., Fallon, P., & Herzog, A. (1991). Learning disabled students' detection of deception. *Learning Disabilities Research and Practice*, **6,** 12–16.

Pearl, R., Bryan, T., & Herzog, A. (1990). Resisting or acquiescing to peer pressure to engage in misconduct: Adolescents' expectations of probable consequences. *Journal of Youth and Adolescence*, **19,** 43–55.

Pearl, R., Donahue, M., & Bryan, T. (1985). The development of tact: Children's strategies for delivering bad news. *Journal of Applied Developmental Psychology*, **6,** 141–149.

Pearl, R., Farmer, T. W., Van Acker, R., Rodkin, P. C., Bost, K. K., Coe, M., & Henley, W. (1998). The social integration of students with mild disabilities in general education classrooms: Peer group membership and peer-assessed social behavior. *Elementary School Journal*, **99,** 167–185.

Perlmutter, B. F., Crocker, J., Cordray, D., & Garstecki, D. (1983). Sociometric status and related personality characteristics of mainstreamed learning disabled adolescents. *Learning Disability Quarterly*, **6,** 21–31.

Prilliman, D. (1981). Acceptance of learning disabled students in the mainstream environment: A failure to replicate. *Journal of Learning Disabilities*, **14,** 344–346.

Putnam, J., Markovchick, K., Johnson, D. W., & Johnson, R. T. (1996). *Journal of Social Psychology*, **136,** 741–752.

Raviv, D., & Stone, C. A. (1991). Individual differences in the self-image of adolescents with learning disabilities: The role of severity, time of diagnosis, and parental perceptions. *Journal of Learning Disabilities*, **24,** 602–611, 629.

Reiff, H. B., Hatzes, N. M., Bramel, M. H., & Gibbon, T. (2001). The relation of LD and gender with emotional intelligence in college students. *Journal of Learning Disabilities*, **34,** 66–78.

Rice, M. (1993). "Don't talk to him; he's weird": A social consequences account of language and social interactions. In A. Kaiser & D. Gray (Eds.), *Enhancing children's communication*, Vol. 2. (pp. 139–158). Baltimore: Brookes Publishing.

Rock, E. E., Fessler, M. A., & Church, R. P. (1997). The concomitance of learning disabilities and emotional/behavioral disorders: A conceptual model. *Journal of Learning Disabilities*, **30,** 245–263.

Rourke, B. P., & Fuerst, D. E. (1996). Psychosocial dimensions of learning disability subtypes. *Assessment*, **3,** 277–290.

Sabornie, E. J., & Kauffman, J. M. (1986). Social acceptance of learning disabled adolescents. *Learning Disability Quarterly*, **9,** 55–60.

Sabornie, E. J. (1994). Social–affective characteristics in early adolescents identified as learning disabled and nondisabled. *Learning Disability Quarterly*, **17,** 268–279.

Sainato, D. M., Zigmond, N., & Strain, P. (1983). Social status and initiations of interaction by learning disabled students in a regular education setting. *Analysis and Intervention in Developmental Disabilities*, **3,** 71–87.

Sale, P., & Carey, D. M. (1995). The sociometric status of students with disabilities in a full-inclusion school. *Exceptional Children*, **62,** 6–19.

San Miguel, S. K., Forness, S. R., & Kavale, K. A. (1996). Social skills deficits in learning disabilities: The psychiatric comorbidity hypothesis. *Learning Disability Quarterly*, **19,** 252–261.

Sater, G. M., & French, D. C. (1989). A comparison of the social competencies of learning disabled and low achieving elementary-aged children. *Journal of Special Education*, **23**, 17–27.

Settle, S. A., & Milich, R. (1999). Social persistence following failure in boys and girls with LD. *Journal of Learning Disabilities*, **32**, 201–212.

Siperstein, G. N., Bopp, M. J., & Bak, J. J. (1978). Social status of learning disabled children. *Journal of Learning Disabilities*, **11**, 98–102.

Siperstein, G. N., & Goding, M. J. (1983). *Social integration of learning disabled children in regular classrooms.* Greenwich, CT: JAI Press.

Smith, D. S., & Nagle, R. J. (1995). Self-perceptions and social comparisons among children with LD. *Journal of Learning Disabilities*, **28**, 364–371.

Sobol, M. P., Earn, B. M., Bennett, D., & Humphries, T. (1983). A categorical analysis of the social attributions of learning-disabled children. *Journal of Abnormal Child Psychology*, **11**, 217–228.

Solomon, D., Watson, M., Battistich, V., Schaps, E., & Delucchi, K. (1996). Creating classrooms that students experience as communities. *American Journal of Community Psychology*, **24**, 719–748.

Stanley, P. D., Dai, Y., & Nolan, R. F. (1997). Differences in depression and self-esteem reported by learning disabled and behavior disordered middle school students. *Journal of Adolescence*, **20**, 219–222.

Stevenson, D. T., & Romney, D. M. (1984). Depression in learning disabled children. *Journal of Learning Disabilities*, **17**, 579–582.

Stiliadis, K., & Wiener, J. (1989). Relationship between social perception and peer status in children with learning disabilities. *Journal of Learning Disabilities*, **22**, 624–629.

Stone, W. L., & La Greca, A. M. (1984). Comprehension of nonverbal communication: A reexamination of the social competencies of learning disabled children. *Journal of Abnormal Child Psychology*, **12**, 505–518.

Stone, W. L., & La Greca, A. M. (1990). The social status of children with learning disabilities: A reexamination. *Journal of Learning Disabilities*, **23**, 32–37.

Swanson, H. L., & Malone, S. (1992). Social skills and learning disabilities: A meta-analysis of the literature. *School Psychology Review*, **21**, 427–443.

Toro, P. A., Weissberg, R. P., Guare, J., & Liebenstein, N. L. (1990). A comparison of children with and without learning disabilities on social problem-solving skill, school behavior, and family background. *Journal of Learning Disabilities*, **23**, 115–120.

Touliatos, J., & Lindholm, B. W. (1980). Dimensions of problem behavior in learning disabled and normal children. *Perceptual and Motor Skills*, **50**, 145–146.

Tur-Kaspa, H. (2002a). Social cognition in learning disabilities. In B. Y. L. Wong & M. L. Donahue (Eds.), *The social dimensions of learning disabilities* (pp. 11–31). Mahwah, NJ: Lawrence Erlbaum Associates.

Tur-Kaspa, H. (2002b). The socioemotional adjustment of adolescents with LD in the kibbutz during high school transition periods. *Journal of Learning Disabilities*, **35**, 87–96.

Tur-Kaspa, H., & Bryan, T. (1994). Social information-processing skills of students with learning disabilities. *Learning Disabilities Research & Practice*, **9**, 12–23.

Tur-Kaspa, H., & Bryan, T. (1995). Teachers' ratings of the social competence and school adjustment of students with LD in elementary and junior high school. *Journal of Learning Disabilities*, **28**, 44–52.

Tur-Kaspa, H., Margalit, M., & Most, T. (1999). Reciprocal friendship, reciprocal rejection, and socio-emotional adjustment: The social experiences of children with learning disorders over a one-year period. *European Journal of Special Needs Education*, **14**, 37–48.

Tur-Kaspa, H., Weisel, A., & Segev, L. (1998). Attributions for feelings of loneliness of students with learning disabilities. *Learning Disabilities Research & Practice*, **13**, 89–94.

Vallance, D. D., Cummings, R. L., & Humphries, T. (1998). Behavior in children with language learning disabilities. *Journal of Learning Disabilities*, **31**, 160–171.

Vaughn, S., & Elbaum, B. E. (1999). The self concept and friendships of students with learning disabilities: A developmental perspective. In R. Gallimore, L. Bernheimer, D. L. MacMillan, D. L. Speece, & S. Vaughn (Eds.), *Developmental perspective on children with high incidence disabilities* (pp. 81–110). Mahwah, NJ: Lawrence Erlbaum Associates.

Vaughn, S., Elbaum, B., & Boardman, A. G. (2001). The social functioning of students with learning disabilities: Implications for inclusion. *Exceptionality*, **9**, 47–65.

Vaughn, S., Elbaum, S. E., & Schumm, J. S. (1996). The effects of inclusion on the social functioning of students with learning disabilities. *Journal of Learning Disabilities*, **29**, 598–608.

Vaughn, S., Elbaum, B. E., Schumm, J. S., & Hughes, M. T. (1998). Social outcomes for students with and without learning disabilities in inclusive classrooms. *Journal of Learning Disabilities*, **31**, 428–436.

Vaughn, S., & Haager, D. (1994). Social competence as a multifaceted construct: How do students with learning disabilities fare? *Learning Disability Quarterly*, **17**, 253–266.

Vaughn, S., Haager, D., Hogan, A., & Kouzekanani, K. (1992). Self-concept and peer acceptance in students with learning disabilities: A four- to five-year prospective study. *Journal of Educational Psychology*, **84**, 43–50.

Vaughn, S., Hogan, A., Kouzekanani, K., & Shapiro, S. (1990). Peer acceptance, self-perceptions, and social skills of learning disabled students prior to identification. *Journal of Educational Psychology*, **82**, 101–106.

Vaughn, S., McIntosh, R., Schumm, J. S., Haager, D., & Callwood, D. (1993a). Social status, peer acceptance, and reciprocal friendships revisited. *Learning Disabilities Research and Practice*, **8**, 82–88.

Vaughn, S., Zargoza, N., Hogan, A., & Walker, J. (1993b). A four-year longitudinal investigation of the social skills and behavior problems of students with learning disabilities. *Journal of Learning Disabilities*, **26**, 404–412.

Wiener, J. (1980). A theoretical model of the acquisition of peer relationships of learning disabled children. *Journal of Learning Disabilities*, **13**, 506–511.

Wiener, J. (2002). Friendship and social adjustment. In B. Y. L. Wong & M. Donahue (Eds.), *The social dimensions of learning disabilities* (pp. 93–114). Mahwah, NJ: Lawrence Erlbaum.

Wiener, J., Harris, P. J., & Shirer, C. (1990). Achievement and social–behavioral correlates of peer status in LD children. *Learning Disability Quarterly*, **13,** 114–127.

Wiener, J., & Sunohara, G. (1998). Parents' perceptions of the quality of friendship of their children with learning disabilities. *Learning Disabilities Research & Practice*, **13,** 242–257.

Wong, B. Y. L., & Donahue, M. (Eds.). (2002). *Social dimensions of learning disabilities: Essays in honor of Tanis Bryan*. Mahwah, NJ: Lawrence Erbaum.

Wong, B. Y., & Wong, R. (1980). Role-taking skills in normal achieving and learning disabled children. *Learning Disability Quarterly*, **3,** 11–18.

Wright-Strawderman, C., & Watson, B. L. (1992). The prevalence of depressive symptoms in children with learning disabilities. *Journal of Learning Disabilities*, **25,** 258–264.

CHAPTER 5

Self-Regulation among Students with LD and ADHD

Karen R. Harris,[*] **Robert R. Reid,**[†] **and Steve Graham**[*]

[*]*University of Maryland*
[†]*University of Nebraska–Lincoln*

I. DEFINING AND UNDERSTANDING SELF-REGULATION

Throughout history, the ability to control and regulate one's behavior has been considered desirable. The philosopher Aristotle, for example, praised the virtues of self-awareness, and Benjamin Franklin was a staunch proponent of self-regulation. Benjamin Franklin described a number of self-regulation procedures he used in his quest for self-improvement (Zimmerman & Schunk, 1989). At one time in his life, he defined 13 virtues, such as temperance and order, that he wished to develop. He kept a record in which he established goals to increase each virtue, monitored his successes and failures, recorded daily results, and established new goals. The Scottish poet Robert Burns considered prudent, cautious self-control to be the root of wisdom, and William Penn, the founder of Pennsylvania, did not consider a person fit for commanding others if they could not "command themselves" (cf. Harris *et al.*, 2003).

Today, the area of self-regulation has become a major focus of research in many areas of education and educational psychology, and an important construct in research and intervention in the areas of learning disability (LD) and attention-deficit hyperactivity disorder (ADHD) (Graham *et al.*, 1992; Schunk & Zimmerman, 2003). While more basic research is still needed, researchers have provided evidence that these students have difficulties with or deficiencies in self-regulation processes (cf. Barkley, 1997; DuPaul & Stoner, 1994; Harris, 1982, 1985, 1986a; Torgesen, 1977, 1980; Zivin, 1979). Both academic and social difficulties encountered by students with LD may arise, in part, from problems in self-regulation of organized, strategic behaviors (Graham *et al.*, 1992; Harris, 1982). Further, in the last decade the conceptualization of ADHD as primarily difficulties with attention, impulsivity, and hyperactivity has been challenged; the current view of ADHD is that this disorder is actually a broader syndrome of deficient self-control (Barkley, 1997; Cutting & Denckla, 2003). Researchers in ADHD have conceptualized self-control as having subdomains, including cognitive control and social-emotional control, and have focused on deficits in executive functions.

While students with LD and those with ADHD are a heterogeneous group, difficulties in self-regulation appear common among students with either disorder. Further, underachievement is common among students with ADHD, with up to 80% of these students exhibiting academic achievement problems and as many as 26% of students with ADHD also diagnosed as having LD (Barkley, 1997; Cutting & Denckla, 2003; DuPaul & Stoner, 1994). Among those students challenged by either or both LD and ADHD, difficulties are strongly evident with inhibition of behavior, delay of gratification, persistence while engaged in activities requiring self-regulation, producing the amount and quality of work they are capable of, maintaining on-task behaviors, following through when given instructions, and planning and directing goal-directed, future-oriented actions.

Given the recent emphasis on the role of self-regulation/self-control in learning and development, and the recognition that students with LD and/or ADHD commonly have deficits in self-regulation, it is not surprising that a great deal of intervention research has been conducted. In fact, intervention research in self-regulation has become evident not only in the areas of LD and ADHD, but across many specialities in education and psychology. Important summaries of this growing body of research are available in the works of Boekaerts, Pintrich, and Zeidner (2000); Diaz and Berk (1992); Schunk and Zimmerman (1994, 1998); Zimmerman and Schunk (1989); and Zivin (1979).

In this chapter, we overview the theoretical bases for research in self-regulation; common self-regulation strategies or processes; the effects of self-regulation interventions on major dependent variables or outcomes; factors that can influence the use and effectiveness of self-regulation among learners, with an emphasis on self-efficacy; and the effects of combining explicit development of self-regulation abilities with strategies instruction. First, however, we turn to definitions of common terms in this area, including self-regulation, self-regulated learning, metacognition, and executive function.

A. Self-Regulation and Self-Regulated Learning

The relatively large number of researchers working in self-regulation across a number of domains has resulted in a plethora of definitions for self-regulation and self-regulated learning; a number of definitions can similarly be found for metacognition and executive function. As research has progressed in these areas, definitions have evolved and been refined, and we expect that this will continue to be the case. Further, there is some ambiguity and overlap among these constructs and their definitions (Boekaerts et al., 2000), which will also continue to be addressed as research and practice evolve. Here, we present definitions currently offered by leading researchers in these areas.

Self-regulation can be defined as the "process whereby students activate and sustain cognitions, behaviors, and affects, which are systematically oriented toward attainment of their goals" (Schunk & Zimmerman, 1994, p. 309), and can be seen as referring to the "degree that individuals are metacognitively, motivationally, and behaviorally active participants in their own learning process" (Schunk & Zimmerman, 1994, p. 3). Self-regulated learning, therefore, encompasses thoughts, feelings, and actions generated by the student and then monitored and adapted by the student over time in order to attain learning goals. Zimmerman (2000) argued that students can self-regulate aspects of their own learning behaviors, environmental conditions, and their cognitive and affective states, and has offered a model of the cyclical phases of self-regulation which includes forethought, performance, and self-reflection. He has identified different subprocesses of self-regulation, such as task analysis, self-motivational beliefs, and self-control processes, that occur during these phases.

The construct, and thus the definition of, self-regulation is obviously complex. Boekaerts et al. (2000) stated that self-regulation involves a number of "integrated microprocesses, including goal-setting, strategic planning, use of effective strategies to organize, code, and store information, monitoring and metacognition, action and volitional control, managing time effectively, self-motivational beliefs (self-efficacy, outcome expectations, intrinsic interest, and goal orientation, etc.), evaluation and self-reflection, experiencing pride and satisfaction with one's efforts, and establishing a congenial environment" (p. 753). We will return to these behavioral, affective, and cognitive components and processes of self-regulation as we continue to discuss research in this area with students with LD and ADHD.

B. Metacognition

Boekaerts *et al.* (2000) noted that the distinction between self-regulation and metacognition is sometimes unclear in the literature and that there is little consensus on the nature of the relationship between these two terms. Meta-cognition is commonly agreed to encompass students' awareness of the skills, strategies, and resources needed to perform a task effectively, as well as their knowledge of how to regulate their behavior in order to successfully complete the task (cf. Boekaerts *et al.*, 2000; Wong, 1982). Or, in somewhat simpler terms, metacognition might be seen as students' knowledge about both learning and how to manage their own learning. Today, many research-ers see self-regulation as the broader term, and define it as encompassing metacognitive knowledge and skills (Boekaerts *et al.*, 2000; Schunk & Zimmerman, 1994, 1998). Self-regulation is seen as going beyond metacog-nition because it incorporates affective/emotional, motivational, and behavioral monitoring and self-control processes.

C. Executive Functioning

The last term to be defined here, executive functioning, has also been seen as overlapping with the terms metacognition and self-regulation, making pre-cise understanding and use of all these terms somewhat challenging. Cutting and Denckla (2003) argued that the term executive functioning should not be elevated to the position of a synonym for metacognition. The term execu-tive function is somewhat more commonly used by cognitive neuropsycholo-gists and cognitive psychologists, whereas the term self-regulation is more commonly used by educational and educational psychology researchers.

Barkley (1997) defined executive function as "the self-directed mental activities that occur during the delay in responding, that serve to modify the eventual response to an event, and that function to improve the long-term future consequences related to that event" (p. 56). He further noted that the term executive function incorporates self-directed actions; organization of behavior across time; the use of self-directed speech, rules, or plans; deferred gratification; and goal-directed, future-oriented, purposive, effortful, or intentional actions, concluding that "executive functions are those types of actions we perform to ourselves and direct at ourselves so as to accomplish self-control, goal-directed behavior, and the maximization of future outcomes" (p. 57). The nuances in the definitions of the terms self-regulation, metacognition, and executive function have much to do with the fields of study from which they have arisen and the times at which these definitions were developed. While the overlap among these terms and the lack of clear distinctions in these constructs may be confusing at first, each view has informed research on self-regulation or self-control. These terms are also related to the different theoretical perspectives of self-regulation, which we turn to next.

II. THEORETICAL BASES FOR RESEARCH ON SELF-REGULATION

While more theoretical perspectives on self-regulation exist, we briefly describe four of the most relevant theories from which research on self-regulation among students with LD or ADHD has evolved: operant theory, information processing theory, social constructivist theory, and social cognitive theory (Schunk & Zimmerman, 2003). More detailed discussion of these theories and their contributions to self-regulation research, as well as contributions from other perspectives, can be found in Schunk and Zimmerman (1994, 1998, 2003) and in Boekaerts *et al.* (2000). Similar to the overlaps and difficulties with clear distinctions noted in the terms previously defined, these theoretical perspectives also have areas of overlap; further, each of these theories continues to evolve and develop. Thus, our portrayal of these theories can be seen only as an overview; careful review of each and its contribution to self-regulation research is recommended for those interested in this area.

Operant Theory

Operant, or behavioral, theorists have traditionally explained human behavior through environmental antecedents and consequences, with research focusing primarily on readily observable and measurable overt behaviors. Radical behaviorists have seen cognitions as having no place in the science of behavior, while more moderate behaviorists do not deny the existence of the mind, yet see cognitive components of behavior as either irrelevant or trivial (Harris, 1982). As early as the 1970s, however, some proponents of behavioral theory began expanding it to include a greater role for cognition. Kanfer and Karoly (1972) wrote an early and extremely influential article regarding self-regulation from a behavioral perspective, entitled, interestingly, "Self-control: A behavioristic excursion into the lion's den." Just two years later, Mahoney and Thoresen (1974) published an influential book that reviewed behavioral and social learning perspectives on self-regulation, entitled, *Self-control: Power to the Person.* These early and important works are must reading for those who want to understand the progression of research in self-regulation.

Schunk and Zimmerman (2003) explained that from an operant theory perspective, a student decides what behaviors to regulate, establishes discriminative stimuli for their occurrence, evaluates performance according to whether or not it meets standards, and administers reinforcement. Key self-regulation processes studied by behavioral researchers include goal-setting, self-instructions, self-monitoring (including both self-assessment and self-recording), and self-reinforcement. These same processes, however, have also been studied by researchers of other theoretical persuasions.

Information Processing Theory

Schunk and Zimmerman (2003) noted that there are several models of information processing but, in general, this theory emphasizes that students need to compare present activities and abilities against standards and then take steps to resolve discrepancies. Metacognition, or knowledge about task demands, personal capabilities, and strategies for the task, is seen as necessary for self-regulated learning. Learning is further seen as the encoding of information into long-term memory; new knowledge is related to existing information in working memory. Self-regulation or self-control processes are used in creating new learning and in moving information from working memory to long-term memory.

Social Constructivist and Social Cognitive Theories

These two theories, as is true of both operant and information processing theories, are complex and cannot be thoroughly described here. Schunk and Zimmerman (2003) described the social constructivist theory of self-regulation as grounded in theories of cognitive development that postulate that human beings are intrinsically motivated, active learners. Mental representations and refinements in understandings develop over time, with reflection, experience, social guidance, and acquisition of new information. Self-regulation, then, is seen by social constructivists as the process of students "acquiring beliefs and theories about their abilities and competencies, the structure and difficulty of learning tasks, and the way to regulate effort and strategy use to accomplish goals" (Schunk & Zimmerman, 2003, p. 66). Students' beliefs and theories are related to their level of development and change due to ongoing development and experiences. The works of Vygotsky, Luria, Flavell, and others are frequently seen as fundamental to this theory, and are also seen as informing social cognitive theory (Harris, 1982, 1990).

Social cognitive theory is grounded in Bandura's (1986) emphasis on the reciprocal nature of interactions between behaviors, environmental factors, and cognition and affect. Self-regulation is seen by social-cognitive theorists as situation specific, and as strongly influenced by students' self-efficacy beliefs (Schunk & Zimmerman, 1994, 1998, 2003). Zimmerman's three-phase model of the cyclical processes of self-regulation (forethought, performance, and self-reflection) mentioned earlier evolved from a social cognitive theoretical base. Various self-regulatory processes are seen as coming into play across the three phases and the interaction of personal, behavioral, and environmental factors. We turn next to components of self-regulation commonly studied across these differing theoretical views of self-regulation: self-monitoring, self-instruction, goal-setting, self-evaluation, and self-reinforcement.

III. COMMON SELF-REGULATION PROCESSES: APPLICATION WITH STUDENTS WITH LD AND ADHD

There are a number of self-regulation processes or strategies that can be effectively taught to students with deficiencies or difficulties in self-regulation to aid in their development of these capabilities. These include self-monitoring (also called self-assessment or self-recording), self-evaluation, self-instruction, goal setting, and self-reinforcement. All of these aspects of self-regulation have been thoroughly researched and classroom tested, and have demonstrated efficacy for students with LD and ADHD (Mace *et al.*, 2001; Reid, 1999). Though we discuss each separately, we stress that these self-regulation procedures are commonly and effectively combined in practice. We also briefly discuss some less commonly used, but potentially effective, approaches to self-regulation. Once we have explained each of these self-regulation procedures, we turn to the major target behaviors, or dependent variables, that have been studied using self-regulation interventions.

A. Self-Monitoring

Self-monitoring is one of the most thoroughly researched self-regulation techniques and has been called one of the most important subprocesses of self-regulated learning (Reid, 1996; Shapiro *et al.*, 2002). It was originally developed as an assessment procedure designed to allow psychologists to gather information from patients regarding behaviors, feelings, or cognitions in order to evaluate effectiveness of interventions (Kanfer, 1977; Shapiro *et al.*, 2002). However, it was found that merely being aware of and recording behaviors caused changes in the frequency of their occurrence (Nelson & Hayes, 1981). This behavior change, termed "reactivity," led to the use of self-monitoring as an intervention in and of itself. Self-monitoring is defined as occurring when an individual first self-assesses whether or not a target behavior has occurred, and then self-records the occurrence, frequency, duration, or so on of the target behavior (Nelson & Hayes, 1981).

For example, in the one of the earliest demonstrations of self-monitoring, researchers taught an eighth-grade student to periodically ask herself whether or not she was working or paying attention in class and to then record the results on a tally sheet, with positive results (Broden *et al.*, 1971). Typically, self-monitoring does not involve the use of external reinforcers; however, in some cases, notably involving children with ADHD, self-monitoring is combined with external reinforcement (Barkley *et al.*, 1980). Teaching a student to use self-monitoring is both quick and straightforward, and procedures are well established (see Graham *et al.*, 1992; Reid, 1993).

B. Self-Evaluation

Self-evaluation is closely related to self-monitoring. Self-evaluation differs from self-monitoring in the use of external comparisons and reinforcers. It has been used frequently and very effectively with children with ADHD (e.g., Shapiro *et al.*, 1998). Self-evaluation requires students to rate a behavior at set intervals (Shapiro & Cole, 1994). For example, students might rate their behavior on a scale of 1 (did not follow directions or finish work) to 5 (followed all directions and finished all work). Students' ratings are then compared to the evaluation of an external observer (e.g., teacher, paraprofessional), and students receive points or tokens based how closely they match the external rating. After students have attained consistently accurate ratings, the external matching is faded and children self-award points based on their self-evaluation.

C. Self-Instruction

Self-instruction techniques involve the use of self-statements to direct or self-regulate behavior (Graham *et al.*, 1992). Put simply, children quite literally learn to "talk themselves through" a task or activity. Self-instruction techniques grew from Vygotsky's (1934/1962) observation that children used overt verbalizations to help regulate behavior. Self-talk (often termed "private speech") is used by children to self-regulate and guide behavior and is a part of the normal developmental process (Harris, 1990). Self-instruction techniques mimic the manner in which language is normally used to self-regulate behavior. Graham *et al.* (1992) identified six basic forms of self-instructions: (1) Problem Definition—defining the nature and demands of a task; (2) Focusing Attention/Planning—attending to task and generating plans; (3) Strategy Related—engaging and using a strategy; (4) Self-Evaluation—error detection and correction; (5) Coping—dealing with difficulties/failures; (6) Self-reinforcement—rewarding oneself.

Teaching students to use self-instruction involves: (a) discussing the importance of verbalizations, (b) teacher and student jointly developing meaningful, individualized task-appropriate self-statements, (c) modeling the use of self-statements, and (d) providing collaborative practice in the use of self-instruction to perform the task (Graham *et al.*, 1992). The ultimate goal is for students to progress from the use of modeled, overt self-statements to covert, internalized speech (Harris, 1990). Self-instruction techniques have a well-demonstrated record of effectiveness for children with LD (Swanson *et al.*, 1999). They are also commonly used as a component in strategy instruction interventions (e.g. Graham & Harris, 1996).

D. Goal-Setting

Effective learners are goal-oriented (Winne, 1997), and goal-setting is viewed as an important aspect of self-regulation (Bandura, 1986). Goals serve important functions for learners. Goals structure effort, provide information on progress, and serve to motivate performance (Schunk, 1990). Goals may be either absolute (i.e., with a fixed standard such as completing 20 math problems correctly in 6 minutes) or normative (i.e., doing as well as another student on the math problems). There is some evidence that the most appropriate goals for children with LD might be normative as these types of goals may enhance self-efficacy and motivation (Schunk, 1987). Students who see satisfactory progress toward a goal are more likely to sustain effort (Bandura, 1986).

There are three salient features of effective goals: specificity, proximity, and difficulty (Bandura, 1988). Specificity refers to how well a goal is defined. Goals which are vague (e.g., do your best on the test) are not as effective as those which are well specified (e.g., achieve at least 80% correct on the test). Proximity refers to temporal aspects of goals. Proximal goals can be completed in the near term (e.g., copy my spelling words 3 times by the end of class), and are generally more effective than distal goals, which can only be completed in the far future (e.g., learn 100 new spelling words by the end of the year). Note, however, that it is possible to use a series of proximal goals to accomplish a distal goal. Difficulty refers to how much challenge a goal poses an individual. Goals which are easily attained do not serve to enhance or maintain effort (Johnson & Graham, 1990). The most effective goals are those which are moderately challenging. That is, those which are neither too easy nor too difficult.

Goal-setting often involves a self-judgment process that entails comparing current performance with a goal (Schunk, 2001). For goal-setting to affect behavior, goals must be valued. If a goal has little or no importance to the student, then it is unlikely to improve performance or maintain motivation or effort. Additionally, attributions (the perceived cause of an outcome) must be considered (Schunk, 2001). Individuals must perceive progress toward a goal as being the primary result of their own efforts rather than simply luck or outside help (e.g., the teacher helped me).

E. Self-Reinforcement

Self-reinforcement occurs when a student selects a reinforcer and self-awards it when a predetermined criterion is reached or exceeded (e.g., when I write 3 pages, I get a break) (Graham *et al.*, 1992). This process is analogous to the natural developmental process where a child learns that meeting expectations often results in positive reinforcement while the opposite typically results in no response or a negative response (Zimmerman & Schunk, 1989). As a result, children learn to self-reinforce (or self-punish) their own behavior. Implementing self-reinforcement involves: (1) determining standards for rewards, (2) selecting a reinforcer, (3) evaluation of performance, and (4) self-awarding reinforcement when criterion is reached. Self-reinforcement is often combined with other self-regulation techniques; it is frequently the final step in a sequence of self-regulation processes and can set the stage for further self-regulation. The notion that individuals can actually engage in self-reinforcement may be seen by some as counter to a strict operant perspective of self-regulation (see Mace *et al.*, 2001, for a detailed critique); regardless, the technique itself is quite effective.

F. Final Thoughts

We have briefly defined and discussed major self-regulation techniques that research indicates are effective for children with LD and ADHD. There are other promising self-regulation techniques. Zimmerman (1998) suggested that use of imagery—the ability to visualize successful task performance—may serve to structure effort and also serve as a useful guide for new learning. Visualization is also used in techniques such as Stop–Think where students imagine a large "Stop" sign to help inhibit impulsive reactions. Another promising technique is correspondence training (e.g., Paniagua & Black, 1990). Correspondence training involves evoking a verbal commitment to perform a particular behavior at a specified level during a defined period (e.g., finish the math worksheet in 10 minutes). After the defined period, children are reminded of the verbal commitment, informed whether their actions corresponded to their commitment, and provided a reinforcer if the behavior corresponded to the verbal commitment. A number of studies have demonstrated effectiveness of correspondence training for children with ADHD. Other techniques, such as strategic planning and self-consequences (Zimmerman, 1998), may also be useful for children with self-regulation difficulties.

Finally, we stress that self-regulation does not take place in a vacuum. The environment is a significant factor in self-regulation from both the social–cognitive and operant perspectives (Mace *et al.*, 2001; Schunk, 2001). At the most basic level, environmental manipulations can enhance or enable self-regulation (e.g., taking a limited amount of cash prevents overspending) (Mace *et al.*, 2001). Students also may self-regulate their environment to enhance performance (e.g., creating a study space that is quiet and free of distractions to enhance studying or improve homework completion). Additionally, the environment can provide feedback on effort, discriminative stimuli to cue self-regulation, and reinforcement for successful self-regulators. Providing children with a structured environment with predictable stable routines is a necessary prerequisite for self-regulation and can greatly increase the likelihood of effective self-regulation. Children with LD or ADHD will likely have some degree of problem with self-regulation even in the best possible environment. In a disordered, chaotic environment, successful self-regulation is doubtful, at best. There are numerous environmental changes that can enhance self-regulation, such as providing students with folders to serve as organizers for assignments, taping prompts to lockers (Did you remember to bring...), or using Job Cards (which list the steps for a task and serve to cue performance) (Pfiffner & Barkley, 1998; Reid, 1999).

IV. SELF-REGULATION AND MAJOR DEPENDENT VARIABLES

Having defined and described each of the most common self-regulation procedures, we turn to the effects of self-regulation interventions on major dependent variables. These include on-task behavior, academic productivity, and academic accuracy. Next, we discuss effects on disruptive behaviors. Finally, we discuss the use of self-regulation techniques in the social context.

A. On-Task Behavior

On-task behavior is the most studied outcome in self-regulation interventions by a wide margin. For example, in a review of self-monitoring research involving children with LD, Reid (1996) noted that of 23 experiments, 22 included on-task behavior as a dependent measure. This is understandable, as increasing on-task behavior is a natural focus for self-regulation interventions among students with LD. Though not sufficient in isolation, attending to a task and maintaining effort are important prerequisites to academic success. Moreover, increasing on-task behavior can have positive effects on classroom climate and the teacher–child relationship (Hallahan & Lloyd, 1987).

Self-monitoring has a long record of effectiveness for increasing on-task behavior for children with LD (Reid, 1996). Over 20 studies with children with LD have reported increased on-task behaviors. The effects of self-monitoring have been demonstrated across age levels and educational settings. The majority of studies used participants in the 9 to 11 age group; however, self-monitoring has been effective for children as young as 7 (e.g., Hallahan *et al.*, 1979, 1982) and as old as 18 (e.g., Blick & Test, 1987; Prater *et al.*, 1991). Self-monitoring is effective across individual, small group, and large group settings (e.g. Hallahan *et al.*, 1979, 1981; Prater *et al.*, 1992). An important factor in self-monitoring intervention is the durable nature of the effects. Several studies have demonstrated that benefits of self-monitoring have been maintained over several months of classroom use (e.g., Harris, 1986b; Harris *et al.*, 1994; Lloyd *et al.*, 1989).

With the notable exception of self-instruction (Abikoff, 1991), self-regulation interventions have also been successful in increasing on-task behavior for children with ADHD (DuPaul & Stoner, 2002). Mathes and Bender (1997) used self-monitoring of attention successfully with three elementary-age, resource students. Harris *et al.* (in press) reported meaning-ful increases in both on-task behavior and spelling study performance using self-monitoring procedures with students with ADHD. Shimabukuro also reported increased on-task behavior for three 12- to 13-year-old students with LD and ADHD (Shimabukuro *et al.*, 1999). Similar results were reported by DeHaas-Warner (1990) for a preschool student during readiness tasks and by Christie *et al.* (1984) for three elementary-school students in the general education classroom. It is noteworthy that self-monitoring resulted in increases in on-task behavior over and above psychostimulant medication in two studies (Mathes & Bender, 1997; DeHaas-Warner, 1990). Other researchers have combined self-monitoring and self-reinforcement to increase on-task behavior for children with ADHD (e.g., Barkley *et al.*, 1980; Edwards *et al.*, 1995).

Self-evaluation techniques have also been used successfully to improve on-task behavior for children with ADHD. For example, Ervin *et al.* (1998) reported improvements for a 14-year-old student in a residential placement; similar results were found by Shapiro *et al.* (1998) for two 12-year-old children, one in general education and one in a self-contained setting. Similarly, self-reinforcement has also demonstrated effectiveness for children with ADHD (Ajibola & Clement, 1995; Bowers *et al.*, 1985).

B. Academic Productivity

The effects of self-monitoring on academic productivity—the amount or rate of academic responding—for children with LD have been documented in a number of studies (Reid, 1996). However, effects are less clear than for on-task behavior. Some early studies found clear effects (e.g., Roberts and Nelson, 1981), while others reported equivocal effects (e.g., Hallahan *et al.*, 1979, 1982) or no effects (Lloyd *et al.*, 1982). Methodological problems and issues in the design of the self-monitoring interventions may have contributed to the lack of effects in these studies. In some studies, new material was introduced without regard to mastery; this is a potential problem because self-monitoring will not affect skills not already in a child's repertoire. Simply put, self-monitoring something a student does not know how to do will not help the student do it better. In other studies, students were required to perform previously mastered tasks for prolonged periods, which may have resulted in resistance or boredom. More recent studies, with stronger treatment validity, have reported that self-monitoring can meaningfully improve academic productivity (e.g., DiGangi *et al.*, 1991; Harris, 1986b; Harris *et al.*, 1994, in press; Lloyd *et al.*, 1989; Maag *et al.*, 1993; Reid & Harris 1993).

Effects of self-regulation interventions on academic productivity have not been well studied for children with ADHD. Self-monitoring increased academic productivity for three 12- to 13-year-old students with ADHD in one study for reading, math, and written expression tasks (Shimabukuro *et al.*, 1999). However, McDougall and Brady (1998) did not find that self-monitoring improved productivity for a fourth grade student on a math task. Ajibola and Clement (1995) used self-reinforcement to increase the academic productivity for six children with ADHD on a reading comprehension task.

We were unable to locate any research on self-evaluation with children with ADHD which targeted academic productivity. Because of the well-documented difficulties of children with ADHD in academic productivity and assignment completion (e.g., DuPaul & Stoner, 1994), this is an area that should receive increased research attention.

1. Self-Monitoring of Attention vs Self-Monitoring of Performance for On-Task and Academic Performance

Harris *et al.* (in press) reported the first study on the relative effects of both self-monitoring of performance and self-monitoring of attention among students with ADHD on on-task behavior and spelling study performance. Both self-monitoring of attention and self-monitoring of performance had positive effects on students' on-task and spelling study behaviors. While improvements in on-task behavior were comparable across the two self-monitoring interventions, however, self-monitoring of attention produced substantially higher gains in spelling study behavior among four of the six elementary students in their study. While this is the first study to investigate differential effects of these two self-monitoring interventions among students with ADHD, previous studies of differential effects among students with LD found the opposite result—self-monitoring of performance tended to result in higher rates of spelling study than did self-monitoring of attention (Harris, 1986b; Harris *et al.*, 1994; Reid & Harris, 1993). Clearly, further research on the comparative effects of these two self-monitoring procedures among students with LD and ADHD is needed.

C. Academic Accuracy

There is strong evidence that suggests self-monitoring can increase the rate of academic responding. However, the effects of self-monitoring on academic *accuracy* are not clear-cut. For children with LD, only two studies have reported data on accuracy (Dunlap & Dunlap, 1989; Maag *et al.*, 1993). Both studies involved math computation tasks and both found clear effects on accuracy. Similarly, three studies have reported positive effects on accuracy for children with ADHD (Edwards *et al.*, 1995; Shimabukuro *et al.*, 1999; Varni & Henker, 1979). There is some question, however, as to whether or not self-monitoring alone should result in increased accuracy (Reid, 1996). As previously noted, self-monitoring does not create new behaviors; it only affects behaviors already in a child's repertoire. While self-monitoring may increase awareness of accuracy, theoretically it does not provide a means of improving accuracy in and of itself. Self-monitoring may, however, result in increased practices which could improve accuracy. It may also be combined with a strategy as was the case in the Dunlap and Dunlap (1989) study. Here, students self-monitored the use of correct procedures in solving math problems (e.g., start in ones column, remember to carry). The usefulness of self-regulation techniques for situations that involve new learning is an under researched area. Hallahan and Sapona (1983) speculated that self-monitoring would not be effective for new learning. Interestingly, Reid and Harris (1993) found that, in some situations, the use of self-regulation can actually decrease new learning when there is a mismatch between the task and the self-regulation technique.

D. Disruptive Behavior

Children with LD and ADHD often exhibit problem behavior in the classroom. This may take the form of inappropriate verbalizations, impulsive or inappropriate behaviors, or excessive motor activity. These types of behaviors have a deleterious effect on the classroom learning environment—there is less time spent in instruction and learning activities—and may also have a detrimental effect on teacher–student relationships. Several studies have demonstrated that self-regulation approaches may be useful for disruptive behaviors of children with ADHD. Three studies conducted in hospital and research settings (Barkley *et al.*, 1980; Horn *et al.*, 1983; Kern *et al.*, 2001) used a combination of self-monitoring and external reinforcers to reduce disruptive behaviors. This is noteworthy, as these children had severe behavioral or emotional difficulties.

Studies conducted in the classroom environment have also shown that self-monitoring can reduce disruptive behavior. Christie *et al.* (1984) used self-monitoring in a general education classroom. Similarly, Stewart and McLaughlin (1992) reported reduced off-task behaviors in a self-contained special education setting. In contrast to the studies in hospital settings, neither of these studies used external reinforcers. Self-evaluation has also been effective at reducing problem behaviors in the general education classroom and self-contained settings (Davies & Witte, 2000; Hoff & DuPaul, 1998; Shapiro *et al.*, 1998).

The effectiveness of self-regulation techniques in the general education setting is particularly salient. Most children with LD and/or ADHD will spend the majority of their school day in the general education classroom (Reid *et al.*, 1994). High rates of disruptive behaviors are a barrier to effective inclusion. Methods which reduce these behaviors can improve the chances that these children will be effectively included in the general education setting, and thus are particularly important. Self-regulation interventions are extremely promising because typically they are acceptable to classroom teachers and do not require much additional time from teachers after implementation. However, more research is needed to determine how self-regulation can best be used to integrate children with LD and ADHD into the general education setting (Reid, 1996). Whether there are differences in the magnitude of effects across different interventions (e.g., self-monitoring or self-evaluation) and what behaviors are best targeted (i.e., should interventions focus on reducing inappropriate behavior or on increasing desired behavior?) are important questions for future researchers.

E. Self-Regulation in the Social Context

The difficulties of children with LD for consistency and ADHD are not limited to academics. The social milieu also poses problems for many of these children. In fact, some have proposed that social deficits be included in the definition of LD (Lerner, 2000). Bryan (1997) estimated that over a third of children with LD also have impaired social skills. The problem is even more serious with children with ADHD as many of the symptomatic behaviors reflect difficulty in social functioning. From 40% to 60% of children with ADHD will also develop severe problems that affect social relations, such as Oppositional Defiant Disorder (Barkley, 1998). These socially based problems are not trivial. In fact, Lerner (2000) suggested that deficits in social functioning may be even more disabling than academic difficulties because they are more pervasive.

There is evidence to suggest that, for many children with LD and ADHD, the cause of the social skill problem is not due to a *lack* of social skills, but rather to an inability to activate skills already in the repertoire or to difficulty overcoming impulsive (but inappropriate) behaviors (Barkley, 1998; Bryan & Sonnenfield, 1981). This distinction is important as self-regulation techniques require prerequisite skills to be present if they are to be employed effectively. Unfortunately, the research base on self-regulation for children with LD and ADHD in the social context is sparse (Shapiro *et al.*, 2002). As a result, it's not yet possible to assess how effective self-regulation approaches may be in this area. There have, however, been some successful applications with children with ADHD. In an experimental program, Hinshaw *et al.* (1984) used a combination of self-evaluation and self-evaluation plus medication in a playground setting and found that both were effective for reducing negative social behaviors. In another interesting study, Gumpel and David (2000) taught a 10-year-old to self-monitor his playground behavior. The child was taught to set an inexpensive kitchen timer and to use a small notebook to self-record whether he was engaged in appropriate behaviors (e.g., I succeeded in playing without hitting.) at 4-minute intervals. Self-monitoring effectively decreased the rate of aggressive playground behavior and increased the rate of positive social interactions for an elementary school child. Gains were maintained 6 weeks following cessation of treatment.

V. FACTORS INFLUENCING AND INFLUENCED BY SELF-REGULATION

Researchers from multiple theoretical perspectives and domains have proposed a host of factors that can influence the use and effectiveness of self-regulation among learners and that can, in turn, be influenced by the process of self-regulation. As Zeidner *et al.* (2000) noted, there is as of yet little agreement regarding the "phases or facets in the structure and morphology of self-regulation" (p. 753). Key factors could include environmental determinants and influences (family, social, religious, etc.), affective and motivational factors (self-efficacy, attributions, goal orientation, ability beliefs, achievement values, mood, etc.), and individual differences (gender, age, cognitive ability, personality, etc.).

Multiple models of the temporal placement of these factors and their reciprocal relationships and interactions with each other and self-regulation processes have been suggested, with little research yet available to fully explain the role of any given factor or to support any particular model (Boekaerts *et al.*, 2000; Schunk & Zimmerman, 1994, 1998). In this chapter, we further address one of the constructs researchers have found evidence for in relationship to self-regulation and that has been investigated by researchers in the areas of LD or ADHD: self-efficacy.

A. Self-Efficacy

While the role of self-efficacy in self-regulation and the effects of self-regulation on self-efficacy are not yet clearly established, some researchers view self-efficacy as an integral part of the self-regulation process (Zeidner et al., 2000). The term "self-efficacy" refers to students' pre-task judgments—their expectations or beliefs regarding whether or not they can perform a given task or activity. Some researchers believe that change in self-efficacy is a critical factor in changes in behavior (cf. Zimmerman, 2000). Self-efficacy is believed to have a strong influence on performance as it affects choice of activities, the amount of effort expended, and persistence in the face of difficulty. In other words, individuals who believe they are capable of successful performance are likely to choose challenging activities, work hard, and persist when difficulties are encountered (Harris & Graham, 1996). Thus, strong self-efficacy may lead to greater and more effective self-regulation, while successful self-regulation and completion of a task may, in turn, strengthen self-efficacy.

Interestingly, students with LD may not only experience low self-efficacy regarding some tasks that are within their capabilities; some research indicates that very young children and students with LD frequently exhibit unrealistically high pre-task expectancies—they expect to be able to successfully complete activities they are not yet capable of (Graham & Harris, 1989; Sawyer et al., 1992). Unrealistically high expectations among students with LD may be due to misperceptions of task demands or difficulties in comprehending the task, inaccurate self-knowledge, selective attention to what has been mastered as opposed to what has not, inability to match demands to ability level, or employing a self-protective coping strategy (Sawyer et al., 1992). When unrealistically high pre-task expectancies are followed by failure or extreme difficulties, negative, maladaptive attitudes and beliefs, including lowered self-efficacy, may be the result.

In terms of self-regulation processes, not only must students believe they can perform an appropriate task, but in order to have positive pre-task expectancies for their ability to self-regulate the task, they must also believe that they are using self-regulation processes and skills to assist in reaching their goals (Zeidner et al., 2000). Pintrich (2000) emphasized that not only can learners regulate their cognition and behavior, they can also regulate their motivation and affect. Self-regulation of motivational beliefs can include regulation of goal-orientation; beliefs about the importance, utility, and relevance of the task; personal interest in the task; and self-efficacy (Pintrich, 2000; Boekaerts et al., 2000). Here again, the complex relationships among self-regulation and factors such as self-efficacy are evident, and remain critical targets for future research. While little research regarding self-efficacy and self-regulation has been done among students with ADHD, some research involving the combination of strategies instruction and development of self-regulation of strategic performance and the effects of such intervention on performance and self-efficacy among students with LD has been conducted. We turn next to consideration of the integration of strategies instruction with self-regulation development and the resulting effects among students with LD.

VI. SELF-REGULATION OF STRATEGIC PERFORMANCE

The target behaviors for self-regulation discussed so far have largely been relatively discrete behaviors such as academic productivity or accuracy, and on-task behavior. A number of researchers have noted that one or more self-regulation procedures could also be critical in successful use of more complex learning strategies (cf. Boekaerts *et al.*, 2000; Harris & Graham, 1996; Schunk & Zimmerman, 1994, 1998). In fact, approaches to strategies instruction across a number of fields have been strongly influenced by the seminal work of both Donald Meichenbaum and Ann Brown and her colleagues (Harris, 1982; Harris & Graham, 1992, 1999; Wong *et al.*, 2003). Meichenbaum (1977) noted that a number of self-regulation procedures could be critical in strategy training, and developed guidelines for self-instructional training. Brown and her colleagues (cf. Brown *et al.*, 1981) emphasized the importance of self-control components in strategy learning, which they described as planning and executing the strategy, monitoring strategy use, and evaluating strategy effectiveness and outcomes. Although a substantial body of research exists among students with LD, unfortunately, we were unable to locate any research integrating development of powerful academic and self-regulation strategies in instruction for students with ADHD, making this an important area for future research (Harris & Schmidt, 1997, 1998).

1. SRSD

A review of cognitive strategies instruction research with students with LD is available by Wong *et al.* (2003); space precludes a broad review of the integration of self-regulation with strategies instruction here. Rather, one model, Self-Regulated Strategy Development (SRSD) is described. SRSD has been in development by Harris, Graham, and their colleagues since the early 1980s (Harris, 1982; Harris & Graham, 1992, 1999). In addition to the importance of the work of Meichenbaum and Brown and her colleagues in the development of SRSD, Harris and Graham (1992, 1999) have also noted the foundational influence of the work of Soviet researchers and theorists (including Vygotsky, Luria, and Sokolov) on the social origins of self-control and the development of the mind, as well as the work of Deshler, Schumaker, and their colleagues on the validation of acquisition steps for strategies among adolescents with LD.

While current models of strategies instruction have profited from the many lines of strategies instruction research and have converged in many areas (Pressley & Harris, 2001), in the early stages of its development the SRSD model differed from other strategies instruction models in two important ways (Harris & Graham, 1999; Wong et al., 2003). First, other models of strategies instruction, developed primarily for normally achieving students, did not seek to explicitly teach and support the development of self-regulation abilities—rather, development of self-regulation was implicit in these models. Based in part on the research on expertise in writing and research on children's self-regulation (Harris & Graham, 1992), explicit instruction in and supported development of critical aspects of self-regulation were integrated as critical components throughout the stages of instruction in the SRSD model. These self-regulation components included goal-setting, self-assessment, self-instruction, self-reinforcement, imagery, and managing the writing environment (most of the research with SRSD has been done in the area of composition, although work in reading and math has also been done; see Graham & Harris, 2003).

Second, based again on research as well as their own early experiences with strategies instruction among students with LD, Harris and Graham stressed that while a heterogeneous group, children with LD often face additional challenges related to reciprocal relations among academic failure, social difficulties, self-doubts, learned helplessness, low self-efficacy, maladaptive attributions, unrealistic pre-task expectancies, and low motivation and engagement in academic tasks (Harris, 1982; Harris & Graham, 1992). Therefore, children's attitudes and beliefs about themselves as writers/learners and the strategies instruction they participated in became critical targets for both intervention and assessment during and after strategies instruction. Throughout SRSD instruction, students are explicitly supported in the development of attributions for effort as well as the use of powerful writing strategies, knowledge of writing genres and the writing process, self-efficacy, and high levels of engagement. Further, progression through SRSD instruction is criterion-based rather than time-based; students are given the time they need to attain important component skills and abilities and achieve desired outcomes.

In addition, Harris and Graham (1992) noted that students with LD often experience one or more cognitive difficulties in areas such as attention, impulsivity, memory, or information processing, as well as significant academic difficulties. Thus, they articulated an underlying premise of SRSD early on—children who face significant and often debilitating difficulties in academic areas would benefit from an integrated approach to intervention that directly addresses their affective, behavioral, and cognitive characteristics, strengths, and needs (Harris, 1982; Harris & Graham, 1992). Further, students who face serious struggles with learning will often need to be meaningfully engaged in more extensive, structured, and explicit instruction to develop skills, strategies (including self-regulation strategies), and understandings formed more easily by many of their peers. Thus, development of SRSD has reflected purposeful and explicit integration of knowledge gained from differing theoretical perspectives and lines of research; the further development of SRSD remains open to advancements across multiple lines of research (Harris & Graham, 1992, 1999).

Because SRSD instruction is described in some detail in the chapter in this book entitled "Writing Instruction," we do not offer a description of this complex instructional process here. Greater detail on SRSD in the classroom can be found in Harris and Graham (1996), and an example of the complete stages of instruction can be seen in an inclusive fourth grade classroom in the video, "Using Learning Strategies," produced by the Association for Supervision and Curriculum Development (2002). Rather, we will briefly summarize what research on SRSD has told us about the effectiveness of this approach for students with LD, and particularly on what we have learned about the role of self-regulation development within this model.

2. Outcomes of SRSD

More than 30 studies using the SRSD model of instruction in the area of writing involving LD and normally achieving students in the elementary through secondary grades have been reported since 1985, with several additional studies reported in reading and math (Harris & Graham, 2003). Writing strategies across a number of genres have been developed and researched, typically with the assistance of teachers and their students, including personal narratives, story writing, persuasive essays, report writing, expository essays, and state writing tests (Graham, & Harris, 2003; Harris & Graham, 1996). Research has demonstrated significant and meaningful improvements following SRSD in students' development of planning and revising strategies, including brainstorming, self-monitoring, reading for information and semantic webbing, generating and organizing content, advanced planning and dictation, revising with peers, and revising for both substance and mechanics (Graham & Harris, 2003).

In addition, SRSD has resulted in improvements in four main aspects of students' performance: quality of writing, knowledge of writing, approach to writing, and self-efficacy regarding writing (Graham & Harris, 2003; Harris

& Graham, 1999). The quality, length, and structure of students' compositions have improved across a variety of strategies and genres. In some studies, students with LD have improved to where their performance is similar to that of their normally achieving peers in the same classrooms. Maintenance of these improvements has been found for the majority of students with LD, with some students needing booster sessions for long-term maintenance. Generalization, while not as robust as maintenance, has been found across settings, persons, and writing media. Meaningful improvements have been found for normally achieving students as well as students with LD, making this approach a powerful fit for inclusive classrooms. It is important to note, in addition, that although normally achieving students typically do not need as extensive or scaffolded instruction, research indicates that students with LD do not show meaningful gains unless the complete, scaffolded, and collaborative SRSD instructional stages are implemented (cf. Danoff *et al.*, 1993; Harris & Graham, 1999).

A. Findings Regarding the Self-Regulation Components of SRSD

As noted, a basic premise underlying the SRSD model is that inclusion and explicit development of self-regulation abilities contributes to students' mastery of the strategies they are learning and to the maintenance and generalization of these strategies. One important research objective, then, is to determine the relative contribution of the self-regulation components of SRSD (Harris & Graham, 1999). While further research is needed, Harris, Graham, and their colleagues have reported two studies of the contribution of self-regulation development to the acquisition, maintenance, and generalization of writing strategies (Graham & Harris, 1989; Sawyer *et al.*, 1992).

In the first study, Graham and Harris (1989) provided fifth and sixth graders with LD strategies instruction in planning and writing stories using either the full SRSD instructional approach (including self-regulation) or SRSD minus explicit goal setting and self-assessment, including graphing of progress. However, it is important to note that both conditions included cognitive modeling and development of self-instructions, a powerful self-regulation component. Students in both conditions consistently used the preplanning and story-writing strategy; schematic story structure evidenced significant and meaningful change that was maintained and generalized to a new writing situation for both groups. Improvement in overall quality of stories was also found immediately after instruction among both groups. Importantly, no differences were found between the two groups in terms of strategy use, writing performance, or self-efficacy. Thus, in this study, the inclusion of explicit instruction in goal-setting and self-assessment did not enhance the strategic behavior, beliefs, or writing performance of these students with LD.

However, this first study (Graham & Harris, 1989) did not compare the presence of explicit self-regulation instruction to the absence of such instruction. Not only were self-instructions explicitly developed in both conditions, it is likely that many of the remaining instructional components in SRSD (such as cognitive and collaborative modeling involving the use of self-regulation) generated and induced self-regulatory behavior (Harris & Graham, 1999; Sawyer *et al.*, 1992).

Thus, in a second study, Sawyer *et al.* (1992) investigated the effects of three versions of SRSD on planning and story-writing among fifth and sixth grade students. The first version was the complete SRSD model; the second version removed explicit instruction in goal-setting and self-assessment (including graphing of progress); the third version further removed additional explicit and implicit components that promote self-regulation, including self-instructions and cognitive and collaborative modeling of strategy use involving self-regulation. In all conditions, however, each step of the writing strategy was presented and explained, the goals and benefits of the strategies instruction were discussed, the steps of the strategy were memorized, and mastery was criterion-based, with students continuing instruction until they could use the strategy independently.

The students with LD made meaningful gains in story-writing in all three conditions (Sawyer *et al.*, 1992). However, the contribution of self-regulation components was evident in this study at two points. First, students who received the first and second versions, which included self-instructions and modeling, had significantly higher schematic structure scores than did either students in the third version (where further self-regulation components were removed) or students in a writing practice control condition. Further, students in the first, or full SRSD version, performed significantly better than students in all other conditions on the generalization probe administered in a new setting by the regular classroom teacher. Thus, findings from this study, coupled with the observations that the inclusion of explicit self-regulation development is not costly in terms of either time or materials and that students have consistently reported that the self-regulation components are helpful and desirable, support the use of the full SRSD model with explicit development of self-regulation (Harris & Graham, 1999; Sawyer *et al.*, 1992). Further research, however, is clearly needed.

VII. CONCLUSION

In this chapter, we have taken a look at the importance of self-regulation, which has been described as perhaps one of our most important qualities as humans (Zimmerman, 2000). The term self-regulation, and the related terms self-regulated learning, metacognition, and executive function, were defined and discussed, as were major theoretical bases for self-regulation research. Common self-regulation strategies or processes were explained, and research on their effects on behavioral, academic, and social outcomes were reviewed. Multiple factors that can influence the use and effectiveness of self-regulation among learners were noted, with an emphasis on self-efficacy. Finally, the role of self-regulation processes in the learning and successful use of more complex academic strategies was explored by reviewing the SRSD model of instruction for students with LD and other students who struggle in the classroom.

While research on self-regulation among students with LD, other students with special needs, and their normally achieving peers has virtually exploded in the past 15 years, there remain far more questions than answers in this intriguing area. We have noted directions for further research throughout this chapter, and detailed discussions of the work that has been done and directions and needs in future research have been established in seminal works by Boekaerts *et al.*, 2000; Schunk and Zimmerman, 1994, 1998; and Zimmerman and Schunk, 1989. We close by noting, however, that while a great deal more research is needed, we know enough about the importance of and how to assist in the development of self-regulation among students with LD and ADHD to use this knowledge base in making a difference in the lives of these students.

References

Abikoff, H. (1991). Cognitive training in ADHD children: Less to it than meets the eye. *Journal of Learning Disabilities*, **24**(4), 205–209.

Ajibola, O., & Clement, P. W. (1995). Differential effects of methylphenidate and self-reinforcement on attention-deficit hyperactivity disorder. *Behavior Modification*, **19**, 211–233.

Association for Supervision and Curriculum Development (Producer). (2002). Using learning strategies (Video, "Teaching Students with Learning Disabilities" Series). Alexandria, VA: Association for Supervision and Curriculum Development.

Bandura, A. (1986). *Social foundations of thought and action*. Englewood Cliffs, NJ: Prentice Hall.

Bandura, A. (1988). Self-regulation of motivation and action through goal systems. In V. Hamilton, G. H. Browder, & N. H. Frijda (Eds.), *Cognitive perspectives on emotion and motivation* (pp. 37–61). Dordrecht, The Netherlands: Kluwer Academic.

Barkley, R. A. (1997). *ADHD and the nature of self-control*. New York: Guilford Press.

Barkley, R. A. (1998). *Attention-deficit hyperactivity disorder: A handbook for diagnosis and treatment*. (2nd ed.). New York: Guilford Press.

Barkley, R. A., Copeland, A. P., & Sivage, C. (1980). A self-control classroom for hyperactive children. *Journal of Autism and Developmental Disorders*, 10, 75–89.

Blick, D. W., & Test, D. W. (1987). Effects of self-recording on high-school students' on-task behavior. *Learning Disability Quarterly*, 10, 203–213.

Boekaerts, M., Pintrich, P. R., & Zeidner, M. (Eds.). (2000). *Handbook of self-regulation.* New York: Academic Press.

Bowers, D. S., Clement, P. W., Fantuzzo, J. W., & Sorensen, D. A. (1985). Effects of teacher-administered and self-administered reinforcers on learning disabled children. *Behavior Therapy*, 16, 357–369.

Broden, M., Hall, R. V., & Mitts, B. (1971). The effects of self-recording on the classroom behavior of two eighth-grade students. *Journal of Applied Behavior Analysis*, 4, 191–199.

Brown, A. L., Campione, J. C., & Day, J. D. (1981). Learning to learn: On training students to learn from text. *Educational Researcher*, 10, 14–21.

Bryan, J. H., & Sonnenfield, J. (1981). Children's social ratings of ingratiation tactics. *Journal of Learning Disabilities*, 5, 605–609.

Bryan, T. (1997). Assessing the personal and social status of students with learning disabilities. *Learning Disabilities Research and Practice*, 12, 63–76.

Christie, D. J., Hiss, M., & Lozanoff, B. (1984). Modification of inattentive classroom behavior: Hyperactive children's use of self-recording with teacher guidance. *Behavior Modification*, 8, 391–406.

Cutting, L. E., & Denckla, M. B. (2003). Attention: Relationships between attention-deficit hyperactivity disorder and learning disabilities. In H. L. Swanson, K. R. Harris, & S. Graham, *Handbook of learning disabilities* (pp. 125–139). New York: Guilford Press.

Danoff, B., Harris, K. R., & Graham, S. (1993). Incorporating strategy instruction within the writing process in the regular classroom: Effects on the writing of students with and without learning disabilities. *Journal of Reading Behavior*, 25, 295–322.

Davies, S., & Witte, R. (2000). Self-management and peer-monitoring within a group contingency to decrease uncontrolled verbalizations of children with attention-deficit/hyperactivity disorder. *Psychology in the Schools*, 37, 135–147.

De Haas-Warner, S. (1990). The utility of self-monitoring for preschool on-task behavior. *Topics in Early Childhood Special Education*, 12, 478–495.

Diaz, R. M., & Berk, L. E. (1992). *Private speech: From social interaction to self-regulation.* Hillsdale, NJ: Lawrence Erlbaum.

DiGangi, S. A., Maag, J. W., & Rutherford, R. B. (1991). Self-graphing of on-task behavior: Enhancing the reactivity of self-monitoring on-task behavior and academic performance. *Learning Disability Quarterly*, 14, 221–230.

Dunlap, L. K., & Dunlap, G. (1989). A self-monitoring package for teaching subtraction with regrouping to students with learning disabilities. *Journal of Applied Behavior Analysis*, 22, 309–314.

DuPaul, G. J., & Stoner, G. (1994). *ADHD in the schools: Assessment and intervention strategies.* New York: Guilford Press.

DuPaul, G. J., & Stoner, G. (2002). Interventions for attention problems. In M. R. Shinn, H. M. Walker, & G. Stoner (Eds.), *Interventions for academic and behavioral problems II: Preventive and remedial approaches* (pp. 913–938). Bethesda, MD: NASP Publications.

Edwards, L., Salant, V., Howard, V. F., Brougher, J., & McLaughlin, T. F. (1995). Effectiveness of self-management on attentional behavior and reading comprehension for children with attention deficit disorder. *Child and Family Behavior Therapy, 17,* 1–17.

Ervin, R. A., DuPaul, G. J., Kern, L., & Friman, P. C. (1998). Classroom-based functional and adjunctive assessments: Proactive approaches to intervention selection for adolescents with attention deficit hyperactivity disorder. *Journal of Applied Behavior Analysis, 1,* 65–78.

Graham, S., & Harris, K. R. (1989). A components analysis of cognitive strategy instruction: Effects on learning disabled students' compositions and self-efficacy. *Journal of Educational Psychology, 81,* 353–361.

Graham, S., & Harris, K. R. (1996). Self-regulation and strategy instruction for students who find writing and learning challenging. In C. M. Levy & S. Randall (Eds), *The science of writing: Theories, methods, individual differences, and applications* (pp. 347–360). Mahwah, NJ: Erlbaum.

Graham, S., & Harris, K. R. (2003). Students with LD and the process of writing: A meta-analysis of SRSD studies. In L. Swanson, K. R. Harris, & S. Graham (Eds.), *Handbook of research on learning disabilities* (pp. 323–344). New York: Guilford Press.

Graham, S., Harris, K. R., & Reid, R. (1992). Developing self-regulated learners. *Focus on Exceptional Children, 24,* 1–16.

Gumpel, T. P., & David, S. (2000). Exploring the efficacy of self-regulatory training as a possible alternative to social skills training. *Behavior Disorders, 25,* 131–141.

Hallahan, D. P., & Lloyd, G. W. (1987). A reply to Snider. *Learning Disability Quarterly, 10,* 153–156.

Hallahan, D. P., Lloyd, J. W., Kneedler, R. D., & Marshall, K. J. (1982). A comparison of the effects of self-versus teacher-assessment of on-task behavior. *Behavior Therapy, 13,* 715–723.

Hallahan, D. P., Lloyd, J. W., Kosiewicz, M. M., Kauffman, J. M., & Graves, A. W. (1979). Self-monitoring of attention as a treatment for a learning disabled boy's off-task behavior. *Learning Disability Quarterly, 2,* 24–32.

Hallahan, D. P., Marshall, K. J., & Lloyd, J. W. (1981). Self-recording during group instruction: Effects on attention to task. *Learning Disability Quarterly, 4,* 407–413.

Hallahan, D. P., & Sapona, R. (1983). Self-monitoring of attention with learning disabled children: Past research and current issues. *Journal of Learning Disabilities, 15,* 616–620.

Harris, K. R. (1982). Cognitive–behavior modification: Application with exceptional students. *Focus on Exceptional Children, 15*(2), 1–16.

Harris, K. R. (1985). Conceptual, methodological, and clinical issues in cognitive–behavioral assessment. *Journal of Abnormal Child Psychology, 13,* 373–390.

Harris, K. R. (1986a). The effects of cognitive–behavior modification on private speech and task performance during problem solving among learning disabled and normally achieving children. *Journal of Abnormal Child Psychology, 14,* 63–76.

Harris, K. R. (1986b). Self-monitoring of attentional behavior versus self-monitoring of productivity: Effects on on-task behavior and academic response rate among learning disabled children. *Journal of Applied Behavior Analysis*, **19**, 417–423.

Harris, K. R. (1990). Developing self-regulated learners: The role of private speech and self-instructions. *Educational Psychologist*, **25**, 35–49.

Harris, K. R., Friedlander, B. D., Saddler, B., Frizelle, R., & Graham, S. (in press). Self-monitoring of attention versus self-monitoring of academic performance: Differential effects among students with ADHD in the regular classroom. *Journal of Special Education*.

Harris, K. R., & Graham, S. (1992). Self-regulated strategy development: A part of the writing process. In M. Pressley, K. R., Harris, & J. T. Guthrie (Eds.), *Promoting academic competence and literacy in school* (pp. 277–309). New York: Academic Press.

Harris, K. R., & Graham, S. (1996). *Making the writing process work: Strategies for composition and self-regulation* (2nd ed.). Cambridge, MA: Brookline Books.

Harris, K. R., & Graham, S. (1999). Programmatic intervention research: Illustrations from the evolution of self-regulated strategy development. *Learning Disability Quarterly*, **22**, 251–262.

Harris, K. R., Graham, S., Reid, R., McElroy, K., & Hamby, R. (1994). Self-monitoring of attention versus self-monitoring of performance: Replication and cross-task comparison. *Learning Disability Quarterly*, **17**, 121–139.

Harris, K. R., & Schmidt, T. (1997). Learning self-regulation in the classroom. *The ADHD Report*, **5**(2), 1–6.

Harris, K. R., & Schmidt, T. (1998). Learning self-regulation does not equal self-instructional training. *The ADHD Report*, **6**(3), 7–11.

Hinshaw, S. P., Henker, B., & Whalen, C. K. (1984). Cognitive–behavioral and pharmacologic interventions for hyperactive boys: Comparative and combined effects. *Journal of Consulting and Clinical Psychology*, **52**, 739–749.

Hoff, K. E., & DuPaul, G. J. (1998). Reducing disruptive behavior in general education classrooms: The use of self-management strategies. *School Psychology Review*, **27**, 290–303.

Horn, W. F., Chatoor, I., & Conners, C. K. (1983). Additive effects of Dexedrine and self-control training. *Behavior Modification*, **7**, 383–402.

Johnson, L., & Graham, S. (1990). Goal setting and its application with exceptional learners. *Preventing School Failure*, **34**, 4–8.

Kanfer, F. H. (1977). The many faces of self-control, or behavior modification changes its focus. In R. B. Stuart (Ed.), *Behavioral self-management* (pp. 1–48). New York: Brunner/Mazel.

Kanfer, F. H., & Karoly, P. (1972). Self-control: A behavioristic excursion into the lion's den. *Behavior Therapy*, **3**, 398–416.

Kern, L., Ringdahl, J. E., Hilt, A., & Sterling-Turner, H. E. (2001). Linking self-management procedures to functional analysis results. *Behavior Disorders*, **26**, 214–226.

Lerner, J. (2000). *Learning disabilities: Theories, diagnosis, and teaching strategies* (8th ed). New York: Houghton Mifflin.

Lloyd, J. W., Bateman, D. F., Landrum, T. J., & Hallahan, D. P. (1989). Self-recording of attention versus productivity. *Journal of Applied Behavior Analysis*, **22**, 315–323.

Maag, J. W., Reid, R., & DiGangi, S. A. (1993) Differential effects of self-monitoring attention, accuracy, and productivity. *Journal of Applied Behavior Analysis*, **26**, 329–344.

McDougall, D., & Brady, M. P. (1998). Initiating and fading self-management interventions to increase math fluency in general education classes. *Exceptional Children*, **64**, 151–166.

Mace, F. C., Belfiore, P. J., & Hutchinson, J. M. (2001). Operant theory and research on self-regulation. In B. Zimmerman & D. Schunk (Eds.), *Self-regulated learning and academic achievement* (pp. 39–65). Mahwah, NJ: Lawrence Erlbaum.

Mahoney, M. J., & Thoresen, C. E. (1974). *Self-control: Power to the person*. Monterey, CA: Brooks/Cole Publishing.

Mathes, M. Y., & Bender, W. N. (1997). The effects of self-monitoring on children with attention-deficit/hyperactivity disorder who are receiving pharmacological interventions. *Remedial and Special Education*, **18**, 121–128.

Meichenbaum, D. (1977). *Cognitive behavior modification: An integrative approach*. New York: Plenum Press.

Nelson, R. O., & Hayes, S. C. (1981). Theoretical explanations for reactivity in self-monitoring. *Behavior Modification*, **5**, 3–14.

Paniagua, F. A., & Black, S. A. (1990). Management and prevention of hyperactivity and conduct disorders in 8- to 10-year-old boys through correspondence training procedures. *Child and Family Behavior Therapy*, **12**, 23–56.

Pfiffner, L. J. & Barkley, R. A. (1998). Treatment of ADHD in school settings. In R. A. Barkley (Ed.), *Attention deficit hyperactivity disorder: A handbook for diagnosis and treatment* (2nd ed) (pp. 458–490). New York: Guilford Press.

Pintrich, P. R. (2000). The role of goal-orientation in self-regulated learning. In M. Boekaerts, P. R. Pintrich, & M. Zeidner (Eds.), *Handbook of self-regulation* (pp. 452–502). New York: Academic Press.

Prater, M. A., Hogan, S., & Miller, S. (1992). Using self-monitoring to improve on-task behavior and academic skills of an adolescent with mild handicaps across special education and regular education settings. *Education and Treatment of Children*, **15**, 43–55.

Prater, M. A., Joy, R., Chilman, B., Temple, J., & Miller, S. R. (1991). Self-monitoring of on-task behavior by adolescents with learning disabilities. *Learning Disability Quarterly*, **14**, 164–177.

Pressley, M., & Harris, K. R. (2001). Teaching cognitive strategies for reading, writing, and problem solving. In A. L. Costa (Ed.), *Developing minds: A resource book for teaching thinking*, 3rd ed. (pp. 466–471). Alexandria, VA: Association for Supervision and Curriculum Development.

Reid, R. (1993). Implementing self-monitoring interventions in the classroom: Lessons from research. *Monograph in Behavior Disorders: Severe Behavior Disorders in Youth*, **16**, 43–54.

Reid, R. (1996). Self-monitoring for students with learning disabilities: The present, the prospects, the pitfalls. *Journal of Learning Disabilities*, **29**, 317–331.

Reid, R. (1999). Attention deficit hyperactivity disorder: Effective methods for the classroom. *Focus on Exceptional Children*, **32**(4), 1–20.

Reid, R., & Harris, K. R. (1993). Self-monitoring of attention versus self-monitoring of performance: Effects on attention and academic performance. *Exceptional Children*, **60**, 29–40.

Reid, R., Maag, J. W., Vasa, S. F., & Wright, G. (1994). Who are the children with ADHD: A school-based survey. *Journal of Special Education*, **28**, 117–137.

Roberts, R. N., & Nelson, R. O. (1981). The effects of self-monitoring on children's classroom behavior. *Child Behavior Therapy*, **3**, 105–120.

Sawyer, R. J., Graham, S., & Harris, K. R. (1992). Direct teaching, strategy instruction, and strategy instruction with explicit self-regulation: Effects on learning disabled students' composition skills and self-efficacy. *Journal of Educational Psychology*, **84**, 340–352.

Schunk, D. (1987). Peer models and children's behavioral change. *Review of Educational Research*, **57**, 149–174.

Schunk, D. (1990). Goal setting and self-efficacy during self-regulated learning. *Educational Psychologist*, **25**, 71–86.

Schunk, D. (2001). Social cognitive theory and self-regulated learning. In B. Zimmerman & D. Schunk (Eds.) *Self-regulated learning and academic achievement* (pp. 125–151). Mahwah, NJ: Lawrence Erlbaum.

Schunk, D. H., & Zimmerman, B. J. (1994). *Self-regulation of learning and performance: Issues and educational applications.* Hillsdale, NJ: Lawrence Erlbaum.

Schunk, D. H., & Zimmerman, B. J. (1998). *Self-regulated learning: From teaching to self-reflective practice.* New York: Guilford Press.

Schunk, D. H., & Zimmerman, B. J. (2003). Self-regulation and learning. In W. M. Reynolds & G. E. Miller (Eds.), *Handbook of psychology, Vol. 7* (pp. 59–78). Hoboken, NJ: John Wiley and Sons.

Shapiro, E. S., & Cole, C. L. (1994). *Behavior change in the classroom.* New York: Guilford Press.

Shapiro, E. S., DuPaul, G. J., & Bradley-Klug, K. L. (1998). Self-management as a strategy to improve the classroom behavior of adolescents with ADHD. *Journal of Learning Disabilities*, **31**, 545–555.

Shapiro, E. S., Durnan, S. L., Post, E. E., & Levinson, T. S. (2002). Self-monitoring procedures for children and adolescents. In M. R. Shinn, H. M. Walker, & G. Stoner (Eds.), *Interventions for academic and behavioral problems II: Preventive and remedial approaches* (pp. 433–454). Bethesda, MD: NASP Publications.

Shimabukuro, S. M., Prater, M. A., Jenkins, A., & Edelen-Smith, P. (1999). The effects of self-monitoring of academic performance on students with learning disabilities and ADD/ADHD. *Education and Treatment of Children.* **22**, 397–414.

Stewart, K. G., & McLaughlin, T. F. (1992). Self-recording: Effects on reducing off task behavior with a high school student with attention deficit hyperactivity disorder. *Child & Family Behavior Therapy*, **14**, 53–59.

Swanson, H. L., Hoskyn, M., & Lee, C. (1999). *Interventions for students with learning disabilities.* New York: Guilford Press.

Torgesen, J. K. (1977). The role of non-specific factors in the task performance of learning disabled children: A theoretical assessment. *Journal of Learning Disabilities*, **10**, 27–35.

Torgesen, J. K. (1980). The use of efficient task strategies by learning disabled children: Conceptual and educational implications. *Journal of Learning Disabilities*, **13**, 364–371.

Varni, J. W., & Henker, B. (1979). A self-regulation approach to the treatment of three hyperactive boys. *Child Behavior Therapy*, **1**, 171, 192.

Vygotsky, L. S. (1962). *Thought and language* (E. Hanfmann & G. Vakar, eds. and trans.) Cambridge, MA: MIT Press. (Originally published, 1934.)

Winne, P. H. (1997). Experimenting to bootstrap self-regulated learning. *Journal of Educational Psychology*, **89**, 397–410.

Wong, B. Y. L. (1982). Understanding learning disabled students' reading problems: Contributions from cognitive psychology. *Topics in Learning and Learning Disabilities*, **3**(2), 15–23.

Wong, B., Harris, K. R., Graham, S., & Butler, D. (2003). Cognitive strategies instruction research in learning disabilities. In L. Swanson, K. R. Harris, & S. Graham (Eds.), *Handbook of research on learning disabilities* (pp. 383–402). New York: Guilford Press.

Zeidner, M., Boekaerts, M., & Pintrich, P. R. (2000). Self-regulation: Directions and challenges for future research. In M. Boekaerts, P. R. Pintrich, & M. Zeidner (Eds.), *Handbook of self-regulation* (pp. 749–768). New York: Academic Press.

Zimmerman, B. J. (1998). Developing self-fullfilling cycles of academic regulation: An analysis of exemplary instructional models. In D. Schunk & B. J. Zimmerman (Eds.). *Self-regulated learning: From teaching to self-reflective practice* (pp. 1–19). New York: Guilford Press.

Zimmerman, B. J. (2000). Attaining self-regulation: A social cognitive perspective. In M. Boekaerts, P. R. Pintrich, & M. Zeidner (Eds.), *Handbook of self-regulation* (pp. 13–41). New York: Academic Press.

Zimmerman, B. J., & Schunk, D. (1989). *Self-regulated learning and academic achievement: Theory, research, and practice.* New York: Springer Verlag.

Zivin, G. (Ed.) (1979). *The development of self-regulation through private speech.* New York: John Wiley and Sons.

CHAPTER 6

The Reading Brain in Children and Youth: A Systems Approach

Virginia W. Berninger
University of Washington

Preface

Contemporary neuroscience uses brain imaging tools with living people in order to understand developing brain–behavior relationships without relying, as in the past, only on inferences based on people who lose function or die. See Humphreys and Price (2001) and Wood and Flowers (2000) for the history of this rapidly evolving field and its current challenges. As a result of the advances in functional imaging technology and related cognitive paradigms, the neural architecture for specific cognitive domains, such as reading, is being more precisely specified than was possible two decades ago (e.g., Goldman-Rakic *et al.*, 2000). Since the Decade of the Brain, during which the United States government targeted brain research as a funding priority, a wealth of research findings about brain structure–function relationships in reading and reading disability in living children and adults has emerged, and is increasingly referred to in the literature on learning disabilities. The goal of this chapter is to make this research more accessible for preservice and inservice professionals who work with children and youth with specific learning disabilities affecting their reading.

Some readers may be overwhelmed with the numerous references to specific brain regions. Berninger and Richards (2002) provide, for an audience without prior training in neuroscience, an introduction (written text and graphical illustration) of the brain structures and functions that are involved in reading and between normal and disabled readers; reference to it may help some readers in assimilating the material in Sections II and III, which provide an update on the imaging studies not yet published when Berninger and Richards (2002) went to press. Figures 5.1 and 5.2 from that text are reproduced in this chapter, as Figs. 6–1 and 6–2, respectively, so that readers can locate, in a graphic illustration of the brain, many of the specific brain structures discussed in reference to brain imaging studies. However, the chapter can also be read for the general principles discussed apart from the specific brain structures cited. Research reviewed is restricted to adults and children whose reading development is normal or who have a specific reading disability despite development that otherwise falls generally in the normal range; their reading disabilities are associated with anomalies (rather than damage) in the neural architecture of their brains (reviewed in Berninger & Richards, 2002; Leonard, 2001; Shaywitz & Shaywitz, 2003). The brain basis for reading disorders associated with disease, injury, or development outside the normal range due to prenatal events, perinatal events, or congenital neurogenetic conditions is not covered.

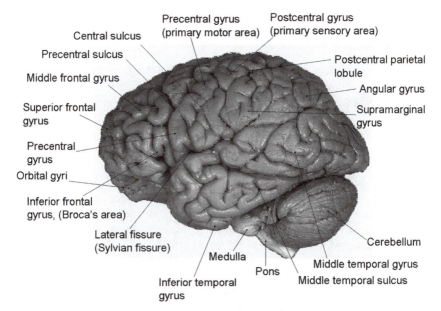

Figure 6–1   Gyri, sulci, and fissures on the surface of the cortex that are often referred to in the *in vivo* brain imaging studies for reading and related systems. Reproduced with permission from V. Berninger & T. Richards (2002). *Brain library for educators and psychologists*, San Diego: Academic Press.

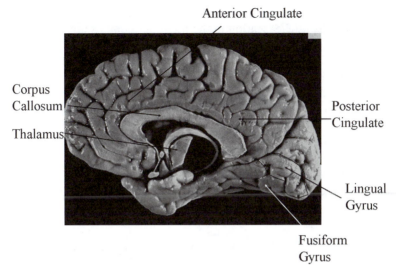

Anterior Cingulate

Corpus Callosum

Thalamus

Posterior Cingulate

Lingual Gyrus

Fusiform Gyrus

Figure 6–2 Brain structures deep in the brain that are often referred to in the *in vivo* brain imaging studies for reading and related systems. Reproduced with permission from V. Berninger & T. Richards (2002). *Brain literary for educators and psychologists.* San Diego: Academic Press.

This chapter has four sections. The first section discusses five theoretical approaches to the brain as a system of coordinated processes and introduces system theory as a conceptual framework for understanding brain function. The second section offers a model of the most important processes in the brain's functional reading system and illustrates the model with findings of recent adult and child imaging studies. In this section, "Triple Word Form Awareness and Mapping Theory," which informs our brain imaging and treatment studies, is introduced. The third section uses this model to organize a review of a growing body of imaging studies that compare children and youth with and without reading disabilities. Following a summary of the first three sections, the fourth section considers the implications of a system approach to reading for understanding the etiology of reading disabilities and designing effective treatment for preventing and remediating specific reading disabilities.

I. BRAIN AS A FUNCTIONAL SYSTEM

A. Five Approaches to System Theory

1. Levels of Construction

In the late nineteenth century, Hughlings Jackson (e.g., Jackson, 1887) startled his colleagues in neurology by proposing that mental processes be studied from the perspective of their level of construction in the nervous system rather than their location in the brain. Although simple sensory and motor functions may be localized to one region of the brain, cognitive functions, which are more complex, are probably not localized to a single brain region. More likely, a set of processes, each activating many localized circuits distributed across brain regions, may be constructed at many levels of the nervous system, including the *unimodal circuits* that code specific sensory and motor functions and the *heteromodal* association areas that integrate multiple sensory and motor codes or create abstractions that do not retain sensory- or motor-specificity. At the beginning of the twenty-first century, findings of brain imaging research are consistent with Jackson's proposal that had been revolutionary at the end of the 19th century.

2. Functional Systems in the Working Brain

A. R. Luria (1962, 1973), the Russian neuropsychologist, extended Jackson's insight. He introduced a more detailed model that specified (1) functional units for arousal in the inner brain, information processing in the rear brain, and programming/regulation in the front of the brain, and (2) how these functional units might draw on different levels of the nervous system. These levels vary in the degree to which they are modality-specific and code specific kinds of sensory and motor information. Luria, who used the clinical method to study the brain at work in living patients, compared their performance on contrasting tasks that shared common processing requirements but also had unique processing requirements. From careful scrutiny of which brain functions were lost and spared followed injury or disease and how patients performed on the contrasting tasks, he concluded that localized processes distributed throughout the brain were orchestrated to achieve the specific goals of the brain at work. The concept of a functional brain system represented a paradigm shift from thinking about one structure–one function to recognizing that the following four principles may more accurately reflect *macro-level brain–behavior relationships*:

- The brain recruits regions distributed throughout it to perform a specific function.
- Different tasks draw on some common regions and not just unique regions.
- The same brain region may participate in more than one functional system.
- Many different brain regions are involved in one functional system.

Results of brain imaging research at the beginning of the twenty-first century are consistent with these principles based on Luria's clinical observations in the mid-twentieth century about functional systems.

3. Society of Minds

Marvin Minsky, one of the founding fathers of artificial intelligence, took yet another approach to understanding organization of brain functions. He used principles of brain organization and child development and built robots that learned. From this engineering exercise in artificial intelligence, he conceptualized a theory—Society of Minds—of how human intelligence develops (Minsky, 1986). To explain his theory to lay people, he consulted with a poet to create metaphors that captured the technical concepts of a multilevel, multisystem organization and wrote a novel to illustrate the principles in creating a thinking machine (Harrison & Minsky, 1992). According to Society of Minds theory, the mind is built from many small processes (agents), which are organized into agencies, which are, in turn, organized into societies in the mind. Not only are the societies organized hierarchically, but also multiple societies exist, creating a heterarchical organization. A typical agent knows its job, which is to switch on other agents using an on–off system, but is typically unaware of the other agents except through connections with them. The agent is typically directly connected to only a few other agents, but through a series of indirect connections (agent 1 is connected to agent 2 which is connected to agent 3 and so on) may have indirect influences on agents far down the communication loop. These metaphors capture the digital all-or-nothing principle that governs the firing of the axon in a neuron that triggers the electrochemical signal that traverses the spatially separated synapse to create a momentary functional connection with another neuron. The receiving neuron is either an excitatory neuron that sends a signal to other neurons or is an inhibitory neuron that prevents further neural communication down the line. Although over the course of development, the communication among the agencies (collections of agents) and societies (collections of agencies) increases, communication of one agency or society with another is always indirect in terms of models the agencies and societies create of one another.

To maintain coordination in such a complex system, timing mechanisms orchestrate the neural architecture distributed in space. A total state of mind is the sum total of the agents that are active (firing) and quiet (not firing) at any moment of time. Mental processes are, therefore, not only the result of sequential transmission of an electrical impulse across a synapse (gap between single neurons or nerve cells) but also the result of the *constellation of neural networks that happen to be firing at a moment in time*, which is momentary time. Compared to real time that is linear, momentary time is nonlinear because each of the agents, agencies, and societies lives in a slightly different time world with a different history of what happened in the past and is happening now. What may seem like a fleeting flash to one agency may seem like an era to another. Only specialized agencies can deal with what might happen next (the future).

Minsky proposed that time blinking—finding the difference between two mental states by activating them in rapid succession and noticing which agents change state—may be the brain's mechanism for synchronizing neural activity throughout the brain, which is a collection of different mechanisms on their own time scales. Time blinking may give rise to brain waves. If Minsky's analysis of the role of timing in brain function is correct, then brain functions rely not only on micro-level, sequential transmission of neural signals across synapses (neural pathways) in real time but also on the macro-level temporal coordination of constellations of neural pathways transmitting in parallel in momentary time. Indeed, current brain imaging techniques often find activation in many brain regions with an unfolding time course that involves both simultaneous and sequential activation of different brain regions (reviewed in Berninger & Richards, 2002). One theory of dyslexia, supported with electrophysiological studies, is that the ortho-graphic and phonological systems underlying word reading are on different time scales and, compared to normal readers, dyslexics take longer to coordinate these systems in real time (Breznitz, 2002).

Given the enormous temporal as well as spatial complexity of the functional architecture of the human mind, Society of Minds theory also considers how such a system might be self-governed to avoid chaos. Rather than a single executive, a set of executive processes oversees and *temporally coordinates* these various agents, agencies, and societies that live in different time zones. For example, if conflicts occur because different mental states (constellations of which agents are firing) are imposed on the same agency in momentary time, the conflict is sent to a high-level agency for managing the societies of mind. Not all executive functions are devoted to managing conflict. Some are devoted to managing the many layers that are created as the brain interacts with the environment and learns. In the simplest kind of learning, the connections are changed by either creating new ones or drop-ping old ones. In another kind of learning, a new layer is created, with connections to an earlier layer or layers. Some layers are designed to detect *world-caused (stimulus events)*, others are designed for *operation on the world (motor output)*, and others are designed to detect *brain-caused (simulus)* events in layers of the brain not directly connected to the outside world. In the course of learning, many layers of brain-created simulus events are constructed with connections to internal layers removed by one or more steps from those layers with direct links to the outside world (input or output). Minds develop as a sequence of many layers of interconnected societies of brain events in multidimensional time.

4. Orchestration of Mind

Michael Posner, a cognitive neuroscientist, was the lead member of the first multidisciplinary team to use brain imaging to study the complex brain system at work during reading (Posner *et al.*, 1988). This team studied brain activation as adults listened to single spoken words and viewed single written words. Distinctly different, nonoverlapping brain regions were activated during auditory and visual presentation of words, consistent with earlier theory of modality-specific sensory coding in unimodal cortex. However, when the task changed from passive listening to vocal repetition of the auditorially or visually presented word, which requires cross-modality integration of sensory and motor codes, the pattern of brain activation shifted, presumably to heteromodal association cortex. Some areas of brain activation were common to both orally repeating aurally presented words and orally reading visual words, presumably because of the oral motor output required.

Posner and colleagues captured the notion of localized processes coordinated throughout the brain in real time with the metaphor of the orchestra. The localized processes are the individual musicians. They are orchestrated at the subgroup level in societies organized by musical instrument (e.g., strings, woodwinds) and at the whole group level by the conductor whose ongoing actions coordinate their varied functions in time. As a result, the individual musicians play in concert with each other and the net effect is the result of distributed activity and not a single individual. Even momentary solos are appreciated best in the context of the whole performance as it unfolds in time.

5. Role of Timing in the Executive Functions for Managing the Brain at Work

Animal studies are increasing our understanding of the role of the prefrontal cortex, especially lateral dorsal prefrontal cortex (LDPFC) in the temporal coordination of the working brain during goal-directed activity. LDPFC has many connections to parietal association areas (Goldman-Rakic *et al.*, 2000) and makes and executes plans. Interference with LDPFC also interferes with planning of temporally extended and sequenced programs of behavior but not with automatic, well-rehearsed acts, which appear to be housed elsewhere. Prefrontal cortex is more likely to be involved in the initial stages of learning procedural knowledge for performing novel acts than in the subsequent performance of well-practiced, automatic acts. Anterior cingulate in the frontal region also activates during planning and appears to play a role in conflict resolution. A supervisory attentional system in the frontal lobes protects the working brain from external and internal distraction through an inhibitory mechanism that suppresses distraction (see Fuster, 1997, for discussion of evidence for these claims).

Fuster (1997) offers the testable prediction that the temporal coordination is accomplished by *cross-temporal contingencies* between the primary sensory cortex and the primary motor cortex. Primary sensory cortex is specialized for different kinds of sensation, is located in posterior regions of the brain, and has the most direct connections with the external world. Primary motor cortex is located in the frontal regions of the brain and is specialized for movement and acting on the world. However, connectivity flow is very different in primary sensory cortex and primary motor cortex. In sensory cortex, the flow is from bottom up, from primary (unimodal) to association (heteromodal) cortex. In motor cortex, the flow is from top down, from high-level LDPFC to midlevel premotor cortex including supplementary motor cortex, onto low-level spinal cord activity. The higher regions specify goal-defined trajectory paths for reaching goals, rather than elementary movements, and the lower regions are focused on specific and concrete movements. In Fuster's model, cross-temporal contingencies are created between primary sensory cortex and primary motor cortex, between unimodal association areas and premotor cortex, and between heteromodal association cortex and the prefrontal cortex. Cortical–subcortical temporal contingencies may also form. All behavior involves a hierarchical ordering of structured units of sensation and action that are coordinated in time. Perception–action cycles, with feedback and feedforward mechanisms, are the basis for the organism's interaction with the environment.

6. Differences in the Computational Mechanisms of Humans and Animals

Brains are electrochemical computers whose computations create inner mental worlds (the mind) and overt interactions with the external world (behavior). Although humans and animals share remarkably similar brain structures, they differ functionally in a substantial way in the functional mental worlds and behaviors their brains *create*. This functional difference is due, in large part, to the larger prefrontal cortex of humans than that of animals. The lateral dorsal prefrontal cortex (LDPFC) manages the cross-temporal contingencies (Fuster, 1997) that create the functional systems in multidimensional space and time that differentiate humans and animals. This ability to compute in multivariate time and space (see Minsky's Society of Mind Theory; Minsky, 1986) gives humans the computational power not only to adapt to their internal and external environments but also to change their environments and create new ones. Sequential, digital, all-or-none transmission of neural signals across the structurally separated synapses in linear time is necessary but not sufficient for the computing power of the human brain, which also depends on the dendritic branches and spines that receive signals from many sources and operate in momentary time.

Dendrites have genetically constrained lower branches and environmentally sensitive upper branches (Diamond & Hopson, 1998; Jacobs *et al.*, 1993) and are *analogue processors* sensitive to graded signals. (See Berninger and Richards (2002), chapter 2, for possible computational operations in human learning that involve both analogue and digital processes.) However, contemporary imaging techniques do not provide a direct way to study either the analogue dendritic or digital axonal processes in the micro-level computations that create the macro-level functional systems in the working brain. That may be possible someday with further developments in mathematical modeling and nanotechnology for studying microscopic units of space and time.

For the purposes of this chapter, all the reader needs to understand is that the results of the brain imaging studies summarized in Sections II and III are expressed in terms of activated brain regions, which have functional significance beyond their location in the brain. Because different brain regions are specialized in terms of the structure and function of neurons in a regional computing center, the location of brain activation may have significance for computational mechanisms that operate either regionally or across regions. The relevance for children and youth with dyslexia is that the computational mechanisms may generally work well but (a) one or more computational mechanisms may not work well and therefore interfere with the overall functioning of the reading system, (b) the timing of these computations on different time scales may not be synchronized so that the various computations can be coordinated in real time, and (c) both the computational mechanisms and their timing may be responsive to instructional treatments.

Most brain imaging studies have focused on whether specific brain regions activate, but a growing number of studies are focusing, in contrast, on the interconnectivity of specific brain regions or computational cross-talk across specific brain regions. These connectivity studies may use statistical techniques (multiple regression) to evaluate which brain regions uniquely predict activation in other brain regions (e.g., Pugh *et al.*, 2000). Alternatively, connectivity studies may use mathematical modeling to evaluate patterns of increased brain activation signal (over noise due to random neural firing) that occur among different brain regions in recurring temporal phases in the brain at rest (Cordes *et al.*, 2000) or during specific reading tasks (Nandy *et al.*, 2003). Specific brain regions participate in many different functional systems. Only through comparisons of the various functions supported by the same brain region will researchers be able to infer the common processes supported by a specific brain region and thus the exact nature of the computation(s) performed by a specific brain region (or area within it). Complete understanding of the functional reading system will require knowledge of regionally specific localized brain activation and interconnectivity of specific regions during the computational processes that create the inner mental worlds and the overt reading behavior of reading brains.

II. IMPORTANT PROCESSES IN THE READING BRAIN

A. Domain-Specific Processes

In Sections II and III, *MRI* refers to structural magnetic imaging, *DTI* refers to diffusion tensor imaging, *fMRI* refers to functional magnetic imaging, *fMRS* refers to functional magnetic spectroscopic imaging, *MSI* refers to magnetic source imaging (a kind of *MEG*), *MEG* refers to magnetoelectroencephalography, and *ERP* refers to event-related potentials. Table 3.5 and Chapter 3 in Berninger and Richards (2002) compare the relative advantages and disadvantages of each of these brain imaging tools.

Visual inspection of the brains of normal and disabled readers reveals no secrets about the structural anomalies that differentiate the neural architecture of those who learn to read easily and those who struggle to learn to read. Structural MRI studies that image the volume or surface size of various brain regions show differences between good readers and dyslexics in neural architecture (reviewed by Leonard, 2001). A DTI study that compared the relative amount of gray to white matter in specific regions showed that the relative gray matter intensity differs between adult dyslexics and controls in multiple specific brain regions, consistent with a systems approach to understanding reading disability (Brown *et al.*, 2001): bilateral occipital lobe, left mesial temporal lobe, left inferior temporal gyrus, left middle temporal lobe, left middle temporal gyrus, bilateral superior temporal gyrus, bilateral angular gyrus, right precentral gyrus, bilateral inferior frontal gyrus, bilateral superior frontal gyrus, left orbital frontal gyrus, bilateral cerebellum, and bilateral caudate and thalamus. Whether these differences in intensity of gray matter are the result of genetic constraints, maturational lags, instruction and reading experiences, or all of the above is unknown.

During functional imaging, the brain of a live person performing a task is scanned and later analyzed. Functional imaging illuminates the differences between dyslexic and nondyslexic brains at work. Table I summarizes functional components of a reading brain, each of which may be supported by many localized and/or distributed brain regions. The sections in Table I on subword and word processes provide the conceptual framework for Triple Word Form Awareness and Naming Theory that informs our imaging and instructional studies. According to this theory, words are coded in three different formats, and learning to read depends on (a) becoming aware of the phonological, orthographic, and morphological units in these word forms and (b) mapping the interrelationships among these units to decode unknown words and access written words automatically (e.g., Berninger & Richards, 2002).

Table I

Selected Domain-Specific, Other Language, and Domain-General Processes Contributing to the Functional Reading System

Domain-Specific (Language by Eye)
Subword
  Phonological awareness
  Morphological awareness
  Orthographic awareness
Word
  Phonological word form
  Morphological word form
  Orthographic word form
  Beginning decoding of novel word forms (orthographic–phonological mapping)
  Advanced decoding of novel word forms (mapping orthography, phonology, and
    morphology)
  Automatic word reading of familiar word forms
Word and Text Comprehension
  Vocabulary understanding
  Sentence (syntax) understanding
  Discourse (genre-specific) understanding
Other Functional Language Systems
  Language by ear
  Language by mouth
  Language by hand
Domain-General
  Working memory for goal-directed jobs
    Temporary networks for storing incoming information from the environment, accessing
      information in long-term memory, and actively constructing new information related to
      goal(s) at hand
    Articulatory loop for maintenance of information in working memory, verbal output, and/
      or verbal mediation for self-regulation of processing or learning
    Executive function (including supervisory attention, conflict detection and resolution,
      metacontrol—planning, monitoring, updating, and revising, and temporal coordination
      of processes)
  Circuits for learning and for automatization

1. Orthographic Awareness

Occipital and inferior posterior regions of temporal cortex are activated during a single-letter detection task performed by adults (Garrett *et al.*, 2000). Comparing matching letters (orthographic processing) and matching lines (nonorthographic visual processing) in an fMRI study with children showed unique activation for orthographic letter processing in the occipital lobes (bilateral middle/superior occipital, right lingual), parietal lobes (left superior parietal lobule and surrounding region, left inferior parietal, and right precentral sulcus), temporal lobe (right lateral sulcus, right superior temporal lobe), and frontal lobes (right superior frontal, left precentral, right inferior frontal/insula, left middle frontal and medial frontal, and right cingulate gyrus), and subcortical regions (bilateral thalamus) (Temple *et al.*, 2001). More brain regions may have activated in the Temple *et al.* study of children compared to the Garrett *et al.* (2000) study of adults because when skills improve and are more efficient, fewer brain regions may need to activate to accomplish the same task. Also, judging whether letters match is a more complex task than merely detecting the presence of a letter. Indeed, letter matching activated a widely distributed neural network, compared to the more focal activation during letter detection. However, neither of these tasks assesses orthographic awareness (for which letter detection and recognition are necessary but not sufficient)—that is, the conscious reflection about spelling units in the orthographic word form that can be applied to decode words. For example, awareness that *orthographic* has eight spelling units (or, th, o, gr, a, ph, i, c) corresponding to phonemes facilitates decoding an unknown word, whereas simply knowing that the word has 12 letters does not.

2. Phonological Awareness

Although it is well established that phonological awareness—reflecting upon and analyzing component phonemes in spoken words—is a critical skill in beginning word decoding (Liberman, 1999), functional imaging researchers have not scanned children while they performed a phonological awareness task, such as phoneme deletion. Rather, brains have been scanned while participants repeated auditorially presented pseudowords, phonologically decoded written pseudowords, or made rhyming judgments about auditorially or visually presented pseudowords or visually presented letters. Children who have phonological awareness can analyze the component phonemes in a spoken word that correspond to alphabet letters and blend sounds corresponding to letters in unknown words to construct a spoken word. For example, the spoken word for orthographic has nine phonemes (/or/, /th/, /o/, /g/, /r/, /a/, /ph/, /i/, /c/), even though it has eight spelling units and 12 letters. Blending the /g/ and /r/ phonemes quickly in time and mapping them onto the *gr* spelling unit has the pedagogical advantage of avoiding the insertion of an artifactual vowel sound after each consonant sound.

3. Morphological Awareness

Morphological awareness is conscious reflection about the word parts (roots; inflectional suffixes that signal tense, number, or comparison; prefixes; or derivational suffixes that mark grammatical function) (see Nagy *et al.*, 1994). Preschoolers have morphological awareness of inflectional suffixes and some prefixes and derivational suffixes but, during the school years, mature morphological awareness emerges later than phonological awareness and has a longer developmental course—through the high school years (Nagy *et al.*, 1993). The word *orthographic*, like the words *phonological* and *morphological*, has morphemes that derive from the Greek layer of the word origin. The first morpheme *ortho*, from *orthos*, means right, straight, correct, or normal, and the second morpheme *graph* means write or record. The *ic* signals that the word is an adjective. Thus, the word orthographic refers to correct writing of letter forms and orthographic word form to all the letters in the correctly spelled word. The word phonological has a morpheme referring to sound (-phono) and to study of (-logy) and is marked as an adjective by the suffixes ic + al. The word morphological has a morpheme referring to meaning (morph) and to study of (logy) and the same suffixes marking it as an adjective (ic + al). The phonological word form is all the sounds in the spoken word. The morphological word form is all the morphemes conveying meaning and/or grammar in the spoken ad writes word forms. Thus, *orthographic* is a word that refers to (describes) correct writing of letter forms. According to Multiple Word Format Awareness and Mapping Theory, recovering the meaning of the whole word or lexical unit requires close attention to and coordination of the spelling units, phonemes, and morphemes in the whole word. Morphological awareness of word parts that convey meaning and grammatical function may develop later than orthographic or phonological awareness because it depends on the more complex coordination or mapping of three kinds of word parts—spelling, sound, and meaning/grammar units—than does orthographic awareness (spelling alone or spelling–phoneme mapping) or phonological awareness (sound alone or spelling–phoneme mapping). Morphological awareness is probably necessary for processing the increasingly complex words (multisyllabic and multimorphemic) encountered in written texts in the upper elementary, middle school, and high school grades.

4. Multiple Word Forms or Internal Codes

Brain imaging studies are showing that words are coded in multiple formats (internal codes) in the brain (Berninger & Richards, 2002). Readers draw on these codes in a flexible way in word decoding and recognition (Berninger, 1994; Pugh *et al.*, 1994). The internal codes for phonological and morphological word forms and their interconnections are constructed as children acquire oral language through listening and oral language through speaking. Orthographic word forms are created as children learn to read and write written language. These orthographic word forms are probably created through complex computations that map the preexisting phonological and morphological word forms onto the newly emerging orthographic word forms. During formal schooling, not only does the nature and quality of these orthographic word forms evolve but the related phonological and morphological word forms may also be transformed in the process (Nagy, personal communication). The details of these mapping procedures underlying Triple Word Form Awarness and Mapping Theory and transformations are being charted at the behavioral level in an ongoing longitudinal study.

In an fMRI study, Booth *et al.* (2001) studied developmental changes between children and adults in brain activation patterns for the orthographic and phonological word forms. Children showed overlap in brain regions activated for orthographic and phonological word forms, especially in Wernicke's region. In contrast, adults showed unique activation in non-overlapping brain regions specific to phonological word forms (superior temporal gyrus) and orthographic word forms (middle temporal gyrus and fusiform gyrus). These results indicate that in the course of constructing a reading brain (a new layer; Minsky, 1986) that incorporates the orthographic word form, the reading brain undergoes functional reorganization. Initially, the newly constructed system draws on multiple interconnections between the orthographic word form and the existing phonological word form (Berninger, 1994); see Table I. However, when the orthographic–phonological mapping process is completed, the preexisting system for phonological word forms (on which the orthographic word form system was bootstrapped) becomes separable from that orthographic word form system in the neural architecture—because the newly created layer containing the multiple mapping operations can be directly accessed and operates on its own. Although the two word form systems are separable in the neural architecture of the brain, they may be functionally integrated during the act of reading in real time.

a. Phonological word form processes. For over a century, the sound form of words has been associated with the region of the brain known as classic Wernicke's area, the posterior superior temporal gyrus (Wernicke, 1874). In a recent fMRI study (Burton *et al.*, 2001), adults were asked to repeat orally auditorially presented single words. Unique brain activation (relative to a control condition in which a digitally reversed spoken word was presented and the participants repeated the same word on each trial) occurred in the left posterior superior temporal gyrus and inferior frontal gyrus and supplementary motor areas, which may all be involved in processing phonological word forms. However, considerable interindividual variability was observed.

Event-related brain potential (ERP) studies have shown that specific cognitive functions tend to occur at predictable times after stimulus onset. For example, phonological word processing tends to occur between 250 and 350 ms, whereas semantic processing linked to sentence context occurs later, around 400 ms (Connolly *et al.*, 2001). These findings indicate that the phonological word form is processed earlier and is separable from semantic orthographic word form activates the left fusiform gyrus but that action here may involve only prelexical processing because this gyrus does t code semantic features (e.g., Dehaene *et al.*, 2002). Because left fusiform rus does not respond to numerical digits, it is thought to be specialized for tter processing (Polk *et al.*, 2002). Cohen *et al.* (2002) defined the Visual ord Form (VWF) area on the basis of its representation of letter strings as ordered set of abstract letter identities. Functional imaging data, based on oth blocked fMRI and event-related fMRI designs, localize the Visual ord Form Area in the left fusiform (extrastriatal cortex), which shares tronger activation to alphabetic strings than checkerboards (nonlinguistic isual stimuli) and to written words than nonpronounceable consonant letter trings. See Polk and Farah (2002) for review of other evidence that this egion responds to written stimuli that are wordlike but not to random letter strings. Evidence based on direct recording on the brain has been reported that orthographic–phonological mapping occurs here (Nobre *et al.*, 1994). Orthographic–semantic mapping may also occur here (Cohen *et al.*, 2002).

Orthographic Word Form area is probably a more appropriate term than Visual Word Form area for an area where visual stimuli becomes linked to language and that processes visible language rather than nonlinguistic visual features (Berninger, 1994; Berninger & Richards, 2002; Cohen *et al.*, 2002). Another reason to refer to it as the Orthographic Word Form is that the left ventral cortex (also referred to as basal temporal cortex), which contains the fusiform gyrus, responds comparably to real words and pseudowords with letters that alternate in case format (Polk & Farah, 2002). Thus, abstract orthographic regularities rather than visual features appear to be coded in this word form area.

d. Word decoding. In an event-related fMRI study, Clark and Wagner (2003) studied the role of a phonological control (executive) process in phonological assembly in working memory during learning of novel written words. Clark and Wagner (2003) tested the hypothesis that the left inferior prefrontal cortex mediates phonological control but that inferior and superior parietal activation reflects on-line storage. While their brains were scanned, 20 adults pressed one of two keys under their left hand to indicate whether visually presented words (English real words, English pseudowords, and foreign Finnish words) had two or three syllables. Following scanning, they were given a recognition memory test and asked whether visually presented words had or had not appeared during scanning. Both English words and pseudowords activated left inferior prefrontal cortex and bilateral inferior and superior parietal cortices. Both English pseudowords and Finnish words elicited greater activation in left inferior prefrontal cortex and bilateral parietal cortices, but English words elicited greater activation in bilateral inferior parietal/angular gyrus, posterior cingulate, and medial

analysis of words. A high-resolution event-related brain
study confirmed that phonologically related activation w:
words and pronounceable nonwords; phonological pro
require lexical access (semantic processing) (Connolly *et a*

Human speech perception imposes categories of sound o
speech signal. Speech researchers differentiate between spee
vary across categories (e.g., /b/ and /d/) and those that vary v
(e.g., phones for the articulatory gestures that vary dependin
word context, as in the slight variations in the /b/ in saying ba
MEG study (Kasai *et al.*, 2001), preattentive perception (be
attention) of across-category change in vowels activated both
brain symmetrically, whereas analysis of within-category chan
features of vowel change activated primarily right brain.

b. Morphological word form processes. In an fMRI study (A
2003), morpheme mapping was assessed on the basis of cor
kinds of judgments: (a) whether a word might "come from" (be :
related to word stems that contained familiar spelling units tha
not function as morphemes—derivational suffixes signaling g
information), and (b) whether two words were or were not synony
general semantic features. An example of a yes response for the c
task is "teacher teach," for which the *er* spelling unit functions
pheme that transforms a verb into a noun. An example of a no re:
the comes-from task is "corner corn," for which the *er* spelling uni
function as a morpheme. An example of a yes response for the syno
is "infant baby." An example of a no response for the synonym tas
boy." For both judgments, words were presented auditorially and vi:
that results did not depend on decoding skill. For children with
reading development, different brain regions activated for morphen
ping and for phoneme mapping (comparing judgments about v
one- and two-letter color-coded spelling units in written pseudowor
stand for the same phoneme and whether two sets of letter strings
exactly). Results provided evidence that (a) morphological word forr
uniquely different from general semantic features for word meaning
(b) the phonological word form and morphological word form map
processes are separable in the neural architecture of the brain.

c. Orthographic word form processes. A number of imaging studies
Berninger & Richards, 2002, for a review of studies through 2001)
providing converging evidence that the brain regions specific to the ortl
graphic word form are sensitive to abstractions about the regularities
written words (letter patterns) rather than the visual features of lette
(Cohen *et al.*, 2002; Polk & Farah, 2002). Imaging studies have shown th:

frontopolar cortices. Thus, left inferior prefrontal and parietal regions differentially engaged brain as a function of phonological familiarity. That the left inferior prefrontal cortex activation was greater for unfamiliar than familiar words shows that this region has a role in (a) constructing unfamiliar phonological word forms, and not just retrieving phonological information for familiar word forms, and (b) translating (decoding) orthographic word forms into unfamiliar phonological word forms.

During pseudoword reading, adult readers, who had a history of problems in learning to read but eventually did learn to read, overactivated in left frontal regions and posterior extrastriatal regions but underactivated in the right angular gyrus, dorsolateral prefrontal cortex, and palladium (Ingvar *et al.*, 2002). These findings imply that those who compensate for their brain differences that initially interfere with reading acquisition may still show brain differences when their reading becomes seemingly normal at the behavioral level. Whether brain differences in compensated adult readers represent a brain signature associated with dyslexia or an alternative pathway to the same behavioral outcome requires additional research.

e. Word reading. Using an innovative, automated meta-analysis technique, Turkeltaub *et al.* (2002) analyzed results of 11 PET studies of single word reading. Regions of significant concordance across PET studies, which were subsequently cross-validated in fMRI studies, included bilateral motor and superior temporal cortices, presupplementary motor areas, left fusiform gyrus, and cerebellum. Many studies report converging evidence for a disruption in the left posterior regions where word forms are processed and automatic word recognition occurs (Shaywitz *et al.*, 1998). Maturation of the neuroanatomy underlying single-word reading may be incomplete at age 10 in some children (Schlagger *et al.*, 2002), resulting in a permanent mismatch between their brains and their school curriculum and a stable deficit rather than a developmental lag. The only antidote to this mismatch may be heroic efforts to monitor when such structures do myelinate and to change the academic curriculum for such students throughout schooling until they are fully compensated.

Schlagger *et al.* (2002) studied normally developing children (7 to 10) and young adults (18 to 25) performing three fMRI event-related tasks for visually presented single words that required a single-word verbal response: generate verb, generate rhyme, and generate opposite. Cross-age comparisons are difficult because test performance may depend on task difficulty, which is not comparable across levels in skill development and general maturational level (age) of person performing the task. Children and adults had common and unique activations in left extrastriatal and frontal cortex, but when participants were matched on performance level, an index of task difficulty for individuals, age-related differences disappeared, pointing to the effects of task difficulty on brain activation. This change in results points to the challenges facing imaging researchers, who have to design tasks that, on one hand, pinpoint contrasts in component reading processes, and, on the other hand, are equated in difficulty across (a) developmental levels for a skill known to improve across development and (b) groups of children with and without reading disabilities.

The *word prediction paradigm* instructs participants to say aloud (overt response) or silently (covert response) the first word that comes to mind (e.g., dream) for the first three letters of a word stem (e.g., dre). Researchers choose three-letter groups that are associated with five highly predictable words. Ojemann et al. (1998) used this task in an fMRI study and a PET study and found increased activation occurred in left frontal and supplementary motor areas and right cerebellum, and decreased activation occurred in medial and right lateral parietal regions and right insula. Dhond et al. (2001), who used this task in a MEG study, reported predictable spatiotemporal stages that had flow from the back to the front of the brain, with some concurrent overlap in time or reactivation of previously activated stages later in time. For the repeated (primed) word stems, the inferior frontal gyrus, which was the last region to be engaged by the novel stimulus, showed the largest response. Because of the previous exposure (familiarity), the initial stages of processing may have been skipped and processing proceeded to a latter stage more quickly and efficiently. The authors concluded that (a) word-specific word form for processing/recognition occurred in visual association cortex, (b) Wernicke's area participated in multimodal coding of written words, and (c) Broca's area participated in word production processes even when they were covert.

5. Comprehension—Vocabulary Understanding

In contrast to the orthographic word form (fusiform gyrus) and phonological word form (superior temporal gyrus), which have modality-specific coding in unimodal cortex, semantic processing for word understanding appears to also be coded in modality-free, heteromodal cortex (left inferior frontal gyrus and left middle temporal gyrus) (Booth et al., 2002). A single-subject MEG study indicated that the brain initially responds to multiple semantic associations in parietal–occipital areas but, subsequently in the time course, codes grammatical categories of words (Pulvermüler et al., 2001). Between 200 and 550 ms after stimulus onset, perceptual and semantic encoding, both of which were followed by a recognition memory test, differed mainly over the left superior temporal and left superior parietal sensors, and semantic judgment (whether word was animate or inanimate) elicited more temporalparietal activation than did perceptual judgment (whether first and last letter of word were in alphabetic order) (Walla et al., 2001). Thus, spreading activation of multiple word meanings, based on word associations, may occur early in processing but categorical/schematic judgments of word meaning may occur later.

Verbal fluency (executive functions that control access to and retrieval from the lexicon) may also influence vocabulary understanding. Holland et al.'s (2001) comparison of covert verb generation for auditorially presented nouns and a control task of overt motor productions showed that for children aged 7 to 18, left lateralized activation occurred in Wernicke's area, Broca's area, cingulate gyrus, and dorsolateral prefrontal cortex (DLPFC). Degree of lateralization increased with age, and only activation in left inferior temporal gyrus correlated positively with increasing age. Left inferior frontal regions may be involved in the initial 30 seconds of a verbal fluency task, but the left middle frontal region may be involved in the next 30 seconds (Wood et al., 2001), suggesting that both of these frontal regions may be involved in retrieval of word meaning but at different temporal stages of processing. However, meaning processing activates posterior as well as frontal regions. In an fMRI study, Baker et al. (2001) reported two findings: (a) both left inferior frontal and left fusiform regions activated more during semantic (classifying words as to whether they are abstract) than nonsemantic (classifying words as to whether they are in uppercase format) decisions, and (b) those regions activated more on the recognition memory test that followed the decision tasks. Patterns of brain activation for a verbal fluency task that requires an overt response (speech) is very similar to tasks requiring a covert (inside voice) response, except that the task requiring speech results in more subcortical activation and more dorsal anterior cingulate activation on the difficult than easy items (Fu et al., 2002).

6. Comprehension—Sentence Syntax

Kann and Swaab (2002) reviewed the four paradigms typically used to study receptive syntactic processing: (a) comparison of complex vs simple syntax; (b) comparison of sentences to lists of unrelated words; (c) comparison of sentences composed of pseudowords to normal sentences or rest conditions; and (d) comparison of syntactically correct sentences with ones containing syntactic errors. They concluded that syntactic processing recruits many regions (especially in left frontal and temporal regions) but no brain region is syntax-specific. Hashimoto and Sakai (2002) localized syntactic processing to the left inferior frontal gyrus and left dorsal prefrontal cortex, but Caplan (2001) localized it to the left inferior frontal cortex. Röder et al. (2002) concluded that syntactic processing depends on partially specialized systems for syntactic processing in the left anterior regions in the front of the brain and on partially specialized systems for lexical processing in perisylvian posterior regions in the back of the brain. Cooke et al. (2001) found that the patterns of brain activation on syntactic tasks depend on both how complex the syntax is and what memory requirements are for the task.

MEG, which is an imaging tool that can be used to track the time course of processing, is shedding light on the time course of syntactic processing in a paradigm that compares the identification of a semantically incongruous word vs a semantically congruous word at the end of a sentence (Halgren *et al.*, 2002). The time course for processing may be characterized as follows: Left activation first occurs at 250 msec in Wernicke's area, then spreads to anterior temporal sites by 270 msec, to Broca's area by 300 msec, to dorsolateral prefrontal cortices by 320 msec, and to anterior orbital and frontopolar cortices by 370 msec. Right activation begins at 370 msec in the right anterior temporal and orbital cortices. Bilateral activation occurs at the peak of the N400 component (400 msec after stimulus onset) and involves widespread left activation in temporal lobe (anterior temporal and perisylvian cortex) and frontal lobe (orbital, frontopolar, dorsolateral prefrontal cortex). Right activation in orbital and right anterior temporal cortices continues beyond 400 msec.

7. Comprehension—Discourse

Increasing the complexity of stimuli and tasks exponentially increases the challenges in interpreting the results of brain imaging research. Gaillard *et al.* (2001) studied normal children (ages 7.9 to 13.3) as they read Aesop fables (6 stories with three paragraphs, ranging from 22 to 34 words in length) and answered riddles (What is a purring household pet?) with silent naming responses (cat). Both tasks activated many of the same brain regions, including middle frontal gyrus and dorsolateral prefrontal cortex. Reading extended discourse (fables) resulted in twice as much activation in left middle temporal gyrus and extended activation into superior temporal gyrus (bilateral but greater on the left).

Keller *et al.* (2001) reported imaging data to support the claims that (a) word reading and comprehension draw on different levels of language (single words and sentence syntax) that activate many brain regions, and (b) the same brain region (e.g., the left perisylvian language area) contributes to more than one level of language. However, they also showed that the computational load associated with each level of language results in an interaction that affects distribution of neural activation in the network. Thus, task difficulty affects allocation of resources in the distributed neural network for language comprehension.

Text coherence may also affect distribution of activation. In an fMRI study, Robertson *et al.* (2000) compared sentences with definite articles and sentences without definite articles to study discourse that was relatively more coherent or less coherent, respectively. The more coherent discourse activated more right frontal regions than did the less coherent discourse. In contrast, processing strings of nonletters produced more left activation at the back of the brain. In another fMRI study, Robertson (2000) showed that brain activation supporting narrative comprehension is separable from brain activation supporting word- or sentence-level processes. This finding is consistent with findings from a number of neurolinguistic studies supporting a neural architecture in which neural networks for different levels of language are spatially separable but temporally coordinated during functions that draw on the various levels of language (see Berninger & Richards, 2002).

B. Relationship with Other Functional Language Systems

The traditional neurolinguistic model, which included separate modular centers for receptive language (listening) in Wernicke's area and for expressive language (speaking or oral expression) in Broca's area, has been questioned and revised (Mesulam, 1990) based on multiple imaging methodologies: electrical stimulation prior to neurosurgery (e.g., Fried *et al.*, 1981), electrophysiological studies (e.g., Brown & Hagoort, 1999), and functional imaging studies (e.g., Binder *et al.*, 2000). Recent functional imaging research shows that not only are more brain structures involved than previously thought, but also structures outside of Wernicke's and Broca's areas. Moreover, language regions appear to activate simultaneously as well as sequentially (Fried *et al.*, 1981); often both right and left hemispheres (Beeman & Chiarello, 1998), both subcortical and cortical regions, and both posterior and anterior regions are activated during language processing in the brain imaging environment. Specific patterns of activation depend on the nature of the target tasks and control tasks, imaging modality, and other factors. Different patterns of brain activation are found for different levels of language (units of analysis, ranging from subword to word to sentence/ syntax to discourse/text levels). For a review of the research supporting these generalizations, see Berninger and Richards (2002).

Contrary to the widely held belief that language is a unitary construct, it is not a single system. Lieberman (1999) had the seminal insight that because language has no end organs of its own, it teams with the sensory and motor organs to achieve its goals. There are at least four functional language systems: (a) language teamed with the auditory sense for listening (Language by Ear); language teamed with the mouth and oral motor pathways for speaking (Language by Mouth); (c) language teamed with the eye and the visual sensory system for reading (Language by Eye); and (d) language teamed with the hand and the grapho–motor system for writing (Language by Hand). These functional language systems learn to work together. For example, in Lieberman's (1999) motor theory of speech perception, Language by Ear draws on the articulatory mechanisms of Language by Mouth to perceive auditory words. Consequently, many imaging researchers (e.g., Corina *et al.*, 2001) find activation in precentral gyrus (the primary motor area) on tasks involving receptive speech. Results of imaging studies show that writing and reading draw on common as well as unique brain structures (reviewed by Berninger & Richards, 2002, and updated by Berninger & Hooper, in press). How connections (cross-talk) among the functional language systems develop is the topic of an in-progress longitudinal study of writing and its links with listening, speaking, and reading.

1. Language by Ear (Listening)

Booth *et al.* (2000) studied auditory sentence comprehension in five adults (20 to 28 years old) and seven children (9 to 12 years old). Although children and adults activated similar networks (e.g., inferior frontal areas), children were more likely to activate inferior visual areas, suggesting that they were relying on mental imaging strategies.

2. Language by Mouth (Speaking)

In general, motor output poses methodological challenges for noninvasive imaging techniques (e.g., fMRI, fMRS) and electrophysiology (e.g., ERPs) because it introduces motor artifact. The few studies that used paradigms requiring spoken responses have been primarily done with single words rather than more complex productions involving syntax and discourse. Methodological innovations under investigation may overcome these challenges in future studies.

3. Language by Hand (Handwriting, Spelling, and Composing)

The posterior end of the left middle frontal gyrus, a region now referred to as Exner's Area (Exner, 1881; Matsuo, Kato, & Ozawa, 2001), and the left superior parietal lobule (Basso *et al.*, 1978; Vernea & Merory, 1975) are writing centers that activate during writing but not necessarily reading tasks. In an fMRI study, Matsuo, Kato, Tanaka (2001) compared four contrasting tasks performed by twelve normal adults: Their results have implications for orthographic–motor integration with and without integration with phonological codes. Results depended on whether the orthographic symbol to be copied could be or could not be coded phonologically. Only one region activated uniquely when the orthographic symbol could be recoded phonologically but many regions activated uniquely when the orthographic symbol could not be recoded phonologically. Integrating two codes—orthographic and phonological—with motor output may reap a benefit in that fewer brain resources are needed for reproducing the orthographic symbol. These results, if replicated with children and English alphabet letters, may have implications for how multisensory instruction is designed for students with learning disabilities (for further discussion, see Berninger & Hooper, in press).

Schulte-Körne *et al.* (1998) used the passive oddball paradigm in an electrophysiological study to evaluate mismatch negativity (MMN) for speech and for nonspeech tone stimuli for 19 children with spelling disability and 15 controls, all in fifth or sixth grade. MMN is the negative ERP component elicited in response to discriminable change in frequency, intensity, or duration of tones or phonetic cues in complex auditory stimuli. Normal and disabled spelling groups, who watched a silent movie while they listened to auditory stimuli presented binaurally through headphones, did not differ in MMN for tones but did for speech stimuli. This result for tone judgments replicated prior PET (Rumsey *et al.*, 1992), fMRS (Richards *et al.*, 1999), and fMRI (Corina *et al.*, 2001) findings for dyslexics who have word spelling as well as word reading problems. Schulte-Körne *et al.*'s conclusion—that preattentive speech processes during speech perception may play a role in spelling by influencing the quality and preciseness of the phonological representations available for learning to map phonemes onto alphabet letters—is consistent with the reported finding of an independent genetic pathway from preciseness of phonological word form representation to spelling (orthographic word form production) in dyslexics (Hsu *et al.*, 2002).

An fMRI study provides further evidence for the relationship of speech to spelling (Poldrack *et al.*, 2001). Eight normal adults listened to sentences presented at four rates of compressed speech that varied rate of acoustic changes while maintaining spectral features of the speech signal. Based on regions-of-interest (brain areas that uniquely activate for a specific task) and conjunction analyses (brain areas that activate across different tasks that share a common component process), the investigators concluded that pars triangularis was sensitive to both transient acoustic features in speech perception and phonological decoding. Size of pars triangularis (one of the structures in Broca's area) obtained in a structural MRI study was correlated with behavioral measures of phonological skills and also differentiated dyslexics from verbal IQ- and age-matched controls (Eckert *et al.*, 2003). These dyslexics, like other dyslexics, had significant spelling as well as word reading problems.

In an fMRI study (Kircher *et al.*, 2001), seven normal adults completed a word generation task (producing a word orally to complete a 7-word sentence stem in which the final low-frequency word was missing) and two control tasks (decision—choosing one of two words to complete the sentence stem, which controlled for planning a response; and reading aloud the word completing the sentence stem, which controlled for the oral motor response of saying the word). Comparison of the word-generation task with the decision or reading task revealed unique activation in these regions: left middle frontal, anterior cingulate, precuneus, and right lateral temporal cortex. Comparison of the word generation with the decision task showed the greatest signal change during word generation in the right precuneus and anterior/posterior cingulate, right posterior cerebellar cortex, insula, and lingual/fusiform gyral region, and bilateral middle/superior temporal gyrus. During the decision task, only the left fusiform showed greater signal change. Comparison of the word generation and the reading task showed overall greater right than left activation, with the greatest signal change during word generation in the right superior temporal gyrus, anterior cingulate gyrus, left precuneus, posterior cerebellar cortex, middle frontal gyrus, inferior parietal lobule, and right frontal operculum. Comparison of the decision and the reading control tasks revealed unique activation in the left inferior frontal and middle/superior temporal cortex bilaterally. The investigators concluded that the left hemisphere has more narrow semantic fields, which are constrained by specific, immediate linguistic context, and the right hemisphere has more wide-reaching semantic fields, which are tailored to broad linguistic context, including multiple word meanings and multiple sentence interpretations.

C. Relationship with Domain-General Processes

Domain-general systems that the functional reading system may draw upon include specific sensory systems (auditory, visual, kinesthetic), fine motor systems for the mouth and hand, attentional systems, networks of supervisory executive functions, the limbic system, and the higher-level thinking and problem solving system (Berninger & Richards, 2002). During goal-directed activity, the word storage regions, articulatory loop involving the oral–motor system, and the attentional/supervisory system may be orchestrated together as a functional working memory system. Just as the introduction of *in vivo* brain imaging techniques resulted in findings that changed understanding of the language system from that based solely on autopsy studies, brain imaging studies are expanding knowledge of the working memory system beyond the initial models proposed by Baddeley and colleagues, who are also revising their initial models (Baddeley *et al.*, 1998).

1. Working Memory

a. Storage systems. Recent studies do not support a clear distinction between a phonological store and a visual spatial sketchpad and central executive in working memory. Zurowski *et al.* (2002) reported evidence for a common working memory network for processing speech (phonological features) or spatially coded speech (serial syllables) and phonological working memory: activation in superior frontal sulcus, posterior parietal cortex, left inferior frontal gyrus, precuneus, and bilateral middle frontal gyrus. They failed to find evidence for a localized phonological working memory and concluded that localization of verbal working memory to left prefrontal cortex may really reflect the phonological strategies used in verbal working memory tasks. Left inferior frontal gyrus was activated whether the task was phonological judgment (0-back) or phonological working memory (2-back). Using a novel mental writing task, Sugishita *et al.* (1996) found regionally specific activation for graphic visual imagery in left frontal cingulate and bilateral intraparietal regions. This result suggests that there may be a storage buffer in working memory specific to letter forms.

b. Articulatory loop. Increasingly, the role of the phonological loop is expanding beyond mere rehearsal for maintenance in working memory (an idea grounded in early models of short-term memory) to its role in language learning (Baddeley *et al.*, 1998). Baddeley *et al.* (1998) proposed that the articulatory loop may serve as a phonological control mechanism that regulates phonological operations involved in learning new words. The right cerebellum and bilateral pars triangularis in Broca's area (inferior frontal gyrus) may be structural correlates of the articulatory loop in children (Eckert *et al.*, 2003).

c. Supervisory attentional/executive functions. Tasks that induce conflict (e.g., due to competing responses as on a Stroop test) tend to increase activation in anterior cingulate and left prefrontal cortex, but there does not seem to be a simple distinct network for monitoring or resolving conflict; rather, specific kinds of conflict activate different neural networks or locations in a distributed network (Fan *et al.*, 2003). Shaywitz *et al.* (2001) studied three kinds of attentional control processes (selective attention, divided attention, and executive function) during language tasks emphasizing meaning judgments with words coded in auditory or visual sensory systems. Selective attention was associated with increased activation in left parietal and inferior frontal regions. Divided attention was associated with increased activation in these same regions bilaterally. Executive functions increased activation in frontal regions. Clearly, the frontal lobe plays an important role in the executive functions involved in reading (Denckla, 1996), and the working memory system is a critical part of a functional reading system, especially in supporting reading comprehension processes (Oakhill *et al.*, 1998).

In an fMRI study, Wagner *et al.* (2001) asked 14 normal adults to make word choices (deciding which of two words most closely related to a target word). They investigated the relationships between semantic distance (choices strongly or weakly resembled the target word) and the number of choices (two or four). Results showed that left inferior prefrontal cortex (LIPC) plays a role in controlled access to goal-directed retrieval of semantic knowledge from long-term memory and use of semantic knowledge in working memory. Whether retrieval had to deal with competing options seemed to be irrelevant.

In contrast to the prior exclusive emphasis on the space (capacity) limitations of working memory, the timing mechanisms of working memory are increasingly being considered (Berninger, 1999). Fuster's (1997) animal model makes testable predictions about how the prefrontal cortex governs the temporal organization of many layers of cortex and subcortical regions in coordinating a goal-directed activity. This temporal coordination includes both set (forward in time and mostly motor attention directed toward preparation for action) and short-term memory (retrospective in time and geared to storing incoming sensory-coded information from the environment). Thus, working memory is attention directed to the internal representations that work with short-term storage systems (past time) and set (future time) to reconcile the past and future in the present momentary time.

In humans who can read, the supervisory/attentional system may play an important role in *temporal coordination of the various codes for word form storage*. For example, the middle frontal gyrus, which typically activates in studies of working memory, is strongly activated in logographic reading, probably to coordinate the extensive visuospatial, semantic, and phonological analysis needed to read logographs (Tan *et al.*, 2001). Corina *et al.* (2001) found significant differences between child dyslexics and controls in middle frontal gyrus whether the task was to attend to phonology alone or both phonology and semantics suggesting that the child dyslexics had difficulty not only in processing phonological information but also in the executive control processes for coordinating language codes. These investigators proposed the code coordination hypothesis of dyslexia, not as an alternative to the phonological core hypothesis, but as an additional explanatory mechanism involving executive functions that work specifically with functional language systems.

   d. *Reconciling the phonological core deficit and working memory deficit theories for dyslexia.* Swanson and Siegel (2001) synthesized a growing body of evidence in support of a working memory deficit of dyslexia. Functional systems theory, as articulated in this chapter, offers a viable way to reconcile these contrasting views. Within a functional working memory system, multiple components work together to support goal-directed activity: word form storage to support temporary processing, an articulatory loop for maintaining activation or regulating the word learning process (that depends on mapping the interrelationships among three word forms), and an executive control network for monitoring and managing conflict and for planning and achieving goals. Each of these components may have a phonological component—storage of phonological word forms, phonological processes involved in articulation (phonology involved in oral–

motor function), and executive control processes involved in retrieval of phonological word forms. An individual who has selective impairment in any of these phonological processes is also likely to have an impaired working memory system. From a systems theory perspective, the individual suffers from both a phonological deficit and a working memory deficit. In a multilevel neural architecture, causal mechanisms may exist at multiple levels, thereby complicating the scientific endeavor of inferring a single causal etiology.

2. Circuits for Learning and for Automatization

Different circuits appear to activate during learning a motor skill than during performance of an automatized motor skill. Learning motor skills changed activation patterns in supplementary motor areas and cerebellum (Mazziotta *et al.*, 1991; van Mier *et al.*, 1998), but basal ganglia activated only after overlearning (automatization) (Mazziotta *et al.*, 1991). Frontal areas activated more in early learning of a visual–motor sequence, parietal areas more after practice (Sakai *et al.*, 1998). Cerebellum activated during both novel tasks being learned (motor sequence of key presses) and practiced tasks (Nicholson *et al.*, 1999) but different cerebellar circuits may activate during learning than when executing an automatic motor skill (van Mier *et al.*, 1998). Cerebellar circuits may participate in the computations involved in the precise timing mechanisms governing motor learning (Ivry & Keele, 1989). This research on grapho–motor learning might be extended to study oral motor learning involved in oral reading. Scanning the brains of individuals performing different kinds of rapid automatized naming (RAN) tasks, for example, for letters and for objects, is also adding knowledge about the brain's role in automatizing familiar processes (Misra *et al.*, in press).

III. IMAGING STUDIES OF CHILDREN AND YOUTH WITH AND WITHOUT READING DISABILITIES

In this section, the emerging literature on brain imaging of children and youth that compares normal and disabled readers is reviewed. Such studies are best interpreted in light of the set of tasks that are used, the imaging modality used, and the characteristics of the participants. Given the complexity of functional systems, conclusions should be restricted to the tasks given and the control task(s) used, with acknowledgement that the exact patterning of results may change as a function of the set of processes studied, which is always a subset of the processes in the complete functional reading system. Also, published results do not reflect the sum of all activation detected but only the relative patterning (what was statistically unique compared to the control task or other comparisons among tasks). Many aspects of neural architecture may be necessary but not activated sufficiently to result in unique activation. Each imaging modality has strengths and weaknesses, and conclusions should also be restricted to the neural substrate assessed. Only as the various sets of tasks are studied with many imaging modalities will a full understanding of the reading brain system be achieved.

In general, studies vary considerably in how they define reading disability. This definitional issue poses serious problems for interpretation of brain imaging results (Bishop, 2002) because samples may differ as to whether children have dyslexia (specific deficit in word-reading processes in the context of otherwise normal language and cognitive development) or a variety of aural/oral language processing problems in addition to their reading problems (reading problems not specific to reading and spelling written words). Considerable evidence is mounting that reading problems that do and do not have a basis in underlying aural/oral language disability have a different genetic basis (Bartlett *et al.*, 2002; Lai *et al.*, 2001; SLI Consortium, 2002; Raskind, 2001; Thomson & Raskind, 2003) and a different neuroanatomical basis (Leonard 2001). Brain imaging results may be confounded by samples that are really not comparable in the nature of the reading disabilities represented. This problem goes beyond the thorny issue of IQ–achievement discrepancy as a definition or the use of verbal IQ versus nonverbal IQ in establishing expected level of reading achievement. At stake is how functional brain systems are constructed differently based on the internal context in which the various components are orchestrated (all the relevant components of a functional reading system), which may be different for different kinds of profiles of readers. Adding on interactions of internal components with the external environment adds yet another layer of complexity.

In Bishop's (2002) view, researchers who study dyslexia and other reading disorders should describe their samples more completely on a full profile of language, motor, and cognitive skills. Such precision in characterizing samples is likely to lead to faster progress in understanding the neural basis of the functional reading system and the genetic etiology of deficits in the structural and functional neural architecture. The cutting edge of neural science is integrating molecular genetics and neural architecture (Vandenbergh, 2000). Current genetic methods assume *genetic epigenesis* (non-interacting components at a genetic level) but the possibility of *behavioral epigenesis* (interactions among components in a complex, functional system like the reading brain) has not been investigated empirically.

In this review, a succinct description of tasks is provided, but interested readers are encouraged to go to the original publications for more complete information. This review is organized by imaging modality and begins with fMRI because this noninvasive technique is becoming the most widely used imaging technique for localizing differences in the functional neural architecture. In interpreting activation patterns, it is also helpful to understand that nonactivation may reflect nonengagement of a brain region, whereas during the course of learning, a pattern is often observed of hyperactivation (overengagement of a brain region) in the early stages, followed by reduced activation (less engagement of a brain region) when a process becomes more efficient. Current imaging techniques do not distinguish between activation of excitatory or inhibitory neurons; so localizing activation within the neural architecture does not indicate how the neural activity contributes to the computational process—by causing other neurons to fire (excitation) or to remain silent (inhibitory). Mathematical modeling and advances in nano-technology are needed to sort out the full significance of brain activation for understanding the neural computation of the brain at work in creating the human mind and human behavior. Despite these challenges, some themes are emerging from the various imaging studies with children and youth.

A. Differences between Dyslexics and Normal Readers

1. fMRI

Georgiawa *et al.* (1999), who conducted the first fMRI study of reading in children, administered four hierarchically organized tasks: silent viewing of letter strings (the control task), silent reading of nonwords, silent reading of high-frequency real words, and phonological transformations of words (moving first letter to end of a word and adding suffixes). Comparing the last three tasks to the first task, which served as a common baseline, showed that dyslexics had a different pattern of brain activation than controls in (a) nonword reading (in the left temporal and left inferior frontal regions) and (b) phonological transformations (in the left inferior frontal gyrus and left thalamus). These results are interesting because the participants were German-speaking and the German language has highly regular spelling–sound correspondence, so the phonological processing problems of the dyslexic children cannot be attributed to properties of the written language.

   In another fMRI study, Corina *et al.* (2001) gave two auditorially pre-sented language tasks to English-speaking dyslexic boys (age 9 to 12) and age-matched and verbal IQ-matched controls: phonological (Do these words rhyme?) and lexical (Are both words real words?). The same pairs of words were used for both tasks (Appendix of Serafini *et al.*, 2001) so results cannot be attributed to differences in stimuli. The phonological task required select-ive attention to the phonological codes but selective disregard of semantic codes, whereas the lexical task required selective attention to retrieved semantic and phonological codes but selective disregard of similiarity of phonological codes across word pairs. Dyslexics and controls did not differ on the common control, a tone judgment task, but did on both the phono-logical and lexical tasks. Because neither of these tasks required reading, the differences in brain activation could not be explained solely on the basis of performance differences between dyslexics and controls in reading ability. Significant interactions among group (dyslexic or control), tasks (phonological rhyme judgment—attend to phonology and ignore semantics; lexical judgment—attend to meaning and phonology) occurred in inferior temporal gyrus, precentral gyrus, middle frontal gyrus, and orbital frontal cortex. From a systems perspective, the dyslexics showed brain differences in mapping phonology and meaning, in articulatory awareness for word units, in maintaining words in working memory while linguistic codes were manipulated, and in the executive control for coordinating linguistic codes.

Left inferior temporal gyrus is a region where mapping between phonology and semantics is thought to occur. Adult dyslexics differed from controls in this brain region (Paulesu *et al.*, 1996, 2001). With one exception, individual control brains consistently activated in this region during the phonological rhyme judgment but individual dyslexic brains consistently did not activate (see Berninger & Richards, 2002).

The precentral gyrus is the primary motor zone and may be where articulatory gestures involved in speech perception are processed (see Section II). In the left precentral gyrus, dyslexics overactivated when the task was to attend to sublexical phonology and make rhyme judgments and underactivated when the task was to attend to meaning and phonology of the whole word. This result supports the clinical observation that too much emphasis on articulating small sound units in isolation during decoding without equal emphasis on naming whole words may interfere with dyslexics developing automatic pronunciation of whole words.

Dyslexics underactivated on both tasks, but more so on lexical tasks, in left middle frontal gyrus, which is associated with working memory and processing meaning. This result suggested that they had difficulty with maintaining word forms in working memory while manipulating them.

Dyslexics overactivated on the lexical task and underactivated on the phonological task in left orbital frontal cortex, which is part of the executive system for dealing with conflict. This result suggested that dyslexics had difficulty in (a) attending to sound when it was relevant and ignoring meaning when it was irrelevant; and (b) attending to meaning *and* sound when both were relevant.

Temple *et al.* (2001) used fMRI to compare English-speaking child dyslexics and age-matched dyslexics in the 8 to 12 age range. The experimental paradigm teased apart the orthographic and phonological processing requirements for tasks sharing the same stimuli. The phonological processing task required pressing the button if the names of two capital letters rhymed. The orthographic task required pressing the button if two capital letters matched. The control task was a nonlinguistic line orientation judgment. The results showed that both orthographic and phonological processes are disrupted in dyslexia. In the left temporo–parietal cortex, dyslexics showed no activation during the rhyme task, but showed more activation and a different pattern of activation than control children did in inferior frontal gyrus. Dyslexics had similar activation on both the phonological and orthographic tasks, whereas control children showed more activation on the phonological than the orthographic task. Dyslexics did not activate in occipital–parietal regions and differed from control children in four regions during the orthographic task: left middle/superior occipital gyrus, bilateral cingulate gyrus, right inferior temporal gyrus, and right precuneus.

Georgiawa *et al.* (2002) used fMRI and event-related potentials (ERPs) to study German-speaking dyslexic and age- and IQ-matched controls as they read real words and pseudowords. Published results do not address any differences in brain activation for the two kinds of words. On fMRI activation, dyslexics and controls differed significantly in inferior frontal gyrus, where the dyslexics hyperactivated. Dyslexics also activated in (a) a cluster including the inferior frontal gyrus (Broca's area), the left insula, and anterior left temporal superior gyrus, (b) posterior left thalamus, and (c) left nucleus caudate. ERP differences occurred between the dyslexics and controls in left frontal electrodes at 250–600 msec after stimulus onset for nonword reading.

Shaywitz *et al.* (2002) conducted the largest fMRI study of English-speaking children to date, with 144 children (aged 7 to 18 years), half of whom were dyslexics. Participants completed five hierarchically organized tasks: nonlinguistic, visual judgment of line orientation; letter case judgment; letter rhyming judgment; pseudoword rhyming judgment; and semantic judgment of decoded words. Dyslexic and control group brain activation differed only for the last three tasks that required phonological analysis and not for the first two tasks that required visual analysis. (The case judgment task depends more on visual cues than the letter matching task used by Temple *et al.* (2001) which depends more on orthographic cues.) On the phonological tasks, controls activated more than dyslexics in left sites (inferior frontal gyrus, superior temporal sulcus, middle temporal gyrus, and middle occipital gyrus) and right sites (inferior frontal gyrus, superior temporal sulcus, superior temporal gyrus, middle temporal gyrus, and medial orbital gyrus). Activation in left occipitotemporal regions correlated modestly but significantly with a psychometric measure of pseudoword reading, consistent with a systems model in which this region is important, but not the only region involved, in phonological decoding.

The authors interpret their results for children (and adults) in light of a theory of dyslexia in which disruption to the posterior reading system results in compensatory shifting to anterior systems, for example, in inferior frontal gyrus (Broca's area). This theory is gaining increasing support from a number of studies reviewed in this chapter and in Berninger and Richards (2002). Note that the authors do not localize the problem to a single location but rather to a network of structures. They (also see Pugh *et al.*, 2000; Shaywitz & Shaywitz, 2003) have adopted a systems perspective and emphasize that three systems, primarily on the left side, are disrupted in dyslexia: (a) a ventral occipitotemporal (including middle occipital gyrus and middle temporal gyrus, (b) a dorsal parietotemporal system (including angular gyrus, supramarginal gyrus, and posterior portions of superior temporal gyrus), and (c) an anterior system (including left inferior frontal region). A consensus is emerging among many imaging researchers that these three systems are disrupted in dyslexia.

In an fMRI study, Aylward *et al.* (2003) administered two tasks to infer phoneme mapping: (a) match/mismatch for correspondences between 1 or 2 letters in a pseudoword and a phoneme and (b) match/mismatch of letter strings. They gave two other tasks to infer morpheme mapping: (a) comes from judgments for word pairs that are morphologically related (farmer and farm) or are not (mother and moth), even though they share a common spelling unit (er), and (b) synonym judgments for word pairs that do or do not have the same meaning. Child dyslexics and age- and verbal IQ-matched controls differed in brain activation on both phoneme mapping and morpheme mapping, showing that the language problems of dyslexics are more pervasive than in processing the phonological word form alone. Dyslexics showed less activation than did controls on phoneme mapping in left middle and inferior frontal gyri, right superior frontal gyrus, left middle and inferior temporal gyri, and bilateral superior parietal regions. Dyslexics showed less activation than the controls during morpheme mapping in left middle frontal gyrus, right superior parietal, and right fusiform/occipital gyrus.

2. fMRS and Comparison of fMRI and fMRS

Using fMRS, a kind of functional imaging that detects chemical activation during energy utilization in neural metabolism, Richards *et al.* (1999) found differences between child dyslexics and controls (age 9 to 12) in lactate activation in left frontal regions during a phonological task and replicated this finding on another sample of children of the same age (Richards *et al.* 2002). The dyslexics produced more lactate activation than did age- and IQ-matched controls during the same phonological judgment task used in Corina *et al.* (2001), suggesting that their phonological processing was less efficient at a neural level. Serafini *et al.* (2001) showed comparability of fMRI Blood Oxygenation Level Dependent (BOLD) response and fMRS lactate activation on the lexical judgment task. Richards *et al.* (submitted) compared fMRI and fMRS on the lexical judgment task in word form areas and found fMRI/fMRS convergence in a phonological word form area in good readers but not in dyslexics during a lexical judgment task; fMRS detected abnormal lactate activation in a brain structure associated with attention to different sensory codes.

3. ERP and EP

In a unique series of longitudinal studies, Molfese and Molfese (e.g. Molfese 2000) have collected auditory evoked potentials (EPs) in newborns and studied their language development during the preschool years and reading development during the school years. Quantitative parameters in the newborn EPs predict classification of children's later language ability (high or low) at age 3, verbal IQ (high, average, or low) at age 8, and reading (normal, low, or dyslexic) at age 8 (see Molfese, 2000). Such findings suggest that early intervention might improve outcomes, if research can identify developmentally appropriate early interventions for infants and toddlers.

Flynn et al.'s (1992) event-related potential (ERP) study invalidated the popular myth that dyslexics can be subtyped on the basis of a modality-specific auditory or visual learning style. However, another ERP study validated two subtypes in adolescent readers (McPherson et al., 1998). One subtype has difficulty in phonological decoding—translating orthographic word form into a phonological word form. The other subtype has trouble with rate of reading and response preparation, which may be related to deficiencies in phonological short-term memory. In another ERP study, child dyslexics (aged 9 to 10) were slower in both visual/orthographic and auditory/phonological processessing, and even relatively slower in the phonological processing, compared to controls (Breznitz, 2002). In addition, the dyslexics had larger gaps between their orthographic and phonological rates than did the controls. These gap scores correlated significantly with behavioral measures of decoding.

4. MEG (MSI)

MEG is more sensitive to temporal parameters in brain processing than is fMRI, which provides more precise spatial localization information. In the first MEG study with children, Heim et al. (1999) used a passive oddball paradigm to study processing of rapidly changing speech sounds. Dyslexics (mean age 13) and good readers (mean age 12) were asked to ignore binaurally presented just noticeable consonant vowel syllable contrasts (/ba/ and /da/) as they watched a silent videotape. Dyslexics and controls differed at 100 msec after syllable presentation in that the controls showed left–right asymmetries in brain activation and dyslexics did not. Over time, activation in right auditory cortex increased in controls, but activation in left auditory cortex increased in dyslexics.

MSI is a kind of MEG that provides a real-time spatiotemporal map of brain activity reflecting electrical currents in neuronal aggregation during task performance. Simos et al. (2000) administered an auditory and written word recognition task to dyslexic children (mean age 12) and age-matched controls in an MSI imaging study. On the auditory word task, all dyslexics had greater left than right tempoparietal activation, but on the visual word task, only one dyslexic had greater left than right tempoparietal activation. On the visual word activation task, controls showed a sequential pattern of activation of left basal regions (fusiform and lingual gyri) followed by activation of left tempoparietal regions; but dyslexics, who showed the same initial pattern in left basal regions, showed a contrasting second pattern in that they activated right rather than left tempoparietal regions. This pattern suggested that dyslexics had a problem in functional connectivity between the *ventral* visual association cortex and the *dorsal* left temporal parietal areas. That the dyslexics showed the normal left–right asymmetry on the auditory task, but not the visual word task, suggests that they had difficulty with processing orthographic word forms in left ventral regions, which results in a downstream problem in the dorsal tempoparietal regions. (See previous discussion in Section III on ventral, dorsal, and anterior systems in word reading.)

Simos *et al.* (2000) asked children to judge whether a pair of written pseudowords rhymed during MSI imaging. As in the just described study, the child dyslexics and controls did not differ in left basal regions in the initial stage of processing, but did differ in the subsequent stage when the dyslexics showed a lack of activation in left temporoparietal areas and a corresponding increase in homologous right hemispheric activation but controls showed left activation. The pattern for nonword reading was similar to that observed for real words in the previously described study by this research group. This study did find longer latencies in right basal temporal cortex (fusiform gyrus and lingual gyrus) in child dyslexics, consistent with other reports in the literature.

This research group's paradigms for studying real words and pseudowords may be particularly sensitive to detecting anomalies in parietal regions that support on-line processing of phonological retrieval and control processes (see Clark & Wagner, 2003) at a subsequent stage after initial word form processing. Dyslexics have great difficulty not only with initial processing of phonological word forms in left posterior regions (ventral system), but also subsequent phonological processing in the parietal regions (dorsal system). Clock drawing is a clinical measure that is very sensitive to impairment in this parietal system involved in phonological processing (Eden *et al.*, 2003), which may be part of the working memory system that supports word decoding.

Simos *et al.* (in press) compared kindergartners at-risk and not at-risk for reading disability during MSI imaging on a task that required them to give the most common sound associated with each letter. Brain activity on this task was reliably localized to seven regions in both hemispheres (superior temporal gyrus, middle temporal gyrus, supramarginal gyrus, angular gyrus, inferior frontal gyrus, basal temporal cortices, and mesial temporal cortices). Children who were not at-risk had significantly greater left than right superior temporal gyrus activity compared to the at-risk children. Following explicit, intensive literacy training, the at-risk, profiles were not significantly different from the not at-risk profiles, providing evidence that early intervention can lead to normalization of brain function.

B. Plasticity of Brain—Dyslexic Response to Instruction

Currently controversial topics in research that combines brain imaging and instruction are (a) whether instruction changes the dyslexic brain, and (b) if so, how (Rosenberger & Rottenberger, 2002). There are two competing hypotheses. The compensatory hypothesis predicts that new brain circuits are established, presumably bypassing the faulty circuits. The normalization hypothesis predicts that aberrant brain circuits are repaired and the same ones are used by normal readers and dyslexics who are remediated. One complicating factor is that preexisting differences between dyslexics and good readers may be eliminated for a number of reasons—for example, dyslexics may go from being nonresponsive to being responsive (hence, increasing activation), and good readers may improve in the efficiency of their processing (hence, decreasing activation); however, this differential change in activation could not account for all the observed normalization following instructional intervention (Aylward et al., 2003). The results to date indicate that the brain is responsive to instructional treatments of as little as 3 to 8 weeks duration. However, there is a very long developmental stage between novice and skilled reader for normally developing children without learning disabilities; so it is important not to draw the premature conclusion that there is a quick fix to curing dyslexia because the brains of dyslexics are responsive to instruction. Although research to date provides support for the normalization hypothesis, considerably more research is needed until a definitive resolution of these issues is possible.

1. MRI

In the Aylward et al. (2003) study, both the dyslexics and controls were scanned twice—at the beginning and end of the summer. During the summer, the dyslexics received 3 weeks (2 hours a day for 14 days) of comprehensive reading instruction (linguistic awareness, decoding, fluency, and comprehension described in Berninger et al., 2003) when they were receiving no other reading instruction. The pretreatment differences between the dyslexics and controls were reported earlier in Section III. Following treatment, the regions that showed significant changes from first to second scan in the dyslexics on both phoneme and morpheme mapping were identified and the dyslexics and controls were compared on these in the second scan. On phoneme mapping, dyslexics increased activation in many regions following treatment, but the increased activation in left inferior frontal gyrus and middle frontal gyrus after treatment was significant and robust and resulted in elimination of most significant differences between dyslexics and controls on the second scan. On morpheme mapping, dyslexics increased activation in many regions but significantly in right fusiform gyrus and right superior parietal regions after treatment and were no longer significantly different from the controls in these regions on the second scan.

Nearly all pretreatment brain activation differences between dyslexics and controls, not just the ones that showed the strongest treatment effects for the dyslexics, disappeared on both the phoneme mapping and morpheme mapping tasks on the second scan, indicating the possibility of near normalization following short-term treatment. These results are not just the consequence of generalized attentional mechanisms because both the pretreatment differences and changes after treatment were specific to different kinds of language functions—phoneme mapping or morpheme mapping. These results show that dyslexia is a treatable disorder but not that this complex disorder is cured after a short-term intervention. Full compensation may well depend on long-term, explicit, but highly intellectually engaging instruction in all academic curricula throughout schooling.

Temple *et al.* (2003) administered the same tasks as in Temple *et al.* (2001) to 20 dyslexics (8- to 12-year-olds) before and after 8 weeks of computerized training in aural/oral language skills. Changes on psychometric language and reading tasks and in fMRI brain activation are reported but are difficult to interpret because comparable results are not reported for controls. It is mentioned that controls were scanned twice but results are not reported for comparisons between dyslexics and controls before or after treatment of the dyslexics.

2. fMRS

Richards *et al.* (2000) imaged child dyslexics with fMRS before and after they received a 28-hour intervention, which emphasized phonological awareness and working memory skills and multiple decoding strategies. They also reimaged the controls at the same time the dyslexics were reimaged. Pretreatment differences (Richards *et al.*, 1999) were not found after treatment, suggesting that the brain is both a dependent variable that is responsive to instruction and an independent variable that influences instructional needs. In contrast to Richards *et al.* (2000) in which all dyslexics received the same treatment, the Richards *et al.* (2002) study randomly assigned children to one of two 28-hour treatments in order to make causal inferences about treatment effects—phonological or morphological awareness training embedded in an instructional protocol that had common decoding, fluency, and comprehension components. In Richards *et al.* (2002), the morphological treatment, but not the phonological treatment, was significantly associated with (a) a reduction in lactate activation in left anterior regions during a phonological judgment task, and (b) significant improvement on a behavioral measure of phonological decoding rate for pseudowords. Results were interpreted on the basis of Triple Word Form Awareness and Mapping theory—teaching morphological awareness had a benefit for mapping the interrelationships among phonology, orthography, and morphology, which jointly contribute to the decoding process of unfamiliar words (i.e., pseudowords).

3. MEG (MSI)

Simos *et al.* (2002) obtained MSI imaging in child dyslexics (aged 8 to 17) and controls before and after 80 hours of intensive phonological training. Before intervention, on a visual pseudoword rhyme matching task (judge whether a pair of pseudowords rhyme), dyslexics had little or no activation in left superior temporal gyrus and had increased right activation in this region. Following intervention, performance on behavioral measures of reading improved and activation increased in the left superior temporal gyrus. However, even after treatment, the peak in left superior temporal gyrus activation was later in dyslexics than controls.

SUMMARY OF SECTIONS I, II, AND III

Section I reviewed five systems theories of brain function. The common theme that unifies these theories was that brain function depends on the coordination of multilevel processes in time. Section II explained how the reading brain draws on domain-specific reading processes, other functional language systems, and domain-general processes shared across many functional systems. The point was made that different brain circuits and computational mechanisms are involved in learning a new skill and in executing a practiced, automatic skill. In either case, a neural architecture for working memory supports goal-directed behavior such as reading. Working memory has storage mechanisms, an articulatory loop for learning new words or maintaining familiar words in working memory, and a supervisory attentional system. Each of these processes has a phonological component—the phonological word form for storage, the phonological mediation and word production processes of the articulatory loop, and the executive control processes for retrieving phonological word forms, managing the mapping procedures for interrelating the three word forms (see Table I), and inhibiting irrelevant inhibiting irrelevant information during phonological processing. Thus, the phonological core deficit theory of dyslexia and the working memory deficit theory of dyslexia are not incompatible.

Section III reviewed results of recent brain imaging studies of children and youth with and without reading disabilities, with attention to the various methodological challenges facing imaging researchers—such as equating tasks on difficulty level for different ages and groups and creating tasks that can be compared and interpreted in meaningful ways. These challenges include the definition of what a reading disability is. The brain's response to instructional intervention may well depend on etiology of the reading disability—the specific genetic or neurological factors underlying it or the student's overall profile of abilities. Children who are mildly at risk may be very responsive to early intervention. Those who show persisting signs of dyslexia (specific to reading written words, see Shaywitz, 2003) may also be responsive to instructional intervention. Those with more pervasive language learning disability affecting many aspects of their language functions and ability to use language to learn may be slower to respond to instructional interventions. The issues of defining reading disabilities and effective instructional intervention are now discussed from the perspective of systems theory and the recognition that many different processes in a multilevel, temporally constrained brain architecture are relevant.

IV. IMPLICATIONS FOR ASSESSMENT AND INSTRUCTIONAL INTERVENTION

A. Normal Variation, Atypical Development, and Brain-Based Differential Diagnosis

The IQ–achievement discrepancy definition used in most states for qualifying students for special education services has been problematic for a number of reasons (Fletcher et al., 2002), including the fact that it relies only on an exclusionary definition of what a learning disability is not (not related to sensory, motoric, or intellectual deficit or cultural difference). If reading is a functional brain system (Luria, 1962/1980, 1973), then it should be possible to define specific reading disabilities based on inclusionary criteria of what they are. Such criteria would specify which processes in an individual student's profile are or are not impaired or underdeveloped, for the domain-specific reading system and for the related domain-general systems. In describing an individual student's profile within and across systems, it is important not to confuse learning differences within the normal range (attributed to normal variation) with learning disabilities that are outside the normal range. Learning differences and learning disabilities should be defined on the basis of an individual profile (pattern of component processes in a system) and not on the basis of a single skill. For this reason, the University of Washington research group studied normal variation in reading and writing development using multiple reading and writing and reading-related, writing-related, skills before studying specific reading or writing disabilities.

If the multisystem profile in which low reading achievement occurs influences component processes within and across brain systems, then it is important to define reading disability on the basis of a comprehensive assessment of many functional brain systems and not just low performance on isolated reading skills. Domains that are especially relevant to reading functioning are cognition and memory, receptive and expressive language, visual–spatial, fine and gross motor, attention, executive function, and social and emotional behavior. Only by comparing patterns across domains of functioning, as well as relative performance within a domain, can neuropsychologists evaluate whether children are exhibiting normal variation (learning differences), learning disabilities (specific to a certain system and process and not expected on the basis of developmental level of all other systems, relative to the population mean), or atypical development (disabilities that are not specific to a certain system or process because other systems are significantly outside the normal range, relative to the population mean) (see Berninger, 2001, in press; Berninger & O' Donnell, in press).

The cause of a learning disability (etiology), the most effective treatment for it, and the prognosis (most probable long-term learning outcome) may not be related in a simple one-to-one way (Berninger et al., 2003). The cause of a reading problem is most likely different if it occurs in the profile of a student who also has (a) mental retardation, (b) pervasive developmental disorder with autistic spectrum features, (c) primary language disability, (d) dyslexia (impaired reading and spelling), or (e) dysgraphia (impaired handwriting and/or spelling) with no reading impairment. Not only are the genetics and neurological mechanisms probably different, as already discussed, but also how reading procedures are created (during construction of the functional reading system) is probably different for these various prototypical profiles. For any reading problem, the cause may be univariate, but the most effective treatment is likely to be multivariate and aimed at all levels of language and at nonreading functions as well (Berninger & Abbott, 2003; Berninger & Richards, 2002; Carlisle & Rice, 2003; Wolf & Kennedy, 2002). The most effective treatment for teaching reading to students with each of the prototypical profiles probably shares some common, but also has many unique, features. For example, the kind of vocabulary knowledge that can be used in teaching reading skills will be very different, and the way in which transfer to independent reading can be taught will also vary greatly across these profiles. Moreover, with appropriate instruction, the eventual student learning outcome is likely to be higher for the last two profiles than for the first three profiles, in which more processes fall outside the normal range. Longitudinal research is needed for the etiology, most effective treatments, and prognosis for each of these prototypical profiles.

B. Instructional Implications of Functional Brain Systems

1. Enhancing Teachers' Task Analysis Abilities

Teachers are given little or no training in task analyzing processes needed to learn specific reading skills in the curriculum, in troubleshooting why certain students may have difficulty with learning selected components of curriculum, or in generating alternative solutions should the current instructional approach not be effective. Educating teachers about the reading brain at work provides a conceptual foundation for such diagnosis and generation of instructional approaches.

2. Cross-Level Coordination

In Fuster's (1997) model, all behavior may be described on the basis of a hierarchial ordering of structured units of sensation and action that differ in whether they are coded in sensory or motor modalities or more abstract representations and must be coordinated with one another in a cross-level, bottom-up, top-down fashion. One implication of this hierarchical arrangement is that instructional treatment of written language disorders, like dyslexia and dysgraphia, may need to be aimed more broadly at cross-level, coordinated lower-order and higher-order processes in the hierarchy than is typical in the classic multisensory approach recommended for treating dyslexia. In fact, limiting intervention to multiple sensory codes may restrict rate of reading growth—students may benefit from instruction aimed at motor planning and language processing as well. That is why reading instruction should be aimed at all levels of language close in time in a temporally coordinated fashion (Berninger & Richard, 2002; Berninger & Abbott, 2003).

3. Timing

Minsky (1986), Fuster (1997), and Wolf (2001) make eloquent cases for the role of timing in managing complex mental activity, such as that required for reading. The implication of the importance of timing in orchestrating the various components of a reading brain at work is that more attention should be given to how instructional components are packaged in the classroom. All too often instructional services for students with learning disabilities are fragmented across the school day. For children with vulnerable working memories, which are temporally constrained, the way in which instruction is delivered within the lesson, within the school day, within the school week, and across the school year may influence whether they integrate instruction in a way that allows them to become readers, that is, to rely on a reading system of interconnected components that work together to support effortless accomplishment of reading goals at school and outside school.

4. Multiple Word Forms and Mapping Procedures

Brain imaging research has provided evidence for phonological word forms, orthographic word forms, and morphological word forms in the functional reading system. Reading instruction should, in developmentally appropriate ways, teach phonological, orthographic, and morphological awareness and ways to map interrelationships among the phonological, orthographic, and morphological word forms explicitly (see Berninger *et al.*, 2003; Berninger & Richards, 2002; Carlisle & Rice, in press; Wolf & Kennedy, 2002).

5. Articulatory Loop

Dyslexics may have a structural deficit in the neural architecture supporting the articulatory loop used in learning new words (see Section II). If so, additional research is needed on the most effective methods of teaching phonological decoding and oral reading and to students with dyslexia, given that they may have deficits in (a) the phonological word form storage system, (b) mapping phonology onto other word forms or their constituent units, (c) the phonological word analysis and production system, and/or (d) the executive control processes for managing procedures involving phonological codes or operations.

6. Executive Functions

In our instructional experience, dyslexics need considerable assistance in developing executive functions for self-regulating the learning process. They learn well when a knowledgeable teacher structures the learning environment, makes linguistic principles explicit, and monitors and other-regulates the instructional activities. They learn less well when left to navigate language learning with less explicit instruction and less one-to-one monitoring and other-regulation from teachers. Research is also needed to devise the most effective ways to assist dyslexics with the executive functions involved in language learning both in the general education environment and in the individual or small group tutorial.'

7. Working Memory for Goal-Related Activities

Reading instruction should be designed as optimally as possible for the working memory system. *Many components (linguistic awareness, word forms, the articulatory loop, executive functions, sentence- and text-level language processes, and reading goals) in a multilevel functional system with cross-level, bottom-up, top-down contingencies must be coordinated in time. That is, the Real Whole Language* (see Part III, Berninger & Richards, 2002). Using these instructional design principles, we were able to show significant differences between treatment and control groups in reading growth of first graders (Lesson Set 1), second graders (Lesson Set 6 and 9), and dyslexics

(Lesson Set 13); handwriting growth of first graders (Lesson Set 3); spelling growth of second graders (Lesson Set 4); spelling and composing growth of third graders (Lesson Set 7); handwriting, spelling, and composing growth of third graders (Lesson Set 8); composing growth of fourth graders (Lesson Set 10); maintenance of gains the following year and continued gains in reading (Lesson Set 2) or in spelling (Lesson Set 5); and reading growth for dyslexics who served as their own controls (Lesson Sets 11, 12, 14, and 15) (Berninger & Abbott, 2003).

C. Summary Thoughts on a Systems Approach

As is probably now evident, a systems approach poses many challenges for scientific research. Identifying a single causal mechanism is unlikely in a complex, multilayered system; seeking constraints at specific levels in the system is a more reasonable scientific goal (Berninger, 1994; Berninger & Richards, 2002). Scientists may have to settle for many small theories about different aspects of a system rather than a general theory that accounts for all aspects of a complex biological system designed to interact with a changing environment (Minsky, 1986). Moreover, as researchers are able to develop computational models to understand the nature of the specific kinds of computations performed by the various gyri and sulci referred to frequently throughout this chapter, they will probably have to alter radically their understanding of the processes contributing to the behaviors (Churchland, 1986). For example, the deficit in the fast visual system first documented by Eden *et al.* (1996), which has been replicated by several other groups, may point to a deficit in processing change across elements in a linear array in visual elements. While the rationale for a deficit in processing fast visual motion of arrows on a screen may not be readily apparent at the behavioral level, at a physiological level this task may tap the same processes that support readers' ability to deal with letter elements in a word that change more rapidly than word or lexical units do in written text. This ability to process sequential letters and spelling units in written words and written text poses challenges for many students with reading disabilities whose physiological deficits may interfere with orthographic processing of written text.

D. Closing Words for Skeptics and Critics

Among educational and psychological researchers, there are those who believe that instructional research and practice has managed well without knowing anything about the brain and there is no reason to turn to brain research now to inform either educational research or practice. At the same time, there are many general education and special education teachers who are eager to learn more about the brain in order to understand better the enormous individual differences they observe in children in their classrooms and to implement instructional practices that might help all children, even those with specific learning disabilities, to learn to read well. Apart from the fact that noneducators are astonished to find out that teachers, who are entrusted with the goal of nurturing the brain—the biological organ of learning—receive no instruction in the compositions and (structure and function) workings of the brain as part of teacher preparation, there are many other good reasons for sharing the wealth of research emerging from cognitive neuroscience with educators. One important reason is that if scientists do not take a leading role in this process, journalists, who love to tell stories, are happy to do so. Both journalists and teachers have intellectual curiosity about the brain and will continue to tell and consume good stories based on myth rather than scientific facts unless brain researchers take a more proactive role in getting the results of current cognitive neuroscience research to educators.

Before the technology of brain imaging was available and the Decade of the Brain produced a wealth of previously unavailable knowledge, it may have been tolerable for educational researchers and trainers of educational practitioners to question the relevance of brain research to understanding learning and learning disabilities. However, in the following decade, the burden of defense is on those educational researchers and trainers of educational professionals to explain why they would ignore this growing body of knowledge. It is a rapidly expanding knowledge base and will be revised from time to time, as is always the case in scientifically based information, but that is no excuse for ignoring it, even if it means that professionals will have to take time to learn a new field of knowledge. At the beginning of the twentieth century, B. F. Skinner rebelled against armchair philosophy that was not based on measurable data. He developed time-tested approaches to measuring human behavior apart from the default "black box" that intervenes between brain and behavior but was not measurable at that time. Now that the technology for measuring the intervening variable (which is no longer black and yields intriguing, colorful images) is available, I suspect that Skinner himself, if alive today, would advise these educational researchers and trainers to move on . . . and to embrace a new era in which advances are being made in understanding the interactions within brain systems and between brain systems and instructional environments. Hopefully, this burgeoning knowledge base will continually improve the educational services offered students with specific learning disabilities throughout the twenty-first century.

Acknowledgment

Grant Nos. HD25858-12 and P50 33812-07 from the National Institute of Child Health and Human Development (NICHD) supported the preparation of this chapter, the brain imaging and instructional research at the University of Washington, and the collaboration between the University of Florida and the University of Washington. The author thanks the current brain imaging team in the University of Washington Multidisciplinary Learning Disabilities Center (UWLDC) (Dr. Todd Richards, Principal Investigator; Dr. Elizabeth Aylward, Co-principal Investigator; Dr. Dietmar Cordes, Dr. Rajesh Nandy, Dr. Stephen Dager, Dr. Kenneth Maravilla, Anne Richards, Katherine Field, Aimee Grimme, Larissa Stanberry, and Dr. William Nagy), their collaborators at the University of Florida Gainesville (Drs. Christiana Leonard and Mark Eckert), and past members of the UWLDC (Drs. David Corina, Steven Cramer, and Sandra Serafini).

References

Aylward, E., Richards, T., Berninger, V., Nagy, W., Field, K., Grimme, A., Richards, A., Thomson, J., & Cramer, S. (2003). Instructional treatment associated with changes in brain activation in children with dyslexia. *Neurology*. **61,** 212–218.

Baddeley, A., Gathercole, S., & Papagno, C. (1998). The phonological loop as a language learning device. *Psychological Review*, **105,** 158–173.

Baker, J., Sanders, A., Maccotta, L., & Buckner, R. (2001). Neural correlates of verbal memory encoding during semantic and structural processing tasks. *NeuroReport*, **12,** 1251–1256.

Bartlett, C., Flax, J., Logue, M., Vieland, V., Bassett, A., Tallal, P., & Brzustowicz, L. (2002). A major susceptibility locus for specific language impairment is located on 13q21. *American Journal of Human Genetics*, **71,** 45–55.

Basso, A., Taborelli, A., & Vignolo, L. (1978). Dissociated disorders of speaking and writing in aphasia. *Journal of Neurology, Neurosurgery, and Psychiatry*, **41,** 556–563.

Beeman, M., & Chiarello, C. (1998). Complementary right- and left-hemisphere language comprehension. *Psychological Science*, **7,** 2–8.

Berninger, V. (1994). *Reading and writing acquisition: A developmental neuropsychological perspective.* Madison, WI: WBC Brown & Benchmark Publishing. Reprinted 1996, Westview Press, Boulder, CO.

Berninger, V. (1999). Coordinating transcription and text generation in working memory during composing: Automatized and constructive processes. *Learning Disability Quarterly*, **22,** 99–112.

Berninger, V. (2000). Development of language by hand and its connections to language by ear, mouth, and eye. *Topics in Language Disorders*, **20,** 65–84.

Berninger, V. (2001). Understanding the lexia in dyslexia. *Annals of Dyslexia*, **51,** 23–48.

Berninger, V. (in press). Understanding the graphia in dysgraphia. In D. Dewey & D. Tupper (Eds.), *Developmental motor disorders: A neuropsychological perspective* New York: Guilford.

Berninger, V., & Abbott, S. (2003). *PAL research-supported reading and writing lessons.* San Antonio, TX: The Psychological Corporation.

Berninger, V., & Hooper, S. (in press). A developmental neuropsychological perspective on writing disabilities in children and youth. In D. Molfese & V. Molfese (Eds.), *Handbook of child neuropsychology*. Mahweh, NJ: Lawrence Erlbaum.

Berninger, V., Nagy, W., Carlisle, J., Thomson, J., Hoffer, D., Abbott, S., Abbott, R., Richards, T., & Aylward, E. (in press). Effective treatment for dyslexics in grades 4 to 6. In B. Foorman (Eds.), *Preventing and remediating reading difficulties: Bringing science to scale*. Timonium, MD: York Press.

Berninger, V., O'Donnell, L. (in press). Research—Supported differential diagnosis of specific learning disabilities. In A. Prifitera, D. Saklofske, L. Weiss, & E. Rolfus (Eds.), *WISC-IV Clinical Use and Interpretation*. San Diego, CA: Academic Press.

Berninger, V., & Richards, T. (2002). *Brain literacy for educators and psychologists*. New York: Academic Press.

Binder, J., Frost, J., Hammeke, T., Bellogowan, P., Springer, J., Kaufman, J., & Possing, E. (2000). Human temporal lobe activation by speech and nonspeech sounds. *Cerebral Cortex*, **10**, 512–528.

Bishop, D. (2002). Viewpoint. Cerebellar abnormalities in developmental dyslexia: Causes, correlates, and consequences. *Cortex*, **38**, 491–498.

Booth, J., Burman, D., Meyer, J., Gitelman, D., Parrish, T., & Mesulam, M. (2002). Modality independence of word comprehension. *Human Brain Mapping*, **16**, 251–261.

Booth, J., Burman, D., Van Santen, F., Harasaki, Y., Gitelman, D., Parrish, T., & Mesulam, M. (2001). The development of specialized brain systems in reading and oral language. *Child Neuropsychology*, **7**, 119–141.

Booth, J., MacWhinney, B., Thulborn, K., Sacco, K., Voyvodic, J., & Feldman, H. (2000). Developmental and lesion effects in brain activation during sentence comprehension and mental rotation. *Developmental Neuropsychology*, **18**, 139–169.

Breznitz, Z. (2002). Asynchrony of visual–orthographic and auditory–phonological word recognition processes: An underlying factor in dyslexia. *Journal of Reading and Writing*, **15**, 15–42.

Brown, W., Menon, V., Rumsey, J., White, C., & Reiss, A. (2001). Preliminary evidence of widespread morphological variations of the brain in dyslexia. *Neurology*, **56**, 781–783.

Brown, C., & Hagoort, P. (Eds.) (1999). *The neurocognition of language*. New York: Oxford University Press.

Burton, M., Noll, D., & Small, S. (2001). The anatomy of auditory word processing: Individual variability. *Brain and Language*, **77**, 119–131.

Caplan, D. (2001). Functional neuroimaging studies of syntactic processing. *Journal of Psycholinguistic Research*, **30**, 297–320.

Carlisle, J., & Rice, M. (2002). *Improving reading comprehension. Research-based principles and practices*. Baltimore, MD: York Press, Inc.

Churchland, P. (1986). *Neurophilosophy. Toward a unified science of mind/brain*. Cambridge, MA: MIT Press.

Clark, D., & Wagner, A. (2003). Assembling and encoding word representations: fMRI subsequent memory effects implicate a role for phonological control. *Neuropsychologia*, **1503**, 1–14.

Cohen, L., Lehéricy, S., Chochon, F., Lemer, C., Rivaud, S., & Dehaene, S. (2002). Language-specific tuning of visual cortex? Functional properties of the Visual Word Form Area. *Brain*, **125**, 1054–1069.

Connolly, J., Service, E., D'Arcy, R., Kujala, A., & Alho, K. (2001). Phonological aspects of word recognition as revealed by high-resolution spatio-temporal brain mapping. *NeuroReport*, **12**, 237–243.

Cooke, A., Zurif, E., DeVita, C., Alsop, D., Koenig, P., Detre, J., Gee, J., Pinãngo, M., Balogh, J., & Grossman, M. (2001). Neural basis for sentence comprehension: Grammatical and short-term memory components. *Human Brain Mapping*, **15**, 80–94.

Cordes, D., Haughton, V., Arfanakis, K., Wendt, G., Turski, P., Moritz, C., Quigley, M., & Meyrand, E. (2000). Mapping functionally related regions of brain with functional connectivity MRI (fcMRI). *American Journal of Neuroradiology*, **21**, 1636–1644.

Corina, D., Richards, T., Serafini, S., Richards, A., Steury, K., Abbott, R., Echelard, D., Maravilla, K., & Berninger, V. (2001). fMRI auditory language differences between dyslexic and able reading children. *NeuroReport*, **12**, 1195–1201.

Dehane, S., Le Clec' H, G., Poline, J-B., Bihan, D., & Cohen, L. (2002). The visual word form area: A prelexical representation of visual words in the fusiform gyrus. *Brain Imaging*, **13**, 321–325.

Denckla, M. B. (1996). A theory and model of executive function. In G. R. Lyon & N. A. Krasnegor (Eds.), *Attention, memory, and executive function* (pp. 263–278). Baltimore, MD: Paul H. Brookes Publishing Co.

Dhond, R., Buckner, R., Dale, A., Marinkovic, K., & Halgren, E. (2001). Spatio-temporal maps of brain activity underlying word generation and their modification during repetition priming. *The Journal of Neuroscience*, **21**, 3564–3571.

Diamond, M., & Hopson, J. (1998). *Magic trees of mind. How to nurture your child's intelligence, creativity, and healthy emotions from birth through adolescence.* New York: Penguin Books.

Eckert, M., Leonard, C., Richards, T., Aylward, E., Thomson, J., & Berninger, V. (2003). *Anatomical correlates of dyslexia: Frontal and cerebellar findings Brain*, **126** (no. 2), 482–494.

Eden, G., Van Meter, J., Rumsey, J., Maisog, J., Woods, R., & Zeffiro, T. (1996). Abnormal processing of visual motion in dyslexia revealed by functional brain imaging. *Nature*, **382**, 66–69.

Eden, G., Wood, F., & Stein, J. (2003). Clock drawing in developmental dyslexia. *Journal of Learning Disabilities*, **36**, 216–228.

Exner, S. (1881). *Untersuchungen über die lokalisation der funktionen in der gross-shirnrinde des menschen.* Vienna, Austria: Wilhelm Braumuller.

Fan, J., Flombaum, J., McCandliss, B., Thomas, K., & Posner, M. (2003). Cognitive and brain consequences of conflict. *NeuroImage*, **18**, 42–57.

Fletcher, J., Lyon, G. R., Barnes, M., Stuebing, K., Francis, D., Olson, R., Shaywitz, S., & Shaywitz, B. (2002). Classification of learning disabilities: An evidence based evaluation. In R. Bradley, L. Danielson, & D. Hallahan (Eds.), *Identification of learning disabilities. Research to practice* (pp. 185–250). Mahweh, NJ: Lawrence Erlbaum.

Flynn, J., Deering, W., Goldstein, M., & Rahbar, M. (1992). Electrophysiological correlates of dyslexic subtypes. *Journal of Learning Disabilities*, **25**, 133–141.

Fried, F., Ojemann, G., & Fetz, E. (1981). Language related potentials specific to human language cortex. *Science*, **212**, 353–356.

Fu, C., Morgan, K., Suckling, J., Williams, S., Andrew, C., Vythelingum, G., & McClure, P. (2002). A functional magnetic resonance imaging study of over letter verbal fluency using a clustered acquisition sequence: Greater anterior cingulate activation with increased task demand. *NeuroImage*, **17**, 871–879.

Fuster, J. (1997). *The prefrontal cortex. Anatomy, physiology, and neuropsychology of the frontal lobe, 3rd ed.* (pp. 209–252).

Gaillard, W., Pugliese, M., Grandin, C., Braniecki, S., Kondapaneni, P., Hunter, K., Xu, B., Petrella, J., Balsamo, L., & Basso, G. (2001). Cortical localization of reading in normal children. An fMRI language study. *Neurology*, **57**, 47–54.

Garrett, A., Flowers, D. L., Absher, J., Fahey, R., Gage, H., Keyes, J., Porrino, L., & Wood, F. (2000). Cortical activity related to accuracy of letter recognition. *NeuroImage*, **11**, 111–123.

Georgiawa, P., Rzanny, R., Hopf, J., Knab, R., Glauche, V., Kaiser, W., & Blanz, B. (1999). fMRI during word processing in dyslexic and normal reading children. *NeuroReport*, **10**, 3459–3465.

Georgiawa, P., Rzanny, R., Gaser, C., *et al.* (2002). Phonological processing in dyslexic children: A study combining functional imaging and event related potentials. *Neuroscience Letters*, **318**, 5–8.

Goldman-Rakic, P., Scalaidhe, S., & Chafee, M. (2000). Domain specificity in cognitive systems. In M. S. Gazzaniga, M. (Ed.), *The new cognitive neurosciences* (pp. 733–742). Cambridge, MA: MIT Press.

Halgren, E., Dhond, R., Christensen, N., Van Petten, C., Marinkovic, K., Lewine, J., & Dale, A. (2002). N400-like magnetoencephalography responses modulated by semantic context, word frequency, and lexical class in sentences. *NeuroImage*, **17**, 1101–1116.

Harrison, H., & Minsky, M. (1992). *The Turing option.* New York: Warner Books.

Hashimoto, R., & Sakai, K. (2002). Specialization in the left prefrontal cortex in sentence comprehension. *Neuron*, **35**, 589–597.

Heim, S., Eulitz, C., & Elbert, T. (1999). Alternations in functional organization of the auditory cortex in children and adolescents with dyslexia. *NeuroImage*, **9**, S568.

Holland, S., Plante, E., Byars, A., Strawsburg, R., Schmithorst, V., & Ball, W. (2001). Normal fMRI brain activation patterns in children performing a verb generation task. *NeuroImage*, **14**, 837–843.

Humphreys, G., & Price, C. (2001). Cognitive neuropsychology and functional brain imaging: Implications for functional and anatomical models of cognition. *Acta Psychologia*, **107**, 119–153.

Hsu, L., Berninger, V., Thomson, J., Wijsman, E., & Raskind, W. (2002). Familial aggregation of dyslexia phenotypes: Paired correlated measures. *American Journal of Medical Genetics/Neuropsychiatric Section*, **114**, 471–478.

Ingvar, M., Trampe, P., Greitz, T., Erikkson, L., Stone-Elander, S., & von Eiler, C. (2002). Residual differences in language processing in compensated dyslexics revealed in simple word reading tasks. *Brain and Language*, **83**, 249–267.

Ivry, R., & Keele, S. (1989). Timing functions of the cerebellum. *Journal of Cognitive Neuroscience*, **1**, 136–152.

Jackson, J. H. (1887). Remarks on evolution and dissolution of the nervous system. *Medical Press and Circular ii*, **46,491**, 511, 586, 617. (Reprinted in James Taylor (Ed.), (1958). *Selected writings of Johns Hughlings Jackson*, Vol. 2, New York: Basic Books).

Jacobs, B., Schall, M., & Schiebel, A. (1993). A qualitative dendritic analysis of Wernicke's area in humans. II. Gender, hemispheric, and environmental factors. *The Journal of Comparative Neurology*, **327**, 97–111.

Kaan, E., & Swaab, T. (2002). The brain circuitry of syntactic comprehension. *Trends in Cognitive Sciences*, **6**, 350–356.

Kasai, K., Yamada, J., Kamio, S., Nakagome, K., Iwanami, A., Fukada, M., Itoh, K., Koshida, I., Yumoto, M., Iramina, K., Kato, N., & Ueno. S. (2001). Brain lateralization for mismatch response to across- and within-category change of vowels. *NeuroReport*, **12**, 2467–2471.

Keller, T., Carpenter, P., & Just, M. (2001). The neural basis of sentence comprehension: A fMRI investigation of syntactic and lexical processing. *Cerebral Cortex*, **11**, 223–237.

Kircher, T., Brammer, M., Andreu, N., Williams, S., & McGuire, P. (2001). Engagement of right temporal cortex during processing of linguistic context. *Neuropsychologia*, **39**, 798–809.

Lai, C., Fisher, S., Hurst, J., Vargha-Khaden, F., & Monaco, A. (2001). A forkhead-domain gene is mutated in a severe speech and language disorder. *Nature*, **413**, 519–555.

Leonard, C. (2001). Imaging brain structure in children. *Learning Disability Quarterly*, **24**, 158–176.

Liberman, A. (1999). The reading researcher and the reading teacher need the right theory of speech. *Scientific Studies of Reading*, **3**, 95–111.

Luria, A. R. (1962, Russian translation; 1980, English translation). *Higher cortical functions in man* (2nd ed.). New York: Basic Books.

Luria, A. R. (1973). *The working brain*. New York: Basic Books.

Matsuo, K., Kato, C., Ozawa, F., Takehara, Y., Isoda, H., Isogai, S., Moriya, T., Sakahara, H., Okada, T., & Nakai, T. (2001). Ideographic characters call for extra processing to correspond with phonemes. *NeuroReport*, **12**, 2227–2230.

Matsuo, K., Kato, C., Tanaka, S., Sugio, T., Matsuzawa, M., Inui, T., Moriya, T., Glover, G., & Nakai, T. (2001). Visual language and handwriting movement: Functional magnetic resonance imaging at 3 tesla during generation of ideographic characters. *Brain Research Bulletin*, **55**, 549–554.

Mazziotta, J., Grafton, S., & Woods, R. (1991). The human motor system studied with PET measurements of cerebral blood flow: Topography and motor learning. In N. Lassen, D. Ingvar, M. Raichle, & L. Friberg (Eds.), *Brain work and mental activity. Alfred Benzon Symposium*, **31**, 280–290.

McPherson, W., Ackerman, P., Holcomb, P., & Dykman, R. (1998). Event-related brain potentials elicited during phonological processing differentiate subgroups of reading disabled adolescents. *Brain and Language*, **62**, 163–185.

Mesulam, M. (1990). Large-scale neurocognitive networks and distributed processing for attention, language, and memory. *Annals Neurology*, **28**, 597–613.

Minsky, M. (1986). *The society of mind*. New York: Simon & Schuster.

Misra, M., Katzir, T., Wolf, M., & Poldrack, R. (in press). Neural systems for rapid automatized naming (RAN) in skilled readers: Unraveling the puzzle of RAN-reading relationship. *Brain and Language*.

Molfese, D. (2000). Predicting dyslexia at 8 years of age using neonatal brain responses. *Brain and Language*, **72**, 238–245.

Nagy, W., Diakidoy, I., & Anderson, R. (1993). The acquisition of morphology: Learning the contribution of suffixes to the meaning of derivatives. *Journal of Reading Behavior*, **25**, 155–170.

Nagy, W., Osborn, J., Winsor, P., & O'Flahavan, J. (1994). Structural analysis: Some guidelines for instruction. In F. Lehr & J. Osburn (Eds.), *Reading, language, and literacy* (pp. 45–58). Hillsdale, NJ: Erlbaum.

Nandy, R., Cordes, D., Berninger, V., Richards, T., Aylward, E., Stanberry, L., Richards, A., & Maravilla, K. (2003, June). *An fMI approach to the diagnosis of dyslexia using CCA and a phoneme mapping task*. New York: Human Brain Mapping.

Nicholson, R., Fawcett, A., Berry, E., Jenkins, I., Dean, P., & Brooks, D. (1999). Association of abnormal cerebellar activation with motor learning difficulties in dyslexic adults. *The Lancet*, **353**, 1662–1667.

Nobre, A., Allison, T., & McCarthy, G. (1994). Word recognition in the human inferior temporal lobe. *Nature*, **372**, 260–263.

Oakhill, J., Cain, K., & Yuill, N. (1998). Individual differences in children's comprehension skill: Towards an integrated model. In C. Hulme & M. Joshi (Eds.), *Reading and spelling: Development and disorder*. Mahwah, NJ: Erlbaum.

Ojemann, J., Buckner, R., Akbudak, E., Snyder, A., Olinger, J., McKinstry, R., Rosen, B., Petersen, S., Raichle, M., & Conturo, T. (1998). Functional MRI studies of word-stem completion: Reliability across laboratories and comparison to blood flow imaging with PET. *Human Brain Mapping*, **6**, 203–215.

Paulesu, E., Demonet, J., Fazio, F., McCrory, E., Chanoine, V., Brunswick, N., Cappa, S., Cossu, G., Habib, M., Frith, C., & Frith, U. (2001). Dyslexia: Cultural diversity and biological unity. *Science*, **291**, 2165–2167.

Paulesu, E., Frith, U., Snowling, M., Gallagher, A., Morton, J., Frackowiak, R., & Frith, C. (1996). Is developmental dyslexia a disconnection syndrome? Evidence from PET scanning. *Brain*, **119**, 143–157.

Piaget, J. (1970). Piaget's theory. In P. H. Mussen (Ed.). *Carmichael's manual of child psychology*, Vol. 1, 3rd ed. (pp. 703–732). New York: Wiley.

Poldrack, R., Temple, E., Protopapas, A., Nagarajan, S., Tallal, P., Merzenich, M., & Gabrieli, J. (2001). Relations between the neural bases of dynamic auditory processing and phonological processing: Evidence from fMRI. *Journal of Cognitive Neuroscience*, **13**, 687–697.

Polk, T., & Farah, M. (2002). Functional MRI evidence for an abstract, not perceptual, word form area. *Journal of Experimental Psychology: General*, **131**, 65–72.

Polk, T., Stallup, M., Aguirre, G., Alsop, D., Esposito, M., Detre, J., & Farrah, M. (2002). Neural specialization for letter recognition. *Journal of Cognitive Neuroscience*, **14**, 145–159.

Posner, M., Petersen, S., Fox, P., & Raichle, M. (1988). Localization of cognitive operations in the human brain. *Science*, **240**, 1627–1631.

Pugh, K., Mencl, W., Jenner, A., Katz, C., Frost, S., Lee, J., Shaywitz, S., & Shaywitz, B. (2000). Functional neuroimaging studies of reading and reading disability (developmental dyslexia). *Mental Retardation and Developmental Disabilities Research Review*, **6**, 207–213.

Pugh, K., Mencl, W., Shaywitz, B., Shaywitz, S., Fullbright, R., Constable, R., Skudlarski, P., Marchione, K., Jenner, A., Fletcher, J., Liberman, A., Shankweiler,

D., Katz, L., Lacadie, C., & Gore, J. (2000). The angular gyrus in developmental dyslexia: Task-specific differences in functional connectivity within posterior cortex. *Psychological Science*, **11**, 51–56.

Pugh, K., Rexer, K., & Katz, L. (1994). Evidence of flexible coding in visual word recognition. *Journal of Experimental Psychology: Human Perception and Performance*, **20**, 807–825.

Pulvermüller, F., Assadollahi, R., & Elbert, T. (2001). Short communication: Neuromagnetic evidence for early semantic access in word recognition. *European Journal of Neuroscience*, **13**, 201–205.

Raskind, W. (2001). Current understanding of the genetic basis of reading and spelling disability. *Learning Disability Quarterly*, **24**, 141–157.

Richards, T., Dager, S., Corina, D., Serafini, S., Heidel, A., Steury, K., Strauss, W., Hayes, C., Abbott, R., Kraft, S., Shaw, D., Posse, S., & Berninger, V. (1999). Dyslexic children have abnormal chemical brain activation during reading-related language tasks. *American Journal of Neuroradiology*, **20**, 1393–1398.

Richards, T., Berninger, V., Aylward, E., Richards, A., Thomson, J., Nagy, W., Carlisle, J., Dager, S., & Abbott, R. (2002). Reproducibility of proton MR spectroscopic imaging: Comparison of dyslexic and normal reading children and effects of treatment on brain lactate levels during language tasks. *American Journal of Neuroradiology*, **23**, 1678–1685.

Richards, T., Corina, D., Serafini, S., Steury, K., Dager, S., Marro, K., Abbott, R., Maravilla, K., & Gerninger, V. (2000). Effects of phonologically-driven treatment for dyslexia on lactate levels as measured by proton MRSI. *American Journal of Radiology*, **21**, 916–922.

Richards, T., Dager, S., Corina, D., Maravilla, K., & Berninger, V. (2004, submitted). *Combining functional MRI and functional MR spectroscopic imaging to understand the the lexical deficit in dyslexia.*

Robertson, D. (2000, Dec.). Functional neuroanatomy of narrative comprehension. *Dissertation-Abstracts-International: Section B—The Sciences and Engineering*, **61**, (5-B): 2793.

Robertson, D., Gernsbacher, M., Guidotti, S., Robertson, R., Irwin, W., Mock, B., & Campana, M. (2000). Functional neuroanatomy of the cognitive process of mapping during discourse comprehension. *Psychological Science*, **11**, 255–260.

Röder, B., Stock, O., Neville, H., Bien, S., & Rösler, F. (2002). Brain activation modulated by the comprehension of normal and pseudoword sentences of different processing demands: A functional magnetic resonance imaging study. *NeuroImage*, **15**, 1003–1014.

Rosenberger, P., & Rottenberg, D. (2002). Does training change the brain? *Neurology*, **58**, 1139–1140.

Rumsey, J., Andreason, P., Zametkin, A., Acquino, T., King, C., Hamburger, S., Pikus, A., Rappoport, J., & Cohen, R. (1992). Failure to activate left temporoparietal context in dyslexia. *Archives Neurology*, **49**, 527–534.

Sakai, K., Hikosaka, O., Miyauchi, S., Takino, R., Sasaki, Y., & Putz, B. (1998). Transition of brain activations from frontal to parietal areas in visuomotor sequence learning. *Journal of Neuroscience*, **18**, 1827–1840.

Schlaggar, B., Brown, T., Lugar, H., Vissher, K., Miezin, F., & Petersen, S. (2002). Functional neuroanatomical differences between adults and school-age children in the processing of single words. *Science*, **296**, 1476–1479.

Schulte-Körne, G., Deimel, W., Barling, J., & Remschmidt, H. (1998). Auditory processing and dyslexia: Evidence for a specific speech processing deficit. *NeuroReport*, **9**, 337–340.

Serafini, S., Steury, K., Richards, T., Corina, D., Abbott, R., & Berninger, V. (2001). Comparison of FMRI and FMR spectroscopic imaging during language processing in children. *Magnetic Resonance in Medicine*, **45**, 217–225.

Shaywitz, S. (2003). *Overcoming dyslexia*. New York: Alfred A. Knopf.

Shaywitz, S., & Shaywitz, B. (2003). Neurobiological indices of dyslexia. In H. L. Swanson, K. Harris, and S. Graham (Eds.), *Handbook of research on learning disabilities* (pp. 514–531). New York: Guilford.

Shaywitz, S., Shaywitz, B., Pugh, K., Fulbright, R., Constable, T., Mencl, W., Shankweiler, D., Liberman, A., Skudlarksi, P., Fletcher, J., Katz, L., Marchione, K., Lacadie, C., Gatenby, C., & Gore, J. (1998). Functional disruption in the organization of the brain for reading in dyslexia. *Proceedings of the National Academy of Science USA*. **95**, 2636–2641.

Shaywitz, B., Shaywitz, S., Pugh, K., Fulbright, R., Skudlarski, P., Menel, W., Constable, R. T., Marchione, K., Fletcher, J., Klorman, R., Lacadie, C., & Gore, J. (2001). The functional neural architecture of components of attention in language-processing tasks. *NeuroImage*, **13**, 601–612.

Shaywitz, B., Shaywitz, S., Pugh, K., Mencl, W., Fulbright, R., Skudlarski, P., Constable, T., Marchione, K., Fletcher, J., Lyon, R., & Gore, J. (2002). Disruption of posterior brain systems for reading in children with developmental dyslexia. *Biological Psychiatry*, **52**, 101–110.

Simos, P., Breier, J., Fletcher, J., Bergman, E., & Papanicolaou, A. (2000). Cerebral mechanisms involved in word reading in dyslexic children: A magnetic imaging approach. *Cerebral Cortex*, **10**, 809–816.

Simos, P., Breier, J., Fletcher, J., Foorman, B., Bergman, E., Fishback, K., & Papanicolaou, A. (2000). Brain activation profiles in dyslexic children during non-word reading. A magnetic source imaging study. *Neuroscience Letters*, **290**, 61–65.

Simos, P., Fletcher, J., Bergman, E., Breier, J., Foorman, B., Castillo, E., Davis, R., Fitzgerald, M., & Papanicolaou, A. (2002). Dyslexia—specific brain activation profile becomes normal following successful remedial training. *Neurology*, **58**, 1203–1213.

Simos, P., Fletcher, J., Foorman, B., Francis, D., Castillo, E., Davis, R., Fitzgerald, M., Mathes, P., Denton, C., & Papanicolaou, A. (in press). Brain activation profiles during the early stages of reading acquisition. *Journal of Child Neurology*.

The SLI Consortium (2002). A genomewide scan identifies two novel loci involved in specific language impairment. *American Journal of Human Genetics*, **70**, 384–398.

Sugishita, M., Takayama, Y., Shino, T., Yoshikawa, T., Takahashi, Y. (1996). Functional magnetic resonance imaging (fMRI) during mental writing with phonograms. *NeuroReport*, **7**, 1917–1921.

Swanson, H. L., & Siegel, L. (2001). Learning disabilities as a working memory deficit. *Issues in Education*, **7**, 1–48.

Tan, L., Liu, H., Perfetti, C., Spinks, J., Fox, P., & Gao, J. (2001). The neural system underlying Chinese logograph reading. *NeuroImage*, **13**, 836–846.

Temple, E., Deutsch, G., Poldrack, R., Miller, S., Tallal, P., Merzenrich, M., & Gabrielli, J. (2003). Neural deficits in children with dyslexia ameliorated by behavioral remediation: Evidence from functional MRI. *Proceedings of National Academy of Science USA*, **100**, 2860–2865.

Temple, E., Poldrack, R., Protopapas, A., Nagarajan, S., Salz, T., Tallal, P., Merzenich, M., & Gabrieli, J. (2000). Disruption of the neural response to rapidly transient acoustic stimuli in dyslexia: Evidence from fMRI. *Proceedings of the National Academy of Sciences, USA*, **97**, 12907–13912.

Temple, E., Poldrack, R., Salidis, J., Deutsch, G., Tallal, P., Merzenich, M., & Gabrieli, J. (2001). Disrupted neural responses to phonological and orthographic processing in dyslexic children: An fMRI study. *NeuroReport*, **12**, 299–307.

Thomson, J., & Raskind, W. (2003). Genetic influences on reading and writing disabilities. In H. L. Swanson, K. Harris, and S. Graham (Eds.), *Handbook of learning disabilities* (pp. 256–270). New York: Guilford.

Turkeltaub, P., Eden, G., Jones, K., & Zeffiro, T. (2002). Meta-analysis of the functional neuranatomy of single-word reading: Method and validation. *NeuroImage*, **16**, 765–780.

van Mier, H., Temple, L., Perlmutter, J., Raichle, M., & Petersen, S. (1998). Changes in brain activity during motor learning measured with PET: Effects of hand performance and practice. *Journal of Neurophysiology*, **80**, 2177–2199.

Vandenbergh, D. (2000). Techniques of molecular genetics. In M. Ernst & J. Rumsey (2000). *Functional neuroimaging in child psychiatry*. Cambridge, UK: Cambridge University Press.

Vernea, J., & Merory, J. (1975). Frontal agraphia (including a case report). *Proceedings of Australian Association of Neurology*, **12**, 93–99.

Wagner, Q., Paré-Blagoev, E. J., Clark, J., & Poldrack, R. (2001). Recovering meaning: Left prefrontal cortex guides controlled semantic retrieval. *Neuron*, **31**, 329–338.

Walla, P., Hufnagl, B., Lindinger, G., Imhof, H., Deecke, L., & Lang, W. (2001). Left temporal and tempoparietal brain activity depends on depth of word encoding: A magnetoencephalographic study in healthy young subjects. *NeuroImage*, **13**, 402–409.

Wernicke, C. (1874). *Der aphasische symptomenkomplex*. Brelau, Germany: Cohn & Weigert.

Wolf, M. (2001). Preface: Seven dimensions of time. *Dyslexia, fluency, and the brain* (pp. ix–xix). Timonium, MD: York Press.

Wolf, M., & Kennedy, R. (2002, December). How the origins of written language instruct us to teach: A response to Stephen Strauss. *Educational Researcher*.

Wood, A., Saling, M., Abbott, D., & Jackson, G. (2001). A neurocognitive account of frontal lobe involvement in orthographic lexical retrieval: An fMRI study. *NeuroImage*, **14**, 162–169.

Wood, F., & Flowers, L. (2000). Dyslexia: Conceptual issues and psychiatric comorbidity. In M. Ernst & J. Rumsey (2000). *Functional neuroimaging in child psychiatry*. Cambridge, UK: Cambridge University Press.

Zurowski, B., Gostomzyk, J., Grön, G., Weller, R., Schirrmeister, H., Neumeier, B., Spitzer, M., Reske, S., & Walter, H. (2002). Dissociating a common working memory network from different neural substrates of phonological and spatial stimulus processing. *NeuroImage*, **15**, 45–57.

Instructional Aspects of Learning Disabilities

Difficulties in Reading Comprehension for Students with Learning Disabilities

Lorraine Graham and Anne Bellert
University of New England

I. INTRODUCTION

The percentage of students identified with learning disabilities (LD) continues to increase. Currently, about 7% of the school-age population in North America are considered to have some form of learning disability (Gersten *et al.*, 2001). In Australia and New Zealand where the definition of LD is broader and includes students with various learning difficulties, at least 20% of school students are considered to have problems in academic areas. Of these students, 5% are considered to have specific learning disabilities in academic areas, most commonly, reading (Westwood & Graham, 2000).

Definitions of learning disabilities and learning difficulties vary and controversies over identification procedures, particularly the notion of a discrepancy between individuals' potential and their actual performance, persist (e.g., Fuchs & Fuchs, 1998). However, in broad terms, it is agreed that students with learning disabilities have significant and pervasive problems acquiring and using some combination of listening, speaking, reading, writing, reasoning, or mathematical skills due to underlying difficulties involving their use of language and manipulation of abstract concepts (e.g., Swanson & Hoskyn, 1998). These difficulties may be associated with

Learning about Learning Disabilities, Third Edition

attention and behavior problems. However, they are not considered to result from sight or hearing problems, intellectual disabilities, emotional disorders, or cultural differences. Of all the students who are identified as having learning disabilities, the vast majority experience problems in reading, not only in terms of decoding deficiencies but also in terms of their abilities to construct understandings and draw inferences (Carlisle, 1999; Tractenberg, 2002).

Reading comprehension is a necessary skill throughout schooling and a vital component of the successful transition to adult responsibilities. It is the complex outcome of the process of constructing meaning from print. Reading comprehension can be conceptualized as an interactive process requiring the dynamic combination of a reader's background knowledge with the information decoded from text. Successful comprehension requires students to coordinate many complex skills and to actively participate in their own learning. Students' success in comprehension is influenced by how interesting and relevant they find the text they are reading, their competencies in recognizing, decoding, and pronouncing words fluently and accurately, their awareness of the different purposes associated with reading, and facility with comprehension monitoring strategies (Gersten *et al.*, 2001; Swanson, 1999). The effective comprehension of printed material is also related to text-based factors, such as the structure and quality of texts, and the familiarity or complexity of the concepts presented and the vocabulary used (Raben *et al.*, 1999).

Various theories have been put forward to explain how comprehension occurs. The bottom-up model emphasizes the teaching of discrete skills that combine to result in meaning and comprehension. The top-down model advocates reading instruction that de-emphasizes skills and focuses instead on a holistic approach to reading connected text and the value of immersing children in a literate environment. Interactive models such as Rumelhart's (1976) combine both these theoretical approaches and characterize readers as active and strategic learners who are engaged in predicting, questioning, confirming, and self-correcting their interpretations of texts. In the interactive model, readers apply aspects of bottom-up or top-down processing as appropriate, depending on the type of comprehension breakdown experienced by the reader and whether the material being read is familiar or unfamiliar (Manzo & Manzo, 1993). Whatever the theoretical perspective that helps interpret a reader's actions, comprehension involves recognizing the words on the page (computer screen, television, billboard, or package) fluently and accurately, together with understanding and interpreting the ideas being conveyed in the context of the whole text and the individual's background knowledge.

In the first section of this chapter, we discuss the difficulties in reading comprehension commonly experienced by students with learning disabilities.

Because comprehending narrative texts requires some different strategies than comprehending factual texts, the next section of this chapter offers a synthesis of research findings related to effective instruction for improving students' understanding of these types of text. In the final part of the chapter, we present what we consider to be continuing dilemmas in reading research and promising future directions for addressing the comprehension difficulties faced by students with learning disabilities.

II. STUDENTS' DIFFICULTIES IN READING COMPREHENSION

Reading comprehension is an important academic skill. It underpins school learning and becomes increasingly important in all subject areas as students progress through the grades. Students with learning disabilities have more difficulty comprehending what they read than students without disabilities, even when differences in decoding skill are taken into account (Englert & Thomas, 1987; Taylor & Williams, 1983).

In general, students with learning disabilities experience poor comprehension due to their failure to read strategically and to spontaneously monitor their understanding while reading. Despite the volume of research on teaching comprehension strategies, instructing students with learning disabilities to use active and efficient reading strategies in a flexible and personalized way remains a challenge. Students with learning disabilities can experience comprehension problems because of difficulties in (a) using their background knowledge appropriately; (b) decoding and word recognition; (c) vocabulary knowledge; (d) fluency; (e) strategy use and metacognitive skills; and (f) in differentiating between common text structures. The next sections address, in turn, each of these difficulties that may be experienced by students with learning disabilities.

A. Appropriate Use of Background Knowledge

The appropriate use of background knowledge is a crucial element in extracting meaning from text. Current research indicates that students benefit most from activities that assess, activate, and develop their background knowledge before reading (e.g., Brownell & Walther-Thomas, 1999; Jitendra et al., 2000; Raben et al., 1999). Structured pre-reading activities serve to make the text accessible to students and enable them to remember what they have learned. Indeed, the activation of background knowledge can mean the difference between being able to understand and apply new concepts and confusion and lack of comprehension.

When students are not familiar with the topic of a text, they are likely to find the concepts presented in it difficult and confusing. For example, the ease of understanding and drawing an appropriate inference from the following pairs of sentences (Kintsch & Kennan, 1973) is quite dramatic.

1. The burning cigarette was carelessly discarded. The fire destroyed many acres of forest.
2. An abnormally low amount of hydrocele was found. The spermatic cord was quite dry.

Because the reader is likely to know the consequences of throwing a burning cigarette into dry bush land, comprehension of these sentences is almost assured. However, the words *hydrocele* and *spermatic cord* are not likely to be in the background knowledge of most readers. Therefore, the comprehension of the second pair of sentences is much more effortful and potentially unsuccessful.

As Rumelhart (1980) pointed out, background knowledge and comprehension interact in several ways. The reader may simply not have the background knowledge to link to the text. The more limited students' general knowledge and vocabulary skills are, the more difficulty they have in activating appropriate knowledge to assist in comprehending text. Alternatively, textual cues may not be recognized as clues to link to or activate the knowledge the reader already has, or comprehension failures can occur because the reader may construct an interpretation of the text that is not the one intended by the author.

Students with learning disabilities may experience difficulties in activating appropriate knowledge or in developing background knowledge when it is missing or uncertain. These students may have knowledge about a topic but they do not necessarily bring this known information to the experience of reading and comprehending (Paris *et al.*, 1983). Pre-reading activities such as brainstorming, developing a graphic organizer, questioning activities, and writing related to the topic can help activate knowledge. When students lack the background knowledge necessary to understand a particular text, decisions need to be made regarding what specific knowledge will be provided, how much time can be allocated for knowledge development activities, and what specific activities will best facilitate students' understanding. In general, the more students know about a topic, the more motivated they are to learn and the easier it is for them to integrate their background knowledge with text information, and to organize the new information in memory, available for later retrieval.

B. Decoding and Word Recognition

Decoding and word recognition skills are implicated in comprehension difficulties because they are related to the core deficit that is assumed to underlie learning disabilities. As Swanson (1999, p. 505) states, the assumption has emerged in recent years that students with learning disabilities have "specific processing deficits localized in phonological processing, particularly at the word-recognition level...(Shaywitz *et al.*, 1996; Seigel, 1992; Stanovich & Seigel, 1994)." This view is widely accepted because reading problems are so pervasive in students with learning disabilities and because of the large volume of research suggesting that phonological coding deficits underlie their reading difficulties, particularly in sight word recognition (Seigel, 1993). Although there is some evidence that other factors such as naming speed are also important in understanding the difficulties experienced by readers with learning disabilities (Wolf, 2002), phonological processing remains conceptualized as a core deficit at the heart of learning disabilities.

When students do not decode quickly and accurately, their available cognitive resources and limited working memory capacity are used for identifying words and not for constructing meaning at the sentence and text level. Some readers labor so much over decoding and word recognition that by the time they struggle to the end of a sentence, they have forgotten what happened at the beginning. Such effortful and inefficient decoding obviously affects students' comprehension and, as a consequence, their motivation to read. Some students must work so hard to decode text that they experience reading as neither engaging nor enjoyable.

Automatic decoding is an important component of Stanovich's (1980) interactive–compensatory model of reading. Stanovich illustrates his model by describing a poor reader who is deficient in word recognition skills. In order to make sense of text, this reader uses known words and guesses unknown words based on semantic and syntactic knowledge and other contextual clues. Stanovich concludes that compensating for poor decoding and word identification skills in this way is unlikely to lead to fluent and accurate reading. if beginning readers and those with learning disabilities are to become proficient readers, they must develop the ability to recognize words independent of context clues in a rapid and automatic fashion.

Competent readers' skills in context-free word recognition and effective phonological decoding combine to produce fluent reading (Carlisle & Rice, 2002). Rapid and accurate decoding seems a necessary, but not sufficient, condition for comprehension to occur. It reduces memory demands for word identification and releases limited working memory resources for the construction of meaning. However, this does not ensure that meaning will be constructed successfully. Students need to establish a bank of words they know instantly by sight so that they gain confidence and enjoyment from reading. Because students with learning disabilities can have memory difficulties and may forget words that they seemed to know the day before, systematic practice of word recognition skills and vocabulary development activities are of benefit (Westwood, 2001). The more frequently encountered and practiced words are, the more likely learners will remember them and use their stored knowledge when reading and comprehending connected text.

C. Vocabulary Knowledge

A lack of vocabulary knowledge or a mismatch between the reader's vocabulary and that of the text can also be a cause of reading comprehension difficulties. McCormick (1999) uses the following example to illustrate how the ease of comprehension is affected by an individual's knowledge of word meanings.

1. Apprehension of the semantic fields of morphological units is pivotal for deriving semantic content when reading. This seems to be consummately plausible and most preceptors' ripostes to this attestation would predictably be, "Inexorably so!"
2. Knowledge of word meanings is important for reading comprehension. This seems to be quite logical and most teachers' responses to this statement would be, "Of course!"

These contrasting paragraphs convey the same message but use very different vocabulary words to do so. Text that contains many unfamiliar words leads students to experience a high error rate in reading due to their inability to link text to their background knowledge, thus impacting their comprehension and contributing to a sense of frustration and loss of motivation. Birsh (1999) indicates that successful reading comprehension is closely related to an individual's oral language comprehension and vocabulary skills.

Perfetti (1984, p. 87) also notes that vocabulary differences make an important contribution to reading ability because "knowing word meanings enables the reader to assemble and integrate propositions" from text and make sense of what is read. When words are not known, readers' initial representations of text can be incomplete and the further integration of ideas becomes problematic. Just as a lack of vocabulary knowledge can hamper comprehension, so can a lack of knowledge of syntax and sentence structure related to the sequence of words in phrases and sentences. As a consequence, most students with learning disabilities benefit from explicit instruction regarding how various connecting and signal words, such as prepositions, can change the meaning of text and how pronouns relate to their referents.

D. Fluency Related to Reading Comprehension

Fluency related to reading is most often conceptualized in terms of speed and accuracy (Chard *et al.*, 2002). There seems to be an optimum rate of fluency that allows the smooth processing of information by the reader. Automaticity in reading through smooth effortless decoding and word identification frees cognitive capacity so that the reader's attention can be focused on meaning (Perfetti, 1977, 1985). Slow reading makes it difficult to retain information in working memory long enough for meaning to be constructed and restricts students to low levels of processing by focusing on letters and words rather than on concepts and how they link together. In contrast, reading that is too fast may result in the neglect of important detail in text.

Students with learning disabilities often struggle to read fluently (Meyer & Felton, 1999). Common problems are related to sight reading words, decoding words, and reading phases and sentences automatically and with meaning. Slow reading is debilitating because it prevents students thinking about the text while reading. Both rapid reading of high frequency words and the speedy application of decoding skills appear critical for optimal reading development (Chard *et al.*, 2002). As students with learning disabilities are so commonly dysfluent readers, Wolf (2000) and her colleagues (e.g., Bowers & Wolf, 1999) have put forward the double deficit hypothesis, which theorizes that students with learning disabilities have core difficulties in the naming speed of words as well as in the phonological processing of letters and sounds. The implication of this thoroughly researched and increasingly influential hypothesis is that students who are able to decode need ample opportunities to practice reading connected text in order to become fluent readers. As students become fast and accurate readers, they often take more delight in reading and may even begin to reverse the consequences of lack of reading practice, which Stanovich (1986) has termed the Matthew Effects.

Stanovich (1986) describes how students with learning disabilities experience delayed phonological awareness and subsequent difficulty in attaining automaticity of decoding and word recognition. Because laborious decoding is a drain on cognitive resources, poor comprehension follows and students become mired in low-level processing. As able readers continue to develop their reading proficiency, they tend to read more and develop the benefits of extended practice opportunities as well as exposure to new words and ideas. In contrast, students who encounter difficulties with reading are generally less inclined to read. As a result, students with learning disabilities practice reading skills significantly less than their peers and the cycle of Matthew Effects in reading, which Stanovich (1986) characterizes as "the rich get richer and the poor get poorer," continues. As students progress through school, the gap between able and struggling readers widens.

Interestingly, interventions focused on enhancing reading fluency may have the potential to reverse Matthew Effects over time. A study conducted by Graham *et al.* (2001) indicated that an emphasis on word recognition, repeated reading, and students' strategy use resulted in improved measures of speed and accuracy, as well as in gains on standardized vocabulary and comprehension tests. In addition, students maintained their improvement in fluency up to one year after the completion of the intervention (Pegg *et al.*, 2002). During the intervention, students made comments such as "I didn't know I could read like that. I sound just like the good kids!", indicating increased confidence and enjoyment of reading. The implication of this finding is that providing opportunities for repeated readings and the motivated practice of word recognition skills improves students' automaticity of word recognition and reading fluency and this frees cognitive resources to focus on comprehension of text. The essential change here is a shift in cognition from a concentration on lower levels of processing, such as decoding letters and words, to processing higher-order aspects of text, such as conceptual understandings and inferred meaning.

Stanovich (1986) used a biblical passage (Matthew 25:29) to illustrate the effects of lack of practice on readers. Similarly, increasing fluency through interventions that emphasize word recognition and repeated readings may have effects on readers akin to that described in the Wisdom of Solomon (16:11), "For they were pricked, that they should remember thy words; and were quickly saved, that not falling into deep forgetfulness, they might be continually mindful of thy goodness." Overall, it appears that fluency is a critical but neglected factor in many reading programs (Kamenui & Simmons, 2001). Accurate decoding is not enough; readers need to remember words and read quickly if they are to understand the connections between ideas in print and "not fall into deep forgetfulness."

E. Strategy Use and Metacognition

An area of focus in comprehension research is strategy instruction and metacognition, which is concerned with students' awareness of their own thinking and their ability to regulate strategy use while working to comprehend printed material. It is important for students to monitor their own comprehension and to take steps to regain clarity of understanding when meaning breaks down or becomes confused. Comprehension strategies can explicitly teach students how to draw inferences from text, summarize information, predict what will happen next in a narrative, formulate and answer questions about text, and visualize what they read in order to improve comprehension (see Table I).

Table I

Metacognitive Strategies for Making Meaning during Reading

Inferring	Questioning	Clarifying	Predicting	Visualizing
"But the answer is not there!" How to find an unstated answer in a text:	**Readers generate questions and respond through self-talk or "think alouds"**	**Clarify when an unknown word is encountered**	**Make a prediction when**	**Encourage students to create a picture in their minds**
• Join information together (synthesize)	• Who is ___?	• Sound the word out. Is it at all familiar?	• Headings are provided	• Describe the picture
• Try to make a reasonable guess (draw a conclusion) based on the information at hand	• What is/does ___? • When is ___? • Where is ___?	• Use context clues to help work out the meaning	• The author asks a question in the text	• How does the picture change over time?
	• Why is ___ important?	• Look for a definition elsewhere in the text	• The text suggests what will be discussed next	• What events or information cause the picture to change?
• Make connections, generalize from specific text to real life experiences	• Why does ___ happen? • What are the parts of ___?	• Look for word roots or other word parts that may be familiar	• A previous prediction is confirmed or confounded	**Explore imaginings and emotional responses**
• Read between the lines to detect an underlying message	• How is ___ an example of ___?	• Consider the need to use a dictionary or glossary – now or later?	• A nuance or implication is detected	• When I read this, I imagine . . .
	• How do ___ and ___ compare?	• Ask someone	**Predict outcomes and themes**	• As I read in my mind, I see . . .
• Relate cause and effect; apply reason when facts are not specifically stated	• How are ___ and ___ different?	**Clarify when meaning is unclear**	• Adjust and change predictions, anticipate endings	• Reading this reminds me of . . .
• Recognize and explore supporting details	• How does ___ happen? • What is most important, ___ or ___?	• Read ahead to see if the text makes sense anyway	• Where does the narrative seem to be heading?	• This makes me feel like . . .
• Make comparisons	• What is my opinion of ___?	• Reread the section that is confusing	• Is the factual text true to topic or form? Is there an underlying message?	**Develop a graphic organizer to illustrate cause and effect or to explore relationships**
• Sense motives		• Change pace of reading, slow down to get more clues, speed up to get "the big picture"	• What is the purpose of this part of the text?	• Concept maps
• Make judgments about characters, relationships, validity of the text	• How many subheadings are there?	• Reconsider original predictions	• How does this relate to the main idea of the text?	• Grids, tables, charts, graphs, etc.
• Infer information from visual cues including layout	• Does this section finish soon?	• Evaluate material being read—is it accurate, is it biased?	*Predicting content and outcomes is an important pre-reading activity but successful comprehension requires readers to continue to make and adjust predictions during reading as well.*	• Venn diagrams
• Monitor text structure; detect the main idea in each section	• What will the next section be about?	• Ask someone		• Sociograms
Infer—to conclude by reasoning from evidence; to deduce, to imply	*Peer modeling of self-questioning during reading is a powerful means of demonstrating this strategy to students with LD.*	*Students with LD may need cues and prompts to ask for clarification (e.g., "What I don't understand is . . ." or "This is the part that's confusing me . . .").*		• Theme charts *Students with LD often need visual representation of information to reinforce spoken or written sources.*

In light of findings from research investigating students' metacognition and strategy use, conceptions of the nature of learning disabilities have changed. Although the notion of an underlying processing difficulty still stands, in terms of strategy use, the present view is that inefficiencies rather than deficiencies characterize the difficulties experienced by students with learning disabilities (Gersten et al., 2001). These students could possess the strategies necessary to approach the comprehension of text in a planned and strategic way but may fail to use them at the appropriate time or may apply these strategies in an inefficient or incomplete manner.

The primary function of reading is extracting meaning from text. If children do not notice that comprehension has broken down, they will fail to take steps to fix whatever the problem is. Students need to monitor the success and failure of their attempts to construct meaning from text in order to be strategic and successful readers. Comprehension monitoring is key in the development of this kind of independent and self-regulated reading for meaning. While some reading tasks, such as following directions, are more likely to elicit comprehension monitoring than other reading situations, comprehension monitoring is important in processing all types of text. In fact, recent comprehensive syntheses literature indicates that instruction focused on comprehension monitoring and strategy training is one of the most effective instructional techniques for students with learning disabilities (Forness, 1997; Gersten et al., 2000, Swanson, 1999).

Given the complexity of effective strategy use and the necessity of developing a repertoire of strategies appropriate for different purposes, it is essential that instruction be specific, long-term, and directly address issues of transfer and generalization of strategies to other reading tasks. Instruction in reading comprehension strategies appears to be most effective when it aims to increase metacognitive skills (Chan & Cole, 1986; Graves, 1986; Malone & Mastropieri, 1992), includes ample opportunities for practice (Pressley et al., 1989), and attributes success to effort and strategy use (Borkowski et al., 1988; Schunk & Rice, 1992). An important general finding in many strategy training studies has been that students are more successful and more likely to transfer strategy use to new situations when the strategic procedure includes self-monitoring questions (Graves, 1986; Malone & Mastropieri, 1992; Wong & Jones, 1982).

Many effective strategies direct students to reread or look back in the text if they cannot respond confidently to the questions that they learn to ask themselves. Simply rereading and returning to the text in a random way, however, does not help students with learning disabilities improve their comprehension; rather, these students have to learn to reread strategically. For example, Graham and Wong (1993) compared self-instructional training to the more traditional teaching of a question–answer relationship strategy. Their results indicated that instructing students with learning disabilities to ask themselves three focus questions as a strategy to guide rereading was more effective and resulted in better maintenance of learning.

The three self-monitoring questions used in this study were: (1) How will I answer this question? *(Select a strategic approach)* (2) What kind of question is this? *(literal, inferential, or creative)*, and (3) Is my answer correct? *(Justify or prove the answer)*. The 3H strategy, displayed in Figure 7–1 has been successfully used by students in Canada and Australia as a self-instruction strategy to guide rereading and answering questions.

Likewise, Swanson's (1999) meta-analysis of reading research related to students with learning disabilities assembles convincing evidence to show that such strategies are beneficial to students with learning disabilities. Gersten *et al.* (2001) in their review of teaching reading comprehension strategies also conclude that many of the strategic inefficiencies experienced by students with learning disabilities can be ameliorated and that instruction can significantly improve their strategic processing. Strategy instruction, combined with direct instructional techniques, appears to yield the highest effect sizes, indicating the most positive influence on students' reading comprehension performance.

1. Head First!

Before reading	What do I know?
During reading	What don't I understand?
After reading	What do I need to find out?

Ask for help if you need to.
Content?
Vocabulary?
How to?

Use the 3Hs to remind you where the answers to questions are found:

2. HERE In one sentence from the passage.

3. HIDDEN Join together. The answer is in two or more parts of the passage. Or the answer comes from joining together information from the passage and information that you already know.

4. In my HEAD Use what you already know to answer the question. Just you or the passage and you.

5. Check Your Answers. Reread each question and your answer to see if they fit together. How confident are you of your answer? After you have finished all the questions, return to any answers you are not sure of. Go through the 3H strategy and check these answers again. You should have a reason for each of your answers. You do? Well done!

Figure 7–1 The 3H Strategy for Answering Comprehension Questions after a Passage.

F. Differentiating between Common Text Structures

Research during the 1980s established that students with learning disabilities have difficulty recognizing many task demands related to comprehension activities, including how to differentiate between, and strategically approach, different types of text (e.g., Englert & Thomas, 1987; Taylor & Samuels, 1983; Wong & Wilson, 1984). Students with learning disabilities tend to be unsure of the characteristics of common narrative and factual texts, and consequently experience difficulties using their knowledge of text structures and recognition of the different purposes of texts as an aid to comprehension. As more narratives tend to be used in schools, general comprehension strategies were initially taught to suit these story-oriented texts. In recent times, however, increased awareness that specific strategies apply more to one text type than another has meant that differentiating among types of text has become increasingly important.

Students in today's schools encounter a variety of texts such as poems, plays, stories, novels, essays, reports, descriptions, and textbook expositions that are presented through traditional and electronic media. The two most common of these text structures are narrative and factual. With experience, most students gradually develop awareness of the different structures used in written texts; however, it is particularly important that teachers facilitate this awareness for students with learning disabilities. These students tend to be delayed in their comprehension of the different text structures used in factual or informational texts (Weisberg & Balajthy, 1989) and in their awareness of the basic elements of narratives (Montague et al., 1990).

The elements of a narrative are organized into what can be described as "story grammars," consisting of setting, characters, events, and eventual outcome. Students typically develop an awareness of the story grammar appropriate to narrative text (e.g., fiction, fairy tales, myths, fiction, fables, plays, and legends) as they listen to and read stories during their early years of life. Students who struggle with reading, however, are slower to develop a sense of the importance of elements such as main characters, setting, the problem, the complication, and the resolution of a plot. This is evident from the stories that these students tell and their comprehension of those they read. For example, Montague et al. (1990) gave students, with and without learning disabilities, tasks that required the students to retell and write stories. They found that students with learning disabilities did not perform as well as their peers did in terms of amount and type of information included in their recounts and written stories. Compared to their peers, students with learning disabilities demonstrated less developed understanding of the conventions of a narrative.

In contrast to narrative texts, the purpose of factual writing is to impart new information and develop students' general knowledge about the world and natural phenomena. Factual texts use one or more patterns of text structure, such as cause and effect, problem and solution, temporal sequencing, enumeration, or comparison and contrast (Anderson & Armbruster, 1984). Factual or expository text structure can also include embedded definitions, explanations of technical processes, and procedural sequences, as well as labeled diagrams, graphs, and charts that need to be "read" and interpreted.

In the same way that awareness of the conventions of narratives affects student's comprehension, awareness of structures used in factual texts affects students' understanding and recall. For example, Taylor and Samuels (1983) investigated how students' awareness of text structure impacts on their comprehension by comparing recall of well-organized passages with that of passages consisting of randomly ordered sentences. They found that the fifth and sixth grade students who were aware of text structure recalled more from the well-organized passages. The students who were less aware of text structure, however, performed in a similar way on both the randomly ordered and the well-organized passages. In this and other related research, students with learning disabilities seemed unaware of their inability to comprehend and used no strategies to monitor their understanding of text (Englert & Thomas, 1987; Taylor & Williams, 1983).

Gersten et al.'s (2001) review of reading comprehension research presents the following three major research findings related to students' awareness of text structure and their comprehension of factual texts. From the literature, it appears (1) that awareness of text structure increases developmentally (Brown & Smiley, 1977), (2) that some text structures are more obvious and easier to recognize than others (Englert & Hiebert, 1984), and (3) that skill at discerning text structures, and then using knowledge about them appropriately, is an important factor in comprehending factual text (Taylor & Beach, 1984; Taylor & Samuels, 1983). Acquiring an awareness of text structure seems particularly important for readers with learning disabilities. It appears to foster an appreciation of the organizational factors that underlie factual texts and provides a way for students to remember new information. The strategy of analyzing the structure of texts may also lead to more active processing and a greater effort on the part of students to understand and remember what is read (Carlisle & Rice, 2002). While an awareness of text structure is not likely to address all the problems associated with understanding different types of texts that are experienced by students with learning disabilities, it is clearly likely to enhance the coherence of students' comprehension.

G. Summary of Students' Difficulties in Reading Comprehension

Students with learning disabilities can experience comprehension problems for a range of reasons which can generally be conceptualized as a lack of mastery of the component knowledge and skills that make up effective reading comprehension. For students with learning disabilities, reading comprehension problems often feature difficulties in recognizing and appropriately applying background knowledge, poor decoding and word recognition skills, limited vocabulary knowledge, underdeveloped reading fluency, a less than strategic approach to comprehension, including the use of ineffective or inefficient strategies, and limited understandings about common text structures. Frequently, these reasons do not operate independently of one another; rather, there exists a reciprocal causation between the component skills of reading comprehension, resulting in potentially complex and debilitating reading comprehension problems. Nonetheless, students' difficulties with reading comprehension can be ameliorated by focused and effective instruction.

Swanson's (1999, p. 522) meta-analysis indicated that the most important instructional components associated with improvements in reading comprehension were:

1. *Directed response questioning*, which included the teacher directing students to ask questions, the teacher and students engaging in dialogue, and/or the teacher asking questions.
2. *Controlling the difficulty of the processing demands of tasks* so that activities were generally short, with the level of difficulty controlled, the tasks appropriately sequenced, and the teacher providing necessary assistance through demonstration.
3. *Elaboration*, which occurred when additional or redundant explanations were made about the concepts, procedures, or steps in a strategy.
4. *Modeling by the teacher of steps* so that the teacher demonstrated the processes that the students were to follow.
5. *Small group instruction*, either with students and a teacher or between students.
6. *Strategy cues* that included reminders to use strategy steps, the teacher verbalizing the procedures, and the use of "think aloud" models with the teacher presenting the benefits of strategy use and its applicability to certain reading situations.

Obviously, there is no quick fix to difficulties with reading comprehension for students with learning difficulties. However, well-considered instruction delivered over an extended period of time, and integrated across the curriculum, will support students to improve and develop their skills and enable them to better participate in learning at school and in the wide variety of "real life" experiences that require effective and efficient reading comprehension.

III. EFFECTIVE READING COMPREHENSION INSTRUCTION

Before discussion of the role of specific strategies in improving the comprehension of narrative and factual texts, general approaches to implementing effective instructional interventions for students with learning disabilities will be outlined. This is an important area to address because considerable progress has been made in designing, implementing, and evaluating effective interventions that target these students' performance difficulties in academic areas (e.g., Vaughn *et al.*, 2000).

For instance, one of the prevailing criticisms of special education for students with learning disabilities is "its overemphasis on the 'basics' with the exclusion of any creative or cognitively complex activities," which consequently limits these students to a sparse intellectual diet (Gersten, 1998, p. 163). This type of instruction reflects the belief that the development of basic skills precedes any complex cognitive activity. Swanson's (1999) meta-analysis of reading research, however, suggests that providing many practice opportunities can actually minimize the difficulties experienced by students with learning disabilities, as long as the practice takes place in small, interactive groups and is accompanied by direct questioning and careful control of the difficulty level of tasks.

Similarly, Vaughn *et al.*'s (2000) meta-analysis, which examined the components of interventions associated with high effect sizes, found that the strongest impact on students' learning came from interactive, small-group instruction coupled with controlled task difficulty which, together, ensured students' success. Vaughn and her colleagues (2000) also found that effective interventions focused on key learning areas and used a style of "direct response teaching" which is interactive and invites dialogue between the teacher and students, and among peers, through posing questions and encouraging students to think aloud about text.

In their analysis of reading comprehension research for students with learning disabilities, Mastropieri *et al.* (1996) also concluded that self-questioning strategies had a positive impact on students' learning. Similarly, Gersten *et al.* (2001) in their review categorized effective strategy interventions as either "comprehension monitoring" or "text structuring." In both these types of studies, students were taught to generate questions and to think aloud about what they read before, during, and after they interact with text. Table II presents some of the self-questions students can ask as they work towards constructing and clarifying the meaning of a passage.

To summarize, in effective reading comprehension interventions, students are encouraged to articulate their thoughts while teachers provide feedback or ask follow-up questions based on the students' responses to text. This interactive dialogue accelerates the comprehension process and moves students with learning disabilities toward the ultimate goal of the internalization of more sophisticated thinking skills that can be used appropriately as they read. The role of the teacher is to explicitly teach students how to apply appropriate strategies. This instruction should be overt and should include

Table II

Self-Questions Asked Before, During and After Reading

Before reading	During reading	After reading
What will this text be about? Make predictions based on the cover, title, context of book, prior info about the author, etc.	*What is important information?* Underline important parts of the passage in order to remember where important information is.	*Can I retell the story or restate the main points in my own words?* Summarize and self-question.
What do I already know about this topic? Relate and explore in terms of background knowledge. Make connections.	*Where does the information fit into my graphic organizer?* Formulate an ongoing graphic overview. Consider relationships and connections to what I already know.	*What connections does this text have with my life and background knowledge?* Make links with what I already know.
What don't I understand about this text? Skim to identify any words that may be difficult. Clarify their meanings.	*What is the author going to say next?* Make predictions based on your reading so far.	*What do I need to find out?* Skimming for a date or name, and looking for a key word or a particular phrase, involves knowing about text structure and layout
What type of text is this? Getting a grip on text structure can help me understand the purpose of the text and know what to expect from it.	*What will I do if I encounter an unfamiliar word or if I realize I don't understand what I have read?* Apply "fix-up" strategies:	*How will I answer comprehension questions after a passage?* Use a strategy like the 3H Strategy. The answers are either Here, Hidden, or in my Head.
What type of graphic organizer would be appropriate for this text? Concept map, matrix, cause and effect diagram, numbered steps, etc.	- Sound out the word. Have I heard it before? - Read ahead. - Reread the section that is confusing me. - Vary my pace of reading to better enable comprehension (slow down) or fluency (speed up) - Ask someone to help.	*How can I remember information from the passage?* Complete the graphic overview

multiple opportunities for students to practice under quality feedback conditions with the teacher or with able peers before they use strategies on their own. Students should also be taught that there are some instances where strategies are only somewhat useful and other situations where strategies do not fit particular passages. Interactive dialogue is an essential component of strategy instruction. It provides ongoing and systematic feedback to assist students in understanding what they read.

A. Improving Students' Comprehension of Narrative Text

Proficient readers set their own purposes for reading, engage in active questioning, and understand when to reread or apply other fix-up strategies. As we have already discussed, students with learning disabilities can be taught these strategic ways of approaching comprehension tasks. Strategic readers make decisions based on their purposes for reading. For example, if reading for pleasure, they can approach the task in any manner, including reading as fast or as slowly as desired and even skipping over sections of the text. However, if students are reading to learn, they need to use effective strategies that will vary depending on whether the text is narrative or expository. In general terms, strategic readers start by thinking about what they are going to read and then use the sort of self-questions and fix-up strategies already outlined in Table II.

Although this discussion of the strategies appropriate to different text structures is separated into narrative and factual sections, in actuality, many of the instructional procedures that facilitate comprehension of narratives can also ease the interpretation of factual texts and vice versa. There are some special features of each type of text, however, that merit separate consideration. Graesser et al. (1991) suggest that several characteristics of narratives make them easier to comprehend than factual texts, mainly because the topics covered and the organizational strategies used in narratives tend to be more familiar than those employed in, for instance, textbooks. Table III contains a range of strategies that specifically support students' comprehension of narrative texts.

Question–Answer Relationships and Reciprocal Teaching are two general comprehension strategies that can be applied to narrative texts. While strategic readers attempt to visualize the action of the story and ask themselves questions focusing on narrative elements (such as setting, characters, and motives, the main events of the plot, the problem presented in the story, and its resolution), students with learning disabilities are generally not so active in processing text. Question–Answer Relationships (QARs), then, are useful in reminding teachers and students of the variety of questions that can be asked about any text. QARs focus on three particular types of comprehension questions that can be asked after reading. These are text-explicit questions

Table III

Strategies that Support Students' Comprehension of Narrative Texts

Types of text	Strategy
• *Stories*	Focus on descriptive passages featuring noun groups, adjectives, and adverbs that illustrate characters and settings.
• *Drama*	
• *Poetry*	Develop understandings about story grammar. Explain how narratives are typically structured in terms of orientation, complication, and resolution.
• *Fairy tales*	
• *Myths*	Develop appropriate graphic organizers. For example:
• *Fables*	• sociograms to plot understandings about characters and relationships
• *Legends*	• storymaps to clarify the sequence of events.
	Look for nuances, hints of future events, and the implications of happenings. These are often key clues to what will happen in the narrative.
	Identify main characters and secondary characters. Consider their roles. Explore the relationships between characters.
	Consider, explore, and visualize the setting. Relate it to the characters.
	Derive meaning from figurative language. Deconstruct similes, metaphors, and descriptions.
	Verbalize and reflect on "the movie in your head" (i.e., students' visualization of the narrative). How and why does it change as the text is read?
	Identify temporal words that connect happenings to clarify the sequence of events.
	Retell or recount the text using "who, what, when, where, why" questions as a guide.

that are answered using literal information from one sentence in the passage, text-implicit or inferential questions, and script-implicit questions that rely on students' background knowledge. The 3H strategy, depicted in Figure 7–1, is an example of a QAR strategy. Question–Answer Relationship strategy instruction requires a considerable amount of teacher modeling and collaborative work if students are to understand different question types and their importance to effective comprehension processing.

Another strategy that also encourages students to "relate information in the text to their own experiences" (Au, 1999) is reciprocal teaching. In this strategy, the adult and students take turns assuming the role of teacher (Palincsar, 1986). Using a reciprocal teaching framework, the teacher and students interact by predicting, questioning, summarizing, and clarifying information from text. When students predict what will happen or what information the author wants them to understand from what they are about to read, they are activating their background knowledge. They also learn to use the structure of the text to help them make defensible predictions. Students are, therefore, using and consolidating their knowledge of the structure of text when engaged in reciprocal teaching activities.

The questioning part of the reciprocal teaching strategy, which can also be incorporated into the 3H strategy, provides students with opportunities to identify the kind of information that is the basis of a good question, to frame their own questions (whether Here, Hidden, or in my Head), and then engage in asking themselves and their peers what their answers might be. In this way, reciprocal teaching empowers students and gives them agency in what and how they learn. It also allows students to practice identifying important information in a passage.

In a similar way, reciprocal teaching fosters summarizing skills. Summarizing is a difficult task for students with learning disabilities. They find it difficult to condense information and to determine which parts of a text are important and which can be omitted without losing key concepts. Teaching summarizing requires much modeling and practice before students with learning disabilities experience independent success.

Clarifying is the final aspect of the reciprocal teaching strategy. This section encourages students to preview difficult vocabulary in a passage and gives them practice at implementing fix-up strategies to address comprehension breakdowns. This strategic approach to comprehension monitoring is of particular importance to students with learning disabilities who are likely to have a history of comprehension difficulties. Once students are taught in a structured and direct way to clarify their understanding of text through rereading, reading ahead, using pictures or structural clues, and asking for help, the conditions are set for them to read meaningfully and to engage thoughtfully with both narrative and factual texts.

B. Improving Students' Comprehension of Expository Text

Compared to narrative texts, many students find factual texts less familiar and less engaging (Gersten *et al.*, 2001). Because factual texts are written to communicate information, they are more likely to incorporate a greater variety of text structures (e.g., analysis, cause and effect, classification, comparison and contrast, definition, description, enumeration, identification, illustration, problem and solution, and sequence) and, therefore, to require the use of multiple comprehension strategies. Table IV presents a number of strategies that specifically support students' comprehension of factual texts. This section will specifically describe the utility of graphic organizers, the KWL strategy, and SQ3R in supporting students' effective comprehension of factual texts.

The use of graphic organizers is a general strategic approach to teaching reading comprehension that is particularly applicable to factual texts because they can alert students to the organization of the passage, the central concepts, and the relationships among the ideas presented in the text. Graphic organizers are also known as semantic maps, semantic webs, concept maps, frames, or thematic maps. In essence, graphic organizers are representations of what has been read. They can take various forms, such as a Venn diagram

Table IV

Strategies that Support Students' Comprehension of Factual Texts

Types of text	Strategies
• *Reports* • *Arguments* • *Procedures* • *Descriptions* • *Explanation* • *Response* • *Discussion* • *Recounts* • *Personal responses*	Build up knowledge of text types in order to understand the social purposes of text and identify important organizational structures & features. Focus on keywords, technical terms, and their synonyms. This key strategy requires development of vocabulary skills. "Read" charts, graphs, pictures, headings, and other graphics. Use graphic organizers. Concept maps, definition maps, flow charts, and structured overviews are all useful organizers for factual texts. Make judgments and be critical. For example: Is this an argument or an information report? Is this a realistic procedure? How concrete are these "facts"? Develop skills in skimming, scanning, and summarizing for understanding text organization and for locating information. Use contents, glossary, indexes, dictionary, and other sources to gather information and clarify vocabulary knowledge.

of similarities and differences between two countries described in a magazine article, a matrix which organizes attributes of different minerals along two or more dimensions, or a flowchart marking the events of a significant period of history. Graphic organizers not only help to make text comprehensible, but they also assist in the memorization, storage, and analysis of information. As well, they can encourage students to engage in critical thinking activities and improve recall of factual information. Graphic organizers are particularly helpful to students who have limited vocabulary knowledge because they can serve as mental maps that allow students to draw and visualize the complex relationships between concepts in any content area.

Another frequently used strategy for understanding factual text is the K-W-L method. This strategy is based on research that emphasizes the importance of activating students' background knowledge in order to assist them in constructing meaning from purposeful reading (e.g., Anderson, 1977; Slater, 1989; Steffensen, 1978). This strategy makes use of a chart divided into three categories:

What we already know (K)   What we want to learn (W)
What we learned (L)

After the teacher introduces the topic in a general way, students are instructed to complete the first column of the chart. The teacher then leads a class discussion on what students think they already know about the topic and writes down every response the students offer. No judgment about the validity of responses is made at this time. After the brainstorming session is complete, the teacher elicits and lists comments from students about what they want to find out about the chosen topic. At the completion of the activity, students can direct the teacher to cross out the things they thought they knew but which proved inaccurate during their exploration of the topic. During the time set aside to record what was learned, students can clarify vocabulary, categorize new knowledge, and reflect on the amount of learning that has occurred (Ogle, 1989).

SQ3R (Survey, Question, Read, Recite (or Record), Review) is a well-known study method (Robinson, 1961) that helps students work actively with content material. The process provides a systematic format for reading that helps students interact with the text by asking questions and then looking for answers. The steps of this strategy are:

1. *Survey.* Students examine the titles, headings, subheadings, captions, charts, and diagrams to get the "big picture."
2. *Question.* Formulate questions for each title, heading, subheading, caption, chart, or diagram.
3. *Read.* Students read and make notes about each section in order to answer the questions formulated from reading the titles, headings, subheadings, captions, charts, or diagrams.
4. *Record.* After reading the selection, students attempt to answer the questions without looking back at the material.
5. *Review.* Students reread to verify answers and to make sure they have understood the main points of the text.

As the students become more proficient at using SQ3R, they formulate their own questions and guide their own study of text. The time students spend practicing and being guided to learn this strategy benefits them when they begin to use this strategic approach independently. Carlisle and Rice (2002) note, however, that, "Although SQ3R is often advocated as a useful comprehension strategy for poor readers, research on the technique over the years, most of which involved college students, has yielded mixed results." (p. 197) Indeed, most of the studies investigating this technique have focused on normally achieving students, not those with learning difficulties. It is clear from the current research on comprehension strategy instruction, however, that students with learning disabilities need modeling and explicit instruction to master the prerequisites of strategic reading, such as *how* to formulate good questions and *how* to locate the main idea of a passage. Such instruction must accompany strategies like SQ3R if they are to be of maximum use to students with comprehension difficulties.

Researchers from the University of Kansas developed a strategy called MULTIPASS, based on SQ3R (Schumaker *et al.*, 1982), which takes into account the particular needs of students with learning disabilities. In this strategy, readers are taught to make several purposeful "passes" over a passage from a textbook. The innovation Deshler, Schumaker, and team made in developing this strategy and many others appropriate to content-area reading was not so much in the technique itself but in the teaching method they used. Students experienced instruction that was very explicit and intense, and practiced on materials of controlled difficulty before applying the strategy to grade-appropriate textbook passages. Under these conditions, there was clear improvement in comprehension for adolescents with learning disabilities. These findings suggest that, for students with learning disabilities, strategy instruction needs to be systematic and sustained over time, with many opportunities to practice and extend the use of strategies to a variety of reading situations.

In summary, explicit instruction is an essential feature of effective interventions that aim to improve the comprehension of both narrative and factual texts for students with learning disabilities. The elements of appropriate strategies should be identified and demonstrated to students using examples and providing models of strategy use and interactive dialogue. Ample opportunities for teachers to provide formative feedback and to shape students' practice and habit of using comprehension strategies are necessary.

IV. FUTURE DIRECTIONS

Although strategy instruction for students with learning disabilities has undoubtedly been successful in improving reading comprehension performance, considerable work still remains in order to explore how students come to "own" and to modify, over time, the strategies they are taught. Importantly, future research will also need to grapple with how strategy instruction can be incorporated into schools and classrooms to better support students with learning disabilities. Unless these challenges related to understanding and implementing comprehension strategy research are met, the situation described by Trent *et al.* (1998, p. 303) will continue, that is, "Children who have always learned despite our paradigmatic shifts, structural reforms, and policy changes will continue to learn, and the children who have always failed will continue to fail. We must strive to do better."

Because students with learning disabilities perform at a level considerably below that of their age peers on academic tasks, it is vital to make full use of valuable learning time. Yet, little is known about how to get students to "own" their strategies, personalize them, and apply them spontaneously to new contexts. Further research into these issues is necessary because, as Garner (1986) points out, the changes that students make to strategies after an intervention do not always work in their favor. Alterations and modifications to strategies, as well as the ways students personalize strategies, need to be monitored to ensure that students' strategic plans remain effective.

Comprehension instruction for students with learning disabilities appears to be most effective when it is explicit and intensive and also attends to some of the basic elements of academic skill, such as speed of reading and decoding words (Chard *et al.*, 2002). In striving to better understand students' reading comprehension strategy use though, it will also be necessary to investigate the importance of the control of task difficulty and its underlying relationship to students' task persistence and motivation. The various organizers and strategies that assist students with learning difficulties to actively comprehend narrative and factual texts may help them understand the purposes of comprehension and critical literacy in relation to their own life goals and sense of agency in the world. Students with learning disabilities need to be motivated to persist, and may persist longer in what can be for them the arduous task of comprehension, when they take an active role in learning.

While the instructional adaptations that meet the needs of students with learning disabilities may benefit others in a regular classroom setting, the dilemma of providing the intensity of instruction required by this population remains. The small group and explicit nature of the effective instructional approaches identified by recent meta-analyses seems at odds with moves toward the inclusion of all students in the regular classroom, in-class models of support for learning difficulties, and the lack of success students with learning disabilities can experience in resource room pull-out reading programs. Schumm *et al.*'s (2000) finding that appropriate and successful interventions are an effective means of improving the self-concepts of elementary school children further highlights the importance of small-group instruction. Although comprehension strategies designed for students with learning disabilities may benefit all learners, their use in the regular classroom belies the intensity of instruction that is necessary to make a lasting change to the comprehension performance of individuals with learning disabilities.

The implementation of procedures for the spread of information about comprehension strategies requires a great deal of coordination and cooperation between researchers, school system personnel, principals, teachers, and parents. For example, it is important to consider the impact of classroom factors, such as classroom goal structure, the view of knowledge and intelligence held by teachers and students, and students' attributional patterns on strategy use (Borkowski *et al.*, 1989; Garner, 1987). As Palincsar and David (1992) observed, successful classroom interventions must take into account

"(1) the culture of the classroom; (2) the place of the intervention in the total curriculum; and (3) the match between the instructional goals of the research and the outcomes to which assessment systems hold teachers and children accountable." (p. 77) As such, whether strategy instruction is effective or not is subject to a myriad of classroom factors, and, in addition, must fit closely with current models of special education service delivery.

Unless the challenge of incorporating strategy instruction productively into school systems is met, we will continue to experience the situation where "many of the instructional practices that have the most potential to make a meaningful difference for students with LD and other poor readers are seldom employed" (Carlisle & Rice, 2002). Whole-class undifferentiated instruction still seems to be the norm in both regular classrooms (Schumm et al., 2000) and resource settings (Moody et al., 2000). Gersten et al. (1997) found that when strategy instruction is used in schools, the quality of instruction can be poor and implementation erratic, with essential elements, such as the fostering of active participation from students with learning disabilities, omitted. It is clear that we must strive to do better. Children need well-designed instruction in comprehension in order to reach the levels of reading achievement necessary to meet the demands of life in our increasingly technologically oriented society. Researchers and teachers must work together to foster critical thinking, motivation, and comprehension competence for all.

What better testimony to the possibilities of effective strategy instruction than the comments of a student who learned a reading comprehension strategy during a successful intervention:

> Before I couldn't answer very many questions. Only one like, "What's the title?" or something like that. I couldn't do any of the others. It was hard for me to understand. I didn't know what the heck to do. I was scared of it. I *know* what to do now!

References

Anderson, R. C. (1977). *Schema-directed processes in language comprehension* (Tech. Rep. No 50). Urbana-Champaign, IL: University of Illinois, Centre for the Study of Reading.

Anderson, T. H., & Armbruster, B. B. (1984). Content area textbooks. In R. C. Anderson, J. Osborne, & R. J. Tierney (eds.), *Learning to read in American schools* (pp. 193–226). Hillsdale, NJ: Erlbaum.

Au, K. H. (1999). A multicultural perspective on policies for improving literacy achievement: Equity and excellence. In M. L. Kamil, P. B. Mosenthal, P. D. Pearson, & R. Barr (eds.), *Handbook of reading research* (Vol. 111, pp. 835–851). Mahwah, NJ: Erlbaum.

Birsh, J. R. (1999). *Multisensory teaching of basic language skills.* Baltimore, MD: Paul H. Brookes.

Borkowski, J. G., Estrada, M. M., & Hale, C. A. (1989). General problem-solving skills: Relations between metacognition and strategic processing. *Learning Disability Quarterly*, **12**, 57–70.

Borkowski, J. G., Weyhing, R. S., & Carr, M. (1988). Effects of attributional retraining on strategy-based reading comprehension in learning disabled students. *Journal of Educational Psychology*, **80**, 46–53.

Bowers, P. G., & Wolf, M. (1999). Theoretical links between naming speed, precise timing mechanisms, and orthographic skill in dyslexia. *Reading and Writing: An Interdisciplinary Journal*, **5**, 69–85.

Brown, A. L., & Palincsar, A. S. (1987). Reciprocal teaching of comprehension strategies: A natural history of one program for enhancing learning. In J. Borkowski & J. D. Day (eds.), *Intelligence and cognition in special children: Comparative studies of giftedness, mental retardation, and learning disabilities.* New York: Ablex.

Brown, A. L., & Smiley, S. S. (1977). Rating the importance of structural units of pose passages: A problem of metacognitive development. *Child Development*, **48**, 1–8.

Brownell, M. T., & Walther-Thomas, C. (1999). An interview with Dr. Marilyn Friend. *Intervention in School and Clinic*, **37**(4), 223–228.

Carlisle, J. F. (1999). Free recall as a test of reading comprehension for students with learning disabilities. *Learning Disabilities Quarterly*, **22**, 11–22.

Carlisle, J. F., & Rice, M. S. (2002). *Improving reading comprehension: Research-based principles and practices.* Baltimore, MD: York Press.

Chan, L. K. S., & Cole, P. G. (1986). The effects of comprehension monitoring training on the reading competence of learning disabled and regular class students. *Remedial and Special Education*, **7**, 33–40.

Chard, D. J., Vaughn, S., & Tyler, B. (2002). A synthesis of research on effective interventions for building reading fluency with elementary students with learning disabilities. *Journal of Learning Disabilities*, **35**(5), 386–406.

Englert, C. S., & Hiebert, E. H. (1984). Children's developing awareness of text structures in expository materials. *Journal of Educational Psychology*, **76**, 65–75.

Englert, C. S., & Thomas, C. C. (1987). Sensitivity to text structure in reading and writing: A comparison between learning disabled and non-learning disabled students. *Learning Disability Quarterly*, **10**(2), 93–105.

Forness, S. (1997). Mega-analysis of meta-analyses: What works in special education services. *Teaching Exceptional Children*, **29**(6), 4–9.

Fuchs, L. S., & Fuchs, D. (1998). Treatment validity: A unifying concept for reconceptualizing the identification of learning disabilities. *Learning Disabilities Research and Practice*, **13**, 204–219.

Garner, R. (1987). *Metacognition and reading comprehension.* Norwood, NJ: Ablex.

Garner, R. (1986). Children's knowledge of structural properties of expository text. *Journal of Educational Psychology*, **78**(6), 411–416.

Gersten, R. (1998). Recent advances in instructional research for students with learning disabilities: An overview. *Learning Disabilities Research and Practice*, **13**, 162–170.

Gersten, R., Fuchs, L. S., Williams, J. P., & Baker, S. (2001). Teaching reading comprehension strategies to students with learning disabilities: A review of research. *Review of Educational Research*, **71**(2), 279–320.

Gersten, R., Vaughn, S., Deshler, D., & Schiller, E. (1997). What we know about using research findings: Implications for improving special education practice. *Journal of Learning Disabilities*, **30**, 466–476.

Graesser, A. C., Golding, G. T., and Long, V. B. (1991). *Advances in discourse processes: Structures and procedures of implicit knowledge*. Norwood, NJ: Ablex.

Graham, L., & Wong, B. Y. L. (1993). Comparing two modes in teaching a question-answering strategy for enhancing reading comprehension: Didactic and self-instructional training. *Journal of Learning Disabilities*, **26**(4), 270–279.

Graham, L., Bellert, A. M., & Pegg, J. E. (2001). *Enhancing the automaticity of basic academic skills for middle school students*. Paper presented at the annual meeting of the Australian Association of Special Education, October, Melbourne, Australia.

Graves, A. W. (1986). Effects of direct instruction and metacomprehension training on finding main ideas. *Learning Disabilities Research*, **1**(2), 90–100.

Jitendra, A. K., Hoppes, M. K., & Xin, Y. P. (2000). Enhancing main idea comprehension for students with learning problems: The role of summarization strategy and self-monitoring instruction. *Journal of Special Education*, **34**, 127–139.

Kamenui, E. J., & Simmons, D. C. (2001). Introduction to this special issue: The DNA of reading fluency. *Scientific Studies of Reading*, **5**, 203–210.

Kintsch, W., & Kennan, J. M. (1973). Reading rate and retention as a function of the number of propositions in the base structure of sentences. *Cognitive Psychology*, **5**, 257–279.

Malone, L. D., & Mastropieri, M. A. (1992). Reading comprehension instruction: Summarization and self-monitoring training for students with learning disabilities. *Exceptional Children*, **58**, 270–279.

Manzo, A. V., & Manzo, U. C. (1993). *Literacy disorders: Holistic diagnosis and remediation*. Fort Worth, TX: Harcourt Brace Jovanovich.

Mastropieri, M. A., Scruggs, T. E., Bakken, J. P., & Whedon, C. (1996). Reading comprehension: A synthesis of research in learning disabilities. In *Advances in learning and behavioural disabilities*, T. E. Scruggs & M. A. Mastropieri (eds.), Vol. 10, pp. 201–223. Greenwich, CT: JAI Press.

McCormick, S. (1999). *Instructing students who have literacy problems*. New Jersey: Prentice-Hall.

Meyer, M. S., & Felton, R. H. (1999). Repeated reading to enhance fluency: Approaches and new directions. *Annals of Dyslexia*, **49**, 283–306.

Montague, M., Maddux, C. D., & Dereshiwsky, M. I. (1990). Story grammar and comprehension and production of narrative prose by students with learning disabilities. *Journal of Learning Disabilities*, **23**, 190–197.

Moody, S. W., Vaughn, S., Hughes, M. T., & Fischer, M. (2000). Reading instruction in the resource room: Set up for failure. *Exceptional Children*, **66**, 305–316.

Ogle, D. M. (1989). K-W-L: A teaching model that develops active reading of expository text. *The Reading Teacher*, **39**, 564–570.

Palincsar, A. M., & Brown, A. L. (1984). Reciprocal teaching of comprehension-fostering and comprehension-monitoring activities. *Cognition & Instruction*, **1**, 117–175.

Palincsar, A. M., & Brown, A. L. (1986). Interactive teaching to promote independent learning from text. *Reading Teacher*, **39**(8), 771–777.

Palincsar, A. S., & David, Y. M. (1992). Classroom-based literacy instruction: The development of one program of intervention research. In B. Y. L. Wong (ed.), *Contemporary intervention research in learning disabilities: An international perspective* (pp. 65–80). New York: Springer-Verlag.

Paris, S. G., Lipson, M. Y., & Wixson, K. K. (1983). Becoming a strategic reader. *Contemporary Educational Psychology*, **8**, 293–316.

Pegg, J. E., Graham, L. J., & Bellert, A. M. (2002). An analysis of long-term effects of an intervention program designed for low-achieving middle-school students. Paper presented at the Annual Meeting of the International Psychology in Mathematics Association, July, Honolulu, Hawaii.

Perfetti, C. A. (1977). Language comprehension and fast decoding: Some psycholinguistic prerequisites for skilled reading comprehension. In J. T. Guthries (ed.), *Cognition, curriculum, and comprehension* (pp. 20–41). Newark, DE: International Reading Association.

Perfetti, C. A. (1984). Some reflections on learning and not learning to read. *Remedial and Special Education*, **5**(3), 34–38.

Perfetti, C. A. (1985). *Reading ability*. New York: Oxford University Press.

Pressley, M., Goodchild, F., Fleet, J., Zajchowski, R., & Evans, E. D. (1989). The challenges of classroom strategy instruction. *Elementary School Journal*, **89**, 301–342.

Raben, K., Darch, C., & Eaves, R. C. (1999). The differential effects of two systematic reading comprehension approaches with students with learning disabilities. *Journal of Learning Disabilities*, **32**(1), 36–47.

Robinson, H. M. (1961). The major aspects of reading. In H. A. Robinson (ed.), *Reading: Seventy-five years of progress*. Chicago: University of Chicago Press.

Rumelhart, D. E. (1980). Schemata: The building blocks of cognition. In R. J. Spiro, B. C. Bruce, & W. F. Brewer (eds). *Theoretical issues in reading comprehension* (pp. 33–58). New Jersey: Lawrence Erlbaum.

Rumelhart, D. E. (1976). Toward an interactive model of reading. In S. Dornic (Ed.), *Attention and performance* (Vol. VI, pp573–603). Hillsdale, NJ: Erlbaum.

Schumaker, J. B., Deshler, D., Alley, G. Warner, L., & Denton, T. (1982). Multipass: A learning strategy for improving reading comprehension. *Learning Disabilities Quarterly*, **5**(3), 295–304.

Schumm, J. S., Moody, S. W., & Vaughan, S. (2000). Grouping for reading instruction. Does one size fit all? *Journal of Learning Disabilities*, **33**(5), 477–488.

Schunk, D. H., & Rice, J. M. (1992). Verbalization of comprehension strategies: Effects on children's achievement outcomes. *Human Learning*, **4**(1), 1–10.

Seigel, L. S. (1992). An evaluation of the discrepancy definition of dyslexia. *Journal of Learning Disabilities*, **25**, 618–629.

Seigel, L. S. (1993). The cognitive basis of dyslexia. In M. Howe & R. Pasnak (eds.), *Emerging themes in cognitive development* (pp. 33–52). New York: Springer Verlag.

Shaywitz, B. A., Stuebing, J. M. Shaywitz, S. E., & Fletcher, J. (1996). Intelligent testing and the discrepancy model for students with learning disabilities. *Learning Disabilities Research and Practice*, **13**(4), 295–304.

Slater, M. D. (1989). *Messages as experimental stimuli: Design, analysis, and inference.* Paper presented at the annual meeting of the Association for Education in Journalism and Mass Communication, August, Washington, DC.

Stanovich, K. E. (1980). Toward an interactive-compensatory model of individual differences in the development of reading fluency. *Reading Research Quarterly*, **16**, 32–71.

Stanovich, K. E. (1986). Cognitive processes and the reading problems of learning disabled children: Evaluating the assumption of specificity. In J. K. Torgesen & B. Y. L. Wong (eds.), *Psychological and educational perspectives on learning disabilities* (pp. 87–131). Orlando, FL: Academic Press.

Stanovich, K. E. (1986). Matthew effects on reading: Some consequences of individual differences in the acquisition of literacy. *Reading Research Quarterly*, **21**, 360–407.

Stanovich, K. E., & Seigel, L. S. (1994). Phenotypic performance profile of children with reading disabilities: A regression-based test of the phonological-core variable difference model. *Journal of Educational Psychology*, **86**, 24–53.

Steffensen, M. S. (1978). Satisfying inquisitive adults: Some simple methods of answering yes/no questions. *Journal of Child Language*, **5**(2), 221–236.

Swanson, H. L. (1999). Reading research for students with LD: A meta-analysis of intervention outcomes. *Journal of Learning Disabilities*, **32**(6), 503–534.

Swanson, H. L., & Hoskyn, M. (1998). Experimental intervention research on students with learning disabilities: A meta-analysis of treatment outcomes. *Review of Educational Research*, **68**, 277–321.

Taylor, B. M., & Beach, R. W. (1984). The effects of text structure instruction on middle grade students' comprehension and production of expository text. *Reading Research Quarterly*, **19**, 134–146.

Taylor, B. M., & Samuels, S. J. (1983). Children's use of text structure in recall of expository material. *American Educational Research Journal*, **20**, 517–528.

Taylor, M. B., & Williams, J. P. (1983). Comprehension of learning-disabled readers: Task and text variations. *Journal of Educational Psychology*, **75**, 743–751.

Tractenberg, R. E. (2002). Exploring hypotheses about phonological awareness, memory, and reading achievement. *Journal of Learning Disabilities*, **35**(5), 407–424.

Trent, S. C., Artiles, A. J., & Englert, C. S. (1998). From deficit thinking to social constructivism: A review of theory, research, and practice in special education. *Review of Educational Research*, **23**, 277–307.

Vaughn, S., Gersten, R., & Chard, D. J. (2000). The underlying message in LD intervention research: Findings from research syntheses. *Exceptional Children*, **67**(1), 99–114.

Weisberg, R., & Balajthy, E. (1989). Improving disabled readers' summarization and recognition of expository text structure. In N. D. Padak, T. V. Rasinski, & J. Logan (eds.), *Challenges in reading* (pp. 141–151). Provo, UT: College Reading Association.

Westwood, P. (2001). *Reading and literacy difficulties: Approaches to teaching and assessment.* Victoria, Australia: ACER.

Westwood, P., & Graham, L. (2000). How many children with special needs in regular classes: Official predictions vs teachers' perceptions in South Australia and New South Wales. *Australian Journal of Learning Disabilities*, **5**(3), 24–35.

Wolf, M., & Bowers, P. (2000). "The double-deficit hypothesis" for the developmental dyslexias. *Journal of Educational Psychology*, **91**(3), 1–24.

Wolf, M. (1996). "The double-deficit hypothesis for the developmental dyslexias." Paper presented at the meeting of the Orton Dyslexia Society, Boston, MA.

Wolf, M. (2002). The second deficit: An investigation of the independence of phonological and naming speed deficits in developmental dyslexia. *Reading and Writing: An Interdisciplinary Journal*, **15**(2), 43–72.

Wong, B. Y. L., & Jones, W. (1982). Increasing meta-comprehension in learning disabled and normally achieving students through self-questioning training. *Learning Disability Quarterly*, **5**(2), 228–238.

Wong, B. Y. L., & Wilson, M. (1984). Investigating awareness of and teaching passage organization in learning disabled children. *Journal of Learning Disabilities*, **17**, 477–482.

CHAPTER 8

Writing Instruction

Steve Graham,[*] Karen R. Harris,[*]
and Charles MacArthur[†]

[*]University of Maryland
[†]University of Delaware

INTRODUCTION

This chapter reviews what is known about teaching writing to students with learning disabilities (LD). First, we establish why the mastery of writing is so important for these students. Second, the processes involved in effective writing, as well as how students with LD write, are examined. Third, specific instructional recommendations for teaching writing to students with LD are presented. These recommendations are based on our current understanding of the writing process and the needs of students with LD. Whenever possible, recommendations are based on empirically validated procedures. We did not limit our discussion just to evidence-based practices, however. Promising practices are emphasized as well.

I. WRITING IS CRITICAL TO CHILDREN'S SUCCESS IN SCHOOL AND BEYOND

More than 5000 years ago, the Sumerians devised the first known system of writing, called cuneiform (Diamond, 1999). Using a wedge-shape reed stylus, they made impressions on a moist clay tablet. This allowed them to keep track of various goods, such as amounts of grains and numbers of sheep. From this humble beginning, the application of writing has undergone an

Learning about Learning Disabilities, Third Edition
281

incredible metamorphosis, becoming one of the most influential inventions of all time.

One contribution of writing is that it lets us communicate with others who are removed by distance or time. This allows us to maintain personal links with family, friends, and colleagues even when we are unable to be with them. Writing connects more than just our immediate circle of associates and loved ones, however. It can also foster and preserve a sense of heritage and purpose among larger groups of people. For instance, the Chinese promoted a sense of national unity by adopting a standard system of writing in the third century B.C. (Swedlow, 1999).

Another contribution of writing is that it provides a flexible tool for persuading others. This was demonstrated by an employee who solved an irritating problem at work (Hines, 2000). She replaced an ineffective sign, "Alarm Will Sound If Door Opened," with the sign, "Wet Paint," which produced the desired effect of keeping people from going out the emergency exit.

Writing's power further resides in its ability to convey knowledge and ideas (Diamond, 1999). Writing makes it possible to gather, preserve, and transmit information widely, with great detail and accuracy. As a result, writing is integrated into virtually all aspects of our society. Order is maintained through a series of written and codified laws. Job seekers must complete one or more written applications and are likely to use manuals and other print material to learn new occupational skills. Scientists and other academics share their findings and ideas in journals and on the Web. Even everyday tasks, such as cooking a microwave dinner or paying a bill, involve following written directions.

Although writing was once the province of the elite and the clergy, this is no longer the case. Over 5 billion people now write (Swerdlow, 1999), 85% of the world's population. People who do not write are at a disadvantage in today's world. They lose a valuable tool for communication, learning, and self-expression. Poor writing skills also restrict opportunities for employment and further education.

Mastery of writing is also critical to school success. One of the most common uses of writing in educational settings involves evaluation (Graham, 1982). Writing is the major means by which students demonstrate their knowledge in school, and the primary instrument that teachers use to evaluate academic performance.

Writing is further used as a tool for gathering, remembering, and sharing subject matter (Durst & Newell, 1989). One of the primary purposes of note-taking, for instance, is to help students cull and organize the most significant information from lectures or text, so that it will be available for later review and study. Writing a summary serves a similar purpose, as the student must consolidate the available information to reflect the basic essence or gist of the discourse (Hidi & Anderson, 1986). The process of deciding what to include and eliminate, what integration of ideas makes sense, and what restructuring (if any) is necessary makes the summarized information more memorable.

An additional contribution of writing is embodied in E.M. Forster's observation, "How can I know what I think until I see what I say" (Burnham, 1994). His quote acknowledges that writing provides a useful instrument for helping children explore, organize, and refine their ideas about subject matter (Applebee, 1984). For example, analytic or persuasive writing, a common classroom tool, forces students to go beyond the available information, to construct and present their own interpretations about a topic. This reformulation can lead to new insights and a more complex understanding of the information.

Another goal of writing in school is to provide students with the opportunity for self-exploration. Children are encouraged to examine their interests, feelings, and experiences through writing. Activities like journal writing, autobiographies, and personal narratives are used to promote such self-reflection.

Finally, Stephen King, the reigning master of the horror genre, tells his fans that he writes "such gross stuff" because "I have the heart of a small boy—and I keep it in a jar on my desk" (Brodie, 1997). For Mr. King, writing is not only a profession, but it provides a personal means for self-expression. Schools emphasize the artistic and creative aspects of writing as well. Children write plays, poetry, and stories, using their imagination and personal experiences to craft a virtual experience for their intended audience (Durst & Newell, 1989).

II. WHAT ARE THE INGREDIENTS INVOLVED IN LEARNING TO WRITE

An extensive literature on the development of expertise, including research on writing (Alexander *et al.*, 1998; Hayes & Flower, 1986; Scardamalia & Bereiter, 1986), suggests that writing development depends upon changes that occur in students' knowledge, strategies, skills, and will. This includes knowledge of writing and writing topics, skills for producing and crafting text, processes for energizing and directing thoughts and actions, and strategies for achieving writing goals and overcoming barriers. All of these—knowledge, skill, will, and self-regulation—are evident in skilled writing.

Take, for instance, knowledge of writing topics. Skilled writers typically generate more ideas than they need when writing, culling and eliminating less productive ones as they compose. Raymond Carver, the popular mystery writer, for example, cut the first drafts of his stories in half as he edited them (Burnham, 1994). Perhaps more importantly, when skilled writers are not knowledgeable about a topic, they devise effective and sometimes ingenious methods for obtaining information. Sue Hubble, a writer of children's books about insects, indicated that at the start of a new writing project, she visits the Library of Congress and spends several weeks reading everything she can about her topic. She then talks to entomologists who are experts on the subject, and if she can find no expert, she obtains the needed information by raising and observing the insects of interest herself (Hubble, 1996).

Skilled writers are also adept with the basic skills for translating language into print, such as handwriting and spelling. These skills are so well mastered by most skilled writers that they have little or no influence on the writing process (Scardamalia & Bereiter, 1986). This is not the case for all of the skills involved in producing and crafting text, however. Writers must make decisions about word choice, textual connections, syntax, clarity, and so forth. This can be both taxing and time consuming, even for a skilled writer. For instance, Theodore Geisel (Dr. Seuss) indicated that, "Every sentence is like a pang of birth. *The Cat in the Hat* ended up taking well over a year" (Brodie, 1997).

Many skilled writers further develop routines, rewards, or goals to motivate themselves to write. Jack Kerouac, author of *On the Road*, used a variety of rituals to help him compose, including kneeling and praying before starting to write and lighting a candle and composing by its light. (Plimpton, 1967) Sophie Burnham, author of *For Writers Only*, indicated that she promises herself an ice cream cone or a call to a friend as an inducement to finish a section she is working on (Burnham, 1994). Philip Dick, the famed science fiction writer, regulated his writing output by setting a goal to write two novels a year (Sutlin, 1989).

Finally, skilled writers employ a variety of strategies to help them achieve their writing goals and overcome difficulties they encounter while writing. These include strategies for planning, generating information, evaluating, revising, environmental structuring, and so forth. R. L. Stine, creator of the popular children's series, *Goosebumps*, indicated that he outlines every book in advance of writing it (Associated Press, 1995). Likewise, J. K. Rowling, author of the *Harry Potter* series, spends several months planning each book, filling several boxes with notes and ideas (Shapiro, 2000).

III. THE WRITING OF STUDENTS WITH LD

A recent book, *Snoopy's Guide to the Writing Life* (Conrad & Schultz, 2002), employs one of the most popular comic page characters of all time, Charlie Brown's mercurial dog Snoopy, to illustrate the difficulties involved in writing. Snoopy will also serve as our guide, as we examine the writing of children with LD.

Although Snoopy enjoyed a rich fantasy life, involving many personas, ranging from litigious lawyer to hapless golfer, it was not uncommon to find him sitting on top of his doghouse with typewriter at paw in many of the *Peanuts* cartoons. On one such occasion, we find him starting his masterpiece with his most famous line, "It was a dark and stormy night." He goes on to write that, "Suddenly, a shot rang out!" This is followed by, "Then another! And another! And then some more." He ends with, "Shots, that is."

Snoopy's approach to writing is similar to the approach employed by many students with LD. In contrast to more skilled writers, they employ an approach to composing that minimizes the role of planning, revising, and other self-regulation strategies (Graham, 1997; Graham & Harris, 1994). Like Snoopy, children with LD typically convert writing tasks into tasks of telling what one knows, doing little planning or reflection in advance or during writing (Graham, 1990; McCutchen, 1988). Information that is somewhat topic appropriate is gathered from memory and written down, with each preceding idea stimulating the generation of the next idea. Little attention is directed to the needs of the audience, the organization of text, the development of rhetorical goals, or the constraints imposed by the topic.

In another *Peanuts* cartoon, we see Snoopy intently staring at his typewriter. After a few moments, he declares that, "Sometimes when you are a great writer, the words come so fast you can hardly put them down on paper." Despite this claim, he continues to stare at the typewriter until he finally says, "SOMETIMES."

Like Snoopy, students with LD often have difficulty finding enough to say when they write. Their papers are inordinately short, containing little detail or elaboration, and once an idea is generated, they are very reluctant to discard it (Graham *et al.*, 1991).

There are several possible reasons why these children generate so little content when writing. One, they may be unknowledgeable or uninterested in the topics they write about. Two, they may terminate the composing process too soon, before accessing all they know. In one study (Graham, 1990), children with LD spent only 6 or 7 minutes writing an opinion essay, but when prompted to write more, generated 2 to 4 times more text, with at least half of the prompted material being new and useful. Three, they may lose or fail to generate possible content because of interference from poorly developed text production skills. In contrast to skilled writers, many students with LD struggle with the mechanics of writing, producing papers full of spelling, capitalization, punctuation, and handwriting miscues (Graham *et al.*, 1991).

Once again on the top of his doghouse, we find Snoopy sharing a completed manuscript with Lucy, his most virulent critic. She tells him that his stories are stupid and that there is not anything at all good about his writing. Never at a loss for a response, Snoopy says, "I have neat margins."

Like Snoopy, students with LD often have a very restrictive view of what constitutes good writing. They are less knowledgeable about writing and the writing process than their normally achieving peers (Englert *et al.*, 1988), and are more likely to emphasize form, rather than substance, in their writing (Graham *et al.*, 1993b). For instance, a student with LD who struggled with writing told us that good writers "spell all of their words correctly, make all of their letters the same height, and write neatly." In contrast, a good writer in this child's class told us that good writers "brainstorm ideas...then think about it and then write about it...look it over to see how to make it all fit right...then they do a final copy and go over that; and then if it is still not right, they do it again."

Finally, we find Snoopy opening a letter from a publishing house that has just reviewed his latest story. They inform him that they are returning his worthless story and ask him not to "...send us any more. Please, Please, Please!" This brings a smile to Snoopy's face, as he "loves to hear an editor beg."

Snoopy is consistently resilient in the face of repeated rejection. His confidence should be shaken, but it is not. His motto is, "Never listen to the reviewers." Students with LD also appear to be more confident than is warranted. When we assessed the self-efficacy of 10- to 14-year-old children with LD, they were just as confident about their writing capabilities as their better writing peers (Graham *et al.*, 1993b). They reminded us of another student who declared, "I am the best they is in English" (Linkletter, 1962). Although an unrealistically high estimate of ability may promote persistence in spite of a history of poor performance (Sawyer *et al.*, 1992), there is a down side. Students who overestimate their capabilities may fail to allocate the needed resources and effort, believing it to be unnecessary.

An important goal in writing instruction for students with LD, therefore, is to help them develop the knowledge, skills, and strategies used by more skilled writers. Methods for fostering motivation for writing and sharpening self-efficacy are important as well, as children are less likely to engage in the types of mental activities that epitomize skilled writing if they do not value writing or if they overestimate their abilities (Graham & Harris, 1994). Impressive changes in the writing of students with LD have been obtained when instruction has emphasized the development of these factors (Berninger *et al.*, 1995; Englert *et al.*, 1995, 1991; Graham *et al.*, 1991; MacArthur *et al.*, 1995).

The rest of this chapter examines how schools can help students with LD become skilled writers. The construction of programs that support this development is challenging, as it cannot be limited to a single grade or teacher. Instead, it requires a coherent, coordinated, and extended effort, because writing problems are not transitory difficulties that are easily fixed (Graham & Harris, 2001). Although writing development is a complex and somewhat uncertain process, it depends upon changes that occur in knowledge about writing, motivation, strategic behaviors, and writing skills (Alexander *et al.*, 1998). Consequently, an effective program must incorporate catalysts that amplify students' knowledge, skill, will, and self-regulation. Writing instruction for students with LD must further emphasize both prevention and intervention; respond to the specific needs of each child; maintain a healthy balance between meaning, process, and form; and employ both formal and informal learning methods (Graham & Harris, 1997). Principles for actualizing these recommendations are presented next.

IV. PRINCIPLES OF WRITING INSTRUCTION

A. Provide Exemplary Writing Instruction

An essential tactic in preventing writing difficulties is to provide exemplary writing instruction right from the start, beginning in first grade and continuing through high school. Providing students with consistent quality instruction in writing is advantageous for three reasons. One, it maximizes the writing development of children in general. Two, it minimizes the number of students who develop writing problems as a result of poor instruction. Three, it helps to ameliorate the severity of writing difficulties experienced by children whose primary problems are not instructional, such as children with learning disabilities.

Although quality writing instruction will differ somewhat from grade to grade, processes that shape and transform students' writing knowledge, skill, will, and self-regulation should be emphasized at each succeeding level. Just as importantly, exemplary writing instruction should be based on the empirical analysis of effective writing practices. This includes research on the practices of highly effective writing teachers (e.g., Wray *et al.*, 2000) as well as the outcomes of experimental treatment studies conducted with both good (e.g., Hillocks, 1986) and poor writers (e.g., Graham & Harris, 1998a). Finally, this empirical knowledge should be combined with knowledge gained through clinical and practical experience (e.g., Scott, 1989). We recently completed such an analysis (Graham & Harris, 2001) and developed a list of features for an exemplary writing program. The list is presented as a checklist in Table I, providing teachers with an instrument for assessing the general quality of classroom writing instruction.

Table I

Checklist for Classroom Writing Instruction

My students...

___ Write daily and work on a wide range of writing tasks for multiple audiences, including writing at home.

___ Help each other plan, draft, revise, edit, or publish their written work.

___ Share their work with each other, receiving praise and critical feedback on their efforts.

___ Use writing as a tool to explore, organize, and express their thoughts across the curriculum.

___ Assess their progress as writers.

I make sure that I...

___ Develop a literate classroom environment where students' written work is prominently displayed and the room is packed with writing and reading material.

___ Establish a predictable writing routine where students are encouraged to think, reflect, and revise.

___ Hold individual conferences with students about their current writing efforts, helping them establish goals or criteria to guide their writing and revising efforts.

___ Make writing motivating by setting an exciting mood, creating a risk-free environment, allowing students to select their own writing topics or modify teacher assignments, developing assigned topics compatible with students' interests, reinforcing children's accomplishments, specifying the goal for each lesson, and promoting an "I can do" attitude.

___ Provide frequent opportunities for students to self-regulate their behavior during writing, including working independently, arranging their own space, and seeking help from others.

___ Conduct periodic conferences with parents, soliciting their advice and communicating the goals of the program as well as their child's progress as a writer.

To help students progress as writers I...

___ Model the process of writing as well as positive attitudes toward writing.

___ Provide instruction on a broad range of skills, knowledge, and strategies, including phonological awareness, handwriting and spelling, writing conventions, sentence-level skills, text structure, the functions of writing, and planning and revising.

___ Deliver follow-up instruction to ensure mastery of targeted writing skills, knowledge, and strategies.

___ Monitor students' progress as writers as well as students' strengths and needs.

___ Adjust my teaching style and learning pace as needed, conduct mini-lessons responsive to current student needs, and provide individually guided assistance with writing assignments.

Note: Place a check next to each item that describes a feature of writing instruction in your classroom. Determine if the actualization of any **unchecked items** would improve the quality of writing instruction in your class. Source: Graham & Harris (2002).

An example of an instructional program that incorporates many of the principles listed in Table I is the Early Literacy Project (ELP), designed by Englert and her colleagues (Englert *et al.*, 1995). With this program, writing and reading instruction occurs as part of a thematic unit. For a thematic unit on wolves, for instance, students read narrative and expository material about these animals and then use writing as a means for responding to these texts as well as a mechanism for gathering additional information about wolves. Instruction on specific writing skills, such as spelling, and strategies for planning and revising text, occurs within the context of the unit and is supported by teacher modeling, discussion, and guided practice. Opportunities to engage in meaningful writing are plentiful, as students not only respond in writing to their reading materials, but generate personal experience stories, maintain a journal detailing their observations and thoughts, and write reports. Teachers further assist students by scaffolding their reading and writing experiences. For instance, word banks, pictionaries, and planning sheets are often used as temporary aids to support students' writing efforts. A positive classroom environment is created by encouraging children to share their work and collaborate with each other. For example, students work together to apply strategies taught by their teacher, frequently talk with each other about what they are doing, and share their writing with the class. Finally, the ELP program is supplemented by more conventional instruction, as students are explicitly and systematically taught skills such as phonemic awareness, phonics skills, and spelling.

Systematic evaluations of the ELP program demonstrate that such instruction can have a positive impact on the writing performance of some of the most difficult-to-teach children. Over the course of a year, Englert *et al.* (1995) examined whether the program improved the writing of students with special needs in grades one through four. In comparison to a group of similar children receiving instruction in a literature-based literacy program, students taught by veteran ELP teachers made greater gains in writing: their papers contained fewer spelling miscues, were longer, and better organized. In addition, Mariage (1993) found that two to three years of such instruction, starting in the primary grades, was enough to bring some students with special needs up to grade-level performance.

B. Tailor Writing Instruction to Meet the Needs of Struggling Writers

A critical element in providing effective writing instruction to students with learning disabilities is to tailor instruction so that it is responsive to their needs. Such adaptations are a regular part of the practices of highly effective teachers. For instance, Pressley *et al.* (1996) found that outstanding literacy teachers provided qualitatively similar instruction for all students, but that children experiencing difficulty with literacy learning received extra teacher support. This included extra help learning critical skills, more explicit teaching, and more individually guided assistance.

A nationwide survey by Graham *et al.* (2003) revealed that teachers make a variety of adaptations to tailor instruction to meet the needs of struggling writers. The most frequent adaptations involved extra one-on-one help, including individual assistance from the teacher, adult tutors or volunteers, or older and same-age peers (including collaborative planning, writing, or revising with a peer). Adaptations to meet handwriting and spelling difficulties were also quite common. In the area of spelling, for instance, teachers created personalized spelling lists for weaker writers, directly helped them spell unknown words, or employed word banks and other aids to facilitate correct spelling. In contrast, some teachers sought to bypass transcription difficulties by allowing struggling writers to dictate their compositions or write with a keyboard (e.g., Alpha Smart). A third set of adaptations focused on supporting the thinking and creative processes involved in writing. To illustrate, teachers facilitated the planning of weaker writers by having them draw what they planned to write about, talk out their ideas in advance of writing, or use webs or graphic organizers to generate and sequence ideas. Revising efforts were supported through the use of revising checklists or by the teacher or a peer directly helping the child revise. Other adaptations included helping weaker writers select writing topics, making writing assignments shorter or easier, and assigning additional writing homework.

Teachers further indicated they devoted more attention to teaching handwriting, phonics for spelling, and punctuation and capitalization skills to weaker writers than to average writers. They were also more likely to reteach writing skills to struggling writers, provide mini-lessons responsive to their needs, and conference with these children about their writing.

Unfortunately, almost 20% of the participating teachers indicated that they made no adaptations for struggling writers. Another 24% of the teachers made only one or two adaptations, and some of the adaptations made by teachers were not necessarily positive ones. In comparison to average writers, for example, teachers were less likely to let weaker writers share their writing with peers, help others, select their own writing topics, or complete writing assignments at their own pace. Teachers are unlikely to maximize the success of students with learning disabilities or other struggling writers, however, if they make no adjustments or their modifications limit children's participation or decisionmaking.

C. Explicitly and Systematically Teach Strategies for Planning and Revising Text

Students with LD typically do little planning or revising when writing (Graham *et al.*, 1991). They focus most of their planning efforts on generating ideas while they write. Their revising efforts concentrate primarily on changing one word to another and fixing mechanical errors. This stands in marked contrast to skilled writers, who spend one-half or more of their writing time planning and revising their paper (Gould, 1980; Kellogg, 1987). An obvious means for addressing this problem is to help students with LD upgrade or even replace their existing writing strategies with more sophisticated ones, those requiring the same self-regulatory procedures used by skilled writers.

One well-known example of a program for explicitly teaching writing strategies to students with LD is the Cognitive Strategies Instruction in Writing program (CSIW) (Englert *et al.*, 1991). In CSIW, "think sheets" that provide prompts for carrying out specific activities are used to direct students' actions during the following writing processes: planning, organizing information, writing, editing, and revising. For example, for the writing task, "providing directions for completing an activity," the think sheet for organizing information includes prompts to identify where the activity will take place, what materials are needed, and what steps are involved. To help students internalize the strategies and the framework incorporated in the think sheets, a variety of features common to effective strategy instruction are used, including an emphasis on teachers' modeling of an inner dialogue on how to use the think sheets; assisted teaching in using the procedures until such coaching is no longer needed; and guiding students to understand what they are learning, why it is important, and when it can be used. In a study including fourth and fifth grade students with and without LD, children who received CSIW instruction wrote papers that were qualitatively better, contained more ideas, and were more sensitive to the needs of the reader than did children participating in Writers' Workshop (Graves, 1983).

Another example of strategy instruction in writing involves the work done by Wong and her colleagues (Wong, 1997). Wong *et al.* (1994) taught adolescents with LD how to use a variety of planning and revising strategies (i.e., searching memory for relevant topics and ideas, revisualizing events, reexperiencing emotions, detecting and diagnosing writing problems, and evaluating the clarity of the central theme of the paper) when writing reportive essays. To teach the strategies, the instructor first modeled their use and then helped students learn how to use them by providing collaborative assistance in their application. Instruction in these strategies resulted in more clearly written essays with better developed themes.

Writing strategies have also been taught to adolescents with LD by Deshler and his colleagues (Deshler & Schumaker, 1986). They have developed strategies for generating different types of sentences and paragraphs as well as a strategy for writing a theme consisting of five paragraphs. Their most widely used writing strategy, however, is a self-directed routine for editing a paper for errors of capitalization, organization, punctuation, and spelling. After learning to use this strategy, students with LD were able to detect and correct more mechanical errors in both their own writing and that of others (Schumaker *et al.*, 1982).

Self-Regulated Strategy Development

We have also been involved in teaching writing strategies to students with LD, using an approach we refer to as Self-Regulated Strategy Development

(SRSD). This approach is designed to help students master the higher-level cognitive processes involved in composing; develop autonomous, reflective, self-regulated use of effective writing strategies; increase knowledge about the characteristics of good writing; and form positive attitudes about writing and their capabilities as writers (Harris & Graham, 1996).

These goals are achieved through various forms of support in the SRSD model.[1] One form of support is inherent in the writing strategies students are taught—a strategy provides structure that helps one organize and sequence behavior. A second form of support involves helping children acquire the self-regulation skills needed to use writing strategies successfully, manage the writing process, and replace unproductive behaviors with constructive ones. This includes teaching students to use self-regulatory procedures such as goal setting, self-assessment, and self-instructions.

Additional support is provided through the methods used to teach the writing strategies and accompanying self-regulation procedures. As students initially learn to use these processes, the teacher supports them through modeling, explaining, reexplaining, and assisting when necessary. This assistance is gradually withdrawn as students become more able to use these processes independently. Writing capabilities are further strengthened by increasing students' knowledge about themselves, writing, and the writing process. Model compositions are used to introduce students to the characteristics of good writing. Goal-setting, self-monitoring, and teacher feedback help students acquire knowledge of their writing capabilities and how to regulate the composing process.

Stages of Instruction

Six instructional stages provide the framework for SRSD (Harris & Graham, 1996). These stages provide a "metascript" or general guideline that can be reordered, combined, or modified to meet student and teacher needs. In some instances, a particular stage may not be needed at all. For example, students may have already acquired the background knowledge (stage 1) needed to use the writing strategies and self-regulation processes targeted for instruction. Similarly, the types of self-regulatory procedures (self-instructions, goal setting, self-monitoring, and so forth) taught to students is determined on an individual basis.

The first stage of instruction (Develop Background Knowledge) involves helping students develop the preskills, including knowledge of the criteria for good writing, needed to understand, acquire, and use the writing strategies targeted for instruction. During the second stage (Discuss It),

---

[1]Many of these same kinds of support are evident in the other strategy instructional approaches reviewed in this chapter.

students examine and discuss their current writing performance as well as the strategies they use to accomplish specific writing assignments. The target writing strategies are then introduced, and their purpose and benefits, as well as how and when to use them, are examined by the students. At this point, students are asked to make a commitment to learn the strategies and act as collaborative partners in this endeavor. The teacher may also decide to explore with students any negative or ineffective self-statements or beliefs that currently affect their writing.

In the third stage (Model It), the teacher models, while thinking out loud, how to use the writing strategies using appropriate self-instructions, including problem definition, planning, strategy use, self-evaluation, coping and error correction, and self-reinforcement statements. After analyzing the teacher's performance, teacher and students may collaborate on changing the strategies to make them more effective. Students then develop and record personal self-statements they plan to use during writing.

During stage four (Memorize It), the steps of the writing strategies, any mnemonics for remembering them, and personalized self-statements are memorized. Although students paraphrase the steps when memorizing them, care is taken to ensure the original meaning is maintained. This stage is not needed by all students, and is typically included for children who have severe memory problems.

In stage five (Support It), students and teachers use the strategies and self-instructions collaboratively to complete specific writing assignments. Self-regulation procedures, including goal-setting and self-assessment, may be introduced at this time. Students set goals to improve specific aspects of their writing and use the strategies and self-instructional procedures to mediate their performance. They evaluate their success in meeting these goals by monitoring and evaluating their written products as well as what they do. During the final stage (Independent Performance), students use the strategies independently. If students are still using goal-setting or self-assessment, they may decide to start phasing them out. Students are also encouraged (if they are not already doing so) to say their self-statements covertly, "in their head."

Procedures for promoting maintenance and generalization, including the use of self-reflection (see Harris, & Graham, 1999), are integrated throughout the stages of instruction. These include identifying opportunities to use the writing strategy and self-regulation procedures, analyses of how these processes might need to be modified with other tasks and in new settings, and evaluation of the success of these processes during instruction and subsequent application.

To date, 24 studies using SRSD to teach writing strategies have been conducted (Graham & Harris, 2003). The model has been used to teach a variety of planning and revising strategies, including brainstorming

Table II

Strategies for Writing a Persuasive Essay and a Story

Persuasive Essay Writing Strategy (De La Paz & Graham, 1997)
THINK - Who will read this?
   Why am I writing this?
STOP - Suspend judgement (Generate ideas for each side of the issue)
   Take a side (Decide your position)
   Organize ideas (Select ideas to include and order them for writing)
   Plan more as You Write (Continue planning while writing)
DARE - REMEMBER
   Develop your topic sentence
   Add supporting ideas
   Reject arguments for the other side
   End with a conclusion
Story Writing Strategy (Graham & Harris, 1989)
1. Think of a story that you would like to share with others.
2. Let your mind be free.
3. Write down the story part reminder:
   W - W - W   The Story Part Reminder is a reminder to make notes for these questions:
   WHAT = 2   Who is the main character; who else is in the story?
   HOW = 2   When does the story take place?
                   Where does the story take place?
                   What does the main character want to do; what do the other characters
                   want to do?
                   What happens when the main character tries to do it; what happens with
                   the other characters?
                   How does the story end?
                   How does the main character feel; how do other characters feel?
4. Make notes of your ideas for each part.
5. Write your story—use good parts, add, elaborate, or revise as you write or afterwards, and
   make sense.

(see Harris & Graham, 1985), self-monitoring of productivity (see Harris *et al.*, 1994), reading for information and semantic webbing (see MacArthur *et al.*, 1996), generating and organizing writing content using text structure (see Graham & Harris, 1989; Sawyer *et al.*, 1992), goal setting (see Graham *et al.*, 1995, 1992), MacArthur, Schwartz, revising using peer feedback (see MacArthur *et al.*, 1991), and revising for both mechanics and substance (see Graham & MacArthur, 1988). SRSD has led to changes and improvement in four aspects of students' performance: quality of writing, knowledge of writing, approach to writing, and self-efficacy (cf. Graham *et al.*, 1991; Graham & Harris, 2003; Harris & Graham, 1996). Evaluations of SRSD by teachers and students have also been positive. Examples of two writing strategies taught using the SRSD procedure are presented in Table II.

Additional Comments

Although strategy instruction has been presented as a curricular option in and of itself (Deshler & Schumaker, 1986), we believe that it is much more powerful when it is integrated as part of the regular program. In the area of writing, for example, teaching students a peer-revising strategy that can be used as an integral part of the process approach to writing provides an excellent means for promoting collaboration and improving students' planning skills (see MacArthur *et al.*, 1991).

It should further be noted that well-taught and well-learned strategies may not be used regularly and effectively by students with LD (Graham & Harris, 1998b). Although students may possess the know-how, they may not possess the will to use the strategies or may use them in a careless fashion (Wong, 1994). Consequently, teachers should consider students' goal orientations and attitudinal dispositions when developing and providing strategy instruction, and employ instructional procedures that facilitate mindful use of the inculcated strategies (see Graham & Harris, 1998b; Wong, 1994). It is equally important to monitor if students continue to use the strategies over time and if they adapt their use to new situations. While provisions for promoting maintenance and generalization should be a routine part of good strategy instruction, teachers may need to use booster sessions to promote continued and adaptive strategy use (Harris & Graham, 1996).

D. Explicit and Systematic Basic Writing Skills for Text Production

There is a strong relation between the fluency and quality of children's writing and their proficiency with text production skills such as handwriting and spelling (Graham, 1990; Graham *et al.*, 1997). Moreover, efforts to improve such skills can also result in corresponding improvements in writing performance (Berninger *et al.*, 1997, 1998; Graham *et al.*, 2000, 2002; Jones & Christensen, 1999). Consequently, we recommend that teachers devote instructional time to teaching text production skills, especially handwriting and spelling, to students with LD (Graham, 1999). Such instruction should not dominate the writing program, however, and should focus on those skills that are most likely to make a difference.

Handwriting

The basic goals of handwriting instruction are to help students develop writing that is legible and can be produced quickly with little conscious attention. This involves teaching students an efficient pattern for forming individual letters as well as how to hold their pen or pencil and position the paper they are writing on (Graham, 1999). This does not require hours of time practicing individual letters. Instead, once a letter is introduced, students should spend a short time carefully practicing the letter, receive help as needed (including subsequent review), and evaluate their own efforts. Fluency in handwriting is best promoted through frequent writing and develops gradually over time (Graham & Weintraub, 1996).

Table III presents a checklist for evaluating the quality of handwriting instruction. The checklist is based on the findings from comprehensive reviews of the empirical literature (Graham, 1999; Graham & Weintraub, 1996). It emphasizes both effective instructional procedures and productive adaptations for struggling writers.

We would also like to point out that providing extra handwriting instruction to young children experiencing difficulty with this skill may help to prevent later writing problems. For instance, Graham *et al.* (2000) provided first grade children (who had slow handwriting and generally poor writing skills) with approximately 7 hours of additional handwriting instruction. Three times a week, each child met with a tutor for 15 minutes of instruction. Each 15-minute lesson involved four activities. For the first activity, Alphabet Warm-up, students learned to name and identify the letters of the alphabet. With the second activity, Alphabet Practice, three lower-case letters sharing common formational characteristics (e.g., l, i, and t) were introduced and practiced. The tutor modeled how to form the letters, followed by the student's practicing each letter by tracing it three times, writing it three times inside an outline of the letter, copying it three times, and circling the best formed letter. Three lessons were devoted to mastering each letter set, with the second and third sessions primarily involving letter practice in the context of single words (e.g., lit) or hinky-pinks (rhyming words such as itty-bitty). The third activity, Alphabet Rockets, involved asking the child to copy a short sentence quickly and accurately for a period of three minutes. The sentence contained multiple instances of the letters that were emphasized in Alphabet Practice during that lesson (e.g., **Little kids like to get letters.**). The number of letters written was recorded on a chart and during the next two lessons, students tried to beat their previous score by writing at least three more letters during the specified time period. With the fourth activity, Alphabet Fun, the student was taught how to write one of the letters from Alphabet Practice in an unusual way (e.g., as long and tall or short and fat) or use it as part of a picture (e.g., turning an i into a butterfly or an s into a snake). Students who received this extra instruction became quicker and better handwriters than peers assigned to a contact control group receiving instruction in phonological awareness. They also evidenced greater gains in their ability to craft sentences and generate text when writing a story.

Table III

Checklist for Handwriting Instruction

I teach children how to write each letter by...
___ Showing them how it is formed.
___ Describing how it is similar and different from other letters.
___ Using visual cues, such as numbered arrows, as a guide to letter formation.
___ Providing practice tracing, copying, and writing the letter from memory.
___ Keeping instructional sessions short, with frequent reviews and practice.
___ Asking children to identify or circle their best formed letter or letters.
___ Encouraging them to correct or rewrite poorly formed letters.
___ Monitoring their practice to ensure that letters are formed correctly.
___ Reinforcing their successful efforts and providing corrective feedback as needed.

I help children become more fluent in handwriting by...
___ Providing them with plenty of opportunities to write.
___ Eliminating interfering habits that may reduce handwriting fluency.
___ Having them copy a short passage several times, trying to write it a little faster each time.

I promote handwriting development by...
___ Making sure that each child develops a comfortable and efficient pencil grip.
___ Encouraging children to sit in an upright position, leaning slightly forward, as they write.
___ Showing them how to place or position their paper when writing.
___ Teaching children to identify and name the letters of the alphabet.
___ Teaching them how to write both upper- and lower-case letters.
___ Allotting 75 to 100 minutes per week to handwriting instruction (grades 1 through 4).
___ Providing children with plenty of opportunities to use different types of writing instruments and paper.
___ Asking children to set goals for improving specific aspects of their handwriting.
___ Implementing appropriate procedures for left-handed writers, such as how to properly place or position their paper when writing.
___ Monitoring students' handwriting, paying special attention to their instructional needs in letter formation, spacing, slant, alignment, size, and line quality.
___ Dramatizing children's progress in handwriting through the use of charts of graphs, praise, or posting neatly written papers

I assist students who are experiencing difficulty by...
___ Organizing my class so that I can provide additional handwriting instruction to children who need it.
___ Coordinating my handwriting instruction with the efforts of other professionals, such as an occupational therapist.
___ Placing special emphasis on the teaching of difficult letters, such as *a, j, k, n, q, u,* and *z,* as well as reversals (see Graham *et al.,* 2001).
___ Ensuring that they master one style of handwriting before a second style is introduced.
___ Considering if an alternative to handwriting, such as an Alpha Smart keyboard, is warranted.
___ Helping them develop a positive attitude about handwriting.
___ Talking with their parents about my handwriting program and soliciting advice.

I make sure that I...
___ Encourage students to make all final drafts of papers neat and legible.
___ Maintain a balanced perspective on the role of handwriting in learning to write.

Note: Place a check next to each item that describes a feature of handwriting instruction in your class. Determine whether the actualization of any **unchecked items** would improve your handwriting instruction (Graham & Harris, 2002).

Spelling

The basic goal of spelling instruction is to help students become proficient and fluent in spelling words they are likely to use in their writing. This involves learning the common regularities and patterns underlying English orthography; the correct spelling of frequently used words; and strategies for studying new words, applying knowledge of spelling (e.g., spelling by analogy), and proofreading (Graham *et al.*, 1996). Frequent reading and writing contribute to spelling development, as they serve as a source for additional learning, a context for practicing newly learned skills, and a reminder on the importance of correct spelling in practical and social situations. Children also need to become familiar with external aids to spelling such as the dictionary, thesaurus, spell checkers, or asking another person for help.

Table IV presents a checklist for evaluating the quality of spelling instruction. The checklist is based on the findings from comprehensive reviews of the empirical literature (Graham, 1983, 1999; Graham & Miller, 1979). It emphasizes both effective instructional procedures and productive adaptations for struggling writers.

As with handwriting, providing extra spelling instruction to young children experiencing difficulty with this skill may help to prevent later writing problems. For example, Graham *et al.* (2002) provided second grade children who were poor spellers and writers with approximately 12 hours of additional spelling instruction. Pairs of students met with a tutor 3 times a week for 20 minutes each lesson. Instruction involved 6 units with 6 lessons each, and each unit contained five instructional activities

During the first lesson of each unit, children completed a word sorting activity (activity one) that focused on the spelling patterns taught in that unit (these primarily centered on long or short vowel patterns). With the tutor's help, students first sorted word cards into two or three spelling pattern categories. Each category was represented by a master word (e.g., the words "made," "maid," and "may" were the master words for the three patterns representing the long /a/ sound), and children placed each word card in the appropriate category. If the children placed a word in the wrong category, the tutor corrected the mistake and modeled out loud how to decide where the word should be placed. Once all words were placed, the tutor helped students state rules for the patterns emphasized in that word sort (e.g., When you hear a long /a/ in a small word, the "a" is often followed by a consonant and silent "e."). Students then generated words of their own that matched the patterns. Next, the word cards were reshuffled and students completed the word sort again, getting help and feedback as needed. At the end of each lesson, students were encouraged to hunt for words that fit the target patterns (activity two).

Table IV

Checklist for Spelling Instruction

I help children learn new spellings by ...

___ Teaching them how to spell words they are likely to use when writing.

___ Encouraging them to use spell checkers, dictionaries, and so forth to determine the correct spelling of unknown words.

___ Modeling correct spelling when I write.

___ Having them build words from letters or letters and phonograms (e.g., **c–at**).

I help children learn their spelling list words by ...

___ Administering a pretest to identify which words need to be studied.

___ Teaching them an effective strategy for studying words.

___ Having them practice their words together.

___ Keeping instructional sessions short, with frequent practice and review.

___ Administering a posttest to determine which words were mastered.

___ Asking that words misspelled during testing are corrected.

___ Monitoring whether they continue to correctly spell mastered words over time.

___ Providing additional study for words that were not mastered or maintained over time.

___ Reinforcing the correct spelling of taught words in their writing.

I promote spelling development by ...

___ Making sure that each child can segment words into sounds as well as add, delete, and substitute sounds.

___ Showing students how the sounds in a word are related to print.

___ Teaching them common sound/symbol associations, spelling patterns, and helpful spelling rules.

___ Teaching them strategies for determining the spelling of unknown words.

___ Providing instruction and practice in proofreading.

___ Allotting at least 60 to 75 minutes per week to spelling instruction.

I assist students who are experiencing difficulty by ...

___ Organizing my class so that I can provide additional spelling instruction to those who need it.

___ Adjusting the number of words that they have to study each week.

___ Providing them with a personalized list of words to study.

___ Asking them to set goals for how many new words they will learn to spell each week.

___ Setting aside time for them to study their spelling words at school.

___ Presenting only a few words to be studied at a time.

___ Testing their daily progress on the words they are studying.

___ Encouraging them to monitor their study behavior and subsequent spelling performance.

___ Using spelling games and computer programs to reinforce the learning of spelling words and skills.

___ Teaching them spelling mnemonics for words that are especially difficult to spell.

___ Providing a personalized dictionary containing words the child is likely to misspell.

___ Placing spelling demons and other difficult words on wall charts.

___ Dramatizing spelling progress through the use of charts or graphs, praise, and so forth.

___ Reteaching skills and strategies that they did not master.

___ Helping them develop a positive attitude about spelling.

___ Talking with their parents about my spelling program and soliciting advice.

I make sure that I ...

___ Encourage students to correct misspellings in all final drafts of papers.

___ Maintain a balanced perspective on the role of spelling in learning to write.

Note: Place a check next to each item that describes a feature of spelling instruction in your class. Determine whether the actualization of any **unchecked items** would improve your spelling instruction (Graham & Harris, 2002).

During the second lesson and continuing through lesson five, students studied 8 new spelling words (activity three). These were words that students had misspelled previously, and each word matched one of the spelling patterns emphasized in that unit. Students used two basic procedures to study these words. One procedure, "Graph Busters," involved students recording the number of times they correctly practiced the words during a lesson using a traditional study strategy. The second procedure involved studying words while playing a game with a peer partner. Spelling Road Race was one of the games. It consisted of a laminated board with a racing track divided into 30 segments. When children correctly spelled one of the spelling words, they moved a place for each letter or word.

Also starting in the second lesson and continuing through lesson five, students practiced sound–letter associations for consonants, blends, diagraphs, and short vowels (activity four). Using flash cards with a picture on one side (e.g., a "cat") and the corresponding letter on the other side ("c"), students practiced 9 to 16 associations during each lesson.

Students completed a word-building activity (activity five) during lessons two through five. This involved building words with rhymes that fit the target spelling patterns. They were asked to create as many real words as they could from a rhyme (e.g., "ay") and 18 different consonants, blends, and digraphs.

In the final lesson of each unit, students completed three tests. One test was on the 8 words they studied, a second was on words that were studied in the previous two units, and a third was on words that matched the rhymes used during the word-building activity. Students not only learned and maintained almost all of the words taught, but their performance on two standardized tests of spelling improved dramatically as well. Even more importantly, there was a corresponding improvement in their writing and reading skills.

Sentence Writing Skills

In addition to developing fluent handwriting and spelling skills, students with LD need to develop proficiency in framing their text within a variety of sentence formats (e.g., expressing their thoughts within the context of a complex sentence). Sentence combining, the practice of building more complex sentences from simpler ones, has proven to be a highly effective technique for promoting such skills (Hillocks, 1986; Saddler, 2002). Other traditional procedures for improving students' sentence building skills include arranging and rearranging word cards to form sentences, completing sentences from which specific words or phrases have been deleted, and encouraging students to imitate the patterns in exemplary sentences. In addition, Schumaker and Sheldon (1985) developed a strategy designed to help students generate 14 different types of sentences. For each sentence type, students use a formula to guide the process of building the sentence and selecting words. Students are also taught to identify and define a host of grammatical structures that are relevant to the parts included in the various formulas.

E. Help Students Increase Their Knowledge about Writing and Different Writing Genres

The most common means for acquiring knowledge about writing is through exposure to specific literary examples, either through reading or the presentation of models that embody a specific pattern. Although the practice of imitating written models can have a positive impact on writing, it should be used judiciously, as the effects are quite modest (Hillocks, 1984). Students also acquire some rhetorical knowledge through reading, but the extent of such learning is not known (Bereiter & Scardamalia, 1982). Consequently, teachers should play an active role in guiding the process of acquiring rhetorical knowledge through reading. As students read a particular book, for example, the teacher can encourage discussion, focusing attention on important features of text, such as the use of dialogue, plot development, foreshadowing, and so forth (Bos, 1988).

Students' knowledge about writing can also be increased through explicit instruction (see the section on teaching planning and revising strategies). Fitzgerald and Teasley (1986), for instance, reported that children who received instruction in narrative structure (i.e., specific story elements and their interplay) improved both the organization and quality of their papers. Fitzgerald and Markham (1987) obtained similar results for revising, indicating that students became more knowledgeable and effective revisers after receiving instruction on how to revise.

F. Work to Increase Students' Writing Motivation

Table I presented a variety of suggestions for making writing more motivating. These included setting an exciting mood, creating a risk-free environment, allowing students to select their own writing topics or modify teacher assignments, developing assigned topics compatible with students' interests, reinforcing children's accomplishments, and specifying the goal for each lesson.

Another important aspect of enhancing motivation for writing involves fostering students' sense of competence. This can be promoted (at least in part) by treating children as capable learners. Or in other words, viewing each student as one who can learn to work productively and independently in the classroom.

Just as students with LD need to believe that they are capable writers, so do teachers. Too often teachers view children with learning disabilities negatively, setting low expectations for their performance and limiting their exchanges with them (Graham & Harris, 2001). Such negative views may take the form of more criticism, less attention and praise, and briefer and less informative feedback (Johnston & Winograd, 1985). Children with writing difficulties may be viewed as so challenging by some teachers that a form of pedagogical paralysis occurs, as they are uncertain about what to do with these students or lack confidence in their own capabilities to teach them (Kameenui, 1993). Teachers are not powerless, however, as the findings from the Englert *et al.* (1995) study reviewed earlier showed. Children with learning disabilities can be taught to write well.

G. Take Advantage of Technological Tools for Writing

Computers are flexible writing tools that can enhance the writing of students with LD in many ways. Word processing and related technology can support the basic skills of producing legible text with correct mechanics as well as the more complex cognitive processes of planning, drafting, and revising text and the social processes of collaboration and communication with an audience.

Word Processing

Fairly extensive research has been conducted on instructional use of word processing with nondisabled students; a meta-analysis of this research (Bangert-Drowns, 1993) found a positive, though modest, impact on student writing. Recent research on the use of word processing on statewide accountability assessments (Russell, 1999) has found that nondisabled students who are accustomed to using word processing perform better on accountability tests requiring writing when permitted to use a word processor than when required to write by hand. Less research has been conducted with students with LD. However, a few studies have shown that word processing in combination with effective writing instruction enhances the writing of students with LD (MacArthur *et al.*, 1995, 1996).

Word processors offer several capabilities that may influence the writing process. First, they support the process of revision by easing the physical burden of recopying and the mess of erasing; text can be easily moved, deleted, added, or substituted. The editing capabilities of word processing can be a great boon to writers if they can take advantage of its capabilities. However, simple access to word processing has little impact on the revising behavior of students with LD, who generally have a limited view of revision as correcting errors. For example, MacArthur and Graham (1987) found no difference in revisions made using paper and pencil or word processing by students with LD.

To take advantage of the editing power of word processing, students with LD need instruction and support in learning to revise for meaning as well as errors. The revising skills of students with LD can be improved by instruction in strategies for evaluating and revising their writing. Several studies have combined word processing and strategy instruction in teaching revision, resulting in increases in the number of substantive and mechanical revisions made by students with LD as well as improvement in the quality of their texts (Graham & MacArthur, 1988; MacArthur *et al.*, 1991; Stoddard & MacArthur, 1993). In the cooperative revision strategy developed by MacArthur *et al.* (1991), students work in pairs using the steps presented in Table V.

In addition to supporting revision, word processors enhance publishing by making it possible to produce neat, printed work in a wide variety of professional-looking formats, including newsletters, illustrated books, business letters, and signs and posters. The motivation provided by printed publications may be especially important for students with LD who often struggle with handwriting and mechanics. For classrooms that have just one or two computers, the best use of that equipment may be for publishing projects. Students can work together on a class newsletter or other project, or they can select their best writing for inclusion in a literary magazine.

A final consideration in using word processing is that students must develop some proficiency in typing and must learn to operate the software. Although typing can be considerably easier than handwriting for many students, students with LD should not be expected to develop typing skills without instruction and practice. A variety of software programs are available to provide such practice.

Basic Writing Skills

The difficulties that students with LD have with basic writing skills or mechanics—spelling, capitalization, punctuation, and usage—are well

Table V
Peer Revising Strategy Expressed as Directions to the Peer Editor
(MacArthur *et al.*, 1991)

---

1. LISTEN and READ along as the author reads the story.
2. TELL what it is about and what you liked best.
3. READ it to yourself and make NOTES about:
    A. CLARITY? Is there anything you don't understand?
    B. DETAILS? What information/details could be added?
4. DISCUSS your suggestions with the author.
5. Author: Make changes on the computer.

Note: Evaluation questions in step 3 can be tailored to the ability of the students and to ongoing instruction.

documented. Computer tools, such as spelling and grammar checkers, speech synthesis, word prediction, and speech recognition, have potential to compensate for problems in these areas.

The most widespread tools to support basic writing skills are spelling checkers. Nearly all current word processors include integrated spelling checkers that scan a document for errors and suggest correct spellings. Spelling checkers will not, however, automatically result in error-free documents. MacArthur and his colleagues (MacArthur *et al.*, 1996) found that students with LD were able to correct about one-third of their spelling errors using a spelling checker. The most significant limitation of spelling checkers was that they failed to identify about one-third of errors because the errors were other "real words" correctly spelled, including homonyms and others (e.g., "whet" for "went"). Furthermore, spelling checkers suggested the correct spelling for only one-half to two-thirds of the errors that they did find. Finally, students with LD in this study sometimes failed to recognize the correct spelling in the list of suggestions provided, though this problem was not as common as the preceding problems. Instruction in strategies for using a spelling checker effectively (e.g., trying alternate spellings and proofing for other real words) has been shown to improve performance (McNaughton *et al.*, 1997). Despite their limitations, spelling checkers are clearly important tools for students with LD.

Speech synthesis, another tool with potential to enhance writing skill, includes software or hardware that translates text into speech. It does not sound as natural as digitized speech, which is recorded, but has the advantage that it can be used to speak any text. Word processors with speech synthesis capabilities enable students to hear what they have written and read what others have written. Speech synthesis may help students monitor the adequacy of their writing, including spelling and grammar. Limited research exists on the use of speech synthesis to support writing for students with and without disabilities. Borgh and Dickson (1995) compared word processing with and without speech with fifth grade nondisabled students. Raskind and Higgins (1995) found that speech synthesis helped college students with LD to find more errors than they could find on their own. One promising way to use speech synthesis is to use it after a spell checker to find those other real words not identified as errors by the spelling checker.

A third software tool, word prediction, has the potential to enhance the basic writing skills of students with severe spelling problems. Word prediction was originally developed for individuals with physical disabilities to reduce the number of keystrokes required to type words. As the user begins to type a word, the software predicts the intended word and presents a list of words from which the user can choose. Depending on the sophistication of the software, predictions are based on spelling, word frequency, individual word frequency, and syntax. Generally, speech synthesis is available to read the word choices. MacArthur (1998, 1999) found that word prediction resulted in substantial improvements in the readability and spelling accuracy of writing by students with LD with severe spelling problems. In choosing word prediction software, it is critical to select a program that permits the user to choose dictionaries of different sizes to adapt the program to individual users.

A fourth computer tool that is often mentioned as an aide for students with LD is grammar or style checkers. Students with LD could benefit from software that checked their grammar, capitalization, punctuation, and usage. Unfortunately, current software is designed for older writers and often misses more basic grammatical and mechanical errors, and the feedback provided is often difficult to comprehend.

Finally, speech recognition software has finally reached the stage of development where it can provide a significant benefit to many students with LD. Speech recognition makes it possible for a user to dictate to the computer. In a recent study, MacArthur and Cavalier (in press) taught 35 tenth grade students (25 with LD) to use speech recognition software and had them use it to dictate essays similar to those required on the state accountability tests. Only one of the 35 students was not able to learn to use the system to produce readable essays. Students also composed essays via handwriting and by dictating to a human scribe. Essays composed with speech recognition were of significantly higher quality than those written by hand; essays dictated to scribes were rated even more highly. Using an earlier generation of speech recognition software, Higgins and Raskind (1995) found similar results.

Effective training in the use of speech recognition software involves training students to speak clearly and training the system to recognize their speech and teaching students how to monitor and correct errors. In addition, planning strategies become more important because a good plan facilitates smooth dictation. One of the difficult practical issues in using speech recognition is that it does not work well in a classroom setting because of background noise; thus, schools must provide separate facilities or support use at home.

Planning Processes

Students with LD often have difficulty with planning processes such as setting goals, generating content, and organizing their ideas. Computer applications that support outlining and semantic mapping, programs that prompt students in planning, and multimedia software all have potential to enhance planning processes.

Outlining and semantic mapping are common practices for organizing ideas prior to writing both in schools and among experienced writers. As discussed earlier in this chapter, planning strategies based on text structure and semantic mapping have been shown to be effective ways of improving the writing of students with LD. Many word processors include outlining capabilities, and software is now available for semantic mapping. Outlining and semantic mapping is more flexible and easier to revise on computers than on paper. Despite the promise of computerized semantic mapping, little research has been conducted.

The interactive capabilities of computers can be used to develop programs that prompt writers to engage in planning processes. The most common programs present a series of questions based on text structures to help students generate ideas prior to writing. Although we are not aware of any research on such programs with students with LD, there is research indicating that simple text structure prompts may enhance the writing of students with LD (Montague et al., 1991).

The potential of multimedia software to enhance writing processes is just beginning to be explored as new tools are developed. For young children, "writing" often begins with drawing. Software that permits children to draw pictures and write about them can motivate students to write and help them generate ideas for stories. New CD-ROM "books" provide a link between reading and writing activities; children read the books or have the computer read to them, and then write their own stories using pictures and words from the story. Older students can use more sophisticated multimedia software that permits them to integrate visuals, sounds, and writing to create new forms of communication. Multimedia can also be used to provide background knowledge and as a research source for writing projects.

Collaboration and Communication on Networks

Computer networks, whether local area networks within a classroom or school or the Internet, can offer expanded opportunities for collaborative writing and communication with diverse audiences. Two examples will illustrate some of the possibilities. Batson (1993) used a network within a classroom to teach writing classes for deaf students in which all discussion and interaction were conducted in writing. For the deaf students, the network provided an immersion approach for mastering English. Similar networks have potential in writing instruction for students with LD by providing a natural connection between conversation and formal writing. An entire pre-writing class discussion can be captured for later use in writing. Riel (1985) used e-mail to link students from diverse cultures in collaborative production of a newspaper. Since students from Alaska and California did not share the same cultural knowledge, they struggled to communicate clearly, which provided opportunities to learn about writing and revising. The rapid expansion of Internet resources has opened up new opportunities for communication and collaboration on writing projects.

Special educators are now required to consider assistive technology as an accommodation for individual students with disabilities. A number of extremely promising technology tools have been developed to support writing, and research has begun to demonstrate that these tools can have a positive impact on the learning and performance of students with LD. In particular, applications such as word processing, word prediction, and speech recognition can have a positive impact on students' performance on state accountability tests. Special educators must take the responsibility of advocating for the acceptance of technological accommodations in the classroom and on tests. They must also ensure that they assess their own students and provide them with the technology that could help them. In addition, the field must take up the challenge of continuing development and research on effective educational methods which will enable students with disabilities to use the power provided by these tools.

V. CONCLUDING COMMENTS

The success of schools in teaching writing should be judged not only in terms of how well students develop the skills necessary for meeting academic and occupational demands; the students' desire and ability to use writing for the purpose of social communication and recreation must also be considered. In our efforts to improve the writing of students with LD, we do not want to lose sight of the critical goals of helping students learn to appreciate writing and to enjoy doing it. In this chapter, we have presented a variety of procedures that, when applied in concert, should help students realize all of these goals.

Finally, if we are to improve in any meaningful way how and what students with LD write, we must be dedicated to the importance of writing. Too often special education teachers have made writing instruction the stepchild to reading or math. In allocating time for instruction, it is not unusual to find teachers giving maximum priority to teaching reading, with little emphasis on teaching writing (Leinhart *et al.*, 1980). Similarly, we have found through our own experiences in working with schools and teachers that they are often hesitant and sometimes resistant to allocating sufficient time for writing instruction; they often fear that making such a commitment will have negative consequence because students will get less of something *really important*, such as reading. We would argue that writing is as important as reading. Therefore, we encourage teachers to provide at least four days of writing instruction a week, to look for ways of promoting increased writing across the curriculum, and to attempt to engage students in meaningful and purposive writing activities.

References

Alexander, P., Graham, S., & Harris, K. R. (1998). A perspective on strategy research: Progress and prospect. *Educational Psychology Review*, **10**, 129–154.

Applebee, A. (1984). Writing and reasoning. *Review of Educational Research*, **54**, 577–596.

Associated Press. (1995). This man gives children "Goosebumps" and "Fear Street." *Valdosta Daily Times*, Dec. 27, 1995, B 1.

Bangert-Drowns, R. L. (1993). The word processor as an instructional tool: A meta-analysis of word processing in writing instruction. *Review of Educational Research*, **63**, 69–93.

Batson, T. (1993). The origins of ENFI. In B. C. Bruce, J. K. Peyton, & T. Batson (eds.), *Network-based classrooms: Promises and realities.* New York: Cambridge University Press.

Bereiter, C., & Scardamalia, M. (1982). From conversation to composition: The role of instruction in a developmental process. In R. Glaser (ed.), *Advances in instructional psychology.* (Vol. 2, pp.1–64). Hillsdale, NJ: Lawrence Erlbaum.

Berninger, V., Abbott, R., Whitaker, D., Sylvester, L., & Nolen, S. (1995). Integrating low- and high-level skills in instructional protocols for writing disabilities. *Learning Disability Quarterly*, **18**, 293–310.

Berninger, V., Vaughn, K., Abbott, R., Abbott, S., Rogan, L., Brooks, A., Reed, E., & Graham, S. (1997). Treatment of handwriting problems in beginning writers: Transfer from handwriting to composition. *Journal of Educational Psychology*, **89**, 652–666.

Berninger, V., Vaughn, K., Abbott, R., Brooks, A., Abbott, S., Rogan, L., Reed, E., & Graham, S. (1998). Early intervention for spelling problems: Teaching functional spelling units of varying size with a multiple-connections framework. *Journal of Educational Psychology*, **90**, 587–605.

Borgh, K., & Dickson, W. P. (1992). The effects on children's writing of adding speech synthesis to a word processor. *Journal of Research on Computing in Education*, **24**, 533–544.

Bos, C. (1988). Process-oriented writing: Instructional implications for mildly handicapped students. *Exceptional Children*, **54**, 521–527.

Burnham, S. (1994). *For writers only.* New York: Ballantine.

Brodie, D. (1997). *Writing changes everything: The 627 best things anyone ever said about writing.* New York: St. Martin Press.

Conrad, B., & Schultz, M. (2002). *Snoopy's guide to the writing life.* Cincinnati, OH: Writer's Digest.

De La Paz, S., & Graham, S. (1997). Effects of dictation and advanced planning instruction on the composing of students with writing and learning problems. *Journal of Educational Psychology*, **89**, 203–222.

Deshler, D. D., & Schumaker, J. B. (1986). Learning strategies: An instructional alternative for low-achieving adolescents. *Exceptional Children*, **52**, 583–590.

Diamond, J. (1999). *Guns, germs, and steel: The fates of human societies.* New York: Norton.

Durst, R., & Newell, G. (1989). The uses of function: James Britton's category system and research on writing. *Review of Educational Research*, **59**, 375–394.

Englert, C., Garmon, A., Mariage, T., Rozendal, M., Tarrant, K., & Urba, J. (1995). The early literacy project: Connecting across the literacy curriculum. *Learning Disability Quarterly*, **18**, 253–277.

Englert, C., Raphael, T., Anderson, L., Anthony, H., & Stevens, D. (1991). Making strategies and self-talk visible: Writing instruction in regular and special education classrooms. *American Educational Research Journal*. **28**, 337–372.

Englert, C., Raphael, T., Fear, K., & Anderson, L. (1988). Students' metacognitive knowledge about how to write informational text. *Learning Disability Quarterly*, **11**, 18–46.

Fitzgerald, J., & Markham, L. (1987). Teaching children about revision in writing. *Cognition and Instruction*, **4**, 3–24.

Fitzgerald, J., & Teasley, A. (1986). Effects of instruction in narrative structure on children's writing. *Journal of Educational Psychology*, **78**, 424–432.

Gould, J. (1980). Experiments on composing letters: Some facts, some myths, and some observations. In L. Gregg & E. Steinberg (eds.), *Cognitive processes in writing* (pp. 97–127). Hillsdale, NJ: Erlbaum.

Graham, S. (1982). Composition research and practice: A unified approach. *Focus on Exceptional Children*, **14**, 1–16.

Graham, S. (1983). Effective spelling instruction. *Elementary School Journal*, **83**, 560–568.

Graham, S. (1990). The role of production factors in learning disabled students' compositions. *Journal of Educational Psychology*, **82**, 781–791.

Graham, S. (1997). Executive control in the revising of students with learning and writing difficulties. *Journal of Educational Psychology*, **89**, 223–234.

Graham, S. (1999). Handwriting and spelling instruction for students with learning disabilities: A review. *Learning Disability Quarterly*, **22**, 78–98.

Graham, S., Berninger, V., Abbott, R., Abbott, S., & Whitaker, D. (1997). The role of mechanics in the composing of elementary school students: A new methodological approach. *Journal of Educational Psychology*, **89**, 170–182.

Graham, S., & Harris, K. R. (1989). A component analysis of cognitive strategy instruction: Effects on learning disabled students' compositions and self-efficacy. *Journal of Educational Psychology*, **81**, 353–361.

Graham, S., & Harris, K. R. (1994). The role and development of self-regulation in the writing process. In D. Schunk B. Zimmerman (eds.), *Self-regulation of learning and performance: Issues and educational applications* (pp. 203–228). New York: Lawrence Erlbaum.

Graham, S., & Harris, K. R. (1997). It can be taught, but it does not develop naturally: Myths and realities in writing instruction. *School Psychology Review*, **26**, 414–424.

Graham, S., & Harris, K. R. (1998a). Writing instruction. In B. Wong (ed.), *Learning about learning disabilities* (Vol. 2, pp. 391–423). San Diego, CA: Academic Press.

Graham, S., & Harris, K. R. (1998b). Writing and self-regulation: Cases from the self-regulated strategy development model. In D. Schunk & B. Zimmerman (eds.),

Self-regulated learning: From teaching to self-reflective practices (pp. 20–41). New York: Guilford.

Graham, S., & Harris, K. R. (2001). Prevention and intervention of writing difficulties for students with learning disabilities. *Learning Disabilities Research & Practice*, **16**, 74–84.

Graham, S., & Harris, K. R. (2002). Prevention and intervention for struggling writers. In M. Shinn, H. Walker, & G. Stoner (eds.), *Interventions for academic and behavior problems II: Preventive and remedial approaches* (pp. 589–610). Bethesda, MD: NASP Publications.

Graham, S., & Harris, K. R. (2003). Students with learning disabilities and the process of writing: A meta-analysis of SRSD studies. (pp. 383–402) In L. Swanson, K. R. Harris, & S. Graham (eds.), *Handbook of research on learning disabilities*. New York: Guilford.

Graham, S., Harris, K. R., & Fink, B. (2000). Is handwriting causally related to learning to write? Treatment of handwriting problems in beginning writers. *Journal of Educational Psychology*, **92**, 620–633.

Graham, S., Harris, K. R., & Fink, B. (2002). Contributions of spelling instruction to the spelling, writing, and reading of poor spellers. *Journal of Educational Psychology*, **94**, 669–686.

Graham, S., Harris, K. R., Fink, B., & MacArthur, C. (2003). Primary grade teachers' instructional adaptations for struggling writers: A national survey. *Journal of Educational Psychology*, **95**, 279–293.

Graham, S., Harris, K. R., & Loynachan, C. (1993a). The basic spelling vocabulary list. *Journal of Educational Research*, **86**, 363–368.

Graham, S., Harris, K.R., & Loynachan, C. (1996). The directed spelling thinking activity: Application with high frequency words. *Learning Disabilities Research & Practice*, **11**, 34–40.

Graham, S., Harris, K. R., MacArthur, C., & Schwartz, S. (1991). Writing and writing instruction with students with learning disabilities: A review of a program of research. *Learning Disability Quarterly*, **14**, 89–114.

Graham, S., & MacArthur, C. (1988). Improving learning disabled students' skills at revising essays produced on a word processor: Self-instructional strategy training. *Journal of Special Education*, **22**, 133–152.

Graham, S., MacArthur, C., & Schwartz, S. (1995). Effects of goal setting and procedural facilitation on the revising behavior and writing performance of students with writing and learning problems. *Journal of Educational Psychology*, **87**, 230–240.

Graham, S., MacArthur, C., Schwartz, S., & Page-Voth, V. (1992). Improving the compositions of students with learning disabilities using a strategy involving product and process goal setting. *Exceptional Children*, **58**, 322–334.

Graham, S., Schwartz, S., & MacArthur, C. (1993b). Knowledge of writing and the composing process, attitude toward writing, and self-efficacy for students with and without learning disabilities. *Journal of Learning Disabilities*, **26**, 237–249.

Graham, S., & Miller, L. (1979). Spelling research and practice: A unified approach. *Focus on Exceptional Children*, **12**, 1–16.

Graham, S., & Weintraub, N. (1996). A review of handwriting research: Progress and prospects from 1980 to 1994. *Educational Psychology Review*, **8**, 7–88.

Graham, S., Weintraub, N., & Berninger, V. (2001). Which manuscript letters do primary grade children write legibly. *Journal of Educational Psychology*, **93**, 488–497.

Graves, D. (1983). *Writing: Teachers and children at work*. Exeter, NH: Heinemann.

Harris, K. R., & Graham, S. (1985). Improving learning disabled students' composition skills: Self-control strategy training. *Learning Disability Quarterly*, **8**, 27–36.

Harris, K. R., & Graham, S. (1996). *Making the writing process work: Strategies for composition and self-regulation*. Cambridge, MA: Brookline.

Harris, K. R., & Graham, S. (1999). Programmatic intervention research: Illustrations from the evolution of self-regulated strategy development. *Learning Disability Quarterly*, **22**, 251–262.

Harris, K. R., Graham, S., Reid, R., McElroy, K., & Hamby, R. (1994). Self-monitoring of attention versus self-monitoring of performance: Replication and cross-task comparison studies. *Learning Disability Quarterly*, **17**, 121–139.

Hayes, J., & Flower, L. (1986). Writing research and the writer. *American Psychologist*, **41**, 1106–1113.

Hidi, S., & Anderson, V. (1986). Producing written summaries: Task demands, cognitive operations, and implications for instruction. *Review of Educational Research*, **56**, 473–494.

Higgins, E. L., & Raskind, M. H. (1995). Compensatory effectiveness of speech recognition on the written composition performance of postsecondary students with learning disabilities. *Learning Disability Quarterly*, **18**, 159–174.

Hillocks, G. (1986). *Research on written composition: New directions for teaching*. Urbana, IL: National Conference on Research in English.

Hines, L. (2000). *Reader's Digest*, p. 54.

Hubble, S. (1996). News from an uncharted world. *Washington Post Bookworld*, p. 1.

Johnston, P., & Winograd, P. (1985). Passive failure in reading. *Journal of Reading Behavior*, **17**, 279–301.

Jones, D., & Christensen, C. (1999). The relationship between automaticity in handwriting and students' ability to generate written text. *Journal of Educational Psychology*, **91**, 44–49.

Kameenui, E. (1993). Diverse learners and the tyranny of time: Don't fix blame; fix the leaky roof. *The Reading Teacher*, **46**, 376–383.

Kellogg, R. (1987). Effects of topic knowledge on the allocation of processing time and cognitive effort to writing processes. *Memory & Cognition*, **15**, 256–266.

Leinhart, G., Zigmond, N., & Cooley, W. (1980, April). *Reading instruction and its effects*. Paper presented at the Annual Meeting of the American Educational Research Association, Boston.

Linkletter, A. (1962). *Kids sure rite funny! A child's garden of misinformation*. New York: Random House.

MacArthur, C. A. (1996). Using technology to enhance and support the writing processes of students with learning disabilities. *Journal of Learning Disabilities*, **29**, 344–354.

MacArthur, C. A. (1998). Word processing with speech synthesis and word prediction: Effects on the dialogue journal writing of students with learning disabilities. *Learning Disability Quarterly*, **21**, 1–16.

MacArthur, C. A. (1999). Word prediction for students with severe spelling problems. *Learning Disability Quarterly*, **22**, 158–172.

MacArthur, C. A., & Graham, S. (1987). Learning disabled students composing under three methods of text production: Handwriting, word processing, and dictation. *Journal of Special Education*, **21**, 22–42.

MacArthur, C. A., Graham, S., Haynes, J. A., & De La Paz, S. (1996). Spelling checkers and students with learning disabilities: Performance comparisons and impact on spelling. *Journal of Special Education*, **30**, 35–57.

MacArthur, C., & Cavalier, A. (in press). Dictation and speech recognition technology as accommodations in assessments for students with learning disabilities. *Exceptional Children*.

MacArthur, C., Graham, S., Schwartz, S., & Schafer, W. (1995). Evaluation of a writing instruction model that integrated a process approach, strategy instruction, and word processing. *Learning Disability Quarterly*, **18**, 276–291.

MacArthur, C., Schwartz, S., & Graham, S. (1991). Effects of a reciprocal peer revision strategy in special education classrooms. *Learning Disability Research & Practice*, **6**, 201–210.

MacArthur, C., Schwartz, S., Graham, S., Molloy, D., & Harris, K. R. (1996). Integration of strategy instruction into a whole language classroom: A case study. *Learning Disabilities Research & Practice*, **11**, 168–176.

Mariage, T. (1993, December). *The systemic influence of the Early Literacy Project curriculum: A four-year longitudinal study of student achievement from first to fourth grade.* Paper presented at the Annual Meeting of the National Reading Conference, Charleston, SC.

McCutchen, D. (1988). "Functional automaticity" in children's writing: A problem of metacognitive control. *Written Communication*, **5**, 306–324.

McNaughton, D., Hughes, C., & Ofiesh, N. (1997). Proofreading for students with learning disabilities: Integrating computer use and strategy use. *Learning Disabilities Research and Practice*, **12**, 16–28.

Montague, M., Graves, A., & Leavell, A. (1991). Planning, procedural facilitation, and narrative composition of junior high students with learning disabilities. *Learning Disabilities Research and Practice*, **6**, 219–224.

Plimpton, G. (ed.) (1967). *Writers at work: The Paris Review interviews* (Third Series). New York: Viking Press.

Pressley, M., Wharton-McDonald, R., Rankin, J., Mistretta, J., & Yokoi, L. (1996). The nature of outstanding primary-grades literacy instruction. In E. McIntyre & M. Pressley (eds.), *Balanced instruction: Strategies and skills in whole language* (pp. 251–276). Norwood, MA: Christopher-Gordon.

Raskind, M. H., & Higgins, E. (1995). Effects of speech synthesis on the proofreading efficiency of postsecondary students with learning disabilities. *Learning Disability Quarterly*, **18**, 141–158.

Riel, M. M. (1985). The computer chronicles newswire: A functional learning environment for acquiring literacy skills. *Journal of Educational Computing Research*, **1**, 317–337.

Russell, M. (1999). Testing writing on computers: A follow-up study comparing performance on computer and on paper. *Educational Policy Analysis Archives*, **7**(20).

Saddler, B. (2002). *An analysis of the effects of sentence combining practices on the writing of students with average and above-average sentence-combining skills.* Unpublished dissertation, University of Maryland.

Sawyer, R., Graham, S., & Harris, K. R. (1992). Direct teaching, strategy instruction, and strategy instruction with explicit self-regulation: Effects on the composition skills and self-efficacy of students with learning disabilities. *Journal of Educational Psychology*, **84**, 340–352.

Scardamalia, M., & Bereiter, C. (1986). Written composition. In M. Wittrock (ed.). *Handbook of research on teaching* (3rd ed., pp. 778–803). New York: MacMillan.

Schumaker, J., Deshler, D., Alley, G., Warner, M., Clark, F., & Nolan, S. (1982). Error monitoring: A learning strategy for improving adolescent performance. In W. M. Cruickshank & J. Lerner (eds.), *Best of ACLD* (Vol. 3, pp. 179–183). Syracuse, NY: Syracuse University Press.

Schumaker, J., & Sheldon, J. (1985). *The sentence writing strategy.* Lawrence, KS: University of Kansas.

Scott, C. (1989). Problem writers: Nature, assessment, and intervention. In A. Kamhi & H. Catts (eds.), *Reading disabilities: A developmental language perspective* (pp. 303–344). Boston: Allyn & Bacon.

Shapiro, M. (2000). *J. R. Rowling: The wizard behind Harry Potter.* New York: St Martin's Griffin.

Stoddard, B., & MacArthur, C. A. (1993). A peer editor strategy: Guiding learning disabled students in response and revision. *Research in the Teaching of English*, **27**, 76–103.

Swedlow, J. (1999). The power of writing. *National Geographic*, **196**, 110–132.

Sutlin, L. (1989). *Divine invasions: A life of Philip K. Dick.* New York: Harmony.

Wong, B. (1997). Research on genre-specific strategies in enhancing writing in adolescents with learning disabilities. *Learning Disability Quarterly*, **20**, 140–159.

Wong, B. (1994). Instructional parameters promoting transfer of learned strategies in students with learning disabilities. *Learning Disability Quarterly*, **17**, 100–119.

Wong, B., Butler, D., Ficzere, S., Kuperis, S., Corden, M., & Zelmer, J. (1994). Teaching problem learners revision skills and sensitivity to audience through two instructional modes: Student–teacher versus student–student interactive dialogues. *Learning Disabilities Research and Practice*, **9**, 78–90.

Wray, D., Medwell, J., Fox, R., & Poulson, L. (2000). The teaching practices of effective teachers of literacy. *Educational Review*, **52**, 75–84.

CHAPTER 9

Instructional Interventions in Mathematics for Students with Learning Disabilities

Margo A. Mastropieri, Thomas E. Scruggs, Tracy Davidson, and Ritu K. Rana

George Mason University

I. INTRODUCTION

Over much of the nineteenth and twentieth centuries, mathematics has been taught as simply a set of facts, rules, and procedures for dealing with problems involving quantity. In 1989, the National Council of Teachers of Mathematics (NCTM) initiated reform in mathematics education, resulting in the *Curriculum and Evaluation Standards for School Mathematics* (NCTM, 1989; see also NCTM 1991, 1995; Rivera, 1997). These standards were revised in 2000 to become the *Principles and Standards for School Mathematics* (NCTM, 2000). These standards provided six overarching principles to describe features of high-quality mathematics education: equity, curriculum, teaching, learning, assessment, and technology. The standards were proposed for all students K–12 in each of the following areas:

- Number and Operations
- Algebra
- Geometry
- Measurement
- Data analysis and Probability

- Problem Solving
- Reasoning and Proof
- Communication
- Connections
- Representations

For example, the NCTM Standard with respect to Number and Operations specifies that all students must *understand numbers, understand meanings,* and *compute fluently.* Of course, expectations for these standards are different for different grade levels. For students in third to fifth grade, expectations for understanding meanings include "understand various meanings of multiplication and division", "understanding the effects of multiplying and dividing whole numbers", and "understand and use properties of operations, such as the distributivity of multiplication over addition" (NCTM, 2000, p. 148; see also Mastropieri & Scruggs, 2004).

In recent years, the NCTM standards have been seen to have exerted a significant effect on school mathematics programs (Pressley & McCormick, 1995). One major problem of the 1989 standards was that they provided no overt reference to students with disabilities, and therefore were mute on the issue of how the individual needs of students with disabilities were to be addressed (Rivera, 1998).

Many special education professionals expressed concern about the 1989 NCTM standards as applied to students with disabilities (for example, Hofmeister, 1993; Kameenui *et al.*, 1996; Montague, 1996c; Rivera, 1993, 1997). Some of these concerns were based on fears that constructivist methods (e.g., "discovery," "inquiry") which require independent insight on the part of the learner will not be as effective for students with disabilities, for whom insight or deductive inference can be relative weaknesses (e.g., Mastropieri *et al.*, 2001). Another concern about the 1989 standards was that they appeared to rely on theory more than research literature for their conclusions about instruction. Bishop (1990) noted

> It is a little surprising that there is not much reference to the research literature concerning mathematics learning and teaching. There is no impression of the existence of a substantial body of research on which, for example, the proposals in the Standards are based. (p. 366)

NCTM did address the area of disabilities in the 2000 version of the standards, as part of their Equity Principle:

> All students, regardless of their personal characteristics, backgrounds, or physical challenges, must have opportunities to

study—and support to learn—mathematics. Equity does not mean that every student should receive identical instruction; instead, it demands that reasonable and appropriate accomodations be made as needed to promote access and attainment for all students. (NCTM, 2000, p. 11)

NCTM suggested that students with disabilities and other special needs may require accomodations in the form of language support, increased time, oral rather than written assignments, peer mentoring, and cross-age tutoring (NCTM, 2000). However, as in the previous version, little research evidence was provided to support their recommendations. In this chapter, we describe the results of recent intervention research aimed at improving the performance for students with learning disabilities in mathematics.

II. LEARNING DISABILITIES AND MATHEMATICS ACHIEVEMENT

Previous research has suggested that students with learning disabilities can lag far behind other students in the area of mathematics. Scruggs and Mastropieri (1986) reported that mean scores by grade level for 619 primary grade students with learning disabilities ranged between the 18th and 34th percentiles on the Total Math subtest of the Stanford Achievement Test. Parmar *et al.* (1996) reported that a sample of 197 students with learning disabilities and behavioral disorders, in grades 3 through 8, scored as much as 4 years below their nondisabled peers on tests of math problem solving. McLeskey and Waldron (1990) reported that 64% of 906 students in the state of Indiana from ages 5 to 19 were achieving below grade level in mathematics.

That students with learning disabilities frequently underperform in mathematics, however, says little about why this may be so. Montague (1996b) summarized the types of difficulties many students with learning disabilities may exhibit in the area of mathematics (see also Miller & Mercer, 1997):

- Memory and strategic deficits can differentially affect mathematics performance, causing some students to experience difficulty conceptualizing mathematical operations, representing and automatically recalling math facts, conceptualizing and learning algorithms and mathematical formulae, or solving mathematical word problems.
- Language and communication disorders may interfere with students' functioning when they are expected to read, write, and discuss ideas about mathematics.

- Deficiencies in processes and strategies specifically associated with solving mathematical word problems also can interfere with students' conceptual understanding of problem situations and how to address those situations mathematically.
- Low motivation, poor self-esteem, and a history of academic failure can arrest a student's desire to value mathematics and to become confident in his or her ability to become mathematically literate (Montague, 1996b, p. 85).

Montague and Applegate (2000) compared the problem-solving performance of students with learning disabilities, average-achieving students, and gifted students. Their results suggested that students with learning disabilities rated problems as significantly more difficult and scored significantly lower than did both average and gifted students. Students with learning disabilities used significantly fewer problem-solving strategies than did other students.

Cawley *et al.* (1979) described several factors contributing to poor math performance, including (a) problems related to other deficits, such as reading (see also Englert *et al.*, 1987); (b) ineffective or inappropriate instruction; and (c) deficits in psychological processes, such as memory, attention, encoding, or organizational skills. De Bettencourt *et al.* (1993) described deficits of students with learning disabilities in understanding of derived strategies for basic facts. Researchers such as Montague (1996a,b,c) and Lucangeli *et al.* (1998a,b) have provided evidence that students with learning disabilities exhibit lower levels of metacognitive awareness in mathematics than do normally achieving peers.

What intervention strategies have been previously shown to be effective with students with learning disabilities? Mastropieri *et al.* (1991) reviewed research conducted between 1975 and 1989, the year the NCTM Standards were published. They located 30 intervention research studies that documented effective treatments involving reinforcement and goal-setting, specific strategies for computation and problem solving, mnemonic strategies, peer mediation, and computer-assisted instruction. Most intervention strategies focused on computation and employed direct instruction or behaviorally oriented treatments. However, no conclusions can be drawn from that review about research that has been conducted since 1989. More recently, Jitendra and Xin (1997) reviewed mathematics interventions for students with learning disabilities published between 1986 and 1995. Although some significant progress was noted in teaching mathematics, this review was not comprehensive, focusing instead on 14 individual studies concerned with word problem solving involving students with learning and other disabilities, students "at risk," and students receiving remedial instruction. Maccini and Hughes (1997) reviewed mathematics interventions for students with learning disabilities from 1988 to 1995, but confined their review to 20 studies that dealt specifically with adolescents. More recently, Kroesbergen and Van Luit (2003) completed a meta-analysis on math interventions for students with special needs that included studies conducted with students with learning disabilities as well as other at-risk populations.

In a chapter for a previous edition of this volume, Mastropieri *et al.* (1998) reviewed 38 studies of mathematics interventions for students with learning disabilities that had been published between 1988 and 1996. They concluded that a variety of behavioral, cognitive, and metacognitive approaches had been found to be effective in improving mathematics performance of students with learning disabilities. Noteworthy was research demonstrating the effectiveness of metacognitive strategy training across an expanding array of tasks and types of training. Also noted were some novel studies in peer mediation, particularly in goal-setting and homework completion. A number of investigations of computer-assisted instruction (CAI) were also noted, although the results appeared to be inconsistent. Overall, however, the disproportionate representation of research on mathematical computation was noted as a relative weakness, given the amount of such research in the past, and the emphasis of the new NCTM standards on conceptual development. Also given as a concern was the relative shortage of research in higher-level math, such as algebra.

The purpose of the present chapter is to review and summarize intervention research on mathematics performance of students with learning disabilities, in grades K through 12, that has occurred since the research reported by Mastropieri *et al.* (1998). Such a review can provide important information on the present state of knowledge regarding mathematics interventions for students with learning disabilities, and how such information informs previous research, as well as the new NCTM standards. In addition, it is thought that such a review could provide direction for future research efforts in this area.

A. Search Procedures

A systematic literature search was conducted through two computer-based databases, Education Resources Information Center (ERIC) and PsycINFO, to locate articles published from 1997 to 2002 (however, we also included some earlier investigations that were not identified at the time of the previous review). This search procedure used the following descriptors: research or intervention in mathematics, arithmetic, computation, problem solving, or word/story problems in learning disabilities or mildly handicapped individuals. The reference lists of all obtained articles were examined for further sources. Previous reviews (e.g., Gersten *et al.*, in press) were also examined for relevant sources. Finally, a hand search of relevant journals (e.g., *Journal of Learning Disabilities, Learning Disabilities Research & Practice, Exceptional Children*) was conducted.

Articles which met the following criteria were included: First, the target population involved students with learning disabilities enrolled in grades K through 12. Second, the investigation examined the effects of interventions on mathematics performance, as evaluated through experimental or quasi-experimental designs. Third, articles were published from January, 1997, through December, 2002, in order to extend a previous review paper on mathematics interventions for students with learning disabilities, which reviewed studies published prior to December, 1996 (Mastropieri *et al.*, 1998). However, in some cases, studies from 1996 were included if they had not been available for the previous review. As the result of the search procedure, 18 studies from 17 articles were identified which met all selection criteria. These research reports were subdivided into the following topics: instruction referenced to NCTM standards, interventions on computation skills, cognitive strategy instruction, use of manipulatives, and peer mediation, including peer tutoring and cooperative learning.

III. INSTRUCTION REFERENCED TO NCTM STANDARDS

A. Curriculum Comparisons

Some recent research has examined teaching practices consistent with the NCTM standards. Some of this research reflects a departure from more traditional models of instruction in special education, which has emphasized more behavioral, skills-based approaches. Woodward and Baxter (1997) conducted an evaluation of instruction in mathematics incorporating the *Everyday Mathematics* program (Bell *et al.*, 1993), a program that is compatible in many respects with the NCTM standards. Students in inclusive third grade classrooms in two schools employed the *Everyday Mathematics* program while third-graders in another school employed a more traditional basal approach served in the comparison condition. Since the number of students with learning disabilities was small in all classrooms, Woodward and Baxter included academically low-achieving students, so that the total of low-achieving students and students with learning disabilities was 22.

Everyday Mathematics emphasizes concept acquisition and innovative problem solving over computation and procedures. Problems are more in-depth and are taken from either the student's everyday world or information from other curriculum areas, such as geography or life science. Few of the problems appear in the traditional one- or two-step formats that are common in traditional basal and remedial approaches. Consistent with the NCTM standards, students spend a great deal of time identifying patterns, estimating, and developing number sense. In contrast, the traditional basal used in the comparison condition employed many fact or procedurally based examples, and emphasize facts and algorithms, with separate sections devoted to problem solving.

The programs continued throughout the school year, with the students being tested in October and May. Posttests administered at the end of the year revealed that students using *Everyday Mathematics* overall statistically outperformed traditional basal condition students on the concepts subtest of the Iowa Test of Basic Skills, but scores of the two conditions were statistically equivalent on computation, problem solving, and total test score. For higher achieving students, results were more pronounced, with *Everyday Mathematics* condition students statistically outperforming traditional basal condition students on the concepts and the problem solving subtests. However, for lower-achieving students and students with learning disabilities, no statistically meaningful differences were observed on any subtest or total test score. Overall, *Everyday Mathematics* condition students scored higher on a test of problem-solving ability, but the differences were less pronounced for the low-achieving students. In spite of these results, however, Woodward and Baxter (1997) did not conclude that the results supported special educators' concerns about the NCTM standards. Students with learning disabilities and low-achieving students performed as well in the *Everyday Mathematics* program as did similar students in the traditional basal program. In fact, teachers had more difficulty reaching the lowest-achieving students in both conditions; and if one problem in the *Everyday Mathematics* condition reflected the structure and content of the curriculum, other problems included limited educational resources, including personnel, time, and specialized instructional techniques. Such problems are commonly found in most inclusive classrooms.

B. Videodisc-Based Learning

Bottge and colleagues incorporated several principles of the NCTM standards in videodisc-based instruction for eighth grade students with learning disabilities and other low achieving students in math. Bottge *et al.* (2001) employed the Kim's Komet program (Cognition and Technology Group at Vanderbilt University, 1997) to help students develop informal understandings of prealgebraic concepts, including nonlinear functions, independent and dependent variables, rate of change expressed as slope, and measurement error. These are all concepts recommended by the NCTM standards.

In the "anchor" from Kim's Komet, two girls, named Kim and Darlene, compete in a model soapbox derby. Students are required to help Kim create a graph to predict where on the derby ramp she should release her car in order to negotiate successfully several stunts at the end of a straightaway, including a long jump, a loop, and a banked curve. The video presents several challenges to students to compute relative rates of speed and to construct a graph to predict the speed of Kim's car. In this investigation, the teacher built the ramp and track for students to make and test their predictions. In the comparison condition, students practiced a number of problems involving distance, rate, and time. In this investigation, students in a remedial math and a prealgebra class received the videodisc and enhanced anchored instruction (EAI), and two prealgebra classes received traditional problem instruction (TPI). All classes included students with learning disabilities; however, the groups were not comparable overall, since the EAI condition included a remedial math class that was lower-functioning than the TPI condition classes.

Results indicated that the students in the remedial math class scored lower than the prealgebra classes on problem solving at pretest, but did not differ significantly from the prealgebra classes at posttest. However, students in the prealgebra EAI class did not score differently from students in the prealgebra TPI classes. No impact overall of instruction was noted on the computation test.

Bottge *et al.* (2002) evaluated the effectiveness of EAI and TPI again, this time in the context of seventh-grade students with and without disabilities in inclusive classes. Students were assigned at random to EAI or TPI groups. The sample included seven students with learning disabilities. In this investigation, the enhanced anchor instruction was named Fraction of the Cost, and involved three students discussing how they can afford to build a skateboard ramp. They determine the needed material and equipment, and students are asked to determine how they can afford to build the ramp with the money they have. Students then spent six days in the technology education classroom planning and building wooden benches to be used at a new high school. Students in the TPI condition covered the same content in a series of single- and multistep text-based problems. In this investigation, it was found that students in the EAI condition outperformed students in TPI on a contextualized problem test and a transfer test; however, differences were not observed on computation and word problem tests. Data were not analyzed separately for students with disabilities, perhaps because of the small sample size; however, descriptive analysis suggested the effects were somewhat less pronounced on the contextualized test for the students with disabilities.

IV. INTERVENTIONS ON COMPUTATION SKILLS

A. Cover–Copy–Compare

Stading and Williams (1996) examined the effects of the Cover–Copy–Compare procedure for learning multiplication facts in an 8-year-old girl with learning disability. The procedure was evaluated using a multiple baseline procedure across math tables, and was implemented by a parent at home. After baseline data were collected, the student reviewed flashcards with math facts, and completed 16 multiplication facts on a sheet. Then the student was taught to look at the multiplication problem, read it aloud, and answer the problem as she was copying it onto her paper. Then she covered the problem and answer, as she wrote them a second time, and compared the written answer to the example. At the end of the study period, the student was presented with a probe sheet with 16 multiplication facts. After 5 to 14 days of baseline data over all tables and 5 to 15 days of treatment, it was found that the student demonstrated improvement during the procedure across all sets of problems, ranging from 0 to 35% correct in baseline, to 75 to 100% correct during intervention.

B. Training in Cognitive Reflection

Naglieri and colleagues developed training procedures based upon a modern view of intelligence following the analyses of brain structures by Luria (e.g., 1966). These structures have been said to involve three functional units: "(a) cortical arousal and attention; (b) simultaneous and successive information processes; and (c) planning, self-monitoring, and structuring of cognitive activities" (Naglieri & Gottling, 1997, p. 513). These units formed the basis of the PASS theory on which their investigations have been based.

Naglieri and Gottling (1997), arguing that planning processes "provide for the programming, regulation, and verification of behavior and are responsible for behavior such as asking questions, problem solving, and self-monitoring" (p. 514), hypothesized there would be a differential effect when instruction designed to facilitate planfulness was implemented with students rated low and high in planning. This investigation was intended to replicate an earlier investigation (Naglieri & Gottling, 1995), but to have instruction delivered by the general classroom teacher and conducted over a longer period of time. After identifying elementary grade students with learning disabilities as high or low in planning, according to the Cognitive Assessment System (CAS; Naglieri & Das, 1997), all students were exposed to 21 intervention sessions in which students attempted to solve 54 mathematics problems presented in a worksheet within 10 minutes.

Self-reflection sessions were designed to prompt recognition of the student's need to be planful and to use an efficient strategy when completing math problems. Teachers encouraged students to determine how they completed their worksheets, discuss their ideas, consider how their methods worked, and to be self-reflective. To promote self-reflection, teachers asked questions such as the following:

Can anyone tell me anything about these problems?
Why did you do it that way?
What could you have done to get more correct?
What did it teach you? (Naglieri & Gottling, 1997, p. 516)

In response, students said such things as,

When I get distracted, I'll move my seat.
I'll do the easy ones first.
I have to remember to add the numbers after multiplying.
I have to keep the columns straight.
Be sure to get them right, not just get them done. (Naglieri & Gottling, 1997, p. 516)

Naglieri and Gottling identified four students low in planning and four students high in planning. After the instructional intervention, data analysis revealed that all students gained in performance; however, students low in planning appeared to make differential gains as a result of training.

More recently, Naglieri and Johnson (2000) conducted a similar investigation intended to determine whether instruction to facilitate planning would have differential effects depending on the specific cognitive characteristics of each student, including planning, attention, simultaneous, and successive (PASS) characteristics. Nineteen students, 12 to 14 years of age, who had been placed in special education settings for math instruction, were provided with assessments on the CAS which identified students as low in planning (target condition), or low in attention, simultaneous, or successive processing, or not low on any PASS score. All students were provided with baseline assessments, then provided with an intervention in which they completed worksheets, engaged in discussions about the strategies they found to be most effective, and completed another worksheet. After the intervention was completed, student performance was evaluated with respect to their PASS scores. It was found that students with low planning scores improved from 63 to 338% over baseline. Overall, this group improved 167% over baseline. However, students with cognitive weaknesses in other areas, or no weaknesses as assessed on the PASS (e.g., low in attention, simultaneous, or successive processing), improved much less from the intervention; students with lower scores in simultaneous processing deteriorated slightly (−10%). Results provided support for instructional strategies tailored to students' cognitive characteristics.

V. COGNITIVE STRATEGY INSTRUCTION

A. Schema-Based Instruction

Jitendra and Hoff (1996) investigated the effectiveness of a schema-based direct instruction strategy on word problem-solving performance of three third- and fourth-grade students with learning disabilities, based on an earlier report by Jitendra and Hoff (1995). After assessing baseline performance on simple story problems, students were taught a strategy for solving the problems. First, students were taught to recognize features of the semantic relations in the problem, and to identify different problem types, including "change," "group," and "compare" problems. For example, change problems could involve an individual who has a beginning amount of some objects (e.g., marbles) and a different amount of the same objects at the end. Group problems refer to those in which more than one individual has a set of objects. Compare problems identify individuals who have different quantities of the same objects. After being taught to identify types of problems, students were taught to create schematic representations of the problem. For example, for a change problem, a diagram could be created to represent a beginning amount, a change amount, and an ending amount. Next, students were taught to map critical problem elements onto the schemata diagrams and to highlight the missing element with a question mark. Students were then taught to identify from the verbal text the specific change word that indicated whether the beginning amount became more or less. If the change caused the ending amount to be more, the word *total* was written under the ending amount in the schema diagram. Otherwise, the word *total* would be written under the beginning amount. Students were then taught a simple rule to determine whether to add or subtract: When the total was unknown, the other numbers were added; when the total and one of the other numbers were known, the problem required subtraction. Results suggested that the intervention successfully promoted accuracy in solving word problems. In addition, the problem-solving skills were seen to maintain for 2 to 3 weeks after the study was completed. Interviews administered after the final probe suggested that students found the strategy useful in helping them solve word problems.

Potential shortcomings with the Jitendra and Hoff (1996) investigation include the small number of participants and the lack of an alternative treatment condition. Jitendra *et al.* (1998) compared the effectiveness of the explicit schema-based strategy with a traditional-basal strategy on the acquisition, maintenance, and generalization of mathematical word problem solving. Twenty-five students from grades 2 through 5 with mild learning, developmental, or emotional disabilities and 9 students of the same age at risk for mathematics failure were randomly assigned to schema-based or traditional-basal instruction. Students in the traditional-basal condition received instruction on problem solving using a 5-step checklist procedure taken from a mathematics basal program. Students in both conditions received instruction in all three problem types. After 17–20 days of instruction, it was reported that the performance of both groups increased after treatment. Additionally, according to generalization and maintenance tests, students were able to maintain their use of word problem-solving skills and generalized the strategy effects to novel word problems. However, differences between groups on the posttest, delayed posttest, and generalization test favored students in the schema condition. Students in the schema condition scored similarly to an additional normally achieving peer group on the immediate and delayed posttest. Finally, student interviews suggested that students in the schema condition appreciated the usefulness of the procedures in solving word problems and rated their condition more highly than did those in the traditional-basal condition.

B. Strategies for Algebra Learning

STAR Strategy

In two studies, Maccini and colleagues (Maccini & Hughes, 2000; Maccini & Ruhl, 2000) implemented similar procedures to teach algebra problem solving to secondary students with learning disabilities. Both studies employed single-subject designs in which three and six students participated in the studies. Both studies taught students a cognitive strategy—STAR— and used a teaching sequence based on concrete to semiconcrete to abstract in instruction. Concrete applications employed algebra tiles, and semiconcrete applications employed two-dimensional representations of algebra tiles on paper. STAR represented steps, including Search the problem, Translate the problem into words or pictures, Answer the problem, and Review the problem. In the Maccini and Hughes (2000) investigation, six students with learning disabilities learned the strategy, which was evaluated by means of a single-subject multiple baseline research design. Students received training for 40 minutes each day for one to two months, depending on the time needed to obtain 80% accuracy on each assessment. All students had scored below 80% prior to training. Students were taught using the Strategic Math Series (STAR), which consisted of the following elements:

1. Provide an advance organizer (identify new skills and provide rationale for teaching it);
2. Describe and model think-aloud protocols involving the STAR procedure: (a) Search the word problem (read the problem, ask what facts are known and unknown, write down the facts), (b) Translate the words into

an equation in picture form (choose a variable, identify the operation, represent the problem, draw a picture, and write an algebraic equation), (c) Answer the problem, and (d) Review the solution (reread the problem, ask the question, "Does the answer make sense and why?" and then check the answer).

Students were also provided with guided practice and independent practice. They then received a posttest and positive and corrective feedback on their performance.

When students reached mastery, they were given 10 more complex word problems. Results suggested that five of the six participants improved in (a) percent of correct problem representation, (b) percent correct on solution and answer, and (c) percent of strategy usage from baseline to instructional phase. The sixth student was frequently absent and could not complete many of the objectives. The participants improved percent of accuracy on problem representation from baseline to maintenance. Results of the Maccini and Ruhl (2000) investigation were similar, although only one of the three students in that study demonstrated successful transfer performance.

Self-Instruction Training

Lang *et al.* (in press) conducted an investigation intended to determine the effects of self-instructional training on the algebra problem solving performance of students with learning disabilities, students for whom English is a second language, and students who were at risk of failing algebra. Four classes of 74 students, including 17 with learning disabilities, 37 who spoke English as a second language, and 20 who were considered at-risk for math failure, were assigned randomly to either a self-instructional training condition or a traditional instructional condition. All students were administered pretests, immediate posttests, and delayed posttests of algebra problem solving, as well as pre- and post-strategy usage questionnaires and attitude measures. Students were trained daily over a two-week period.

Traditional instruction condition students were provided with procedures for problem solution typically represented in algebra textbooks. Students were not provided with any specific self-instruction strategy training. In the strategy condition, students were given two worksheets containing the self-instruction strategy steps. On the first worksheet, students wrote out each step of the strategy. This worksheet was used during the first four days of training. The second worksheet was a simple checklist that was given to students as they became more comfortable with the strategy steps. The steps included the following:

(a) if I use this strategy, I will be successful,
(b) read the problem,

(c) what is known?
(d) what is not known?
(e) represent the knowns,
(f) represent the unknowns,
(g) do I need more than one equation?
(h) what is the equation?
(i) substitute the knowns into the equation,
(j) solve the equation, and
(k) have I checked my answer? (Lang *et al.*, in press, Appendix A).

Analysis of results revealed that the performance of both groups increased significantly from pretest to immediate posttest and delayed posttest, but no statistically significant difference was found between groups. However, the self-instruction group significantly outperformed the traditional instruction group on reported independent strategy use. Moreover, strategy usage and immediate and delayed posttest scores were found to be significantly correlated, indicating that students who successfully learned the strategy had better performance on the math problem solving tests. No significant differences were found across groups in attitude change.

VI. USE OF MANIPULATIVES

Cass *et al.* (2002) investigated the effect of manipulative instruction on the acquisition and maintenance of problem solving involving perimeter and area by students with learning disabilities in math. Three secondary-level students were provided with instruction using geoboards as an aid to problem solution. The teacher first defined perimeter and demonstrated with concrete examples on the geoboard. The teacher demonstrated how to create shapes on the geoboard and determine their perimeters. Problems from the math text were also given, first with prompts, then with no prompts. For problem solving involving area, the teacher first defined area, then used the geoboard to determine the area of different shapes. Students were then given problems from the math text to solve, first with teacher prompts as necessary to assist students with problem solving, and then with no teacher prompts. Daily tests were provided, followed by maintenance checks, administered twice a week in each of three consecutive weeks following treatment. A multiple baseline design across students and across behaviors (perimeter and area) was employed. Results revealed that none of the students were able to solve any of the area or perimeter problems during baseline; however, all three students reached criterion (80% or greater problems solved correctly on three consecutive days) within 7 days of intervention. Maintenance checks revealed that the behavior maintained over three weeks. The authors concluded that concrete manipulatives facilitated acquisition of math skills.

VII. STUDIES INVOLVING PEER MEDIATION

A. Peer Tutoring

Task-Focused Goals

Fuchs *et al.* (1997) investigated the effects of incorporating task-focused goals (TFG) with low-achieving students and students with learning disabilities on math performance in third-grade general education classrooms. The design employed a control classroom, which incorporated basal math instruction on the same topics, and two experimental conditions. Both experimental conditions incorporated peer-assisted learning strategies (PALS), employed twice a week, and curriculum-based measurement (CBM) to monitor student progress. Both experimental conditions received biweekly computerized feedback on their progress. In the task-focused goals treatment, however, students maintained their own charts and set goals for the next two weeks. After approximately 20 weeks of instruction, students took posttests. Results suggested that low-achieving students had benefited differentially from the TFG condition, while students with learning disabilities benefited approximately equally in all conditions. All students in the TFG condition made a greater change in effort than in the other conditions; however, for students with learning disabilities, this change of effort did not translate into higher performance. No effects were found for condition on student motivation. Students in the TFG condition reported enjoying and benefiting from the task-focused goals.

Peer Tutoring and Math Strategies

Owen and Fuchs (2002) examined the effectiveness of strategy instruction on the problem-solving skills of third grade students with learning disabilities. Twenty-four students participated, whose teachers were assigned at random to one of four conditions: control, acquisition (of the strategy), low-dose acquisition plus transfer, and full-dose acquisition plus transfer. In the three experimental conditions, students were explicitly taught a strategy for solving word problems involving the skill of finding half. Students were taught a six-step strategy, similar to the previously described schema-based strategy employed by Jitendra and colleagues, which included the following steps:

(a) read the problem;
(b) draw small circles to represent the number of which the student will find half;

(c) draw a rectangle, then divide in half;

(d) cross out circles one at a time, as each circle is crossed out, place it in alternating boxes;

(e) check by counting to determine there are the same number of circles in each box;

(f) count the circles in one box and write this number with the correct word label as the answer to the problem.

The acquisition condition students received four lessons that provided instruction, modeling, and feedback on use of the strategy. The low-dose acquisition plus transfer condition students received training on transferring the skill to related problems for the third and fourth lessons. The high-dose acquisition plus transfer condition students received four acquisition and two transfer lessons. Students received instruction in general education classrooms of about 20 students. All experimental condition students with learning disabilities were paired with higher-achieving peers to practice the skills during the course of the lessons. The control condition students received basal mathematics instruction on problems involving halves. Results indicated that students in the full-dose acquisition plus transfer condition outscored students in the low-dose acquisition plus transfer and the control conditions. For amount of work showing steps taught in the treatment, the two transfer conditions outperformed the control condition students. Student and teacher attitudes were positive toward working with partners and using the strategy. The authors concluded that strategy instruction can be productively incorporated in peer tutoring configurations to increase math skills for students with learning disabilities.

Teaching for Transfer Using Tutoring and Computers

Fuchs *et al.* (2002) investigated the effectiveness of problem-solving tutoring, which integrated explicit teaching of problem-solving rules and transfer, in improving math problem solving for fourth grade students with mathematics disabilities. Students were randomly assigned to problem-solving tutoring or not, and then to computer-assisted practice, or not. This resulted in four conditions: problem-solving tutoring, computer-assisted practice, problem-solving tutoring plus computer-assisted practice, or a control condition. All conditions received the same curriculum. In conditions incorporating problem-solving tutoring, students were taught the underlying concepts within, and concepts for solving, each of four problem structures: problems involving shopping lists, problems involving halves (see Owen & Fuchs, 2002), "bag" problems in which a quantity of items is included in a single bag, and pictograph problems in which each picture represents a specific quantity. Students practiced solving these problems in tutoring pairs. Students in these conditions also received explicit teaching for transfer, in which transfer was explained, and students were shown how a problem could be represented differently but still retain its structure or solution. Students practiced these problems in tutoring pairs. Students receiving computer-assisted practice were given practice in real-life problem situations that nevertheless mirrored the four problem structures taught within the tutoring conditions. The computer read the text, showed a video that depicted the problem-solving solution, and provided an item bank of words, numbers, and symbols, along with space and tools for building students responses. Students could also create responses on the keyboard. Tutoring condition students and computer condition students received two lessons per week over 12 weeks; tutoring plus computer condition students received four lessons per week over 12 weeks. After the training, all students were tested on story problems, transfer story problems, and real-world problem solving. For story problems and transfer story problems, the tutoring and tutoring plus computer condition students outgained students in the computer and control conditions. Also for the transfer story problems, computer condition students outgained control condition students. Condition-specific differences were not observed on the transfer to real-world problem solving tests. Additionally, it was observed that students in the computer-assisted instruction did descriptively outperform control condition students by a substantial amount; however, the results were not found to be statistically significant.

Peer Tutoring in Algebra

Alsopp (1997) compared classwide peer tutoring with independent practice on algebra learning. In this investigation, 262 eighth grade students in 14 different general mathematics classes participated either in a classwide peer-tutoring condition or a condition in which students completed independent practice activities after instruction on algebra content. Participants included 99 students considered "at risk," including a small number ($n = 10$) of students with disabilities. The nature of disability was not specified, but presumably many of these were students with learning disabilities. Classes were assigned at random to instructional condition. After 5 weeks of intervention, it was found that tutoring and independent study groups did not differ in academic achievement. Students at risk were not seen to benefit differentially from the experimental treatment, nor were students with disabilities, who were not evaluated separately.

Cooperative Learning

Xin (1996) investigated the effects of cooperative learning including computer-assisted instruction in mathematics in inclusive classrooms. In the first study, 118 third grade students, 25 of whom had learning disabilities, were randomly assigned to either a cooperative learning or a whole-class instructional condition. In the cooperative learning condition, students were grouped in teams of four, and two pairs in each team worked at computers using commercially produced computer software covering math computation and application at the third grade level. When the pairs completed a worksheet at the computer, they met as a team to check the answers, where other team members offered help to those having difficulty. After the session was completed, students took a quiz. Students with learning disabilities took quizzes at their appropriate level. At the end of the week, teams received team certificates based upon their quiz scores, identifying them as a "Super Team," "Great Team," or "Good Team" based on their scores. In the whole-class condition, the teacher provided whole-class instruction on the same content. Students worked at the computer and completed worksheets individually. The amount of time spent in instructional activities and the curriculum materials used were the same in both conditions. Analysis of results revealed that students in the cooperative learning condition statistically outperformed students in the whole-class condition. However, no differences were observed on a measure of attitude toward math or on a measure of general education students' acceptance of students with disabilities. Interviews with students with learning disabilities revealed that students provided more positive responses to the inclusive classroom than did students with learning disabilities in the whole-class condition.

In the second study, 92 fourth grade students, 16 of whom had learning disabilities, were randomly assigned to cooperative or individual learning conditions. The cooperative learning classrooms employed the same procedures as those of the first study, while the individual learning condition employed small group or whole-class teaching in addition to individual work on computers and worksheets. In this study, however, significant differences were not observed between conditions on the achievement measure and, in fact, greater descriptive gains were observed in the individual learning condition. Few meaningful differences were observed on the measures of attitude or social acceptance. Interviews of special education students revealed negative responses toward their inclusion in the regular classrooms in both conditions.

Xin offered few explanations for the lack of a positive finding for cooperative learning in the second study. One possibility given was that the students in the second study were older (fourth grade) than students in the first study (third grade), but exactly why this difference could be expected to explain the differential outcomes was not stated. Another possibility given was the fact that a smaller sample size was used in the second investigation. However, the sample size seemed sufficient for this investigation, and in any case, observed descriptive differences favored the individual condition, suggesting that the lack of results had little to do with statistical power. Further research could help clarify such inconsistent outcomes.

VIII. DISCUSSION

In 1998, Mastropieri *et al.* reviewed recent research in mathematics instruction for students with learning disabilities. They concluded that, overall, behavioral, cognitive, and metacognitive interventions had been effective. They noted some novel uses of peer mediation (for example, incorporating goal setting and homework completion) and computer-assisted instruction.

However, 65% of the studies from that period focused on basic computation skills. A variety of treatments was examined, including reinforcement, teacher presentation variables, peer tutoring, self-monitoring, academic strategies, and computer-assisted instruction. This focus contrasted sharply with the recommendations of the NCTM, who have deemphasized computation in favor of applications on real-world problem solving. Further, when problem solving strategies interventions were conducted, they often tended to involve relatively simple and straightforward problems of the sort typically found in math workbooks. Such problems did not generally correspond to the NCTM (1989) emphasis on "word problems of varying structures" (p. 20), such as problems that require analysis of the unknown, problems that provide insufficient or incorrect data, and problems that can be solved in more than one way or that have more than one correct answer. Mastropieri *et al.* (1998) concluded that additional research in solving different types of problems, perhaps using calculators to assist in calculations, would be helpful in the future, particularly as students with learning disabilities are included more in regular class instruction.

The results of the present review are different in several ways from those of the Mastropieri *et al.* (1998) review. First, even though the earlier review covered a similar period of research, the number of reports identified was considerably smaller. Although the reasons for this are unknown, one possibility is the increased emphasis on reading and phonological processes in identification and treatment of learning disabilities that has been seen in recent years (e.g., Bradley *et al.*, 2002; Snow *et al.*, 1998). If true, this is unfortunate, since a very substantial number of students with learning disabilities exhibit substantial difficulties in mathematics, and it seems unlikely that the source of these difficulties in all cases is the consequence of deficits in reading subskills (see Scruggs & Mastropieri, 2003). At any rate, additional research is urgently needed on all aspects of mathematics learning of students with learning disabilities.

Another significant difference from the previous review is the emphasis of the research topics. Very few studies identified for this review focused exclusively on computation, and those that did were more likely to employ higher-order strategies, such as self-reflective thinking, rather than drill and practice or reinforcement. A number of more recent studies involved algebra learning of students with learning disabilities—an area nearly entirely omitted until recently. Several of the problem solving investigations incorporated manipulative materials, while other investigations focused on approaches to mathematics learning that were directly compatible with NCTM standards. The fact that these latter investigations—employing compatible curriculum or technological components—did not produce differentially positive outcomes for students with learning disabilities suggests that further research is needed in this area. Since many special educators are wary of "discovery" or constructivist approaches for their students (e.g., Mastropieri *et al.*, 1997), additional empirical evidence would be of great benefit.

Compared with previous years, the research reviewed here is also notable for its complexity. In fact, it was difficult to combine separate research reports into simple categories, as, for example, peer tutoring interventions also included goal setting or strategy instruction. Cooperative learning interventions included computer-assisted instruction, and more constructivist procedures also included videodisc technology. Interventions on computation included self-reflective strategy training, and training of algebra skills and concepts was undertaken with manipulative materials and strategy training. Such investigations demonstrate an interest in evaluating more broadly based procedures, incorporating computers, manipulatives, and strategy training within instructional formats.

Finally, many of the investigations in this review are notable for the equivocal findings realized in the research (see also Gersten *et al.*, in press). Specific learning strategies, such as cover–copy–compare or schema-based strategies, produced positive results, much as in previous reviews. However, contemporary NCTM-based math curriculum or "Enhanced Anchored Instruction" failed to produce outcomes greater than traditional instructional conditions did. Tutoring involving task-focused goals failed to outperform comparison conditions, and students who participated in interventions involving peer tutoring and/or computer-assisted instruction did not outperform control condition students on tests of "real-world" learning. Nevertheless, target experimental conditions always performed at least as well as controls, and all investigations provided information of interest.

With respect to algebra learning, some interesting contrasts were observed. In two single-subject investigations with small numbers of students, interventions on algebra skills were successful. However, in two group design studies with larger numbers of students, strategy training and classwide peer tutoring did not reliably increase performance over controls. One possible explanation is that single-subject investigations can describe more intensive individualized instruction, and are more likely to realize benefits compared with pre-intervention baseline instruction. Another possibility is that the group design studies compared target interventions with alternative treatments, rather than pre-intervention baseline data, and therefore the test on interventions is much more rigorous. At any rate, the outcomes of all studies are promising and provide implications for future research.

Overall, it can be stated that research in mathematics education for students with learning disabilities is progressing steadily, although much important research still remains to be conducted. The research from this review demonstrates more sophisticated, more complex treatments, often undertaken with contemporary considerations of general education initiatives in inclusive settings. Future researchers and practitioners will be able to benefit greatly from the insights gained from the present research, in planning future research investigations that can help resolve important issues involving constructivist learning, inclusive classrooms, and instructional delivery systems such as computers, videodiscs, and peer mediation. These insights can produce positive gains in mathematics learning for students with learning disabilities.

References

Allsopp, D. H. (1997). Using classwide peer tutoring to teach beginning algebra problem-solving skills in heterogeneous classrooms. *Remedial and Special Education*, **18**, 367–379.

Bell, M., Bell, M., & Hartfield, R. (1993). *Everyday mathematics*. Evanston, IL: Everyday Learning Corporation.

Bentz, J. L., & Fuchs, L. S. (1996). Improving peers' helping behavior to students with learning disabilities during mathematics peer tutoring. *Learning Disability Quarterly*, **19**(4), 202–215.

Bishop, A. J. (1990). Mathematical power to the people. *Harvard Educational Review*, **60**, 357–369.

Bottge, B. A., Heinrichs, M., Chan, S., & Serlin, R. C. (2001). Anchoring adolescents' understanding of math concepts in rich problem-solving environments. *Remedial and Special Education*, **22**(5), 299–314.

Bottge, B. A., Heinrichs, M., Mehta, Z. D., & Hung, Y. (2002). Weighing the benefits of anchored math instruction for students with disabilities in general education classes. *The Journal of Special Education*, **35**(4), 186–200.

Bradley, R., Danielson, L., & Hallahan, D. P. (2002). *Identification of learning disabilities: Research to practice*. Mahwah, NJ: Lawrence Erlbaum Associates.

Cass, M., Cates, D., Jackson, C. W., & Smith, M. (2002). *Facilitating adolescents with disabilities understanding of area and perimeter concepts via manipulative instruction*. (ERIC Document Reproduction Service No. ED461238).

Cawley, J. F., Fitzmaurice, A. M., Shaw, R. A., Kahn, H., & Bates, H. (1979). LD youth and mathematics: A review of characteristics. *Learning Disability Quarterly*, **2**, 29–44.

Chard, D., & Gersten, R. (1999). Number sense: Rethinking arithmetic instruction for students with mathematical disabilities. *Journal of Special Education*, **33**(1), 18–28.

Cognition and Technology Group at Vanderbilt University (1997). *The Jasper project: Lessons in curriculum, instruction, assessment, and professional development.* Mahwah, NJ: Lawrence Erlbaum Associates.

deBettencourt, L. U., Putnam, R. T., & Leinhardt, G. (1993). Learning disabled students' understanding of derived fact strategies in addition and subtraction. *Focus on Learning Problems in Mathematics*, **15**(4), 27–43.

Englert, C. S., Culatta, B. E., & Horn, D. G. (1987). Influence of irrelevant information in addition word problems on problem solving. *Learning Disability Quarterly*, **10**, 29–36.

Fuchs, D., Roberts, H., Fuchs, L. S., & Bowers, J. (1996). Reintegrating students with learning disabilities into the mainstream: A two-year study. *Learning Disabilities Research & Practice*, **11**, 214–229.

Fuchs, L. S., Fuchs, D., Hamlett, C. L., & Appleton, A. C. (2002). Explicitly teaching for transfer: Effects on the mathematical problem-solving performance of students with mathematics disabilities. *Learning Disabilities Research and Practice*, **17**, 90–106.

Fuchs, L. S., Fuchs, D., Karns, K., Hamlett, C. L., Katzaroff, M., & Dutka, S. (1997). Effects of task-focused goals on low-achieving students with and without learning disabilities. *American Educational Research Journal*, **34**, 513–543.

Funkhouser, C. (1995). Developing number sense and basic computational skills in students with special needs. *School Science and Mathematics*, **95**, 236–239.

Gersten, R., Chard, D. J., Baker, S., & Lee, D. S. (in press). Experimental and quasi-experimental research on instructional approaches for teaching mathematics to students with learning disabilities: A research synthesis. *Review of Educational Research*.

Hofmeister, A. M. (1993). Elitism and reform in school mathematics. *Remedial and Special Education*, **14**, 8–13.

Jitendra, A. K., Griffin, C. C., McGoey, K., Gardill, M. C., Bhat, P., & Riley, T. (1998). Effects of mathematical word problem solving by students at risk or with mild disabilities. *The Journal of Educational Research*, **91**, 345–354.

Jitendra, A. K., & Hoff, K. E. (1995). *Schema-based instruction on word problem solving performance of students with learning disabilities.* East Lansing, MI: National Center for Research on Teacher Training. (ERIC Document Reproduction Service No. ED 381 990).

Jitendra, A. K., & Hoff, K. (1996). The effects of schema-based instruction on the mathematical word problem-solving performance of students with learning disabilities. *Journal of Learning Disabilities*, **29**, 422–431.

Jitendra, A. K., & Xin, Y. P. (1997). Mathematical word problem-solving instruction for students with mild disabilities and students at risk for math failure: A research synthesis. *Journal of Special Education*, **30**, 412–438.

Kameenui, E. J., Chard, D. J., & Carnine, D. W. (1996). The new school mathematics and the age-old dilemma of diversity: Cutting or untying the Gordian knot. In M. C. Pugach & C. L. Warger (eds.), *Curriculum trends, special education, and reform: Refocusing the conversation* (pp. 94–105). New York: Teachers College Press.

Kroesbergen, E., & Van Luitt, J. E. H. (2003). Mathematics interventions for children with special needs: A meta-analysis. *Remedial and Special Education*, **24**, 97–114.

Lang, C. R., Mastropieri, M. A., & Scruggs, T. E. (in press). In T.E. Scruggs & M. A. Mastropieri (Eds.). Advances in learning and behavioral disabilities. *Research in secondary settings*: Oxford, UK: Elsevier Science/JAI Press

Lucangeli, D., Coi, G., & Bosco, P. (1998a). Metacognitive awareness in good and poor math problem solvers. *Learning Disabilities Research & Practice*, **12**, 219–244.

Lucangeli, D., Cornoldi, C., & Tellarini, M. (1998b). Metacognition and learning disabilities in mathematics. In T. E. Scruggs & M. A. Mastropieri (eds.), *Advances in learning and behavioral disabilities* (vol. 12, pp. 219–244). Oxford, UK: Elsevier Science/JAI Press.

Luria, A. R. (1966). *Human brain and psychological processes*. New York: Harper & Row.

Maccini, P., & Hughes, C. A. (1997). Mathematics interventions for adolescents with learning disabilities. *Learning Disabilities Research & Practice*, **12**, 165–176.

Maccini, P., & Hughes, C. (2000). Effects of a problem-solving strategy on the introductory algebra performance of secondary students with learning disabilities. *Learning Disabilities Research & Practice*, **15**, 10–21.

Maccini, P., & Ruhl, K. L. (2000). Effects of a graduated instructional sequence on the algebraic subtraction of integers by secondary students with learning disabilities. *Education & Treatment of Children*, **23**, 465–470.

Mastropieri, M. A., & Scruggs, T. E. (2004). *The inclusive classroom: Strategies for effective teaching* (2nd ed.). Columbus, OH: Prentice Hall.

Mastropieri, M. A., Scruggs, T. E., Boon, R. T., & Carter, K. (2001). Correlates of inquiry learning in science: Constructing density and buoyancy concepts. *Remedial and Special Education*, **22**, 130–137.

Mastropieri, M. A., Scruggs, T. E., & Butcher, K. (1997). How effective is inquiry learning for students with mild disabilities? *Journal of Special Education*, **31**, 199–211.

Mastropieri, M. A., Scruggs, T. E., & Chung, S. (1998). Instructional interventions for students with mathematics learning disabilities. In B. Y. L. Wong (ed.), *Learning about learning disabilities* (2nd ed., pp. 425–451). New York: Academic Press.

Mastropieri, M. A., Scruggs, T. E., & Shiah, S. (1991). Mathematics instruction with learning disabled students: A review of research. *Learning Disabilities Research & Practice*, **6**, 89–98.

McLeskey, J., & Waldron, N. L. (1990). The identification and characteristics of students with learning disabilities in Indiana. *Learning Disabilities Research*, **5**, 72–78.

Miller, S. P., & Mercer, C. D. (1997). Educational aspects of mathematics disabilities. *Journal of Learning Disabilities*, **30**, 47–56.

Montague, M. (1996a). Assessing mathematical problem solving. *Learning Disabilities Research & Practice*, **11**, 238–248.

Montague, M. (1996b). Student perception, mathematical problem solving, and learning disabilities. *Remedial and Special Education*, **18**(1), 46–53.

Montague, M. (1996c). What does the "New View" of school mathematics mean for students with mild disabilities? In M. C. Pugach & C. L. Warger (eds.), *Curriculum trends, special education, and reform: Refocusing the conversation* (pp. 84–93). New York: Teachers College Press.

Montague, M., & Applegate, B. (2000). Middle school students' perceptions, persistence, and performance in mathematical problem solving. *Learning Disability Quarterly*, **23**, 215–227.

Naglieri, J. A., & Das, J. P. (1997). *Cognitive assessment system*. Chicago: Riverside.

Naglieri, J. A., & Gottling, S. H. (1995). A study of planning and mathematics instruction for students with learning disabilities. *Psychological Reports*, **76**, 1343–1354.

Naglieri, J. A., & Gottling, S. H. (1997). Mathematics instruction and PASS cognitive processes: An intervention study. *Journal of Learning Disabilities*, **30**(5), 513–520.

Naglieri, J. A., & Johnson, D. (2000). Effectiveness of a cognitive strategy intervention in improving arithmetic computation based on the PASS theory. *Journal of Learning Disabilities*, **33**, 591–597.

National Council of Teachers of Mathematics (1989). *Curriculum and evaluation standards for school mathematics*. Reston, VA: Author. (ERIC Document Reproduction Service No. ED 304 336).

National Council of Teachers of Mathematics (1991). *Professional standards for teaching mathematics*. Reston, VA: Author.

National Council of Teachers of Mathematics (1995). *Assessment standards for school mathematics*. Reston, VA: Author.

National Council of Teachers of Mathematics (2000). *Principles and standards for school mathematics*. Reston, VA: Author.

Owen, R. L., & Fuchs, L. S. (2002). Mathematical problem-solving strategy instruction for third-grade students with learning disabilities. *Remedial and Special Education*, **23**, 268–279.

Parmar, R. S., Cawley, J. F., & Frazita, R. R. (1996). Word problem-solving by students with and without mild disabilities. *Exceptional Children*, **62**, 415–429.

Pressley, M., &McCormick, C. (1995). Advanced educational psychology for educator, researchers, and policy makers. New York: HarperCollins.

Rivera, D. (1993). Examining mathematics reform and the implications for students with mathematics disabilities. *Remedial and Special Education*, **14**, 24–27.

Rivera, D. P. (1997). Mathematics education and students with learning disabilities: Introduction to the special series. *Journal of Learning Disabilities*, **30**, 2–19.

Rivera, D. P. (1998). Mathematics education and students with learning disabilities. In D. Rivera (ed.), *Mathematics education for students with learning disabilities* (pp. 1–31). Austin, TX: Pro-Ed.

Scruggs, T. E., & Mastropieri, M. A. (1986). Academic characteristics of behaviorally disordered and learning disabled children. *Behavioral Disorders*, **11**, 184–190.

Scruggs, T. E., & Mastropieri, M. A. (2003). Issues in the identification of learning disabilities. In T. E. Scruggs & M. A. Mastropieri (eds.), *Identification and assessment of learning disorders: Advances in learning and behavioral disabilities* (Vol. 16). Oxford, UK: Elsevier Science/JAI Press.

Snow, C. E., Burns, M. S., & Griffin, P. (eds.) (1998). *Preventing reading difficulties in young children.* Washington, DC: National Academy Press.

Stading, M., & Williams, R. L. (1996). Effects of a copy, cover, and compare procedure on multiplication facts mastery with a third grade girl with learning disabilities in a home setting. *Education & Treatment of Children,* **19,** 425–434.

Swanson, H. L., O'Shaughnessy, T. E, McMahon, C. M., Hoskyn, M., & Sachse-Lee, C. M. (1998). A selective synthesis of single subject intervention research on students with learning disabilities. In T. E. Scruggs & M. A. Mastropieri (eds.), *Advances in learning and behavioral disabilities* (Vol. 12, pp. 79–126). Oxford, UK: Elsevier Science/JAI Press.

Wilson, R., Majsterek, D., & Simmons, D. (1996). The effects of computer-assisted versus teacher-directed instruction on the multiplication performance of elementary students with learning disabilities. *Journal of Learning Disabilities,* **29,** 382–390.

Woodward, J., & Baxter, J. (1997). The effects of an innovative approach to mathematics on academically low-achieving students in inclusive settings. *Exceptional Children,* **63,** 373–388.

Xin, F. (1996). *The effects of computer-assisted cooperative learning in mathematics in integrated classrooms for students with and without disabilities. Final Report.* Report for the U. S. Department of Education, Office of Special Education Programs. Rowan College of New Jersey, Glassboro. (ERIC Document Reproduction Service No. ED412696).

CHAPTER 10

Social Competence/Social Skills of Students with Learning Disabilities: Interventions and Issues

Sharon Vaughn,[*] **Jane Sinagub,**[†] **and Ae-Hwa Kim**

[*]*University of Texas at Austin*
[†]*University of Miami*
Dankook University

I. SCOPE AND OBJECTIVES

Students with learning disabilities (LD), by definition, experience learning problems that interfere with their academic success in the classroom. Many students with LD, however, exhibit substantial difficulties in social competence as well (Gresham *et al.*, 2001). A number of professionals have addressed the importance of social competence difficulties of students with LD (Gresham, 1992; Gresham & Elliott, 1989, 1990; La Greca & Stone, 1990).

This chapter provides an overview of social competence and focuses on instructional methods for enhancing the social competence of students with LD. Specific interventions developed for and evaluated with students with LD are described, as are social skills interventions that can be used with students of other populations. Also, findings from syntheses of research on social interventions for preschoolers with disabilities are presented. The chapter further addresses issues that are relevant to teaching children and adolescents with LD social skills. Finally, directions for future research in the area of social skills intervention for students with LD and other disabilities are discussed.

After reading this chapter, the reader will be able to meet each of the following objectives:

1. Define "social competence" and "social skills."
2. Explain why many students with LD need to be taught social skills and why teachers may not emphasize teaching social skills in their curricula for students with LD.
3. Summarize the procedures and critical comments concerning empirically substantiated social skills interventions for students with LD. These interventions include a social skills program for adolescents (ASSET), an interpersonal problem solving intervention, cooperative learning, and mutual interest discovery.
4. Summarize the findings from a meta-analysis of school-based interventions to enhance the self-concepts of students with LD.
5. Summarize procedures and critical comments regarding empirically substantiated social skills interventions with other populations. These interventions include structured learning, social decision making, and peer social initiations.
6. Summarize the findings from syntheses of research on social interventions for preschoolers with disabilities, including (a) social skills interventions and (b) toys and group composition.
7. Explain several key issues related to teaching social skills to students with LD.
8. Discuss future directions for research related to social competence of students with LD and other disabilities.

II. OVERVIEW OF SOCIAL COMPETENCE/SOCIAL SKILLS

A. What are Social Competence and Social Skills?

Defining social competence and social skills has been approached by many researchers and proven to be an enigmatic task. As a result, various models to conceptualizing social competence have been proposed. Vaughn and Hogan (1990) proposed that the construct of social competence is multifaceted, encompassing several individual components. Although these components are described separately, social competence is best understood as a combination of these components. The four components included in Vaughn and Hogan's (1990) model are: (a) social skills (e.g., the ability to initiate and respond appropriately to others), (b) relationships with others (e.g., friendships, peer acceptance), (c) age-appropriate social cognition (e.g., the ability to problem solve and to recognize and monitor social situations), and (d) the absence of behaviors associated with social maladjustment (e.g., absence of aggressive behavior, attention problems, acting out, withdrawal). In this model, Vaughn and Hogan (1990) stressed the need to look at social skills as part of a higher-order construct—social competence.

Another model for conceptualizing social competence, a social validity model, differentiates social competence, a trait, from social skill, a behavior (Bruck, 1986; Curran, 1979; Gresham, 1983, 1998; Wolf, 1978). Social competence as a trait represents an evaluation of individual social behavior based on the competent performance of social tasks in a given situation (McFall, 1982). In contrast, social skills as behaviors are viewed as specific, observable behaviors that an individual demonstrates in order to perform competently on specific social tasks (McFall, 1982). Social skills are viewed as specific behaviors, and social competence is a judgment about those behaviors.

Lastly, social competence is conceptualized as a function of the student's processing social environmental clues in a social exchange model (Dodge, 1986; Dodge *et al.*, 1986). In this model, the construct of social competence consists of three components: (a) perceiving, decoding, and interpreting environmental clues; (b) selecting an appropriate response; and (c) appropriately implementing the social response.

In sum, although there has not been a complete conceptualization of social competence, most researchers agree that conceptually social competence has changed from a global concept referring to the overall adequacy of a person's social performance (Kratochwill & French, 1984) to a multidimensional construct composed of several interacting components (e.g., social skills, self-concept; Vaughn & Hogan, 1990).

B. Why Teach Social Skills to Students with LD?

Traditionally, the rationale has been that social skills are a means to enhancing the social and academic success of students. Many researchers have recognized the importance of social competence in the academic and social development of all students. A meta-analysis by Kavale and Forness (1996) revealed that 75% of students with LD manifested social incompetence that differentiated them from normal developing students. Due, at least in part, to social incompetence, students with LD are less accepted and more frequently rejected by their classmates than are their non-LD peers (NLD; i.e., average- and high-achieving students) (Haager & Vaughn, 1995; Stone & La Greca, 1990; Swanson & Malone, 1992; Vaughn *et al.*, 1998, 1993a; Wiener, 1987; Wiener & Harris, 1997).

Although there is a positive correlation between academic underachievement and peer rejection (Vaughn *et al.*, 1991), rejection of students with LD is not solely a function of their academic difficulties, as illustrated in the following studies. In the studies by Bryan and colleagues (1979, 1980), strangers observed students on videotape for only a few minutes. Despite being kept unaware of which students were LD and which were NLD, the strangers were more likely to perceive the students with LD more negatively than the NLD students. In another study, the social skills, peer acceptance, and self-perceptions of students with LD prior to identification were compared with their NLD peers (Vaughn *et al.*, 1990). Results revealed that as early as 8 weeks after entering kindergarten, students at risk for LD who were later identified as LD differed significantly from their NLD peers on social variables and behavior problems (e.g., social skills, self-perceptions of social acceptance, peers' ratings of acceptance, teacher ratings of behavior problems).

Addressing social incompetence of students with LD is critical because students who experience peer rejection are at greater risk for a myriad of negative outcomes, including later adjustment difficulties, school dropout, loneliness, and juvenile delinquency (for review, see Kupersmidt *et al.*, 1990; Parker & Asher, 1987; Roff *et al.*, 1972). Although many students with LD exhibit social incompetence that manifests as low peer acceptance and low popularity, social skills instruction often is not a high priority in the curricula (Baum *et al.*, 1988). Similarly, although teachers believe that many students are in need of social skills instruction, they often do not address this need in the goals or objectives of students' IEPs (Baum *et al.*, 1988).

Since peer relationships are highly valued by our society and associated with many positive outcomes, why is it that so few teachers teach interpersonal skills? The answer to this question may be that teachers are aware that students with LD have social incompetence, but do not value social skills as an important element of the curricula. In other words, educators may view the teaching of social skills as "taking away" from a student's academic program. Conversely, some teachers may highly value the importance of teaching social skills but perceive that social skills are not valued by the school system and/or parents; thus, they do not teach them.

Perhaps too, some teachers believe social skills are important and wish that their students demonstrated more prosocial behaviors but do not believe it is the school's responsibility to teach social skills. These teachers believe that positive social behaviors should be learned at home, and it is the family's duty to ensure the acquisition and mastery of these behaviors. Also, some educators consider social skills something that is acquired incidentally through the "growing up" process. They think of social skills more as a "characteristic" of the youngster rather than as behaviors that are amenable to change. Fortunately, many youngsters learn appropriate social behaviors without direct, systematic instruction. Social skills, however, are best strengthened through structured intervention programs.

Finally, the rationale to which the greatest number of educators subscribe may be that social skills are not taught because teachers do not know how to teach them. Teachers take courses that focus on teaching language arts, math, reading, and the academic subjects for which they are responsible and may even take courses on how to structure and manage behaviors in the classroom. Very few teachers, however, take courses that provide opportunities for learning how to teach social skills to their students. Teaching social behaviors requires that the teacher understand the development and acquisition of social behavior. Few teachers have confidence in their understanding of the "scope and sequence" of social development or their ability to identify and teach necessary social skills to their students. A first step, then, to providing appropriate social skills instruction for students with LD is to adequately equip teachers with the knowledge and skills of research-based instructional methods to promote social competence/social skills of students with LD.

III. INSTRUCTIONAL METHOD

Students with LD are disproportionately overrepresented as rejected and underrepresented as popular (Vaughn et al., 1990; Wiener & Harris, 1997). The number of students with LD who are rejected by their peers is considerably greater than the number of NLD students who are rejected. In fact, approximately 50% of students with LD are identified as poorly accepted (Stone & La Greca, 1990; Vaughn et al., 1991). Similarly, Vaughn et al., (1990) found that 60% of students with LD were rejected by peers.

Increasing positive peer interaction and peer acceptance for students with LD requires careful planning of the interventions that provide systematic instruction in appropriate social skills, or provide opportunities for students with LD and their NLD classmates to spend structured time together and get to know each other better. Efforts involving merely grouping youngsters with LD with their NLD classmates failed to improve peer acceptance ratings, In fact, in some cases, the peer acceptance ratings of the students with LD actually decreased after the grouping effort (for review, see McIntosh et al., 1991). This chapter describes empirically substantiated interventions that have demonstrated increased peer ratings for participating students.

A. Empirically Substantiated Interventions with Students with LD

Three interventions will be discussed in this section: (a) a social skills program for adolescents, (b) an interpersonal problem-solving intervention, and (c) cooperative learning. An introduction to each intervention will be provided as well as procedures for implementing each intervention and evaluative comments.

1. A Social Skills Program for Adolescents (ASSET)

A Social Skills Program for Adolescents (ASSET) is designed to teach adolescents the social skills they need to interact successfully with peers and adults. Research has documented ASSET's positive effects for adolescents with LD and adjudicated youth (Hazel *et al.*, 1981). ASSET is based on eight social skills considered fundamental to creating and maintaining relationships with others: (a) giving positive feedback, (b) giving negative feedback, (c) accepting negative feedback, (d) resisting peer pressure, (e) problem solving, (f) negotiation, (g) following instructions, and (h) starting and maintaining conversation. The focus on these skills derives from the belief that many adolescents do not exhibit desirable behaviors because they do not know how to perform desirable behaviors, not because they are not motivated to do so. The program's teaching procedures are based on success, successive approximations, mastery, and multiple exemplars. Materials include videotapes of eight teaching sessions, skill sheets, home notes, and criterion checklists.

Each ASSET lesson is taught in a small group and involves nine basic steps. Step one focuses on the review of previously learned skills, including reviewing homework. Step two focuses on explaining the skill on which the lesson focuses. This is either a description of the skill being taught or an overview of a new skill. Step three focuses on "hooking" the student into learning the skill by providing a convincing rationale for its importance. Step four focuses on discussing example situations in which the target skill can be used. The situations must be specific and believable and be related to adolescent life. Students can also volunteer their own examples. Step five focuses on examining the steps or subskills necessary to carry out the target skill. A skill sheet provides the step-by-step sequence of subskills needed to effectively implement each target skill. Step six focuses on modeling the skill itself. Videotapes model how a student can implement particular skills. Activities for students to demonstrate and model specific skills are also provided. Step seven focuses on verbal rehearsal that familiarizes students with the sequence of steps associated with the target skill and provides a procedure for memorizing these steps. Step eight focuses on behavioral rehearsal and criterion performance that provides an opportunity for the students to practice the skills and demonstrate that the criterion for exhibiting each of the delineated skills is met. Step nine focuses on assigning homework. It may include a home note for recording how a student practices and uses skills outside of the instructional setting, particularly at home. Through the implementation of these nine steps, each of the eight skills is taught.

Comments.   In a study by Hazel *et al.* (1982), eight students with LD were taught six of the eight skills delineated in the ASSET program: giving positive feedback, giving negative feedback, accepting negative feedback, resisting peer pressure, negotiation, and personal problem solving. Following program implementation, the students were tested using behavioral role-play situations on each of the six skills. Students with LD who participated in the intervention demonstrated increases in the use of social skills during role-play situations. When compared with two other groups, however, NLD and court-adjudicated youth, the students with LD made only slight gains on cognitive problem solving.

Due to ASSET's delineation of subskills within each target skill, it is useful for teachers who seek a structured curriculum for teaching social skills. When teaching social skills to adolescents with LD, teachers are advised to "apply the same careful systematic procedures used in teaching academic skills" (Zigmond & Brownlee, 1980, p. 82). ASSET provides the guidelines and curriculum for applying such systematic procedures.

Further research with the ASSET program, however, is needed to determine the extent to which skill acquisition demonstrated during structured situations (e.g., role plays) generalizes to nonstructured situations. For example, do students who display increased social skills in a role-play "testing" situation apply those same social skills in real-life settings? Also needed is further information on how target students perceive ASSET instruction. For instance, it is likely that students who believe the intervention is effective are more likely to apply and generalize the learned skills.

2. An Interpersonal Problem-Solving Intervention

Social skills need to be considered in light of multiple contexts, including family, school, and peer contexts. Fundamental to this perspective is the belief that teaching social skills in isolation is unlikely to provide significant and long-lasting change. A social strategy training program based on this belief and emphasizing a problem-solving approach has been developed and evaluated by Vaughn and colleagues (McIntosh *et al.*, 1995; Vaughn & Lancelotta, 1990; Vaughn *et al.*, 1988, 1991). The following procedures outline this model:

1. The training program begins with a school-wide sociometric assessment in which each student rates her or his same-sex classmates on the extent to which he or she would like to be friends with them.
2. Students who receive few "friendship" votes and many "no friendship" votes form the "rejected group" (i.e., students who need support to make friends); students with many "friendship" and few "no friendship" votes comprise the "popular group" (i.e., students who need less support to make friends).

3. "Social skills trainers" for each participating class consist of a rejected student with LD and a highly popular NLD classmate.
4. Social skills trainers from each participating class are removed from their classrooms several times (e.g., 2–3 times) each week for approximately 30 minutes each session to learn specific social skills strategies.
5. The first social skills strategy taught is the *FAST* strategy (McIntosh *et al.*, 1995). The four steps associated with *FAST* are:
   a. *FREEZE AND THINK!* Do not act too quickly. Stop and think: What is the problem?
   b. *ALTERNATIVES?* What are all of the possible solutions?
   c. *SOLUTION EVALUATION.* What are the likely consequences of each solution? What would happen next if I do...? Select the best solution(s) for the long run as well as the short run.
   d. *TRY IT!* What do I need to do to implement the solution? If it does not work, what else can I try?
6. In addition to the *FAST* strategy, social skills trainers are taught to address solutions in terms of long-run and short-run consequences, and to accept negative feedback by learning the *SLAM* strategy (McIntosh *et al.*, 1995). This strategy uses coaching and role-playing to promote the understanding of lessons and to practice skills. The four components of the *SLAM* strategy are:
   a. *STOP!* Stop whatever you're doing.
   b. *LOOK!* Look the person in the eye.
   c. *ASK!* Ask the person a question to clarify what she or he means.
   d. *MAKE!* Make an appropriate response to the person.
7. Each classroom is given its own problem-solving box (e.g., a decorated shoebox) and the teacher and social skills trainers explain the purpose of the problem-solving box to the class. While social skills trainers are learning the social strategies, other students begin to write problems that they have with other children, at home or on the playground, and store these problems in the box. Problems submitted by students are used by the social skills trainers and the entire class to practice their social problem-solving skills and for discussion.
8. After the social skills trainers have learned a particular strategy (e.g., *FAST*) and rehearsed it using real-life problems, they present the strategy to their classmates with backup and support from the researcher and classroom teacher.
9. In subsequent weeks, the social skills trainers leave the classroom for only one session per week, and review the skill strategy (e.g., *FAST*) with classmates at least once per week. These reviews include large-group explanations and small-group problem-solving exercises using the problems from the problem-solving box.

10. At the end of the training program, social skills trainers are recognized by the principal in front of their classes or schools. Social skills trainers wear special buttons while at school that indicate they are social skills trainers for that school. Other students in the school are asked to consult these social skills trainers when they have interpersonal difficulties.

Comments. This social strategy training program proposed by Vaughn and colleagues has been conducted successfully with a female student with LD in a case study design (Vaughn *et al.*, 1988) as well as with a group of students with LD who were identified by their peers as socially rejected (Vaughn *et al.*, 1991). Many of the students who participated in these studies demonstrated increases in peer acceptance following the intervention. In the case study, the female student with LD, who was identified as "rejected" at pretest, was identified as "popular" at the posttest. In the group intervention, all 10 students with LD were identified as "rejected" at pretest but only 5 were identified as "rejected" at posttest and follow-up. Students who participated in the intervention received significantly more positive nominations at posttest than at pretest. Future work needs to examine the characteristics of students for whom this intervention is successful and those for whom it is not so successful. An additional line of future research could entail extending this model to be used with older children because, as yet, it has only been used with elementary-aged students with LD.

3. Cooperative Learning

Cooperative learning is an instructional approach in which students of different ability levels work together in small groups, using a variety of learning activities to improve their understanding of a subject (Cohen, 1994). Since students in cooperative groups have interdependent goals, each member of the group is responsible not only for completing the task assigned to him or her but also for helping other members complete their assignments (Cohen, 1994; Johnson & Johnson, 1989). There are four key elements of cooperative learning: (a) heterogeneous groups (Slavin, 1990), (b) positive interdependence through shared goals and group rewards (Johnson & Johnson, 1989; Slavin, 1983), (c) accountability for one's own learning (Mainzer *et al.*, 1993), and (d) collaborative and interpersonal skills (Bryant & Bryant, 1998).

While the primary purpose of this intervention is to improve academic skills, cooperative learning has also been used to integrate students with and without disabilities and to increase the social acceptance of children in a group. The cooperative atmosphere, as well as the increased exposure of students to each other in the classroom, is expected to increase peer acceptance. Johnson and Johnson (1986) suggest that classrooms can be organized so students work together in small groups or pairs with an emphasis on helping each other to accomplish goals and learn material. Cooperative learning involves the following procedures:

1. High-, average-, and low-achieving students are assigned to four- or five-member teams. Students who are identified as receiving special education or resource help are assigned randomly to these teams.
2. Students are pretested in the academic area of focus and placed in an individualized program based on their test performance.
3. Students complete the following steps to finish their individualized academic work.
   a. Students bring their skill sheets and answer sheets into pairs or triads within their teams.
   b. Students exchange answer sheets with partners.
   c. Students read the instructions and begin working on their own skill sheet.
   d. When a students completes the first four problems, they check each other's work against answer sheets and help each other with any problem. If the first four problems are answered correctly, he or she goes on to the next skill sheet. If any items are wrong, he or she continues with the next problems.
   e. When the student completes the final skill sheet, he or she takes an exam, which is later scored by a teammate. If the student passes the exam, he or she goes to the next more difficult set of problems. If the student does not pass, the teacher will provide instruction.
4. Teams who meet criteria are rewarded with certificates at the end of the week.
5. During this whole process, the teacher works on specific skills with individuals or small groups of students.

Comments. While the positive effects of cooperative learning on academic and social outcomes for students without disabilities have been well-documented (Newmann & Thompson, 1987; Sharan, 1980; Slavin, 1991), the effects of cooperative learning on the social competence of students with LD has not been as thoroughly examined. Although further research examining these effects for social outcomes for students with LD is needed, some researchers have conducted such research and found positive effects for cooperative learning on social outcomes for students with LD. Johnson *et al.* (1986) examined how different levels of cooperation affected interactions among intermediate grade students, including students with LD. Results revealed that pure cooperation promoted more frequent interaction than did a mixture of cooperation and competition, and it also promoted more constructive interaction than did an individualistic approach. Prater *et al.* (1998) compared three teaching approaches to teach social sills (i.e., teacher-directed instruction, structured natural approach, student-generated cooperative group rule) to teach social skills to students with disabilities, including LD, who also participated in cooperative learning. While students in the teacher-directed instruction group improved their social skills on all three measures used, students in the structured natural approach and the student-generated cooperative group rule groups made minimal gain or no gain, respectively. These results imply that students with disabilities may need social skills instruction that teaches necessary social skills for successful integration prior to being placed in cooperative learning groups. Goodwin (1999) also argued that students need to be taught prerequisite social skills in order to work together successfully in cooperative groups.

B. School-Wide Interventions to Promote Self-Concept for Students with LD

Self-concept can be viewed as a component of social competence (Vaughn & Hogan, 1990). The terms "self-concept," "self-perception," and "self-esteem" refer to how an individual judges and perceives him- or herself (Elbaum & Vaughn, 2001). Two widely used models for conceptualizing self-concept are: (a) Harter's model (Harter, 1985; 1996) and (b) Marsh's model (Marsh, 1992; Marsh & Hattie, 1996). In Harter's model, self-concept is conceptualized as encompassing specific domains such as academic competence, social acceptance, physical appearance, and behavioral conduct, and a global domain. In Marsh's model, self-concept is conceptualized as comprising academic competence (divided into specific content areas) and nonacademic competence (including social, personal/emotional, and physical self-concepts).

How students feel about themselves is important not only for their academic/social development but also for their psychological well-being (Bednar *et al.*, 1989; Harter, 1993; Parker & Asher, 1993; Swann, 1996). Students with negative self-concepts are vulnerable to a host of emotional, social, behavioral, and learning problems (Brendtro *et al.*, 1990). Furthermore, a negative self-concept is resistant to change (Swann, 1996). Unfortunately, students with LD are especially at-risk for having negative self-concepts, particularly in the academic domain (Chapman, 1988; Kavale & Forness, 1996; Prout *et al.*, 1992; Serafica & Harway, 1979; Thurlow, 1980).

Considering the importance of developing a positive self-concept during the school years and the difficulties that students with LD have in this regard, validated interventions that enhance self-concept for this population need to be designed and provided to these students.

Elbaum and Vaughn (2001) conducted a meta-analysis of 64 intervention research studies focusing on school-age students with LD (i.e., elementary, middle, high school students) and measuring self-concept as an outcome. Each school-based intervention included in this meta-analysis was categorized as: (a) a counseling intervention, (b) an academic intervention, (c) a mediated intervention (in which teachers or parents of students received the intervention), (d) a physical intervention (e.g., fitness program, physical recreation), (e) a sensory–perceptual intervention (e.g., sensory integration, perceptual–motor therapy), or (f) an "other" intervention, one that did not fit any of the other categories. The self-concept domains assessed by these intervention studies included: (a) general (e.g., general global, overall), (b) academic (e.g., academic, scholastic, intellectual, school), (c) social (e.g., affiliation, parents, peers, popularity, social maturity), (d) personal/emotional (e.g., affective, anxiety, happiness, behavior, competence), and (e) physical (e.g., athletic, appearance).

Across 82 samples of students with LD included in this meta-analysis, the mean weighted effect size was 0.19. Although the mean weighted effect size was relatively small, it was reliably different from 0. This finding suggests that school-based interventions can enhance the self-concept of students with LD. Additionally, this meta-analysis revealed that intervention effects were moderated by several variables. First, a student's grade level was an important moderator of intervention outcomes—middle school students benefited more from interventions than did elementary or high school students. Additionally, the type of intervention that was most effective varied by grade level for students with LD. Whereas counseling interventions were most effective for middle and high school students with LD, the most effective interventions for elementary school students with LD focused on improving students' academic skills. This finding encourages secondary schools to have counseling services available to students. Elementary educators can improve students' self-concept by providing the students with appropriate instruction and helping them experience genuine academic success.

Second, the domain of self-concept was another important moderator of intervention outcomes—interventions had a greater effect on students' academic self-concepts (d = 0.28) than on other self-concept domains. It may suggest that academic self-concept is more easily changeable than other domains of self-concept. Third, there was evidence of an alignment of intervention types and intervention outcomes. For instance, physical interventions influenced physical self-concept and academic interventions had a significant effect on academic self-concept. This finding supports Marsh's argument (Marsh & Yeung, 1998) for tailoring outcomes measures to the goals of an intervention.

C. Empirically Substantiated Interventions with Other Populations

1. Structured Learning

Structured learning, also referred to as skillstreaming, is one of the first social skill training approaches to teaching prosocial skills to children (McGinnis & Goldstein, 1990, 2000) and adolescents (Goldstein & McGinnis, 1997). Teachers, social workers, psychologists, or school counselors can use this approach to help students with and without disabilities who have not learned to interact with others in socially appropriate ways.

The psychoeducational, behavioral format of structured learning contains four components: (a) modeling, (b) role-playing, (c) performance feedback, and (d) transfer of learning (Goldstein, 1993). Each of the components is necessary but not sufficient for teaching prosocial skills; therefore, the combination of these components will lead to improved prosocial skills (Goldstein *et al.*, 1994). Each component is described here.

1. *Modeling.* The trainer describes the skill, provides a behavioral description of the steps that compose the skill, and role-plays these steps. Later modeling provides a portrayal of the complete skill's implementation.
2. *Role-playing.* The trainer encourages the students to relate the skill modeled in the first component to their own lives. Use of the skill in specific situations both present and future are discussed. Students then participate in role-plays while being coached and cued by the trainer. Observers (e.g., other students) are also encouraged to look for specific behaviors.
3. *Feedback.* Feedback after each role-play provides specific responses to the role-play. The trainer provides encouragement and feedback on the effective aspects of the role-play while also modeling and role-playing skills that were not role-played as effectively.
4. *Transfer of learning.* During this component, students have opportunities to practice the steps and skills in real-life settings. One way to promote transfer is the Homework Report, which requests detailed information about the implementation of a skill sequence outside the instructional setting.

The structured learning program designed for elementary students contains 60 prosocial skills arranged into five groups: (a) classroom survival skills, (b) friendship-making skills, (c) skills for dealing with feelings, (d) skill alternatives to aggression, and (e) skills for dealing with stress. The structured learning skills for adolescents include 60 skills arranged into six groups: (a) beginning social skills (e.g., listening, saying "thank you," giving a compliment); (b) advanced social skills (e.g., asking for help, following instructions, convincing others); (c) skills for dealing with feelings (e.g., knowing your feelings, dealing with someone's anger, dealing with fear); (d) skill alternatives to aggression (e.g., asking permission, negotiating, using self-control, keeping out of fights); (e) skills for dealing with stress (e.g., making a complaint, standing up for a friend, responding to failure or persuasion, getting ready for a difficult conversation); and (f) planning skills (e.g., deciding on something to do, setting a goal, making a decision, concentrating on a task).

Steps for teaching each of the 60 skills are provided within a lesson format that includes the steps for performing the skill, notes for discussing each step in the skill, suggested situations for role-playing the skill, and comments about the skill. The lesson format for each social skill can easily be used by teachers and other professionals interested in teaching social skills.

Comments. Positive effects of structured learning on social outcomes have been demonstrated for students with behavior disorders (Sasso *et al.*, 1990; Miller *et al.*, 1992), mental retardation (Fleming & Fleming, 1982; Kiburz *et al.*, 1984), and students without disabilities (Farmer-Dougan *et al.*, 1999). In the studies, participants generally increased their prosocial behaviors and reduced their negative behaviors. Furthermore, the acquired social skills often were maintained and generalized to other settings (Kiburz *et al.*, 1984; Sasso *et al.*, 1990). In the late 1990s, Farmer-Dougan *et al.* (1999) examined how different approaches to consulting with teachers can influence the effectiveness of a skillstreaming approach. They compared two types of teacher consultation: (a) directed and specific consultation regarding the use of skillstreaming approach and (b) consultation not specifically addressing the skillstreaming approach and only providing materials for the approach. Results demonstrated that when a teacher was provided direct and specific support regarding the use of the skillstreaming approach, students increased using prosocial behaviors more than when a teacher was merely provided materials for the approach. This finding suggests how important explicit teacher training and ongoing classroom support are for successful implementation of the skillstreaming approach (i.e., increasing students' use of prosocial behaviors). Given its success with students with behavior disorders, mental retardation, and normally achieving students, further research examining the efficacy of using structured learning with students with LD is warranted.

2. Social Decision-Making

The social decision-making approach is a classroom-based intervention developed for children and adolescents to teach decision-making and interpersonal problem-solving skills (Elias & Clabby, 1989, 1992; Elias & Kress, 1994). The intervention focuses on three "readiness areas" (i.e., self-control, group participation, and social awareness) and eight steps for social decision-making and problem solving. The basic structure of the social decision-making approach is outlined in Figure 10–1. This approach guide contains sample worksheets, directions for teaching students to role-play, and many other helpful teaching tips.

Comments. The social decision-making approach has been used in elementary and middle schools, and the associated skills have also been taught to parents (Churney, 2001; Clabby & Elias, 1986; Elias *et al.*, 1986; Elias & Kress, 1994). Overall, the social decision-making approach was associated with positive social outcomes for participating students. For instance, students entering middle school who did not participate in the problem-solving instruction identified school stressors such as peer pressure, academic demands, coping with authority figures, and becoming involved in substance abuse as significantly greater problems than did students who participated in the problem-solving instruction (Elias *et al.*, 1986). Recently, Churney (2001) revealed that a social decision-making group demonstrated greater assertiveness skills and more coping and problem-solving strategies compared to a comparison group. While research evidence supports using the

---

When children or adolescents use their social decision-making skills, they are
A. Using self-control skills:
   1. Listening carefully and accurately,
   2. Following directions,
   3. Calming themselves down when upset or under stress, and
   4. Approaching and talking to others in a socially appropriate manner.
B. Using social awareness and group participation skills:
   1. Recognizing and eliciting trust, help, and praise from others,
   2. Understanding others' perspectives,
   3. Choosing friends wisely,
   4. Participating appropriately in groups, and
   5. Giving and receiving help and criticism.
C. Using critical thinking skills for decision-making and problem solving:
   1. Noticing signs of feelings,
   2. Identifying issues or problems,
   3. Determining and selecting goals,
   4. Generating alternative solutions,
   5. Envisioning possible consequences,
   6. Selecting the best solution,
   7. Planning and making a final check for obstacles, and
   8. Noticing what happened and using the information for future decision-making and problem solving.

Figure 10–1 Basic Structure of the Social Decision-Making Approach[a]. *Note:* From Elias, M. J., & Kress, J. S. (1994) Social decision-making and life skills development: A critical thinking approach to health promotion in the middle school. *Journal of School Health*, 64(2), 62–66. Reprinted with permission.

social decision-making approach with students without disabilities, little evidence exists regarding its effects for students with LD.

3. Peer Social Initiations

Peer social initiations is an empirically validated approach to teaching social skills to young children with disabilities (for review, see Odom *et al.*, 1992; Strain & Odom, 1986). The Early Childhood Social Skills Program uses the principles and procedures of peer social initiations to facilitate the development of positive interaction skills in preschoolers with and without social delays (Kohler & Strain, 1993). The successful implementation of peer social initiations involves four components:

1. Selecting specific peer initiations that are most likely to yield a positive response from the student. For instance, sharing, showing affection, and giving assistance are likely to receive positive responses from peers (Strain, 1983).
2. Arranging the physical environment to promote interaction requires that materials be available to facilitate interaction. For example, with preschoolers some materials such as toy wagons, toy cars, and blocks are likely to promote peer interactions, whereas materials like puzzles, crayons, and paints are more likely to produce solitary play.
3. Selecting students (i.e., confederates) who are desirable playmates as well as willing participants and instructing them to implement the intervention. Prior to implementing the initiation skills with a target peer, confederates practice and rehearse the skills through multiple role-plays in order to know how to encourage student response as well as how to handle students who do not respond. Figure 10–2 provides a sample script for training confederates over a portion of the intervention.
4. Structuring the interactions between the target student and the confederate through the step-by-step process of daily intervention sessions. In a small group that includes a confederate and a target peer, the teacher describes the activity and materials to be used. The target peer initiates the activity while the teacher takes the confederate aside and prompts her or him as to which social initiations she or he should implement during the activity with the target student. The teacher continues to prompt and reinforce the confederate's and target child's interactions as the activity continues.

Comments. The peer social initiations intervention has been systematically implemented across numerous settings and populations. Positive impacts on both confederates and target students have been demonstrated. Populations who have successfully participated in the intervention include

Adult: "Today you are going to learn how to be a good teacher. Sometimes your friends in your class do not know how to play with other children. You are going to learn how to teach them to play. What are you going to do?"

Child: "Teach them to play."

Adult: "One way you can get your friend to play with you is to share. How do you get your friend to play with you?"

Child: "Share."

Adult: "Right! You share. When you share, you look at your friend and say, 'Here,' and put a toy in his/her hand. What do you do?" [Repeat this exercise until the child can repeat these three steps.]

Child: "Look at your friend and say, 'Here,' and put the toy in his/her hand."

Adult: "Now, watch me. I am going to share with _____. Tell me if I do it right." [Demonstrate sharing.] "Did I share with _____? What did I do?"

Child: "Yea! _____ looked at _____, and said 'here _____' and put a toy in his hand."

Adult: "Right. I looked at _____ and said, 'here _____' and put a toy in his hand. Now watch me. See if I share with _____." [Move to the next activity in the classroom. This time provide a negative example of sharing by leaving out the "put in hand" component. Put the toy beside the role player.] "Did I share?" [Correct if necessary and repeat this example if child got it wrong.] "Why not?"

Child: "No. You did not put the toy in _____'s hand."

Adult: "That's right. I did not put the toy in _____'s hand. I have to look at _____ and say, 'here _____' and put the toy in his hand." [Give the child two more positive and two more negative examples of sharing. When the child answers incorrectly about sharing, repeat the example. Vary the negative examples by leaving out different components: looking, saying 'here,' putting in hand.]

Adult: "Now _____, I want you to get _____ to share with you. What do you do when you share?"

Child: "Look at _____ and say, 'here _____,' and put a toy in his hand."

Adult: "Now, go get ___ to play with." [For these practice examples, the role playing should be responsive to the child's sharing.] (To the other confederates:) "Did _____ share with _____? What did he/she do?"

Child: "Yes/No. Looked at ___, and said, 'here' _____, and put a toy in his hand."

Adult: [Move to the next activity.] "Now, _____, I want you to share with _____." Introduce persistence

Adult: "Sometimes when I play with a friend, he/she does not want to play back, and I have to keep on trying. What do I have to do?"

Child: "Keep on trying."

Adult: "Right, I have to keep on trying. Watch me. I am going to share with ___. Now I want to see if I keep on trying." [Role player will be initially unresponsive. Teacher should be persistent until child finally responds.] "Did I get _____ to play with me?"

Child: "Yes."

Adult: "Did he want to play?"

Child: "No."

Adult: "What did I do?"

Child: "Keep on trying."

Adult: "Right, I kept on trying. Watch. See if I can get _____ to play with me this time." [Again, the role player should be unresponsive at first. Repeat above questions and correct if necessary. Repeat the example until the child responds correctly.]

Figure 10–2 Session 1: Introduction to System-Share Initiation-Persistence. *Note:* From Strain, P. S., & Odom, S. L. (1986). Peer social initiations: Effective intervention for skills development of exceptional children. *Exceptional Children*, **52**, 543–551. Copyright (1986) by The Council for Exceptional Children. Reprinted with permission.

preschool-aged youngsters with disabilities and elementary-aged students with mental retardation, behavior disorders, or visual impairments. Positive outcomes include increases in positive social responses, increases in responses to initiations, increased length of social exchanges, and cross-setting generalization of responses (Odom et al., 1992; Strain & Odom, 1986).

One concern about this intervention, however, is the limited generalization and maintenance of treatment effects. A likely explanation for this limited generalization and maintenance of treatment effects is that the environments to which students returned did not have socially responsive peers with whom to initiate and maintain the target behaviors. When responsive peers were present, greater generalization and maintenance effects have been documented (Shafer et al., 1984).

In general, this intervention has been effective and applicable in a wide range of settings. Furthermore, it does not require a special curriculum or a teacher's guide. Yet, because this intervention has not been systematically tested with students with LD, further research is needed before its efficacy with this population is known. More information regarding social skills interventions for preschoolers with disabilities is provided in the next section.

D. Syntheses of Interventions to Enhance Social Competence for Preschoolers with Disabilities

1. Social Skills Interventions for Preschoolers with Disabilities

Over the past two decades, interest in the social competence of students with disabilities has increased. Deriving from accumulated research addressing the social functioning of students with disabilities, several reviews have summarized the results of social skills interventions for students with disabilities; however, these reviews primarily focused on social skills interventions for school-age students. Because social functioning manifests differently across developmental periods (Guralnick & Neville, 1997), effective social skills interventions for school-age students may not be effective for preschoolers. Thus, Vaughn and her colleagues (Vaughn et al., 2003) conducted a synthesis of research studies that address the social competence of preschoolers (i.e., 3- to 5-year-old children) with any identified disabilities.

An extensive search of the professional literature yielded a total of 23 group design intervention studies that met the criteria for inclusion in the synthesis (see Vaughn et al., 2003). Social skills interventions for preschool children are often delivered in intervention packages, with each package containing a combination of various intervention features considered effective for enhancing specific behaviors. The synthesis revealed that the following intervention features were commonly included in social intervention packages for preschool children with disabilities:

1. *prompting*, when a teacher either verbally or physically reminded children to use the social skills they had learned;
2. *rehearsal or practice*, in which children practiced the taught social skills;
3. *play-related activities or play-related centers*, which were designed to elicit delayed or absent social behaviors;
4. *free play generalization*, in which children played with untrained peers or new toys during a posttest or follow-up session, in order to determine whether learned social behaviors generalized to other settings;
5. *reinforcement of appropriate social skills*, which provided a positive response, such as a hug, smile, kind words, stickers, or a cookie, provided by a teacher to a child who showed appropriate use of social behaviors;
6. *modeling of social skills*, when a teacher demonstrated appropriate social skills, such as sharing or greeting;
7. *social skills-related storytelling*, in which the person implementing the treatment read or presented stories on social functioning to children;
8. *direct instruction*, in which a teacher taught appropriate social skills such as sharing, or understanding of emotional expression;
9. *imitation*, when a mother or peer engaged in exactly the same behavior as the target child or vice versa;
10. *time-out*, in which a child who engaged in an inappropriate behavior was placed in a time-out chair for one minute.

Based on analysis of effect size outcomes in relation to the primary studies' critical features, positive outcomes were associated with a range of interventions, including modeling, play-related activities, rehearsal and practice, and/or prompting (Antia *et al.*, 1993; Dawson & Galpert, 1990; Ferentino, 1991; Fewell & Vadasy, 1989; Jenkins *et al.*, 1989; Koenigs & Oppenheimer, 1985; LeBlanc & Matson, 1995; Matson *et al.*, 1991; Rogers *et al.*, 1986). The large range of interventions including these features provides insight into the various ways that the social competence of preschoolers with disabilities could be improved. This range included: (a) teachers' using social skills programs embedded in their general education programs (Antia *et al.*, 1993; Ferentino, 1991; Fewell & Vadasy, 1989; Jenkins *et al.*, 1989; Koenigs & Oppenheimer, 1985); (b) interventions that combined instruction in social skills with behavioral contingencies (LeBlanc & Matson, 1995; Matson *et al.*, 1991); (c) programs that provided integrated/social interaction groups for children with and without disabilities (Jenkins *et al.*, 1989), (d) interventions that trained parents or peers as models to promote appropriate social behaviors (Dawson & Galpert, 1990; Strain, 1985); and (e) an intensive social skills program (Rogers *et al.*, 1986).

2. Manipulation of Toys and/or Group Composition Effects on Social Competence of Preschoolers with Disabilities

Preschool children often manifest social competence through play activities that facilitate the development of social, cognitive, affective, physical, and language abilities (McCabe *et al.*, 1999; Torrey, 1987); however, the play of children with disabilities differs from that of typically developing peers. Children with disabilities engage in more solitary and less cooperative play and nonplay behaviors when compared to their typically developing peers. Also, they have more difficulty spontaneously interacting with other children (Devoney *et al.*, 1974; Federlein, 1979; Guralnick & Groom, 1987; Mindes, 1982). Furthermore, relative to typically developing children, children with disabilities are more likely to engage in lower cognitive levels of plays (i.e., functional play) than higher cognitive levels of plays (i.e., constructive and dramatic play; Guralnick *et al.*, 1995; Johnson & Ershler, 1985). These differences in social behaviors may be significant enough to deter typically developing peers from choosing a child with a disability as a play partner (Dunn, 1991; Peck & Cooke, 1983).

In response to these results demonstrating the inappropriate play behaviors of preschool children with disabilities, attention, in recent years, has been focused on identifying factors that enhance their play behaviors. Most research related to play as a means of promoting social competence of children with disabilities has revolved around their social interactions and cognitive levels of play (Beckman & Kohl, 1984; Dunn, 1991; McCabe *et al.*, 1999; Torrey, 1987; Villarruel, 1990). Because children with disabilities often have difficulties with spontaneous social interaction and engage in lower levels of cognitive play, efforts have been made to design strategies to help them circumvent these difficulties. One way to promote more appropriate play behaviors in this population is manipulating environmental variables (e.g., manipulating of toys and/or group composition). In order to draw some conclusions from the literature, Kim and her colleague (Kim *et al.*, 2003) conducted a synthesis regarding the manipulation effects of two environmental variables (i.e., toys and/or group composition) on play and social behaviors of preschoolers with disabilities.

An extensive search of the professional literature published between 1975 and 1999 (June) yielded a total of 13 intervention studies that met the inclusion criteria for the synthesis (see Kim *et al.*, 2003). An analysis of study outcomes is provided for three effects: (a) toy effect, (b) group composition effect, and (c) toy effect combined with group composition effect.

1. *Toy effect.* Studies included in this analysis compared: (a) the effects of playing with "social" toys (e.g., blocks, balls) vs playing with "isolate" toys (e.g., books, art) on social outcomes (Kallam & Rettig, 1991; Rettig *et al.*, 1993); and (b) the effects of playing with different types of toys (i.e., computer programs, puzzles, free blocks, model blocks) on social outcomes (Villarruel, 1990).
2. *Group composition effect.* Studies included in this analysis compared: (a) the effects of unmixed groups (i.e., groups consisting of children with disabilities) with mixed groups (i.e., groups consisting of children with and without disabilities) on social outcomes (Guralnick, 1981; Guarlnick & Groom, 1988); and (b) the effects of pairing chronologically age-matched children without disabilities with pairing children with disabilities on social outcomes (Guralnick & Groom, 1987).
3. *Toy effect combined with group composition effect.* Studies included in this analysis compared: (a) the effects of playing with "social" toys and "isolate" toys in mixed and unmixed groups on social outcomes (Beckman & Kohl, 1984; Martin *et al.*, 1991); (b) the effects of playing with "social" toys and "isolate" toys in balanced (i.e., equal number of children with and without disabilities) and unbalanced groups (i.e., one child with and three children without disabilities) on social outcomes (Dunn, 1991); and (c) the effects of playing with three different types of toys (i.e., functional, constructive, dramatic) in mixed and unmixed groups on social outcomes (McCabe *et al.*, 1999).

Overall, findings from this synthesis revealed: (a) playing with social toys increased positive social outcomes more than playing with isolate toys for children with disabilities, and (b) play groups in which children with and without disabilities were mixed resulted in positive social outcomes for children with disabilities.

Although playing with social toys and in mixed groups positively affected the social behaviors of children with disabilities, these environmental variables were associated still with moderate amounts of isolated/parallel play (Dunn, 1991), and playing with isolate toys and in unmixed groups resulted in moderate amounts of social interaction (Beckman & Kohl, 1984; Martin *et al.*, 1991). These findings suggest that manipulating toys and group composition may not be sufficient to promote positive social behaviors for all children with disabilities. Thus, it is reasonable to expect that other interventions may be needed to improve the social skills of some children with disabilities, especially children who have severe delays.

IV. ISSUES

The most effective programs are tailored to the specific needs of the identified population (Coie, 1985). The notion of fitting the intervention to the population's needs should be further explored with students with LD whose social competence, for example, is associated with several areas that on the surface may appear to be unrelated to social competence (e.g., academic performance). If the goal is to increase the social acceptance of students, a model that solely emphasizes teaching social skills to the student in isolation is likely to be insufficient. Rather, models that include academic tutoring, peer involvement, social skills instruction, and perhaps even teacher training are needed. In addition, it may be necessary to develop specific interventions for youngsters with social skills difficulties based on whether they exhibit behavior problems. For example, youngsters with externalizing behavior problems (e.g., aggression) may need interventions that include prohibitions as well as social skills instruction.

An important issue in social skills interventions with students with LD is the inclusion of peers without LD in the intervention. Sancilio (1987) reviewed the literature on peer interaction as a method of therapeutic intervention with children and concluded that peers can serve as effective change agents with other peers. However, merely increasing opportunities for peer interaction without efforts to improve the target child's social skills are less likely to be successful (Sancilio, 1987). The interventions need to be highly structured and focused on improving the target child's social skills. Structured peer interactions usually take one of two forms: peers as social reinforcers or peers as trained initiators. As social reinforcers, peers may provide positive reinforcement such as "good," and "I like playing with you when you share" to target children. Peers can be trained to ignore negative behaviors while still reinforcing positive behaviors (Solomon & Wahler, 1973). As trained initiators, peers may try to get target children to play with them and initiate social interactions with them.

A second issue relates to the need for social skills interventions to be part of the curriculum rather than brief, one-shot lessons. In a discussion of their research involving a 6-week intervention with students with LD who had poor social skills, La Greca and Mesibov (1981) caution,

> It is not reasonable to expect that longstanding social problems can be entirely remediated within the span of six weeks, although definite inroads can be made. Thus, it is suggested that future investigators consider issues such as examining the effects of longer and more comprehensive intervention programs, as well as exploring the possibility of including social-skills instruction in the school curriculum, so that instruction can be accomplished on a regular, ongoing basis. (p. 238)

V. FUTURE DIRECTIONS FOR SOCIAL SKILLS INTERVENTION RESEARCH

Overall, social skills interventions for students require further empirical evidence of their effectiveness for enhancing the social competence of students with LD as well as the acceptance and positive perceptions of these youngsters by significant others (e.g., peers, teachers, parents). Meta-analysis studies have revealed that overall effect sizes associated with social skills interventions for students with LD were small to medium (Elbaum & Vaughn, 2001; Forness & Kavale, 1996). Researchers have attempted to provide probable explanations for these relatively small overall effect sizes. For example, small effect sizes may stem from the fact that there are several different types of social skills difficulties—social skills acquisition difficulties, social skills performance difficulties, and social skills fluency difficulties (Gresham, 1981a, b)—and that each of these difficulties may require specific intervention strategies. Social skills acquisition difficulties refer either to the absence of knowledge for executing an appropriate social skill under an optimal condition or to a failure in recognizing an appropriate social skill for a specific situation. Social skills performance difficulties refer to knowing the appropriate social skills but failing to perform the skills in a specific situation. Social skills fluency difficulties refer to the awkward performance of social skills. Gresham (1998) argued that interventions to promote social skills acquisition should differ from interventions to help with performance or fluency difficulties; however, many social skills interventions to date have not considered the students' specific social skills difficulties (Gresham et al., 2001). Thus, mismatches between students' specific difficulties and the social skills interventions may result in the small to medium effect sizes demonstrated by the intervention research.

A second reason for these effect sizes may be related to many of the intervention studies failing to report fidelity of implementation data. Fidelity of implementation data is concerned with the accuracy and consistency with which interventions are implemented as planned. Without fidelity of implementation data, it is not clear whether the interventions are ineffective because of poor implementation or poor interventions. The absence of fidelity of implementation data makes it difficult to draw conclusions regarding the intervention effects on social competence for students with LD. Also, few valid and reliable assessments exist that can measure adequately the social competence of students with LD (Gresham et al., 2001; Vaughn & Sinagub, 1997).

Another reason for these effect sizes may be that most of the social skills interventions in the studies focused on developing isolated, discrete social skills without considering students' social systems/environments (e.g., interactions between the student and other individuals, classroom contexts, task-related variables; Gresham *et al.*, 2001). To support this reasoning, Smith and Travis (2001) argued that the lack of conclusive evidence across studies in this area may result from social skills interventions being developed from an incomplete conceptual framework devoid of context. For students with LD, especially those with significant social difficulties, teaching isolated social skills may not be sufficient to improve their social competence, which requires comprehensive interventions that take into consideration their social systems/environments. In addition, given that the social skills difficulties of students with LD generally persist for relatively long periods of time, and that these difficulties are resistant to change, the intensity and duration of most social skills interventions may not be sufficient to help students with LD deal with these difficulties.

These probable explanations provide insights for future social skills intervention research. First, further research should match social skills interventions with students' specific social skills difficulties. Second, intervention studies should carefully monitor and report fidelity of implementation. Third, efforts should be made to develop more adequate measures for assessing the social competence (e.g., self-concept, peer acceptance, social skills, behavior adjustment) of students with LD. Fourth, interventions should take into consideration students' social systems and their efficacy with students with LD needs to be investigated. Fifth, future research should systematically investigate the effects of different duration and intensity levels in social skills interventions on social competence for students with LD. Finally, these interventions' long-term effects on social competence and their efficacy in natural settings (i.e., outside of the classroom or clinic) need to be evaluated.

VI. SUMMARY

This chapter has provided an overview of interventions designed to enhance the social competence of students with LD (e.g., social skills, peer acceptance, self-concept). Definitions of social competence and social skills were presented, and background was provided on why students with LD need social skills interventions and what barriers exist to discourage or prevent the teaching of social skills.

We then described several intervention studies conducted specifically with students with LD. These descriptions provided procedures for implementing the interventions as well as comments to assist trainers or others using the programs in knowing when and with whom to use the interventions. We also presented findings for school-based interventions created to enhance the self-concept of students with LD. In addition, social interventions evaluated with other populations were presented. Our discussion also led to an evaluation of social interventions specifically designed for preschoolers with disabilities. Finally, this chapter provided an overview of issues relevant to teaching social skills to students with LD and future directions for social skills intervention research.

References

Antia, S. D., Kreimeyer, K. H., & Eldredge, N. (1993). Promoting social interaction between young children with hearing impairments and their peers. *Exceptional Children*, **60**(3), 262–275.

Baum, D., Duffelmeyer, F., & Geelan, M. (1988). Resource teacher perceptions of the prevalence of social dysfunction among students with learning disabilities. *Journal of Learning Disabilities*, **21**(6), 380–381.

Beckman, P. J., & Kohl, F. L. (1984). The effects of social and isolate toys on the interactions and play of integrated and nonintegrated groups of preschoolers. *Education & Training of the Mentally Retarded*, **19**(3), 169–174.

Bednar, R. L., Wells, M. G., & Peterson, S. R. (1989). *Self-esteem: Paradoxes and innovations in clinical theory and practice*. Washington, DC: American Psychological Association.

Brendtro, L. K., Brokenleg, M., & Van Bockern, S. (1990). *Reclaiming youth at risk: Our hope for the future*. Bloomington, IN: National Education Service.

Bruck, M. (1986). Social and emotional adjustments of learning disabled children: A review of the issues. In S. J. Ceci (ed.), *Handbook of cognitive, social, and neuropsychological aspects of learning disabilities* (pp. 361–380). Hillsdale, NJ: Erlbaum.

Bryan, T., & Perlmutter, B. (1979). Female adults' immediate impressions of learning disabled children. *Learning Disabilities Quarterly*, **2**, 80–88.

Byan, T., & Sherman, R. (1980). Immediate impressions of nonverbal ingratiation attempts by learning disabled boys. *Learning Disability Quarterly*, **3**, 19–28.

Bryant, D. P., & Bryant, B. R. (1998). Using assistive technology adaptations to include students with learning disabilities in cooperative learning activities. *Journal of Learning Disabilities*, **31**(1), 41–54.

Chapman, J. W. (1988). Learning disabled children's self-concepts. *Review of Educational Research*, **58**(3), 347–371.

Churney, A. H. (2001). Promoting children's social and emotional development: A follow-up evaluation of an elementary school-based program in social decision-making/social problem-solving. *Dissertation Abstracts International*, **62**(1-A), 75.

Clabby, J. F., & Elias, M. J. (1986). *Teach your child decision making*. New York: Doubleday.

Cohen, E. G. (1994). Restructuring the classroom: Conditions for productive small groups. *Review of Educational Research*, **64**(1), 1–35.

Coie, J. D. (1985). Fitting social skills intervention to the target group, In B. H. Schneider, K. H. Rubin, & J. E. Ledingham (eds.), *Children's peer relations: Issues in assessment and intervention* (pp. 141–156). New York: Springer-Verlag.

Curran, J. C. (1979). Social skills: Methodological issues and future directions. In A. Bellack & M. Hersen (eds.), *Research and practice in social skills training* (pp. 319–354). New York: Plenum Press.

Dawson, G., & Galpert, L. (1990). Mothers' use of imitative play for facilitating social responsiveness and toy play in young autistic children. *Development and Psychopathology*, **2**, 151–162.

Devoney, C., Guralnick, M. J., & Rubin, H. (1974). Integrating handicapped and nonhandicapped preschool children: Effects on social play. *Childhood Education*, **50**(6), 360–364.

Dodge, K. A. (1986). A social information processing model of social competence in children. In M. Perlmutter (ed.), *Cognitive perspectives on children's social and behavioral development* (pp. 77–125). Hillsdale, NJ: Erlbaum.

Dodge, K. A., Pettit, G. S., McClaskey, C. L., & Brown, J. (1986). Social competence in children. *Monographs of the Society for Research in Child Development*, **44**(2, Serial No. 213).

Dunn, L. B. (1991). Effects of toy and group composition on the social play of young children with and without handicaps. *Master's Abstracts International*, **31**(02), 552.

Elbaum, B., & Vaughn, S. (2001). School-based interventions to enhance the self-concept of students with learning disabilities: A meta-analysis. *Elementary School Journal*, **101**(3), 303–329.

Elias, M. J., & Clabby, J. F, (1989). *Social decision-making skills: A curriculum guide for the elementary grades*. Rockville, MD: Aspen.

Elias, M. J., & Clabby, J. F. (1992). *Building social problem-solving skills: Guidelines from a school-based program*. San Francisco: Jossey-Bass.

Elias, M. J., Gara, M., Ubriaco, M., Rothbaum, P., Clabby, J., & Schuyler, T. (1986). Impact of a preventive school problem-solving intervention on children's coping with middle-school stressors. *American Journal of Community Psychology*, **14**(3), 259–275.

Elias, M. J., & Kress, J. S. (1994). Social decision-making and life skills development: A critical thinking approach to health promotion in the middle school. *Journal of School Health*, **64**(2), 62–66.

Farmer-Dougan, V., Viechtbauer, W., & French, T. (1999). Peer-prompted social skills: The role of teacher consultation in student success. *Educational Psychology*, **19**(2), 207–219.

Federlein, A. C. (1979). A study of play behaviors and interactions of preschool handicapped children in mainstreamed and segregated settings. *Dissertation Abstracts International*, **40**(02), 642.

Ferentino, S. C. (1991). Teaching social skills to preschool children in a special education program. (Doctoral dissertation, Hofstra University, 1991). *Dissertation Abstracts International*, **52**, 4490.

Fewell, R., & Vadasy, P. (1989). Play as an intervention strategy with young children with deaf–blindness. In M. Bullis (ed.), *Research on the communication development of young children with deaf–blindness* (pp. 105–122). (ERIC Document Reproduction Service No. ED 328007).

Fleming, E. R., & Fleming, D. C. (1982). Social skill training for educable mentally retarded children. *Education and Training of the Mentally Retarded,* **17**(1), 44–50.

Forness, S. R., & Kavale, K. (1996). Treating social skill deficits in children with learning disabilities: A meta-analysis of the research. *Learning Disability Quarterly,* **19,** 2–13.

Goldstein, A. P, (1993). Interpersonal skills training interventions. In A. P. Goldstein & C. R. Huff (eds.), *The gang intervention handbook* (pp. 87–157). Champaign, IL: Research Press.

Goldstein, A. P., Harootunian, B., & Conoley, J. C. (1994). *Student aggression: Prevention, management, and replacement training.* New York: Guilford.

Goldstein, A. P., & McGinnis, E. (1997). *Skillstreaming the adolescent: New strategies and perspectives for teaching prosocial skills* (revised ed.). Champaign, IL: Research Press.

Goodwin, M. (1999). Cooperative learning and social skills: What skills to teach and how to teach them. *Intervention in School and Clinic,* **35**(1), 29–33.

Gresham, F. M. (1981a). Assessment of children's social skills. *Journal of School Psychology,* **19,** 120–134.

Gresham, F. M. (1981b). Social skills training with handicapped children: A review. *Review of Educational Research,* **51,** 139–176.

Gresham, F. M. (1983). Social validity in the assessment of children's social skills: Establishing standards for social competency. *Journal of Psychoeducational Assessment,* **1,** 297–307.

Gresham, F. M. (1984). Social skills and self-efficacy for exceptional children. *Exceptional Children,* **51**(3), 253–261.

Gresham, F. M. (1998). Social skills training: Should we raze, remodel, or rebuild? *Behavioral Disorders,* **24,** 19–25.

Gresham, F. M. (1992). Social skills and learning disabilities: Causal, concomitant, or correlational. *School Psychology Review,* **21,** 348–360.

Gresham, F. M., & Elliott, S. N. (1989). Social skills as a primary learning disability. *Journal of Learning Disabilities,* **22,** 120–124.

Gresham, F. M., & Elliott, S. N. (1990). *Social skills rating system.* Circle Pines, MN: American Guidance Service.

Gresham, F. M., Sugai, G., & Horner, R. H. (2001). Interpreting outcomes of social skills training for students with high-incidence disabilities. *Exceptional Children,* **67**(3), 331–344.

Guralnick, M. J. (1981). The social behavior of preschool children at different developmental levels: Effects of group composition. *Journal of Experimental Child Psychology,* **31,** 115–130.

Guralnick, M. J., Connor, R. T., Hammond, M., Gottman, J. M., & Kinnish, K. (1995). Immediate effects of mainstreamed settings on the social interactions and social integration of preschool children. *American Journal on Mental Retardation,* **100**(4), 359–377.

Guralnick, M. J., & Groom, J. M. (1987). The peer relations of mildly delayed and nonhandicapped preschool children in mainstreamed playgroups. *Child Development*, **58**, 1556–1572.

Guralnick, M. J., & Groom, J. M. (1988). Peer interactions in mainstreamed and specialized classrooms: A comparative analysis. *Exceptional Children*, **54**(5), 415–425.

Guralnick, M. J., & Neville, B. (1997). Designing early intervention programs to promote children's social competence. In M. J. Guralnick (ed.), *The effectiveness of early intervention* (pp. 579–610). Baltimore, MD: Paul H. Brookes.

Haager, D., & Vaughn, S. (1995). Parent, teacher, peer, and self-reports of the social competence of students with learning disabilities. *Journal of Learning Disabilities*, **28**(4), 205–215.

Haager, D., & Vaughn, S. (1997). Assessment of social competence in students with learning disabilities. In J. Lloyd, E. Kameenui, & D. Chard (eds.), *Issues in educating students with disabilities* (pp. 129–152). Mahwah, NJ: Erlbaum.

Harter, S. (1985). *Manual for the Self-Perception Profile for Children*. Denver: University of Denver.

Harter, S. (1993). Causes and consequences of low self-esteem in children and adolescents. In R. Baumeister (ed.), *Self-esteem: The puzzle of low self-regard* (pp. 18–37). New York: Plenum.

Harter, S. (1996). Historical roots of contemporary issues involving self-concept. In B. Bracken (ed.), *Handbook of self-concept: Developmental, social, and clinical considerations* (pp. 1–37). New York: Wiley.

Hattie, J. (1992). *Self-concept*. Hillsdale, NJ: Erlbaum.

Hazel, J. S., Schumaker, J. B., Sherman, J. A., & Sheldon, J. (1981). *ASSET: A social skills program for adolescents*. Champaign, IL: Research Press.

Hazel, J. S., Schumaker, J. B., Sherman, J. A., & Sheldon, J. (1982). Application of a group training program in social skills and problem solving to learning disabled and non-learning disabled youth. *Learning Disability Quarterly*, **5**, 398–408.

Interagency Committee on Learning Disabilities. (1987). *Learning disabilities: A report to congress*. Washington, DC: Department of Health and Human Services.

Jenkins, J., Odom, S., & Speltz, M. (1989). Effects of social integration on preschool children with handicaps. *Exceptional Children*, **55**(5), 420–428.

Johnson, J. E., & Ershler, J. L. (1985). Social and cognitive play forms and toy use by nonhandicapped and handicapped preschoolers. *Topics in Early Childhood Special Education*, **5**, 69–82.

Johnson, D. W., & Johnson, R. T. (1986). Mainstreaming and cooperative learning stragies. *Exceptional Children*, **52,** 553–561.

Johnson, D., & Johnson, R. (1989). Cooperative learning: What special education teachers need to know. *Pointer*, **33**(2), 5–10.

Johnson, D. W., Johnson, R. T., Warring, D., & Maruyama, G. (1986). Different cooperative learning procedures and cross-handicap relationships. *Exceptional Children*, **53**(3), 247–252.

Kallam, M., & Rettig, M. (1991). *The effect of social and isolate toys on the social interaction of preschool-aged children in a naturalistic setting* (ERIC Document Reproduction Service No. ED 349 118).

Kavale, K. A., & Forness, S. R. (1996). Social skill deficits and learning disabilities: A meta-analysis. *Journal of Learning Disabilities*, **29**(3), 226–237.

Kiburz, C. S., Miller, S. R., & Morrow, L. W. (1984). Structured learning using self-monitoring to promote maintenance and generalization of social skills across settings for a behaviorally disordered adolescent. *Behavioral Disorders*, **10**(1), 47–55.

Kim, A., Vaughn, S., Elbaum, B., Hughes, M. T., Sloan, C. V. M., & Sridhar, D. (2003). Effects of toys and/or group composition on social behaviors of preschool children with disabilities: A synthesis. *Journal of Early Intervention* **25**(3), 189–205.

Koenigs, A., & Oppenheimer, L. (1985). Development and training of role-taking abilities with emotionally disturbed preschoolers: A pilot study. *Journal of Applied Developmental Psychology*, **6**(4), 313–320.

Kohler, F. W., & Strain, P. S. (1993). The early childhood social skills program. *Teaching Exceptional Children*, **25**(2), 41–42.

Kratochwill, T. R., & French, D. C. (1984). Social skills training for withdrawn children. *School Psychology Review*, **13**(3), 331–338.

Kupersmidt, J. B., Coie, J. D., & Dodge, K. A. (1990). The role of poor peer relationships in the development of disorder. In S. R. Asher & J. D. Coie (eds.), *Peer rejection in childhood* (pp. 274–308). Cambridge, UK: Cambridge University Press.

La Greca, A. M., & Mesibov, G. B. (1981). Facilitating interpersonal functioning with peers in learning-disabled children. *Journal of Learning Disabilities*, **14,** 197–199, 238.

La Greca, A. M., & Stone, W. (1990). Children with learning disabilities: The role of achievement in social, personal, and behavioral functioning. In H. L. Swanson, & B. Keogh (eds.), *Learning disabilities: Theoretical and research issues* (pp. 333–352). Hillsdale, NJ: Erlbaum.

LeBlanc, L. A., & Matson, J. L. (1995). A social skills training program for preschoolers with developmental delays: Generalization and social validity. *Behavior Modification*, **19**(2), 234–246.

Mainzer, R. W., Mainzer, L. K., Slavin, R. E., & Lowry, E. (1993). What special education teachers should know about cooperative. *Teacher Education and Special Education*, **16**(1), 42–50.

Marsh, H. W. (1992). Content specificity of relations between academic achievement and academic self-concept, *Journal of Educational Psychology*, **84**(1), 35–42.

Marsh, H. W., & Hattie, J. (1996). Theoretical perspectives on the structure of self-concept. In B. Bracken (ed.), *Handbook of self-concept: Developmental, social, and clinical considerations* (pp. 38–90). New York: Wiley.

Marsh, H. W., & Yeung, A. S. (1998). Top-down, bottom-up, and horizontal models: The direction of causality in multidimentional, hierarchical self-concept models. *Journal of Personality and Social Psychology*, **75**(2), 509–527.

Martin, S. S., Brady, M. P., & Williams, R. E. (1991). Effects of toys on the social behavior of preschool children in integrated and nonintegrated groups: Investigation of a setting event. *Journal of Early Intervention*, **15**(2), 153–161.

Matson, J. L., Fee, V., Coe, D. A., & Smith, D. (1991). A social skills training program for developmentally delayed preschoolers. *Journal of Clinical Child Psychology*, **20**(4), 428–433.

McCabe, J. R., Jenkins, J. R., Mills, P. E., Dale, P. S., & Cole, K. N. (1999). Effects of group composition, materials, and developmental level on play in preschool children with disabilities. *Journal of Early Intervention*, **22**(2), 164–178.

McFall, R. M. (1982). A review and reformulation of the concept of social skills. *Behavioral Assessment*, **4**, 1–33.

McGinnis, E., & Goldstein, A. P. (1990). *Skillstreaming in early childhood: Teaching prosocial skills to the preschool and kindergarten child*. Champaign, IL: Research Press.

McGinnis, E., & Goldstein, A. P. (2000). *Skillstreaming the elementary school child: New strategies and perspectives for teaching prosocial skills* (revised ed.). Champaign, IL: Research Press.

McIntosh, R., Vaughn, S., & Bennerson, D. (1995). FAST social skills with a SLAM and a RAP: Providing social skills training for students with learning disabilities. *Teaching Exceptional Children*, **28**(1), 37–41.

McIntosh, R., Vaughn, S., & Zaragoza, N. (1991). A review of social interventions for students with learning disabilities. *Journal of Learning Disabilities*, **24**(8), 451–458.

Miller, M. G., Midgett, J., & Wicks, M. L. (1992). Student and teacher perceptions related to behavior change after skillstreaming training. *Behavioral Disorders*, **17**(4), 291–295.

Mindes, G. (1982). Social and cognitive aspects of play in young handicapped children. *Topics in Early Childhood Special Education*, **2**(3), 39–52.

Newmann, F. M., & Thompson, J. A. (1987). *Effects of cooperative learning on achievement in secondary schools: A summary of research*. (ERIC Document Reproduction Service No. ED 288 853).

Odom, S. L., McConnell, S. R., & McEvoy, M. A. (1992). *Social competence of young children with disabilities: Issues and strategies for intervention*. Baltimore: Brookes.

Parker, J. G., & Asher, S. R. (1987). Peer relations and later personal adjustment: Are low accepted children at risk? *Psychological Bulletin*, **102**(3), 357–389.

Parker, J. G., & Asher, S. R. (1993). Friendship and friendship quality in middle childhood: Links with peer group acceptance and feelings of loneliness and social dissatisfaction. *Developmental Psychology*, **29**, 611–621.

Peck, C. A., & Cooke, T. P. (1983). Benefits of mainstreaming at the early childhood level: How much can we expect? *Analysis & Intervention in Developmental Disabilities*, **3**(1), 1–22.

Prater, M. A., Bruhl, S., & Serna, L. A. (1998). Acquiring social skills through cooperative learning and directed teacher instruction. *Remedial & Special Education*, **19**(3), 160–172.

Prout, H. T., Marcal, S. D., & Marcal, D. C. (1992). A meta-analysis of self-reported personality characteristics of children and adolescents with learning disabilities. *Journal of Psychoeducational Assessment*, **10**(1), 59–64.

Rettig, M., Kallam, M., & McCarthy-Salm, K. (1993). The effect of social and isolate toys on the social interactions of preschool children. *Education and Training in Mental Retardation*, **29**(3), 252–256.

Roff, M., Sells, S., & Golden, M. (1972). *Social adjustment personality development in children*. Minneapolis: University of Minnesota Press.

Rogers, S. J., Herbison, J. M., Lewis, H. C., Pantone, J., & Reiss, K. (1986). An approach for enhancing the symbolic, communicative, and interpersonal functioning of young children with autism or severe emotional handicaps. *Journal of the Division for Early Childhood*, **10**(2), 135–145.

Sancilio, M. F. M. (1987). Peer interaction as a method of therapeutic intervention with children. *Clinical Psychology Review*, **7**, 475–500.

Sasso, G. M., Melloy, K. J., & Kavale, K. (1990). Generalization, maintenance, and behavioral co-variation associated with social skills training through structured learning. *Behavioral Disorders*, **16**, 9–22.

Serafica, F. C., & Harway, N. I. (1979). Social relations and self-esteem of children with learning disabilities. *Journal of Clinical Child Psychology*, **8**(3), 227–233.

Shafer, H. S., Egel, A. L., & Neef, N. A. (1984). Training mildly handicapped peers to facilitate changes in the social interaction skills of autistic children. *Journal of Applied Behavior Analysis*, **17**, 461–476.

Sharan, S. (1980). Cooperative learning in small groups: Recent methods and effects on achievement, attitudes, and ethnic relations. *Review of Educational Research*, **50**, 241–271.

Slavin, R. (1983). When does cooperative learning increase student achievement? *Psychological Bulletin*, **94**, 429–445.

Slavin, R. (1990). *Cooperative learning: Theory, research, and practice.* Englewood Cliffs, NJ: Prentice-Hall.

Slavin, R. (1991). Synthesis of research of cooperative learning. *Educational Leadership*, **48**(5), 71–82.

Smith, S. W., & Travis, P. C. (2001). Conducting social competence research considering conceptual frameworks. *Behavioral Disorders*, **26**(4), 360–369.

Solomon, R. W., & Wahler, R. G. (1973). Peer reinforcement control of classroom problem behavior. *Journal of Applied Behavior Analysis*, **17**, 461–476.

Stone, W. L., & La Greca, A. M. (1990). The social status of children with learning disabilities: A reexamination. *Journal of Learning Disabilities*, **23**, 32–37.

Strain, P. S. (1983). Identification of peer social skills for preschool mentally retarded children in mainstreamed classes. *Applied Research in Mental Retardation*, **4**, 543–551.

Strain, P. S. (1985). Programmatic research on peers as intervention agents for socially isolate classmates. *Pointer*, **29**(4), 22–29.

Strain, P. S., & Odom, S. L. (1986). Peer social initiations: Effective intervention for social skills development of exceptional children. *Exceptional Children*, **52**, 543–551.

Swann, W. B. (1996). *Self-traps: The elusive quest for higher self-esteem.* New York: Freeman.

Swanson, H. L., & Malone, S. (1992). Social skills and learning disabilities: A meta-analysis of the literature. *School Psychology Review*, **21**, 427–443.

Thurlow, M. L. (1980). *Preliminary evidence on information considered useful in instructional planning* (Report No. IRLD-RR-27). Minneapolis: Institute for Research on Learning Disabilities. (ERIC Document Reproduction Services No. ED 131 716).

Torrey, C. C. (1987). Environmental effects on the social play behavior of handicapped and nonhandicapped preschoolers. *Dissertation Abstracts International,* **48**(10), 2534.

Vaughn, S., Elbaum, B. E., Schumm, J. S., & Hughes, M. T. (1998). Social outcomes for students with and without learning disabilities in inclusive classrooms. *Journal of Learning Disabilities,* **31**(5), 428–436.

Vaughn, S., & Hogan, A. (1990). Social competence and learning disabilities: A prospective study. In H. L. Swanson & B. K. Keogh (eds.), *Learning disabilities: Theoretical and research issues* (pp. 175–191). Hillsdale, NJ: Erlbaum.

Vaughn, S., & Hogan, A. (1994). Social competence of students with LD over time: A within-individual examination. *Journal of Learning Disabilities,* **27**(5), 292–303.

Vaughn, S., Hogan, A., Kouzekanani, K., & Shapiro, S. (1990). Peer acceptance, self-perceptions, and social skills of LD students prior to identification. *Journal of Educational Psychology,* **82**, 101–106.

Vaughn, S., Kim, A., Sloan, C. V. M., Hughes, M. T., Elbaum, B., & Sridhar, D. (2003). Social skills interventions for young children with disabilities: A synthesis of group design studies. *Remedial and Special Education,* **24**(1), 2–15.

Vaughn, S., & Lancelotta, G. X. (1990). Teaching interpersonal social skills to low accepted students: Peer-pairing versus no peer-pairing. *Journal of School Psychology,* **28**(3), 181–188.

Vaughn, S. R., Lancelotta, G. X., & Minnis, S. (1988). Social strategy training and peer involvement: Increasing peer acceptance of a female, LD student. *Learning Disabilities Focus,* **4**, 32–37.

Vaughn, S., McIntosh, R., Schumm, J. S., Haager, D., & Callwood, D. (1993a). Social status and peer acceptance revisited. *Learning Disabilities Research and Practice,* **8**(2), 82–88.

Vaughn, S., McIntosh, R., & Spencer-Rowe, J. (1991). Peer rejection is a stubborn thing: Increasing peer acceptance of rejected students with learning disabilities. *Learning Disabilities Research and Practice,* **6**(2), 83–88.

Vaughn, S. R., McIntosh, R., & Zaragoza, N. (1992). Social interventions for students with learning disabilities: Towards a broader perspective. In S. Vogel (ed.), *Educational alternatives for students with learning disabilities* (pp. 183–198). New York, NY: Springer-Verlag.

Vaughn, S., & Sinagub, J. M. (1997). Social assessment of at-risk populations: Implications for students with learning disabilities. In S. M. Clancy Dollinger & L. DiLalla (eds.), *Assessment and intervention issues across the lifespan* (pp. 159–180). Hillsdale, NJ: Erlbaum.

Vaughn, S., Zaragoza, N., Hogan, A., & Walker, J. (1993b). A four-year longitudinal investigation of the social skills and behavior problems of students with learning disabilities. *Journal of Learning Disabilities,* **26**(6), 404–412.

Villarruel, F. (1990). Talking and playing: An examination of the effects of computers on the social interactions of handicapped and nonhandicapped preschoolers. *Dissertation Abstracts International,* **51**(11), 3630.

Wiener, J. (1987). Peer status of learning disabled children and adolescents: A review of the literature. *Learning Disabilities Research,* **2**(2), 62–79.

Wiener, J., & Harris, P. J. (1997). Evaluation of an individualized, context-based social skills training program for children with learning disabilities. *Learning Disabilities Research*, **12,** 40–53.

Wolf, M. M. (1978). Social validity: The case for subjective measurement or how applied behavior analysis is finding its heart. *Journal of Applied Behavior Analysis*, **11,** 203–214.

Zigmond, N., & Brownlee, J. (1980). Social skills training for adolescents with learning disabilities. *Exceptional Education Quarterly*, **12,** 77–83.

CHAPTER 11

Strategic Academic Interventions for Adolescents with Learning Disabilities

Martha J. Larkin[*] and Edwin S. Ellis

*State University of West Georgia
University of Alabama*

I. INTRODUCTION

The ultimate goal of working with adolescents with learning disabilities (LD) is to ensure that they become self-reliant, confident, competent, well-adjusted adults who generally are happy and productive citizens. The process of attaining such a quality of life often is a considerable journey, both for the individuals with LD and for those who are attempting to facilitate this success. For the individuals with LD, the journey began long before the onset of adolescence, and these individuals tend to change a great deal as they travel the path from early childhood to adolescence and eventually to adulthood. Since LD usually is a chronic condition, most young children with this disability eventually become adults with LD. Having LD, however, does not preclude attaining self-reliance and some degree of independence, though it certainly can make the journey arduous.

A body of research focuses upon highly successful adults with LD with particular emphasis on the characteristics that have helped them to be successful (see Gerber *et al.*, 1992; Kershner *et al.*, 1995; Reiff *et al.*, 1996; Spekman *et al.*, 1992). An examination of these characteristics may provide substantial guidance for what educators should be doing to prepare

Learning about Learning Disabilities, Third Edition

adolescents with LD to attain similar success (Polloway *et al.*, 1992; Reiff *et al.*, 1995). Gerber et al. (1992) interviewed 46 highly successful and 25 moderately successful adults with LD in the United States and Canada to determine how vocational success was achieved. The study noted that many adults with LD experienced years of failure until they *made conscious decisions to take control of their lives* (i.e., internal decisions) and *adapted and shaped themselves to move ahead* (i.e., external manifestations) (see Table I). You may want to read the autobiographies of some of the many successful adults with LD, such as Christopher Lee (Lee & Jackson, 1992) and Rob Langston (Langston, 2002), who describe their journeys from failure to success.

As would be expected, the ideal characteristics of successful adults with LD vs adolescents with LD often are very different. In order to provide effective interventions for adolescents with LD, it is important to understand who they are and the environments in which they must function while, at the same time, keeping in mind the long term goals for self-reliance and independence. Larkin and Ellis (1998) used a framework in the academic, cognitive, motivational, and social areas to illustrate the characteristics of adolescents with LD and the corresponding school setting expectations. Such a framework shows how the characteristics of adolescents with LD contrast greatly with what is expected of all students in traditional school settings (see Table II). This chapter focuses on the academic and cognitive areas with some mention of motivation. The purpose of showing all four areas in Table II is to convey the complexity of being an adolescent with LD.

In order to provide successful strategic academic interventions for adolescents with LD, educators must consider both the characteristics of these individuals and their environments. Adolescents with LD may be considered successful in their environment outside of school. Peers may see these adolescents as talented athletes, musicians, or even gang members. Parents

Table I
Characteristics of Highly Successful Adults with Learning Disabilities

Internal decisions
1. Have the desire to excel in order to excel.
2. Consciously set explicit goals for themselves.
3. Reframe or reinterpret the LD experience in a more positive or productive manner.
External manifestations—Adaptability
1. Persist or work hard because it is a way of life.
2. Try to fit to environments in which their skills and abilities can be optimized.
3. Display learned creativity (i.e., strategies, techniques) to enhance their ability to perform.
4. Surround themselves with supportive and helpful people and upgrade skills by designing personal improvement programs.

Adapted from Gerber *et al.* (1992).

Table II

Characteristics of Adolescents with LD and School Expectations

Areas	Characteristics of LD	School Expectations
Academic	■ Lack basic academic skills (e.g., read, listen and take notes, write, take tests, solve problems) ■ Fail to use skills systematically ■ Use ineffective/inefficient learning strategies ■ Lack prerequisite knowledge ■ Do not use learning enhancers	■ Read to gain information ■ Listen and take notes ■ Write ■ Take tests ■ Solve problems ■ Apply effective/efficient learning strategies ■ Possess content knowledge ■ Use learning enhancers
Cognitive	■ Have poor language skills ■ Lack knowledge of thinking strategies ■ Are prone to memory problems ■ Are not aware of their own thinking	■ Use background knowledge ■ Apply effective/efficient thinking strategies ■ Remember information ■ Be aware of own thinking and use higher-order thinking
Motivational	■ Experience great stress ■ Fail to see relationship of appropriate effort and success ■ Have difficulty in making a commitment to learn or perform ■ May avoid challenging tasks & give up easily after initial setbacks	■ Expend effort needed for success ■ Value effort & performance ■ Have independent work habits ■ Create effective and efficient work plans
Social	■ May lack basic social skills ■ Misinterpret nonverbal communication ■ Participate in social activities less than peers ■ Lack understanding of culture's moral principles ■ Are poor social problem solvers	■ Respect authority & follow rules ■ Accept criticism & assistance ■ Work collaboratively with others ■ Participate in social activities & conversations ■ Resist inappropriate peer pressure ■ Maintain a pleasant social manner ■ Actively participate in class

Adapted from Larkin and Ellis (1998).

or guardians may see these adolescents as functioning well at home where reading and academics are not emphasized. When these individuals with LD enter school where the focus is on academics, then the cycle of failure begins. You may have encountered some elementary school students who, based on their past history in school, do not believe they can be successful. If individuals with LD are not given instruction and interventions that take into consideration both their characteristics and their environment, then the cycle of failure likely will continue into adolescence and adulthood. Thus, the key to successful instruction and intervention for adolescents with LD is contained in the following formula:

$$\text{Success } f \text{ Individual } \times \text{ Environment}$$
$$(S f I \times E)$$

This formula, "Success (S) is a function (f) of the individual (I) times ($\times$) the environment (E)," provides a powerful message. Educators should keep in mind that they might not be able to change the characteristics of the individuals (i.e., students) with whom they work, but they can consider those characteristics and modify the environment or make adaptations in order to help their students be successful in academics.

II. EMPOWERMENT STRATEGIES FOR ACADEMIC SUCCESS AND INDEPENDENCE

One of the highest priorities of the teacher of students with LD should be creating an academic environment that reinforces in these students the idea of taking responsibility for their lives, gaining independence, and being in control of their own destinies. Specific strategies for creating such an environment include: (a) clarify who is in control, (b) facilitate goal setting and self-reinforcement, (c) communicate and teach confidence, and (d) emphasize personal effort and application of effective and efficient strategies.

A. Clarify Who is in Control and Self-Monitoring

Many students with LD perceive themselves as passive recipients of "whatever life dishes out" and as having little control over their own destinies. To address these debilitating beliefs, effective teachers invest considerable time counseling their students about who is in control of their lives in order to help them realize that they already are making adult decisions in their lives and to capitalize on this power to take control more actively. This concept of who is in control permeates the instructional atmosphere on a daily basis. The language used by effective teachers of students with LD consistently communicates this concept, and the manner of instructional delivery reinforces it.

Students with LD often become dependent on their teachers to mediate their success. They expect their teachers to keep track of their assignments and to "spoon feed" them the information needed for the assignments, and to evaluate whether the assignments have been completed successfully in a timely manner. Such beliefs are counterproductive to facilitating student goal setting and independence. To change these beliefs, effective teachers frequently reiterate the role of special education in relation to facilitating independence (see Field, 1996) over the long term (e.g., teaching skills that can be used widely now and in the future), as opposed to assuring short-lived success (e.g., tutoring a student so that she passes a test), and always relate what is being learned to how it will help students with LD become more independent.

One way of helping students to become more independent is facilitating the use of self-monitoring behaviors in the classroom and encouraging students to generalize such behaviors to other settings and situations. Self-monitoring helps students to determine whether or not a particular behavior has occurred and then to record the results. This especially is useful for adolescents with LD to reinforce the idea that they are in control of their own behaviors (King-Sears & Cummings, 1996) and that the positive behavior can lead to positive outcomes (Rankin & Reid, 1995). King-Sears and Cummings advocated the use of self-management techniques such as self-monitoring for the following reasons: (a) to alleviate problem behaviors in general education classrooms as a prereferral intervention, (b) to precede or follow more intrusive behavior management systems, (c) to assist students in focusing attention on specific academic and social behaviors, (d) to promote students' responsibility for and control of their behavior, and (e) to provide natural consequences and opportunities for generalization of appropriate behaviors.

Self-monitoring procedures especially are appropriate for secondary students (Carter, 1993) due to increased student–teacher ratios and increased demands on student productivity (Prater et al., 1991). If students in secondary special education placements are taught to self-monitor their behavior, then their chances of being mainstreamed into the general education setting are increased. Prater et al., in five single-subject studies of adolescents with LD, concluded that these youth can implement self-monitoring procedures successfully in both special and regular education settings to improve their on-task behavior. These researchers also found that self-monitoring works well in settings where much time is spent in independent seatwork. Reinforcement was teamed with self-monitoring in some of the studies, but results indicated that both could be faded effectively and removed without affecting the students' on-task behavior.

Reid (1996) reported that research on self-monitoring has shown positive results not only in on-task behavior, but also in academic productivity (i.e., the amount or rate of academic responding) and accuracy. Trammel et al., (1994) found that adolescents with LD in grades 7 through 10 could be taught how to use self-monitoring procedures to increase the number of daily homework assignments completed (i.e., academic productivity) and graph their homework completion data. This helped the students to understand the importance of homework completion and the students began to receive higher daily grades. Martin and Manno (1995), in a study of middle school boys with learning and behavior problems, found that students' story compositions were more complete (i.e., accurate) when they were taught how to use a check-off system to ensure that essential elements were included in their narratives.

Dunlap *et al.* (1991) outlined the following steps for self-monitoring procedures to increase student independence: (a) define target behavior so that it is understood clearly by the student, (b) identify functional reinforcers and allow the student to select them, (c) design the self-monitoring method/ device, (d) teach the student to use the device (e.g., through teacher and/or student modeling), and (e) fade the use of the self-monitoring device. Carter (1993) suggested the following additional steps in the self-monitoring procedure once the student has been taught how to use the recording device: (a) choose a strategy for ensuring accuracy (e.g., student has opportunity to match his or her record with the teacher's), (b) teacher and student select goal and contingencies, and (c) review goal and student performance. Also, once fading the use of the self-monitoring device begins, there should be a plan in place for generalization and maintenance.

B. Facilitate Goal Setting and Self-Reinforcement

Luckner (1994) noted that responsible people set goals and determine steps to achieve them. Teachers can help students learn this essential life skill by talking about goals and assisting students to set and strive for achievable personal goals. Spekman *et al.*, (1992) recommended that interventions focus on goal setting and self-directedness along with the academic curriculum.

> We need to help individuals face their learning disability, accommodate their goals accordingly, accept responsibility for their actions, and prepare for appropriate careers. Experiences need to be meaningful and a safe environment provided to review failures and setbacks. Perseverance and proactivity can be nurtured in this context. (p. 169)

Bender (1994) noted that students can be trained to attribute their successes positively. Duchardt *et al.*, (1995) evaluated the BELIEF strategy, a task-specific strategy designed to teach students with LD how to understand, identify, discuss, and transform ineffective beliefs. They found that students with LD can be taught to apply the BELIEF strategy effectively. In other words, students are able to examine the elements of existing beliefs and alter them independently if the beliefs are perceived to be incompatible with personal needs and goals.

Adolescents with LD often do not use effective self-motivation strategies such as making self-coping and affirmation statements, establishing their own goals, and providing themselves with reinforcement, and must be taught these strategies explicitly. The overriding purpose of self-motivation training is to promote in students a perception of self-efficacy and personal control (McCombs, 1984). These perceptions underlie the ability of students to take positive self-control and change negative attitudes and orientations toward learning.

Many teachers teach goal setting as both a skill and a philosophy. For example, they teach their students how to set annual goals for learning and how to present these goals at their Individual Education Planning (IEP) conferences in such a way that the goals are included in their formal educational plans (VanReusen *et al.*, 1987; Van Reusen & Bos, 1990). Considerable time is spent with students discussing goals and teaching them how to determine long-term (i.e., post-secondary, yearly, and semester), weekly, and even daily performance goals and how these goals relate to each other. For example, potential strategies to be taught are presented as a "vehicle to realize personal goals" (Lenz, 1991, p. 17), and students subsequently participate in decisions regarding which strategies to learn. If students express the desire to learn a specific strategy, their subsequent commitment to the task is stronger and more enduring.

Effective teachers help students write these commitments in the form of goal statements that reflect intended real-life future applications of the to-be-learned strategy (Ellis *et al.*, 1993). Moreover, conversations between teachers and the students with LD constantly reflect a goal-setting orientation. Students are encouraged to collaborate with teachers in the evaluation of the effectiveness of the strategy in helping them meet specific tasks in their settings. Each week specific time is allotted for discussing students' long-term goals, how they are being met, and progress toward meeting them. On a daily basis, students are encouraged to set performance goals and teachers should provide time at the end of class for students to assess whether their goals were met. Lenz *et al.*, (1991) suggested that beginning with goal-setting applications that students face daily may be more appropriate because goal attainment applied to weekly, monthly, yearly, or longer applications could be too abstract. They found that training in goal attainment increased the rate of project completion for adolescents with LD. In short, student goals permeate the atmosphere of effective LD classrooms (Lenz *et al.*, 1996).

In addition to teaching goal-setting strategies, effective teachers also teach students with LD to make positive affirmations, and self-coping statements to motivate themselves as they work though a task, to evaluate their own performances, to use self-reinforcement and self-correction procedures, and to monitor progress toward their goals (Seabaugh & Schumaker, 1981). Thus, the instructional process in highly effective special education programs is driven by student goals, *not* teacher goals. For example, Ellis (1989) taught students prior to the beginning of a content lesson to set content learning goals by: (a) writing a question about the content that they hope will be answered in the upcoming lesson and (b) noting goals for participating in class. At the end of the content lesson, students with LD were taught to think back and determine whether their question had been answered and whether they had met their participation goals. Ellis reported that, as a result, the level of student participation significantly increased during the class and that teachers perceived that students with LD were more interested in the subject matter.

C. Communicate and Teach Confidence

Many students with LD who have a history of failure experiences have little confidence in their own abilities (see Licht & Kistner, 1986). They often attribute their successes to variables beyond their control (e.g., attribute a successful outcome to good luck—"The teacher made the test easy this time") and their failures to their own perceived ineptitudes (e.g., "I failed because I'm not good at taking tests"). Many students also crucify themselves with negative self-statements (e.g., "I'm too dumb for this"). In a study examining the motivation techniques employed by expert master teachers, effective teachers of students with LD frequently communicated confidence in their students, using such statements as "I know you can do it" or "Now you're ready for a more difficult problem because you'll be able to handle it." Expert teachers also teach students to communicate their confidence to peers. For example, when using cooperative learning techniques during group practice activities, one student in each group is designated as the encourager. The role of the encourager is to encourage and reinforce others, as well as to communicate confidence in others during difficult or frustrating circumstances.

D. Emphasize Personal Effort and Application of Effective and Efficient Strategies

Because many adolescents with LD seem to believe that their successes are due largely to factors beyond their personal control (e.g., "I did well on the test because the test was easy"), the role of personal effort as a key factor in any formula for success should be emphasized continuously when teaching these students. Successful problem solving, in the simplest terms, is related to one's choosing a strategy that can address the demand of the setting and making a concerted effort to use the strategy effectively. Ellis and Lenz (1996) noted that students with LD should be taught that the key elements in the formula for successful problem solving in an academic setting are the following:

> Appropriate Chosen Learning Strategy + Personal Effort =
> Successful Problem Solving

Referring frequently to this formula when discussing progress and providing feedback enhances students' understanding that personal effort must be exerted to ensure success is enhanced as well as their understanding of the learning process. Likewise, students are taught to attribute failure experiences to use of less effective and/or efficient strategies. Emphasis is placed on encouraging students to try harder to use the *best* strategy (i.e., the most effective and efficient strategy) for the task.

Scruggs and Mastropieri (1992) and Fulk (1994) noted the importance of "attribution training" or stressing the importance of effort combined with effective strategies to help students be successful. Although a number of studies have examined the effects of focusing students' attention on the importance of effort and attribution retraining on students with histories of failure, only a few have focused specifically on students classified as LD (see Anderson & Jennings, 1980; Licht & Kistner, 1986). Frequently encouraging students to make positive attribution and affirmation statements also can, over time, help students to use more effective motivation strategies.

To facilitate more positive beliefs, teachers can employ a form of attribution retraining by requiring students to acknowledge the positive attributions (e.g., "You got a B on the test. One of the reasons you got a B instead of a lower grade was because you really were trying to use a good strategy for preparing for the test, right?") or to make the positive choice between negative and positive attributions (e.g., "You got a B on the test. Was it because the teacher made the test easy or because your studying hard made it easy?"), and then facilitate the student's selection of the choice that reflects self-control. Because some students with LD frequently use counterproductive negative self-talk (e.g., "I can't do this, I'm too dumb"), teachers can teach students to make positive affirmation statements prior to and during difficult tasks. For example, students can be taught to write at the top of the first page of their tests a positive affirmation statement (e.g., "I'm going to smoke this test") before beginning the test (Hughes *et al.*, 1993).

III. STRATEGIC INSTRUCTIONAL PRACTICES

Helping students become empowered for academic success and independence is only one aspect of teaching adolescents with LD. Effective teachers for these students must consistently employ strategic instructional practices, such as: (a) connect instruction to assessment, (b) employ a systematic lesson structure, (c) provide explicit instruction and (d) scaffold instruction.

A. Connect Instruction to Assessment

Mertler (2003) noted that accurately and consistently assessing and evaluating the performance of students is essential for classroom teachers. The assessment process involves collecting, synthesizing, and interpreting information to aid in educational decision making (Airasian, 2000). This might include tests, homework assignments, class activities, group projects, and/or informal observations (Mertler, 2003). Evaluation involves making value judgments about students' capabilities and the merits of their performance. A great deal of professional decision making required in evaluation has the potential for important repercussions; therefore, evaluation should occur only after sufficient assessment information has been collected, analyzed, and synthesized.

The instructional process is composed of three basic components: (a) planning instruction, (b) delivering instruction, and (c) assessing instruction (Airasian, 2000). Mertler (2003) noted that although the steps of this process may appear circular in nature, in actuality they are integrated throughout the process. Thus, the effective teacher plans instruction with not only delivery in mind but also assessment. Likewise, instructional delivery impacts planning of future lessons as well as current and future lesson assessment. Also, the effective teacher considers assessment information to plan and deliver future lessons.

The first author of this chapter (Larkin) found that some novice teachers of students with LD construct beautiful lesson plans with emphasis on delivery and little consideration of assessment. "Oh, I will ask my students to turn in their worksheets for a grade, or I will give them a test at the end of the lesson," the novice teacher may say. When Larkin further examined the novice teacher's lesson plan, she found that the end-of-lesson test or worksheet might not have any connection to the lesson objective(s) stated. Therefore, it is crucial that all teachers, including those of adolescents with LD, integrate all components (i.e., planning, delivery, and assessment) of the instructional process and, in particular, make sure that assessment is tied closely to instruction.

Essentially, effective teachers determine precisely what students are expected to know about a topic by examining national, state, and local standards as well as IEP objectives. Then teachers must assess what their students already know about the topic. For students who already know the information, a brief review may be all that is necessary before moving on to new and/or more difficult information. Students who have limited or no knowledge of the topic need more intensive instruction and, of course, assessment tailored to that instruction. Assessment should always follow the teaching of new information to determine what students now know. Then future instruction should be based on these assessment results.

B. Employ a Systematic Lesson Structure

Novice teachers, as well as some more experienced teachers, may have a tendency to get into the body of a lesson quickly with little or no thought to preparing students to focus on the lesson. The lesson may end with the bell signaling time to change classes or with students working independently on assignments with little or no attempt to bring closure to the lesson. Although, different educators may use different terminology, essentially a lesson should have a beginning, middle, and end. This is a good practice to use with all students, but especially those with LD because they may need extra assistance to make connections among new information and tie the main ideas of new information to already known information in a meaningful and memorable way.

Silbey (2001) suggested that a lesson should have the following four distinct features: (a) a 5- to 10-minute *bridge* to connect previous work to the newly learned information, (b) a 3- to 5-minute *goal setting introduction* to introduce the lesson objectives and focus students' attention on the learning outcomes, (c) a 30- to 40-minute *lesson body* that contains the work that students will do to reach the learning goals, and (d) a 5- to 10-minute *closure/preview* that reflects on the day's learning and previews how the learning will be used in the future. During the closure, goals posted from the lesson introduction should be reviewed to determine whether they have been met. If so, then a previewing bridge for the next lesson can be provided.

Other popular terms for lesson beginnings are "advance organizers" and for lesson closure, "post organizers." Deshler *et al.* (1996) indicated that an advance organizer consists of verbal or written information (or both) that is presented to students before the lesson body. The purpose of an advance organizer is to help students gain some initial understanding of the lesson content, and to become familiar with the lesson organization and purposes for learning. According to Lenz *et al.* (1987), the key components that should be included in the advance organizer are: (a) information about the lesson topics and subtopics, (b) background information and concepts to be learned, and (c) rationale and expected outcomes for learning. Adolescents with LD typically do not have the store of background knowledge of their normally achieving peers or they may not recognize when and how to activate the background knowledge that they do have. Therefore, the use of advance organizers in the classroom can be beneficial to all students, but particularly those with LD.

Lesson post organizers also can be helpful to all students, but particularly those with LD. Middle and high school textbooks for each subject may contain 500 pages or more. It is an amazing feat for students without disabilities to remember much of the information in these texts, and likely to be even more difficult for the students with LD to read, make sense of, and remember this information. Post organizers can be brief (5–10 minutes), but can do a world of good in helping students to focus on and remember key ideas and their relationships. Also, students can connect the essential new information (i.e., minus the confusing details) to previously learned information in order to keep the learning process meaningful. Meaningful learning can guard against what Ellis (the second author of this chapter) refers to as "intellectual bulimia" (i.e., study and/or cram for the exam, purge the information for the exam, and then forget the information within a short time period). A good post organizer gets students actively involved in sharing information they have learned and/or their perspectives on what they have learned. For example, a student's "ticket out of class" (i.e., required assignment before leaving class for the day) may be to share one thing he or she has learned from the lesson or students may construct a web of key ideas learned. Another possibility to encourage reflection is having students THINK of a key idea from the day's lesson, PAIR with a peer, and each SHARE their selected key ideas (i.e., THINK, PAIR, SHARE).

So far, we have emphasized the lesson beginning through the use of an advance organizer and the lesson ending through the use of a post organizer. Although experienced teachers may feel more comfortable planning the lesson body, there still are a few important principles to keep in mind. The concept of the lesson planning pyramid developed by Schumm et al. (1994) employs a graphic of a pyramid cut into three sections. The bottom or largest section contains what all students should learn. The middle section is smaller than the bottom section and contains what most students will learn. The top section of the pyramid is the smallest section and contains what some students will learn. Students with LD have average to above average intelligence, but struggle with their learning. Therefore, their learning likely will fit best in the bottom to middle section of the pyramid. In other words, the focus of the lesson body for students with LD should be on what all, or perhaps most, students will learn.

The Lesson Planning Routine developed at the University of Kansas Center for Research on Learning assists teachers in planning lessons for diverse groups of learners including those with disabilities (Lenz et al., 1993). This routine uses a graphic device called the Lesson Organizer which helps teachers to share with students: (a) the lesson content, (b) student expectations, (c) the relationship of the current lesson to the unit lesson, (d) the lesson parts and their relationships, (e) useful background knowledge or vocabulary, and (f) self-test questions for review.

C. Provide Explicit Instruction

Although there are a number of instructional models with growing popularity that might be effective when teaching adolescents with LD (e.g., whole language or holistic instruction, discovery learning, thematic instruction, reciprocal teaching), those that focus on making instruction as explicit as possible have received the most research scrutiny and have, by far, the greatest empirical support as a means of effectively teaching adolescents with LD. Although the relative effectiveness of less explicit instructional models is unknown due to limited research in this area, the effectiveness of using explicit instruction is *well* documented. Deciding to employ less explicit instructional techniques should be carefully deliberated in light of insufficient evidence to warrant their use. Teachers who choose to provide a less explicit approach to teaching their students should monitor and measure carefully the degree to which students are actually learning what it is they need to learn. Less explicit approaches to instruction often *create an illusion that students are learning* when, in fact, they may not be.

Explicit instruction means that the teacher ensures that students are well informed about what is expected, what is being learned, why it is being learned, and how it can be used. Students also are informed about the instructional techniques that will be used to help them learn and why these techniques are useful in helping them master what is being taught. For example, if the teacher was teaching a textbook reading strategy to students, the purpose for learning the strategy, when and where the strategy can be used, the rationale and function for each strategy step as well as the behaviors that are expected to result from performing the step are explained explicitly to students. Clear explanations of the mental actions that are to take place when performing each of the strategy steps are provided. Students are taught not only how to perform the strategy, but also how to be in control of key cognitive processes when using the strategy. To explicitly model how the strategy is used, teachers think aloud while performing the strategy so that students can witness effective use of self-regulation processes. In addition, students are informed about what they will be doing during each stage of the learning process and how these activities will help them master the strategy and use it in their regular classes to be more successful.

1. Making Covert Processing More Explicit

In order to meet specific task demands (e.g., writing an essay, reading a textbook chapter), students systematically must apply problem-solving processes. Although the results of performing some of these processes are readily observable, the processes themselves often are covert, and thus not readily observable. For example, many processes involve the use of *cognitive strategies*, such as visual imagery, prioritizing, hypothesis generating, relating new information to prior knowledge or paraphrasing; and *metacognitive strategies* such as problem analysis, decision making, goal setting, task analysis, and self-monitoring (Ellis & Lenz, 1996). An aspect of teaching that tends to be the least explicit is instruction in the covert processes that take place when performing tasks. For example, teachers may model and remodel the overt processes associated with writing a short essay and then prompt students to write their own essays. Often, students are required to *infer the mental processes that take place* when performing the task. They must infer what must be thought (a) prior to the beginning the task (e.g., the thinking processes associated with analyzing the task requirements, reflecting on prior experiences with similar tasks, considering how best to approach the task, using self-motivation strategies), (b) while performing the task (monitoring the effectiveness of the strategy they are using, monitoring stress levels, etc.), as well as (c) after the task has been completed (reflecting on the effectiveness of the strategy employed, using self-reinforcement, etc.). Research has demonstrated that making covert processes more explicit for adolescents with LD greatly increases effectiveness of instruction (Ellis *et al.*, 1993). For example, when teaching a reading comprehension strategy that involves paraphrasing the main ideas of a paragraph, an effective teacher will explain and demonstrate the cognitive processes one might use to find and state the main idea. This teacher also would coach students to enable them to perform these cognitive processes effectively and efficiently. Roehler and Duffy (1984) called instruction that emphasizes covert processing "direct explanation" (p. 265). In short, they argue that effective teachers focus not only on the mechanical aspects of learning and performing, but also on directly teaching students to understand and use the covert processes used in the task. A less effective teacher, on the other hand, might simply instruct the student to perform the covert behavior while providing *no* explanation or demonstration of the covert behaviors and then the teacher would provide feedback with regard to whether the desired outcome was attained. In sum, adolescents with LD seem to learn best when instruction is explicit. Therefore, the covert processes they are expected to master must be explained explicitly.

2. Modeling Procedures and Processes

Modeling important procedures and processes should be considered the "heart of instruction" (Schumaker, 1989). Unfortunately, teachers tend to model more overt procedures and *tell* students what they are doing (e.g., "Now I'm going to find the main idea of this paragraph. Let's see...the main idea is...traveling light—it's important to travel light when backpacking."), as opposed to "thinking aloud" during the overt procedures to model more covert processes (Brown, 1978; Duffy & Bursuck, 1994; Fulk, 1994; Palincsar & Brown, 1984).

The result of modeling the covert processes is that students with LD can witness how effective problem solvers think. Thus, effective teachers not only need to thoroughly explain covert processes to adolescents with LD, they also need to explicitly model them. Schumaker (1989) identified three major phases of instruction involving modeling. In Phase I, teachers provide an organizer for the lesson that, among other things, alerts students to the fact that modeling will be provided and cues students to attend to the covert processes being modeled as they think aloud and ask students to imitate them. In Phase II, the teacher demonstrates the procedures and processes while thinking aloud and emphasizing the cognitive processes involved. The teacher demonstrates self-instruction and self-monitoring processes while performing the task. In Phase III, students are prompted to gradually perform more and more of the required thought processes and physical acts themselves; that is, they become the demonstrators. Initially, students can be prompted to name the next step of the task. Once mastered, they should be prompted to say what they would say as they: (a) check their progress, (b) evaluate their performance, (c) make adjustments, and (d) problem-solve. By involving students, the teacher can check their understanding of the procedures and processes involved in performing their tasks. Ellis *et al.* (1993) noted that forcing students to think aloud before they are ready could bog instruction down and make the task difficult. Students should participate in the modeling at a level that will prompt maximum involvement but still assure success.

D. Scaffold Instruction

Scaffolding or mediated scaffolding is "temporary support for students to learn new material" (Kame' enui *et al.*, 2002). It optimizes learning by providing "the systematic sequencing of prompted content, materials, tasks, and teacher and peer support..." (Dickson *et al.*, 1993, p. 12). The scaffolding concept (Bruner, 1975) stems from Vygotsky's work in which he found that children who received adult assistance could perform tasks that they ordinarily could not accomplish independently. In an academic setting, support is given to students until they can apply independently new skills and strategies that they learn (Rosenshine & Meister, 1992). Students need more assistance when they are learning new or difficult tasks or information. Scaffolding requires the "routine application of 'calibrated assistance'" (Wong, 1998, p. 340), in which students receive the amounts and kinds of support needed. The key to successful scaffolding is removing gradually the support as students begin to demonstrate task mastery in order to move the responsibility for learning from the teacher to the students (Larkin, 2002).

1. Scaffolding Model

Several researchers described models of scaffolded instruction in which students gradually are moved from more assistance to less assistance in order to achieve independence (see Beed *et al.*, 1991; Ellis, 1993, 2000; Kameenui & Carnine, 1998; Mercer *et al.*, 1996). Essentially, the process is the same for these models; the difference lies in the terminology used and the number of steps required to move from teacher assistance to student independence. The four-stage scaffolding process based on the work of Ellis (1993, 2000) works well for adolescents with learning disabilities in academic settings (See Figure 11–1).

During the initial *Teacher* stage of the scaffolding process, the teacher introduces and models the task for students (work through the steps of a learning strategy, use a graphic organizer, tune a small engine carburetor, etc.). For example, the teacher may have a partially completed graphic organizer on an overhead transparency; as completion of the graphic organizer is being modeled by the teacher, he or she "thinks aloud," describing the information and how the relationships among the items of information are illustrated on the graphic organizer.

In the second stage, *Class*, the teacher and the class co-construct or co-perform the task because the task is still too new or difficult and the teacher anticipates that the students will need a great deal of assistance. To continue with the graphic organizer example, the teacher may display a partially completed organizer on an overhead transparency while students have paper copies of the same organizer at their desks. The teacher facilitates a discussion of the information and guides the students. They fill in the blanks on their organizers while the teacher simultaneously completes the organizer on the transparency. To guide students' thinking and mediate connections to background knowledge, the teacher may ask many questions of the students and encourage them to become less dependent on the teacher to supply the answers.

The third stage, *Group*, gives students an opportunity to work with a partner or in a small cooperative group (i.e., 4–6 students) to complete a different version of the same task completed in stage 2. For example, the teacher gives the student groups a partially completed or totally blank graphic organizer on a different topic than that used in stage 2 and provides directions for the task. During this in-class activity, the teacher moves around the room to monitor students' progress and provide assistance or feedback when needed. Both the *Class* and *Group* stages are forms of guided practice, although the former is teacher-mediated and the latter is peer-mediated practice. Peer-mediated practice is just as important as teacher-mediated practice. Because students with LD may learn as much

Figure 11–1   Four-stage process for scaffolding instruction (from Ellis 1993, 2000).

from their peers as they do from teachers about how a procedure is performed, it is important to provide opportunities for students to interact and dialogue among themselves about various aspects of performing the task. Students participating in peer-mediated practice activities should need less teacher mediation and feedback, but more opportunities to practice the task to build fluency.

The last stage, *Individual*, refers to students working independently on the task. This form of student-mediated practice gives students the opportunities to practice the task to build fluency, so that both the overt and covert behaviors associated with the task can be performed automatically and quickly. This may be done as an in-class activity where students can still receive teacher assistance or feedback if needed. Therefore, students in the graphic organizer example individually would practice completing graphic organizers similar to those used in the previous three stages. Later, these students may be given a homework assignment in which they are to complete independently another similar graphic organizer.

2. Scaffolding Guidelines and Tools

Individual student needs can be accommodated through scaffolding (Kame'enui *et al.*, 2002). In a literature summary, Hogan and Pressley (1997) described the following eight essential elements of scaffolded instruction that teachers can use as a guide. These elements do not have to occur in this order.

- Become pre-engaged with the student and the curriculum by considering curriculum goals and student needs to select tasks.
- Establish shared goals with the student to promote motivation and investment in learning.
- Actively diagnose student needs and understandings to plan appropriate instruction.
- Provide tailored assistance to meet student needs.
- Help the student to maintain pursuit of his or her goals.
- Give feedback to help the student learn to monitor progress and recognize behaviors that contribute to success.
- Control for frustration and risk by creating an environment in which the student is comfortable taking risks with learning.
- Assist the student to generalize learning and to become an independent learner by practicing tasks in a variety of contexts.

Larkin (1999, 2001) noted the following guidelines for successful scaffolding:

- Begin with what students can do because they need to know their strengths and feel positive about what they can do independently.

- Help students achieve success quickly, so that they do not become too frustrated and shut down.
- Help students to exhibit academic and social characteristics similar to those of their peers in order to promote their self-esteem and foster their motivation for learning.
- Know when it is time to stop because students with LD become discouraged and may make more errors during extremely long practice sessions.
- Help students to be independent when they have command of the task, because they may receive less assistance as they move from elementary to middle and secondary school and then into the postsecondary or vocational world.

Also, Larkin (1999, 2001) found that all of the teachers participating in her study used a variety of scaffolding tools (see Figure 11–2) during their instruction and attempted to select tools to meet individual student needs.

IV. TEACHING HIGH-IMPACT STRATEGIES

Ultimately, the ideal educational programming for students with LD results in both confidence and competence necessary for autonomous functioning in the adult world and fosters a sense of belonging. There is no typical student with LD (Mercer, 1997; Reiff *et al.*, 1996), which means that no one method of addressing particular learning styles or needs will be appropriate for many or all of these students. Although adolescents with LD comprise a heterogeneous group, a great deal has been learned in the last few decades about how to improve the effectiveness of interventions for these students.

As noted earlier in this chapter, *success is a function of the individual interacting with the environment*. In order for their students (i.e., individuals) to be successful in the academic environment, effective teachers must not only

---

Scaffolding Tools

- Model and think aloud
- Invite student participation
- Maximize frequency of correct responses
- Cue and prompt
- Analyze critical features
- Question
- Explain and elaborate
- Verify and clarify understanding
- Summarize and synthesize

Figure 11–2   Scaffolding tools (from Larkin, 1999, 2001).

be familiar with individual student needs but also with environmental or setting demands. This information helps teachers to plan effective learning strategy instruction for their students. A strategy is *"an individual's approach to a task... when it includes how a person thinks and acts when planning, executing, and evaluating performances on a task and its outcomes."* (Lenz *et al.*, 1996, p. 5). Both skills and strategies consist of a set of steps or procedures, but only strategies take into account how individuals plan, think about their observable and nonobservable behaviors, or evaluate their processes.

It is important to distinguish between *teaching strategies* and *learning strategies*. As a teacher, you use many strategies to perform your job of teaching. You have certain approaches to planning, executing, and evaluating your teaching performance on various tasks. You use teaching strategies to help you perform your job. In comparison, learning strategies are what you teach your students to help them learn to perform particular tasks. You hope that your students will learn the strategies well enough and find them useful enough to remember and use them at other times and in other settings.

The intent of learning strategy instruction is to teach strategies effectively (i.e., the student learns and generalizes the strategy) and efficiently (i.e., the student learns the strategy to an optimal level with minimal effort by both the teacher and student) (Lenz *et al.*, 1996). Students who are struggling need to learn strategies to help them improve their task performance. If a student already knows how to perform a task effectively and efficiently, then there is no need for the student to learn a strategy for that task. On the other hand, the student who spends a great deal of time trying to perform a task with unsuccessful results could benefit from a strategy to meet his or her needs in performing that task. Although strategy instruction will not harm students, teaching the same strategy to all students does not guarantee that an individual student's needs are met. In other words, strategy instruction should not be assumed to be *one strategy fits all*, but should instead be differentiated. Gregory and Chapman (2002) stated that differentiated instruction is a philosophy that teachers embrace to reach each learner's unique needs. It assists learners at their level, but still offers challenging, appropriate options to help them be successful.

A number of research-validated learning strategies appropriate for adolescents with LD have been developed at the University of Kansas Center for Research on Learning. A few of their strategies will be highlighted in this chapter, but you may wish to visit their web site at http://www.ku-crl.org to obtain more information about these and other learning strategies. Some of the Kansas Strategies require that you participate in training prior to purchasing the manuals, while others require no training. In this section, you will be introduced to a few learning strategies in the following areas:

(a) reading comprehension, (b) remembering, (c) written expression, (d) competence, and (e) mathematics.

A. Reading Comprehension

In order to comprehend, an individual must relate actively what is being read to his or her background knowledge about the topic. The National Reading Panel noted that teaching reading strategies helps struggling readers to "reason strategically" when they encounter barriers to their understanding (NICHD, 2000, p. 14). Middle and high school students are bombarded with so much information that it is difficult for adolescents with LD to learn and remember what they have read. Paraphrasing, summarizing, question answering, and self-questioning are beneficial strategies to teach these students if they do not currently perform them.

1. Paraphrasing and Summarizing

The Paraphrasing Strategy (Schumaker *et al.*, 1993) was developed and validated at the University of Kansas Center for Research on Learning to help students recall the main ideas and important details of what they have read. The strategy is based on the first-letter mnemonic RAP:

Read a paragraph

Ask a question to identify the main idea and details

Put the main idea and details into your own words.

During the first step, students read the paragraph silently (Bos & Vaughn, 2002). In the second step, they ask themselves a question to identify the main idea and important details of what they have read. Finally, they put the main idea and details into their own words to help them remember the information. You may want to encourage your students to provide at least two details related to each main idea. Schumaker *et al.* indicated that good paraphrases must: (a) contain a complete thought with a subject and verb, (b) be accurate, (c) make sense, (d) contain useful information, and (e) be in the student's own words. Students with LD who learned and used the Paraphrasing Strategy increased their comprehension on grade-level materials from 48 to 84% (Schumaker *et al.*, 1984).

Similar to the Paraphrasing Strategy, gist summaries help students to summarize information contained in a single paragraph. The challenge of gist summaries is to use a single sentence for the summary (Swanson & DeLaPaz, 1998). Teacher modeling shows students how to restate information read using the fewest number of words possible. At first, students may summarize two sentences of a paragraph in 15 words or less. Then you can challenge them to summarize the entire paragraph in 15 words or less. Adolescents with LD will need teacher feedback to determine the most crucial information to report. Gist summaries also can give students practice with their goal setting (e.g., maximum number of words to use in one sentence to summarize a paragraph).

2. Question Answering and Self-Questioning

When students are asked questions about what they have read, they need to recognize where and how they will find the information necessary to answer the questions. Raphael (1982) identified the following questioning strategies: (a) right there, (b) think and search, (c) author and you, and (d) on my own (p. 378). Casteel *et al.* (2000) adapted these strategies by adding a statement to further assist students in locating the appropriate information to answer the questions:

> *Right There*—I can find the answer in one place in the book.
> *Think and Search*—I can find the answer in the book, but all of the answer won't be in the same place.
> *Author and Me*—I have to use what the author wrote and what I know to answer the question. I have to "read between the lines."
> *On My Own*—I can answer the questions by using what I already know about the topic.

Another important comprehension strategy is that of self-questioning. Vacca and Vacca (2002) noted that ReQuest originally was designed for one-on-one instruction, but can be adapted easily for a class to help students think while they read. In ReQuest, teacher and students silently read the same text passage. Note that you may want to select short passages, particularly for students who struggle with comprehension. Second, the students question the teacher after the teacher closes the book. The teacher may ask students for clarification of their questions and the teacher may model how he or she may not always know the answer. Also, the students may take turns asking the teacher questions or may work in teams to ask the teacher questions. In the third step, the teacher and students exchange roles. In other words, the teacher asks the students about the text passage read. Students can indicate that they do not know an answer to a question, but must explain why they do not know the answer. During this step, the teacher can model asking a variety of kinds of questions to help students learn to ask good questions. These three steps can be repeated for each section of text read. Then students make predictions about the remainder of material to be read and justify why they made the predictions that they did. This is a time for you to encourage students to take a risk with their predictions.

After making predictions, the students silently read the remainder of reading material followed by a teacher-facilitated class discussion (Vacca & Vacca). The ReQuest strategy is a good way to introduce students to the notion of self-questioning. Then they can be encouraged and shown how to self-question as they read selections (see McKenna & Robinson, 2002).

B. Remembering

Secondary school demands require that students know the meaning and spelling of numerous vocabulary words. In addition, students often are asked to show that they understand the meaning of the vocabulary words through essay writing, worksheet exercises, experiments, projects, and so on. This can be a most difficult task for some adolescents with LD. Students may be able to put the vocabulary meanings into short-term memory (i.e., about 20 seconds), but too often the information is quickly forgotten (Hughes, 1996), partly because many students use less efficient and effective learning strategies, such as repetition or verbal rehearsal (i.e., saying information over and over) in an attempt to remember the words. Verbal rehearsal may be appropriate for remembering briefly a telephone number to call a friend, but the approach is usually a very poor long-term memory strategy.

Many adolescents with LD greatly benefit from instruction in a more efficient and effective strategy for learning vocabulary. In other words, they need to be able to use the vocabulary information in working memory (i.e., "held in mind") and file away the information in long-term memory for retrieval later (Hughes, 1996). For many adolescents with LD, retrieving the information from long-term memory can be just as difficult as learning the information in the first place. Therefore, an appropriate vocabulary strategy will aid not only the students in learning the information, but also in retrieving it.

Mnemonics are remembering devices that help to make meaningful connections from seemingly unconnected information. Such connections aid in memory storage and later retrieval (Hughes, 1996). Although there are several kinds of mnemonics, keyword is one variety that is often used for learning vocabulary. Keywords are familiar concrete words that visually or acoustically resemble an obvious portion of the unfamiliar word (Bulgren & Lenz, 1996). Brigham, et al. (1995) found that students with LD recalled significantly more feature locations of American Revolutionary War battles using keyword and pictorial mnemonics than students who were given only drawing of actual features pertaining to battle sites. They further noted that positive effects occur for students with LD because concreteness is enhanced. Mastropieri et al. (1997) stated that mnemonic instruction for students with

LD produced positive effects on learning information about U.S. presidents. Bulgren *et al.* (1995) found that students with LD instructed in a paired associates strategy involving mnemonics made substantial improvement in the creation of study cards and in test performance. (See Greene [1994] for a discussion of how mnemonics can be applied to various content areas.) Evers and Bursuck (1995) suggested mnemonics as a way for students with LD in technical classes to remember machine parts, the steps to complete a task, or shop procedures.

1. LINCS Vocabulary

The LINCS Vocabulary Strategy (Ellis, 1995) is one of the University of Kansas strategies that provides powerful memory enhancement techniques to help students learn the meaning of new vocabulary words. In LINCS, the strategy steps cue students to focus on the critical concept elements, employ visual imagery, make connections with prior knowledge, and try keyword mnemonic devices to create a study card. Then students are given instructions on how to study the card to improve their comprehension and concept recall.

LINCS (Ellis, 1995) is based on the keyword mnemonic method (Figure 11–3). Each letter of the word "LINCS" cues students to perform a step to aid in learning vocabulary. For example, to perform the first step, *List the parts*, students determine important words and information to record on an index card. The word is written and circled on the front of the card, and a short definition is written on the back. For example, this may be done for the vocabulary word, *fief* and its definition, land given by a king for fighting in his army.

For the second step, *Imagine a picture*, students begin to use memory-enhancing devices and create a mental image of the term and its meaning. They describe that image to themselves or to someone else. For example, a student's mental image may be of a king giving a knight a piece of land in return for the knight's agreeing to serve in the king's army.

To perform the third step, *Note a familiar reminding word*, students identify from their background knowledge a common word that is similar acoustically to the new vocabulary word. In the example, *life* (a familiar word from the student's background knowledge sounds like *fief*). Therefore, the rhyming word *life* is written on the lower one-half of the front of the index card.

The fourth step, *Construct a "LINCing" story*, requires that the student make an association between the vocabulary word *fief* and the rhyming or LINCing word *life*. For example, the student might think, "For life refers to the period of time someone exists. When the knight returns from fighting, he will be in charge of his land for life."

A Close-up of the LINCS Strategy

Step 1:   List the parts
- List the word on a study card.
- List the most important parts of the definition on the back of the study card.

Step 2:   Imagine a picture
- Create an image in your mind of what the word is about.
- Describe the image.

Step 3:   Note a "Reminding Word"
- Think of a familiar word that sounds like the new word or part of the new word.

Step 4:   Construct a LINCing story
- Make up a short story about the meaning of the new word that includes the Reminding Word.
- Change your image to include your story.

Step 5:   Self-test
- Self-test "forward":
    1. Say the new word.
    2. Say the Reminding Word.
    3. Think of the LINCing Story.
    4. Think of the image.
    5. Say the meaning of the new word.
    6. Check to see if you're correct.

- Self-test "backwards":
    1. Say the new word.
    2. Say the Reminding Word.
    3. Think of the LINCing Story.
    4. Think of the image.
    5. Say the meaning of the new word.
    6. Check to see if you're correct.

Figure 11–3   LINCS: a vocabulary-learning strategy (from Ellis, 1995).

The fifth and final step in LINCS is *Self-test*, in which the student uses forward (i.e., vocabulary word to LINCing word to LINCing story to definition) and backward (i.e., definition to LINCing story to LINCing word to vocabulary word) retrieval methods. Students are reminded of the chain analogy and encouraged to make strong LINCS. In other words, a chain is only as strong as its weakest link. Good LINCing words and stories are what make this vocabulary strategy successful.

The LINCS vocabulary strategy was used with students with LD in a sixth grade social studies class. The students with LD gained 24% after learning the strategy (Wedel *et al.*, 1992). Results indicate that students with LD are capable of learning a vocabulary memory strategy, and some are able to generalize its use to other subjects and settings. This study indicated that teacher-created mnemonics seemed to be more effective and efficient than those that were student-generated, for unknown reasons. More research needs to be conducted as to how to instruct students to consistently and proficiently generalize this technique (Hughes, 1996).

2. FIRST-Letter Mnemonics

The FIRST-Letter Mnemonic Strategy (Nagel *et al.*, 1994) is another University of Kansas learning strategy whose purpose is to help students to memorize lists of information. In this strategy, students are taught to design mnemonics or memorization aids while finding and making lists of important information. The strategy consists of LISTS, which is an overall strategy, and the substrategy FIRST that is used for making the mnemonic device. The steps in LISTS include:

Look for clues.

Investigate the items.

Select a mnemonic device, using FIRST.

Transfer the information to a card.

Self-test.

In the first step of LISTS, students look for clues in class notes and textbooks to find important lists of information. Then they think of a heading that is appropriate for each list. When students investigate the items (i.e., step two), they determine which items should be included in the list. In step three, students select a mnemonic device using the FIRST substrategy (which will be explained) to construct a mnemonic. For step four of LISTS, students transfer the information to a card; that is, they write the mnemonic and list on the back side of the card and the heading on the front side. Finally, students self-test, which means that they study by looking at the heading and try to use their mnemonic to recall the list items without looking at the list.

The substrategy, FIRST, consists of:

Form a word.

Insert a letter(s).

Rearrange the letters.

Shape a sentence.

Try combinations.

In the first step of the substrategy, students use uppercase letters and write the first letter of each word in the list. They try to see if an acronym or a recognizable word or a nonsense word can be made. In step two, students insert letter(s) to determine whether adding letters helps to form a word. Lowercase letters are added to indicate that these letters do not represent an item on the list (e.g., CaRT). For step three, students rearrange the letters to determine if a word can be made. In the next step, students shape a sentence by using the first letter of each list word to construct a sentence (i.e., an acrostic). Finally, students try combinations of the aforementioned steps to create the mnemonic.

C. Written Expression

Wong *et al.* (1989) found that adolescents with LD performed similar to younger students rather than same-age classmates with regard to essay writing. The essays of students with LD were less interesting and shorter, contained less clarity in communication of written goals, used inferior word choices, and exhibited more spelling errors. Many students with mild LD produce as little as possible to meet the demands of the task. Students whose writing demonstrates a disorganized flow of ideas and poor paragraph structure can benefit from explicit instruction in paragraph and essay writing. Writing strategy instruction enables students "to use an efficient, effective approach to expository writing and to facilitate students' use of self-regulation—self-motivation, self-reinforcement, and goal-directed self-speech—during the prewriting production process, and revising" (Ellis & Colvert, 1996, p. 173). Writing is thinking on paper, so students must use logical methods of organization in order for their writing to make sense to others.

Zipprich (1995) indicated that teaching students with LD a strategy to assist with the planning and organization of writing was beneficial. She found that students who lacked a strategy for planning produced stories that were more poorly written and often were not aware of the component parts of a story. Wong *et al.* (1997) found that adolescents with LD who were taught a writing strategy for compare-and-contrast essays improved the quality of their essays substantially after the training. Particular areas of improvement noted were clarity, appropriateness, and organization of ideas. Hallenbeck (1996) affirmed the value of a writing approach for adolescents with LD that incorporates cognitive strategy instruction within process writing. He found that junior high and high school students with LD improved in the areas of paragraph structure, inclusion of introductions and conclusions, and development of author voice after writing strategy training and practice for a year.

Modeling of process writing to adolescents with LD helped them to be more willing to share their written work with others (Milem & Garcia, 1996), and goal setting could be combined with a strategy to improve students' writing (Voth & Graham, 1993). MacArthur (1994) noted that writing strategies, word processing, and peers were powerful in helping students to revise their writing. Bergen (1994) found that electronic spelling devices were useful for younger students to determine the correct spelling of a word during the editing stage of writing. One writing area that seemed to be more problematic was for students with LD to develop adequate metacognition about their audience's needs. Wong *et al.* (1991) found that interactive teaching (i.e., instructional dialogues with the teacher) improved the clarity and thematic salience of students' expository essays, but the students still had much to learn about adequate revision.

1. Sentence Writing and Paragraph Writing

The University of Kansas Sentence Writing Strategy (Schumaker & Sheldon, 1985) helps students to learn the basic principles of sentence construction and expression. The *Fundamentals in the Sentence Writing Strategy* starts with concepts of subject, verb, infinitive, and preposition. The *Proficiency in the Sentence Writing Strategy* teaches students to recognize and generate four sentence types: simple, compound, complex, and compound–complex.

The mnemonic PENS helps students remember the steps for writing sentences:

Pick a sentence type and formula.

Explore words to fit the formula.

Note the words.

Search for verbs and subjects and check.

PENS also is used in the University of Kansas Paragraph Writing Strategy (Schumaker & Lyerla, 1991) to assist students in writing a topic sentence, detail sentences, and a clincher sentence to form a paragraph. In this strategy, students learn how to write well-organized, complete paragraphs by making an outline of ideas, selecting a perspective and tense, sequencing ideas, and checking their paragraph. Students learn to write various kinds of paragraphs including sequential, descriptive, expository, and compare–contrast.

2. Error Monitoring

The Error Monitoring Strategy (Schumaker *et al.*, 1994) also was developed at the University of Kansas Center for Research on Learning. This strategy was designed to teach students a process for detecting and correcting writing errors and helps them to produce a neater written product. This strategy teaches students how to locate errors in paragraph organization, sentence structure, capitalization, overall editing and appearance, punctuation, and spelling. Error finding is accomplished by having students ask themselves a series of questions. Then students correct their errors and rewrite their passage. The Error Monitory Strategy uses the mnemonic COPS:

C   Have I **C**apitalized the first word and proper nouns?

O   How is the **O**verall appearance? (spacing, legibility, paragraph indents, neatness, and complete sentences)

P   Have I put in commas, semicolons, and end **P**unctuation?

S   Have I **S**pelled all the words correctly?

Mercer (1997) suggested that the teacher review COPS periodically and encourage students to use it daily so that its use will become a habit. Also, the teacher may require students to use COPS on all of their papers prior to turning them in for a grade.

D. Competence

Adolescents with LD often become discouraged with themselves and have their teachers look unfavorably on them because they often do not complete assignments and perform poorly on tests. When the truth is known, these students may not know how to approach an assignment and complete it in a timely manner. Also, they may do poorly on tests because they have test anxiety based on previous failures on exams. Therefore, these adolescents can benefit from being taught competence strategies such as assignment completion and test-taking.

1. Assignment Completion

The Assignment Completion Strategy (Hughes *et al.*, 1995) from the University of Kansas Center for Research on Learning teaches students to monitor their assignments from the time they are assigned until they are completed and submitted to the teacher. In this strategy, students learn to write down and analyze assignments, schedule and complete subtasks, and submit the completed assignment.

Hughes *et al.* (2002) used a multiple-probe across-students design to evaluate the effects of teaching students with LD a comprehensive, independent assignment completion strategy. They wanted to determine if the students could master the strategy and improve their assignment completion rate, quality of assignment products, grades, and teacher satisfaction with their work in general education classrooms. The researchers also wanted to study whether the changes would be maintained over time. Nine middle school students were taught an assignment completion strategy, called the PROJECT Strategy. The steps in this mnemonic device included:

> **P**repare your forms
> **R**ecord and ask (i.e., record assignments and ask questions about unclear aspects)
> **O**rganize
>> **B**reak the assignment into parts
>> **E**stimate the number of study sessions
>> **S**chedule the sessions
>> **T**ake your materials home
> **J**ump to it
> **E**ngage in the work
> **C**heck your work
> **T**urn in your work (Hughes *et al.*, 2002, p. 4).

Hughes *et al.* found that eight of the nine participants in the study mastered the use of the strategy. Their homework completion rates and the quality of products completed as part of their assignments given in the general education classroom improved. Also, the students' grades increased and teacher ratings of the quality of their assignments improved. The researchers concluded that students must be given appropriate assignments and be motivated to complete them and students must be able to master the required skills.

2. Test Taking

Students with LD may not perform well in testing situations because they do not know how to take tests effectively. Often, they may think that "studying hard" is the only thing they have to do get a good grade. A history of poor test performance naturally leads to test anxiety and an "I don't care" coping attitude. Test-taking strategies can be taught to students to assist them in performing better on tests and reducing anxiety. Students must be cautioned that learning a test-preparation strategy does not mean that they are free from studying (Hughes, 1996). Rather, it is a test-taking strategy in combination with good study habits that provide a formula for success in testing situations.

PIRATES (Hughes, Schumaker *et al.*, 1993) is a University of Kansas strategy (Figure 11–4) that helps students to allocate time and carefully read test instructions and questions. Students learn to either answer a question or abandon it for later consideration. The strategy teaches eliminating answers that are obviously wrong and making reasonable guesses from the remaining choices. Students are taught to make sure that they survey the entire test for unanswered questions.

Adolescents with LD and those with behavior problems have used the strategy successfully (Hughes, Ruhl *et al.*, 1993; Hughes & Schumaker 1991a,b). The first step, *Prepare to succeed*, helps to establish a proactive frame of mind (Hughes, 1996). Students who put their name and PIRATES on the test determine the order in which they wish to work test items and the

Prepare to succeed

Put name on test.
Allot time & order sections.
Say something positive.
Start within 2 minutes.

Inspect instructions

Read whole questions.
Underline how and where to respond.
Notice special requirements.

Read, remember, reduce

Read whole questions.
Remember with memory strategies.
Reduce choices.

Answer or abandon

Turn back

Estimate

Avoid absolutes.
Choose longest or most detailed answer.
Eliminate choices.

Survey to ensure all questions are answered

Figure 11–4   PIRATES: A test-taking strategy (from Hughes, Schumaker *et al.*, 1993)

time that should be allotted to each, as well as saying some affirmations, and begin the test within 2 minutes (Hughes, 1996). Order of items is a matter of preference. Some students choose the harder items first while others choose the easy ones.

The second step, *Inspect the instructions*, cues students with LD to focus on directions, something they otherwise may fail to do (Hughes, 1996). This step has a substep RUN, which stands for **R**ead *instructions carefully*, **U**nderline *what to do and where to respond*, and **N**otice *special requirements*. Students are taught the importance of reading directions and how to read them. Then students are to notice whether letters are to be circled or underlined and whether they are to indicate the correct answer or one that is not correct.

Step three, *Read, remember, and reduce*, encourages students to read the question in its entirety before answering rather than acting like eager game show contestants who blurt out an answer before the question is finished. Students also are taught to read all possible choices before answering. *Remember* cues students to remember what they have learned and studied that would help them to answer the item. The students reduce the number of possible choices by eliminating obviously incorrect ones and crossing them out.

Step four, *Answer or abandon*, reminds students to answer the question if they are relatively sure of the answer or abandon the item if they are unsure. Abandoned items should be marked in a way that they cannot be mistaken for answers, but will be easily recognized later. Steps 2, 3, and 4 are repeated for each section of the test until all sections have been attempted.

In step five, *Turn back*, students return to abandoned items to see whether they can remember anything that would help them to answer the questions. Relevant knowledge may have been found in another item. If they still do not know the answer and will not be penalized for guessing, then they can apply three guessing strategies, as cued by the mnemonic ACE, in the sixth step (*Estimate*): (a) **A** stands for avoid absolutes (specific determiners); (b) **C** means choose the longest, most detailed option; and (c) **E** or eliminate (cross off) similar options.

The seventh step, *Survey*, ensures that students have responded to all items and that they have responded to all items in the way in which they intended. Students are taught that changing answers is appropriate only if they are sure that the choice is correct. If they are unsure, it is better to remain with the original choice (Hughes, 1996).

E. Mathematics

Students who struggle with mathematics may dislike math and find the processes laborious because they do not understand the concepts involved. Therefore, it may not be unusual to find middle school and high school adolescents with LD who do not know their math facts or how to solve word problems. Bos and Vaughn (2002) stated that teachers cannot assume that if students learn basic math facts, they will no longer have difficulty with other math operations and problems. Learning math facts does not help students to analyze or understand the application of math operations, but may aid in the fluency and accuracy of performing math operations. Students who do not know their math facts spend so much time computing a small segment of the problem that they likely will be much slower and less accurate than their peers who know their math facts. Although learning math facts is important, teaching students with LD problem solving may be the most important skill, according to Bos and Vaughn. Students with LD lack the metacognitive knowledge about math problem solving strategies, whereas other students can apply math operations to real-world problems.

1. Math Facts

The Strategic Math Series is a component of the Strategic Instruction Model (SIM) developed by the University of Kansas Center for Research on Learning. Mercer and Miller (1998) noted that this series helps students to understand math concepts by using the concrete–representational–abstract teaching sequence systematically and explicitly. Concrete-level lessons use manipulative devices (i.e., three-dimensional objects) such as blocks, counters, etc. Representational-level lessons use drawings and tally marks to represent quantities. Abstract-level lessons use number symbols without objects or drawings. Mnemonic devices such as FIND (for place value), DRAW (for computation), and FAST DRAW (for word problems) cue students how to approach difficult problems and solve word problems. The steps in DRAW (Mercer & Miller, 1992) include:

Discover the sign

Read the problem

Answer, or draw and check

Write the answer

In the first step, *Discover the sign*, the student looks at the operation sign and determines whether to add, subtract, multiply, or divide. For the second step, the student says the problem (e.g., "three times four equals___."). In step three, the student answers the problem if he or she knows it. If the student does not know the answer, then he or she can draw three horizontal lines to represent groups and four vertical tallies to represent the objects in each group. Then all the tallies are counted and recounted for accuracy.

$$1\_\_1\_\_1\_\_1$$
$$1\_\_1\_\_1\_\_1$$
$$1\_\_1\_\_1\_\_1$$

In the fourth step, the student writes the answer to the problem in the answer space (e.g., $3 \times 4 = 12$).

2. Word Problem-Solving

The FAST DRAW word problem-solving strategy also is part of the Strategic Math Series from the University of Kansas. The steps in FAST DRAW (Mercer & Miller, 1992) are:

Find what you're solving for.

Ask yourself, "What are the parts of the problem?"

Set up the numbers.

Tie down the sign.

Discover the sign.

Read the problem.

Answer, or draw and check.

Write the answer.

In the first step of FAST DRAW, the student looks for questions in the problem. Next, the student asks a question to find out the parts of the problem.

Sample Problem: Ted has 4 cans of tennis balls with 3 tennis balls in each can.

Sandy has 2 tennis racquets. How many total tennis balls are there?

The student would need to identify cans as the "group" because they have something in common. Then the student would identify the tennis balls as "objects per group" because there are 3 in each can or group. The student then would multiply "group" (i.e., 4) by "objects per group (i.e., 3) to determine the total (i.e., 12). In step three, the student writes the numbers:

$$\begin{array}{r} 4 \text{ cans} \\ \text{of } 3 \text{ tennis balls} \\ \hline \text{tennis balls} \end{array}$$

In step four, the student writes the problem with the operation sign:

$$
\begin{array}{r}
4 \text{ cans} \\
\times\ 3 \text{ tennis balls} \\
\hline
\text{tennis balls}
\end{array}
$$

Then the student is ready to solve the problem from memory or by using the DRAW strategy described earlier.

V. CONCLUSION

Concluding this chapter is bittersweet. It is bitter in the sense that we have only just begun to convey the wealth of research-validated strategic academic interventions that have been shown to be successful for adolescents with LD. There is so much more that we would have liked to mention, but limited time and space prohibit that. For example, there is another body of literature on graphic organizers, many of which are nice complements to some learning strategies. Graphic organizers help students to summarize and synthesize the important information by recognizing the relationships among concepts or ideas. These graphic organizers assist students in recognizing new concepts and sequence as well as text structures such as hierarchical (e.g., main idea[s] and details), compare–contrast, etc. Conducting an internet search on graphic organizers can provide several good web sites with reproducible graphic organizer forms and examples. Ellis has information regarding graphic organizers and a number of additional learning strategies not mentioned in this chapter at his website www.graphicorganizers.com. The sweet part of concluding this chapter is that in the past few decades we have learned so much about what works for students with LD in order to help them become successful in academic settings. There are so many strategies that can be used and have been shown to be effective with adolescents with LD. The beauty of these strategies is that many can be tailored to individual needs and are strategies that teachers can implement relatively easily.

References

Airasian, P. W. (2000). *Assessment in the classroom: A concise approach* (2nd ed.). Boston: McGraw-Hill.

Anderson, C. A., & Jennings, D. L. (1980). When experiences of failure promote expectations of success: The impact of attributing failure to ineffective strategies. *Journal of Personality*, **48**, 393–407.

Beed, P. L., Hawkins, E. M., & Roller, C. M. (1991). Moving learners toward independence: The power of scaffolded instruction. *The Reading Teacher*, **44**, 648–655.

Bender, W. N. (1994). Social-emotional development: The task and the challenge. *Learning Disability Quarterly*, **17**, 250–252.

Bergen, R. (1994). Improving the writing performance of students with learning disabilities through the use of electronic reference devices. *LD Forum*, **19**(2), 26–27.

Bos, C. S., & Vaughn, S. (2002). *Strategies for teaching students with learning and behavior problems* (5th ed.). Boston: Allyn and Bacon.

Brigham, F. J., Scruggs, R. E., & Mastropieri, M. A. (1995). Elaborative maps for enhanced learning of historical information: Uniting spatial, verbal, and imaginal information. *The Journal of Special Education*, **28**(3), 440–460.

Brown, A. L. (1978). Knowing when, where, and how to remember: A problem of metacognition. In R. Glaser (ed.), *Advances in instructional psychology*, (Vol. 7, pp. 55–113). Hillsdale, NJ: Erlbaum.

Bruner, J. S. (1975). The ontogenesis of speech acts. *Journal of Child Language*, **2**, 1–40.

Bulgren, J. A., Hock, M. F., Schumaker, J. B., & Deshler, D. D. (1995). The effects of instruction in a paired associated strategy on the information mastery performance of students with learning disabilities. *Learning Disabilities Research & Practice*, **10**(1), 22–27.

Bulgren, J., & Lenz, K. (1996). Strategic instruction in the content areas. In D. D. Deshler, E. S. Ellis, & B. K. Lenz (eds.), *Teaching adolescents with learning disabilities: Strategies and methods* (2nd ed., pp. 409–473). Denver, CO: Love.

Carter, J. F. (1993). Self-management: Education's ultimate goal. *Teaching Exceptional Children*, **25**(3), 28–32.

Casteel, C. P., Isom, B. A., & Jordan, K. F. (2000). Creating confident and competent readers: Transactional strategies instruction. *Intervention in School and Clinic*, **36**(2), 67–74.

Deshler, D. D., Ellis, E. S., & Lenz, B. K. (1996). *Teaching adolescents with learning disabilities: Strategies & methods*. Denver: Love.

Dickson, S. V., Chard, D. J., & Simmons, D. C. (1993). An integrated reading/writing curriculum: A focus on scaffolding. *LD Forum*, **18**(4), 12–16.

Duchardt, B. A., Deshler, D. D., & Schumaker, J. B. (1995). A strategic intervention for enabling students with learning disabilities to identify and change their ineffective beliefs. *Learning Disability Quarterly*, **18**, 186–201.

Duffy, M. L., & Bursuck, W. D. (1994). Adapting the secondary curriculum: Considerations for teachers. *LD Forum*, **19**(2), 18–21.

Dunlap, L. K., Dunlap, G., Koegel, L. K., & Koegel, R. L. (1991). Using self-monitoring to increase independence. *Teaching Exceptional Children*, **23**(3), 17–22.

Ellis, E. S. (1989). A metacognitive intervention for increasing class participation. *Learning Disabilities Focus*, **5**(1), 36–46.

Ellis, E. S. (1993). Integrative strategy instruction: A potential model for teaching content-area subjects to learning disabled adolescents. *Journal of Learning Disabilities*, **26**(6), 358–383.

Ellis, E. S. (1995). *LINCS: The vocabulary strategy* (2nd ed.). Lawrence, KS: Edge Enterprises.

Ellis, E. S. (2000). *Strategic graphic organizer instruction.* Tuscaloosa, AL: Masterminds, LLC.

Ellis, E. S., & Colvert, G. (1996). *Writing strategy instruction* (2nd ed., pp. 127–207). Denver, CO: Love.

Ellis, E. S., Deshler, D. D., Schumaker, J. B., Lenz, B. K., & Clark, F. L. (1993). An instructional model for teaching learning strategies. In E. Meyen, G. A. Vergason, & R. Whelen (eds.), *Educating students with mild disabilities* (pp. 151–187). Denver, CO: Love Publishing Co.

Ellis, E. S., & Lenz, B. K. (1996). Perspectives on instruction in learning strategies. In D. D. Deshler, E. S. Ellis, & B. K. Lenz (eds.), *Teaching adolescents with learning disabilities: Strategies and methods* (2nd ed., pp. 9–60). Denver, CO: Love.

Evers, R. B., & Bursuck, W. D. (1995). Helping students succeed in technical classes: Using learning strategies and study skills. *Teaching Exceptional Children,* **28**(3), 22–27.

Field, S. (1996). Self-determination instructional strategies for youth with learning disabilities. *Journal of Learning Disabilities,* **29**(1), 40–52.

Fulk, B. M. (1994). Mnemonic keyword strategy training for students with learning disabilities. *Learning Disabilities Research & Practice,* **9**(3), 179–185.

Gerber, P. J., Ginsberg, R., & Reiff, H. B. (1992). Identifying alterable patterns in employment success for highly successful adults with learning disabilities. *Journal of Learning Disabilities,* **25**(8), 475–487.

Greene, G. (1994). The magic of mnemonics. *LD Forum,* **19**(3), 34–37.

Gregory, G. H., & Chapman, C. (2002). *Differentiated instructional strategies: One size doesn't fit all.* Thousand Oaks, CA: Corwin Press, Inc.

Hallenbeck, M. J. (1996). The cognitive strategy in writing: Welcome relief for adolescents with learning disabilities. *Learning Disabilities Research & Practice,* **11**(2), 107–119.

Hogan, K., & Pressley, M. (eds.). (1997). *Scaffolding student learning: Instructional approaches & issues.* Cambridge, MA: Brookline Books.

Hughes, C. A. (1996). Memory and test-taking strategies. In D. D. Deshler, E. S. Ellis, & B. K. Lenz (eds.), *Teaching adolescents with learning disabilities: Strategies and methods* (2nd ed., pp. 209–266). Denver, CO: Love.

Hughes, C. A., Ruhl, K. L., Deshler, D. D., & Schumaker, J. B. (1993). Test-taking strategy instruction for adolescents with emotional and behavior disorders. *Journal of Emotional and Behavior Disorders,* **1**, 189–198.

Hughes, C. A., Ruhl, K. L., Deshler, D. D., & Schumaker, J. B. (1995). *The assignment completion strategy.* Lawrence, KS: Edge Enterprises.

Hughes, C. A., Ruhl, K. L., Schumaker, J. B., & Deshler, D. D. (2002). Effects of instruction in an assignment completion strategy on the homework performance of students with learning disabilities in general education classes. *Learning Disabilities Research & Practice,* **17**(1), 1–18.

Hughes, C. A., & Schumaker, J. B. (1991a). Reflections on test-taking strategy instruction for adolescents with learning disabilities. *Exceptionality,* **2**, 237–242.

Hughes, C. A., & Schumaker, J. B. (1991b). Test-taking strategy instruction for adolescents with learning disabilities. *Exceptionality,* **2**, 205–221.

Hughes, C. A., Schumaker, J. B., Deshler, D. D., & Mercer, C. D. (1993). *The test-taking strategy.* Lawrence, KS: Edge Enterprises.

Kameenui, E. J., & Carnine, D. W. (1998). *Effective teaching strategies that accommodate diverse learners.* Upper Saddle River, NJ: Merrill.

Kame'enui, E. J., Carnine, D. W., Dixon, R. C., Simmons, D. C., & Coyne, M. D. (2002). *Effective teaching strategies that accommodate diverse learners* (2nd ed.). Upper Saddle River, NJ: Merrill Prentice Hall.

Kershner, J., Kirkpatrick, T., & McLaren, D. (1995). The career success of an adult with a learning disability: A psychosocial study of amnesic-semantic aphasia. *Journal of Learning Disabilities,* **28**(2), 121–126.

King-Sears, M. E., & Cummings, C. S. (1996). Inclusive practices of classroom teachers. *Remedial and special education,* **17,** 217–225.

Langston, R. (2002). *For the children: Redefining success in school and success in life.* Austin, TX: Turnkey Press.

Larkin, M. J. (1999). Teachers' perspectives of learning disabilities pedagogy (Doctoral dissertation, The University of Alabama, 1999). *Dissertation Abstracts International,* **60,** 1981.

Larkin, M. J. (2001). Providing support for student independence through scaffolded instruction. *Teaching Exceptional Children,* **34**(1), 30–34.

Larkin, M. J. (2002). *Using scaffolded instruction to optimize learning.* (ERIC Digest No. 639). Arlington, VA: ERIC Clearinghouse on Disabilities and Gifted Education. (ERIC Document Reproduction Service No. EDO EC 02 17).

Larkin, M. J., & Ellis, E. S. (1998). Adolescents with learning disabilities. In B. Y. L. Wong (ed.), *Learning about learning disabilities* (2nd ed.). San Diego: Academic Press.

Lee, C., & Jackson, R. (1992). *Faking it: A look into the mind of a creative learner.* Portsmouth, NH: Boynton/Cook.

Lenz, B. K. (1991). In the spirit of strategies instruction: Cognitive and metacognitive aspects of the Strategies Intervention Model. In S. Vogel (ed.), *Proceedings of the Second Annual Conference of the National Institute of Dyslexia.* White Plains, NY: Longman.

Lenz, B. K., Alley, G. R., & Schumaker, G. R. (1987). Activating the inactive learner: Advance organizers in the secondary content classroom. *Learning Disability Quarterly,* **10**(1), 53–67.

Lenz, B. K., Boudah, D. J., Schumaker, J. B., & Deshler, D. D. (1993). *The lesson planning routine: A guide for inclusive lesson planning (Tech. Rep. No. 124).* Lawrence, KS: University of Kansas Center for Research on Learning.

Lenz, B. K., Ehren, B. J., & Smiley, L. R. (1991). A goal attainment approach to improve completion of project-type assignments by adolescents with learning disabilities. *Learning Disabilities Research & Practice,* **6,** 166–176.

Lenz, B. K., Ellis, E. S., & Scanlon, D. (1996). *Teaching learning strategies to adolescents and adults with learning disabilities.* Austin, TX: Pro-Ed. Learning Strategies.

Licht, B. C., & Kistner, J. A. (1986). Motivational problems of learning disabled children: Individual differences and their implications for treatment. In J. K. Torgesen & B. Y. L. Wong (eds.), *Psychological and educational perspectives on learning disabilities.* New York: Academic Press.

Luckner, J. (1994). Developing independent and responsible behaviors in students who are deaf or hard of hearing. *Teaching Exceptional Children*, **26**(2), 13–17.

MacArthur, C. (1994). Peers + word processing + strategies = A powerful combination for revising student writing. *Teaching Exceptional Children*, **27**(1), 24–29.

Martin, K. F., & Manno, C. (1995). Use of a check-off system to improve middle school students' story compositions. *Journal of Learning Disabilities*, **28**(3), 137–149.

Masterminds. www.graphicorganizers.com.

Mastropieri, M. A., Scruggs, T. E., & Whedon, C. (1997). Using mnemonic strategies to teach information about U.S. presidents: A classroom-based investigation. *Learning Disability Quarterly*, **20**, 13–21.

McCombs, B. L. (1984). Processes and skills underlying continuing intrinsic motivation to learn: Toward a definition of motivational skills training interventions. *Educational Psychologist*, **19**(4), 199–218.

McKenna, M. C., & Robinson, R. D. (2002). *Teaching through text: Reading and writing in the content areas* (3rd ed.). Boston: Allyn and Bacon.

Mercer, C. D. (1997). *Students with learning disabilities* (5th ed.). Upper Saddle River, NJ: Merrill.

Mercer, C. D., Lane, H. B., Jordan, L., Allsopp, D. H., & Eisle, M. R. (1996). Empowering teachers and students with instructional choices in inclusive settings. *Remedial and Special Education*, **17**(4), 226–236.

Mercer, C. D., & Miller, S. P. (1992). Strategic math series: Instructional procedures and field test results. *Strategram*, **4**(3), 1–3.

Mercer, C. D., & Miller, S. P. (1998). Teaching students with learning problems in math to acquire, understand, and apply basic math facts. In E. L. Meyen, G. A. Verguson, & R. J. Whelen (eds.), *Educating students with mild disabilities* (pp. 177–205). Denver CO: Love.

Mertler, C. A. (2003). *Classroom assessment: A practical guide for educators*. Los Angeles, CA: Pyrczak Publishing.

Milem, M., & Garcia, M. (1996). Student critics, teacher models: Introducing process writing to high school students with learning disabilities. *Teaching Exceptional Children*, **28**(3), 47–48.

Nagel, B. R., Schumaker, J. B., & Deshler, D. D. (1994). *The FIRST-letter mnemonic strategy* (rev. ed.). Lawrence, KS: Edge Enterprises.

National Institute of Child Health and Development. (2000). *Report of the National Reading Panel. Teaching children to read: An evidence-based assessment of the scientific research literature on reading and its implications for reading instruction.* Retrieved May 23, 2002, from http://www.nichd.nih.gov/publications/nrp/smallbook.htm.

Palincsar, A. M., & Brown, A. L. (1984). Reciprocal teaching of comprehension fostering and monitoring activities. *Cognition and Instruction*, **1**, 117–175.

Polloway, E. A., Schewel, R., & Patton, J. R. (1992). Learning disabilities in adulthood: Personal perspectives. *Journal of Learning Disabilities*, **25**(8), 520–522.

Prater, M. A., Joy, R., Chilman, B., Temple, J., & Miller, S. R. (1991). Self-monitoring of on-task behavior by adolescents with learning disabilities. *Learning Disability Quarterly*, **14**, 164–167.

Rankin, J. L., & Reid, R. (1995). The SM rap—Or, here's the rap on self-monitoring. *Intervention in School and Clinic*, **30**(3), 181–188.

Raphael, T. (1982). Questioning–answering strategies for children. *The Reading Teacher*, **37**, 377–382.

Reid, R. (1996). Research in self-monitoring with students with learning disabilities: The present, the prospects, the pitfalls. *Journal of Learning Disabilities*, **29**(3), 317–331.

Reiff, H. B., Gerber, P. J., & Ginsberg, R. (1996). What successful adults with learning disabilities can tell us about teaching children. *Teaching Exceptional Children*, **29**(2), 10–16.

Reiff, H. B., Ginsberg, R., & Gerber, P. J. (1995). New perspectives on teaching from successful adults with learning disabilities. *Remedial and Special Education*, **16**(1), 29–37.

Roehler, L. R., & Duffy, G. G. (1984). Direct explanation of comprehension processes. In G. G. Duffy, L. R. Roehler, & J. Mason (eds.) *Comprehension instruction: Perspectives and suggestions* (pp. 265–280). New York: Longman.

Rosenshine, B., & Meister, C. (1992). The use of scaffolds for teaching higher-level cognitive strategies. *Educational Leadership*, **49**(7), 26–33.

Schumaker, J. B. (1989). The heart of strategies instruction: Effective modeling. *Strategram*, **1**(4), 1–5.

Schumaker, J. B., Denton, P. H., & Deshler, D. D. (1993). *The paraphrasing strategy* (rev. ed.). Lawrence, KS: University of Kansas.

Schumaker, J. B., & Lyerla, K. D. (1991). *The paragraph writing strategy*. Lawrence, KS: University of Kansas Center for Research on Learning.

Schumaker, J. B., Nolan, S. M., & Deshler, D. D. (1994). *The error monitoring strategy*. Lawrence, KS: University of Kansas Center for Research on Learning.

Schumaker, J. B., & Sheldon, J. (1985). *The sentence writing strategy*. Lawrence, KS: University of Kansas Center for Research on Learning.

Schumm, J. S., Vaughn, S., & Leavell, A. G. (1994). Planning pyramid: A framework for planning for diverse student needs during content area instruction. *The Reading Teacher*, **47**(8), 608–615.

Scruggs, T. E., & Mastropieri, M. A. (1992). Classroom applications of mnemonic instruction: Acquisition, maintenance, and generalization. *Exceptional Children*, **58**(3), 219–229.

Seabaugh, G. O., & Schumaker, J. B. (1981). *The effects of self-regulation training on the academic productivity of LD and non-LD adolescents* (Research Report #37). Lawrence, KS: The University of Kansas Institute for Research in Learning Disabilities.

Silbey, R. (2001). Putting it all together: Lesson plans that do the job of linking past, present, and future learning. *Instructor*, **111**(1), 39–40, 72.

Spekman, N. J., Goldberg, R. J., & Herman, K. L. (1992). Learning disabled children grow up: A search for factors related to success in the young adult years. *Learning Disabilities Research & Practice*, **7**, 161–170.

Swanson, P. N., & DeLaPaz, S. (1998). Teaching effective comprehension strategies to students with learning and reading disabilities. *Intervention in School and Clinic*, **33**(4), 209–218.

Trammel, D. L., Schloss, P. J., & Alper, S. (1994). Using self-recording, evaluation, and graphing to increase completion of homework assignments. *Journal of Learning Disabilities*, **27**(2), 75–81.

University of Kansas Center for Research on Learning. http://www.ku-crl.org

Vacca, R. T., & Vacca, J. L. (2002). *Content area reading: Literacy and learning across the curriculum* (7th ed.). Boston: Allyn and Bacon.

VanReusen, A. K., & Bos, C. S. (1990). I PLAN: Helping students communicate in planning conferences. *Teaching Exceptional Children*, **22**, 30–32.

VanReusen, A., Bos, C., Deshler, D., & Schumaker, J. (1987). *The educational planning strategy (I-PLAN)*. Lawrence, KS: Edge Enterprises.

Voth, V. P., & Graham, S. (1993). The application of goal setting to writing. *LD Forum*, **18**(3), 14–17.

Wedel, M., Deshler, D. D., Schumaker, J. B., & Ellis, E. S. (1992). *Effects of instruction of a vocabulary strategy in a mainstream class.* Lawrence, KS: Institute for Research in Learning Disabilities.

Wong, B. Y. L. (1998). Analyses of intrinsic and extrinsic problems in the use of the scaffolding metaphor in learning disabilities intervention research: An introduction. *Journal of Learning Disabilities*, **31**, 340–343.

Wong, B. Y. L., Butler, D. L., Ficzere, S. A., & Kuperis, S. (1997). Teaching adolescents with learning disabilities and low achievers to plan, write, and review compare-and-contrast essays. *Learning Disabilities Research & Practice*, **12**(1), 2–15.

Wong, B. Y. L., Wong, R., & Blenkinsop, J. (1989). Cognitive and metacognitive aspects of learning disabled adolescents' composing problems. *Learning Disability Quarterly*, **12**, 300–322.

Wong, B. Y. L., Wong, R., Darlington, D., & Jones, W. (1991). Interactive teaching: An effective way to teach revision skills to adolescents with learning disabilities. *Learning Disabilities Research & Practice*, **6**(117–127).

Zipprich, M. A. (1995). Teaching web making as a guided planning tool to improve student narrative writing. *Remedial and Special Education*, **16**(1), 3–15.

CHAPTER 12

Social Competence of Adolescents with Learning Disabilities: Interventions and Issues

Nancy L. Hutchinson, John G. Freeman, and Derek H. Berg
Queen's University

I. INTRODUCTION

During the past 30 years, there has been growing interest in enhancing the social competence of children and adolescents with learning disabilities (LD). In adolescence especially, social competence is complex and multifaceted and involves much more than social skills. As we show in this chapter, social competence encompasses several related components central to full participation in and enjoyment of life. These components include (a) positive relations with peers, (b) age-appropriate social cognition, and (c) effective social skills (Vaughn & Hogan, 1990; Wong & Donahue, 2002). Research suggests that many adolescents with LD would benefit from interventions that were tailored to their needs and effective in enhancing specific components of social competence (e.g., Hutchinson *et al.*, 2002).

Lacking social competence can cause adolescents to feel isolated and to be denied opportunities to grow socially, cognitively, and physically through "hanging out" with friends, working in collaborative learning groups, and engaging in their interests with peers. The developmental challenges

Learning about Learning Disabilities, Third Edition

of adolescence are considerable (Buhrmester, 1996), and it is becoming apparent that social interventions for adolescents must embrace, rather than ignore, these developmental issues (Inderbitzen-Pisaruk & Foster, 1990). Social competence is highly context-dependent and most often used in situations where interests are shared (Prenzel, 1992). Socially competent adolescents recognize and exploit the affordances for appropriate social participation in these contexts (Hartup & Stevens, 1997). This suggests that a contextualist perspective may be essential for developing effective interventions to enhance the social competence of adolescents with LD. This chapter reviews research that informs the development of such interventions and makes recommendations for teachers and researchers.

A. Historical Perspective

We have recognized for some time that social factors influence events in the classroom and in the home because we have understood that teaching, learning, and living are essentially social processes. Pioneers like Orton (1937), Kirk (1963), and Johnson and Myklebust (1967) acknowledged that social competence was a challenge for many individuals with LD. However, the publication of two groundbreaking studies in 1974 put social competence on the LD research agenda. Bryan (1974a) reported classroom observations that showed the classroom was a less positive and less responsive environment for children with LD than for their nondisabled peers. In the same year, Bryan (1974b) found that children with LD received fewer peer nominations for positive social characteristics and more peer nominations for negative social characteristics than their classmates without LD. She compared peer ratings on sociometric measures for 84 children with LD in 62 classrooms, grades 4 to 6, to ratings for nondisabled children matched on gender, race, and classroom. These findings were replicated in a study the following year, with the same children with LD in different classrooms (Bryan, 1976). Bryan suggested that "whatever factors lead a child to have a learning disability might also affect a child's social learning" and "might hinder the child in detecting critical cues or making inferences about people" (1974b, p. 311). In 1976, Bryan was the first person to advocate that interventions for students with LD focus on social and affective competence as well as cognitive and achievement goals. At the Chicago Institute of Research on Learning Disabilities, Bryan led a growing group of researchers who focused on many facets of social competence in children and adolescents with LD. They developed an interactional framework which assumed that "characteristics of children interact in significant ways with characteristics of teachers, classrooms, and families" (Bryan, 1983, p. 1). Although the pioneering research on social competence and LD was carried out with children (Bryan, 1974a,b), developmental studies of normally developing adolescents and of adolescents with LD have shown that social competence is even more critical during adolescence (Buhrmester, 1996; Cosden *et al.*, 2002).

Since 1974, most published studies about the social competence of children and adolescents with LD have been quantitative studies that report ratings of social status or social skills by teachers, peers, or the students themselves (Chan, 2000). However, these ratings of social status have left us little closer than Bryan was in 1974 to understanding the social competence of youth with LD or to having a library of interventions we can rely on to consistently enhance the social competence of adolescents with LD (Vaughn & Sinagub, 1998). This chapter addresses the issues about the social competence of adolescents with LD that have been raised in this section.

B. Organization of the Chapter

The remainder of this chapter is organized in five sections. Section II reviews research that describes the social competence of adolescents with LD. This is followed in the third section by a description and critical review of selected interventions intended to enhance the social competence of adolescents with LD. We argue that, while many have suggested that research move from a deficit perspective and an interactional framework to a contextualist perspective, this shift is not apparent even in recent intervention research. In Section IV, our search for alternatives to the current approach to understanding and enhancing the social competence of adolescents with LD shows the complexity of this endeavor. We describe a population of cases about the social competence of adolescents with LD emerging from our program of qualitative research. Theoretical and empirical work on interest, on the social competence of adolescents in the general population, and on contextualist frameworks is also reviewed. Issues emerge in this discussion that inform the design of research on the nature of social competence and the development of interventions to enhance the social competence of adolescents with LD. These implications form Section V, followed by a brief summary and conclusion.

II. REVIEW OF DESCRIPTIVE STUDIES OF SOCIAL COMPETENCE OF ADOLESCENTS WITH LD

Within this section, we review studies that report on the social competence of adolescents with LD. These descriptive studies are organized under headings that reflect three of the components within social competence: (a) relations with peers, (b) social cognition, and (c) social skills.

A. Relations with Peers

The research on the peer relations of adolescents with LD focuses on two distinct issues. The first issue is their social status or popularity, "a unilateral construct in that it refers to the view of the group toward the individual" (Bukowski *et al.*, 1993, p. 25). The second issue is their friendships. Friendship is "a bilateral construct in that it refers to the relationship between two persons" (Bukowski *et al.*, 1993, p. 25), to reciprocal relationships where there is mutual valuing of companionship.

1. Social Status of Adolescents with Learning Disabilities

Many studies have reported that children with LD experience lower levels of acceptance by peers than their normally achieving classmates (e.g., LaGreca & Stone, 1990; Wiener *et al.*, 1990). It is often assumed that the same is true of adolescents with LD. However, much less research has been conducted on adolescents with LD and the findings are not consistent. For example, four of the most frequently cited studies that report on the social status of adolescents with LD suggest that the social status of these adolescents varies greatly. Two of these studies reported lower status (Conderman, 1995; Perlmutter *et al.*, 1983), and two showed no group differences from peers without LD (Sabornie & Kauffman, 1986; Vaughn *et al.*, 1993).

Conderman (1995) used sociograms completed by 905 classmates to compare 74 adolescents with LD with 74 peers without LD randomly chosen from the same grade 6 and 7 social studies classes. The sociogram included nominations for which boys and which girls (a) one would most like to work with on a school project, (b) one would least like to work with on a school project, (c) one would consider most physically attractive, and (d) one would consider best in sports. Students with LD received fewer positive votes, a greater number of negative votes, and fewer attractive and athletic votes. This pattern was especially evident in the sample of girls with LD, who received the fewest number of positive votes and the greatest number of negative votes. The researchers derived categories (Asher & Wheeler, 1985; Coie & Kupersmidt, 1983) which showed that about 60% of the boys with LD and over 50% of the girls with LD ranked either in the accepted or popular social status classifications. The results of this study suggest that, as a group, adolescents with LD have lower social status, but at least half experience acceptable social standing.

In an earlier study, Perlmutter and his colleagues (1983) reported similar findings when they compared 55 adolescents with LD to 107 adolescents without LD on a sociometric measure on which individuals rated the extent to which they liked or disliked each classmate on a 5-point scale. All were in grade 10 at the time. Peers without LD reported liking classmates without LD more than peers with LD. Again, a subgroup of adolescents with LD was as well liked as the most popular students without LD. Other peer-referenced assessment conducted at the same time suggested that the well-liked students with LD were judged to be subdued and reserved, while those who were less popular were judged to be loud and boisterous.

In another early study, Sabornie and Kauffman (1986) found no differences when they compared the sociometric ratings of 46 adolescents with LD to those of 46 matched classmates without LD on a 5-point scale from "very, very best friends" to "dislike them." They also recorded the extent to which the subjects were rated "not known" by their peers. The two groups did not differ significantly on either measure. The adolescents were in grades 9 to 12, and all data were collected in physical education classes. Similarly, in a widely cited study, Vaughn and her colleagues (1993) reported liking and knowing on a 4-point scale for 202 students from grade 3 to grade 10. Students with LD did not differ on knowing or liking from their classmates without LD (high achieving, average achieving, and low achieving). However, only 18 of the 202 students had LD and of those only 10 were in middle school and high school.

A number of literature reviews and meta-analyses have concluded that students with LD have lower social status on peer ratings than their classmates without LD (e.g., Kavale & Forness, 1996; Ochoa & Olivarez, 1995). However, Kavale and Forness (1996) reviewed only studies of children's social status, and their reference list did not include any of the four studies of adolescents described here. Similarly, only 2 of the 17 studies in Ochoa and Olivarez's (1995) meta-analysis were on adolescents (Perlmutter et al., 1983; Sabornie & Kauffman, 1986). Thus, we must conclude that there is considerable variation—some adolescents with LD are ascribed low social status by their peers and as many as half are accepted.

2. Friendships of Adolescents with Learning Disabilities

Friendships are an integral part of social development for adolescents and can be distinguished conceptually and empirically from social status or peer acceptance (Asher et al., 1996). Friendships reflect reciprocated companionship and liking (Furman & Buhrmester, 1985). There are few studies of the friendships of adolescents with LD. In the 1993 study already described, which included only 18 students with LD (10 in middle school or high school), Vaughn et al. reported that students with LD did not differ significantly from other achievement groups on the number of reciprocal friendships reported. Vaughn and Elbaum (1999) reported on the friendships of more than 4000 students with LD, from elementary school through high school. Across all ages, 96% of students with LD listed at least one best friend, with about 67% listing six or more friends. In a study of friendship in children with LD, having even one friend (reciprocal positive nomination) served as a buffer against the status ascribed by others and was associated with high self-perceptions of social acceptance (Bear *et al.*, 1993).

While it appears that many adolescents with LD have friends, what is unknown is the quality of those friendships. Berndt (1999) has argued persuasively that friendship quality is critical. Zetlin and Murtaugh (1988) conducted observations and interviews of 32 mildly learning handicapped adolescents (most had LD) and 32 adolescents without disabilities in high schools, using field notes but no tape recordings. They focused on the degree of intimacy, empathy, and stability in the relationships. The adolescents with disabilities had fewer friendships and spent less time with their friends outside of school, although they talked on the telephone to a comparable extent. The researchers concluded that their relationships showed less intimacy, empathy, and stability and more conflict than did the relationships of nondisabled adolescents. Also, 38% of those with disabilities nominated cousins or siblings as their best friends whereas relations were never nominated by adolescents without disabilities. Vaughn and Elbaum (1999) reported that the perceived quality of friendships for students with LD remained the same throughout the years from elementary into high school, while it tended to improve with age for students without LD, and was higher at every age for the nondisabled students.

Wiener and Sunohara (1995) interviewed children and adolescents (10 to 14 years of age) to obtain self-reports on friendship quality and reported that the 16 youth with LD frequently chose other exceptional students, younger students, and people who did not attend their school as friends. They also reported lower friendship quality than the comparison group without LD, especially on intimacy and conflict resolution. In 1998, Wiener and Sunohara published a qualitative study based on interviews with the parents of these 16 youth with LD about their perceptions of the quality of friendship of their 10- to 14-year- old offspring. Parents reported that 7 of the 16 had a close stable mutual friend of approximately the same age in their classes or neighborhoods, 7 had relationships that were not mutual, not stable, or involved little companionship (sometimes with much younger children). Two were described as having idiosyncratic relationships with people with whom they had little in common. The parents characterized many of the relationships as acquaintanceships rather than friendships. While there are few studies of friendship in either children or adolescents with LD, the small extant literature suggests that friendship quality may be low, especially for adolescents with LD.

B. Social Cognition

A second aspect of social competence is described as social cognition. This includes social perception (e.g., Stiliadis & Wiener, 1989), social problem solving (e.g., Larson & Gerber, 1987), and other aspects of processing social information, verbal and nonverbal.

Social perception involves reading and interpreting verbal and nonverbal social cues in interactions with others. For example, in an early study, Axelrod (1982) showed that grade 8 and 9 students with LD were significantly lower in nonverbal social perception than a comparison group without LD of the emotions communicated in film clips. A developmental study using the same measures (Profile of Nonverbal Sensitivity (PONS) and Four Factor Test of Social Intelligence) found that both LD and non-LD students improved with age (11, 14, and 17 years). However, at every age, the adolescents with LD were lower than the comparison group (Jackson et al., 1987). Using only the PONS with adolescents of 14, 16, and 18 years of age, Sisterhen and Gerber (1989) confirmed previous findings that adolescents with LD were not as adept at understanding nonverbal social information regardless of whether the information was visual or multisensory in nature. In another study, students with and without LD (junior high, senior high, and college students) were assessed in 30-minute interviews for their accuracy in interpreting the thoughts and feelings of actors in tape-recorded stories depicting adults in happy, angry, anxious, and sad interactions (Jarvis & Justice, 1992). The data showed that students with LD at all ages were significantly less accurate at interpreting social situations than their nondisabled peers.

A series of more contextualized descriptive studies extends the validity and relevance of these findings about social perception. A 1980s paper (Bryan et al., 1981) and a later replication (Bryan et al., 1989) showed that when junior high students with LD were pressured to conform in prosocial and antisocial actions, they indicated more willingness than their nondisabled classmates to engage in antisocial actions. Although these studies assessed only expressed dispositions and not actual behavior, they suggest poor social judgment and vulnerability to peer pressure in adolescents with LD. Other indicators of poor social judgment include the lower likelihood of adolescents with LD recognizing when someone was deliberately deceptive in audiotaped stories (Pearl et al., 1991), and their expectation that invitations to engage in misconduct would be straightforward (Pearl & Bryan, 1992). When interviewed about scenarios, and faced with accepting or evading consequences for misconduct, adolescents with LD were more likely to suggest evading responsibility and less likely to propose accepting responsibility than nondisabled peers (Pearl & Bryan, 1994). The researchers suggested that when faced with real situations analogous to those simulated in this series of studies, with little time to reflect, such social–cognitive deficits may render adolescents with LD more susceptible to poor social decisions.

Social problem solving has been the focus of a number of descriptive studies of adolescents with LD. For example, Schneider and Yoshida

(1988) found that grade 7 and 8 adolescents with LD performed at a significantly lower level than peers without LD in recognizing a social problem, generating alternative solutions to interpersonal problems, means–end problem solving of scenarios, and suggesting causes of social problems. All measures came from the Interpersonal Cognitive Problem-Solving Skills measure (Platt & Spivack, 1977) and were administered in individual interviews. In a later study, Hartas and Donahue (1997) audio-taped adolescents as they role-played an advisor and a caller in simulated telephone conversations. Dyads consisted of two adolescents (grades 7 and 8) with LD, two adolescents without LD, and mixed dyads. Discourse analysis revealed that adolescents with LD (in both types of dyads) experienced difficulties generating solutions to interpersonal problems, although they were as likely as nondisabled peers to produce ignore/avoid and third-person advice statements, which are considered less assertive than advising direct action. While there were no observed differences between the girls' groups, boys with LD produced fewer statements reflective of antisocial intervention (e.g., "Get him in trouble") and mediation intervention (e.g., "Talk to your friends") than boys without LD.

Whatever the measure—paper and pencil, hypothetical scenarios, or simulations of authentic tasks—the research on social cognition finds that whenever there are differences between adolescents with and without LD, the differences favor adolescents without LD. And every study reports differences on most measures. Unlike the research on social status, there are consistent findings of lower social competence in this aspect, social cognition.

C. Social Skills

It is thought that social interactions become more complex and intense through adolescence into adulthood (Harter, 1993). We use social skills to refer to the behaviors required to be effective in these complex and intense interactions. However, in spite of the conceptual work of Vaughn and Hogan (1990) and many others (e.g., Bukowski *et al.*, 1993), papers about adolescents with LD continue to use social skills to refer to all aspects of social competence (e.g., Kavale and Forness, 1996; Swanson & Malone, 1992).

Individuals who lack interactive skills may be restricted in many ways in their day-to-day life with peers and others. Some studies have focused on conversational skills. For example, in a study already described, Hartas and Donahue (1997) used discourse analysis to report on the conversational skills of adolescents (grades 7 and 8). They found that adolescents with and without LD were equally skilled at requesting advice on a simulated telephone hotline. Tur-Kaspa and Bryan (1994), however, reported that both children and adolescents with LD (up to grade 9) showed less competent solutions to social problems in conversational format. Other studies suggest that adolescents with LD were less likely to talk to others about their problems and more often sought assistance from individuals who were not judged as good sources of information (e.g., Morrison *et al.*, 1992). Junior high students with LD, when confronted with academic or interpersonal problems, typically had a smaller group of peers to enlist for social support compared to their peers without LD, and more often used avoidance strategies to cope with academic stress. In a study of middle school students, Wenz-Gross and Siperstein (1997) showed the significance of social support. The 40 middle school students with mild handicaps (LD or mild mental handicaps), who were compared to 396 students without learning problems, experienced more stress, less peer support, more adult support, and poorer adjustment. Deficits in social skills, such as difficulties in conversing with peers, may mean that adolescents with LD are less able to seek or find the social support from peers which can enhance adjustment and reduce stress.

D. Summary of Descriptive Studies

The descriptive studies suggest that many adolescents with LD are not as adept at social competence as their classmates. While some do not experience social status difficulties, many have lower friendship quality, most show lower social cognition, and many demonstrate lower social skills, especially in conversation. In an interview study of parents of exceptional adolescents (mainly adolescents with LD), Kolb and Hanley-Maxwell (2003) found that parents wanted schools to help exceptional adolescents develop social competence. The parental interviews included references to the need for schools to intervene and enhance all of social status, peer relations, social cognition, and social skills. The parents were aware of the challenges their adolescents with LD faced in all aspects of social competence, and they advanced many recommendations for how schools could intervene effectively by modifying curriculum, addressing individual needs, and involving parents. The research on social competence interventions is the topic of the next section.

III. REVIEW OF INTERVENTION RESEARCH TO ENHANCE SOCIAL COMPETENCE OF ADOLESCENTS WITH LD

A. Introduction

Given the recognition that social competence represents an area of difficulty for a number of young people with LD (Wong & Donahue, 2002), there have been increasing calls for interventions that target social competence (Bryan,

1999; Omizo *et al.*, 1986). However, despite these calls, there has been limited systematic research into what such interventions should include.

An extensive research program conducted by Sharon Vaughn and her colleagues has examined the social competence, primarily social skills, of children with LD and possible interventions (e.g., McIntosh *et al.*, 1995; Vaughn *et al.*, 1991; Vaughn & Sinagub, 1998). In general, these interventions involved pairing children with LD with popular peers without LD. Both students were taught mnemonic strategies for dealing with social situations in a pull-out context over an extended period, and then the two students acted as trainers for other students (thereby giving the student with LD increased status). Success of the intervention was measured in terms of greater peer acceptance of the children with LD.

While these interventions have been effective for children with LD, they have limited applicability for enhancing the social competence of adolescents with LD. Programs designed for children do not suit adolescents in at least four ways. First, the social skills taught do not match the developmental needs of adolescents. Adolescents increasingly rely on social cognition to understand people around them and need to develop mechanisms for interpreting subtle social cues (McDevitt & Ormrod, 2002). Second, while the contextual factors of a secondary school might allow the withdrawal of adolescents with LD for an extended period, they certainly would not permit the continued absence from class of a nonidentified peer for the same length of time. Third, the "informant" status of the students as they teach strategies to their classmates would not be valued in the adolescent subculture, where a degree of anonymity is preferred, particularly in early adolescence (McDevitt & Ormrod, 2002). Finally, increased peer acceptance is not as valuable an outcome for adolescents as the related, but different, concept—friendship (Bukowski *et al.*, 1987).

Beginning with the premise that the most comprehensive program of research on social interventions for students with LD has limited applicability for adolescents, we sought interventions specifically designed to meet the social needs of this group and the contextual demands of secondary schools. An extensive search of relevant databases (most prominently, ERIC and PSYCINFO) revealed few readily accessible interventions. Among this small group of studies, we discovered little empirically substantiated information on how to intervene to enhance the social competence of adolescents with LD.

For example, in a preliminary report, Stevens and Shenker (1991) described individualized intervention programs for adolescents with LD. Each student's intervention was customized based on a file of needs, as determined by extensive pretesting. Posttesting gauged effectiveness on measures of academic and cognitive functioning, and social and personal adjustment. Compared to controls, the treatment group improved across a range of indicators. However, this preliminary report (at the end of the second year of a three-year study) has not been subsequently updated in the research literature. In addition, the published material gave few details about the nature of the interventions.

Kish (1991), in an article primarily addressed to counselors, detailed the necessary components of a successful intervention for LD adolescents coping with emotional and social development. His primary recommendation was that goal-setting should be a prominent feature of social interventions with these adolescents. However, this recommendation was based on a literature review and his experiences as a special education teacher, rather than on empirical research he had conducted.

In a 2000 article, Anderson explained how social cognition might become a component of instruction within a high school English classroom. The centerpiece of the instruction was a structured worksheet on which students interpret the events of a selected literature passage (e.g., a scene in a Shakespearean play), interpret feelings and signals, and develop alternate outcomes. There was also a space on the worksheet for students to have their ideas cross-checked by the teacher or a peer. Although Anderson did not provide any evidence for the effectiveness of the program, she did indicate how it might be implemented when teaching "Romeo and Juliet".

B. Social Interventions for Adolescents with Learning Disabilities

Despite the general lack of research on the topic, we found three research programs focusing on social interventions for adolescents with LD which we feel are worth highlighting within this chapter. These three interventions represent possibilities for the future. Each program, as we note, has strengths and weaknesses.

1. A Social Skills Program for Adolescents (ASSET)

a. Description of program. The earliest comprehensive program we located was *A Social Skills Program for Adolescents* (ASSET; Hazel *et al.*, 1981, 1982, 1996). Their program trained six social skills: giving positive feedback, giving and accepting negative feedback, resisting peer pressure, negotiating, and solving of personal problems (Schumaker & Hazel, 1984), although two additional skills (following instructions and making/maintaining conversation) were in the original model (Vaughn & Sinagub, 1998). For each social skill, the teacher first described appropriate behavior by explaining the skill, providing a rationale for the skill, giving examples, examining the steps within the skill, and finally providing a model of the behavior. Then the teacher gave the students an opportunity to rehearse the behavior, first verbally and then through role-playing, and finally provided opportunities outside the classroom for students to practice the new skills (Schumaker & Hazel, 1984).

One study (Hazel *et al.*, 1982) has reported ASSET's effectiveness. In this study, students with LD who had participated in the intervention were able to demonstrate the taught skills in novel role-play situations. On the posttest, their role-play behavior was indistinguishable from that of nontrained peers without LD. A later study by Prater *et al.* (1999) used three skills based on ASSET (giving positive feedback, accepting negative feedback, and contributing to discussions) in combination with a peer tutoring model. Sustained gains were obtained for positive feedback and contributing to discussions.

b. Strengths/weaknesses. The major strength of the program is in its isolation and understanding of vital components of social competence. These basic skills are fundamental for adolescents to master if they are to be successful in social interactions. Through using a variety of teaching and learning mechanisms, including videotaping, the program provides reinforcement for adolescent skill development. In addition, the procedures described are comprehensive and include a feedback loop of adolescents practicing the skills in contexts outside school. Therefore, the program explicitly recognizes the necessity of generalizability.

However, the isolation of social skills, which is the program's greatest strength, is also arguably its greatest weakness. In real-life contexts, adolescents are not able to separate social skills so discretely but need to employ them in conjunction with each other and use social cognition to understand situations when such skills would be applied. In addition, explicit attempts to convince adolescents of the value of the social skills would not be necessary if the intervention began with the interests of the adolescents themselves. Finally, given that the program has been readily available for over 20 years, it seems to have had a relatively small long-term impact.

2. Pathways

a. Description of program. In the early 1990s, we developed the *Pathways* program (Hutchinson & Freeman, 1994b). The program consists of five instructional modules, which help adolescents, especially adolescents with LD, understand, access, and maintain careers. Two of the modules address social competence within the employment setting: *Solving problems on the job* (Hutchinson & Freeman, 1994c) and *Anger management on the job* (Hutchinson & Freeman, 1994a). This program responds well to calls (Elksnin & Elksnin, 2001) for greater emphasis on occupational social competence intervention. Although it is clearly not the only program targeting occupational social competence (see, for example, CONNECTIONS by Bullis *et al.*, 2001), having developed it ourselves, we are better able to describe it here.

In the seven "lessons" of the problem-solving module (Hutchinson & Freeman, 1994c), students moved from discussion of job-related social problems to rehearsed, then unrehearsed, role-playing of similar problems, using a structured worksheet to help them analyze the problems and assess possible solutions. Activities were scaffolded in such a manner that teacher involvement and reliance on the worksheet were diminished, as students become more competent problem-solvers. Scenarios given to the students were based on the kinds of situations adolescents are likely to encounter in the workplace. Many of the problems required students to balance competing demands (work vs personal), deal with unexpected crises (e.g., broken equipment), and negotiate social situations (e.g., developing relationships at work). Lessons could be spread over multiple class periods, depending on the learning pace of the group.

The anger management module (Hutchinson & Freeman, 1994a), consisting of eight lessons, was similar in format to the problem-solving module with two notable exceptions. Instead of using structured worksheets to think through situations, students employed a mnemonic ("CALMER") to help them reflect on their anger management issues. In addition, problem situations were derived from students' experiences rather than from a list.

The five modules were evaluated during an intensive 3-year research and development phase (see Freeman & Hutchinson, 1994; Freeman *et al.*, 1991; Hutchinson & Freeman, 1994b). Pencil-and-paper evaluations indicated that students who participated in the interventions were able to think more expansively about problem-solving and anger management situations and their solutions.

b. Strengths/weaknesses. Pathways has three primary strengths as a social intervention. First, it is context-specific in placing the social interactions solidly within the area of careers, helping students develop complex social cognitions that will be beneficial in the workplace. Second, the program was devised with the needs of inclusive classrooms in mind. Its explicit goal was to develop interventions that could be useful for all students, regardless of disabilities. Finally, the program benefited from a collaborative process that involved teachers, researchers, and students in creating instruction that would be of maximal benefit to students.

The weaknesses of Pathways likewise lie in three areas. First, the context-specificity, which contributes to its utility in employment settings, detracts from its applicability to the other contexts where adolescents engage socially. Second, although the program was evaluated on numerous occasions, the assessments for social competence, in particular, relied exclusively on pencil-and-paper assessments that may not represent real-life situations. Finally, while there was an attempt to match the program to students' interests, especially in the anger management module, not enough attention was paid to the vital role of interest in constructing adolescents' friendships and social exchanges.

3. The STAR Project

a. Description of program. Goldsworthy *et al.* (2000) developed a series of interactive, multimedia vignettes through which students can develop social problem-solving competence. The platform for the program was an aerospace school to pique student interest, but the scenarios themselves concerned problems adolescents routinely encounter in everyday life. To aid the students in tackling the problems, they were taught a mnemonic device (STAR: Stop, Think, Act, Reflect).

A prototype of the technology was tested with early adolescents who had attention deficit hyperactivity disorder (ADHD) to see the effects the program had on students' ability to solve text-based and video-based problems. The authors also wanted to know whether there were noticeable differences in behavior post-intervention as seen by teachers, parents, and the students themselves. Students were randomly assigned to one of three groups: STAR intervention, therapy intervention, and attention-control, each of which met for eight sessions (first and last sessions were devoted to testing). While students in the STAR group evidenced greater pretest–posttest growth on the video-based problems as compared to the attention-control group, there were no other significant differences, perhaps as a result of the small sample size (40 students across the three conditions at posttest).

b. Strengths/weaknesses. With the high comorbidity between ADHD and LD (Cantwell & Baker, 1991), a social intervention designed for the former group will likely be applicable to the latter. This intervention also has intriguing aspects in that it tries to place the scenarios in an appealing context; the software program would be readily manageable by a busy teacher in an inclusive classroom; and the situations and mnemonic device should prove interesting to students.

Based on this one article, it is difficult to tell whether such a multimedia package would be successful in promoting improved social competence for adolescents with LD. The intervention was short (only six sessions), and the positive results limited. Furthermore, the authors readily recognized that a multimedia, interactive program cannot be the whole means for changing social competence. It must be used as a supplement to or component of a larger effort.

C. Summary

While recent meta-analyses have examined interventions for students with LD (e.g., Swanson, 1999; Swanson & Sachse-Lee, 2000) and social interventions for children with LD (e.g., Forness & Kavale, 1996), no comparable research has been conducted on social interventions for adolescents with LD. However, there have been some thoughtful suggestions for the development of social interventions for adolescents with LD (e.g., Anderson, 2000; Kish, 1991; Stevens & Shenker, 1991). While there are also some promising intervention programs (e.g., ASSET, Pathways, The STAR Project), there is still a need for a more comprehensive understanding of what constitutes an effective social intervention for adolescents with LD. We cannot simply transfer proven interventions from children to adolescents, as tempting as that prospect might be, because children and adolescents, whether they have LD or not, have different developmental needs. In addition, high schools offer very different social contexts, for social interventions, from the contexts of middle and elementary schools. To develop more effective social interventions, we must use what we know about adolescents with LD, build upon intervention elements that have proven successful in the past for this population, and extend our scope by learning from relevant literature on the social competence of adolescents in general.

IV. INFORMING THE SEARCH FOR ALTERNATIVE APPROACHES

In this section, we review literature that may inform the development of alternate approaches to social interventions for adolescents with LD. We begin by describing some of the findings of our program of research in which we are developing a population of cases about the social inclusion of adolescents with LD in classrooms. This is followed by a review of theories and research in three areas: (a) interest, sometimes referred to as engagement; (b) social competence (especially friendship) in youth without LD; and (c) the contextualist, or social–constructivist, perspective, in which we include the role of the teacher. The literature in these areas can inform the search for effective approaches to social interventions for adolescents with LD.

A. Our Program of Research

A population of cases—that is developing in the research of John Freeman, Nancy Hutchinson, and their graduate students at Queen's University—provides starting points for interventions to enhance the social competence of adolescents with LD in inclusive classrooms (see Hutchinson *et al.*, 2002). These starting points are structured activities based in student interest, the understanding of adolescent friendship in the general population, and the role of context and of teachers. Brief examples from our case studies illustrate why we believe these factors must be considered in developing social interventions.

1. Interest

The role of interest in the friendships of adolescents with LD was highlighted in the case of Lynn. Lévesque (1997) observed and interviewed Lynn at school. Lynn described how she hid her learning disability from her classmates. Her written work was barely decipherable; a peer tutor helped her to edit written assignments before submitting them. However, Lynn was a member of the cheerleading squad at her high school and had close friends on the squad with whom she talked on the phone every evening. Lynn described how she went to school to be with her cheerleading friends: "Friends are what gets me through school . . . always there to support me."

Attending the same resource room was Matt, whose learning disability and attention deficit disorder interfered with his oral and written communication (Lévesque, 1997). Interviews and observations revealed that Matt had no friends to talk with at lunch, usually sat alone, and occasionally talked "at" a classmate about the computer game, "Quake," his only interest. The classmate, knowledgeable about computer applications, did not share Matt's interest in "Quake," and walked away when Matt dominated the conversation. Matt even took up smoking for a short time so he could "stand with the smokers," implicitly demonstrating his need for a shared interest.

Interests shared with peers also played a role in the retrospective accounts we heard from adults with LD who had graduated from high school on schedule (Freeman *et al.*, in press). They described taking part in structured, extracurricular activities with friends during high school, including bands, choirs, drama groups, and teams. They also described joining their friends in structured activities outside of school (e.g., Scouts, martial arts, church groups). In comparison, adults with LD, who had dropped out and later returned to complete high school, described joining friends who had already dropped out of school for informal activities, including "skipping," playing pool, and taking drugs. Structured activities based on interests shared with other students appear to be a basis for developing and maintaining adolescent friendships at school.

2. Adolescent Friendship in the General Population

Our cases have also suggested the importance of understanding the typical development of adolescent friendship in enhancing the social competence of adolescents with LD. For example, Lévesque (1997), in analyzing the social competence and peer relations of Lynn and Matt, demonstrated the applicability of Buhrmester's (1996) four interpersonal competencies necessary for dyadic friendship in early adolescence. These are: (a) initiating and sustaining conversation, (b) making plans to spend time together, (c) self-disclosing personal thoughts and providing emotional support, and (d) working through conflicts. Lévesque also demonstrated that other factors, in the literature on the general adolescent population, are valuable in understanding these cases—reputational bias (Hymel *et al.*, 1990) and adolescent social norms (Evans & Eder, 1989).

3. Role of Context

The contribution of context to understanding the social competence of adolescents with LD was highlighted in the case of Zak (Stoch, 2000). Based on extensive interviews, Stoch described how this young man had so many social conflicts with classmates in integrated classrooms that his mother was called to the school almost daily. Yet at camp, where many, but not all, adolescents had LD and where the researcher first met him, the counselors described Zak as a leader with many friends, who won awards for his kneeboarding and made other campers feel at ease. At home, he was protected by his single mother, not allowed to participate in sporting activities the way he did at camp, and showed little if any of the social competence for which he won awards at camp. Stoch described Zak as "almost a different person" in these different social contexts.

A number of our cases also emphasized the teacher as a key part of the context when considering adolescent social competence. For example, Edwards (2000) observed and interviewed high school teachers exemplary at including adolescents with LD. One teacher, Lauren, talked about adapting teaching for a student: "Mostly, with him, I think it's social things that we should be working on...he doesn't work well with people." She described "insisting that he cooperate with his lab partner...it's the whole interaction, teamwork [that he is learning]." Another science teacher in Edwards' study, Gary, reported in interviews that he used hands-on activities so students were "doing" rather than listening, because this kind of teaching engaged adolescents socially as well as cognitively. Edwards observed Gary creating a safe, supportive learning environment where students with learning disabilities participated fully in activities within cooperative groups and in whole-class discussions. Lévesque (1997) described a classroom teacher who created a social context within which Matt, already described, could participate. This teacher translated Matt's poorly articulated but thoughtful contributions to class discussions for the rest of the class. In this one class, Matt sat up, listened to discussion, made comments, and was a full social participant. In every other class that Lévesque observed, Matt read his science fiction book, ignored the teacher, ignored his classmates, and felt isolated from the content and the context. Cases like these suggest that teachers are an important part of the context within which social competence can develop.

Our case study research has shown us the necessity of understanding interest, friendship, and context, including the teacher, as starting points for developing social interventions for adolescents with LD. Here, we explore what each of these might contribute to our understanding of such interventions.

B. Theories and Research on Interest

Interest is a key motivational variable that has significance in understanding how and why adolescents remain engaged in social relations (Freeman *et al.*, 2002; Hidi & Harackiewicz, 2000). While interest is well understood by nonresearchers, its definition has proven elusive to researchers (e.g., Gardner, 1998; Prenzel, 1992). However, there is agreement that interest lies in a confluence between an individual person and an object (Rathunde, 1993, 1998). In addition, there is a value component to interest (e.g., Renninger, 1998; Schiefele, 1998). We therefore understand an object of interest in relation to the person who holds that interest and values that object. If, for example, I indicate I am interested in classical music, the interest resides neither in me nor in classical music but in a space between. As well, my interest in classical music indicates that I value it.

Interest has generally been divided into two areas: situational and individual (Hidi, 1990). Situational interest relates to an object that appeals to a wide variety of individuals. For example, a chemical explosion representing a volcano would be of situational interest to most students in grade 9. Individual interest refers to a relatively long-lasting attraction between a person and an object. In this sense, an adolescent might be interested in horses or video games or family history. Ainley *et al.* (2002) suggest a third kind of interest: topic interest. In their view, this interest is distinct from both individual and situational interest. It refers to the interest elicited among readers by a word or paragraph presenting a topic.

Interest has at least three functions in relation to the social competence of adolescents. First, John Dewey, in his seminal work, *Interest and Effort in Education* (1913), postulated four types of educative interest: physical, discovery, intellectual, and social. These interests develop as the person develops and encounters different situations. Physical interest is first observed among babies as they explore their own bodies. As the babies grow, they become aware of tools around them that they can manipulate to aid in the discovery of their environment. Although all interest involves a degree of thinking, intellectual interest is specifically concerned with the quest for knowledge through asking questions. Young children are particularly inquisitive and ask adults about the surroundings. Finally, social interest gains prominence as children seek to relate to others and understand them better. By adolescence, social interest is the primary educative interest for most individuals. Therefore, social interest must be viewed as an underlying foundation of all forms of learning in adolescents.

Second, individual interest provides a context for interpersonal relationships (Buhrmester, 1996). When people meet, they tend to converse about areas of mutual interest. Indeed, there is a tendency for adolescent friendships to develop along lines of mutual interests, such as cheerleading (Lévesque, 1997). Adolescents who have limited interests, who do not understand the nature of their interests, or who are unable to convey their interests are at a disadvantage in negotiating social interactions and in developing friendships with peers.

Finally, interest is a major component of extracurricular activity selection. Extracurricular activities, whether in the school or outside, may provide a means of keeping students engaged in school and of strengthening their social competence (Freeman, Stoch, et al., 2002). Furthermore, extracurricular activities, all of which tend to be structured around mutual interests—sports, drama, religious activities, outdoors activities, etc.—have developmental advantages in the social realm (Eccles & Templeton, 2002). One of the particular social advantages associated with some extracurricular activities is the growth of leadership abilities. Extracurricular activities are also associated with the acquiring of appropriate social norms (Eccles & Templeton, 2002). Without knowledge of their own interests and how to use them, adolescents are unable to access appropriate extracurricular activities, a means of maintaining and enhancing their social competence.

Successful social competence interventions for adolescents must start by recognizing the predominant role social interest plays for adolescents. Next, such interventions must help adolescents identify and learn to articulate their interests so they can successfully interact in social situations and develop mutual friendships with individuals whose company they are most likely to enjoy. Finally, successful interventions must help adolescents use their recognized interests to access extracurricular activities that are developmentally appropriate and socially beneficial.

C. Theories and Research on Social Competence in Youth without Learning Disabilities

We frequently remind ourselves that youth with LD are youth first, who also have a disability. But too rarely do we ensure that theory and research on adolescents in the general population inform our work on adolescents with LD. In this section, we do just that—turning our attention to what we can learn from theories and research on social competence in adolescents in the general population. Much of the literature on adolescents in the general population has focused on one aspect of social competence—relations with peers (which, as we saw earlier, is composed primarily of social status and friendship). By the early 1990s, researchers had made considerable progress in understanding the emergence, maintenance, and consequences of social status of children and adolescents in the general population (Asher & Coie, 1990). By 2000, the same could be said about the social status of children and adolescents with LD (Vaughn & Elbaum, 1999). However, research on social status has not proven helpful in developing interventions to enhance adaptation to peers of adolescents with or without LD; greater attention is needed to adolescents' ability to form and maintain satisfying and supportive dyadic friendships.

What is friendship? Friendship has both a deep structure and a surface structure (Hartup & Stevens, 1997). The deep structure refers to its essence or meaning—friendship is always characterized by reciprocity and mutuality; that is, a symmetrical relationship. Friendship fulfills the need for enjoyable companionship. The surface structure refers to the nature or focus of the social exchanges within the reciprocal, companionable relationship. Developmental theorists argue that at every age, there are preoccupying concerns to which people attend. For example, influenced by changes in cognition, by puberty, and by sociocultural context, adolescence is characterized by emergent concerns with self-clarification, self-validation, and obtaining coping assistance (Buhrmester & Prager, 1995; Sullivan, 1953). These concerns shape the surface structure of friendship—its social exchanges; specifically, these concerns can be linked to adolescents' "hanging out," self-disclosing, engaging in supportive problem solving, and seeking self-defining activities among friends (Buhrmester, 1996). Buhrmester argues, as we noted earlier, that four interpersonal competencies follow from these developmental concerns as essential for dyadic friendships during adolescence. These are: (a) initiating and sustaining conversation, (b) making plans to spend time together, (c) self-disclosing personal thoughts and providing emotional support, and (d) working through conflicts.

Since friends are typically preoccupied with similar developmental issues, friendships provide unique opportunities to wrestle with issues of most central concern to both individuals. This implies that adolescents need at least one supportive peer (i.e., dependable, understanding, and accepting) who is a trustworthy confidant in order to deal with their preoccupying concerns. There is evidence to support reciprocal relationships between intimacy in adolescent friendships and both personal adjustment and the development of interpersonal competence (a measure of the four competencies needed for dyadic friendship described in Buhrmester, 1996). In a study of 172 10- to 16-year-olds, Buhrmester (1990) averaged self- and reciprocal friend-reports of intimacy of the friendship and correlated them with self-and friend-reports of interpersonal competence and self-reports of adjustment. Correlations, especially for the relationship between intimacy of reciprocal friendship and interpersonal competence, were higher for 13- to

16-year-olds than for 10- to 13-year-olds. This study adds to the corpus of research on adolescents in the general population that has reported for some time that, during adolescence, having quality friendships is central to developing social competence.

It is thought, however, that different "cultures" or contexts are manifest in male and female peer relations (Tannen, 1990). Interactions between female adolescents place priority on the building of interpersonal connections and less emphasis on agentic concerns. Adolescent females report more frequent interactions of an intimate and supportive nature with female friends than do males with male friends (Maccoby, 1990). On the other hand, interactions between adolescent males focus more on agentic concerns and less on communal concerns, and have been described as "side-by-side" interactions, referring to the focus on doing things together, chiefly sports and competitive games (Wright, 1982). Their supportive discussions often address the accomplishments of sports teams and individuals, and it may be that such interactions meet needs for achievement, recognition, and power.

Some data support the notion of different socializing contexts for adolescents according to gender. Buhrmester and Carbery (1992) interviewed 200 12- to 15-year-old adolescents by telephone each evening over a 5-day period. The adolescents were asked to reconstruct the social events of the preceding 24 hours. For each interaction lasting longer than 10 minutes, the interviewer recorded the types of partners present (i.e., same-sex friends, parents, siblings, etc.) and then asked subjects to rate the extent of self-disclosure and emotional support that took place using a 7-point scale. Females reported somewhat more frequent interactions with friends than males did, and they reported substantially higher levels of self-disclosure and emotional support than males did in daily interactions. These are not necessarily inherent differences but may reflect youth seeking societal gender models and following them (Buhrmester, 1996). Thus, while it is important to consider the role of friendship to interventions in social competence, it is also critical to honor gender differences in this role.

D. Contextualist Perspective

One of the issues pushing educational researchers to think seriously about the social competence of adolescents with LD is the widespread adoption of inclusion. An expectation of inclusive practice is that students with disabilities will benefit cognitively and socially from opportunities to interact with their nondisabled peers in regular classrooms. Such an expectation is bolstered by contextualist perspectives (e.g., Bredo, 1994) and social–constructivst theories (see Trent et al., 1998) that suggest learning occurs in classroom communities where peer interactions are the driving force. Indeed, recommendations for social interventions that emerge from the literature on the peer relations of students with LD often include suggestions for implementing cooperative learning strategies, cross-age tutoring, and structured group activities (e.g., Farmer *et al.*, 1999; Hamre-Nietupski *et al.*, 1994).

Bredo (1994) argued that, in a contextualist or situated perspective, knowledge is inseparable from the context and activities of which it is a part. Deficits lie not within the individual, but in the intersection of the individual and the affordances of the context. This is why an adolescent with LD, like Zak, can look like a different person in different social contexts (Stoch, 2000). Learning is mediated by the immediate situation and the actions of the learner have implications for the situation. This perspective seems particularly relevant when one considers the learning of social competence with peers in highly social contexts like high schools, where "interpretation and meaning vary with the context" (Bredo, 1994, p. 32).

In making their case for complementing existing paradigms with contextual perspectives, Trent *et al.* (1998) argued that four implications, which follow from Vygotsky's sociocultural theory (1978), can enhance interventions for students with mild disabilities. First, social competence is best constructed in meaningful, purposeful contexts. Second, such students need to have the meta-level strategies that are valued in schools (by fellow students as well as adults) made explicit (O'Connor, 1996), including the social cognition that others seem to develop effortlessly. Third, in these social interactions, peers and teachers must gradually transfer the regulation of cognition and actions to the learners. Fourth, learning and development unfold in everyday activities within communities that hold shared understanding. In adopting contextualist perspectives, research and practice would be forced to acknowledge individual developmental processes, the role of teachers and peers in the development of social competence, and a broader sense of what it means to be different and to be socially competent.

It is likely that current views of the benefits of contextualist approaches are somewhat naive. O'Connor (1996) argued that we cannot assume that discussion or collaboration among peers is an "unproblematic pathway to higher order thinking practices" (p. 496); to that, we would add that such discussion and collaboration are not likely to be an unproblematic route to greater social competence. Indeed, our own case studies suggest that the views of adolescents with LD are not always valued by their peers, and that adults will have to be quite insightful in identifying and using the affordances of meaningful social contexts as interventions. O'Connor reminds us that adults do not expect their own social or task-related interactions "to be free of hidden agendas and the sequelae of past interpersonal experiences" (p. 507). Contextualist approaches emphasize teachers and students making thinking explicit in social interactions and in collaborative activities with peers. However, adolescents with LD who are not accepted by their peers or who lack the experience of security (and other aspects of development enhanced in close friendships) may face obstacles in participating fully in these contexts unless activities are mindfully orchestrated by adults.

The research on social competence of adolescents with LD is mixed and suggests that many of them lack peer acceptance. However, it also suggests that many have friendships (e.g., Lévesque, 1997; Vaughn *et al.*, 1993), even if some of these friendships are found to be impoverished or atypical (e.g., Wiener & Sunohara, 1998). Studying these friendships, in contexts where they are found and in contexts where they are facilitated, may provide information about how to tap the strengths of adolescents with LD and about the affordances in these contexts. This is especially important in a contextualist approach that aims to use strengths and contextual affordances as foundations for intervention (Trent *et al.*, 1998).

Some recent research on self-worth of youth with LD suggests that same-age friends may not provide the only source of self-affirmation (Vaughn & Elbaum, 1999). Other sources of support may be parents, siblings, other adults, and teachers. Inasmuch as the classroom context is shaped by the teacher who sets the conditions under which peer relations take place, awareness of the characteristics and actions of teachers who foster friendships between adolescents with LD and their nondisabled peers may also further research on peer relations and social competence. Teachers define what peer treatment is acceptable, and they often form the groups that sit together and learn together during class. In this sense then, teachers contribute to a zone of proximal development for peer relations and social competence in the classroom.

Recently, researchers in LD and social competence, including Tanis Bryan (1991) and Sharon Vaughn (Vaughn & Sinagub, 1998), have called for a move from interactionist to contextualist approaches to social intervention. The contexts in which adolescents use, develop, and even lack social competence are diverse and complex. Responding to this call for a new approach by researchers and practitioners is bound to be challenging; however, the limitations apparent in a review of the extant research on social interventions suggest that such a change in perspective is critical.

V. IMPLICATIONS FOR PRACTICE AND RESEARCH ON SOCIAL COMPETENCE INTERVENTIONS

A. Implications for Practice

In reviewing the social competence of adolescents with LD, interventions that target this population, and related research with other adolescents, we have derived five principles that need to be remembered in developing any future social interventions for youth with LD.

1. Principle One

The interests, needs, and strengths of the particular adolescents must be paramount in designing interventions for adolescents with LD. Interests are cornerstones of satisfying friendships, they provide entrée into desirable extracurricular activities where adolescents can practice their social skills, and they allow young people to grow into more fully developed social beings. In addition, unless adolescents see the meaningfulness of an intervention, that is, are interested in it, they will not put forth sufficient effort for the intervention to succeed.

Understanding interests, to ensure meaningfulness, is helped by understanding individual needs and strengths. Not all youth with LD have social deficits and those who have needs in this area vary in their social relations, social cognition, and social skills. Failure to recognize the unique characteristics of adolescents with LD will result in interventions that have less than desirable results. Even should they participate fully, if the intervention does not target their needs and build on their strengths, these students are not likely to improve in social competence.

2. Principle Two

Building friendships must be a fundamental component of any social intervention. Friendships are an essential part of adolescents' social lives. They provide a critical source of support as adolescents seek their own identities and act as a buffer against negative life experiences. However, developing friendships can be a complex process for which LD adolescents' social competencies are inadequate. Therefore, strategies for beginning and maintaining friendships must be a part of social interventions for adolescents with LD.

3. Principle Three

Be constantly aware of contextual issues surrounding social interventions. There are two types of contexts that need to be considered. First, there is the context in which the instruction is being delivered. Interventions that might prove successful in the middle school context (Elliott *et al.*, 2001) might well not be possible in the secondary school, where heavy curricular demands and a rotating group of teachers for any one student make certain interventions unfeasible. Furthermore, schools are now more inclusive of a range of students, and inclusion may influence the possibility of targeting social competence interventions to any one population.

The second context refers to the places where the social competence will be used. Recognizing that the competence required in one setting may not match that required in another setting and that students learn the context while learning the competence means that an array of meaningful contexts must be included in any intervention.

4. Principle Four

The role of the teacher must be addressed in the social intervention. Teachers provide an essential resource for adolescents with LD. They can promote successful social inclusion, or they can unknowingly institute practices that isolate and stigmatize exceptional students. Therefore, all teachers who work with a student must be aware of the intervention—not necessarily directly involved in teaching the intervention—involved as knowledgeable facilitators who provide a coordinated effort to effect change.

5. Principle Five

Interventions must target discrete social skills, the integration of such social skills, and the social cognition of when to use the skills. It is not enough, as the ASSET program has done, to help students perform isolated skills or, as we have done in Pathways, to ignore such skills in favor of holistic approaches to social competence. Interventions must combine both with teaching about the understanding of how and when they should be used.

By following these five principles, we feel that better social interventions that truly benefit those adolescents with LD who need them can be developed. However, the success of these principles can only be verified by systematic research by multiple independent researchers.

B. Implications for Research

We recognize the difficulties in researching the success of social interventions designed for adolescents with LD. The true measure of their success will only come through the increased ability of the students to interact in multiple contexts, both inside and outside of school. The opportunity to access these multiple contexts is beyond the scope of most researchers. Therefore, rather than making the familiar plea for more longitudinal studies to discover the true effects of the interventions, we offer four practical, less costly suggestions that should be implemented in this field.

1. Suggestion One

Analyze social intervention effects separately by gender. Perhaps because of the low number of participants involved in most interventions for adolescents with LD, the practice of describing results by gender is less common than might be expected. Because females and males experience quite different social contexts in adolescence, it would seem that an intervention might be successful for one gender but not successful for the other.

2. Suggestion Two

Include tracking indicators to monitor program effectiveness. If a social intervention has been successful, changes should be observed in related student behaviors. For example, adolescents who are more socially competent should have fewer referrals to the office for misbehaving. Similarly, if they have friends at school, they are more likely to attend regularly. If these youth have successful social relations, they have a greater chance of school success, as measured by graduation and course completion. Tracking school records thus offers an inexpensive proxy measure of social competence to supplement the usual measures.

3. Suggestion Three

Use multiple methods of gathering data about social competence. In addition to tracking mechanisms, three types of information are relatively easy to obtain: self-report pencil-and-paper measures, role-play scenarios, and teacher ratings. Pencil-and-paper measures can tap social cognition and report on social relations, but may not indicate how adolescents use social skills in real-life situations. Role-plays approximate, but do not match, the variety of contexts adolescents encounter that demand social relations, social cognition, and social skills, perhaps in combination. Teacher ratings, based on observations of students, may be useful for all aspects of social competence, but can be influenced by reputational bias. Using multiple methods compensates for the weaknesses of individual methods while combining their benefits.

4. Suggestion Four

Employ qualitative research techniques more extensively. Case studies focusing on single adolescents or on collectives of adolescents with LD provide information for designing more tailored interventions that honor individual differences in social competence and in context. A population of such cases would build a greater understanding of the relationships among social needs, strengths, contexts, and successful intervention elements. When combined with traditional quantitative research findings, qualitative studies will give us a stronger sense of what does and does not work in meaningful social contexts.

Collectively, use of these suggestions would move the field forward and allow us to understand the complex effects social interventions might have for adolescents with LD.

VI. SUMMARY AND CONCLUSION

In summary, we have briefly characterized research on social competence and LD with the focus on interventions and issues. Three components of social competence are emphasized: relations with peers (social status and friendship), social cognition, and social skills. Inconsistent findings in the research describing the social status of adolescents with LD demonstrate that some adolescents with LD are ascribed low social status by their peers and a smaller number are as well accepted as their best-liked nondisabled peers. On the other hand, most of the few studies on friendship quality suggest low quality characterizes friendships of LD adolescents. Similarly, most studies of social cognition and social skills (particularly conversational skills) show adolescents with LD perform lower than their nondisabled peers. There are few validated interventions that researchers can recommend to practitioners to enhance social competence. A number of principles related to social competence interventions emerged from our review of literature. These principles focus on interest, friendship, a contextualist perspective (with emphasis on the role of the teacher), and the need for social cognition about when to employ aspects of social competence. Researchers would benefit from remaining mindful of the role of gender, school indicators, multiple data sources, and qualitative research in the development and validation of interventions to enhance the social competence of adolescents with LD.

Acknowledgments

This research was supported by a grant from the Social Sciences and Humanities Research Council of Canada, "Enhancing the school engagement of adolescents with learning disabilities: Interest and peer relations" (John Freeman and Nancy Hutchinson, investigators). We acknowledge the contribution of Michelle Levac, Elsa Mihotic, and Karen Burkett.

References

Ainley, M., Hidi, S., & Berndorff, D. (2002). Interest, learning, and the psychological processes that mediate their relationship. *Journal of Educational Psychology*, **94,** 545–561.

Anderson, P. (2000). Using literature to teach social skills to adolescents with LD. *Intervention in School and Clinic*, **35,** 271–279.

Asher, S. R., & Coie, J. D. (eds.). (1990). *Peer rejection in childhood.* Cambridge, MA: Cambridge University Press.

Asher, S. R., Parker, J. G., & Walker, D. L. (1996). Distinguishing friendship from acceptance: Implications for intervention. In W. M. Bukowski, A. F. Newcomb, & W. W. Hartup (eds.), *The company they keep: Friendship in childhood and adolescence* (pp. 366–405). New York: Cambridge University Press.

Asher, S., & Wheeler, V. (1985). Children's loneliness: A comparison of rejected and neglected peer status. *Journal of Consulting and Clinical Psychology*, **53,** 500–505.

Axelrod, L. (1982). Social perception in learning disabled adolescents. *Journal of Learning Disabilities*, **15**, 610–613.

Bear, G. G., Juvonen, J., & McInerney, F. (1993). Self-perceptions and peer relations of boys with and boys without learning disabilities in an integrated setting: A longitudinal study. *Learning Disability Quarterly*, **16**, 127–136.

Bredo, E. (1994). Reconstructing educational psychology: Situated cognition and Deweyian pragmatism. *Educational Psychologist*, **29**(1), 23–35.

Berndt, T. J. (1999). Friends' influence on students' adjustment to school. *Educational Psychologist*, **34**, 15–28.

Bryan, T. (1974a). An observational analysis of classroom behaviors of children with learning disabilities. *Journal of Learning Disabilities*, **7**, 26–34.

Bryan, T. (1974b). Peer popularity of learning disabled children. *Journal of Learning Disabilities*, **7**, 621–625.

Bryan, T. (1976). Peer popularity of learning disabled children: A replication. *Journal of Learning Disabilities*, **9**, 307–311.

Bryan, T. (1983). Learning disabled children and youth's social competence. *Thalamus*, **2**, 125.

Bryan, T. (1991). Assessment of social cognition: Review of research in learning disabilities. In H. L. Swanson (ed.), *Handbook on the assessment of learning disabilities: Theory, research, and practice* (pp. 285–311). Austin, TX: Pro-Ed.

Bryan, T. (1999). Reflections on a research career: It ain't over till it's over. *Exceptional Children*, **65**, 438–447.

Bryan, T., Donahue, M., & Pearl, R. (1981). Learning disabled children's peer interaction during a small group problem-solving task. *Learning Disability Quarterly*, **4**, 13–22.

Bryan, T., Pearl, R., & Fallon, P. (1989). Conformity to peer pressure by students with learning disabilities: A replication. *Journal of Learning Disabilities*, **22**, 458–459.

Buhrmester, D. (1990). Intimacy of friendship, interpersonal competence, and adjustment during preadolescence and adolescence. *Child Development*, **61**, 1101–1111.

Buhrmester, D. (1996). Need fulfillment, interpersonal competence, and the developmental contexts of early adolescent friendship. In W. M. Bukowski, A. F. Newcomb, & W. W. Hartup (eds.), *The company they keep: Friendship in childhood and adolescence* (pp. 158–185). New York: Cambridge University Press.

Buhrmester, D., & Carbery, J. (1992, March). *Daily patterns of self-disclosure and adolescent adjustment*. Paper presented at the biennial meeting of the Society for Research on Adolescence, Washington, DC.

Buhrmester, D., & Prager, K. (1995). Patterns and functions of self-disclosure during childhood and adolescence. In K. J. Rotenberg (ed.), *Disclosure processes in children and adolescents*. New York: Cambridge University Press.

Bukowski, W. M., Hoza, B., & Boivin, M. (1993). Popularity, friendship, and emotional adjustment during early adolescence. In B. Laursen (ed.), *Disclosure processes in children and adolescents* (pp. 10–56). New York: Cambridge University Press.

Bukowski, W. M., Newcomb, A. F., & Hoza, B. (1987). Friendship conceptions among early adolescents: A longitudinal study of stability and change. *Journal of Early Adolescence*, **72**, 143–152.

Bullis, M., Walker, H. M., & Sprague, J. R. (2001). A promise unfulfilled: Social skills training with at-risk and antisocial children and youth. *Exceptionality*, **9**, 67–90.

Cantwell, D. P., & Baker, L. (1991). Association between attention deficit–hyperactivity disorder and learning disorders. *Journal of Learning Disabilities*, **24**, 88–95.

Chan, J. S. (2000). *The social skills of two elementary students with learning disabilities: A participant observational study across seven contexts.* Unpublished master's thesis, Queen's University, Kingston, Ontario, Canada.

Coie, J. D., & Kupersmidt, J. (1983). A behavioral analysis of emerging social status in boys' groups. *Child Development*, **54**, 1400–1416.

Conderman, G. (1995). Social status of sixth and seventh grade students with learning disabilities. *Learning Disability Quarterly*, **18**, 13–24.

Cosden, M., Brown, C., & Elliott, K. (2002). Development of self-understanding and self-esteem in children and adults with learning disabilities. In B. Y. L. Wong & M. Donahue (eds.), *The social dimensions of learning disabilities* (pp. 33–51). Mahwah, NJ: Lawrence Erlbaum Associates.

Dewey, J. (1913). *Interest and effort in education.* Cambridge, MA: Riverside.

Eccles, J. S., & Templeton, J. (2002). Extracurricular and other after-school activities for youth. *Review of Research in Education*, **26**, 113–180.

Edwards, K. L. (2000). *They can be successful too!: Inclusive practices of secondary science teachers.* Unpublished master's thesis, Queen's University, Kingston, Ontario, Canada.

Elksnin, N., & Elksnin, L. K. (2001). Adolescents with disabilities: The need for occupational social skills training. *Exceptionality*, **9**, 91–105.

Elliott, S. N., Malecki, C. K., & Demaray, M. K. (2001). New directions in social skills assessment and intervention for elementary and middle school students. *Exceptionality*, **9**, 19–32.

Evans, C., & Eder, D. (1989, August). *"No exit": Processes of social isolation in the middle school.* Paper presented at the American Sociology Association Meeting, San Francisco.

Farmer, T. W., van Acker, R. M., Pearl, R., & Rodkin, P. C. (1999). Social networks and peer-assessed problem behavior in elementary classrooms: Students with and without learning disabilities. *Remedial and Special Education*, **20**, 244–256.

Forness, S. R., & Kavale, K. A. (1996). Treating social skill deficits in children with learning disabilities: A meta-analysis of the research. *Learning Disability Quarterly*, **19**, 2–13.

Freeman, J. G., & Hutchinson, N. L. (1994). An adolescent with learning disabilities. Eric: The perspective of a potential dropout. *Canadian Journal of Special Education*, **9**(4), 131–147.

Freeman, J. G., Hutchinson, N. L., & Porter, B. (1991). Improving problem solving on the job: Strategy instruction for youth with learning disabilities. *Exceptionality Education Canada*, **1**, 45–65.

Freeman, J. G., McPhail, J. C., & Berndt, J. A. (2002). Sixth graders' views of activities that do and do not help them learn. *Elementary School Journal*, **102**, 335–347.

Freeman, J. G., Stoch, S. A., Chan, J. S. N., & Hutchinson, N. L. (in press). Staying in school: A retrospective study of adults with learning disabilities. *Alberta Journal of Educational Research.*

Furman, W., & Buhrmester, D. (1985). Children's perceptions of the personal relationships in their social networks. *Developmental Psychology*, **20**, 925–933.

Gardner, P. L. (1998). The development of males' and females' interests in science and technology. In L. Hoffmann, A. Krapp, K. A. Renninger, & J. Baumert (eds.), *Interest and learning* (pp. 41–57). Kiel, Germany: Institut für die Pädagogik der Naturwissenschaften an der Universität Kiel.

Goldsworthy, R. C., Barab, S. A., & Goldsworthy, E. L. (2000). The STAR Project: Enhancing adolescents' social understanding through video-based, multimedia scenarios. *Journal of Special Education Technology*, **15**(2), 13–26.

Hamre-Nietupski, S., Hendrickson, J., Nietupski, J., & Shokoohi-Yekta, M. (1994). Regular educators' perceptions of facilitating friendships of students with moderate, severe, or profound disabilities and nondisabled peers. *Education and Training in Mental Retardation and Developmental Disabilities*, **29**, 102–117.

Hartas, D., & Donahue, M. L. (1997). Conversational and social problem-solving skills in adolescents with learning disabilities. *Learning Disabilities Research and Practice*, **12**, 213–220.

Harter, S. (1993). Causes and consequences of low self-esteem in children and adolescents. In R. F. Baumeister (ed.), *Self-esteem: The puzzle of low self-regard* (pp. 87–116). New York: Plenum Press.

Hartup, W. W., & Stevens, N. (1997). Friendship and adaptation in the life course. *Psychological Bulletin*, **121**, 355–370.

Hazel, J. S., Schumaker, J. B., Sherman, J. A., & Sheldon, J. (1982). Application of a group training program in social skills and problem solving skills to learning disabled and non-learning disabled youth. *Learning Disability Quarterly*, **5**, 398–408.

Hazel, J. S., Schumaker, J. B., Sherman, J. A., & Sheldon, J. (1996). *ASSET: A social skills program for adolescents.* Champaign, IL: Research Press.

Hazel, J. S., Schumaker, J. B., Sherman, J. A., & Sheldon-Widgen, J. (1981). *ASSET: A social skills program for adolescents.* Champaign, IL: Research Press.

Hidi, S. (1990). Interest and its contribution as a mental resource for learning. *Review of Educational Research*, **60**, 549–571.

Hidi, S., & Harackiewicz, J. M. (2000). Motivating the academically unmotivated: A critical issue for the 21st century. *Review of Educational Research*, **70**, 151–179.

Hutchinson, N. L., & Freeman, J. G. (1994a). *Pathways: Anger management on the job.* Toronto, ON: Nelson Canada.

Hutchinson, N. L., & Freeman, J. G. (1994b). *Pathways: Program overview.* Toronto, ON: Nelson Canada.

Hutchinson, N. L., & Freeman, J. G. (1994c). *Pathways: Solving problems on the job.* Toronto, ON: Nelson Canada.

Hutchinson, N. L., Freeman, J. G., & Steiner Bell, K. (2002). Children and adolescents with learning disabilities: Case studies of social relations in inclusive classrooms. In B. Y. L. Wong & M. Donahue (eds.), *The social dimensions of learning disabilities* (pp. 189–214). Mahwah, NJ: Lawrence Erlbaum Associates.

Hymel, S., Wagner, E., & Butler, L. J. (1990). Reputational bias: View from the peer group. In S. R. Asher & D. J. Coie (eds.), *Peer rejection in childhood* (pp. 156–186). Cambridge, MA: Cambridge University Press.

Inderbitzen-Pisaruk, H., & Foster, S. L. (1990). Adolescent friendships and peer acceptance: Implications for social skills training. *Clinical Psychology Review*, **10**, 425–439.

Jackson, S. C., Enright, R. D., & Murdock, J. Y. (1987). Social perception problems in learning disabled youth: Developmental lag versus perceptual deficit. *Journal of Learning Disabilities*, **20**, 361–364.

Jarvis, P. A., & Justice, E. M. (1992). Social sensitivity in adolescents and adults with learning disabilities. *Adolescence*, **27**, 977–988.

Johnson, D., & Myklebust, H. (1967). *Learning disabilities: Educational principles and practices*. New York: Grune & Stratton.

Kavale, K. A., & Forness, S. R. (1996). Social skill deficits and learning disabilities: A meta-analysis. *Journal of Learning Disabilities*, **29**, 226–237.

Kirk, S. A. (1963). Behavioral diagnosis and remediation of learning disabilities. *Proceedings of the Conference Exploring the Problems of Perceptually Handicapped Children*, **1**, 1–23.

Kish, M. (1991). Counseling adolescents with LD. *Intervention in School and Clinic*, **27**, 20–24.

Kolb, S. M., & Hanley-Maxwell, C. (2003). Critical social skills for adolescents with high incidence disabilities: Parental perspectives. *Exceptional Children*, **69**, 163–179.

LaGreca, A. M., & Stone, W. L. (1990). Children with learning disabilities: The role of achievement in their social, personal, and behavioral functioning. In H. L. Swanson & B. Keogh (eds.), *Learning disabilities: Theoretical and research issues* (pp. 333–352). Hillsdale, NJ: Lawrence Erlbaum Associates.

Larson, K. A., & Gerber, M. M. (1987). Effects of social cognitive training for enhancing overt behavior in learning disabled and low achieving delinquents. *Exceptional Children*, **54**, 201–211.

Lévesque, N. (1997). *Perceptions of friendships and peer groups: The school experiences of two adolescents with learning disabilities*. Unpublished master's thesis, Queen's University, Kingston, Ontario, Canada.

Maccoby, E. E. (1990). Gender and relationships: A developmental account. *American Psychologist*, **45**, 513–520.

McDevitt, T. M., & Ormrod, J. E. (2002). *Child development and education*. Upper Saddle River, NJ: Pearson Education.

McIntosh, R., Vaughn, S., & Bennerson, D. (1995). Fast social skills with a slam and a rap. *Teaching Exceptional Children*, **28**(1), 37–41.

Morrison, G. M., Laughlin, J., Smith, D., Ollansky, E., & Moore, B. (1992). Preferences for sources of social support of Hispanic male adolescents with mild learning handicaps. *Education and Training in Mental Retardation and Developmental Disabilities*, **27**, 132–144.

O'Connor, M. C. (1996). Managing the intermental: Classroom group discussion and the social context of learning. In D. I. Slobin, J. Gerhardt, A. Kyratzis, & J. Guo (eds.), *Social interaction, social context, and language: Essays in honor of Susan Ervin-Tripp* (pp. 495–512). Mahwah, NJ: Lawrence Erlbaum Associates.

Ochoa, S. H., & Olivarez, A. (1995). A meta-analysis of peer rating sociometric studies of pupils with learning disabilities. *The Journal of Special Education*, **29**, 1–19.

Omizo, M. M., Lo, F. G., & Williams, R. E. (1986). Rational–emotive education, self-concept, and locus of control among learning-disabled students. *Journal of Humanistic Counseling, Education, & Development*, **25**(2), 58–69.

Orton, S. (1937). *Reading, writing, and speech problems in children*. New York: Norton & Co.

Pearl, R., & Bryan, T. (1992). Students' expectations about peer pressure to engage in misconduct. *Journal of Learning Disabilities*, **25**, 582–585, 597.

Pearl, R., & Bryan, T. (1994). Getting caught in misconduct: Conceptions of adolescents with and without learning disabilities. *Journal of Learning Disabilities*, **27**, 193–197.

Pearl, R., Bryan, T., Fallon, P., & Herzog, A. (1991). Learning disabled students' detection of deception. *Learning Disabilities Research and Practice*, **6**, 12–16.

Perlmutter, B. F., Crocker, J., Cordray, D., & Garstecki, D. (1983). Sociometric status and related personality characteristics of mainstreamed learning disabled adolescents. *Learning Disability Quarterly*, **6**, 20–30.

Platt, J., & Spivack, G. (1977). *Measures of interpersonal cognitive problem-solving: A manual*. Philadelphia: Hahnemann Community Mental Health/Mental Retardation Center, Department of Mental Health Sciences.

Prater, M. A., Serna, L., & Nakamura, K. K. (1999). Impact of peer teaching on the acquisition of social skills by adolescents with learning disabilities. *Education and Treatment of Children*, **22**(1), 19–35.

Prenzel, M. (1992). The selective persistence of interest. In K. A. Renninger, S. Hidi, & A. Krapp (eds.), *The role of interest in learning and development* (pp. 71–98). Hillsdale, NJ: Lawrence Erlbaum Associates.

Rathunde, K. (1993). The experience of interest: A theoretical and empirical look in its role in adolescent talent development. *Advances in Motivation and Achievement*, **8**, 59–98.

Rathunde, K. (1998). Undivided and abiding interest: Comparisons across studies of talented adolescents and creative adults. In L. Hoffmann, A. Krapp, K. A. Renninger, & J. Baumert (eds.), *Interest and learning* (pp. 367–376). Kiel, Germany: Institut für die Pädagogik der Naturwissenschaften an der Universität Kiel.

Renninger, K. A. (1998). What are the roles of individual interest, task difficulty, and gender in student comprehension? In L. Hoffmann, A. Krapp, K. A. Renninger, & J. Baumert (eds.), *Interest and learning* (pp. 228–238). Kiel, Germany: Institut für die Pädagogik der Naturwissenschaften an der Universität Kiel.

Sabornie, E. J., & Kauffman, J. M. (1986). Social acceptance of learning disabled adolescents. *Learning Disability Quarterly*, **9**, 55–60.

Schiefele, U. (1998). Individual interest and learning: What we know and what we don't know. In L. Hoffmann, A. Krapp, K. A. Renninger, & J. Baumert (eds.), *Interest and learning* (pp. 91–104). Kiel, Germany: Institut für die Pädagogik der Naturwissenschaften an der Universität Kiel.

Schneider, M., & Yoshida, R. K. (1988). Interpersonal problem-solving skills and classroom behavioral adjustment in learning-disabled adolescents and comparison peers. *Journal of School Psychology*, **26**, 25–34.

Schumaker, J. B. H., & Hazel, J. S. (1984). Social skills assessment and training for the learning disabled: Who's on first and what's on second? Part II. *Journal of Learning Disabilities*, **17**, 492–499.

Sisterhen, D. H., & Gerber, P. J. (1989). Auditory, visual, and multisensory non-verbal social perception in adolescents with and without learning disabilities. *Journal of Learning Disabilities*, **22**, 245–249, 257.

Stevens, R. S., & Shenker, L. (1991). A multidimensional treatment program for learning disabled adolescents: A preliminary report. *Canadian Journal of Special Education*, **7**(1), 60–66.

Stiliadis, K., & Wiener, J. (1989). Relationship between social status and peer status in children with learning disabilities. *Journal of Learning Disabilities*, **22**, 624–629.

Stoch, S. A. (2000). *Zak: An adolescent with learning disabilities at home, at camp, and at school.* Unpublished master's thesis, Queen's University, Kingston, Ontario, Canada.

Sullivan, H. S. (1953). *The interpersonal theory of psychiatry.* New York: Norton.

Swanson, H. L. (1999). *Interventions for students with learning disabilities: A meta-analysis of treatment outcomes.* New York: Guilford Press.

Swanson, H. L., & Malone, S. (1992). Social skills and learning disabilities: A meta-analysis of the literature. *School Psychology Review*, **21**, 427–443.

Swanson, H. L., & Sachse-Lee, C. (2000). A meta-analysis of single-subject–design intervention research for students with LD. *Journal of Learning Disabilities*, **33**, 114–136.

Tannen, D. (1990). Gender differences in topical coherence: Creating involvement in best friends' talk. *Discourse Processes*, **13**, 73–90.

Trent, S. C., Artiles, A. J., & Englert, C. S. (1998). From deficit thinking to social constructivism: A review of theory, research, and practice in special education. *Review of Research in Education*, **23**, 277–307.

Tur-Kaspa, H., & Bryan, T. (1994). Social information-processing skills of students with learning disabilities. *Learning Disabilities Research and Practice*, **9**, 12–23.

Vaughn, S., & Elbaum, B. E. (1999). The self-concept and friendships of students with learning disabilities: A developmental perspective. In R. Gallimore, L. Bernheimer, D. L. MacMillan, D. L. Speece, & S. Vaughn (eds.), *Developmental perspectives on children with high incidence disabilities* (pp. 81–110). Mahwah, NJ: Lawrence Erlbaum Associates.

Vaughn, S., Elbaum, B. E., & Boardman, A. G. (2001). The social functioning of students with learning disabilities: Implications for inclusion. *Exceptionality*, **9**, 47–65.

Vaughn, S., Elbaum, B. E., Schumm, J. S., & Hughes, M. T. (1998). Social outcomes for students with and without learning disabilities in inclusive classrooms. *Journal of Learning Disabilities*, **31**, 428–436.

Vaughn, S., & Hogan, A. (1990). Social competence and LD: A prospective study. In H. L. Swanson & B. K. Keogh (eds.), *Learning disabilities: Theoretical and research issues* (pp. 175–191). Hillsdale, NJ: Lawrence Erlbaum Associates.

Vaughn, S., McIntosh, R., Schumm, J. S., Haager, D., & Callwood, D. (1993). Social status, peer acceptance, and reciprocal friendships revisited. *Learning Disabilities Research and Practice*, **8**, 82–88.

Vaughn, S., McIntosh, R., & Spencer-Rowe, J. (1991). Peer rejection is a stubborn thing: Increasing peer acceptance of rejected students with learning disabilities. *Learning Disabilities Research and Practice*, **6**(2), 83–88.

Vaughn, S., & Sinagub, J. (1998). Social competence of students with learning disabilities: Interventions and issues. In B. Y. L. Wong (ed.), *Learning about learning disabilities* (2nd ed., pp. 453–487). San Diego, CA: Academic Press.

Vygotsky, L. S. (1978). *Mind in society*. Cambridge, MA: Harvard University Press.

Wenz-Gross, M., & Siperstein, G. N. (1997). Importance of social support in the adjustment of children with learning problems. *Exceptional Children*, **63**, 183–193.

Wiener, J., Harris, P. J., & Shirer, C. (1990). Achievement and social-behavioral correlates of peer status in LD children. *Learning Disability Quarterly*, **13**, 114–127.

Wiener, J., & Sunohara, G. (1995, March). *Friendship selection and quality in children with and without learning disabilities*. Paper presented at the meeting of the Society for Research in Child Development, Indianapolis, IN.

Wiener, J., & Sunohara, G. (1998). Parents' perceptions of the quality of friendship of their children with learning disabilities. *Learning Disabilities Research and Practice*, **13**, 242–257.

Wong, B. Y. L., & Donahue, M. (eds.). (2002). *The social dimensions of learning disabilities*. Mahwah, NJ: Lawrence Erlbaum Associates.

Wright, P. H. (1982). Men's friendships, women's friendships, and the alleged inferiority of the latter. *Sex Roles*, **8**, 1–20.

Zetlin, A. G., & Murtaugh, M. (1988). Friendship patterns of mildly learning handicapped and nonhandicapped high school students. *American Journal on Mental Retardation*, **92**, 447–454.

CHAPTER 13

The Science of Schooling for Students with Learning Disabilities: Recommendations for Service Delivery Linking Practice with Research

Jean B. Crockett
Virginia Polytechnic Institute and State University

Almost all of us have gone to school. Most of us have gone to public schools. This seems to qualify us in our minds as experts on public education. We all seem to have an opinion on how children should be taught, how schools should be run, and how teaching should be improved. There is nothing more public than public education. At the same time, there sometimes seems nothing so hidden as the science of schooling, the field of educational research. (Forness, 2002, p. v)

"The science of schooling" means the work of educational research, with its unglamorous and incremental contributions to our knowledge of how children learn best. In his work as both a scholar and a school administrator, Steven Forness (2002) promoted service delivery linking instructional

Learning about Learning Disabilities, Third Edition

practices with the results of empirical research in the field of special education. Research has told us much, he said, about the power of direct skill instruction in teaching children to read and about the critical influences of family and home environment on educational success. Regrettably, research has also demonstrated the likelihood that children with disabilities will experience less success in school, even when provided with strong support, than children without such individual differences.

As Forness (2002) suggested, we would all like to believe that the opposite is true. It really is more exciting and inspirational to imagine "that we can just ignore individual differences, treat all children the same, and thus make disabilities disappear. These beliefs all make for better stories and thus are more likely to be what we see or hear from the media" (p. v). But educators entrusted with the responsibility of teaching students with learning disabilities (LD) cannot afford to confuse popular appeal with the science of schooling. Science may not be the only means to understanding educational phenomena, but its rational and logical approach is "the best trick we know so far for solving our most pressing problems" (Sasso, 2001, p. 190).

Vaughn and Dammann (2001) defined science as "an approach to the development of a consistent, documented system of knowledge based on rigorous, systematic, objective observations that lead to hypotheses or theories that are then tested and refined in an iterative process." (p. 22) In discussing the meaning of science and empirical rigor in the social sciences (see Crockett, 2001b), they pointed out why special education, more than other areas of education, needs to proceed by relying on science for its usefulness in improving educational practice.

> Whereas typically achieving students can make up for lost time, learn well independently, and make up for mistakes made by educators, special education students cannot. The influence of research and evidence on decision-making has even greater value for those students with disabilities who most require precision in their instructional and behavioral plans. These are the students who can least afford to recover from practices that ignore research findings. (Vaughn & Dammann, 2001, p. 27)

Success, for these students, depends on sound decisions about instructional interventions by educators and parents and the availability of evidence to support those decisions.

Students with LD, in particular, are characterized by extreme individual differences that often pose significant academic and social challenges. Successful schooling for them relies on a distribution of labor, with school-based practitioners utilizing research knowledge and researchers capturing, refining, and documenting the dynamic craft of instruction. In this way, "science does not belong to the researchers, nor does practice belong to the teachers" (Vaughn & Dammann, 2001, p. 27). Instead, both kinds of work influence service delivery decisions. The science of observing teaching and learning as they occur simultaneously in complex classroom contexts for students with LD "actually returns special education to its roots—understanding individual differences and the support students with disabilities need to accelerate their learning." (Schiller & Malouf, 2000, p. 258)

The exploration of the science of schooling in this discussion draws on this tradition and attends to the importance of delivering high-quality instruction to students with LD in schools challenged by reforms and political accountability. This chapter examines current realities and legal parameters of service delivery and views the knowledge base supporting effective practices for students with LD through contemporary syntheses of special education research. Environmental factors in elementary and secondary schools are also explored to see if these students are receiving the interventions they need and if their teachers are getting the support they require to be successful as a result of efforts to redesign instructional delivery. In conclusion, recommendations are made to assist educational decision-makers in enhancing service delivery for students with LD by linking school practice with educational research.

I. SCIENCE AND SCHOOLING FOR STUDENTS WITH LD

The field of special education is probably known more for its social policies addressing the equitable education of students with disabilities than for its scholarship supporting their effective instruction. To the general public, special education is often considered to be synonymous with the term *inclusion*, an educational strategy that emphasizes educating students with disabilities in general education classrooms. Although the democratic nature of social inclusion captures the public spirit, instructional *intervention* is the centerpiece of special education research. Williams (2000) remarked that "in many situations special education students need a distinctive approach to instruction, involving a slower pace, a more elaborated sequence of steps, extensive practice, and clear feedback.... In special education, we look for matches between students and interventions" (p. viii). Kauffman (1999) described this work as special education's historic mission, "seeking reliable, common knowledge about how best to teach students with disabilities—researching and applying instruction that is intensive, urgent, relentless, goal directed according to individual need, and delivered in the setting where it is most effective" (p. 253).

Over time, special education research has contributed to the knowledge base that underlies good teaching and has demonstrated that its application by skillful teachers results in student learning. As a result, the maturing field of special education has established its professional jurisdiction, making it possible for others to "identify the group with the work around which it is organized" (Yinger & Nolen, 2003, p. 389), in this case, the work of enhancing the academic learning and social growth of children and youth with disabilities. According to Gersten *et al.* (2000), special and general educators are eager for guidance in using feasible and sustainable practices and parents "crave instruction that yields documented outcomes for students" (p. 453). As policymakers continue to raise standards for student achievement, parent advocacy organizations can be expected to grow stronger in demanding better services and in holding the field of special education more accountable for its use of effective practices (Greenwood, 2001). These contemporary forces from within and without the field of education increase the urgency for teachers to use research-based interventions for students with LD and for administrators to develop a better understanding of how to implement those interventions within local schools.

The fortunes of service delivery for students with LD are bound to the total educational enterprise as it wrestles with policies that some suggest confuse "the focus on *each* child needing special education with the aphorism of educating *all* children, associated with school reform" (Kaufman & Lewis, 1999, p. 224). Several premises characterize current reforms: standards will be set at a high level and these high standards will apply to all students. According to Kaufman and Lewis, realizing these reforms creates a tension between bottom-up professionalism and top-down accountability and students with disabilities are caught in the middle. Their individualized programs rely on bottom-up decision making to address the unique educational needs resulting from their disability while top-down federal legislation emphasizes their participation and progress in the general education curriculum and in state and national assessments designed for all students. Although the reform agenda is assumed to apply to all students, those who receive special education are often overlooked and "the particular problems of students who can learn the general education curriculum only with extreme difficulty, if at all, are not routinely taken into account" (Kauffman, 2002, p. xi).

A. Current Realities of Service Delivery

Today's public expects educators to achieve basic literacy for all youth and to do so in ways that no child will be "left behind." Reading is regarded as the new civil right (U.S. Department of Education, 2002a) and the No Child Left Behind Act of 2001 (NCLB) requires each state to hold its public schools accountable for making yearly progress toward the goal of "closing the achievement gap and ensuring that every child is proficient in math and reading by the school year 2013–14" (p. 3). If most students with disabilities and students in other traditionally low-performing subgroups in grades 3 through 8 fail to make adequate progress toward reaching 100% proficiency in reading and mathematics, their schools could face remedial actions. For example, teachers and administrators could face job reassignments; school systems could also be required to provide free tutoring programs and to provide parents with vouchers to send their children to private schools. Schools that continue to fail could face the loss of accreditation and possible closure. Although goal setting and monitoring of achievement are familiar practices to special educators, public policies are outpacing research about the effects of high-stakes testing on the achievement of students with disabilities and changing the landscape of their instructional delivery (Crockett, 2001a; Shriner, 2000).

Special education enrollments have risen simultaneously with the increased demands of standards-based reforms. The number of students with disabilities receiving special education, ages 6 through 21, grew by 30% from 4.3 million in 1990–1991 to 5.6 million in 1999–2000. Students with LD make up the majority of this school-age population and, although minorities are not largely overrepresented in this group, the percentage of students with LD varies by age. Students with LD comprise approximately 40% of special education students in elementary schools and 62% of special education students at the secondary level. Close to one-half of the 2.8 million students with LD across age and grade levels are assigned to regular classes for at least 80% of their instructional time. Secondary schools have experienced the largest growth in the number of students with LD and the performance of these students in the general education curriculum frequently calls for a special instructional response. For example, in 1998–1999, only 63.3% of students with LD graduated with a standard diploma and 27.1% dropped out before completing high school (U.S. Department of Education, 2001). Dropout factors most frequently mentioned as "pushing" students with LD out of school include grade retention, low academic achievement, and perceptions that school personnel are uncaring and indifferent to their success (Scanlon & Mellard, 2002).

B. Appropriate Education is the Legal Standard for Students with LD

The legal principles that guide the education of students with LD actually encourage educators to be attentive rather than indifferent to students' achievement and personal learning needs. The Individuals with Disabilities Education Act (IDEA) ensures that any student with a disability who needs special education is provided with a free appropriate public education (FAPE) in the least restrictive environment (LRE) and is taught by trained teachers who use effective practices. *Special education* is clearly defined in law as "specially designed instruction, at no cost to parents, to meet the unique needs of a child with a disability including instruction conducted in the classroom, in the home, in hospitals and institutions, and in other settings" (IDEA, § 1401(25)(A)). FAPE is the centerpiece of the IDEA and it is assured through the provision of an individualized education program (IEP). To be appropriate, an IEP must be: (a) individualized to a student's unique educational needs, (b) reasonably calculated to allow for educational benefit, and (c) procedurally correct in its development (Bateman & Linden, 1998).

In providing students with FAPE, Bateman and Linden (1998) emphasized that the IDEA requires school personnel to follow a proper sequence: (a) first finding a student eligible to receive special education, (b) developing the student's IEP, and (c) only then determining the instructional placement that, for this student, constitutes the LRE. The LRE requirements of the IDEA set out the factors to consider in educating students with and without disabilities together to the maximum extent appropriate. The law presumes that the least restrictive appropriate placement for any student is the regular class. However, this presumption can be rebutted if decision-making teams find a mismatched relationship between a student's learning needs and the ecological elements affecting his or her appropriate instruction in the regular setting. For this reason, school systems are legally required to make a full continuum of alternative learning environments available that range from regular classes, special classes, separate schools, residential facilities, and hospitals to home settings.

The IDEA Amendments of 1997 grafted the school reform agenda to each student's IEP with stipulations addressing access to the general education curriculum. The term "specially designed instruction" was explicitly defined in the law as appropriately adapting the content, methodology, or delivery of instruction to eligible students for two reasons: (1) to address the unique needs of the student that result from the disability and (2) to ensure access to the general curriculum so that he or she can meet the local educational standards that apply to all children. The sequence of these requirements is important to follow because the secondary imperative, to ensure access to the general curriculum, depends upon the primary directive—to address the disability-related needs of the child. In other words, the best hope for schools in meeting state standards and national goals adequately rests with their vigilance in meeting the needs of students with disabilities appropriately.

With regard to service delivery for students with LD, it is important to note that participation in the general curriculum does not mean the same thing as inclusion in regular classes. Sharp and Patasky (2002) emphasized the distinction that "inclusion in a regular classroom concerns the setting where a student with a disability is educated. . . . Participation in the general curriculum concerns what a student learns" (p. 3). The law expects that students for whom the LRE is not the regular classroom will be taught the general curriculum to the maximum extent appropriate to their learning wherever they receive instruction.

C. Coming to Consensus about Learning Disabilities

Controversies surrounding the identification of students with LD and the provision of service systems to address their learning are perennial, perhaps because these issues are of fundamental concern to shareholders. Anticipated changes in public policies prompted more than 200 researchers, practitioners, policymakers, and parents of students with LD to attend the Learning Disabilities Summit in August 2001. Their task was to review research on major issues in the field and to find common ground on which to build improved programs. Following the Summit, the Learning Disabilities Roundtable, coordinated by the National Center for Learning Disabilities (NCLD), developed statements of consensus representing the views of member organizations of the National Joint Committee on Learning Disabilities (NJCLD). These statements outlined what should be valued and what should be promoted with regard to the nature of learning disabilities, the identification process, eligibility criteria, intervention, and professional development (U.S. Department of Education, 2002b).

According to consensus, the concept of specific learning disabilities is valid, supported by converging evidence that such disabilities are neurologically based and intrinsic to individuals who show intra-individual skills and abilities. Learning disabilities are not due primarily to other disabling conditions and they are evident across the ethnic and economic spectrum, persisting at varying levels of intensity throughout a person's lifespan. The identification process should be student-centered and comprehensive, using efficient problem-solving approaches. Decisions about eligibility for services are to be made by an interdisciplinary team in a timely manner and based on information collected from the comprehensive evaluation using multiple methods and relevant sources of data. Eligibility decisions, however, should not rely on ability–achievement discrepancy formulas because there is no evidence that this approach can be applied in ways that are consistent and educationally reliable and valid. The responsibility for delivering high-quality instruction, research-based interventions, and prompt identification of individuals at risk belongs to general educators collaborating with special education and related services personnel (U.S. Department of Education, 2002b).

Statements of consensus regarding interventions and professional development centered on the premise that "regular and special education must be coordinated as part of a coherent system which is held accountable for the educational outcomes of students with SLD" (U.S. Department of Education, 2002b, p. 30). Interventions should be scientifically based, with the prelude to any intervention being high-quality instruction provided in the general education classroom where most of these students begin their schooling. Educators should have information about these practices because students with LD require intensive, explicit, and frequently monitored instruction to achieve academic success. Students with LD require a continuum of intervention options offered through regular and special education across all grade levels. Regardless of setting, interventions must be timely and specifically matched to the student's learning and behavioral needs and they are most effective when they are employed consistently, faithfully, and with a sufficient level of intensity and duration. The consensus statements also addressed changes in professional development to increase "the staff and school capacity" (p. 30) to participate in comprehensive evaluations, team problem-solving, the delivery of effective interventions, and collaboration among regular and special education personnel (U.S. Department of Education, 2002b).

D. Dilemmas of Service Delivery for Students with LD

The statements of consensus that emerged from the Learning Disabilities Roundtable helped to clarify important issues of identification and programming. They also raised questions about the primary role of special education in this coherent system. Many strategies promoted in the statements are foreign to the general education culture and expectations were clear that special education personnel would need to provide consultative assistance to their colleagues as they selected and implemented unfamiliar approaches. However, this assistance poses a potential dilemma for service delivery. If special education devolves into a generic support program, it runs the risk of offering more the illusion than the reality of help to students with specific learning issues that cannot be addressed in the regular classroom (see Ellis in Casareno, 2002).

A shortage of qualified personnel also threatens the quality of special education service delivery. More than 12,000 special education teaching positions were left vacant or filled by substitutes in 1999–2000, and 8% of the special educators who were employed were not fully certified for their roles. Administrators cited shortages of qualified applicants and insufficient salary and benefits as the greatest barriers to filling these positions (U.S. Department of Education, 2001). Once they were hired, some special educators attributed their inability to teach students effectively to reasons such as (a) role ambiguity and competing responsibilities, (b) overwhelming paperwork, (c) high caseloads and lack of time for individualized instruction, and (d) insufficient administrative support. As a result of frustrations, many special educators leave their positions for general education assignments or leave teaching completely (CEC, 2000).

The availability and preparation of general educators for their roles, both in teaching and in administrating schools, provides another challenge. Most general educators teaching for six or fewer years have no preparation in adapting instruction for special education students (Study of Personnel Needs in Special Education, 2001). Most school administrators have limited knowledge about the educational needs of students with disabilities (Crockett, 2002) and, in addition, there is a greater demand for special education administrators than can be met by the current supply (Lashley & Boscardin, 2002).

These shortages of qualified personnel pose serious threats to service delivery at a time when some parents of students with LD have given up on unresponsive schools, removing their children from public programming at increasing rates and attributing learning gains to instructional methods used in private schools (Bhat *et al.*, 2000). The policy context surrounding the education of students with LD in the United States is expected to reflect the preference of the No Child Left Behind Act for parental choice. For special education, this could mean contention about federally funded vouchers and school choice programs for students with disabilities (Goldstein, 2002). Despite perennial controversies over service provision, however, the field of LD has steadily followed its mission of determining which instructional interventions yield the most positive outcomes. In other words, special education's continuing attention to the science of schooling has quietly proceeded, hidden in the shadow of more public concerns.

II. IDENTIFYING EFFECTIVE INSTRUCTION FOR STUDENTS WITH LD

As pressures have risen to provide visible results for students with LD, so have opportunities to turn to practices with a record of success, particularly in the area of reading. For over three decades, special education researchers have tested multiple academic and social interventions to see "what works" best for students in particular circumstances. A knowledge base is emerging from the results of well-conducted syntheses of this research supporting the use of important instructional components that are predictive of positive outcomes for a range of students with LD (Swanson, 2000b). Several of these syntheses are discussed in this section.

According to Vaughn and Dammann (2001), a systematic body of knowledge provides a stronger foundation for a theory of education than do alternatives to science, such as superstition, folklore, and craft. Educational practices have long been influenced by myths of wisdom and local lore about schooling but neither of these approaches can support widely defensible propositions about how students with LD should be taught. Education has developed over time primarily through the use of *craft*—"a goal-oriented body of knowledge developed through trial and error" (p. 24)—rather than *science*. If protected against myth and folklore, craft can contribute useful techniques that lead to acceptable results. But education as a craft sets no standards for assuring that others can replicate strategies and outcomes. In contrast, education as a *science* sets its sights on developing and distributing information about teaching and learning so that others might challenge the evidence or promote the results.

A. The Convergence of Evidence across Studies

The mission of scientific research in special education is to evaluate the worth of interventions to those who receive them so that practical decisions can be made about which interventions best serve which kinds of learners (Mostert & Kavale, 2001). Analytical narrative syntheses provide useful information by discussing and comparing individual studies in detail so that evidence in the form of patterns and consistencies from data sources can converge across studies. Techniques of meta-analysis synthesize evidence from quantitative research studies, measuring the main effects of interventions across multiple trials and providing "usable knowledge that represents hard quantitative evidence about efficacy and efficiency" (p. 61). According to Rumrill and Cook (2001), "meta-analyses can provide an indepth description of research findings and can also serve an explanatory function, because findings observed across numerous related investigations bring with them a deeper level of understanding that may explain the interrelationships of variables" (p. 155).

In conducting a meta-analysis, researchers derive a numerical indicator of the relative effectiveness of the strategy, or intervention, averaged across all studies. This indicator is called the *effect size* (ES). The ES is a standard score that reflects the mean of one group/condition in relation to another. ESs are expressed as a positive or negative decimal number. A positive ES indicates that the group receiving the intervention performed better than the control groups or comparison condition and a negative ES indicates the opposite. Larger numbers, either positive or negative, indicate greater differences between groups. For example, an intervention that produces an ES of 1.00 indicates that the group receiving the intervention outperformed the others by one standard deviation (Rumrill & Cook, 2001). Concepts of statistical power have also been used to suggest that ESs may be classified as small (0.20), medium (0.50), or large (0.80) (Cohen, 1988). Not only does this approach provide a numerical indicator that represents the strength of a particular intervention, ESs can be compared across different approaches used in special education indicating that some interventions have more power than others (Forness *et al.*, 1997).

The results of meta-analyses have become increasingly accessible to decision-makers; however, the quality of the results depends on the use of rigorous procedures (Mostert, 1996, 2001). Those who synthesize special education research must proceed with great care as they confront the challenges posed by the variety of populations, methods, and outcomes in the studies they review. According to Gersten *et al.* (2000), one of the greatest concerns to researchers who conduct meta-analyses, or any other form of research synthesis, is that the results will be taken as being the final word; but "this is virtually never the case" (p. x), as science builds on earlier work in an ongoing struggle to discern valid trends. Forness *et al.* (1997) remarked that any synthesis or meta-analysis should come with the label: "Caution: Students Are All Different" (p. 8). Mean ESs only provide an estimate of an intervention's relative power. There can be considerable variation in the outcomes for different kinds of students within each meta-analysis. With these caveats in mind, conclusions can be drawn across a body of studies indicating practices that are relatively established as effective and practices that require further research. Educators can then combine these data with their own knowledge of practice to make more rational decisions.

Kavale and Forness (2000) provided numerous examples of meta-analyses relevant to students with LD. Some of these syntheses address settings for instruction, others address the instruction that goes on within those settings. The importance of evaluating for which students and under what circumstances approaches are effective becomes apparent within the larger discussion of where teaching takes place.

B. Knowledge about the Settings for Instruction

The knowledge base supporting the effectiveness of including students with LD in regular classes for instruction is weak and inconclusive. There are few studies empirically documenting outcomes for students with LD in different instructional settings and those that exist fail to present conclusive evidence for preferred service delivery (Crockett & Kauffman, 1998). Hallahan *et al.* (1996) suggested that efficacy research based on instructional settings has done little but demonstrate how difficult it can be to do this type of research. Some studies did not use multiple variables or investigate multiple outcomes for students in their designs. Students and teachers were not randomly assigned, and control groups were established on the assumption that different schools were more alike than not because of their demographic similarities rather than their contextual differences. Some outcome studies have been compromised by the means with which they measured students' gains.

Numerous studies, from the past to the present, have attempted to compare whether regular class placement for instruction yielded better academic achievement, social adjustment, or classroom behavior than resource rooms or self-contained classes. In short, they might have been measuring the outcomes for students who were socially and academically stronger from the beginning with lower performing students in specialized settings. They might also have been misconstruing placement itself as an instructional treatment (Kavale & Forness, 2000).

Data have been equivocal on the worth of inclusive programming and placements for a variety of reasons (Crockett & Kauffman, 1999). Frequently, these reasons have to do with what is actually being measured in various studies: Is increased inclusion being measured or increased student performance? Are positive perceptions being measured or positive results? For which students are the results positive, and under what conditions were the results obtained? In reviewing studies of inclusive practices, decision makers are advised to ask the following questions:

1. *Who* is being studied? Results vary by disability classification as well as by individuals. This variability among groups and individuals demands that detailed information be provided in studies about the abilities of the students and the contextual conditions of the differing instructional placements.
2. *What* is being studied? Results vary with the focus of the study, whether findings address social outcomes, academic outcomes, or both. Results also vary with the interventions employed and the measures used to assess improved performance. Objective measures are preferable to more subjective assessments such as teachers' grades or students' feelings.
3. *Where* is inclusion being studied? The instructional context makes a difference in the outcomes of research on inclusion. Educational programming differs by district, by school, by level of schooling, and so the application of studies across sites and grade levels should be approached with caution. There is little commonality among both students and classroom ecologies at the preschool, elementary, middle, and high school levels.
4. *How* is inclusion being studied? Conditions under which a study is implemented also make a difference. Many studies of instructional inclusion have been conducted under optimal conditions with the support of federal grants and the guidance of university faculty. The exigencies of crowded classes, insufficient funding, and understaffing rarely play a role in the research literature.

In the past decade, syntheses were conducted across several placement studies that had been carefully designed to evaluate inclusive building-level models. These elementary schools were restructured with university or grant support so that students with LD received their instruction in regular classes. Manset and Semmel (1997) compared outcomes across eight of these models that included schoolwide interventions *requiring* specialized instructional programming in regular classes rather than merely *suggesting* changes in practice. They reviewed in detail the program characteristics and quantified outcomes in reading and mathematics for students with mild disabilities, low achievers, and average achievers, in studies published between 1984 and 1994. Common elements across models included elementary classrooms redesigned to more closely resemble special education settings with low student–teacher ratios, intensive basic skills instruction, close monitoring of performance, and opportunities for one-on-one instruction. These model classrooms were redesigned to discourage pull-out instruction, although some students with mild disabilities who were included for instruction during the full school day were often "pulled-aside" (p. 164) to receive additional attention.

Special education students in these schools were expected to achieve better academic outcomes than in traditional pull-out programs because extraordinary resources supported these inclusive efforts. However, only two studies yielded positive findings in reading and only two out of five researchers whose models derived outcomes for mathematics reported a statistically significant impact for their approach. Collectively, conclusions could not be drawn from this narrative synthesis about the superiority of inclusive over pull-out programming. Instruction in inclusive placements was consistently positive for normally achieving students and effective for some students with mild disabilities and low achievers but not for all. Manset and Semmel (1997) pointed out that consultation services did not make a significant impact in these models. "This suggests that returning students with mild disabilities to the mainstream and providing general education teachers with only additional training or consulting may not be sufficient" (p. 175).

Zigmond *et al.* (1995) also compared restructured elementary schools, compiling students' reading gains from three collaborative models of service delivery for students with LD that developed a common database in an effort to enhance information beyond the scope of individual studies. Each was a university initiative that sought to alter learning environments by increasing the capacity of teachers to accommodate learning activities for a wider range of students' needs. In each model, academic achievement was the measure of effectiveness. Because the achievement level of students with LD is typically well below that of average achievers, analysis focused on the size of the reading gains they registered. In order to maintain or reduce the gap, gains needed to match or exceed grade-level peers. Results indicated that after one year of fully integrated educational programs and services, only 37% of the students in these programs made average gains and 63% did not. Even more discouraging was that 40% of the LD sample made gains that were less than half the size of the grade-level averages. According to Zigmond *et al.* (1995), "findings from these three studies suggest that general education settings produce achievement outcomes for students with learning disabilities that are neither desirable nor acceptable" (p. 539).

Vaughn *et al.* (2001) argued that the social dimensions of placement should also be considered because the social problems of many students with LD have consequences for their successful instruction in inclusive settings. In this regard, Elbaum (2002) suggested that placement studies relying on group-comparisons overshadow the importance of individual effects. Elbaum conducted a meta-analysis of 38 empirical studies conducted from 1975 to 1999 comparing the self-concept of groups of students with LD receiving instruction in different educational placements. The studies resulted in a total of 65 different placement comparisons with no systematic association found between self-concept and educational place-ment. Comparative placements in more or less restrictive settings yielded the following mean weighted effect sizes: regular class vs resource room, ES = 0.05; regular class vs self-contained, ES = 0.05; resource room vs self-contained ES = 0.01; self-contained vs special school ES = -0.39; and regular class vs special school, ES = 0.14. In this analysis, a minus score favored the more restrictive setting, indicating that students served in self-contained classes in regular schools had lower self-concepts than students served in special schools.

Contrary to those who assume students feel stigmatized in more restrictive settings, "students with LD placed in regular classrooms for all their instruc-tion did not, overall, exhibit higher self-concept than students placed in either part-time or full-time special education classrooms" (Elbaum, 2002, p. 222). Elbaum emphasized, however, that this absence of reliable associ-ation between placement and self-concept represents the collective results for *groups* of students with LD; it does not mean that instructional placement is irrelevant to the self-concept of *individual* students. "Indeed, individual students may be profoundly affected by a placement that jeopardizes their self-esteem" (p. 222), meaning placement in either regular or special settings. For Elbaum, the greatest lesson from this synthesis is that further attempts to investigate issues of instructional settings using group-comparison designs are not likely to be very informative. Instead, she recommended designs that examine the variation of individual responses to different placements, relat-ing this variation "to academic and socio-emotional characteristics of indi-vidual students, on the one hand, and characteristics of different educational contexts, on the other" (p. 223).

In summary, placement decisions are complex and the knowledge base supporting them is peppered with problems. According to Swanson (2000a), if intervention research could provide decision makers with systematic knowledge about the outcomes of inclusive schooling, the controversy surrounding student placements might be avoided. However, unless it can be shown that all students with LD do not benefit from separate programs, Swanson argued that the full continuum of alternative placements should be made available. To do otherwise would jeopardize their educational opportunity. Swanson's perspective supports service-delivery policies less obsessed with placement and more concerned with maximizing gains in achievement by minimizing errors in instruction.

C. Knowledge about Instruction within Settings

Placing emphasis on teaching shifts the essential question from *where* instruction should occur to *what kind* of instructional interventions need to occur within settings for students to be successful. Kavale and Forness (2000) addressed this emphasis by distinguishing interventions designed to build skills that supposedly underlie academic learning from those that help students to learn new knowledge by adapting and modifying instructional methods. Their meta-analytic data favored the latter over the former interventions, which included the appealing but disappointing strategies of Perceptual Motor-Training (ES = 0.08), and Modality-Matched Instruction (ES = 0.14), popularly known as teaching to learning styles. (See Kavale & Forness for an in-depth discussion of these data.)

Instructional intervention research over time reflects different conceptualizations of the nature of special education, depending on whether emphasis was placed on *special* or on *education*. In the past 20 years, research has moved away from specialized interventions based on cognitive processes toward investigations of academic domains that influence curriculum and instruction. Kavale and Forness (2000) stressed the primary importance of reading instruction to students with LD, providing examples of meta-analyses that indicate powerful effects for strategies including mnemonic instruction (ES = 1.62), reading comprehension (ES = 1.06), and Direct Instruction (ES = 0.84). Results culled from these syntheses and meta-analyses provide much information relevant to effective school-based instruction and service delivery for students with LD. For Vaughn *et al.* (2000), "these findings represent giant steps forward from the 'underlying process approaches' that characterized early research and conceptualizations in the field" (p. 110).

D. Key Findings from Intervention Research

Swanson, with his colleagues, identified more than 3000 published and unpublished intervention research studies addressing learning disabilities from the inception of the field in 1963 until 1997. From this corpus, 180 studies provided the base for subsequent meta-analyses (Swanson, 2000b; Swanson & Hoskyn, 1998) determining that a combined model of direct instruction and strategy instruction is effective for remediating LD, when compared with other instructional models. Vaughn *et al.* (2000) referred to these meta-analyses in identifying three factors critical for teachers to employ in delivering effective instruction to students with LD:

1. Carefully control the difficulty of tasks by sequencing examples and problems to assure that students maintain high levels of success.
2. Teach students with LD in small, flexible, interactive grouping arrangements of six or fewer students.
3. Build students' skills in directed response questioning.

Directed response questioning procedures teach students to generate questions while reading their assignments or working on mathematical problems. These procedures promote *thinking aloud* and are critical features of teaching approaches that embrace strategy instruction as well as direct instruction. Regardless of the domain being addressed, these three components—small, interactive groups, directed questioning, and carefully controlled task difficulty—"have the potential to work in concert to influence, to the largest degree possible, student learning and students' independent functioning" (p. 101).

With regard to teaching reading to students with LD, Vaughn *et al.* (2000) derived generalizable principles of instruction from intervention research syntheses addressing (a) higher-order processing and problem-solving, (b) reading comprehension, (c) written expression, and (d) grouping practices associated with improved outcomes in reading for students with LD. The five principles proposed by Vaughn *et al.* are summarized below and illustrate that a knowledge base of interventions supporting positive outcomes for students with LD, as well as higher-achieving students, is emerging to guide decisions:

1. *Effective instructional approaches for students with LD consist of visible and explicit components.* Students benefit when teachers identify the elements to be learned and demonstrate them with examples.
2. *Effective instructional practices for students with LD are based on the following knowledge*:
   (a) *Procedures and strategies strengthen higher-order thinking and teach students to develop action plans to guide their learning activities.* Students should be taught overtly how to apply a particular strategy and they should have multiple opportunities to practice the strategy and receive feedback before they are expected to use it on their own

(b) *Small, interactive groups and pairs that facilitate interaction between teacher and student and between students in the form of peer tutoring have been associated with improved outcomes in reading and writing for all students, especially students with disabilities when they serve in the role of tutor.* These small groupings are associated with increased outcomes in self-concept as well as academic gains.

(c) *Interactive dialogue between teacher and student and between students and proficient peers is associated with improved outcomes for students in reading and writing.* Teachers and other students can provide ongoing and systematic feedback to address misunderstandings or revise written work.

3. *Critical variables that influence learning outcomes include task difficulty, task persistence, and motivation to learn.* Students are more motivated to persist when they work on meaningful tasks that challenge them but are not beyond their reach. Those students who meet with some success in school are more likely to engage in educational or work experiences following school.

4. *Effective interventions in reading and writing for students with LD include systematic skill building as well as the development of strategies that address skills and knowledge more broadly.* Improving outcomes in reading and writing for students with LD depends on instruction in the basic and fundamental elements of reading and writing, such as sounding out words or spelling with accuracy.

5. *Effective interventions for students with LD have educational benefits for all learners.* "In all cases where interventions have demonstrated significant positive effects for students with LD, they have resulted in at least as high (and most often higher) effect sizes for all other students in the class, including average and high-achieving students" (p. 108).

Vaughn *et al.* (2000) pointed out that none of these instructional principles is revolutionary and that each holds promise for higher-achieving students. Nonetheless, despite the evidence supporting their effectiveness for a wide range of learners, "these principles are too rarely implemented in classrooms" (p. 111). Heward (2003) characterized this disjuncture between what is known about the science of schooling for students with disabilities and what is practiced in classrooms as a "distressing gap" (p. 188), a gap that Carnine (1997) sought to reduce by making the results of research more trustworthy, useable, and accessible to teachers. Neglecting to use these principles when teaching students with LD in general education classrooms frequently results in instruction that does not provide adequate opportunities to apply knowledge and to practice skills for students who are struggling to learn.

III. ARE STUDENTS WITH LD RECEIVING
SPECIALIZED INSTRUCTION DESIGNED TO BE
EFFECTIVE?

Studies of elementary and secondary schools provide clear descriptions of what special education is like for students with LD and their teachers in the context of inclusive school reforms and heightened accountability. These snapshots illustrate classroom ecologies that influence the delivery of effective instruction, such as student-teacher interactions, the organization of curriculum and instruction, and the management of the learning environment (Speece & Keogh, 1996).

As part of a multi-year research project, Mastropieri and Scruggs (2001) studied attributes of successful inclusive classrooms, identifying seven variables across elementary and secondary grade levels and types of disabilities that appeared to be most meaningful: (a) support from administrators; (b) support from special education personnel, including help with instructional accommodations, co-teaching, and paraprofessionals; (c) an accepting and positive classroom atmosphere; (d) appropriate curriculum delivered with concrete examples, frequent explanations, and practical activities; (e) effective general teaching skills; (f) peer assistance; and (g) disability-specific teaching skills targeting the special learning needs of individuals with exceptionalities (p. 266). These attributes are frequently challenged by the complexities of service delivery, particularly in middle and high school classrooms. Service delivery for students with LD varies across different levels of schooling, adjusting to the developmentally different characteristics of learners and the environments in which they receive their instruction. In this discussion, consideration is given first to how teachers are using scientific evidence to provide specialized instruction designed to be effective for students with LD in the context of elementary schools.

A. The Science of Schooling for Elementary Students with LD

Service delivery for students with LD has been studied most frequently on the elementary level and much of what has been written suggests that instructional components, rather than educational settings, are more relevant to student success. In what were among the first descriptive case studies of full inclusion for students with LD, Baker and Zigmond (1995) examined whether restructured elementary schools provided opportunities for students to learn and for their teachers to provide them with intensive special education in regular classes. These studies have been described in detail elsewhere (see Crockett & Kauffman, 1998) but they are mentioned here because of their importance. These cases illustrated how traditional components of special education, such as "specially designed curriculum, specialized teaching methods, specially trained teachers, and facilitative settings" (Scruggs & Mastropieri, 1995, p. 232), were sacrificed for the unproven benefits of educating students in regular classes. Although Baker's and Zigmond's observations predated public policies that focus contemporary teachers on results, evidence from more recent studies suggests that the meaning and practice of inclusion for elementary students with LD has not changed much in the past decade.

1. Unrealistic Expectations and Insufficient Support

In recent years, the delivery of inclusive instruction has been studied by examining attitudes toward students with disabilities and expectations for those who teach them. According to Cook (2001), the primary responsibility for instruction and educational outcomes for students with LD has increasingly been transferred to general educators. Unlike students with severe disabilities whose differences are extremely atypical, students with LD are assumed to lack meaningful differences from their nondisabled peers. As a result, they are often ignored in regular classes and held to typical and unadjusted group norms. Cook noted the reality that teachers often reject or are indifferent to students with less visible disabilities who demonstrate attitudes and behaviors that interfere with their instruction, suggesting that their inclusion in regular classes should not be a foregone conclusion. He also recommended that "schools emphasize, rather than downplay, the disability status and unique characteristics and needs of students with hidden disabilities when training and preparing general educators for inclusion. Fostering appropriate recognition of disabilities may be particularly imperative in the current environment of 'high stakes' testing" (p. 211). Given the current demands for academic excellence, general educators are less likely to tolerate atypical performance and behavior, even in elementary schools.

First-year special education teachers face special challenges in negotiating their roles alongside their general education colleagues. Some of their responsibilities are written in policies while others—such as fostering the recognition of disabilities—are hidden in the folklore of the workplace. Mastropieri (2001) remarked how personnel problems can occur when administrators fail to recognize differences among students whose disabilities mildly or severely affect their learning. For example, as some districts increase their use of inclusive education models, they are simultaneously raising expectations "for more special education teachers to work with any student with disabilities in any setting" (p. 72). In addition, new teachers frequently find that resources are inadequate to purchase research-based materials and scheduling is built around convenience rather than maximizing instructional time. Mastropieri suggested that problems with scheduling and time "may well be increasing as teachers are stretched to meet standards of learning for competency tests" (p. 73). Faced with unrealistic expectations and insufficient support, success for novice special educators seems to rely on personal dedication and the motivation to be successful in working with students who are difficult to teach. Veteran teachers as well as novices are facing similar challenges in serving students with LD in regular classes without the opportunities to employ instructional principles supported by research.

2. Changing Roles and Responsibilities

In order to clarify the emerging role of the LD inclusion teacher, Klingner and Vaughn (2002) chronicled the experiences of a veteran special educator who made the transition from teaching in resource settings to inclusive elementary classrooms. In this urban school, special education instruction was provided within regular classes and called for this teacher, as an inclusion specialist, to use the following blend of knowledge, skills, and dispositions:

> (a) special education assessment and intervention skills, (b) the ability to creatively adapt and accommodate instructional lessons and assignments to meet the needs of students with LD in a whole-class setting, (c) an understanding of the general education curriculum and goals, (d) the ability to collaborate and co-plan with general education teachers, and (e) commitment and dedica- tion. (p. 29)

According to Klingner and Vaughn, "the extent to which co-teaching is acceptable to teachers is highly relevant and influences their success and satisfaction with their roles in an inclusion model" (p. 29).

Co-teaching, with the concomitant responsibility to adjust to the person- alities and teaching styles of others, was the most obvious difference between teaching in an inclusive classroom or in a separate setting. In the inclusive classroom, individualized plans could be easily eclipsed by curricular imperatives. For example, a resource room teacher might ask, "What is the best way to teach the objectives listed on the IEP and meet this student's individual needs?" (Klingner & Vaughn, 2002, p. 29). The inclusion special- ist, however, must involve the co-teacher in asking, "What is the best way to teach the objectives listed on the IEP and at the same time help the student fit in and be successful in the GE [general education] classroom" (p. 29). In this inclusive setting, the standard curriculum and the goals of the regular classroom largely drove instructional decisions. Despite efforts to provide appropriate instruction within the regular class, Joyce—the veteran special educator—and her co-teachers observed that the lowest-performing students with LD were not receiving sufficient instruction at their level.

In their case studies, Baker and Zigmond (1995) determined that inclusion teachers allowed concerns for the group to eclipse concern for individual students. In this case, Klingner and Vaughn (2002) reported that Joyce kept her focus on the needs of her individual students with LD but that she did so with great difficulty and much effort. Over 7 years, from her initiation as an inclusion teacher to her maturity as an inclusion specialist, Joyce witnessed the deterioration of funds and formalized supports for co-planning. What had begun in this school as a structured process for supporting students with multiple needs in regular classrooms had, within several years, withered into a casual, hit-or-miss, occurrence. This case study captures the confusion of roles among educators and illustrates how pressures for *schools* to do well on standardized tests can displace individually crafted goals that target success for *students* with LD. Ironically, success for these students, especially for those with severe learning needs, depends on the specialized attention too frequently overlooked.

3. Non-Specific IEPs

The delivery of specialized instruction is weakened when IEPs are driven by programmatic goals rather than individual needs. IEPs written by teachers in inclusive elementary programs have been described as relying on more general descriptions of students rather than on specific data regarding such skills as decoding, reading comprehension, and sight word recognition. Espin *et al.* (1998) came to this conclusion after reviewing 108 IEPs of students with mild disabilities (50 in resource settings and 58 in inclusive settings) in grades 1 through 6. The IEPs for students in inclusive settings reflected greater concern with their progress in the general education curriculum and with how they differed in performance from their average-achieving peers. In contrast, the IEPs for students in resource settings were individually tailored to their needs through "a greater variety of goals and more specific test information about the array of skills currently possessed by those students" (p. 171). Resource room IEPs also indicated that more time was allocated for specialized services than in inclusive settings and more long-range goals were set for students to achieve, even though these groups of students were equal in ability.

These findings are consistent with other studies reporting that teachers in resource programs utilize more, and more specific, sources of data in planning, implementing, and evaluating ongoing reading instruction than do their colleagues in inclusive programs. In planning reading instruction, special educators in inclusive programs seemed to rely more on tools used by general educators, such as basal series tests and informal reading inventories. Espin *et al.* (1998) concluded that "services received by students in resource programs are more closely adjusted to their level of need than are services for students in inclusive programs" (p. 172), except in the area of reading. Students whose IEPs reflected the highest amount of service time for reading had greater exposure to reading instruction in inclusive settings. It is likely that these students received a double-dose of reading, both in the regular class and in a pull-out setting. If individual students with LD had been able to benefit from the in-class reading instruction, this might have been an important matter to consider in planning their service delivery. However, there is increasing evidence to suggest that students with severe LD need more intensive instruction than can be provided even within enhanced inclusive classrooms.

4. Mixed Outcomes of Responsible Inclusion

Few studies explore academic outcomes for students across a spectrum of abilities within inclusive classes and Klingner et al. (1998) stressed the importance of such research. Reading was their focus as they described the academic outcomes for students in grades 3 through 6 who were high-achievers, low to average-achievers, and students with LD. The elementary school they attended provided students with LD instruction in the regular classroom with co-teaching for part of the school day. The model implemented at this school was described as being "responsible" inclusion because teachers volunteered to participate, adequate resources were provided including extra computers and paraprofessional assistance, the model was developed at the school level, a continuum of services was maintained, and students' IEPs were regularly monitored and modified. Every teacher who participated in the study received intensive year-long professional development on improving student outcomes in literacy. This school's stakeholders made extraordinary efforts over a 4-year period to transform their delivery system from relying on resource support to more inclusive instruction. As a result of these extensive efforts, however, outcomes for students were variable: "Some students with LD made considerable gains in reading over one school year, many made modest gains, and some made few or no gains" (p. 158). A subset of low-to-average readers similarly did not improve significantly over the school year, suggesting that average students might get lost and not progress in classes with students with disabilities. However, high-achieving students all made reading gains that exceeded the standard error of measurement for their school and reported that they liked their class assignment, helping lower-performing students, and having an additional teacher in the room for part of the day.

Over the school year, 20% of the students with LD did not improve their scores in reading—and these were not the lowest readers in the school. These students were nonreaders or they were reading at the primer level and they made no progress as a group, despite their participation in a "responsible" inclusion program that received considerable support. According to Klingner *et al.* (1998), one explanation was that the literature-based reading instruction used in inclusive classrooms and the techniques taught to teachers were not developed specifically for students with severe reading disabilities. Another explanation pointed to accumulating evidence supporting the notion that a small subgroup of students have severe difficulties learning to read and are often resistant even to the most scientifically based instruction. Klingner *et al.* were unequivocal in their conclusion that full-time, well-funded placements in regular classes with in-class special education support are not sufficient in meeting the needs of learners with severe reading problems. "They require combined services that include in-class support and daily intensive, one-on-one instruction from highly trained personnel. This is an expensive proposition but appears to be the only solution that will yield growth in reading for students with severe reading disabilities" (p. 159).

5. Reflections on Service Delivery at the Elementary Level

Public opinion might contend that students with LD benefit equally from instruction in inclusive classes or resource rooms, but evidence accumulated over the past two decades suggests that many students with LD experience academic difficulty in full-time placements in general education classrooms—even classrooms fortified to support their success. More information is needed about the intra- and inter-individual variations in students with LD, both those who fail and those who succeed in inclusive settings, and about the ecological components that most effectively support their special education instruction.

B. The Science of Schooling for Secondary Students with LD

The ecologies of secondary classrooms pose special considerations for teachers of students with LD "including an emphasis on higher level content knowledge, independent study skills, and the overall pace of general education classroom instruction" (Mastropieri & Scruggs, 2001, p. 266). In addition, the ramifications of high stakes testing often determine whether a student ultimately receives a high school diploma, increasing the pressure to succeed on both students with LD and on those who teach them. Although inclusion in regular classes has the potential to extend social networks for students with LD and to ensure their access to the general education curriculum, this potential is threatened by a scarce knowledge base addressing effective instruction in secondary inclusive classrooms.

Successful high school completion depends on mastering a wide range of content areas. Many students with LD find mastery to be elusive because of their own weak skills and the expertise or expectations of their teachers.

Secondary special educators rarely have expertise that extends across the content areas, and secondary general educators usually have high expectations for students to possess proficient study skills and prerequisite content knowledge (Mastropieri & Scruggs, 2001). Secondary teachers may also feel less sanguine toward inclusive instruction than elementary teachers do because inclusion competes with demands to cover the curricular content in one year's time and to deliver instruction at a rapid pace. For these and other reasons, secondary inclusion efforts are challenged by less than positive attitudes and specially designed instruction is often overlooked.

1. Lack of Support for Struggling Readers

There is particular urgency to the delivery of special education to secondary students with reading disabilities who spend the majority of their day in general education content area classes that emphasize "reading to learn" the curriculum. Recent research examining school-based models for middle school reading instruction suggests that very intensive and highly structured reading programs can make a difference in performance for students with a record of reading failure. However, high-quality intervention programs in reading are rarely in place for struggling adolescent readers, although many students begin middle school unable to read fluently or to learn from text (McCray et al., 2001). Instead, intensive reading instruction is often eclipsed by special education service delivery that favors tutoring students in general curricular content so that they might "survive" in the middle school inclusive classroom.

Bryant et al. (2001) described general educators in middle school inclusive classrooms who were overwhelmed with the diverse learning needs of students and reliant on special educators to help them meet the needs of struggling readers. Unfortunately, the special educators' time was distributed across multiple classrooms, leaving low-performing readers to work independently and content area teachers to work with few options to assist them in meeting the needs of students with LD as they prepared for high-stakes tests. In middle schools, Bryant et al. stressed the importance of interventions including reading strategy instruction, progress monitoring, and flexible grouping "because there will be a small group of students with reading disabilities severe enough to warrant more intensive, adapted instruction (e.g., smaller groupings, more instructional time, modified materials)" (p. 263).

2. Mixed Outcomes for Intervention Strategies in the Content Areas

Intervention strategies for secondary students with LD parallel those found useful for elementary students with LD but require adaptations to reflect differences in instructional content and context. Mastropieri and Scruggs (2001) reviewed the effectiveness of several interventions frequently used to promote successful inclusive teaching of content on the secondary level. Several studies conducted by Deshler, Schumaker and colleagues demonstrated that the effects of strategy instruction, an approach with a record of success in special education settings, were less reliable when used to teach science and social studies in secondary inclusive classrooms. Students with LD did not statistically outperform their control counterparts and one explanation hinged on the low levels of teacher implementation in inclusive classes compared with previous research in special education settings. Secondary teachers reported that pressures to cover content overpowered the process of implementing strategy instruction with more intensity.

Peer tutoring interventions implemented in secondary content area classrooms resulted in mixed outcomes for students with LD, most likely because of ecological factors related to social interactions, curriculum and instruction, and classroom management (Mastropieri & Scruggs, 2001). Several studies demonstrated that tutoring in world history was successful in helping students with disabilities acquire unfamiliar vocabulary and summarize concepts using drill and practice techniques and strategy-based tutoring. However, there were no significant differences observed in their oral reading fluency, although students with disabilities involved in strategy-based tutoring spent significantly more time in oral reading than did traditionally instructed students.

Outcomes of peer tutoring were mixed for students with disabilities in algebra classes and English classes. With regard to algebra, tutoring was not successful for middle school students with LD. Although they enjoyed the experience and thought it was helpful, these students demonstrated no significant differences in their performance from students who were taught traditionally. Teachers were generally positive about classwide peer-tutoring, but found it exhausting to implement. In English literature classes, tutoring was successful for one group of middle school students with disabilities but failed to demonstrate positive results for high school students. Mastropieri and Scruggs (2001) remarked on the insufficiency of research guiding inclusive secondary English instruction and noted how some English teachers viewed the implementation of peer-tutoring procedures and the management of their delivery as a waste of teaching time. Co-teaching relationships may also have interfered with the fruitful implementation of peer tutoring.

Inclusive instruction at the secondary level most frequently relies on practices of co-teaching, but the popularity of this approach overshadows its credibility as a reliable intervention because systematic research on its effects is scarce (Mastropieri & Scruggs, 2001). As of the year 2000, Weiss and Brigham identified more than 700 studies describing co-teaching, but only 23 providing evaluative data. Few of these studies addressed outcomes for secondary students with LD; in some studies, co-teaching resulted in acceptable outcomes for these students but in others the results were less clear. Mastropieri and Scruggs concluded that co-teaching is "an important element of inclusive secondary classrooms. However, it should incorporate instruction in effective learning strategies" (p. 271). This caveat is important because co-teaching alters customary instructional behaviors for both partners, enhancing the use of some research-validated practices and diminishing others (Klingner & Vaughn, 2002; Weiss & Lloyd, 2002).

3. Implications of Co-Teaching for Secondary Students with LD

The cost of co-teaching as a secondary service delivery model bears close scrutiny in assessing opportunities for students with LD to learn and for special educators to provide specially designed instruction. According to detailed descriptions derived from interviews and multiple observations conducted by Weiss and Lloyd (2002), co-teaching differentiated the roles and instructional actions of experienced and well-qualified secondary special educators in co-taught and special education classrooms. These special educators taught differently depending on whether they were co-teaching in classrooms that averaged 4 students with disabilities and 17 nondisabled students, or solo teaching math, English, and study skills to an average of 7 students in resource classrooms. In co-taught classes, they assumed various roles, including monitoring behavior rather than delivering instruction. Some assumed the responsibility of teaching the same content in separate classrooms "because the students with special needs required greater academic modification than was available in the general education classroom" (Weiss & Lloyd, 2002, p. 64). They also assumed a third role by providing instruction to the whole class in a segment of the general curriculum. Only one special educator, at the middle school level, assumed a fourth role by working as part of a teaching team, taking turns with general educators in providing instruction and monitoring students in content area classrooms.

Scheduling was a constraint to co-teaching in regular classes. Despite the use of block scheduling with 90-minute classes, three special educators were split between classes and could only participate in co-teaching for one-half of the class period. Consequently, they had little time "to deliver, modify, or specialize instruction. What the teachers could not do in the co-taught classroom they tried to make up for in the special education classroom" (p. 67), forgoing specialized instruction in another content area so that students could study for tests or complete assignments. When they assumed the role of sole instructor in special settings, these special educators took charge of "controlling instruction, assessment, and feedback" (Weiss & Lloyd, 2002, p. 65). Each teacher reported that the instruction provided in the resource room setting addressed content at a lower level, "broken down into smaller units, delivered at a slower pace, and individualized more than in the general education classroom" (p. 65). Although there were similarities in instructional actions taken within co-taught and special education classes, "teachers' additional instructional actions included more specific explanations, questions, help, and feedback" (p. 66).

These special educators felt pressure to write IEPs prescribing co-teaching at the secondary level because of state-mandated diploma requirements and high-stakes tests. As a result, the specialized support their students needed to succeed was less available to them. In this school system, poorly conceived staff development might have been partially to blame as district administrators arranged for elementary co-teachers to provide training for teachers at all grade levels without specifically addressing secondary school issues and practices. Neither special educators nor administrators in this study reflected a clear understanding of how co-teaching was to be used to deliver specially designed instruction: "We saw little use of special educators' expertise in the co-taught situation. Overall, co-teaching . . . was implemented to get students with disabilities into the general education curriculum without much thought of how or how well" (Weiss & Lloyd, 2002, p. 68).

According to Weiss and Lloyd (2002), co-teaching should not be viewed as the appropriate service-delivery model in all cases. Before co-teaching is implemented, the needs for implementing this model and the expectations for its success should be carefully articulated. Weiss and Lloyd suggested these guiding questions: "(a) What types of instruction do the students need? (b) how can the special educator help the general educator deliver that instruction? (c) what role should the special educator take? and (d) how will the school and the teachers evaluate whether the program is effective?" (p. 68). The implications of co-teaching for quality working conditions should also be considered. As school systems struggle to attract and retain special educators, attention needs to be paid to the costs of supporting co-teaching through sufficient resources, time, and training. Teachers with graduate degrees are not likely to stay in positions where they perform the work of paraprofessionals and their specialized training is overlooked.

4. Reflections on Service Delivery at the Secondary Level

These studies of special education delivery for students with LD describe complexities that help to explain why inclusive interventions on the secondary level, even strategies incorporating validated principles of instruction, might produce mixed results. Accumulating evidence from the science of secondary schooling reflects general educators' perceptions that implementing inclusive procedures requires undue costs of time and effort and interferes with the extensive content coverage required of standards-based reforms. With regard to providing instruction to secondary students with LD, there is much to be learned about cultivating the use of research-based practices and about teaching the general education curriculum effectively in inclusive as well as specialized settings.

In some of these elementary and secondary schools, sound practices were implemented but with disappointing results. In others, special education service delivery seemed to be proceeding casually in meeting its statutory commitments and heedlessly in ignoring the science of schooling. If most students with LD need small, interactive groups, directed questioning, and carefully controlled task difficulty to be successful regardless of instructional domain, then it appeared from some cases that students were not consistently getting what they needed across the grades. According to Heward (2003), "the biggest reason we do not teach more children with disabilities better than we do is not because we do not know enough but because we do not teach them as well as we know how" (p. 201).

IV. RECOMMENDATIONS FOR SERVICE DELIVERY THAT LINKS PRACTICE WITH RESEARCH

Developing and sustaining the use of classroom practices that are based in the science of schooling is far more complicated than announcing the existence of a knowledge base and requiring teachers to use it (Gersten *et al.*, 2000). Only recently has special education research begun to address these important issues and Gersten *et al.* noted that there is much to be understood about "the constellation of factors" (p. 445) that enhance or discourage the sustained use of desirable practices. Some of these factors are related to the organization of schools. Most of what is known about sustainability can be attributed to studies exploring how changes in practices were incorporated into daily use across districts, schools, and classrooms for students at risk for school failure. These studies rendered enough useful information related to teacher beliefs and organizational practices for Gersten *et al.* to offer decision-makers a set of guidelines for professional development efforts that address sustainability. However, more empirical research is needed to develop a better understanding about sustainability as it applies to teachers working with students with disabilities.

As expectations for the increased performance of students with LD mount and the results of their assessments are made public, educators responsible for service delivery decisions have greater reasons for making the science of schooling a more visible component of public education. What follows are four recommendations for service delivery that link school practice to educational research: (a) turn to science as the best trick we know for solving educational problems; (b) specify clearly what we are hoping to achieve; (c) rely on instruction as the best tool we have for improving student performance; and (d) cultivate—and keep—competent and caring personnel.

A. Turn to Science as the Best Trick We Know for Solving Educational Problems

Educational decision-makers must ensure the use of teaching methods that are most effective because the results have real consequences for students with LD. According to Kauffman (2002), "most of us want and expect those who build or fix cars and airplanes, practice medicine, build houses, and so on to use scientific information in their practices. We should expect no less of educators" (p. 232). In seeking scientific guidance, decision-makers are encouraged to turn first to analytical narrative syntheses and meta-analyses of research to gather information across a broad knowledge base. Research employing either quantitative or qualitative methods can provide scientific data as long as procedures for conducting the study and interpreting and disseminating the results have been followed with rigorous precision (Vaughn & Damman, 2001). Methodology matters not because of a philosophical preference but because of what the data allow the research to say about the efficacy and relevance of instructional practices (Feuer *et al.*, Towne, & Shavelson, 2002; Mostert & Kavale, 2001). According to Gersten (2001), "good descriptive research helps *elucidate* problems or issues, which can then be more effectively studied for solutions" (p. 46).

B. Specify Clearly What We Are Hoping to Achieve

According to Bateman (1992), the key for educators in using scientific and systematic procedures effectively is to "specify clearly what it is we are hoping to achieve" (p. 2). For special educators, this means specifying clearly what we hope to achieve with whom and under what circumstances we hope to achieve it. For example, when educators co-teach students with LD in inclusive classrooms, what are they hoping to achieve: (a) are they hoping to provide these students with access to the general education curriculum without doing harm to their academic achievement or (b) are they hoping that they will achieve greater academic gains than they traditionally achieved in resource or separate programs (Zigmond & Magiera, 2002)? These are very different goals and the science of schooling suggests that co-teaching has yet to demonstrate its power as a useful tool in helping teachers to achieve the second goal.

With regard to addressing student achievement, educational decision-makers need to understand the relationship between an *adequate* general education as defined by their locality and an *appropriate* special education as prescribed for each student with LD. Special education law has codified hopes for achievement by specifying clearly that every child with LD is entitled to an appropriate education, based on his unique educational needs, that emphasizes specialized instruction and that prepares him for independent living and employment. In the current reform context, the personalized standard of an individually appropriate education might be conceived as the *value-added* that makes achievement at locally defined levels of performance possible for some students with LD.

C. Rely on Instruction as the Best Tool We Have for Improving Student Performance

Pedagogical decision-making holds the greatest promise of rebutting presumptions about individual students with LD and preventing failure for those students who are falling behind (Crockett, 2001a). Educational decision-makers can become advocates for sound instruction, wherever it occurs, by drawing on the emerging scientific knowledge base that supports effective instruction for students with LD. They can also ensure that students who fall at the far end of the distribution—those whose learning problems are severe—receive intensive support. Gallagher (1999) emphasized that these students require "different strategies of treatment or special education" (p. 250), making attempts to fully include them in regular classes unrealistic. Learning disabilities are chronic conditions that need continuous attention. For many students with LD, "it is not a matter of shaking hands at the schoolhouse door and wishing them well; a failure to follow through with adult services runs the risk of those students losing much of the gains that they made in their school programs" (p. 250).

Educational decision-makers should be aware that generic "learning support programs" (Danielson, 2002) have popular appeal in their goal "to extend extra help to any student who needs it, no questions asked" (p. 100). But a closer look reveals that sometimes no consideration is given to the profound impact of severe LD: "Learning support programs reflect a school's commitment to the successful learning of all students, as well as the belief that all students are natural learners—that any difficulties they encounter are probably short-term and can be addressed with little fanfare" (p. 100). Such rhetoric ignores the science of schooling for students with LD.

Educational decision-makers should also be mindful that the popular myth of educational homogeneity, or believing that good instruction makes students more uniform in their performance, is a fundamentally flawed assumption (Kauffman, 2002). Setting a basic floor of achievement and believing that all students will reach it is a central hope of the standards movement and implicit in the phrase "no child left behind." But Kauffman pointed out the hard evidence that "education that does not stifle the progress of the fastest learners—education that encourages each student, whether fast or slow, to learn as fast and as much as possible—will inevitably have the effect of increasing the differences among students" (p. 131). Equalizing the nation's public through education might be a politically advantageous goal, but it is scientifically impossible. "Understanding why education does not homogenize the population unless it hampers the achievement of the best students or excludes the low achievers may require consideration of normal and skewed statistical distributions" (p. 131), a core component of the science of schooling.

D. Cultivate—and Keep—Competent and Caring Personnel

As a final recommendation, educational decision-makers need to be concerned with two interrelated issues to ensure the integrity of their special education service delivery: (a) ensuring that students with LD get what they need to learn and (b) ensuring that their teachers receive the support they require to do their jobs—and to stay with them. This requires commitment to cultivate competent and concerned professionals who use evidence-based practices with their students and to create positive conditions for these special educators at work.

According to Billingsley (2002b), "one of the most important challenges for the field of special education is to develop a qualified workforce and to create work environments that sustain special educators' involvement and commitment" (p. 1). Over a decade of research suggests that educational decision-makers can address these challenges by hiring certified teachers and using salary and bonus incentives; developing support programs specifically for new special educators; creating positive work environments and increasing administrative support; structuring teachers' roles so that they can focus on their students' learning; and encouraging professional development that focuses on teacher effectiveness. Finally, decision-makers can provide programs to help special education teachers mediate their work-related stress (Billingsley, 2002a). Each of these actions addresses the development of instructional capacity and if teaching is to be considered as desirable and meaningful work, they must be addressed in the context of educational reform. Schools must become hospitable places for adults to work and to develop professionally.

For Elmore (2002), "the brutal irony of our present circumstance is that schools are hostile and inhospitable places for learning. They are hostile to the learning of adults and, because of this, they are necessarily hostile to the learning of students" (p. 2). In his view, something has to change for the concept of accountability to be viewed as an opportunity for the reciprocal development of public schools and the professional growth of educators. That means that if the public wants more accountability for performance results, it has to make financial investments in the knowledge and skills of educators. If educators want "legitimacy, purpose, and credibility for their work" (p. 3), they have to learn to do their work differently and more effectively. This is the price of accountability, said Elmore, and the hope of strengthening public education: "Want to improve schools? Invest in the people who work in them" (p. 1). It might also be said: Want to improve student performance? Invest in the science of schooling with its unglamorous and incremental contributions to our knowledge of how children learn best.

References

Baker, J. M., & Zigmond, N. (1995). The meaning and practice of inclusion for students with learning disabilities: Themes and implications from the five cases. *The Journal of Special Education*, **29**, 163–180.

Bateman, B. D. (1992). *The essentials of teaching*. Creswell, OR: Otter Ink.

Bateman, B. D., & Linden, M. A. (1998). *Better IEPs: How to develop legally correct and educationally useful programs*. Longmont, CO: Sopris West.

Bhat, P., Rapport, M. J., & Griffin, C. (2000). A legal perspective on the use of specific reading methods for students with learning disabilities. *Learning Disabilities Quarterly*, **23**, 283–297.

Billingsley, B. S. (2002a). Improving special education teacher retention: Implications from a decade of research. *Journal of Special Education Leadership*, **15**, 60–66.

Billingsley, B. S. (2002b). *Special education teacher retention and attrition: A critical analysis of the literature*. Gainesville, FL: University of Florida, Center on Personnel Studies in Special Education.

Bryant, D. P., Linan-Thompson, S., Ugel, N., Hamff, A., & Hougen, M. (2001). The effects of professional development for middle school general and special education teachers on implementation of reading strategies in inclusive content area classes. *Learning Disabilities Quarterly*, **24**, 251–264.

Carnine, D. (1997). Bridging the research-to-practice gap. *Exceptional Children*, **63**, 513–521.

Casareno, A. (2002). Ed Ellis: Working to improve education for adolescents with learning disabilities. *Intervention in School and Clinic*, **37**, 292–297.

Council for Exceptional Children. (2000). *Bright futures for exceptional learners: An action agenda to achieve quality conditions for teaching and learning*. Reston, VA: Author.

Cohen, J. (1988). *Statistical power analysis for the behavioral sciences* (2nd ed.). Hillsdale, NJ: Erlbaum.

Cook, B. G. (2001). A comparison of teachers' attitudes toward their included students with mild and severe disabilities. *The Journal of Special Education*, **34**, 203–213.

Crockett, J. B. (2001a). Beyond inclusion: Preventing disabilities from handicapping the futures of our children. In T. O'Brien (ed.), *Enabling inclusion: Blue skies or dark clouds?* (pp. 81–98) London, UK: The Stationary Office.

Crockett, J. B. (2001b). The meaning of science and empirical rigor in the social sciences [Special issue]. *Behavioral Disorders*, **27**, (1).

Crockett, J. B. (2002). Special education's role in preparing responsive leaders for inclusive schools. *Remedial and Special Education*, **23**, 157–168.

Crockett, J. B. & Kauffman, J. M. (1998). Classrooms for students with learning disabilities: Realities, dilemmas, and recommendations for service delivery. In

B. Y. L. Wong (ed.), *Learning about learning disabilities* (pp. 489–525). San Diego, CA: Academic Press.

Crockett, J. B., & Kauffman, J. M. (1999). *The least restrictive environment: Its origins and interpretations in special education.* Mahwah, NJ: Erlbaum.

Danielson, C. (2002). *Enhancing student achievement: A framework for school improvement.* Alexandria, VA: Association for Supervision and Curriculum Development.

Elbaum, B. (2002). The self-concept of students with learning disabilities: A meta-analysis of comparisons across different placements. *Learning Disabilities Research & Practice,* **17**, 216–226.

Elmore, R. (2002). The price of accountability. *Results,* November. Retrieved November 30, 2002, from http://www.nsdc.org/library/results/.

Espin, C. A., Deno, S. L., & Albayrak-Kaymak, D. (1998). Individualized Education Programs in resource and inclusive settings: How "individualized" are they? *The Journal of Special Education,* **32**, 164–174.

Feuer, M. J., Towne, L., & Shavelson, R. J. (2002). Scientific culture and educational research. *Educational Researcher,* **31**, (8), 4–14.

Forness, S. R. (2002). Foreword. In J. M. Kauffman, *Education deform: Bright people sometimes say stupid things about education* (pp. v–vi). Lanham, MD: Scarecrow Press.

Forness, S. R., Kavale, K. A., Blum, I. M., & Lloyd, J. W. (1997). What works in special education and related services: Using meta-analysis to guide practice. *Teaching Exceptional Children,* **29**, (6), 4–9.

Gallagher, J. J. (1999). Knowledge versus policy in special education. In R. Gallimore, L. P. Bernheimer, D. L. MacMillan, D. L. Speece, & S. Vaughn (eds.), *Developmental perspectives on children with high-incidence disabilities* (pp. 245–259). Mahwah, NJ: Erlbaum.

Gersten, R. (2001). Sorting out the roles of research in the improvement of practice. *Learning Disabilities Research & Practice,* **16**, 45–50.

Gersten, R., Chard, D., & Baker, S. (2000). Factors enhancing sustained use of research-based instructional practices. *Journal of Learning Disabilities,* **33**, 445–457.

Gersten, R., Schiller, E. P., & Vaughn, S. (eds.). (2000). *Contemporary special education research: Syntheses of the knowledge base on critical instructional issues.* Mahwah, NJ: Erlbaum.

Goldstein, L. F. (2002). Election results boost special ed. vouchers. *Education Week,* **XXII**, (14), 21, 24.

Greenwood, C. R. (2001). Science and students with learning and behavioral problems. *Behavioral Disorders,* **27**, 37–52.

Hallahan, D. P., Kauffman, J. M., & Lloyd, J. W. (1996). *Introduction to learning disabilities.* Boston: Allyn and Bacon.

Heward, W. L. (2003). Ten faulty notions about teaching and learning that hinder the effectiveness of special education. *The Journal of Special Education,* **36**, 186–205.

Individuals with Disabilities Education Act Amendments of 1997, 20 U.S.C. §1400 *et seq.*

Kauffman, J. M. (1999). Commentary: Today's special education and its messages for tomorrow. *The Journal of Special Education,* **32**, 244–254.

Kauffman, J. M. (2002). *Education deform: Bright people sometimes say stupid things about education.* Lanham, MD: Scarecrow Press.

Kaufman, M. J., & Lewis, L. M. (1999). Confusing each with all: A policy warning. In R. Gallimore, L. P. Bernheimer, D. L. MacMillan, D. L. Speece, & S. Vaughn (eds.), *Developmental perspectives on children with high-incidence disabilities* (pp. 223–244). Mahwah, NJ: Erlbaum.

Kavale, K. A., & Forness, S. R. (2000). Policy decisions in special education: The role of meta-analysis. In R. Gersten, E. P. Schiller, & S. Vaughn (eds.). (2000). *Contemporary special education research: Syntheses of the knowledge base on critical instructional issues* (pp. 281–326). Mahwah, NJ: Erlbaum.

Klingner, J. K., & Vaughn, S. (2002). The changing roles and responsibilities of an LD specialist. *Learning Disabilities Quarterly*, **25**, 19–31.

Klingner, J. K., Vaughn, S., Hughes, M. T., Schumm, J. S., & Elbaum, B. (1998). Outcomes for students with and without learning disabilities in inclusive classrooms. *Learning Disabilities Research & Practice*, **13**, 153–161.

Lashley, C., & Boscardin, M. L. (2002). *Special education administration at a crossroads: Availability, licensure, and preparation of special education administrators.* Gainesville, FL: University of Florida, Center on Personnel Studies in Special Education.

McCray, A. D., Vaughn, S., & Neal, L. I. (2001). Not all students learn to read by third grade: Middle school students speak out about their reading disabilities. *Remedial and Special Education*, **35**, 17–30.

Manset, G., & Semmel, M. I. (1997). Are inclusive programs for students with mild disabilities effective? A comparative review of model programs. *The Journal of Special Education*, **31**, 155–180.

Mastropieri, M. A. (2001). Introduction to the special issue: Is the glass half full or half empty? Challenges encountered by first-year special education teachers. *The Journal of Special Education*, **34**, 66–74.

Mastropieri, M. A., & Scruggs, T. E. (2001). Promoting inclusion in secondary classrooms. *Learning Disabilities Quarterly*, **24**, 265–274.

Mostert, M. P. (1996). Reporting meta-analyses in learning disabilities. *Learning Disabilities Research and Practice*, **1**, 2–14.

Mostert, M. P. (2001). Characteristics of meta-analyses reported in mental retardation, learning disabilities, and emotional and behavioral disorders. *Exceptionality*, **9**, 199–226.

Mostert, M. P., & Kavale, K. A. (2001). Evaluation of research for usable knowledge in behavioral disorders: Ignoring the irrelevant, considering the germane. *Behavioral Disorders*, **27**, 53–68.

Rumrill, P. D., & Cook, B. G. (2001). *Research in special education: Designs, methods, and applications.* Springfield, IL: Charles C. Thomas.

Sasso, G. M. (2001). The retreat from inquiry and knowledge in special education. *The Journal of Special Education*, **34**, 178–193.

Scanlon, D., & Mellard, D. F. (2002). Academic and participation profiles of school-age dropouts with and without disabilities. *Exceptional Children*, **68**, 239–258.

Schiller, E. P., & Malouf, D. B. (2000). Research syntheses: Implications for research and practice. In R. Gersten, E. P. Schiller, & S. Vaughn (eds.). (2000).

Contemporary special education research: Syntheses of the knowledge base on critical instructional issues (pp. 251–262). Mahwah, NJ: Erlbaum.

Scruggs, T. E., & Mastropieri, M. A. (1995). What makes special education special? Evaluating inclusion programs with the PASS variables. *The Journal of Special Education*, **29**, 224–233.

Sharp, K. G., & Patasky, V. M. (2002). *The current legal status of inclusion*. Horsham, PA: LRP.

Shriner, J. G. (2000). Legal perspectives on school outcomes assessment for students with disabilities. *The Journal of Special Education*, **33**, 232–239.

Speece, D., & Keogh, B. (eds.). (1996). *Research on classroom ecologies: Implications for inclusion of children with learning disabilities*. Mahwah, NJ: Erlbaum.

Study of Personnel Needs in Special Education. (2001). *General education teachers' role in special education*. Retrieved, November 4, 2002, from http://www.spense.org.

Swanson, H. L. (2000a). Issues facing the field of learning disabilities. *Learning Disabilities Quarterly*, **23**, 37–50.

Swanson, H. L. (2000b). What instruction works for students with learning disabilities? Summarizing the results from a meta-analysis of intervention studies. In R. Gersten, E. P. Schiller, & S. Vaughn (eds.), *Contemporary special education research: Syntheses of the knowledge base on critical instructional issues* (pp. 1–30). Mahwah, NJ: Erlbaum.

Swanson, H. L., & Hoskyn, M. (1998). A synthesis of experimental intervention literature for students with learning disabilities: A meta-analysis of treatment outcomes. *Review of Educational Research*, **68**, 271–321.

U. S. Department of Education. (2001). *Twenty-third annual report to Congress on the implementation of the Individuals with Disabilities Education Act*. Washington, DC: Office of Special Education Programs, U. S. Government Printing Office.

U. S. Department of Education. (2002a). *The achiever*. Washington, DC: Office of Intergovernmental and Interagency Affairs.

U. S. Department of Education. (2002b). *Specific learning disabilities: Finding common ground*. Washington, DC: Office of Special Education Programs.

Vaughn, S., & Dammann, J. E. (2001). Science and sanity in special education. *Behavioral Disorders*, **27**, 21–29.

Vaughn, S., Elbaum, B., & Boardman, A. G. (2001). The social functioning of students with learning disabilities: Implications for inclusion. *Exceptionality*, **9**, 47–66.

Vaughn, S., Gersten, R., & Chard, D. J. (2000). The underlying message in LD intervention research: Findings from research syntheses. *Exceptional Children*, **67**, 99–114.

Weiss, M. P., & Lloyd, J. W. (2002). Congruence between roles and actions of secondary special educators in co-taught and special education settings. *The Journal of Special Education*, **36**, 58–68.

Williams, J. P. (2000). Foreword. In R. Gersten, E. P. Schiller, & S. Vaughn (eds.), *Contemporary special education research: Syntheses of the knowledge base on critical instructional issues* (pp. vii–viii). Mahwah, NJ: Erlbaum.

Yinger, R. J., & Nolen, A. L. (2003). Surviving the legitimacy challenge. *Phi Delta Kappan*, **84**, 386–390.

Zigmond, N., Jenkins, J., Fuchs, L. S., Deno, S., Fuchs, D., Baker, J. N., Jenkins, L., & Couthino, M. (1995). Special education in restructured schools: Findings from three multi-year studies. *Phi Delta Kappan*, **76**, 531–540.

Zigmond, N., & Magiera, K. (2002). A focus on co-teaching. *Current Practice Alerts*, **6**, Retrieved November 4, 2002, from http://www.dldcec.org/alerts/.

CHAPTER 14

A Community of Practice: Implications for Learning Disabilities

Annemarie Sullivan Palincsar,[*] **Jane N. Cutter,**[†] **and Shirley J. Magnusson**[*]

[*]*University of Michigan*
[†]*University of Prep School*

I remember sitting in this meeting in the fall thinking, 'absolutely not! I am not convinced this IQ score is all this kid is ever going to be.' But at that point, I didn't know her the way I know her now. Now I feel much stronger about what I know. (Ms. Dunbar, focus group interview)

This comment was made by a fourth-grade general educator, reflecting on her experiences participating in a community of practice that was focused on, among other issues, enhancing the engagement and learning of students with disabilities in the course of guided inquiry science instruction. This teacher is among the 95% of general educators in United States classrooms who teach, each year, an average of 3.5 students with disabilities (SPeNSE, 2000). The quote is compelling for several reasons. First, the teacher expresses her wariness of the traditional kinds of evidence that are used to make decisions about the education of students with special needs. Second, she recalls her uncertainty about how to communicate her alternative view of the child. Finally, she voices newfound confidence in her capacity to advocate for the child. What is missing from the print version, of course, is the emotion in the teacher's voice as she recalls how troubled she was by the tone and substance of the meeting at which this child's educational needs and prospects were discussed.

In this chapter, we report our experiences constituting a community of practice with general educators, such as Ms. Dunbar. We begin by providing a rationale for constituting a community of practice whose focus included meeting the needs of included students. We then present the theory undergirding a community of practice model of professional development, illustrating how this model was applied in our work. Finally, we turn to the outcomes and implications of this work.

I. SETTING THE STAGE: TEACHING IN CONTEMPORARY INCLUSIVE SCHOOLS

Contemporary sociopolitical trends in the United States have significant implications for general educators. With the passage of amendments to the *Individuals with Disabilities Education Act* (IDEA, 1997), not only has there has been a substantial increase in the numbers of students who are "included" in the general education classroom setting, but also there is the expectation that these students are entitled to learn the general education curriculum. Concomitantly, national education reform movements press teachers to aspire to increasingly ambitious learning goals for all of their students. Hence, general educators are expected to provide increasingly diverse classrooms of students with ever more challenging curriculum and pedagogy. While, in principle, it is a worthy goal that students with learning disabilities be provided these learning opportunities, there is evidence that students with learning disabilities are not achieving well compared with their typically achieving peers. For example, the U.S. Department of Education 23rd Annual Report to Congress on the Implementation of IDEA (2001) indicated that the high school dropout rate for students with learning disabilities in the U.S. was 27% as compared with an 11% dropout rate for nonidentified students. Furthermore, on average, 30% fewer students with learning disabilities demonstrate proficiency on statewide and national assessments when compared with typically achieving students. These data highlight the importance of identifying means of supporting teachers to better meet the needs of students with learning disabilities.

In fact, research has revealed that teachers have significant misgivings about their preparation and capacity to serve students with disabilities. Vaughn *et al.* (1996), using interviews and focus group discussions regarding general educators' attitudes and beliefs regarding inclusion, determined that teachers reported lacking the specific skills and knowledge requisite to educating students with learning disabilities. This finding was confirmed by Avramidis *et al.* (2000) using survey data.

In a study designed to characterize teachers' dispositions toward meeting the needs of identified students, Vaughn and Schumm (1994) noted a disparity between what teachers believed was desirable as opposed to feasible in meeting the needs of identified students. The participants ($n = 92$), from elementary through secondary grades, completed a survey in which they were asked to rate both the feasibility and desirability of 30 adaptations for included students. While the teachers rated most of the proposed adaptations as *desirable*, they rated significantly fewer of the adaptations as *feasible*; in particular, they rated changing long-range plans, adapting curricula or using alternative curricula, and adapting assessment procedures as the least feasible. Adaptations viewed as the most feasible were those that did not require individualization.

Unfortunately, research that has been conducted investigating the engagement and learning of students with special needs in the context of ambitious instruction suggests that individualization of instruction is often requisite to their success (Dalton *et al.*, 1997; Mastropieri & Scruggs, 1992; Woodward *et al.*, 2001). Hence, we need models, not only of the specific ways in which curriculum and instruction can productively be modified to meet the needs of included students, but also models of how teachers might be supported to implement these modifications. This was the goal of our research. Specifically, we were interested in: (1) characterizing both the opportunities and challenges associated with guided inquiry learning in science, (2) identifying the modifications in instructional practice that would enhance engagement and learning, especially for children with learning disabilities, and (3) investigating the process and outcomes of implementing these modifications. The conduct of this research required a sustained relationship with general educators who would be willing to support the close study of their practice, and who were committed to implementing and evaluating innovative practices. To achieve these goals, we invited a group of 18 general educators (grades K–5) to join us, as university researchers, in the constitution of a Community of Practice.

II. CONSTITUTING AN EDUCATIONAL COMMUNITY OF PRACTICE

Contemporary learning theories speak to the interdependence of social and individual processes in the co-construction of knowledge (John-Steiner & Mahn, 1996; Palincsar, 1998; Rogoff, 1994). From this perspective, thought, learning, and the construction of knowledge are not just influenced by social factors but are, in fact, social phenomena. Hence—in the case of teachers constructing knowledge about their practice—there need to be occasions for interaction, joint deliberation, and the collective pursuit of shared goals. However, teaching (at least in the United States) is typically a private, personal, and individualistic enterprise (Little, 1992) that permits few occasions for teachers to experience sustained collegial and intellectual support as they try out new practices. The literature on communities of practice provides an interesting alternative that is consistent with a sociocultural perspective on learning and educational innovation.

Popularized by Lave and Wenger (1991) and elaborated upon by Wenger (1998), communities of practice are an integral part of our daily lives. Furthermore, we each belong to multiple communities of practice in our personal and professional lives. What distinguishes a community of practice is the "sustained pursuit of a shared enterprise" (Wenger, 1998 p. 45). The practices that characterize a community include the language, roles, tools, values, and procedures that are the signs of membership in a particular community (Wenger, 1998) and that advance the shared enterprise.

Defining practice in an educational community is more challenging than defining practice in other disciplines, in part, because a teacher's practice is expected to vary as a function of her or his context. This notion is captured by the construct of pedagogical content knowledge (PCK), which is the knowledge teachers have to help others learn specific subject matter. PCK develops from the transformation of subject matter knowledge, pedagogical knowledge (which includes knowledge of children, learning, and individual differences in children's learning), and knowledge of context, which includes knowledge of classroom, school, and district contexts.

In our work, we addressed some of this complexity by focusing on a central element of PCK: one's orientation toward teaching—an overarching conception of how to teach a particular subject (Grossman, 1990). An orientation can be thought of as a "conceptual map" that guides instructional decisions about issues such as daily objectives, the content of student assignments, the use of textbooks and other curricular materials, and the evaluation of student learning (Borko & Putnam, 1996). We submit that a teacher's orientation—because it reflects knowledge and beliefs regarding a particular epistemology—provides enough common points with other individuals with the same orientation to facilitate working together in a community and yet leaves room for individual variation in practice due to context differences. Thus, one guiding principle that we employed in constituting our community of practice was to focus at the level of orientation. We describe this orientation below. Furthermore, our common goal was the development of practice consonant with this orientation, rather than promoting a particular set of strategies or a particular pedagogical model.

The goal of producing formal knowledge for the educational community influenced our conceptualization of the diversity needed in the community. We sought diversity in terms of the teachers' self-identified strengths and challenges as teachers, the grade levels they taught, and the communities they served. To ascertain the teachers' strengths and challenges, they completed an application in which they rated their knowledge and skill in such areas as technology, science, classroom management, and coordinating small group work. The inclusion of teachers across the elementary school grades (K–5) reflected our interest in a developmental perspective regarding the nature of science teaching practice in the elementary school. As we developed our knowledge of what the youngest students were capable of learning about science, we could concomitantly adjust our expectations of older students. Our inclusion of teachers whose students ranged from being at high risk with respect to academic failure to those coming from highly advantaged home situations that have enhanced their readiness and ability to learn reflected our belief that these situations have led teachers to diverse experiences and expertise relative to teaching practice. This variety maximized the practical knowledge upon which the community could draw in co-constructing formal knowledge of science teaching practice as it relates to the diversity of students in our schools.

The notion behind a community of practice is that it provides a context that fosters learning and development through individuals' participation in the activities of the community. Community members transform their understandings, roles, and responsibilities as they collaborate with knowledgeable others in carrying out activities that constitute the practices of that community (Lave & Wenger, 1991; Rogoff, 1994). To understand what this means in the context of professional development with teachers, it is important to conceptualize teaching as an intellectual activity that involves complex decision-making and utilizes knowledge from a number of domains as teachers plan, enact, and reflect upon their teaching.

In the next portion of this chapter, we illustrate how these principles informed the design of specific activities designed to engage the community of practice in addressing the needs of included students. However, before proceeding to describe the activities, we elaborate on the orientation to teaching that has been central to our work: Guided Inquiry supporting Multiple Literacies (GIsML).

III. GUIDED INQUIRY SUPPORTING MULTIPLE LITERACIES (GIsML)

We elected to label our orientation Guided Inquiry supporting Multiple Literacies (GIsML) for the following reasons: "Inquiry" reflects our belief that inquiring is fundamental to learning; furthermore, inquiry matches the orientation stipulated in national standards as the desired approach to teaching science. "Multiple literacies" reflects the notion that meaningful inquiry often crosses disciplinary boundaries and that it is often useful to apply tools from multiple disciplines to engage in successful inquiry (e.g., use of mathematical tools in scientific inquiry). Finally, "Guided" reveals our belief that the teacher plays a critical role in facilitating the development of scientific knowledge in an inquiry-based environment. (For a more elaborated description of GIsML, the reader is referred to Magnusson & Palincsar, 1995).

One tool that was introduced to the community of practice was a heuristic (see Figure 14–1), depicting the instruction according to phases set within a particular problem space; that is, a guiding question that is broad and identifies a general conceptual terrain (e.g., How does light interact with matter? Why do things sink and float? What's in soil?). Inquiry proceeds through cycles of investigation guided by specific questions (e.g., How does light interact with mirrors?) or a particular phenomenon (e.g., shaping a ball of clay to hold the most weight). Integral to this orientation is the conception of the classroom as a community of inquiry (cf. The Cognition and Technology Group at Vanderbilt, 1994; Wells, 1995). Hence, the investigations and documentation of data gathered in the course of the investigation are conducted in pairs or small groups. Furthermore, a critical feature in the instruction is the reporting phase, during which the investigative teams share their data, identify the evidence they have gathered to support or refute extant claims, and contribute new claims for the class's consideration. Students experience the same phase repeatedly in the same or different contexts. This is the recursive aspect of instruction that is required to promote meaningful learning—particularly with respect to scientific inquiry. For example, one needs sufficient experiences examining natural relationships among phenomena before one can meaningfully test explanations for these phenomena.

In the course of GIsML instruction, students and teachers participate in two forms of investigation. Through firsthand investigations, children have experiences related to the phenomenon(a) they are investigating. In the

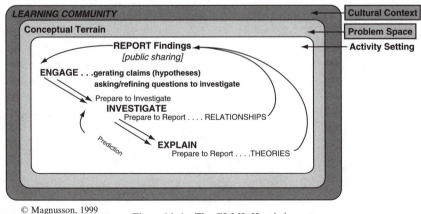

© Magnusson, 1999

Figure 14–1   The GIsML Heuristic.

course of secondhand investigations, children consult text for the purpose of learning about others' interpretations of phenomena or ideas. The ultimate goal of GIsML instruction is to support children's learning of scientific understandings and to enable students to experience, understand, and appreciate the ways in which these understandings have evolved by using the tools, language, and ways of reasoning that are characteristic of scientific literacy (cf. Driver *et al.*, 1985; Lemke, 1990; White & Frederiksen, 1998).

Research investigating the experiences of students with learning disabilities in guided inquiry science instruction is sparse and little of it is classroom-based. Carlisle and Chang (1996) conclude from their classroom research that students with learning problems fare poorly and express doubts about their capacity to perform successfully in these classes. The potential for students with learning disabilities to profit from inquiry-based experiences is signaled in the research of Dalton *et al.* (1997) who found that students showed greater attainment of conceptual understanding in an inquiry-based condition when compared with an activity-based (essentially unguided) condition; however, the students with learning disabilities did not demonstrate the same conceptual growth as their nonidentified peers.

Explanations for the difficulties experienced by students with learning problems in the context of science instruction vary and suggest different forms of intervention. For example, Gersten and Baker (1998) argued that students with learning disabilities must become "fluent with essential factual and conceptual knowledge" (p. 24) before they can profitably engage in inquiry-based instruction. Furthermore, Woodward and Noell (1991) and Mastropieri *et al.* (1997) argue that students with learning disabilities require significant coaching to engage productively in the kinds of reasoning that are typically associated with inquiry-based approaches to science instruction. These findings suggest the following questions: What constitutes helpful guidance for students with learning disabilities in science instruction? How can guided-inquiry instruction promote the conceptual development of students with learning disabilities? What would enable these students to profit from the opportunities guided-inquiry instruction appears to provide students who do not have learning disabilities? These questions guided the design of the case study research conducted with the community of practice in its second year. We turn to this research next.

IV. CONDUCTING CASE STUDIES OF INCLUDED STUDENTS IN GIsML INSTRUCTION

The five fourth and fifth grade teachers from the GIsML community of practice participated in the first phase of this case study research. These teachers were in the second year of membership in the community.

Typically, teachers instructed a GIsML program of study over several weeks (2 to 5 weeks) on a daily basis, for 45 minutes to 2 hours a day (dictated by scheduling constraints and the preferences of the teacher). The research methods employed reflected a range of ethnographic procedures including (a) videotaping, (b) focused observations by participant observers who documented using field notes, (c) debriefings with the teacher following instruction, and (d) structured interviews with the identified children.

Prior to beginning the GIsML program of study, each teacher identified the students for whom there were Individualized Educational Programs. Typically, there were three identified children in each classroom, with an additional two or three children whom the teacher had referred for evaluation or whom the teacher was considering referring, principally because of concerns with academic achievement and/or behavior. The teacher determined how these students were grouped for the purposes of small group work.

A. Observational Research

One focus for the observations was the entire class. This focus was more or less problematic, depending upon the participant structure in place. For example, within GIsML instruction, there are several phases when the participant structure is whole-class presentation and/or discussion (e.g., during the presentation of the question/challenge/problem that will guide the investigation, planning for the investigation, and when the children are reporting and comparing the outcomes of their inquiry). There are other phases when the students are working primarily in small groups (e.g., during the investigation activity, when preparing to share the results of their investigation, and generating claims they wish to make following their investigations). The researcher followed the teacher (using a video camera and field notes) during both whole-class and small-group activity. In addition, there was a sound system adequate for capturing students' participation in these whole-group activities.

During the small group activities, a researcher continued to follow the teacher (who was wired with a remote microphone) while other researchers focused on the activity of the identified students, rotating attention from one child to the next in 15- to 20-minute intervals. If the observer found the child to be totally disengaged in the activity of GIsML instruction for a 5-minute period, the observer intervened for the purpose of exploring procedures for re-engaging the student, starting from low-level intervention and proceeding to more supportive intervention, only to the level necessary to reengage the child. An example of a low-level intervention would be asking the student to explain what he or she is doing. A more high-level intervention would include offering to record the child's thinking if he or she appeared to have writing difficulties. The nature of the support as well as the student's response to the intervention was recorded in the field notes.

In addition to characterizing the opportunities and challenges associated with GIsML instruction, the research was designed to determine how students with special needs responded to these opportunities. Some of the data useful to answering this query result from the classroom data already described. However, to understand what the students, as individuals, acquired in the way of scientific concepts and the ability to engage in scientific reasoning as a function of their GIsML experiences, the classroom data clearly needed to be augmented with additional data. These data included: (a) formal assessments that were administered pre-/post-GIsML instruction, (b) individual interview data, and (c) artifacts that were generated by the students in the course of GIsML instruction (e.g., student notebooks, posters, and other forms of writing).

B. Formal Assessments

There were three formal assessments administered to all student participants in each class: a standardized reading assessment (The Gates–MacGinitie), measuring vocabulary knowledge and comprehension, a pre- and post-assessment of the students' conceptual understandings of the topic of the program of study, and a measure that assessed children's attitudes toward and beliefs about the nature of science and scientific problem solving.

Relative to the identified students, these formal measures were used for several purposes. One purpose was to gather information regarding children's prior knowledge. These data informed the teachers' thinking and decision making as they planned the program of study with the university-based researchers. A second use was to compare the entering knowledge and beliefs of identified children with their unidentified peers. And, of course, a third reason was to be able to assess changes in students' thinking following the program of study. However, these are all fairly static measures that do little to inform the question of how children have come to these attitudes, beliefs, and understandings. The remaining three data sources (individual interviews, artifacts, and video and field notes) were useful to addressing this question.

C. Individual Interviews

Each day, following the instructional session, the identified children were interviewed using the following set of questions; (1) What happened in class today? (2) What did *you* do today? (3) What did you learn about [topic under study], (4) Was there anything helpful to your learning today? (5) Was there anything that was unhelpful to your learning today? (6) What would have been helpful to your learning today? and (7) Is there anything else you would like to tell us?

Engaging the students as informants served the following purposes: The interview provided the occasion to ascertain the child's perspective on the day's events. The child's comments enabled elaboration upon the field notes for the day, and, finally, the child's reflections on the day's events could be juxtaposed with the other records of the day's events.[1]

D. Student Artifacts

The artifacts, including student notebooks and the posters completed by pairs of students, provide another window on the child's thinking and learning throughout the instruction. It was not uncommon for a child in her small group activity to assent to the position of the group on an issue, but to then reveal in her own notebook entry that, in fact, she had a more accurate or complete conception than did her peers. These artifacts were also invaluable to learning more about the mediational means and semiotics that children draw upon in resourceful ways when traditional writing is ineffectual for them.

E. Video Records and Field Notes

Finally, the (partial) video-record and field notes were integral to "getting another look" when trying to fill in the details regarding the day's events or when checking on the relationship between the child's account and the events as they appeared to unfold to an observer.

V. CONSTRUCTING AND ANALYZING THE CASE STUDIES

Following data collection, the next challenge was the preparation of the case studies themselves. Working from the multiple data sources we have described, the goal was to represent the experiences of each child in a manner that captured both the activity of the child and the context in which this activity was unfolding[2]. The cases were constructed by: (a) compiling the assessment data to provide descriptive information regarding each identified

---

[1]We are keenly aware that these individual interviews are themselves a form of intervention. We have frequently observed children using these interviews as occasions for "rehearsing" ideas that they will subsequently bring to the classroom (e.g., the day after the interview).

[2]For additional information regarding the construction of the cases, see Palincsar *et al.* 2000. Case studies of included students in GIsML instruction are presented in Collins (2003), Cutter (2003), and Miller (1999).

child's general achievement level, prior knowledge regarding the topic under investigation, and changes in understanding over the course of the instruction, (b) drawing upon the field notes and video records to write a narrative that captured the child's engagement and participation in both the small group and whole class instruction, (c) synthesizing the interview data to capture the child's reflections on his or her experiences with this instruction, and (d) synthesizing comments made by the teacher relative to the instruction or to the identified child's engagement and learning.

We then conducted across-case analyses for the purpose of identifying patterns in the included students' participation and learning. These analyses revealed that students' challenges clustered into four categories of demand: print literacy, linguistic/conceptual, attention, and social interaction. We describe each of these next.

In GIsML instruction, there were a number of ways in which children could represent and communicate their ideas; to illustrate, we documented identified children using drawing and demonstrations to describe their thinking. Nevertheless, there were also numerous demands for print literacy. For example, there were data tables that were presented by peer groups reporting their findings, and there were notebook entries that the children were asked to make in which they recorded their claims and the supporting evidence, and, of course, in secondhand investigations, the children were reading text. These demands often exceeded the students' capabilities. In some cases, because of the role played by the researchers (described previously), we were able to determine the kinds of support that enabled the students to meet these print literacy demands; for example, providing environmental print to support preparing notebook entries (e.g., posting terms frequently associated with the topic under study, such as *density* and *buoyancy* in the study of floating and sinking objects, or terms used in scientific inquiry, such as *evidence* and *observation*) and transcribing children's writing.

There are numerous conceptual and linguistic demands associated with guided inquiry science instruction. For example, integral to scientific inquiry is an understanding of argumentation—learning how to evaluate the relationship between knowledge claims and the evidence for those knowledge claims, learning how to search for disconfirming evidence, and keeping in mind and comparing competing ideas. The linguistic demands are related to the specificity with which language is used in science and the fact that many of the technical terms used in science are unfamiliar to children.

The demands on children's attention in the context of GIsML are related to some of the features particular to this form of inquiry-based instruction. As has been indicated, there is a significant amount of recursiveness that is integral to this instruction. For example, multiple groups of students investigate the same phenomenon and report data that are typically more similar than different. Children need to attend closely to how others conducted their investigations; they need to listen for how the findings of other groups compare to their own findings, and they need to be thinking about the significance of these similarities and differences in outcomes. Furthermore, cycles of inquiry occur in which students conduct investigations in which they are manipulating one variable at a time (e.g., changing the ramp height in an investigation of mass and momentum). If a student fails to appreciate the ways in which the recursiveness serves to provide multiple opportunities to confirm and refine one's understandings, then the recursiveness can seem repetitive, uninteresting, and unnecessary. Given the frequency with which identified students also exhibit problems of attention, this is a demanding aspect of guided inquiry teaching. At least initially, the demands on the teacher include supporting students to understand why multiple investigations of the same phenomenon are necessary and helping students to focus their attention in productive ways.

The social interaction demands on children are particularly prominent when the class is working in small groups. The roles and responsibilities of the group members need to be negotiated, and compromises need to be made relative to the distribution of resources. The case study research revealed that it was not uncommon for included students to be disenfranchised during small-group work; these students were denied access to the investigation materials, their ideas were not solicited, and—even when their ideas were accurate and would have advanced the group's thinking—they were challenged relative to having their ideas acknowledged.

Recall that the ultimate goal in the construction of these individual cases was to present what we learned through this case study research to the GIsML Community of Practice in order (a) to provide teachers the opportunity to see included student participation in a new way, (b) to promote conversation and collaborative problem solving regarding the opportunities and challenges of guided inquiry science instruction, and (c) to collaboratively design interventions that might be implemented in general education settings that would enhance the learning of included students. To facilitate this, we prepared "vignettes" that, while derived from the case studies, were briefer than the case studies and were also composites, enabling us to feature the areas of challenge we identified in the case study research. Furthermore, the vignettes were also constructed to feature the strengths that included children brought to the instruction (e.g., their skills in using equipment and representing their ideas through drawing). The vignettes were several pages in length. University-based members of the community then planned the reading and discussion of the composite vignettes as the centerpiece of the conversation during two of the meetings of the upper elementary teachers in the community of practice, introducing one vignette at each meeting. The teachers first read through the vignette and then, drawing upon the discourse that they were accustomed to in GIsML instruction, the teachers were encouraged to identify claims they would make about the participation and learning of the child featured in the vignette and the evidence supporting each claim.[3] The reading of the vignettes was followed by a discussion in which the school- and university-based members of the community generated a set of interventions, drawing not only on the vignettes, but also on the teachers' and researchers' experiences in the classrooms. These interventions (identified in Table I) were organized according to the four areas (previously described) that had been identified as areas of challenge for included students.

Following the two vignette conversations, four of the five teachers who had participated in the case study research chose to participate the following year in the next phase of this research—implementing the interventions in a guided inquiry program of study. This phase of the research began with planning conversations that were held with each teacher individually. Meeting with the individual teachers ensured that the planning took into account (among other issues) their unique classroom contexts, the profiles of the individual students enrolled in their classes, and the opportunities and challenges associated with the specific topic(s) their class would be investigating. While there was some variability in the interventions teachers committed to investigating, there was more commonality than difference. Each teacher identified interventions related to print literacy, including: (a) providing students a publicly posted glossary of terms frequently encountered in GIsML instruction (e.g., evidence) or specific to the topic of study they would be implementing (e.g., reflection, absorption, transmission), (b) providing specific writing prompts to support children's writing in their notebooks, and (c) making provisions for children with significant writing problems to have a writing "buddy" to assist with writing challenges. The four teachers also selected an intervention specific to the conceptual/linguistic demands associated with GIsML; namely, encouraging the included students to practice their presentations before they engaged in public reporting to the class regarding their investigation. Two teachers indicated an interest in frequently interviewing included students for the purpose of monitoring more closely the nature of their thinking, particularly during small group investigation time. All of the teachers indicated that they were concerned about the experiences included students were having in the context of the small group investigations (in particular). The social relational problems experienced by identified students were especially prominent in the two vignettes and were referenced in these planning conversations. The teachers proposed: (a) modeling the nature of constructive interactions in small group investigation, (b) paying closer attention to the constitution of small groups, (c) monitoring more closely the interaction of the small groups, and

---

[3]For sample vignettes and analyses of teacher–researcher conversations using the vignettes, see Cutter *et al.* (2002).

Table I

Interventions for Promoting the Engagement/Achievement of Students with Special Needs

Challenges	Strategies
Language/Cognition	1. Engage in close monitoring of the thinking of students (especially during investigations, in preparation for reporting, and following reporting) • observing what these students are doing during their investigation • frequently "checking in" with these students to determine what they are thinking 2. Assign and rotate "intellectual" roles that would support cognitive engagement (e.g., playing the roles of monitoring the clarity of data representation or monitoring the relationship between claims and data) 3. Provide "rehearsal" opportunities, especially prior to reporting 4. Pay explicit attention to technical vocabulary by • engaging students in generating useful definitions (e.g., "what do we mean in this class when we talk about providing evidence?) • assessing students' understanding of terminology 5. Maintain a class/individual glossary of useful terms and post and refer to these terms.
Print literacy	1. Use scaffolded notebook entries that support students' thinking and organization of ideas, and that reduce amount of required writing • employ prompts that focus students' writing (e.g., describe what happened to the CDS when you pressed on the balloon; explain your thinking about why this happened) 2. Provide peer- or adult-assisted writing (i.e., transcription) 3. Provide environmental print supportive of writing in the topic area (e.g., posted claims, glossary) 4. Support students' use of graphic depictions with simple labels • Model use of graphics • Share different representations
Attentional	1. Engage in pacing to optimize attention of class (e.g., employ selective reporting by students, have groups report to one another and then share a comparison of their findings and explanations) 2. Use jigsawing, as appropriate, to maximize use of time and provide more compelling reasons for sharing 3. Assign "intellectual" roles (described previously) to set purposes for listening 4. Provide frequent and specific feedback to these students regarding their engagement and activity, especially with respect to cueing students when they are engaged in productive activity, as well as when they are in need of a change of course toward productive intellectual activity.
Social/Interactional	1. Promote effective interaction during problem-solving activity in small groups by:

continued

Table 1

(Continued)

Challenges	Strategies
	• Explicitly model how to effectively work together to engage in problem-solving activity in small groups. • Monitor small groups to determine how well they are working together effectively such as with turn-taking, sharing materials • Facilitate debriefing in small groups regarding how effectively they worked together during the problem-solving activity. 2. Plan group work mindful of using distributed expertise among students so that they assist one another (e.g., organizational skill, engineering skill, task-focused) 3. Group students mindful of interactional demands (e.g., distributing across groups those students who excel at being helpful to others).

(d) paying more attention to the assignment of roles and responsibilities in the small group activity. Finally, one of the four teachers indicated that she would include as an intervention paying closer attention to issues of pacing so that she did not unnecessarily tax the children's attention spans.

VI. LINKING TEACHER LEARNING AND STUDENT LEARNING

The outcomes of implementing these interventions are reported in Palincsar *et al.* (2001), in which we compare the pre- to post-test performance on the measures of conceptual understanding and scientific reasoning for the year in which we conducted the case study research and for the year in which the teachers implemented the interventions described. We reported the data from each year for included students, low-achieving students, and typically achieving students. We found that, prior to the vignette and planning conversations, identified children did not make significant progress in science content learning, as measured by the paper-and-pencil assessments. In fact, the only students who demonstrated significant learning gains were the typically achieving students. After the vignette-based professional development and implementation of the interventions previously described, the included children made significant or near significant gains in content knowledge in three out of four classrooms. While there are limitations to teasing apart the effects of the interventions, given that they were implemented during the second consecutive year each teacher taught the same program of study, it is worth noting that the pattern of student improvement held across teachers, whether a teacher had two or three years of experience teaching a topic. Furthermore, in the one teacher's class in which we continued to see significant gains accrue only to the typically achieving students, we did not observe the teacher to implement the interventions she had identified in the planning conference with the identified students; in fact, she indicated that she felt drawn to use these interventions with the more capable students, whom, she felt, were in a better position to profit from the interventions.

VII. THE TEACHERS' REFLECTIONS

In this final portion of the chapter, we present some of the teachers' reflections on their participation in the activities of this community of practice, specific to focusing on the engagement and learning of included students. Our data sources include teachers' journals, as well as focus group conversations and interviews that we conducted with the teachers in the course of this research.

A significant theme emerging from the teachers' reflections is the extent to which, in the context of guided inquiry experiences, included students revealed more about their strengths than is typically revealed in more traditional instruction, although they are challenged to share what they know effectively. Ms. Dunbar speaks to this:

> When these children are in science—where they are using both language and hands-on experiences—it's like this floodgate; all of a sudden they can let out all they know. Their knowledge was real scattered, all over the place....The have never been in a position of having all this knowledge come out and so they don't have any idea how to process, or refine it...they have had very little practice doing that. They almost look like my four-year-old...where the world is just your oyster...perhaps if they had done this earlier, they wouldn't be like this.

One theme that emerged from these data was that the interventions that the teachers identified as the most effective were also the most demanding on the teacher. An example was the activity of interviewing the included students for the purpose of monitoring their thinking. However, as Ms. Jentzen describes in the following text, this was also a very effective intervention if for no other reason than the opportunities it afforded her to learn about what these students knew and had not been able to communicate in more traditional ways:

> In one way, it [the intervention of frequently interviewing included students about their thinking] confirmed a lot of things that I had

been thinking all these years as I've been working with students—
mainly with these special, you know, ed students. They know a lot
more than they are ever going to be able to tell you or especially
write. And it really comes out as you do these interviews . . . they
might write a word or maybe nothing on a piece of paper . . . no
matter what you to try to get them to do . . . these students have such
difficulty with reading and writing. But . . . that said . . . they were
really understanding what was going on, and had a lot of material
to contribute and their understanding was pretty impressive. And if
you did not interview these students at these critical stages, you'd
never know that this was happening.

A third theme emerging from the teacher reflection data is the tension
experienced by the teacher who is trying to accommodate students with
special needs at the same time that she is trying to optimize the learning of
her entire class; in essence, planning and conducting instruction that would
accommodate multiple—not necessarily overlapping—zones of proximal
development. Ms. Dunbar speaks to this tension and the way that she
resolved it, which was to permit students a more significant role in determining what course their investigations would take:

I thought it was fabulous that the special ed kids could do this. But
if it is at the expense of other kids making growth. . . . So this year I
really tried hard to find ways that I could be stretching everybody . . . So that it could stretch everybody . . . I had to be willing to let
kids go. Kids did go in all different directions . . . I mean a lot of stuff
I wasn't ready for them to go on to . . . but they did and it was a good
thing. They went beyond our investigation and even took it home
with them.

A final theme is the sense of self-efficacy that teachers derived from
enacting the interventions that they selected. Two teachers, Ms. Dunbar
and Ms. Lacey, spoke to this. First, Ms. Dunbar:

A lot of times you go to the meetings (IEP) and you are just sitting
there and you are a nobody. I mean they are talking around you, and
you as a classroom teacher know that this isn't right, or this doesn't
feel very good . . . but I feel like I'm not the intellectual person, or
I don't have anything to bring to the table. I had Morgan's IEP in the
process of doing GIsML and I felt much more confident that
I clearly got it. It was like . . . Ah, I have this whole new understanding of this kid. And what I could do as a teacher to work with
her . . . and prior to this, she just looked like an out-of-control,

wisecracking, mean little girl. And that's not what's going on here at all. Like I had much more knowledge. Actually, I have more knowledge than the people sitting at the table who are just talking from books. I mean, I am talking about a real kid, sitting here, who...who absolutely can do some of this stuff and you [speaking of the other members of the IEP team] need to help me with this.

A similar sentiment is expressed by Ms. Lacey, who is commenting on the value of implementing GIsML instruction, complete with the interventions, at the beginning of the school year. Ms. Lacey also speaks to the learner and task-specific nature of the intervention implemented:

So the advantage of doing inquiry at the beginning of the year, even though we have always felt that there were advantages to doing it at the end...spending time with those special ed kids and absolutely knowing what you can do to help them. I'm not saying nobody did anything with these kids before...but probably not like this real specific kind of...let's look at what needs to happen here...kind of thing.

VIII. CONCLUSION

This chapter has focused on the ways in which school- and university-based members of a community of practice collaborated in the context of a professional development effort to come to new understandings about how to better support identified students in challenging science instruction. Specifically, case study research, conducted over sustained time and drawing upon multiple sources of data at the level of the teacher, classroom, and individual identified student, led to the design of vignettes that featured composite pictures of included children.

During the group discussions of the vignettes, teachers began to develop a shared sense of both the strengths that identified students brought to this instructional context, and the challenges they encountered. This research and vignette activity revealed that the challenges of included students were not merely a function of the characteristics of the children, but also a function of the features of the context. The availability of physical resources, the interactions with peers, the children's access to the teacher, the culture of the classroom, and many other features influenced the learning opportunities available to included students.

The vignettes presented the findings of the research in specific ways that were highly recognizable by the teachers. We would argue that the vignettes became a powerful tool for the use of this community of practice. What we cannot speak to, of course, is the value of the vignettes outside of the context of a community of practice. Previous research on professional development to enhance the inclusion experiences of students (Schumm & Vaughn, 1995; Marks & Gersten, 1998) suggests that a relationship of trust between researchers and teachers, as well as researchers' respect for teacher perspectives, can make a difference in the professional development context. Our research, although not focused on the issue of trust, might seem to provide additional support for these conclusions.

Our findings also support the conclusions drawn by Vaughn and Schumm (1994) and Boudah et al. (1997) regarding the need for intensive collaboration in professional development efforts that are directed to work of this complexity. In part, the use of case-based vignettes, drawn from the classrooms of participating teachers, enabled the experience to be intensive, collaborative, and sensitive to teacher needs and views. The design features of the vignettes allowed for close examination of particular children in particular instructional contexts, thus creating the possibility for common understandings. The narrative form of the vignette may also have contributed to teachers' interest in and understanding of the contents of the vignettes. Teachers reported that they were able to "see" their own students in the composite student featured in the vignettes.

Through the mediation of discussion prompts, teachers focused on the strengths of the included student in the vignette as well as the challenges faced by that student. From a common understanding of included students' strengths and challenges, strikingly similar strategies designed to support included students were identified and adopted by all participating teachers. As we have presented these findings to other researchers interested in enhancing the experiences of teachers and students in inclusive settings, we have been asked, "How did you get teachers to do all that?" In fact, the teachers decided for themselves what practices would be most helpful, in light of what they knew about their own students and about the instructional context. Conversations around case-based vignettes appear to provide a context in which educators can develop a shared lens for considering the profiles of diverse learners in inclusive settings, and identify approaches to enhancing the participation and achievement of these students.

APPENDIX 1: VIGNETTES FROM EVAN'S EXPERIENCE WITH THE LIGHT PROGRAM OF STUDY

Evan: The Learner

At the time of the Light Program of Study in this fourth grade classroom, Evan was 9 years, 5 months old. Evan is blond with blue eyes, a quiet, always neatly dressed child. He often appears to attend to what is going on in class, but has difficulty understanding some of the more subtle aspects of a whole-class activity. His records indicate a diagnosis of Asperger's Syndrome, which especially challenges Evan's ability to attend and to carry on some social interactions. Nevertheless, Evan has evidenced a willingness to participate wholeheartedly in all the phases of the GIsML instruction, including the secondhand investigation during which the students and teacher participated in Reciprocal Teaching. Although Evan appears to be quiet and indeed somewhat removed and he has evidenced difficulty in small group interactions, he has consistently attempted to make a place for himself as a contributing member of this classroom community. We observed Evan getting support from the teacher or other children. For example, during a whole-class writing activity, the teacher made sure that Evan was able to stay with the rest of the class by either helping him with his writing or suggesting ways for him to abbreviate what he was writing with the idea of coming back to it later.

Evan's scores on the Gates MacGinite Reading Tests, Vocabulary and Comprehension and samples of his writing indicate a student who is struggling with the written word. On the Vocabulary subtest, Evan's raw score was 19, placing him in the 23rd percentile, with a grade equivalence of 3.1. On Comprehension, he scored slightly higher, with a raw score of 24, placing him in the 37th percentile with a grade equivalence of 3.3. His total reading scores were raw score = 43, percentile = 29, and grade equivalent = 3.2. Interestingly, Evan values books and reading. In an interview and on the epistemological measure, he commented positively regarding the helpfulness of books for finding out about things. When asked about what might be additionally helpful in the Light investigation, he reported that he would want to read more about light in a book. We also observed a high level of engagement during the secondhand investigation when the class was reading the scientist's notebook, especially when Evan took the lead during that activity.

This GIsML activity in the classroom took place over several weeks. Through the use of videotapes, fieldnotes, interviews, Evan's journals, and other literacy artifacts, we were able to observe Evan in various activities and participant structures over time. In the following vignettes, we characterize some of Evan's experiences in the Light Program of Study, attending especially to both the challenges and opportunities of the GIsML instruction as they intersect with Evan's cognitive and affective strengths and needs.

Initial Activities: Week 1

The conceptual goals for this inquiry were for the children to advance their understanding about the ways in which light interacts with various materials. The children were introduced to the concepts of absorb, transmit, and reflect. In the first week of the investigation, the children worked in dyads with a flashlight and a bucket filled with 28 different materials: plastic tray, brown paper, white/brown circle, white Styrofoam, black circle, white board, blue Styrofoam, cup, blue spongy object, silver cardboard, aluminum foil, orange tissue paper, yellow windsock material, meat tray, black felt, white felt, small white circle, small square plastic container, plastic baggie, dark blue wrap, Kleenex, white netting, wax paper, bag, light blue wrap, silver/brown wrap, red lid and bucket. The children shined the flashlight on each material, examining and then categorizing the way the light interacted with the material. For example, they would look to see if there was any light coming through the material. The children were given worksheets listing the materials and providing a column for them to organize the materials into categories based on the way light interacted with them. After investigating and then categorizing the materials for two days, each dyad reported their findings to the whole class during public sharing.

During the initial investigation, Evan and his partner, Danny, were engaged in the activity and working cooperatively together. We observed Evan contributing to his partner's ideas and to the whole class discussion. Danny and Evan worked well together at first. Danny took a "mentoring" role (as reported by the teacher) that provided Evan with support and encouragement. Evan reported to one of the researchers that he was Danny's "assistant," a responsibility that seemed to provide a frame for him in terms of what he was expected to do. We also found that the first worksheet given to the students to guide their investigation was particularly helpful to Evan. It kept him focused on the task, while supporting his understanding of what the partners were supposed to do in the first investigation of light interacting with materials. [see worksheets]

We noted that during this investigation, Evan was not only engaged, but understood his role and responsibility as a partner. For example, when the teacher, trying to encourage the children to talk to each other in their dyads or small groups, asks the class what kinds of questions one partner might ask another, Evan responded: "What can we do to support this?"—referring to how to document their findings in order to report it to the class. Again, we observed the teacher asking Evan and Danny about their progress as they prepare their documentation for public sharing. At this point, she asked the boys how they might show evidence for their claims. Evan suggests they can "show 'em with pictures."

When Evan and Danny reported to the class during public sharing, we observed a well-orchestrated presentation. Evan read from one side of the chart, and Danny read the remainder. The chart was made up of categories in which the boys had placed the various materials based on how they interacted with light from a flashlight. Danny took charge, fielding questions from other students. All the while, using a yardstick as a pointer, Evan attempted to choose children who had their hands raised. The boys had chosen interesting terms to describe what the light is doing with the materials, and we can't be sure if Evan contributed to the development of these terms. During the public sharing, Danny reported that some materials were "holey and clear," the light "cuts through," and "half and half" in describing the light going through the material. Evan's partner was helpful in supporting Evan through parts of the investigation. However, over time, Danny took on more of the activity and sometimes seemed to prevent Evan from being fully involved.

The next investigation during week 1 was introduced by the teacher after all the children had reported their findings from the first investigation. At this time, she also presented the standards for investigating and maintaining consistency in the inquiry. The "light catcher" (a piece of white cardboard) was shown to the children and recommended as a tool to see light on the other side of the material being investigated. At this point, the teacher also described reflection of light off an object for the students by comparing a bouncing soccer ball with the reflection of light off an object. During this discussion, we get a sense that Evan understands at least this initial idea of reflecting light. During the whole group discussion, he volunteered and went to the board, diagramming light from a flashlight bouncing off different objects.

During these activities, Evan was engaged and contributing (according to interviews, artifacts, videos). We also have evidence, from the pre- and postconceptual assessments, that his conceptual understanding regarding light absorbing, transmitting, and reflecting was advanced.

Public Sharing

From the videotapes, we have evidence of Evan engaged and participating as a listener during public sharing, particularly in the first two weeks of the GIsML instruction. He consistently raises his hand and contributes or asks questions. When he is called on, his questions and comments are not always clear to the listener, and as a result may not always be followed up on or clarified.

During interviews, Evan indicated that he was listening to what others had to report during public sharing. He commented that he liked to hear what other people were thinking about the investigation. Evan wanted to know more about how they did what they did, and he reported that the charts other students used in their sharing were helpful to him.

The interviews conducted with Evan, especially after public sharing (two occasions in the first week), indicated his developing understanding about how light behaves when interacting with various materials. He reported in the interview that he had learned that day that light reflects, that it can be blocked, and that it can go through materials. He told the interviewer that his new learning that day had been that light can be blocked, but some light can go all the way through. He said he wondered and would want to ask the other students, "How did you do that?" He thought it was helpful to his learning to learn "about all the stuff that people know about light." The same day, Evan wrote in his journal, "Light is blocked by dark material."

Week 2 and Beyond

In Week 2, the children started by getting ready to share and then reporting their findings. During the first day of this week, the teacher introduced the terms "reflect," "absorb," and "transmit", with a definition for each. We have evidence of Evan's understanding in an interaction where he pointed out that all three (absorb, transmit, reflect) are going on at the same time with one material. However, soon after this contribution, it appeared that Evan was not engaged in working with his partner or in getting ready for the reporting the next day. In a discussion with Danny, Evan, and the teacher, the teacher and Danny were interacting, but Evan, although sitting right there, was not participating. A little later, the camera captured Evan walking around the room somewhat aimlessly and at one point going to the teacher to ask if it isn't time for art. At the end of this day, Evan wrote in his journal: "I learned that light can reflect, absorb, and transmit" and "My partner and I aren't getting along." In fact, from our videotape data from that day, Danny and Evan, while they are physically together at the table, are never observed talking to each other at all. We observed Danny taking over more of the activity and Evan just sitting there. Evan contributes during the public sharing the next day by reading part of the chart that Danny had constructed. However, it is Danny who has taken control of the reporting, determining what they will share and calling on students with questions and comments.

During the public sharing the next day, Evan and Danny (with pointers in hand) reported on which materials absorbed, reflected, and transmitted light. Evan added, "Most of it reflected." This was not really heard because Danny called on Ronnie who had a question in the middle of Evan's statement. We seem to have another example here of Evan's engagement in the public sharing phase as both listener and reporter.

During the reflection with mirrors cycle of the GIsML activity, Evan continued to be less engaged and did not contribute at all to his new partnership with Brandon. Furthermore, during whole-group activities such as public sharing, we observed Evan a few steps behind with many of his comments and questions. For example, he repeated a comment about the measurement of angles made by the reflected light presented by two boys who were sharing. The same point had been noted previously by three other children and the teacher, tired of the repetition, said they had heard enough about the angles not adding up to 180 and that it did not need to be mentioned again. Within seconds of her statement, Evan raised his hand and reported that the boys angles did not add up to 180. Laughter erupted and Evan looked around him in utter confusion. Moreover, conceptual measures and artifacts of Evan's work during this time indicate no growth in conceptual understanding of reflection with mirrors.

Secondhand Investigation: Reciprocal Teaching

The remainder of Week 2 was devoted to the secondhand investigation, the text inquiry into Lesley Park's notebook. From the videotape and field notes, we have data that Evan exhibited a high level of engagement and some measure of enthusiasm during RT, especially when he led the activity. In his role as leader on 2/27/98, Evan had specific and predictable "tasks" to perform, and he seemed quite supported by the "script." Evan knew what was expected and what to do next. He understood that in his role as leader he was responsible to his peers to summarize parts of the text, generate questions, make predictions, and check on the need for others to clarify. However, not only was he conscientiously connected to his role as leader, he was also genuinely using the text to further his understanding while performing that role. We have some information that Evan values and enjoys reading (primarily from the epistemology measure), so perhaps it is not surprising that Evan participated fully in this cycle of the GIsML inquiry. During his time as leader, Evan prompted an interesting discussion when he asked the question, "Why is light energy?" In his interview that day, Evan, when asked what questions he had, repeated, "Why does it [light] have energy?" And interestingly, when asked what would help him learn more, Evan suggested that if he could look back through the pages of the text it would help, and that he would like to see Lesley do her investigations. All in all, he found the secondhand investigation that day to be fun. He said, "It was fun" at least twice during the interview.

As the GIsML instruction proceeded and by the time the class gets to the Color inquiry using the secondhand investigation, we have evidence from the videotapes that Evan seldom contributed in a substantive way to advancing his own understanding or to the thinking of his classmates. From the pre- and post-conceptual measures, Evan exhibits no growth in his conceptual understanding of color. Artifacts of Evan's writing would also confirm these observations.

References

Avramidis, E., Bayliss, P., & Burden, R. (2000). Student teachers' attitudes toward the inclusion of children with special educational needs in the ordinary school. *Teaching and Teacher Education*, **16**, 277–293.

Borko, H., & Putnam, R. T. (1996). Learning to teach. In D. C. Berliner & R. C. Calfee (eds.), *Handbook of educational psychology* (pp. 673–708). New York: Macmillan.

Boudah, D., Deshler, D., Schumaker, J., Lenz, B. K., & Cook, B. (1997). Student-centered or content centered? A case study of a middle school teacher's lesson planning and instruction in inclusive classes. *Teacher Education and Special Education*, **20**(3), 189–203.

Carlisle, J. F., & Chang, V. (1996). Evaluation of academic capabilities in science by students with and without learning disabilities and their teachers. *The Journal of Special Education*, **30**(1), 18–34.

Collins, K. (2003). *Ability profiling and school failure: One's child's struggle to be seen as competent.* Mawah, NJ: Lawrence Erlbaum.

Cutter, J. (2003). *Teacher mediation of student learning in an inclusive group during guided inquiry science instruction.* Unpublished doctoral dissertation, University of Michigan, Ann Arbor.

Cutter, J., Palincsar, A. S., & Magnusson, S. J. (2002). Supporting inclusion through case-based vignettes. *Learning Disabilities Research and Practice*, **17**(3), 186–200.

Dalton, B., Morocco, C. C., Tivnan, T. & Mead, P. L. R. (1997). Supporting inquiry science: Teaching for conceptual change in urban and suburban classrooms. *Journal of Learning Disabilities*, **30**(6), 670–684.

Driver, R., Guesne, E., & Tiberghien, A. (1985). *Children's ideas in science.* Philadelphia: Open University Press.

Gersten, R., & Baker, S. (1998). Real world use of scientific concepts: Integrating situated cognition with explicit instruction. *Exceptional Children*, **65**(1), 23–35.

Grossman, P. (1990). The making of a teacher: Teacher knowledge and teacher education. New York: Teacher's College Press.

IDEA (1997). Individuals with Disabilities Educations Act. www.ed.gov/offices/OSERS/IDEA/

John-Steiner, V., & Mahn, H. (1996). Sociocultural approaches to learning and development. *Educational Psychologist*, **31**, 191–206.

Lave, J., & Wenger, E. (1991). *Situated learning: Legitimate peripheral participation.* Cambridge: Cambridge University Press.

Lemke, J. (1990). *Talking science: Language, learning, and values.* Norwood, NJ: Ablex.

Little, J. W. (1992). Opening the black box of professional community. In A. Lieberman (ed.), *The changing contexts of teaching* (pp. 157–178). Chicago: University of Chicago Press.

Magnusson, S. J., & Palincsar, A. S. (1995). Learning environments as a site of science education reform. *Theory into Practice*, **34**(1), 1–8.

Marks, S. U., & Gersten, R. (1998). Engagement and disengagement between special and general educators: An application of Miles and Huberman's cross-case analysis. *Learning Disabilities Quarterly*, **21**(winter), 34–56.

Mastropieri, M., & Scruggs, T. E. (1992). Science for students with disabilities. *Review of Educational Research*, **62**(4), 377–411.

Mastropieri, M. A., Scruggs, T. E., & Butcher, K. (1996). How effective is inquiry learning for students with mild disabilities. *Journal of Special Education*, **31**(2), 99–211.

Miller, M. (1999). *The opportunities and challenges of guided inquiry science experiences for students with special needs.* Unpublished doctoral dissertation, University of Michigan, Ann Arbor.

Palincsar, A. S. (1998). Social constructivist perspectives on teaching and learning. To appear in *Annual Review of Psychology*, **49**, 345–375..

Palincsar, A. S., Collins, K. M., Marano, N. L., & Magnusson, S. M. (2000). Investigating the engagement and learning of students with learning disabilities in Guided Inquiry science. *Language, Speech, and Hearing Services in the Schools*, **31**, 240–251.

Palincsar, A. S., Magnusson, S. M., Collins, K. M., & Cutter, J. (2001). Promoting identified students' understanding of scientific concepts and scientific reasoning in inclusive classrooms. *Learning Disabilities Quarterly*, **24**(1), 15–32.

Palincsar, A. S., Magnusson, S. M., Marano, N. L., Ford, D., & Brown, N. M. (1998). Designing a community of practice: Principles and practices of the GIsML community. *Teaching and Teacher Education*, **14**(1), 5–19.

Rogoff, B. (1994). Developing understanding of the idea of communities of learners. *Mind, Culture, and Activity*, **1**, 209–229.

Schumm, J. S., & Vaughn, S. (1995). Meaningful professional development in accomodating students with disabilities. *Remedial and special education*, **16**(6), 344–353.

SPeNSE (2000). Study of Personnel Needs in Special Education. Ferdig.coe.ufl.edu/spense.investigators.html.

The Cognition and Technology Group at Vanderbilt. (1994). From visual word problems to learning communities: Changing conceptions of cognitive research. In K. McGilly (ed.), *Classroom lessons: Integrating cognitive theory and classroom practice* (pp. 157–201). Cambridge, MA: MIT Press.

U. S. Department of Education (2001). Twenty-third Annual Report on the Implementation of the Individuals with Disabilities Education Act. http:www.ed.gov/offices/OSERS/ OSEP/Prodtcs/OSEP2001AnlRpt/.

Vaughn, S., Schumm, J. S. (1994). Middle school teachers' planning for students with learning disabilities. *Remedial and Special Education,* **15**(3), 152–161.

Vaughn, S., Schumm, J. S., Jallad, B., Slusher, J. & Samuell, L. (1996). Teachers' views of inclusion. *Learning Disabilities Research and Practice*, **11**(2), 96–106.

Wells, G. (1995). Language and the inquiry oriented curriculum. *Curriculum Inquiry,* **25**, 233–269.

Wenger, E. (1998). *Communities of practice: Learning, meaning, and identity.* Cambridge, UK: Cambridge University Press.

White, B., & Frederiksen, C. (1998). Inquiry, modeling, and metacognition: Making science accessible to all students. *Cognition and Instruction*, **16**(1), 3–118.

Woodward, J., & Noell, J. (1991). Science instruction at the secondary level: Implications for students with learning disabilities. *Journal of Learning Disabilities*, **24**(5), 277–284.

Woodward, J., Monroe, K., & Baxter, J. (2001). Enhancing student achievement on performance assessments in mathematics. *Learning Disability Quarterly*, **24**(1), 33–46.

A Lifespan Approach to Understanding Learning Disabilities

Learning Dis/ability as the Intersection of Competing Discourses: Implications for Classrooms, Parents, and Research

D. Kim Reid and Jan Weatherly Valle

Teachers College, Columbia University

I. INTRODUCTION

In its third decade of institutionalization within public education, special education has reached a crossroads. As debates about the overall efficacy of special education rage in both professional and popular literature, larger questions emerge about the purpose of schooling and the role of special education in achieving that purpose (Dudley-Marling, 2001; Andrews *et al.*, 2000; Brantlinger, 1997). What was a noble intention to provide a free and appropriate education in the least restrictive environment for students with dis/abilities[1] now engenders scathing criticisms among some professionals,

---

[1]We use the spelling *dis/ability* to remind our readers that "dis" is always the mirror image of and is co-constructed by our notions of "ability," that what we normalize in our culture and our time in history determines what is viewed as abnormal, however, such dichotomies as normal/abnormal, abled/disabled, healthy/pathological can be misleading and dangerous.

Learning about Learning Disabilities, Third Edition
Copyright © 2004 by Academic Press. All rights of reproduction in any form reserved.

who suggest that special education has become nothing more than "a refugee camp for the casualties of schooling" (Slee & Weiner, 1998, p. 105).

It is neither the presence of debates nor the criticisms leveled at special education that should concern us. Indeed, such debates reflect the work of thinking professionals who care about the educational outcomes for children. It is the current polarization about the direction of special education reform that has the potential to stymie the field and prolong the resolution of issues. Describing this schism as "the special education divide," Andrews *et al.*, (2000) identify two opposing and distinct viewpoints about special education: (1) incremental reformers who uphold the current system of searching out scientifically validated instructional practices and innovations that lead to educational transformations *within the individual* in contrast to (2) the substantial reconceptualists who maintain that the current system is inherently flawed because of assumptions about dis/ability *within both society and schools* that significantly limit the educational outcomes of individuals. In fact, within academic circles, this philosophical divide has materialized in the recent addition of Disability Studies in Education, a new special interest group within the American Educational Research Association (AERA), that stands apart from the Special Education special interest group. Clearly, this is a debate of significance.

The field of learning dis/abilities, with its particular history of enduring debates around what exactly constitutes a learning dis/ability as a differentiated category for *certain* students who display difficulty learning and not others, provides a rich context within which to consider what it means to identify and serve students designated as having "special needs"—special enough to warrant attention apart from the needs of ordinary learners. The very act of making decisions about which children deserve which resources for what purpose constitutes the construction of *meaning-making* about how we conceive a free and appropriate education for *all* children. As Dudley-Marling (2001) argues, "Ultimately, the meaning of learning disabilities is tied closely to the meaning of schooling" (p. 13).

II. DISCURSIVE PRACTICES OF DIS/ABILITY

To better understand the process of meaning-making within the learning dis/abilities field, it is useful for us to conceptualize "the linguistic conventions that structure the meanings assigned to disability and the patterns of response to disability that emanate from, or are attendant upon, those meanings" (Linton, 1998, p. 8). Our discursive perspective is not meant to diminish or call into question the academic difficulties of students labeled as learning dis/abled, but rather to broaden our understandings beyond conventional and naturalized ways of thinking. In this essay, we use the term *impairment* to refer to "variations that exist in human behavior, appearance, functioning, sensory acuity, and cognitive processing" (Linton, 1998, p. 2) and *dis/ability* as the product of the social, political, economic, and cultural structures of society (Corker & Shakespeare, 2002). Furthermore, we hope in making this distinction to bring unintended consequences that result from assumptions within our discipline to the fore. In conceptualizing learning dis/abilities as a discourse that responds to the shifting nature of the culture in which it is embedded (like all other discourses), we are able to consider how dis/ability becomes constructed in the ways we choose to speak about it and practice it.

A. Scientific, Medical, and Psychological Discourses

In that medicine and psychology spawned the field of learning dis/abilities (as well as the institution of special education), it is no surprise that the traditional conceptualization of learning dis/abilities embodies the scientific, medical, and psychological discourses: a scientific expert (e.g., school psychologist, neuropsychologist, clinical psychologist) must make a "diagnosis" based on comparisons with the performance of children thought to be "disability-free." However, as a disciplinary offspring not only of medicine but also of psychology, special education also embraces the inherent assumptions of that parent discipline. We see the basic tenets of science, medicine, and psychology in the centering and privileging of statistically defined "normalcy" (Davis, 1995), individualizing and pathologizing of difference, and adherence to the objective traditions of science (Linton, 1998). Hence, special educators choose *the individual* as the primary unit of analysis.

It is instructive to consider the process by which an ordinary child becomes a *disabled individual*. In current practice, teachers present academic tasks deemed "age-appropriate" with expectations of a specified range of responses that represent mastery. The child whose responses consistently fall outside this specified range eventually will, in most cases, be noticed as "a person with qualities to be discovered by agents of the School" (Varenne & McDermott, 1998, p. 215). Herein, the evolution begins. The child becomes an object of intense observation and documentation, a process reserved *only* for children who perform outside of the specified range of response. In order to confirm or rule out the possibility of learning dis/abilities, a teacher makes a referral so that a psychologist can administer a battery of psychoeducational tests to the child to generate an individualized psychoeducational report based largely upon the results. Soon, a special education committee meets to discuss the test results and to determine eligibility for individualized special education services. If deemed eligible on the basis of "really being" a special education student, an Individualized

Education Plan (IEP) is developed. The transformation from ordinary schoolchild to disabled individual is now complete.

The act of assigning individuals, specifically children, as the unit of analysis reveals much about the "taken-for-granted" assumptions that undergird special education generally and learning dis/abilities specifically. Such assumptions form the basis of a particular *discourse of disability* that, in turn, constructs a particular *individual*—the special needs child. Reliance upon the scientific, medical, and psychological discourses for making meaning of dis/ability precludes any conceptualization other than "deviance from the norm, as pathological condition, as deficit, and significantly, as an individual burden" (Linton, 1998, p. 11).

As a profession, special education relies upon the assumption that it is both legitimate and possible to expose, measure, and categorize normal and abnormal cognitive, emotional, and behavioral phenomena within individuals. Thus, a close relationship exists between psychometrics and special education. Given the origins of special education within medicine and psychology and the close association of psychometrics with the natural sciences, it is unsurprising that special educators embraced the construct of intelligence, giving rise to a widespread use of tests as well as a sustained belief in the capacity of tests to portray accurately how individuals learn and think (Thomas & Loxley, 2001). Consequently, the use of tests to explicate learning or failure-to-learn engenders a particular way of speaking about children. For example, the language of testing provides a host of terms and phrases that might be evoked in explaining a child's struggles to learn—a significant discrepancy between ability and achievement, areas of deficiency, visual and auditory processing problems, evidence of scatter, inattentive behaviors, erratic performance, reluctance to take risks, lack of inhibitory control, performance relative to grade level, and so on. Perhaps as Linton (1998) contends, "The fact that impairment has almost always been studied from a deficit model means that we are deficient in language to describe it any other way than as a 'problem' " (p. 141). Furthermore, the more focused we are on the individual, the more likely it is that the individual will become "determined" and restricted by his or her dis/ability status (Varenne & McDermott, 1998). Or, as Thomas and Loxley (2001) describe this phenomenon, the "disabled child" becomes enveloped in a "cocoon of professional help" (p. 53).

B. Institutional and Legislative Discourses

Because people act intentionally to construct social structures that support and distribute particular discourses, it is relevant to focus on special education as the institution society has constructed in response to children who struggle in school. If we conceive of language as a form of social practice, we more clearly see "conventions routinely drawn upon in discourses [that] embody ideological assumptions which come to be taken as mere 'common sense'" (Fairclough, 1989, p. 77). Thus, our interest lies in examining special education as an institution that speaks about learning dis/abilities in naturalized ways and enacts particular practices for individuals so classified.

Foucault's (1983) analysis of the human sciences is useful to our conceptualization of special education as a social institution. In understanding how an object of discourse (e.g., madness, sex, criminality) becomes "an overall discursive fact," Foucault (1978) considers "who does the speaking, the positions and viewpoints from which they speak, the institutions which prompt people to speak about it and which store and distribute the things that are said" (p. 11). Therefore, what interests Foucault (1973) is not the *truth* of what is said, but rather the *apparatus* itself through which what is said *can be said* in a particular society.

If, like Foucault, we understand special education as a discourse through which a whole system of practices functions in a coherent way, we grasp the ways in which dis/ability is produced and maintained. Special education is a complex apparatus constructed and monitored through law (The Individuals with Disabilities Education Act and its subsequent reauthorizations), enacted through the domain of public education, and financially supported by federal and state governments. As such, IDEA represents the intersection of political beliefs and scientific ideas about dis/ability within the specific cultural context of America at a particular time in history (Kalyanpur & Harry, 1999; Varenne & McDermott, 1998). For example, IDEA's emphasis upon *individuals* with dis/abilities reflects the particularly American value of individualism as does the law's intense focus upon *individual* educational programming (Turnbull & Turnbull, 1997). As Varenne and McDermott (1998) maintain, "The people of the United States tell each other that education is about individuals and their development and that educational practice is legitimate only to the extent that it fosters individual development" (p. 106).

The legal and educational practices underpinning the institution of special education likewise support the scientific, medical, and psychological discourses that select the individual as its unit of analysis. In response to the occasion of a child's failure to learn, a cadre of professionals who together comprise the learning dis/ability service industry (e.g., special education teachers, special education consultants, educational diagnosticians, school psychologists, clinical psychologists, tutors, special education administrators) stand poised and ready to apply their scientific tools to the task of identifying the educational needs of the individual child. Once characterized as having "special needs," the scientific, medical, and psychological discourses reposition the child who fails to learn as a child who *requires* an education that is, by definition, special—so "special" that it may mean an education apart from children without a "special" designation. For in America, the child who fails to learn is living within "a world well organized to label and disable" (Varenne & McDermott, 1998, p. 42). The discursive practices inherent within the present apparatus of special education lead professionals predictably toward the "easy overattribution of events to the dispositions of individuals rather than to the failings of institutions" (Thomas & Loxley, 2001, p. 53; Skrtic, 1991). Given that the current institutional/legislative discourses legitimize *normal* and *abnormal* as naturalized categories of individuals, it is also a discourse whose consequences extend deep within an individual's "most private deliberations about their worth and acceptability" (Linton, 1998, p. 24).

C. Social, Political, and Cultural Discourses

In contrast to the currently operationalized discourses (scientific, medical and psychological, and institutional and legislative) that individualize dis/ability, the newly emerging field of Disability Studies offers a framework for conceptualizing social, political, and cultural discourses. These are discourses that promote understanding of dis/ability as both a function of human variation (as opposed to pathology and deficit) and the meanings attributed to those variations (Linton, 1998). Within such a framework, the external conditions—social, political, and cultural—that contribute significantly to the dis/ability experience share center stage with human variation as the unit of analysis.

In contrast to an understanding of dis/ability solely in terms of deficits located within the individual (what we are calling impairment), these discourses acknowledge that dis/ability may be experienced differently depending upon an individual's race, class, and gender. Typically, in the quantitative studies that dominate the field, these discourses are largely ignored (Reid, 2001). Given the varying combinations of such identity dimensions, however, it follows that there can be no single experience of dis/ability.

If we reconceptualize learning dis/abilities in terms of human variation rather than pathology, it silences the debate about whether *all* children should receive a free and appropriate education in the least restrictive environment, that is, in inclusive[2] educational settings. In this view, variation is addressed through differentiation, not the sorting of children into already available categories. In response to dis/ability, it becomes necessary

---

[2]We must acknowledge that there are serious problems with the ways that what people call "inclusive education" is being carried out. In many instances, students are put into general education classes, but they never become part of the class, that is, they are never truly included. Or, they are put into classes where they are expected to do the grade-level work they cannot do and neither the students nor the teacher are given sufficient supports.

to move beyond assessment and intervention with the *individual* to assessment and intervention of the *context* in which the individual functions.

III. IMPLICATIONS FOR THE CLASSROOM

The link between the perspective we have described and instructional practice lies, for us, in Vygotsky's theory and its associated instructional methods, now widely research-based, and also its compatibility with critical theory. These ways of looking at instruction place emphasis on the *meaning* we give impairment (i.e., an impairment is only an occasion for difficulties and focuses on the impact of context on dis/ability. For far too long, special education has zeroed in on the "disordered child," and only now are some beginning to examine the failures in instructional environments—see, for example, the recent work of Beth Harry and her colleagues (2002)—and on examining who benefits from this arrangement, children and their families or the orderliness of schools. When we focus on what teachers must do to create a welcoming and productive classroom as educational practices interact with the individual characteristics of children, two questions become salient: First, how should teachers' roles differ from what is typical and traditional? And, second, what would classroom instruction look like if we focus on the context as a way to support difference?

A. Teachers and the Context

To create and re-create supportive, efficient, and effective contexts for learning minute by minute and day after day, teachers need to approach their work as *scholar practitioners:*[3] this is that teachers must be able to operate as responsive curriculum-makers and informed decision-makers rather than as technocrats who steadfastly follow directions in textbooks and implement preformulated programs—which are necessarily based on logical task analyses and, because of their built-in structure, cannot address the illogical, psychological realities of fluctuating student needs. To design curriculum and make effective decisions, teachers must know how to ask and answer questions to improve teaching and learning and vigilantly monitor the impact of societal forces as they get played out in classrooms. That is, they must regard teaching as critical inquiry and accept ethical responsibility for social change. Being a scholar practitioner is different from being a

---

[3]We are not talking about every teacher becoming a teacher researcher, although we have no problem with teacher research. The model we have in mind is that teachers continuously observe students, analyze, and keep track of what each student is doing (see Calkins, 1994, for specific and reasonable methods for doing this), and make decisions about what and how to teach the student using the data collected. It is in this way the teacher becomes the curriculum maker.

teacher researcher in the sense that data are collected as an integral part of teaching.

According to Vygotsky's view as well as that of both the dis/ability studies and dis/ability rights movements, the biological impairments—whether neurological, physical, or sensory—are real and can be substantial. What matters, as we have argued earlier, is not so much the fact that impairments exist, but the meaning we give them. As Hall (2000) points out, the problem with categorizing people is that we assign more value to some groups than others, therefore introducing inequitable power dynamics. In this sense, we can conceive of dis/ability as an historical social construction[4] rather than simply a medical fact. Dis/ability, therefore, is always an interaction between the student's characteristics and the demands (and supports) of the current historical and political as well as material environments (Fleischer & Zames, 2001; Longmore & Umansky, 2002; Mitchell & Snyder, 2000; Stiker, 2002). Teachers, then, need to examine both the "realities" of individual diversity (detectable or assumed) and the more textual stories, anecdotes, myths, jokes, and practices of our culture that define dis/ability in ways that serve to marginalize dis/abled people.

We argue that teachers need to accept ethical responsibility for social change not only because of our concern with dis/ability, but also because people with dis/abilities are not "neutral" bodies. We are concerned about the overrepresentation of students of color[5] and students who are English Language Learners (ELL) in special education—as well as their greater likelihood of being placed in segregated settings after they are identified (Losen & Orfield, 2002). Although the data suggest that such students are often underrepresented in the learning dis/abilities category and over-represented in mental retardation and emotional behavioral disturbance, we are aware that underrepresentation and the concomitant denial of services is a problem as well, particularly when Latinos/as, who tend to be under-represented in learning dis/abilities, are sometimes highly overrepresented in the juvenile justice system. Furthermore, as the number of students classified in one category goes down (e.g., in the category of mental retardation after the California courts determined that there was a disproportionate number of African American children labeled as mentally retarded), the numbers in one or both of the other categories goes up (i.e., learning disabilities and emotional disturbance). However, there is little variation in the

---

[4]Disability has carried different meanings in different cultures and in different periods of history. Longmore and Umansky (2001) trace the shifting meanings of dis/ability in American history and culture.

[5]We are well aware that the term "people of color" is problematic, because it makes whiteness invisible—as if white is not a color—at the same time that it centers whiteness as the normal and natural standard (Bartolome & Macedo, 1999). The term "English language learner" functions in a similar way, in that it centers Standard American English.

total number of students assigned to the three categories combined (Kavale & Forness, 1998). Part of the problem is that daily school practices—referrals, evaluations, placements, and instructional practices—are carried out under conditions never intended by the law (Harry *et al.*, 2002; Mehan *et al.*, 1986). Another part of the problem, of course, is that the mostly white teaching force operates on subconscious assumptions about what constitutes knowledge, the purpose of schooling, and appropriate curriculum (Losen & Orfield, 2002) and makes referrals based on those unconscious assumptions.

To counteract these problems in the case of dis/ability means learning to see through labels to perceive and honor the multidimensionality and capabilities of all students, despite their impairment(s). It also implies making serious efforts to learn from students about their situatedness (i.e., their individual positioning determined by the intersectionality of race, class, gender, sexual preference, and age) and what it means to them. To profit from this learning, teachers must have a thorough understanding of the nature of society and the interaction between culture and learning and how they construct and position various persons with dis/abilities. Teachers, particularly with students whose life experiences differ from their own, must ask students about their lives, listen to them, and learn from them. They must also be as knowledgeable about studying and empowering students in a variety of contexts (i.e., home, classroom, playground) as they are about planning and evaluating academic instruction. They must be prepared to collaborate in inclusive communities as well as teach in one-to-one or small-group settings. Teachers need to apply, modify, and invent classroom practices that allow all students to learn side by side in culturally relevant ways.

Culture plays such an important part because learning is an inherently social activity (Nieto, 2002; Vygotsky, 1987/1998, 1993). It is through working with others that one becomes socialized into the strategies and practices of the community, that is, becomes a literate person (Gee, 1999). Schooling is about the acquisition of ways of talking, acting, thinking, strategizing, knowing about knowing, and doing school—for example, different contents such as social studies, science, and mathematics require different languages and practices.[6] These are always associated with a social group, such as the community or the class. In classrooms, often

---

[6]The IRE model is often criticized, because the teacher does most of the talking and holds the lion's share of the power. It also forces students to respond rapidly and with predetermined correct answers, often a problem for students with impairments that manifest as learning dis/abilities. However, this does not mean that this form of instruction should never be used. It can be useful in some kinds of lessons. Certainly, however, it should be used much less often than it currently is. As we differentiate instruction more, we believe that teachers will choose this model less frequently.

"appropriate" ways of behaving are considerably different from those learned by children at home (Heath, 1983). This mismatch is particularly apparent when children from urban or rural settings or nondominant/racial/cultural/linguistic groups enter school and confront the preference teachers typically have for language usage that is narrowly defined by Standard American English (SAE) exposition. We would not argue that students should not be taught SAE, but rather that their home languages and other aspects of culture be accepted and used as the basis for instruction and for crossing boundaries to SAE. That they are not has been largely a political, rather than instructional, decision.

Since learning is internalized through social, most often dialogic, interactions, we consider these languages and practices both the context for and the content of instruction. This means, as Rueda, Gallego, and Moll and others (see Torres-Velasquez, 1999) have pointed out, that what constitutes the least restrictive environment and defines the nature of a free and appropriate education is not static. Curriculum is enacted in each classroom with each teacher and each group of students during each minute of the day. As a consequence, the least restrictive environment is no more a place than is special education. The former is a range of services; the latter shifts minute to minute according to what is being said and done in the material context of the classroom, by whom, and about what. As a consequence, teachers must be prepared to address the ways that classroom participation structures—the IRE model (teacher Initiates, student Responds, and teacher Evaluates), revoicing, structured and conversational instructional groupings (Reid & Fahey, 2000)—can be used to promote learning through dialogic social interaction, learner independence through structured routines, and access to the general education curriculum through differentiated instruction. We should note here that we interpret the 1997 reauthorization of IDEA as well as the No Child Left Behind Act of 2002 as emphasizing access to the general education curriculum over exclusively accelerated (typically, in deficit models, referred to as *remedial*) approaches to instruction.

However, because every student is different—there really are no "types" of students—and learning dis/abilities are, by definition, a heterogeneous group of disorders, we also highlight the need for student-centered, authentic, and contingent instruction. Such instruction requires that teachers design primarily social and holistic (Thomas & Loxley, 2001) tasks that address the curricular goals. Once the tasks have been assigned, they observe and evaluate students' responses, and scaffold the students' behaviors by helping them extend appropriate responses and redirect incorrect or insufficient ones.

Vygotsky (1987/1998, 1993) also argues that teaching must lead development. Teachers, then, must support children as they work within their individual zones of proximal development: that is, beyond what they can do without assistance but within the range of what they can do with support. It is in this way that students grow into the languages and practices of schooling. For example, students learn language by interacting with other language users, science by collectively carrying out experiments, history by researching and writing historical narratives.

To carry out this kind of contingent teaching, teachers must have inquiry tools—they must know how to observe, conference, and interview; generate anecdotal records; take and analyze field notes; lay out sociograms; analyze student work samples and portfolios, etc.—to solve the ongoing problems of teaching, to study an individual student, to collect information to share with parents, and/or to provide evidence to support a position for colleagues and supervisors. Such data can be very important in prereferral trial teaching and in the development of IEPs. It is this kind of close observation and contingent teaching that promotes teachers as curriculum makers and reveals the nature of appropriate academic and culturally relevant responses.

In sum, we see the role of teachers as supportive and interactive inquirers. They observe and guide students, incorporating a gradual release of teacher (and other student) responsibility. As students participate in and progressively acquire appropriate school behaviors, they become increasingly able to act independently. Knowledge is acquired through a reciprocal effect between learners and teachers, who transform the discourse of interest even as they are transformed by it. Clearly, we are not advocating what has become business-as-usual: the general education classroom with a teacher at the front and most students working individually on the same task at the same time, perhaps with students with learning dis/abilities working with a teacher, teacher aide, or paraprofessional over to one side doing one-to-one or remedial instruction. Or, worse yet, situations where students are removed from the classroom for all or part of the day.

B. Our View of Classroom Instruction

We begin with the (democratic, civil rights) assumption, grounded in social justice concerns, that separate is not equal and that all students belong in general education classrooms (Shapiro, 1999). Rather than ask if a student with a learning dis/ability belongs, we ask what the *teacher* must do with the assistance of other team members to make the general education classroom a welcoming, productive, and constructive environment for all students. In our minds, the responsibility for "fitting in" has more to do with changing attitudes and the development of welcoming classroom communities and compensatory and differentiated instructional approaches than with the characteristics of individual learners. Another way to say this is that the focus is on redesigning the context, not on individuals' impairments.

We acknowledge that there is considerable resistance to this position as a result of historical assumptions about dis/ability and the practices and purposes of schooling. We also acknowledge that we need to learn more about how to do inclusion better and that we might never become so sufficiently skilled that we are always able to include 100% of students. Nevertheless, our basic assumption is that social justice is best served through the pursuit of increasingly inclusive practices.

One way of truly including students with dis/abilities (rather than having them in general education classrooms in which they are still marginalized) is to include in the curriculum a variety of ways of knowing. For example, teachers might discuss with students how the privileging of science has served to disempower the voices of persons who do not have formal training—in comparison to experts of the scientific, medical, psychological, institutional, and legal discourses—and begin to expose students to materials that incorporate different ways of knowing. People with dis/abilities, because of reduced life chances, are often among those who are undereducated, although they have a lot to tell us about the experience of being dis/abled, particularly with respect to being in schools and other life settings with a label. So teachers might include in the curriculum personal-experience narratives in the form of autobiographies, interviews, focus groups, essays, etc. and assist students in discovering what we can learn from them. Other useful materials include novels, poems, and other forms of literature as well as films, videos, and TV programs. Teachers can also direct students to the internet, newspapers, magazines, and other popular information sources—both those developed by people with dis/abilities and those in which students with dis/abilities are written about by others. Another avenue for foregrounding nonscience forms of knowing is to invite parents and other people from the community to share their knowledge on relevant topics.

Respect for life experience helps all of us militate against the notion that we and other "experts" have the answers. It helps our students become more sensitive and appreciative of the knowledge that people with dis/abilities have to share and positions them to be more understanding of the dis/ability rights and dis/ability studies movements. We hope that it might also help engender in today's children a stance of solidarity with those dis/abled people who are working so assiduously to improve circumstances for themselves and others, particularly those who are unable to speak for themselves because of poverty, language issues, etc.

The first step in providing a supportive, welcoming, and productive classroom environment is the building of a classroom community. It is a strong community that facilitates academic, social, and emotional growth among students, particularly within communities composed of diverse learners (Peterson & Hittie, 2003; Sapon-Shevin, 1999). Community-building is a conscious and evolutionary process that begins on the first day of school and ends on the last day. It is the foundation that supports cooperative learning, differentiated instruction, and classroom talk. To ensure successful implementation of such strategies, teachers must intentionally create a classroom environment that engenders a sense of safety and belonging, a value for diversity, shared responsibility for the community, and an overall atmosphere of support and caring. What might a community of learners look like in action? Upon entering such a classroom, one would most likely notice movable classroom furniture that is arranged and rearranged to foster active collaboration among students. Bulletin boards are not teacher-made; instead, students "own" and use bulletin boards to reflect life in this particular classroom. Group photographs may be placed around the classroom, depicting students engaged in memorable community activities. In that collaboration is valued over competition, students constantly work together and view one another as valuable sources of knowledge, regardless of differing ability levels, culture, or ethnicity. Class meetings are routine, providing a site in which teacher and students engage in respectful and thoughtful dialogue about their community. Lastly, students take ownership for their community, sharing in leadership roles and active problem-solving.

Another step is the use of differentiated instruction (Tomlinson, 1999, 2001). Differentiated instruction is a flexible system of offering multiple levels/types of instruction around the same key learning goals. Teachers determine what is to be learned by all—let's say one structure for writing an expository paragraph using introductory, supporting, and concluding sentences—and then groups—and regroups, sometimes heterogeneously, sometimes homogeneously and sometimes even as a whole group, depending on the nature of the lesson—students who work collaboratively to help one another achieve that goal, whether the assignment be an individual or group assignment. Teachers may vary the process, product, or content of assignments in order to meet the needs of students working at various levels of familiarity and competence. For example, some students may be asked to write an expository report on some topic they research together; some may be asked to compose an essay using expository paragraphs, but on some familiar topic that does not require research; and some groups may be asked to write a single paragraph. The common instructional goal allows all students to share in large group instruction, discussion, and debriefing. Textbook companies are now producing social studies and other texts that cover the same content at different levels of reading complexity, which can greatly facilitate the implementation of differentiated instruction.

Compensatory instruction, on the other hand, is designed to allow the students access to the general education curriculum in ways that work around their dis/abilities. Students with reading problems might watch a film, listen to a recording, read with a partner, or prepare a text the night before with the help of their families at home in order to enable them to participate in classroom activities. As another example, students having difficulties in writing or spelling may be taught to use computer spell- and grammer-checks. We mention compensatory instruction because it is powerful but seldom used.

What we do not advocate is instructional *accommodations*. This term suggests that classroom instruction be designed for those students who "fit" grade-level requirements and then modified for those who cannot perform well. It is this kind of thinking that continues to marginalize students with dis/abilities, who are nearly always perceived as not fitting in one way or another—academically, socially, physically, etc. Instead, instruction should be designed from the outset with all students in mind. Seldom, then, is it appropriate to conceptualize a classroom as a space in which a single teacher teaches a single lesson to all students at the same time. Instead, it is more productive to think of the classroom as a community of learners and teachers who work together to make certain that everyone is supported in doing work that is appropriate.

Clearly, our approach to classroom practices is more *politically grounded* and *interactive* than that of many teachers and colleagues. Many take for granted, for example, that the deficit is in the child, where we prefer to think of the problem as a sociopolitical one (e.g., curbs and steps, not immobility, cause the handicapping condition, despite the fact of paralysis). Or, for another example, there seems to be an assumption that the law always protects students and their families; we, however, advocate the examination of how legal ideology also functions to stabilize social structures that reproduce inequitable educational outcomes.

We think an honest look at the competing discourses in the field (i.e., scientific, medical, psychological, institutional, legal, social, political, and cultural) and the failures (e.g., disappointing efficacy studies, overrepresentation of students of color) of special education enables teachers to become aware that they have choices and that those choices have real consequences for real children. Focusing on students' impairments leads to much different conceptualizations, assessments, and interventions than does focusing on, for example, the medical, legal, and bureaucratic sets of apparatus that classify them as disabled. The result is that teachers become more thoughtful about what they do, more aware of the impact of their decisions, and, hopefully, assume ethical responsibility for making change where it is needed.

IV. IMPLICATIONS FOR PARENTS (CAREGIVERS)

The Individuals with Disabilities Act (IDEA) mandates collaborative decisionmaking among parents and professionals. Specifically, the law ensures that parents have the right to be informed, the right to be knowledgeable about the actions to be taken, the right to participate, the right to challenge, and the right to appeal (IDEA, 1990, 1997). Thus, parents have the right, by law, to engage with professionals in the special education process. However, upon stepping into the arena of special education to exercise the legal right to participate, parents unwittingly enter an ongoing drama in which the principal players speak the elaborate language of science and law and offer mere walk-on roles to parents.

As established elsewhere in this chapter, special education embodies scientific, medical, psychological, institutional, and legislative discourses. Entrenched within the positionality of "expert," school professionals typically initiate, direct, and terminate special education committee meetings. Parents may struggle to understand the legal and scientific language that circulates among professionals. Their own child, described by professionals as an amalgamation of test scores, discrepancies, deficits, and limitations, sometimes becomes virtually unrecognizable to them (Valle & Aponte, 2002). The parent's knowledge of the child, in contrast, appears informal (i.e., less important) in its lack of scientific verification. Thus, special education discourses that drive and sustain practice may effectively alienate parents from the collaborative process guaranteed by law.

How might we reconceptualize the relationship between professionals and parents to come closer to the kind of collaboration envisioned within IDEA? We must first recognize how scientific, medical, and psychological discourses estrange parents from the process. Special education professionals can begin by refusing the standpoint of objectivity required by science to embrace "other ways of knowing" that may emanate from a subjective and particular standpoint. In opening such a space, parents can participate as experts in their own right. They bring to the table holistic conceptions of the child across time and contexts. The integration of such textured and contextual understandings of the child with educational perspectives would most certainly lead us closer to authentic collaboration. Furthermore, the release of special education professionals from the shackles of objectivity should enable parents and professionals to engage with one another as people with a common interest in the educational welfare of the child—in sharp contrast to performing the "roles" of parent and professional as typically expected within current special education practice. Within a context of shared responsibility, parents and professionals should be able to construct a reciprocal relationship of mutual benefit in which each genuinely learns from the other.

We must also acknowledge that parents may experience the institution of special education differently, depending upon their cultural orientation. For example, Kalyanpur et al. (2000) suggest that "the principle of parent participation is based on ideals that are highly valued in the dominant culture" (p. 122). In other words, parents from cultures other than the white, middle-class culture of the United States may not value the special education guarantee of due process in the quite the same way. For cultures in which the needs of collective society supersede those of the individual, it may be difficult for parents coming from such (sub)cultures to appreciate the emphasis that special education places upon individual performance and intervention (Kalyanpur & Harry, 1999).

As discussed at length elsewhere in this chapter, the discursive practices of special education operate within a scientific, objective framework. Hall (1981) contends that cultures for which objectivity holds great value are "low context" cultures, that is, cultures that rely upon decontextualization as a means to generalization. In contrast, "high context" cultures "accept, even encourage, conclusions that tolerate greater ambiguity" (Kalyanpur & Harry, 1999, p. 7). Thus, parents from high context cultures who question the practices of a low context culture (e.g., America) are at risk for being perceived as ignorant, impertinent, and/or uncooperative. Moreover, the conception of dis/ability as something that resides within the individual and requires treatment may be bewildering to parents from (sub)cultures in which dis/ability "has spiritual causes, is temporary, is group owned, and must be accepted" (Kalyanpur & Harry, 1999, p. 45).

How might we consider differing worldviews within the context of parent/professional collaboration? In order to communicate and collaborate effectively, we contend that the position of the special education professional needs to be that of a listener/learner. To engage in meaningful collaboration with parents means letting go of the alienating expert stance that positions professionals above parents rather than beside them. It is within *mutual* dialogic exchange that authentic collaborative relationships have the possibility to flourish.

V. IMPLICATIONS FOR RESEARCH

Approaching dis/ability as we have suggested obviously implies a revised agenda for our research enterprise as well as our educational one. Thinking of dis/ability as a sociohistorical, scientific, medical, psychological, institutional, and legal construction means that we must begin to research and, when needed, change the sociopolitical and cultural contexts in which individual conditions or impairments play out. It also suggests that we focus more on the variety of potential meanings one might assign to individual impairments that render them hurtful or harmless. We hinted at some needed realignments in our research efforts earlier: studies directed at understanding how the sociohistorical, scientific, medical, psychological, institutional, and legal discourses position students as dis/abled; investigations to determine which and how aspects of instructional environments and professional beliefs and attitudes produce and re-produce dis/ability; exploration of how the myths, stories, anecdotes, and jokes that circulate in our culture have defined and continue to define dis/ability and how we might interrupt effects that are harmful (such as the overrepresentation of students from nondominant-culture linguistic and ethnic/racial groups); and searching for ways of increasing commitment to and processes for improving inclusion, societal and educational. Additional federal and state funds are one part of the solution, but improved teacher education programs that emphasize the rights of all children to be in classrooms and prepare teachers to carry out differentiated instruction are also essential. We need to learn more about how to do this well.

But, important as these issues are, more than new topics and questions are needed. Our fascination as a field with quantitative designs and methods is troubling, given that researchers have employed the procedures of the hard sciences to study humans—now widely believed to be inappropriate (see Denzin & Lincoln (2000) and Thomas & Loxley (2001) for extended arguments). One of the reasons why this has been so troubling is that this work has led almost exclusively to the *comparison of groups*. Group-based methodologies, however,

> by abstracting particular groups' similarities from an understanding of their various complexities (such as differences among them in terms of gender, class, language, locality, age, health, sexual orientation, [ability], etc.), often fall into the trap of *essentializing* (e.g., perceiving all Latinos/as [or students or subgroups of students with learning dis/abilities] to be the same), objectifying (i.e., seeing people as objects of educational policies and practices, rather than as self-determining subjects with a say in their education), or even romanticizing the lives of those on the margins. (Leistyna, 1999, p. 149)

Acceptance of such group-based distinctions is built into the system. American educators share a mindset that we can or should be able to know something about student behavior and achievement from a label, the student's test scores, and sometimes even race/ethnicity or native tongue. In fact, these presuppositions almost never hold true; the picture is always too complicated to allow generalizations. For example, at least some factors, such as academic initiative, are more closely aligned with immigrant status (e.g., how many generations a family has been in the United States or the country of origin) than with racial/ethnic background (Tai, 1999) and yet concerns with immigrant status are virtually absent from our literature. As a consequence, we should be skeptical about educational research that draws conclusions regarding groups without reference to the social positionings of specific individuals within these groups. Reid (2001) argues elsewhere that randomizing these differences away in controlled designs or matching subjects are not adequate solutions. Rather, they serve to obscure important information.

Another problem with group-based studies is that although many demonstrate significant *associations*, eager researchers often interpret these findings as *causal*. Thomas and Loxley (2001), for example, suggest that despite years of research and claims about causality, it is still unclear whether reading (sub)skills, such as phonemic awareness, are the cause of the deficit or the result. Careful reading of the literature confirms the legitimacy of their critique: it is as plausible to assume that students who are experiencing difficulties learning to read, for example, may not be adept at the (sub)skills being assessed because they do not read well as it is to assume that failure to acquire those (sub)skills is the basis for their inability to read. Other problems Thomas and Loxley raise with respect to quantification include the fallacy of reductionism, the metaphorical nature of knowledge, the reification of constructs through the use of the measurement instruments that define them, and the negative effects of labeling on identity and performance. They assert that claims touting the progress of special education over the last 100 years seem to be related more consistently to "changes in the political and social climate than from research in special education" (p. 23). The climate that led to PL94–142 is one case in point, the growing federalization of education another. No wonder we consistently read laments from educational researchers about the gap between research, at least theoretically objective and controlled, and practice, rooted in habits of mind and the spontaneous, intuitive, and local decision-making that grows out of them.

Perhaps educational change is rooted in shifts in the zeitgeist, because administrator, teacher, and student habits of mind—their identities, like all person's identities—are formed and reformed in whatever political, symbolic, and economic conditions dominate society at large. In the context of contemporary capitalist social formations, these conditions are competitive and hierarchical and, in mainstream special education research, treated as if they were static and immutable "truths." What we need, then, is a more dynamic and fluid notion of how we think about difference, a conception that would enable us to examine the more textured nuances of the societal and individual co-construction of meanings, and their material effects, surrounding individual impairments. "Such a perspective of identity would support our efforts to shatter static and frozen notions that perpetuate ahistorical, apolitical, and classless views of [difference as it exists in] culturally pluralistic societies" (Darder & Torres, 1999, p. 177).

Linton (1998) suggests that we turn to the methods of the "new scholarship"—that of the humanities, feminist studies, area studies, and so forth. These are post-positivist in nature, which means that they recognize a relationship between the observer and the observed, and, therefore, eschew objectivity and generalizability. All research is partial; there is no expectation that something stable and final can be said (Lincoln & Denzin, 2000), because every study is situated in a particular point of view. Knowledge is interpretative: it stems from our "reading" of the world. Interviews, ethnographies, case studies, and life histories (Reid, 2001) are some useful methods that constrain neither the questions researchers can ask nor the types of responses that participants can give.

VI. CONCLUSIONS

People with dis/abilities, like the rest of us, are not static "core" selves, but rather each is a "colony of possibilities" (Bruner, 1990). To know them, to teach them properly, we must listen to and respect their voices and their parents' (caregivers') voices and not dismiss or denigrate their knowledge through the scientific, medical, psychological, institutional, and legal discourses that now construct them. We may benefit greatly by expanding the forms of knowledge we consider *to count*. Change efforts must focus on the school rather than the child and on society as the basis for the shifting attitudes and practices of schooling. The history of dis/ability in Western culture indicates that

> considered as a feature of society, difference might be said to enjoy
> mixed fortunes. Sometimes difference is in vogue; it is a thing to be
> welcomed and may be referred to wholesomely in such terms as
> "diversity." On other occasions...it is viewed as something more
> shadowy, even malevolent, with any difference being treated as
> deviant (Munroe, 1977, cited in Thomas & Loxley, 2001, p. 77).

What we have to realize is that things need not be the way they are; as a profession, we have a choice to make. We can continue to sort and segregate students according to the current special education discourses despite the lack of evidence that these are helpful to them. Or, we can work in solidarity with people with dis/abilities to foster a set of different assumptions: not competition, but cooperation; not exclusion, but inclusion, and not disability, but ordinary human diversity.

References

Andrews, J. E., Carnine, D. W., Coutinho, M. J., Edgar, E. B., Forness, S. R., Fuchs, L. S., Jordan, D., Kauffman, J. M., Patton, J. M., Paul, J., Rosell, J., Rueda, R., Schiller, E., Skrtic, T., & Wong, J. (2000). Bridging the special education divide. *Remedial and Special Education*, **21**, 258–260.

Bartolome, L. I., & Macedo, D. P. (1999). Dancing with bigotry: The poisoning of racial and ethnic identities. In R. H. Tai & M. L. Kenyatta (eds.), *Critical ethnicity: Countering the waves of identity politics.* New York: Rowman & Littlefield.

Brantlinger, E. (1997). Using ideology: Cases of non-recognition of the politics of research and practice in special education. *Review of Educational Research,* **74**(4), 425–459.

Bruner, J. (1990). *Acts of meaning.* Cambridge, MA: Harvard University Press.

Calkins, L. M. (1994). *The art of teaching reading.* Portsmouth, NH: Heinemann.

Corker, M. & Shakespeare, T. (2002). *Disability/Postmodernity: Embodying disability theory.* London: Continuum.

Darder, A., & Torres, R. D. (1999). Shattering the "race" lens: Toward a critical theory of racism. In R. H. Tai & M. L. Kenyatta (eds.), *Critical ethnicity: Countering the waves of identity politics.* New York: Rowman & Littlefield.

Davis, L. J. (1995). *Enforcing normalcy: Disability, deafness, and the body.* London, UK: Verso.

Denzin, N. K. & Lincoln, Y. S. (Eds.) (2000). Handbook of qualitative research. Thousand Oaks, CA: Sage Publications.

Dudley-Marling, C. (2001). Reconceptualizing learning disabilities by reconceptualizing education. In L. Denti & P. Tefft-Cousin (eds.), *New ways of looking at learning disabilities* (pp. 5–18). Denver: Love.

Education for All Handicapped Children Act (P. L. 94–142) 1975, amending Education of the Handicapped Act, renamed Individuals with Disabilities Education Act, as amended by P. L. 98–199, P. L. 99–457, P. L. 100–630, & P. L. 100–476, 20 U.S.C., Secs. 1400–1485.

Fairclough, N. (1989). *Language and power.* London, UK: Longman.

Fleisher, D. Z. & Zames, F. (2001). *The disability rights movement: From charity to confrontation.* Philadelphia: Temple University Press.

Foucault, M. (1983). Afterword: The subject and power. In H. L. Dreyfus & P. Rabinow, *Michel Foucault: Beyond structuralism and hermeneutics.* Chicago, IL: University of Chicago Press.

Foucault, M. (1973). *The birth of the clinic: An archaeology of medical perception* (A. Smith, trans.). New York: Vintage Books.

Gee, J. P. (1999). Critical issues: Reading and the new literacy studies. Reframing the National Academy of Sciences report on reading. *Journal of Literacy Research,* **31**, 355–374.

Hall, E. T. (1981). *Beyond culture.* Garden City, NJ: Anchor Press/Doubleday.

Hall, S. (ed.). (2000). *Representation: Cultural representations and signifying practices.* London, UK: Sage.

Harry, B., Klingner, J. K., Sturges, K. M., & Moore, R. F. (2002). Of rocks and soft places: Using qualitative methods to investigate disproportionality. In D. J. Losen and G. Orfield, *Racial inequity in special education.* Cambridge, MA: Harvard University Press.

Heath, S. B. (1983). *Ways with words: Language, life, and work in communities and classrooms.* Cambridge: Cambridge University Press.

Kalyanpur, M., Harry, B., & Skrtic, T. (2000). Equity and advocacy expectations of culturally diverse families' participation in special education. *International Journal of Disability, Development, and Education*, **47**(2), 119–136.

Kalyanpur, M., & Harry, B. (1999). *Culture in special education*. Baltimore, MD: Paul H. Brookes Publishing Co.

Kavale, K. A. & Forness, S. R. (1998). The politics of learning disabilities. *Learning Disability Quarterly*, **21** (4), 245–273.

Leistyna, P. (1999). Racenicity: The relationship between racism and ethnicity. In R. H. Tai & M. L. Kenyatta (eds.), *Critical ethnicity: Countering the waves of identity politics*. New York: Rowman & Littlefield.

Linton, S. (1998). *Claiming disability*. New York: New York University Press.

Longmore, P. K. & Umansky, L. (2001). *The new disability history: American perspectives*. New York: New York University Press.

Losen, D. J., & Orfield, G. (2002). *Racial inequity in special education*. Cambridge, MA: Harvard Educational Press.

Losen, D. J. & Orfield, G. (2002). Racial inequity in special education. Cambridge, MA: Harvard University Press.

Mehan, H., Hartwick, A., & Meihls, J. L. (1986). *Handicapping the handicapped: Decision-making in students' educational careers*. Stanford, CA: Stanford University Press.

Nieto, S. (2002). *The light in their eyes: Creating multicultural learning communities*. New York: Teachers College Press.

Peterson, J. M., & Hittie, M. M. (2003). *Inclusive teaching*. Boston, MA: Allyn & Bacon.

Reid, D. K., & Fahey, K. (2000). *Language development, differences, and disorders*. Austin, TX: Pro-Ed.

Reid, D. K. (2001). Montague and Rinaldi and Meltzer, Katzir-Cohen, Miller, and Roditi: A critical commentary. *Learning Disability Quarterly*, **24,** 99–105.

Sapon-Shevin, M. (1999). *Because we can change the world*. Needham Heights, MA: Allyn & Bacon.

Shapiro, A. (1999). *Everybody belongs: Changing negative attitudes toward classmates with disabilities*. New York: RoutledgeFalmer.

Skrtic, T. M. (1991). *Behind special education: A critical analysis of professional culture and school organization*. Denver, CO: Love.

Tai, R. H. (1999). Investigating academic initiative: Contesting Asian and Latino educational stereotypes. In R. H. Tai & M. L. Kenyatta (eds.), *Critical ethnicity: Countering the waves of identity politics*. New York: Rowman & Littlefield.

Thomas, G., & Loxley, T. (2001). *Deconstructing special education and constructing inclusion*. Buckingham, UK: Open University Press.

Tomlinson, C. A. (1999). *How to differentiate instruction in mixed-ability classrooms*. Alexandria, VA: ASCD.

Tomlinson, C. A. (2001). *The differentiated classroom: Responding to the needs of all learners*. Alexandria, VA: ASCD.

Torres-Velasquez, D. (ed.). (1999). Sociocultural perspectives in special education. Special issue of *Remedial and Special Education*, **20**.

Turnbull, A. P., & Turnbull, H. R. (1997). *Families, professionals, and exceptionality: A special partnership* (3rd ed.). Upper Saddle River, NJ: Merrill/Prentice-Hall.

Valle, J. W., & Aponte, E. (2002). IDEA and collaboration: A Bakhtinian perspective on parent and professional discourse. *Journal of Learning Disabilities*, **35**, 469–479.

Varenne, H., & McDermott, R. (1998). *Successful failure*. Boulder, CO: Westview Press.

Vygotksy, L. S. (1987/1998). *The collected works of L. S. Vygotsky* (Vols. 1–5). New York: Plenum.

Vygotksy, L. S. (1993). *The collected works of L. S. Vygotsky* (Vol. 2). New York: Plenum.

CHAPTER 16

Adolescents with Learning Disabilities: Revisiting *The Educator's Enigma*

B. Keith Lenz and Donald D. Deshler
The University of Kansas

I. INTRODUCTION

Surrounded by controversy and suspicion over the nature of learning disabilities that plague those with learning disabilities at any age, adolescents with LD are further tormented by the turbulence of adolescence. Their experience does not engage the interest and attention of the majority of researchers in the field, who are interested in beginning language, literacy, numeracy, and social development. Similarly, they are not close enough to independence to be of significant interest to the growing number of employers, government agencies, and adult literacy service providers concerned with how adults with learning disabilities navigate the areas of work, family, and community.

Historically, most of the professional literature as well as initiatives in research, program development, and even federal funding were directed at younger students with learning disabilities. The prevailing assumption (or hope) was that if intervention took place at a young age, many of the manifestations of the learning disability would be minimized or avoided

*The authors wish to express our appreciation to Dr. Jean Schumaker, our colleague at the University of Kansas Center for Research on Learning, for her support and assistance in the completion of this manuscript.

altogether in later years (Kirk & Elkins, 1975). However, the field has learned that adolescents and adults with LD have enduring and unique characteristics that manifest in differing ways as development and setting demands change (e.g., Brinckerhoff *et al.*, 1992; Mellard & Deshler, 1991; Schumaker & Deshler, 1984, 1987).

By adolescence, individuals with learning disabilities are unique because they develop layers of secondary characteristics that evolve due to persistent and often unaddressed primary learning disabilities at a time when they are forming a life identity. Repeated and unsuccessful attempts to teach an individual to read lead to more than a persistent reading or learning disability. As adolescents with learning disabilities move to an environment where reading and other skills are assumed, they are more likely to be viewed as being lazy, lacking vocabulary and background knowledge, being poorly organized, and as either having difficulty interacting with others or choosing to associate with the wrong peer group. Simultaneously, they are developing belief systems and images of themselves as workers, students, and as members of families and communities.

The impressive array of data that have emerged during the past 15 years in NICHD-sponsored research on reading and learning disabilities (e.g., Lyon & Fletcher, 2001) has helped make the case for early identification and intervention. While focusing on younger children is of great importance and laudable, there is a potential danger in overemphasizing early treatment *at the expense of* interventions at later ages. That is, the calls for these early intervention efforts may be misinterpreted as implying that by doing the early intervention, most of the problems presented by students with learning disabilities will be addressed. While this is certainly a desired outcome, it is much more likely that while age-specific learning tasks may be addressed, the underlying problems will persist and continue to manifest in new ways and in different learning tasks as students get older and demands increase. Deshler (2002) has argued that there are two primary reasons for not putting all of our eggs in the early identification and intervention basket (Deshler, 2002).

> First, even though an impressive array of reading interventions have been developed for younger students (e.g., Foorman *et al.*, 1991; Torgesen *et al.*, 1992), it is unlikely that these methods will be successfully implemented *to scale* nationally given our schools' poor track record of implementing educational innovations (e.g., Elmore, 1996; Fullan, 1993; Knight, 1998). In spite of the effectiveness of the existing set of interventions, the problems of bringing any innovation to broad-scale implementation with fidelity is remote (Cuban, 1984). Because of the enormous challenges of effecting large-scale implementations, there will be many students who will not receive the intervention and will move on to later grades with significant, unaddressed deficits. Second, even if

children with learning disabilities do receive quality interventions during their early years, in all likelihood, their disability will endure into adolescence and adulthood. The need for equally effective intervention strategies for these older individuals is as great as, if not greater than, the need for interventions for younger children because of all the emotional overlays that generally emerge as individuals mature and continue to encounter significant failure (Shaw *et al.*, 1994). Hence, it is critical that the learning disabilities field has a research and intervention agenda that is designed to address multiple aspects of the condition of learning disabilities across multiple age ranges. As compelling as the case for early intervention can be, if that case is made *at the expense of* addressing the equally problematic and unique set of problems presented by older-aged individuals, the long-term effects of such a policy will be devastating for thousands of individuals with learning disabilities.

Despite the continuing tendency for many in the field of learning disabilities to assume that the characteristics of adolescents with learning disabilities are the same as those of younger children and that the nature and conditions present in elementary schools are more similar than dissimilar from those found in secondary schools, evidence continues to mount to underscore the fact that there are, indeed, significant differences relative to (a) the characteristics of adolescent learners, (b) the conditions of schooling under which they must learn and perform, and (c) the types of interventions required to dramatically impact their performance. Notable progress has been made during the past 25 years in all three of these areas. Decision making relative to programming and policy directives should be carried out in light of what has been learned rather than incorrectly assuming that sound practice for adolescents is simply an extension of what characterizes younger students and how they are taught.

The purpose of this chapter is to (a) provide an historical context within which to understand current practice, challenges, and issues related to meeting the needs of adolescents with learning disabilities; (b) highlight some of the important findings that have emerged through research on older students with disabilities; (c) profile an array of instructional principles that have emerged as being centrally tied to producing significant outcomes for adolescents with learning disabilities; and to (d) discuss important research and policy issues that should be addressed to improve the field's capacity to better meet the needs of these students.

II. HISTORICAL CONTEXT

An important lens through which to understand how adolescents have been viewed, studied, and educated is that of various federal legislative and funding initiatives in the United States. This panoramic view helps to explain where the field currently stands relative to the quality of services it is prepared to provide to these older-aged students.

The landmark passage of P. L. 94–142 in 1975 was instrumental for a broad array of reasons. However, for adolescents with disabilities, this legislation meant that almost overnight schools were under the edict to provide services to a group of students that heretofore had largely been ignored—that is, adolescents with learning disabilities. Until the passage of this legislation, the vast majority of schools which provided services to students with learning disabilities did so at the elementary level but not necessarily during middle school or high school.

In the late 1970s, through Part D of P. L. 94–142, two major funding initiatives directed federal funds to projects that focused on adolescents with learning disabilities. First, the Child Service Demonstration Centers (CSDCs) were designed to provide federal funding for projects that outlined innovative approaches to identifying and providing services to students with learning disabilities in school settings. While the majority of the projects funded were for programs working with elementary-aged students, several awards were given to projects that focused on secondary schools. These projects varied greatly from parallel alternative curricula designed to provide materials from core classes in alternative formats to intensive skill-based classes that afforded students multiple exposures to critical skill sets to learning strategy instruction designed to teach students how to learn (Deshler, 1978). As these programs became established, networks of professionals throughout the country were formed. Through formally scheduled meetings and informal conversations, a critical mass of professionals and activities surrounding adolescents with learning disabilities emerged. It became clear that the challenges and issues facing those charged with providing services to adolescents with learning disabilities in secondary school settings were not only perplexing but they were, in many instances, unique from the challenges presented by younger LD students.

While valuable information emerged from the CSDC initiative, it did not provide to the field the kind of research base that was needed to address basic issues surrounding learning disabilities identification and treatment. Consequently, a second Part D funding initiative was launched by the Bureau of Education for the Handicapped (later renamed the Office of Special Education Programs [OSEP]) to establish five Institutes for Research in Learning Disabilities (IRLDs). The charge to each of these institutes was to develop and validate successful interventions through basic and applied research. The University of Kansas Institute for Research in Learning Disabilities was the first national research center designed to focus exclusively on adolescents with learning disabilities. For the first time in the field's history, several lines of programmatic research were aimed at understanding the unique characteristics of adolescents with learning disabilities as well as designing intervention packages to impact their performance in school and nonschool settings (see Alley *et al.*, 1983; Deshler *et al.*, 1982; Schumaker *et al.*, 1983). One of the most significant outcomes of the five IRLD was a significant cadre of individuals who earned their doctoral degrees while being affiliated with IRLDs. This added significantly to the overall scholarship capacity of the field and created a critical mass of leadership personnel who were prepared to conduct research on populations of individuals with learning disabilities.

The attention directed to carrying out an aggressive research agenda on populations with learning disabilities through the IRLDs, however, was short-lived. In the mid- to late-1980s, federal funding was redirected to other priorities that included Handicapped Children's Model Projects (HCMPs), which were similar in purpose to CSDCs *but* their intent was to address the needs of *all* types of students with disabilities, not just students with learning disabilities. Additionally, during the latter part of the 1980s, considerable attention was directed to issues related to transition from secondary schools to the world of work. Madeline Will, director of the Office of Special Education and Rehabilitative Services, championed the transition movement (Sitlington *et al.*, 1999). Her persuasive leadership was strengthened by several legislative initiatives. During this period of time, the needs of adolescents with learning disabilities were largely seen as being met through effective transition plans. This fact, coupled with a realignment in the internal organization of OSEP, resulted in a limited number of specific funding opportunities to study the unique problems of populations with learning disabilities.

In the early 1990s, the NICHD began supporting a major research effort to study word-recognition problems in young children with learning disabilities. This work, which was heavily funded throughout the 1990s and into the twenty-first century led to significant breakthroughs in understanding the nature of underlying reading problems encountered by children with learning disabilities (e.g., Foorman *et al.*, 1991; Torgesen *et al.*, 1992). Regrettably, hardly any of this research focused on older students. In 2003, however, NICHD, the Office of Vocational and Adult Education (OVAE), the Office of Special Education and Rehabilitative Services (OSERS), and the Institute for Education Sciences (IES) teamed together to commit approximately $2.8 million in FY 2003 to fund four to six new 5-year grants in the area of adolescent literacy. The specific focus of the request for applications was "the discovery of cognitive, perceptual, behavioral, genetic, hormonal, and neurobiological mechanisms that are influential in the continuing development of reading and writing abilities during the adolescent years, and on methods for the identification, prevention, and remediation of reading and writing disabilities in adolescents." This shift in funding priorities is most encouraging given the long dearth of even minimum grant attention and support for the in-depth study of the underlying causes of reading and writing disabilities and how these are manifested in adolescents.

Building on the call in the IDEA Amendments of 1997 for students with disabilities to gain access to the general education curricula, the Office of Special Education Programs (OSEP) funded two institutes to study the needs of adolescents with disabilities (these efforts focused on issues of disabilities as a whole and not the potentially unique problems surrounding adolescents with learning disabilities). One 5-year grant was awarded to the University of Wisconsin–Madison (Research Institute on Secondary Education Reform [RISER]) (Hanley-Maxwell *et al.*, 2001); the other was a jointly funded grant to the University of Kansas and the University of Oregon (the Institute for Academic Access [IAA]) (Deshler *et al.*, 2001). The primary focus of Project RISER was to understand the contextual realities supportive of inclusive education in high school environments. The focus of IAA was to design and validate interventions for improving educational results for high school students with disabilities (including those from high poverty areas and from organizationally and demographically diverse settings). Some of the findings of the IAA research effort will be summarized in the remainder of this chapter.

While these two OSEP-funded initiatives as well as the jointly supported (NICHD/OVAE/OSERS/IES) adolescent literacy initiative are encouraging signs, there remains evidence that the unique (and often perplexing) problems of adolescents are *not* viewed as being major issues in the learning disabilities field. Most significantly, the reauthorization of IDEA in 2003 includes provisions for altering the methodologies used to identify students with learning disabilities. That is, for the first time, schools are allowed to use identification models other than aptitude–achievement discrepancy models to make learning disabilities determination decisions. The alternative model that has captured the strongest support from many researchers, professional organizations, and practitioners is the Responsiveness-to-Intervention (RtI) Model. This model is applied in general education classrooms by using curriculum-relevant tasks. A baseline for student performance is taken to determine current level of functioning. Students who are performing below a designated cut-point are then taught relevant skills using evidence-based instructional practices from the targeted curriculum area. Finally, students are retested to determine their level of "responsiveness" to the intervention. Those who are not responsive may be provided with additional instruction under altered instructional conditions (e.g., increased intensity). If students fail to respond to instruction after several iterations of the instructional routine, they may be deemed candidates for additional assessment for possible designation as having a learning disability.

Nearly all of the research on the RtI Model has been done with early elementary students and the academic tasks that are selected for use in the RtI Model are such things as word lists that are tied to the curriculum, number facts, etc. Selection (and subsequent measurement) of such tasks for younger students is a relatively straightforward task. However, the selection and measurement of tasks that are related to secondary curriculum areas (e.g., social studies, science, etc.) are much more problematic. These issues have largely been ignored by those advocating the RtI approach (e.g., Vaughn & Fuchs, 2003). The prevailing assumption is that if a workable model can be developed for younger children, it will be relatively easy to generalize the findings to older students in secondary settings. This assumption ignores the complexities of secondary curricula and the fact that most secondary teachers do not see their role as being one of conducting repeated probes in basic skill areas to identify students with learning disabilities. While these problems are potentially solvable, it is significant to note that the unique needs of adolescents and the unique dynamics of secondary classrooms are largely being ignored in one of the most significant policy debates in years.

It is encouraging to note that during the past 25 years, headway has been made in turning attention of researchers and program developers to the special challenges presented by adolescents with learning disabilities (Deshler *et al.*, 2001). This work has underscored how vitally important it is to thoroughly understand the unique characteristics of these learners and the schools in which they must survive. Instructional programs must be tailored in light of these factors. However, there remain many more unanswered than answered questions. Long-term, programmatic research is needed to bring about the kinds of breakthroughs that will be required to dramatically improve the outcomes that most adolescents with learning disabilities are currently experiencing.

III. HOW RESEARCH HAS INFORMED PRACTICE

There has been an increase in the amount of research conducted on adolescents judged to be at-risk for academic failure (including those with learning disabilities) that sheds light on how we can improve our educational practices. These research findings can be divided into three areas: (a) learner characteristic variables, (b) setting demand or contextual variables, and (c) intervention variables. A sampling of key findings from each of these areas is highlighted in this section.

A. Learner Characteristic Variables

Over the past 25 years, numerous studies have shown that achievement scores in reading, writing, and mathematics plateau as students move through the secondary school grades (Schmid *et al.*, 1980; Warner *et al.*, 1980; Gregory *et al.*, 1985; Curtis, 2002). These studies indicate that once students move into an instructional environment that emphasizes content mastery over the development of skills, skill development slows and eventually halts for most adolescents with learning disabilities. What is most significant about the line of studies that points to this finding is that very little change overall has occurred over the past 25 years in secondary schools as a result of this knowledge. In other words, our awareness of the problem has not led to significant changes in practice to reverse this trend.

While we have been aware of the failure of secondary schools to address the poor achievement growth of adolescents with learning disabilities, efforts to examine the characteristics of adolescents' literacy development confirms that this achievement plateau is likely to occur across groups of adolescents characterized by reading difficulties. In a review of studies on adolescent literacy across adolescents with a history of reading difficulties, Curtis (2002) reported that growth in word analysis and word recognition skills levels off at the third- to fifth-grade reading levels. Based on these data, it may be possible to conclude that the current structure of secondary schools and the literacy services that they provide are not compatible with conditions required to promote literacy for any students, whether they have a learning disability or not. If this is true, then advocacy for secondary school reform that places literacy improvement as a key goal should be broadened to stakeholder groups outside of the disability community.

Beyond those studies that document underachievement of adolescents with learning disabilities compared to their peers, numerous researchers have demonstrated that adolescents with learning disabilities do not maximize the skills and knowledge that they have acquired through the effective use of learning strategies (see Swanson, 1993, p. 62, for a review). That is, students with learning disabilities don't effectively set goals, make plans, follow plans, monitor plans, monitor progress, reflect, and adjust plans in ways that lead to completion of tasks or resolution of problems commensurate with peers without learning disabilities. Therefore, students with learning disabilities are viewed as poor or inefficient information processors. In response, various researchers have chosen to investigate various dimensions of this difference in processing by investigating student strategy use (e.g., Torgesen & Houck, 1980; Wong & Jones, 1982; Wong *et al.*, 1986; Lenz & Hughes, 1990; Graham & Wong, 1993).

If students with learning disabilities can be characterized by their inefficient use of strategies to process information, then instruction in strategies to compensate for or enhance processing should show interventions based on strategy instruction to be effective. For example, Swanson (2001) in a review of strategy-based interventions selected interventions that included two or more goal-oriented tactics designed to enhance information processing or reduce the complexities of information processing as part of the intervention package (e.g., the use of elaboration combined with verbal dialogue with the teacher or peers to complete a task). To answer the question about which interventions seemed most effective for students with learning disabilities, Swanson (2001) reported that interventions that focused on a learning strategies approach to teaching individuals with learning disabilities, including adolescents with learning disabilities, accounted for most of the variance in his meta-analysis of interventions. These findings not only help us understand which instructional approaches may be most beneficial for these students, but reinforce the importance of considering the impact of inefficient strategy use on learning.

Strategy differences appear to extend beyond academic tasks and into personal and social realms as well. For example, social skills of adolescents with learning disabilities closely resemble adjudicated youth (Schumaker, 1992). As a result, the underlying strategy differences can affect problem solving that youth face in personal and interpersonal dilemmas and may also affect their judgment and decision making in difficult situations, more so than youth who do not have a learning disability. These youth may then become more at-risk for making poor choices about using illegal substances, participating in illegal activities, becoming sexually active, and becoming involved in destructive relationships. Conversely, failure at being able to successfully navigate social situations may make youth with learning disabilities more likely to avoid social relationships of any type (Schumaker, 1992).

The impact of the failure of schooling is also apparent. The National Longitudinal Transition Study (Wagner et al., 1993) reported that a disproportionate number of students with learning disabilities dropped out of school compared to the general population. Prior to dropping out of school, these students evidenced a broad array of other performance and adjustment problems including: (a) higher rates of absenteeism; (b) lower grade-point averages (Schumaker, Deshler, Bulgren et al., 2002); (c) lower scores on state/national achievements tests (Schumaker, Deshler, Bulgren et al., 2002), (d) higher course failure rates than those in the general population (Wagner et al., 1993); (e) feelings of poor self-esteem (Wagner et al., 1993); and (f) higher rates of inappropriate social behaviors (Schumaker, 1992). Predictably, only a small minority of these individuals was found to pursue a post-secondary education (Wagner et al., 1993). In short, students with learning disabilities typically lack the skills needed to succeed in high school, and are not prepared to face the demanding expectations of the globalization of commerce and industry, the dramatic growth of technology, and the dramatic transformation of the workplace and the very nature of work itself (Martin, 1999; Oliver, 1999; Rifkin, 1995).

In summary, two important lines of research have been conducted that have particular merit in helping us understand adolescents with learning disabilities. First, research on the descriptive nature of the population points to their inability to process information in the same way as students who do not have disabilities. Differences in the way that these students approach and handle tasks consistently characterize these students. These differences commonly manifest themselves across academic tasks and affect many aspects of these student's lives. While some students show more discrete areas of processing disability (e.g., specific to a type of task such as learning to read), difficulty processing information whether across areas or in a specific area is a more accurate way of describing students with learning disabilities.

The second line of research focuses on response to intervention. Consistent with the research on descriptive nature of these students, interventions that focus either on compensating for potentially difficult processing tasks or on teaching students with learning disabilities how to process information more efficiently improves their learning. While research based on clinical interventions for both children and adolescents has demonstrated that instruction in learning strategies is effective, discovering how these findings can directly influence learning and performance, given the complex set of circumstances and demands that surrounds adolescents, is more elusive. Intervention variables that have been found to effectively promote learning in a secondary setting are described in the next section.

B. Setting Demands and Contextual Variables

In a series of studies (see Schumaker, Deshler, Bulgren *et al.*, 2002), a broad set of descriptive data were collected from nine high school settings representing urban, suburban, and rural settings. Collectively, these data paint an informative picture of some of the defining features of high school settings and the context within which adolescents with disabilities must survive. A synopsis of some of the major findings that emerged from this research is the following:

1. Enrollment in Rigorous Content Classes

To what extent are adolescents with learning disabilities enrolled in core curriculum classes with their nondisabled peers? Overall, adolescents with disabilities were enrolled in only about 5% of the potential core curriculum classes (English, history, science, mathematics) in which they could be enrolled. For example, for a sample of 153 adolescents with disabilities in an urban high school (assuming that each student could be enrolled in 4 core courses), there would be a potential of 612 rigorous course enrollments ($153 \times 4 = 612$). In this school, the actual number of rigorous general education enrollments was 8. Thus, for the most part, adolescents with disabilities are not included in rigorous course work that leads to a standard high school diploma. Excluding students from these settings places them at a great disadvantage when it comes to being prepared to pass state outcome examinations. In essence, many schools appear to have "written off" adolescents with disabilities by setting low expectations for them relative to their classroom placements.

2. Accommodations are Offered

When students with disabilities are placed in rigorous core courses, can they expect accommodations? A review of practices in the nine high schools studied indicated that students with disabilities couldn't count on their teachers making accommodations to facilitate their learning. Two hundred eighty-five core academic classes were observed across the nine high schools and very few instances of accommodations were observed. In addition to 10 instances of individual attention that were noted, the following accommodations were observed: extra credit (1), enlarged worksheets (2), take tests elsewhere (2), go to resource room for help (2), and work with student before/after school (1). It was interesting to note that in filling out a survey, general education teachers indicated that they frequently adapted their curriculum to provide accommodations for students with disabilities.

3. Attitudes of Teachers and Administrators

Why do these students fail? General education teachers and administrators believe that the major contributors to academic failure for students with disabilities are low student goals, poor student attitudes, and poor student skills and abilities. Simultaneously, they indicated that they believe school-wide structures and policies as well as instructional methods contribute least to student failure. They also indicated that they believe that student progress is satisfactory when about 50% of the students are mastering at least 50% of the curriculum content. In short, these reports indicate that expectations are relatively low for students with disabilities and that the primary explanation for poor performance is centered in the student and not inappropriate instruction, accommodations, or the school structure.

4. Instructional Practices in General Education Classrooms

When general education teachers were observed, they engaged in instruction 59 to 89% of the intervals observed. For the largest portion of these intervals, they were addressing the whole group of students (not just the students with disabilities). They spent the largest portion of instructional time engaged in lecture or reading aloud to students. Other frequently observed teacher activities were giving directions, asking questions, and monitoring students as they worked. They were observed to engage in few motivational behaviors and only rare instances of critical instructional behaviors such as modeling, elaborated feedback, or the use of graphic organizers were observed.

Overall, we can say that while many arenas of education may be changing to respond to the diversity of students and how students need to learn, the instructional culture of high schools has not been affected by this movement. High schools continue to provide poor instruction for most students including students with learning disabilities. While there are exceptions, the teachers and administrators in the high schools that were studied approached education as primarily teacher-centered, viewed change to accommodate learning differences as compromising standards, and viewed most problems in student learning and achievement as student-centered.

C. Intervention Variables

Ever since the emergence of hypotheses suggesting that information processing could be improved by instruction in "how to learn," research has consistently supported this approach. Students with learning disabilities can learn and apply strategies in ways that improve their performance (Swanson, 2001). In addition to the research demonstrating the success of strategy instruction, research has also been conducted on variables that are important during the instructional process. Two major sets of variables have emerged as important in designing interventions for adolescents with learning disabilities: (a) the use of direct instruction to teach learning strategies, and (b) the use of explicit content area teaching routines that can compensate for inefficient strategy use.

1. Direct Instruction of Learning Strategies

A 20-year line of programmatic research conducted by The University of Kansas Center for Research on Learning (KUCRL) staff and others indicates that adolescents with learning disabilities can learn complex packages of cognitive strategies and can apply them to tasks that are required within the high school general education curriculum (see Schumaker & Deshler, 1992, for a partial review). Unfortunately, the instructional methods that are effective in teaching these complex strategies involve the intensive investment of time and resources, typically in pull-out/support-type educational settings. Numerous research studies have indicated that general education teachers' attempted use of these methods is not effective in teaching strategies to students with learning disabilities who have been included in diverse classes, primarily because the teachers (a) have a large amount of content to cover, (b) are unwilling to present numerous opportunities for practicing the strategies, (c) do not have the required time available to evaluate student work related to strategy instruction, and (d) because of the large numbers of students present in the classroom, are unable to provide the individual feedback required by students with learning disabilities to make progress (Beals, 1983; Boudah et al., 1997; Deshler & Schumaker, 1993; Scanlon et al., 1996; Seybert, 1998). In short, core curriculum teachers alone are not able to provide the level of intensity required to ensure that adolescents with learning disabilities will master needed strategies. This is an important point that should guide program planning for adolescents with learning disabilities given the emphasis on providing inclusive education to students in general education settings.

However, instructional situations in which instruction is sufficiently intensive must be created to ensure that students will have an opportunity to learn the strategies needed to reduce the impact of their disability. To address this challenge, the Learning Strategies Curriculum has been developed as part of an ongoing R&D effort associated with the Strategic Instruction Model (SIM). The Learning Strategies Curriculum has undergone extensive field testing with adolescents to validate the efficacy of this instructional approach (e.g., Deshler & Lenz, 1989; Deshler & Schumaker, 1988; Schumaker & Deshler, 1992). Since 1979, school district personnel have tested the instructional procedures and the task-specific learning strategies in a host of different settings with different kinds of students.

Each intervention included in the SIM curriculum includes the instructional procedures and materials needed by the teacher to teach adolescents to acquire and generalize a given strategy. The curriculum has been organized to focus on three major categories of demands presented by various curricula—acquisition, storage, and expression of information. In addition to the content design of the learning strategies (i.e., the overt and covert steps needed to complete a task or meet a challenge, such as how to self question during reading to increase comprehension), another issue that has captured significant attention has been the design of instructional methodology for explicitly teaching learning strategies. Out of this work has emerged an eight-stage working model that incorporates a set of procedures for promoting the acquisition and generalization of a learning strategy (Brownell et al., 1993; Kline et al., 1991). A programmatic series of research studies was conducted to determine whether the eight-stage instructional methodology could be effectively used to teach strategies to at-risk adolescents, including those with learning disabilities (Schumaker & Deshler, 1992).

Two major questions have guided this line of programmatic work: Can adolescents be taught to use the learning strategies and learning strategies curriculum? Does their use of the strategies result in improved performance on academic tasks? Fourteen studies were conducted to address these questions (Schumaker & Deshler, 1992). In general, this research has shown that adolescents dramatically improved use of a particular strategy when the instructional methodology was implemented. In all of the studies, students generalized their application of the strategy across stimulus materials. In the studies focusing on reading strategies (Clark et al., 1984; Lenz & Hughes, 1990; Schumaker et al., 1982) generalization occurred across materials with varying reading and ability levels. Several studies showed that student performance on generalized academic tasks also improved when they used the strategy. For example, when students used The Paired Associates Strategy to find, organize, and memorize paired facts in high school textbooks, their scores improved when they were given the textbook chapter and asked to prepare for a test over the information in the chapter (Bulgren et al., 1995).

The validated instructional procedures for teaching all strategies within the SIM curriculum include eight stages of acquisition and generalization. The seven acquisition stages are: (1) orient to key concepts, assess, and make a commitment to learn, (2) describe the nature of the skills, the potential benefits, and the steps of a strategy, (3) model the behavior and cognition involved in using the strategy, (4) verbal practice of the key information and steps of the strategy, (5) controlled practice of the skills with feedback from peers and/or teacher, (6) advanced practice of the skills with feedback from peers and/or teacher, and (7) posttest and make commitments to generalize the strategies. The eighth stage, generalization, includes four distinct phases: (1) orientation and awareness of situations in which the strategy can be used, (2) activation by preparing for and practicing strategies in content-area classes, (3) adaptation of the strategy for other tasks, and (4) maintenance of the strategy for continued application in a variety of real-life learning and workplace settings. Research has shown that 98% of all the low-achieving students who were taught the strategies mastered them if the eight-stage instructional procedure described here (Ellis et al., 1991; Schumaker & Deshler, 1994) was followed carefully.

Although the strategy curriculum is considered valuable to participants, the unique and most powerful feature appears to be the instructional approach embedded throughout the curriculum and how well the teacher implemented the procedures. Prior to teaching strategies in each of the interventions, instructors undergo professional development in SIM. Part of this professional development effort will provide them an opportunity to practice delivering instruction in a controlled setting with content from the SIM curriculum and to receive feedback on their practice sessions. Proficiency in the instructional components or science of instruction related to strategic instruction is also embedded within the text of the curriculum so that for each new skill, instructors are given examples of how to describe and model the skill, and provide verbal, controlled, advanced practice and generalization activities. In this manner, fidelity to the intervention is greatly enhanced.

2. Teaching Routines to Compensate for Inefficient Strategies

Another line of research has addressed the question: What type of instruction is required to ensure that students acquire critical background knowledge when they do not have the efficient strategies required for independent learning? The line of research, conducted by KUCRL researchers, has focused on routines, called Content Enhancement Teaching Routines, to address this question. These routines are used by general education teachers in core curriculum courses to enhance content and to deliver the content in "learner-friendly" ways, using a variety of sensory modalities and validated instructional principles, such that students can easily understand and remember the content. Each routine is anchored in a graphic organizer or visual that is used to assist in the visual presentation and sorting of information and is implemented via a sequenced set of steps that teachers use to actively engage their students. Routines have been developed and validated for: (a) introducing and organizing teacher-led instruction for lessons, units, and courses (Lenz, 1994; Lenz, 1998) (b) teaching major concepts (i.e., "colonialism," "poetry," "equation") (e.g., Bulgren *et al.*, 1993, 1994; Bulgren, Lenz *et al.*, 1993); (c) teaching interrelated facts (Ellis, 1998); (d) teaching the meaning of vocabulary words and other terms (Ellis, 1992); (e) making content memorable (Schumaker *et al.*, 1998b); (f) introducing a textbook chapter (Deshler *et al.*, 1997); and (g) engaging students in content-rich assignments and projects (Rademacher *et al.*, 1998).

Research has shown that when core curriculum teachers use one of these Content Enhancement Teaching Routines on a consistent basis, the unit test scores of *all* students in the class (including those with disabilities) improve by approximately one letter grade (e.g., Bulgren *et al.*, 1988, 1993, 1994). Moreover, research has shown that most students with learning disabilities who were previously failing course tests can pass those tests if the teaching routine is used to present the content lessons.

Like the instructional procedures developed for instruction in learning strategies, the instructional procedures developed for use by core curriculum teachers were carefully studied by the researchers across the various studies. In each case, teachers did three important things. First, the teacher explicitly taught the class about the graphic device and how the device was used as a part of an instructional routine. Second, the teacher used the routine regularly throughout the targeted content learning period so that students had multiple opportunities to learn how the routine guided learning. Third, the teacher overtly engaged students in a strategic process each time the routine was used in a way that modeled and guided students through the steps of efficient information processing using a graphic organizer to show the student how information was organized. As the class became more familiar with the routine over time, the teacher encouraged students to assume more responsibility for guiding the completion of the device as part of group instruction.

D. Perspectives on Practice

During the 1970s, a theoretical framework emerged for addressing inefficient information processing in adolescents through learning strategy instruction.

In the 1980s, data was generated lending evidence-based support for this link and various models emerged for teaching learning strategies and for applying strategy-based instruction to problems that the adolescent faced beyond academic tasks. Strategy instruction was used in different ways to enhance motivation, social interactions, and transition to out-of-school settings. In the 1990s, researchers in the field of special education continued to demonstrate this link, and research on strategy instruction began to be applied to teacher planning and content area instruction. In the 2000s, we are seeing strategy instruction merge with general education methodologies as part of group instruction provided in the core curriculum.

In large measure, the merging of special education and general education methodologies has been partly due to the growing experiential as well as empirical evidence that instruction that has worked successfully for students with learning disabilities has been shown to work for students without disabilities (Vaughn et al., 2000). As a result, teachers who are responsible for meeting the needs of increasingly diverse groups of students are being urged to adopt methods originally designed to increase the learning of students with learning disabilities as part of group instruction (Lenz & Ehren, 2001).

This movement may be best represented by interest in the application of universal design principles to curriculum development. Universal design represents a movement to develop instructional environments for all students in which a variety of high-impact learning supports are built in to facilitate learning for any student who needs them (Rose & Meyer, 2002). For example, in a collaborative effort between the Center for Applied Special Technologies (CAST) and the University of Kansas Center for Research on Learning (KUCRL), technology, web-based text readers, learning strategy instruction, and content enhancement devices are being blended to develop a prototype for an interactive digital textbook that will provide scaffolded instruction in promoting learning of high school biology. The digital textbook will also provide cues and supports for learning high school biology regardless of a student's learning needs. This blending of technology, strategic supports, and core curriculum content opens the door to new ways of providing universal access to content regardless of a student's level of need. As a result, teachers are provided with new options for individualizing instruction in the context of mainstream education.

The ability to integrate strategic supports into broader learning contexts has only recently become possible because of results from ongoing research on what works under which conditions across a secondary school environment. Six conditions that should guide overall program design appear to be critical. These conditions, include attention to: (a) how strategies for learning are acquired and generalized, (b) how we compensate for inefficient learning strategies during content learning, (c) judiciously selecting which content is critical for all students to really know, (d) developing a continuum of literacy supports that cut across all teachers in a building, (e) establishing academic relationships that give youth voice, and (f) providing nonacademic interventions that promote youth planning and control. These conditions are described here.

1. Attention to How Strategies for Learning are Acquired and Generalized

Those who want adolescents with learning disabilities to learn and use strategies cannot ignore the huge body of research on the type of instruction that has been found to be successful. We know that an effective sequence for strategy instruction includes a process of assessment, student and teacher commitment and goal setting, describing the strategy, modeling the strategy, practice that moves from teacher guided to student guided, and guided support to help the student learn how to generalize the strategy across tasks and settings—at school, at home, and in the community. However, beyond this sequence, we also know that level of explicitness, teacher responsiveness, and the intensity of instruction provided to students as a teacher moves through this sequence is also important. Graphic organizers, frequent reviews, verbal elaboration on strategy elements, ongoing reflection on strategy purpose and applications in the real world, high levels of student response and participation during instruction, scaffolding of practice, opportunities for individual feedback, and opportunities to learn about and to modify the strategy for various learning situations should define the instructional sequence that is used to ensure learning for adolescents with learning disabilities, (see Swanson, 2001, and Vaughn et al., 2000, for a discussion of these variables).

Unfortunately, even though we know how to teach strategies to most students with learning disabilities, few secondary teachers across general and special education programs are even aware of this type of instruction or lack the know-how to provide this type of instruction in the secondary setting. In addition, few administrators or curriculum coordinators are knowledgeable enough about the instructional methodologies required to provide effective strategy instruction to help teachers develop these skills. And in many of those classrooms where strategy instruction is being provided, class size is not sufficiently limited to allow teachers to provide instruction that is intensive enough to bring about the learning outcomes desired nor do teachers have the time to work with other teachers to collaborate on strategy generalization. While there is great flexibility in how instructional methodology can be implemented, it is clear that an overall philosophy of providing intensive and explicit instruction combined with authentic experiences in applying the strategy in obviously successful ways is required. More careful school and program planning needs to be provided to create the instructional conditions needed to accomplish this if academic gains are to be realized for students with learning disabilities.

2. Attention to How We Compensate for Inefficient Learning Strategies during Content Learning

When students have not learned how to apply effective learning strategies independently to content area learning (e.g., mastering vocabulary in biology) or to meet more personal needs (e.g., learning how to operate a piece of equipment at work), the student with learning disabilities is faced with meeting task demands without benefit of needed educational experiences. This is often the challenge that students face as they participate in secondary core curriculum course work. In this instructional situation, the student needs to be taught by experts in the subject knowledge arena who can make relevant content decisions as well as experts in the strategy arena who know how to guide the student in ways to learn the content that can compensate for students' poor strategies. The research on promoting content acquisition in the core curriculum either through teaching the student strategies directly or through the use of content enhancement devices described earlier has demonstrated that guided strategic processing (i.e., verbally walking through the learning process required to complete the task) when combined with graphic organizers (i.e., visually showing the student how the content is manipulated as the steps of the process are completed) helps the student learn the content and models how the content is mastered.

Research on teacher planning for students with disabilities (see Lenz *et al.*, in press, for a review) indicates that core curriculum teachers who are expert in the subject matter have not developed insights into how their subject matter is mastered. However, consistent use of explicit teaching routines that allow teachers to regularly reflect on the insights that they have developed and then to authentically test their decisions in classroom situations is an effective way of helping teachers learn how to do this. For example, Bulgren & Schumaker (in press) reported that prompting core curriculum teachers to regularly select and use a graphic organizer-based teaching device to guide students in a content learning task (e.g., learning a key concept) throughout a course helped teachers move to a more explicit and strategic approach to instruction. Bulgren *et al.* reported that in addition to using the routine, teachers needed to use a process called "Cue–Do–Review" each time they used it. The "Cue" phase involves initially teaching students how the device will be used and then subsequently alerting students to the device and how it will facilitate learning until its use becomes automatic. The "Do" phase involves using the graphic organizer to complete a learning task in partnership with students following a set of steps that represent a strategic approach to the task. The teacher provides scaffolded instruction in helping the student see a link between what they already know about the content and new learning. The "Review" phase involves revisiting what students now know about the content as well a reviewing the underlying strategy associated with the graphic organizer. Eventually, as teachers and students routinely work together through the content enhancement device, both become better at using the tool and are prompted to think more deeply about the content as well as the process for learning the content.

What is most important about this process is that it allows teachers to become more explicit and focused during group instruction. Bulgren *et al.* reported that studies have consistently shown that significant learning gains can be seen for students without disabilities as well as those with disabilities when this instructional process is used. This is important because it increases the odds that teachers will adopt and continue to use research-based approaches because they are effective for a wide variety of students (Lenz, Schumaker, Deshler *et al.*, 1991).

3. Attention to Judiciously Selecting which Content is Critical for All Students to Really Know

We know that Content Enhancement Teaching Routines can significantly increase learning in core curriculum classrooms when students do not have optimum learning strategies. However, the planning needed for this type of instruction requires thoughtfulness that is incompatible with the current mindset commonly found across teachers in secondary schools—which focuses on how quickly large amounts of content can be covered in a course. The greatest battle we face is how to eliminate the academic punishment of students who do learn content that has not been filtered for worth and importance. This does not mean watering down the curriculum or compromising standards, What we must fight for is more careful delineation of which content is critical for *all* students to master (i.e., what is critical for satisfactory performance in life across home, family, job, and social contexts), what content should *most* students master (i.e., what enhances life contexts, but is not critical), and what content should some students master (i.e., what enhances and is personally interesting, but is not critical) (Lenz *et al.*, 2004) The reason that this is so important is that the *time* needed for teachers to enhance the most critical content through teacher-guided instruction does not allow time to be usurped for content that is not critical, especially if students are going to be punished in the grading process. Secondary teachers are not being asked to face this challenge alone. Every educator at every instructional level and in the corporate world must struggle with how to sort through the mass of possible information to be learned to determine how to sort content for different types of learning.

However, this approach to filtering and focusing for content area instruction does not mean that standards are not placed front and center. It means that content-area teachers must find the heart and soul of the standards, ensure that student learning begins at this point, and then work outward. The critical content will be highly focused during instruction; other content may be targeted, but the focus of direct teacher attention will not be directed toward this content, and the grading consequences for students who do not have the background knowledge, skills, or strategies to process this independently will be minimal. This also requires teachers to plan what part of the critical content needs to be committed to memory (e.g., what vocabulary and concept learning is required), what type of thinking is required (e.g., comparative or causal reasoning), and how this information should be generalized for problem solving outside of school.

4. Attention to Developing a Continuum of Literacy Supports that Cut Across All Teachers in a Building

Traditionally, programs for students with learning disabilities have focused on interventions that are effective at a micro-level. However, integration of services for students with learning disabilities into the general education setting has required special educators to think more broadly about how services for adolescents with learning disabilities fit within schoolwide programs and into the school improvement process. Recent initiatives to improve the literacy of students at the secondary level have provided a forum for collaborative planning for literacy-based reform efforts that can benefit adolescents with learning disabilities. Most literacy initiatives have focused on how to improve the reading and overall literacy performance. However, as mentioned at the beginning of this chapter, consideration of the impact on the success of adolescents with learning disabilities in the secondary school environment requires a different approach to developing literacy programs.

Literacy initiatives at the secondary level are most likely to be successful if they can integrate the need for the development of skills, mastery of appropriate learning strategies, and approaches to ensuring mastery of content. Researchers at the KUCRL have adopted a framework for developing literacy services in secondary schools called the Content Literacy Continuum (Lenz & Ehren, 2001). While the Content Literacy Continuum (CLC) provides a framework for implementing the SIM model in schools, it also provides a framework for other literacy programs and meets the needs of adolescents with learning disabilities within the context of schoolwide literacy improvement for all students.

There are five levels of services associated with the CLC (See Figure 16–1). First, core curriculum teachers plan how students will master content regardless of literacy levels. Comprehension is based on shoring up background knowledge and vocabulary and the core curriculum is where this type of literacy develops. A number of interventions might be adopted across school courses to shore up background knowledge and background. However, the Content Enhancement teaching routines mentioned throughout this chapter were specifically designed with the goals of building background knowledge and vocabulary.

Table I

The Content Literacy Continuum for Guiding the Development of School-Wide Literacy Services in Secondary Schools

Level of service	Focus of actions	Example
Level 1 Ensure mastery of critical content	All students learn critical content required in the core curriculum regardless of literacy levels. Teachers compensate for limited literacy levels by using explicit teaching routines, adaptations, and technology to promote content mastery.	Teachers use Content Enhancement Routines, such as The Unit Organizer Routine, to deliver content.
Level 2 Weave shared strategies across classes	Teachers embed selected learning strategies in core curriculum courses through direct explanation, modeling, and required application in content assignments.	Teachers teach the steps of a paraphrasing strategy (RAP), regularly model its use, and then embed paraphrasing activities in course activities throughout the year to create a culture of "reading to retell."
Level 3 Support mastery of shared strategies for targeted strategies	Students who have difficulty mastering the strategies presented in courses by content teachers are provided more instruction in the strategies through specialized, more intensive instruction delivered by support personnel.	When core curriculum teachers notice students having difficulty learning and using strategies such as paraphrasing, they work with support personnel to provide more intensive instruction.
Level 4 Provide more intensive intervention for those who need work on basic literacy elements	Students learn literacy skills through specialized, direct, and intensive instruction in listening, speaking, reading, and writing through carefully designed and delivered courses.	Courses in researched-based reading programs such as the SRA Corrective Reading Program are created for students.
Level 5 Deliver a more intensive clinical option for those who need it	Students with underlying language disorders learn the linguistic, related cognitive, metalinguistic, and metacognitive underpinnings they need to acquire content literacy skills and strategies.	Speech–language pathologists engage students in curriculum-relevant therapy.

From Lenz and Ehren, 2001.

Second, core curriculum teachers plan how to embed instruction in critical learning strategies into their courses. To accomplish this, teachers describe, model, and use key steps and elements of strategies to introduce students to how the subject matter is best learned. When learning strategies such as self-questioning and paraphrasing are introduced and reinforced across teachers and subject areas, students begin to associate the strategies with the content as opposed to associating the strategies with a reading class. In addition, students share common learning goals, see how the strategy is used in an authentic context (i.e., to learn content as opposed to learning an isolated learning strategy), and have sufficient prompts to practice the strategies as a group, in smaller groups, and individually as the teacher requires students to use specific strategies to complete assignments.

Third, unfortunately, while embedding strategy instruction in the core curriculum provides a valuable stage for launching strategy instruction, the type of group instruction that is provided in the general education setting is not sufficiently intensive to provide the level of detail and feedback required to learn strategies for students with limited literacy skills, including many students with learning disabilities. While some studies have begun to show that some of these students can progress in strategy learning (e.g., Scanlon *et al.*, 1996), few studies have been able to move general education teachers to the level of explicitness required for mastery of strategies in general education settings without the assistance of special education or other support teachers. As a result, support services—not necessarily classes—are planned for students who need more intensive strategy instruction and feedback to ensure mastery that cannot be provided in the core curriculum. Returning to the first point addressed in this section, more intensive attention must be given to how learning strategies are acquired and generalized if we want students to actually apply the strategies to comprehend and learn content.

Fourth, course and service options that can help students build the decoding skills and reading fluency necessary for acquiring and generalizing most learning strategies must be planned. In general, most efforts to teach learning strategies in the area of reading to adolescents with learning disabilities focus on comprehension of text. These strategies require that the student have sufficient word analysis skills to read words fluently at a minimum of a fourth grade level. Unfortunately, a significant number of students in secondary schools still need to develop these skills if they are to develop the comprehension strategies needed to navigate the secondary core curriculum. This will require secondary schools—middle and high schools—to develop courses where these skills can be taught. Reading programs such as Corrective Reading, a program that provides intensive direct instruction in these skills and has a long history of research supporting its use with adolescents, can provide the basis for such courses. Then, bridging strategies such as The Word Identification Strategy (Lenz & Hughes, 1990) can be used to help students make the transition to learning strategy classes.

Fifth, the final level of services that need to be developed in secondary schools to promote literacy is the provision of curriculum-relevant therapy that can be provided by speech and language professionals. Speech and language pathologists need to be involved in planning and providing clinical intervention for those youth who have underlying language problems that prevent them from profiting from learning strategy instruction. These services focus on helping these students learn the linguistic, metalinguistic, and metacognitive underpinnings they need to acquire the necessary content, skills, and strategies. For example, a student who has a severe language disorder may not be able to learn to paraphrase a paragraph and may need to work on word retrieval and rephrasing extensively at the sentence level before being able to integrate the multiple sentence paraphrasing required to determine the gist of a full paragraph. Generally, these services are provided by a speech pathologist who delivers one-on-one or small-group curriculum-relevant therapy in collaboration with other support personnel teaching literacy skills. They assist content teachers in making appropriate modifications in content instruction to accommodate severe language disorders. This level of service is important for secondary schools to pay attention to because few secondary schools—especially high schools—engage speech pathologists in planning and providing literacy services.

5. Attention to Nonacademic Interventions That Promote Youth Planning and Control

Educators working to develop programs designed to meet the needs of students with learning disabilities must take a broader look at the purpose of educational programs and the long-term goals of services for these students. Regardless of federal, state, and local school mandates, program leaders need to determine what type of educational experiences will prepare the student to advocate for rights, prepare the student for independent and successful navigation of employment demands, and help the student make a transition to postsecondary learning and work options. While this may include completing graduation requirements, another part of this process includes transferring the strategies that have been used to navigate learning and social demands of the core curriculum to postsecondary life and work experiences. These interventions include teaching students the strategies associated with interacting with others to complete tasks, self-advocacy, and learning a process of goal setting, planning, and monitoring. Special educators and others involved in planning and providing transition-related education and support to adolescents with learning disabilities need to learn how to help students adapt and apply learning strategies that they have learned in academic contexts to nonacademic demands.

6. Attention to Establishing Academic Relationships That Ensure Authentic Communication

Finally, an area that has emerged as a factor that must be addressed in promoting school success is how well we know these students, and more importantly, how known do these students feel. In the wake of publicity over violence in secondary schools, some schools have started to give more attention to helping students feel "known" within the secondary school setting. The movement to create smaller learning communities within larger schools partially reflects this concern. Research on the types of communication and the types of academic relationships that exist between teachers and students in secondary schools shows that most of these students do not feel that teachers know them, care to know them, or that they have ways of communicating concerns to teachers. No matter what outcomes are planned for a student, the ability to communicate and provide a forum for authentic, private, and supportive reinforcement and coaching that can help students meet goals should be part of program planning. Research targeted at improving the academic relationship between students and teachers in the core curriculum classroom indicates that such systems can work in secondary schools. For example, Lenz, Adams *et al.* (2004) analyzed over 25,000 communication exchanges between teachers and students and found that weekly communication that focused on improving academic performance significantly improved the confidence that students had in the teacher and improved students' perception of teacher responsiveness to their learning needs. However, Lenz, *et al.*, (2002) also found that many of the teachers needed to learn ways to coach students to solve learning problems. Many teachers also needed support in learning how to respond to students in a proactive way when students expressed dissatisfaction with classroom instruction. In particular, students with learning disabilities who previously had almost no individual communication with the teacher in comparison to peers, including many who had never raised content or learning questions with teachers before, significantly increased their level of teacher contact when academic relationship coaching was introduced. More importantly, teachers were observed changing their instruction in response to student dialogue and modified pace in response to student comments related to problems learning the content.

IV. FUTURE RESEARCH

In light of what we know about how to teach adolescents with learning disabilities, educational practices in secondary schools must be markedly changed on three fronts: (1) *how students learn, master, and apply* critical content information; (2) *how classroom teachers think about and teach* critical content to academically diverse classes so that *all* students (especially those with disabilities) can learn the information; and (3) *how educational contexts are created and curriculum, teachers, parents, support systems, and resources are coordinated* to meet the unique needs of students with disabilities. All of these changes, however, must be addressed within the context of the broad array of school reform efforts that have had a marked influence on the landscape of secondary schools during the past decade (e.g., Cohen, 1995; Darling-Hammond & Falk, 1997; Wang *et al.*, 1998) as well as how recommendations for students with disabilities will be taken into consideration within these reform efforts (e.g., McDonnell *et al.*, 1997). Little research has focused on how school reform in this standards-driven and high stakes testing environment will shape the education of these students.

Additionally, as solutions are sought that will have the capacity to markedly impact the academic and life-adjustment success of adolescents with learning disabilities, the solutions that emerge through the research process must be evaluated in light of the standards of sustainability and scale (Elmore, 1996). That is, while many interventions have been shown to work in research studies, very few have been shown to withstand the demands that are present when attempts are made to introduce them within the realities of today's schools. This type of research will require researchers to regularly consider factors related to sustainability and bringing interventions to scale.

V. CONCLUSION

It has been over 30 years since *The Educator's Enigma: The Adolescent with Learning Disabilities* (Strother *et al.*, 1971), one of the first books on adolescents with learning disabilities, was published. The authors raise several questions: Who is the learning disabled student? How do we find him/her? How does he feel? How do we teach him? The field has made significant progress since these questions were raised. However, we still do not have adequate answers. The adolescent with learning disabilities is still an enigma, and we still strive to answer these questions. Laura Lehtinen-Rogan ends this book with the following closing perspective that still seems to hold true today for those of us who are interested in helping adolescents with learning disabilities:

> What is the outlook for children with problems like these? Do any of them actually "make it?" The fact is that they do, and a large part of the credit for their success is due to the understanding and extra effort of observant teachers.... Challenge is not new to teachers. There are just new challenges. The efforts of teachers and educators to understand the problem of the child with learning disabilities brings us closer to the very core of how learning itself occurs. This is one of the most exciting challenges of all.

References

Adams, G., Lenz, B. K., Laraux, M., Graner, P., & Pouliot, N. (2002). The effects of ongoing communication between teachers and adolescents with disabilities. Lawrence, KS: The University of Kansas, Center for Research on Learning.

Alley, G. R., Schumaker, J. B., Deshler, D. D., Clark, F. L., & Warner, M. M. (1983). Learning disabilities in adolescents and young adult populations: Research implications (Part II). *Focus on Exceptional Children*, **15**(9), 114.

Beals, V. L. (1983). *The effects of large group instruction on the acquisition of specific learning strategies by learning disabled adolescents.* Unpublished dissertation. University of Kansas, Lawrence.

Boudah, D. J., Schumaker, J. B., & Deshler, D. D. (1997). Collaborative instruction: Is it an effective option for secondary classrooms? *Learning Disability Quarterly*, **20**, 293–316.

Brinckerhoff, L. C., Shaw, S. F., & McGuire, J. M. (1992). Promoting access, accommodations, and independence for college students with learning disabilities. *Journal of Learning Disabilities*, **25**(7), 417–429.

Brownell, M. T., Mellard, D. F., & Deshler, D. D. (1993). Differences in the learning and transfer performance of students with learning disabilities and other low-achieving students on problem-solving tasks. *Learning Disabilities Quarterly*, **16**(23), 137–156.

Bulgren, J., & Schumaker, J. (in press). *Synthesis of research on instructional practices designed to promote success for all students in inclusive secondary content classrooms.* Reston, VA: Council for Exceptional Children.

Bulgren, J. A., Hock, M. A., Schumaker, J. B., & Deshler, D. D. (1995). The effects of instruction in a paired-associates strategy on the information mastery performance of students with learning disabilities. *Learning Disabilities Research and Practice*, **10**(1), 22–37.

Bulgren, J. A., Schumaker, J. B., & Deshler, D. D. (1993). *The concept mastery routine.* Lawrence, KS: Edge Enterprises, Inc.

Bulgren, J. A., Schumaker, J. B., & Deshler, D. D. (1994). *The concept anchoring routine.* Lawrence, KS: Edge Enterprises, Inc.

Bulgren, J. A., Schumaker, J. B., & Deshler, D. D. (1988). Effectiveness of a concept teaching routine in enhancing the performance of LD students in secondary-level mainstream classes. *Learning Disability Quarterly*, **11**(1), 3–17.

Clark, F. L., Deshler, D. D., Schumaker, J. B., Alley, G. R., & Warner, M. M. (1984). Visual imagery and self-questioning: Strategies to improve comprehension of written material. *Journal of Learning Disabilities*, **17**(3), 145–149.

Cohen, D. (1995). What is the system in systemic reform? *Educational Researcher*, **24**(9), 11–31.

Cuban, L. (1984). How teachers taught: Consistency and change in American classrooms 1890–1990. New York: Longman.

Curtis, M. B. (2002). *Adolescent reading: A synthesis of research.* June 20, 2002. (www.nifl.gov/partnershipforreading/adolescent/summary11a.html).

Darling-Hammond, L., & Falk, B. (1997). Using standards and assessments to support student learning. *Phi Delta Kappan*, **77**(6), 191–199.

Deshler, D. D., & Schumaker, J. B. (1988). An instructional model for teaching students how to learn. In J. L. Graden, J. E. Zins, and M. L. Curtis (eds.), *Alternative education delivery systems: Enhancing instructional options for all students* (pp. 391–411). Washington, DC: National Association of School Psychologists.

Deshler, D. D. (1978). Issues related to the education of learning disabled adolescents. *Learning Disability Quarterly*, **1**(4), 2–10.

Deshler, D. D. (2002). Response to "Is 'learning disabilities' just a fancy term for low achievement? A meta-analysis of reading differences between low achievers with and without the label." In R. Bradley, L. Danielson & D. P. Hallah (eds.), *Identification of learning disabilities: Research to practice*. Mahwah, NJ: Lawrence Erlbaum.

Deshler, D. D., & Lenz, B. K. (1989). The strategies instructional approach. *International Journal of Disability, Development, and Education*, **3**(2), 15–23.

Deshler, D. D., Schumaker, J. B., Alley, G. R., Warner, M. M., & Clark, F. L. (1982). Learning disabilities in adolescent and young adult populations: Research implications. *Focus on Exceptional Children*, **15**(1), 1–12.

Deshler, D. D., Schumaker, J. B., Lenz, B. K., Bulgren, J. A., Hock, M. F., Knight, J., & Ehren, B. J. (2001). Ensuring content-area learning by secondary students with learning disabilities. *Learning Disabilities Research and Practice*, **16**(2), 96–108.

Deshler, D. D., & Schumaker, J. B. (1993). Strategy mastery by at-risk students: Not a simple matter. *The Elementary School Journal*, **94**(2), 153–167.

Ellis, E. S. (1992). *LINCS: A starter strategy for vocabulary learning*. Lawrence, KS: Edge Enterprises, Inc.

Ellis, E. S., Deshler, D. D., Lenz, B. K., Schumaker, J. B., & Clark, F. L. (1991). An instructional model for teaching learning strategies. *Focus on Exceptional Children*, **23**(6), 1–24.

Elmore, R. F. (1996). Getting to scale with good educational practice. *Harvard Educational Review*, **66**(1), 1–26.

Foorman, B. R., Francis, D. J., Novy, D. M., & Liberman, D. (1991). How letter-sound instruction mediates progress in first-grade reading and spelling. *Journal of Educational Psychology*, **83**, 456–469.

Fullan, M. (1993). *Changing forces: Probing the depths of educational reform*. New York: The Falmer Press.

Graham, L., & Wong, B. Y. L. (1993). Comparing two modes in teaching a question-answering strategy for enhancing reading comprehension: Didactic and self-instructional training. *Journal of Learning Disabilities*, **26**(4), 270–279.

Gregory, J., Shanahan, T., & Walberg, H. (1985). Learning disabled 10th graders in mainstream settings. *Remedial and Special Education*, **6**(4), 25–33.

Hanley-Maxwell, C., Phelps, L. A., Braden, J., & Warren, V. (2001). Schools of authentic and inclusive learning. *Research Institute on Secondary Education reform brief*, Madison, WI: University of Wisconsin.

Kirk, S., & Elkins, J. (1975). Characteristics of children enrolled in child service demonstration centers. *Journal of Learning Disabilities*, **8**, 630–637.

Kline, F. M., Schumaker, J. B., & Deshler, D. D. (1991). Development and validation of feedback routines for instructing students with learning disabilities. *Learning Disability Quarterly*, **14**(3), 191–207.

Knight, J. (1998). Do schools have learning disabilities? *Focus on Exceptional Children*, **30**(9), 1–14.

Lenz, B. K., & Hughes, C. (1990). A word identification strategy for adolescents with learning disabilities. *Journal of Learning Disabilities*, **23**(3), 149–158, 163.

Lenz, B. K., Schumaker, J. B., Deshler, D. D., & Kissam, B. J. (1991). *Planning in the face of academic diversity: Whose questions should we be answering?* (Research report). Lawrence: University of Kansas, Center for Research on Learning.

Lenz, B. K., with Bulgren, J. A., Schumaker, J. B., Deshler, D. D., & Boudah, D. J. (1994). *The unit organizer routine*. Lawrence, KS: Edge Enterprises.

Lenz, B. K., with Schumaker, J. B., Deshler, D. D., & Bulgren, J. A. (1998). *The course organizer routine*. Lawrence, KS: Edge Enterprises.

Lenz, B. K., Adams, G., Graner, P., & Laraux, M. (2004). *Communication patterns in the development of academic relationships between high school students and their teachers*. (Research report). Lawrence, KS: The University of Kansas Center for Research on Learning.

Lenz, K., & Ehren, B. (2001). Promoting adolescent literacy through a content literacy continuum of services. *Strategram*, **6**(2), 1–4.

Lenz, K., Adams, G., Schumaker, J., Bulgren, J., and Deshler, D. D. (in press). *Issues and research related to influencing teacher planning to ensure that students with disabilities gain access to the high school core curriculum*. Reston, VA: Council for Exceptional Children.

Lenz, K., Bulgren, J., Kissam, B., & Taymans, J. (2004). SMARTER planning for academic diversity. In K. Lenz & Deshler, D. D. (eds.), *Teaching content to all: Evidence-based inclusive practices in middle and secondary schools* (pp. 47–77). Boston: Pearson Allyn & Bacon.

Lyon, G. R., & Fletcher, J. M. (2001, Summer). Early warning system. *Education Matters*, 23–29.

Martin, C. (1999). *Net future*. New York: McGraw-Hill.

McDonnell, L. M., McLaughlin, M. J., & Morison, P. (eds.). (1997). *Educating one & all: Students with disabilities and standards-based reform*. Washington, DC: National Academy Press.

Mellard, D. F., & Deshler, D. D. (1991). Education of exceptional persons: Learning Disabilities. In M. C. Alkin (ed.), *Encyclopedia of educational research, 6th edition*. Washington, DC: American Educational Research Association.

Oliver, R. W. (1999). *The shape of things to come*. New York: McGraw-Hill.

Rademacher, J., Schumaker, J., Deshler, D., & Lenz, B. K. (1998). *The quality assignment routine*. Lawrence, KS: Edge Enterprises.

Rifkin, J. (1995). *The end of work: The decline of the global labor force and the dawn of the post-market era*. New York: Putnam.

Rose, D., & Meyer, A. (2002). *Teaching every student in the digital age: Universal design for learning*. Alexandria, VA: ASCD.

Scanlon, D., Deshler, D. D., & Schumaker, J. B. (1996). Can a strategy be taught and learned in secondary inclusive classrooms? *Learning Disabilities Research & Practice*, **11**(1), 41–57.

Schmid, R., Algozzine, B., Wells, D., & Stoller, L. (1980). *The national secondary school survey*. (Research report). Gainesville, FL: The University of Florida.

Schumaker, D. D., & Deshler, D. D. (1994). Secondary classes can be inclusive, too. *Educational Leadership*, **52**(4), 50–52.

Schumaker, J. B., Deshler, D. D., Alley, G. R., & Denton, P. H. (1982). Multipass: A learning strategy for improving reading comprehension. *Learning Disability Quarterly*, **5**(3), 295–304.

Schumaker, J. B. (1992). Social performance of individuals with learning disabilities. *School Psychology Review*, **21**(3), 387–399.

Schumaker, J. B., & Deshler, D. D. (1984). Setting demand variables: A major factor in program planning for the learning disabilities adolescent. *Topics in Language Disorders Journal*, **4**(2), 22–40.

Schumaker, J. B., & Deshler, D. D. (1987). Implementing the regular education initiative in secondary schools—A different ball game. *Journal of Learning Disabilities*, **2**(1), 36–42.

Schumaker, J. B., & Deshler, D. D. (1992). Validation of learning strategy interventions for students with learning disabilities: Results of a programmatic research effort. In B. Y. L. Wong (ed.), *Contemporary intervention research in learning disabilities: An international perspective* (pp. 22–46). New York: Springer-Verlag.

Schumaker, J. B., Deshler, D. D., Alley, G. R., & Warner, M. M. (1983). Toward the development of an intervention model for learning disabled adolescents: The University of Kansas Institute. *Exceptional Education Quarterly*, **3**(4), 45–74.

Schumaker, J. B., Deshler, D. D., Bulgren, J. A., Davis, B., Lenz, B. K., Grossen, B. (2002). Access of adolescents with disabilities to general education curriculum: Myth or reality? *Focus on Exceptional Children*, **35**(3), 1–16.

Schumaker, J. B., Deshler, D. D., Lenz, B. K., & Bulgren, J. (2002). The Institute for Academic Access (IAA). *The Institute for Academic Access Brief*. Lawrence, KS: University of Kansas Center for Research on Learning.

Schumaker, J., Bulgren, J., Deshler, D., & Lenz, B. K. (1998b). *The recall enhancement routine*. Lawrence: The University of Kansas Center for Research on Learning.

Seybert, L. (1998). *The development and evaluation of a model of intensive reading strategies instruction for teachers in inclusive, secondary-level classrooms*. Unpublished doctoral dissertation. University of Kansas, Lawrence.

Shaw, S. F., McGuire, J. M., & Brinckerhoff, L. C. (1994). College and university programming. In P. J. Gerber & H. B. Reiff (Eds.), *Learning disabilities in adulthood: Persisting problems and evolving issues* (pp. 141–151). Boston: Andover Medical Publishers.

Sitlington, P. L., Clark, G. M., & Kolstoe, O. P. (1999). *Transition education and services for adolescents with disabilities*. Boston: Allyn and Bacon.

Strother, C., Hagin, R., Giffin, M., & Lehtinen-Rogan, L. (1971). *The educator's enigma: The adolescent with learning disabilities*. San Rafael, CA: Academic Therapy Publications.

Swanson, H. L. (1993). An information processing analysis of learning disabled children's problem solving. *American Education Research Journal*, **30**, 861–893.

Swanson, H. L. (2001). Research on intervention for adolescents with learning disabilities: A meta-analysis of outcomes related to high-order processing. *Elementary School Journal*, **101**, 331–348.

Torgesen, J., & Houck, G. (1980). Processing deficiencies in learning disabled children who perform poorly on the digit span test. *Journal of Educational Psychology*, **72**, 141–160.

Torgesen, J. K., Morgan, S. T., & Davis, C. (1992). Effects of two types of phonological awareness training on word learning in kindergarten children. *Journal of Educational Psychology*, **84**, 364–379.

Vaughn, S., & Fuchs, L. S. (2003). Redefining learning disabilities as inadequate response to instruction: The promise and the potential problems. *Learning Disability Research and Practice*, **18**(3), 137–146.

Vaughn, S., Gersten, R., & Chard, D. (2000). The underlying message in LD intervention research: Findings from research syntheses. *Exceptional Children*, **67**(1), 99–124.

Wagner, M., Blackorby, J., & Hebbeler, K., (1993). *Beyond the report card: The multiple dimensions of secondary school performance of students with disabilities. A report from the National Longitudinal Study of Special Education Students* Menlo Park, CA: SRI International.

Wang, M. C., Haertel, G. D., & Walberg, H. J. (1998). Models of reform: A comparative guide. *Educational Leadership*, **55**(7), 66–71.

Warner, M., Alley, G., Deshler, D., & Schumaker, J. (1980). *An epidemiological study of learning disabled adolescents in secondary schools: Classification and discrimination of learning disabled and low-achieving adolescents.* (Research report #20). Lawrence, KS: The University of Kansas Institute for Research in Learning Disabilities.

Wong, B. Y. L., & Jones, W. (1982). Increasing metacomprehension in learning-disabled and normally achieving students through self-questioning training. *Learning Disability Quarterly*, **5**(3), 228–240.

Wong, B. Y. L., Wong, R., Perry, N., & Sawatsky, D. (1986). The efficacy of a self-questioning summarization strategy for use by underachievers and learning-disabled adolescents in social studies. *Learning Disability Focus*, **2**, 20–35.

CHAPTER 17

Adults with Learning Disabilities

Deborah L. Butler
University of British Columbia

*"I will always think of myself as a child with a learning disability. I
don't think it has ever really changed... it is part of my life forever."
(33-year-old adult, as cited in Raskind et al., 2002).*

I. INTRODUCTION

The bulk of research in the field of Learning Disabilities (LD) has been, and
continues to be, focused on the needs of children and adolescents. However,
in the past two decades, researchers have become increasingly sensitive to the
continuing impact of LD on adults, both within and outside educational
settings. Although the study of adult LD was still "in its infancy" in the mid-
1980s (Johnston, 1984, p. 390), research in the past two decades has blossomed, addressing such topics as the challenges facing adults with LD,
outcomes in important life domains, factors associated with more or less
successful outcomes, and approaches to intervention. To summarize what
has been gleaned from this burgeoning literature, this chapter emphasizes
the importance of adopting a lifespan developmental perspective for understanding LD and overviews research in each of these topic areas.

Learning about Learning Disabilities, Third Edition

II. REFOCUSING ON ADULTS WITH LD: AN HISTORICAL OVERVIEW

Gerber (2001) reminds us that the field of LD was founded on early research on acquired brain injury in adults. But by the time the field of LD was formally established in 1963, attention had shifted from acquired brain injury and consequent functional problems to a focus on developmental brain pathology. Conclusions drawn from observed links between neurological damage and skill deficits in adults were extended to infer biologically based problems for children struggling to achieve as expected. The result of this shift in attention was that "the agenda of adolescents and adults was, in effect, put on hold while basic research and subsequent writing weaved together the issues of child development, learning disabilities, and intervention" (Gerber, 2001, p. 168). It is only in the last 20 years, as the cohort of children identified as LD in childhood has moved through adolescence and into adulthood, that researchers and educators have realized that people do not "grow out of LD" and have refocused attention on the needs of adults (Gerber, 2001).

By the mid-1980s, attention to adults with LD was clearly increasing. Position papers were prepared by influential advocacy and professional groups, including the Learning Disabilities Associations in the United States and Canada (LDA, 1994; Wong & Hutchinson, 2001), the National Joint Committee on Learning Disabilities (NJCLD, 1987, 1999; Gajar, 1992), and the Association on Higher Education and Disability (AHEAD; Brinckerhoff et al., 2002). These organizations recognized the need to adopt a lifespan perspective for studying LD, and called for the legislation, policies, and research to direct the development of programs and interventions (Gajar, 1992; Vogel & Reder, 1998b).

A refocusing of attention on adults with LD was also spurred by legislation protecting the rights of individuals with disabilities. For example, in the United States, the Education of All Handicapped Children's Act of 1975 (PL 94–142) guaranteed a free and appropriate education for all students with disabilities from ages 5 to 21 (Gerber, 2001). Young adults with LD were supported under this legislation, at least in school settings. In 1990, PL 94–142 was updated and redefined as the Individuals with Disabilities Education Act (IDEA), and in 1997, amendments to IDEA required the inclusion of transition planning in education of all students with disabilities starting at age 14 (Lerner, 2003). The result was increased anticipation of the demands on young adults with LD in the post-school years, development of transition programs, and interest in post-school outcomes (e.g., Evers, 1996). Simultaneously, U.S. legislation emerged to support the provision of services to adults with LD in postsecondary and vocational settings. For example, the Vocational Rehabilitation Act of 1973 (PL 93–122), section 504, ensures that individuals with disabilities are not excluded from, or discriminated against within, federally funded programs, including colleges and universities. By the mid-1980s, this law was increasingly applied to mandate access to, and necessary accommodations within, postsecondary education for students with LD (Gajar, 1992; Gerber, 2001). In 1990, the Americans with Disabilities Act (ADA) extended protection against discrimination to the public sector and the workplace (Lerner, 2003). Legislative mandates in the United States have had a strong influence on the development of programs for adults with LD, service delivery policies, and the availability of funding for research.

Federal legislation parallel to that in the United States does not exist in Canada. However, protection to individuals with disabilities is provided under the Charter of Rights and Freedoms, and is guided by policies developed at the provincial level. In addition, the coordinated work of the LDAs across the United States and Canada has led to simultaneous development of programs and services within each country (Wong & Hutchinson, 2001). Federally funded programs also have been established in Canada to provide support for adults with LD (Wong & Hutchinson, 2001).

Research on LD in adulthood also has proliferated since the mid-1980s. For example, for her review of research on adolescents and adults with LD published in 1984, Johnston could find very few studies specifically on adults. During a gathering of individuals in 1985 for an "Adult Learning Disabled State-of-the Art meeting" (Gerber, 2001, pp. 171–172), it was concluded that, where research in adult LD was concerned, there was "no state and very little art" (Gerber, 2001, p. 172). But by the time Adelman and Vogel (1998) wrote a review of studies conducted prior to 1992, much more research had been conducted. This chapter integrates findings from previous comprehensive reviews of the literature with findings from more recent research (since 1990) in order to provide an overview of what we know now in the field of adult LD.

III. LD FROM A LIFESPAN PERSPECTIVE

Research on LD in adulthood is not only relevant to researchers, practitioners, community members, and policymakers concerned with adult populations; understanding how LDs play out over time also provides important benchmarks for parents and educators charged with preparing youngsters for the adult years. Further, Gerber's (2001) description of life after formal education as the "other 70 years" provides a sobering reminder of the importance of understanding the impact of LD across the lifespan (Gerber, 2001). As Gerber and Reiff (1991) argue, "the years beyond schooling, which can account for up to seventy-five percent of one's life, need to be studied and understood" (p. 136).

Many researchers are promoting a lifespan developmental perspective for the study of LD (e.g., Gajar, 1992; Gerber, 1994, 2001; Lerner, 2003; Murray, 2003; Polloway *et al.*, 1992; Raskind *et al.*, 1999). These researchers emphasize that how LDs manifest themselves varies across environments (e.g., academic, community, vocational, social), tasks (e.g., reading, using a computer, talking to a patient, answering e-mail), and life phases (e.g., pursuing education or training, employment, starting a family, retirement). Further, as Gerber and Reiff (1991) caution, LD "may not be mitigated with age and may in fact continue to evolve within the various phases of adult development" (p. 136). That is, it is not only possible that the impact of LD may shift over time, but also that the underlying processing problems associated with LD may themselves change. It follows that extrapolating conclusions from research with children in schools may not be useful in understanding the impact of LD on adults within the domains central to adult experience (e.g., educational, vocational, daily living).

Gerber (1994, 2001) argues that development should be considered not just as something that transpires within individuals, but as something that is spurred by the interaction between individuals and environments. In research on LD in children, attention has understandably focused on students' cognitive (dis)abilities in relation to their navigation of academic tasks. Yet, when supporting adolescents with LD (e.g., in transition programs), educators are realizing that it is important, not just to support students' academic success, but also to expand the focus to the "skills and accommodations students with LD will need in their behavior repertoires to succeed in all the societal systems they must interact with in their adult years" (Gerber, 2001, pp. 170–171). Developmental benchmarks for young adults include graduating high school, completing advanced education or training, developing career interests and finding employment, establishing emotional and economic independence from parents and positive social relationships, creating a happy and healthy lifestyle (e.g., with preferred leisure and recreational activities), developing personal values and goals, and assuming the role of a citizen within a community (Gerber, 2001; Lerner, 2003). It follows that understanding LD in adulthood requires examining how LDs impact on individuals' development across life domains (Murray, 2003; Raskind *et al.*, 1999), and within different life phases (Gerber, 1994; Levine & Nourse, 1998).

IV. CHALLENGES FACING ADULTS WITH LD

This section describes research conducted to document challenges, outcomes, and attainments of adults with LD. Many excellent reviews of the research conducted prior to 1992 have already been completed (e.g., Gajar, 1992; Gerber & Reiff, 1991; Levine & Nourse, 1998; Raskind *et al.*, 1999; Adelman & Vogel, 1998). Therefore, in this section, I integrate findings from these previous reviews with results from recent research (see Tables I and II). I start by discussing the types of research that have been conducted in this area. Then I overview challenges faced by adults with LD in four areas: cognitive processing and academic skills, educational attainment, employment, and social/emotional development.

A. Types of Research Documenting Challenges in Adulthood

Three general approaches have been used to examine challenges faced by adults with LD. First, a large number of studies have directly measured individuals' academic or cognitive processing skills. Studies of this type provide important information about the persistence of basic processing difficulties into adulthood. Second, longitudinal follow-up studies have been conducted to trace outcomes for individuals over time. Data from these studies are typically summarized quantitatively and are compared across groups (e.g., LD and non-LD). As a complement to these group-focused follow-up studies, a third type of research has investigated the perspectives of adults with LD about their experiences. A major goal in many of these studies is to account for individual differences in the degree of success achieved.

Six major follow-up studies have provided longitudinal data on outcomes for adults with LD (Table I, column 1). For example, Beitchman *et al.*, (2001) describe findings from the Ottawa Language Study (OLS), a 14-year follow-up study of 236 children diagnosed as having a speech or language impairment at age 5. The researchers observed how many of these children were diagnosed with LD and substance abuse or psychiatric disorders by ages 12 and 19. Blackorby and Wagner (1996) discussed data drawn from

Table I

An Overview of Age-Groups and Data Sources within Various Studies

Follow-up, group-focused studies			Perspectives of LD adults	
Authors	Data	Ages	Authors	Ages
Beitchman *et al.* (2001)	OLS	12–19	Gerber *et al.* (1990)	23–71
Blackorby & Wagner (1996)	NLTS	15–26	Gerber & Reiff (1991)	22–56
Raskind *et al.* (1999)	Frostig	28–35	Gerber *et al.* (1992)	29–67
Rojewski (1999)	NELS	19–21	Shessel & Reiff (1999)	26–60
Vogel & Reder (1998a,b)	NALS	25–64	Polloway *et al.* (1992)	18–40
Werner (1993)	Kauai	0–32	Hellendoorn & Ruijssenaars (2000)	20–39

the National Longitudinal Transition Study (NLTS). They tracked outcomes in employment, education, and residential independence for special education students ($n = 1990$, 350 with LD) both 0 to 2 and 3 to 5 years after leaving high school (at ages 15–26). Raskind *et al.*'s (1999) study followed 41 ex-students from the Frostig Center (a support center for students with learning disabilities) both 10 years (at ages 18 to 25) and 20 years later (at ages 28 to 35). Like other follow-up studies, Raskind *et al.* describe outcomes in employment, educational attainment, and living arrangements for adults with LD. They also compare successful ($n = 21$) and unsuccessful ($n = 20$) participants to identify predictors of success.

Rojeweski's (1999) data derive from the National Education Longitudinal Study (NELS) of 25,000 children who were followed in grades 8, 10, 12, and two years post-high school. He summarizes the educational, vocational, and personal development for a subsample of 11,178 individuals (ages 19–21), 441 of whom had been identified as LD. Vogel and Reder (1998a,b) report

Table II

An Overview of Studies Focused on Cognitive Processing/Academic Achievement
and Interventions

Research on cognitive processing or academic achievement			Research on interventions		
Authors	C/A[a]	Ages	Authors	C/A	Ages
Apthorp (1995)	C	17–28	Butler (1995)	C	18–36
Beers *et al* (1994)	C	21[b]	Butler (1998c)	C	19–48
Bruck (1993)[c]	C	20.5[b] 11[b]	Butler *et al.* (2000)[d]	C	19–55
Cosden & McNamara (1997)	C	22[b]	Butler *et al.* (2000)[e]	C	22–28
Gregg & Hoy (1990)	C	18–25	Kitz & Thorpe (1995)	C	19[b]
Hall *et al.* (2002)	C	19[b]	Lipson (1995)	C	23[b]
Hughes & Suritsky (1994)	C	19–25	Roffman *et al.* (1994)	C	17–25
Leong (1999)	C	28.5[b]	Runyan (1991)	C	18–27
Mosberg & Johns (1994)	C	24[b]	Wilson (1998)	C	18–32
Reiff *et al.* (2001)	C	21.5[b]			
Rubin & Johnson (2002)	C	18–21			
Wilson & Lesaux (2001)	C	18–24			
Gottesman *et al.* (1996)	A	16–63			
Swanson (1994)	A	5–58			
Vogel & Reder (1998b)	A	25–64			

[a] C = college or university students, A = adults, HS = high school students.

[b] Only mean ages reported (average estimated across all groups in the study).

[c] Bruck's study included a grade-6 comparison group, along with college students with and without LD.

[d] Butler, Elaschuk, Poole *et al.* (2000).

[e] Butler, Elaschuk, & Poole (2000).

findings from the National Adult Literacy Survey (NALS) conducted in the United States in 1995. The purpose of the NALS was to determine how the U.S. population (aged 25 to 64 years) fared in terms of functional literacy skills. The final sample included 14,519 individuals, 392 with self-reported LD. Information was collected on participants' functional literacy skills, years of schooling, employment and training, and economic status. Finally, Werner's (1993) research followed the progress of a birth cohort of children born in 1955 on the Island of Kauai. Data were collected before birth and across ages 1, 2, 10, 18, and 32 to identify early risk factors for problems that emerged later, and to track differences in education, employment, and socio-emotional development for children with and without LD.

As a complement to longitudinal studies documenting outcomes at a group level, a number of researchers have adopted qualitative approaches to account for individual differences in outcomes (see Table I, column 2). Many of these studies have been conducted by Paul Gerber and his associates. For example, Gerber et al. (1990) conducted an oft-cited study of 133 moderately successful and successful adults with LD, aged 23 to 71. Their goal was to identify persisting problems of adults with LD based on self-reported, retrospective comparisons of experiences in childhood and adulthood. Gerber and Reiff (1991) conducted an interview study that included 9 LD adults, aged 22 to 56 years. They provide detailed descriptions of these adults' perspectives on their adjustment in education, employment, social–emotional, and daily living domains.

Another influential study was completed by Gerber et al. (1992). This was a retrospective, causal-comparative, interview study of 71 adults with LD, aged 29 to 67 years. Gerber et al. gathered information from participants about outcomes within important life domains, and then compared participants who had achieved high vs moderate levels of success. Unique about this study was the careful matching of highly and moderately successful comparison groups on age, race, gender, LD type and severity, parents' occupations, and family socioeconomic status. This careful matching facilitated isolation of factors that could be associated with greater success. A final example of the work of this team of researchers is provided by Shessel and Reiff (1999), who conducted interviews with 14 adults with LD (aged 26 to 60 years) to find themes related to the experience of LD in adulthood.

Other researchers have also sought the perspectives of adults with LD to enhance understanding regarding their experiences. For example, Polloway et al. (1992) conducted an interview study of 51 adults with LD, aged 18 to 40 years. Similarly, Hellendoorn & Ruijssenaars (2000) sought to replicate Gerber and Reiff's (1991) study with 27 Dutch adults with dyslexia, aged 20 to 39. Taken together, results from group-based follow-up and interview studies provide a rich understanding of LD in adulthood. While follow-up studies have identified long-term outcomes for adults with LD in academic achievement and across multiple life domains, complementary interview studies more deeply portray the quality of individuals' lived experience. Further, integrating findings across the two types of studies uncovers a multiplicity of factors related to the level of success that adults with LD might achieve.

B. Academic Achievement and Cognitive Processing

Several comprehensive literature reviews have documented that the cognitive processing and academic skill deficits that define LD in childhood persist for adults with LD (e.g., Adelman & Vogel, 1998; Gajar, 1992; Johnston, 1984). For example, in an early review, Johnston (1984) found that problems persisted in reading (e.g., imprecise reading, difficulties skimming and pulling out main ideas, phonics), writing, rapid notetaking, spatial–temporal sequencing, and reading social cues. Similarly, Gajar's (1992) review revealed continuing struggles with reading, spelling, listening to lectures, taking accurate notes, and written expression, in addition to problems in learning foreign languages, time management, completing tasks, and using effective study skills. Adelman and Vogel (1998) documented persistent problems for adults with LD in math, spelling, writing (e.g., in punctuation, quality of text, development of ideas, writing style, and sentence construction), and reading (e.g., problems with decoding, oral reading, phonological segmentation, vocabulary, and reading comprehension). Thus, considerable research supports the conclusion that LDs do not subside with age.

However, substantial inter- and intra-individual differences exist in the problems experienced (Adelman & Vogel, 1998). Further, Gajar (1992) noted that, in the research she reviewed, most participants were young adults with LD. Such a narrow focus is problematic, because understanding LD in adulthood requires examining how cognitive processing problems impact on adult functioning across domains and ages. Unfortunately, consistent with Gajar's (1992) finding, of the 15 studies collected for this post-1990 review that directly assessed cognitive or academic skills, 80% included college student samples (see Table II). Only a few studies directly examined the cognitive or academic skills of older adults with LD within or outside of school settings (Gottesman et al., 1996; Swanson, 1994; Vogel & Reder, 1998b), although a few additional studies investigated the experience of cognitive processing problems for adults with LD using self-report measures (e.g., Gerber et al., 1990; Hellendoorn & Ruikjssenaars, 2000; Shessel & Reiff, 1999).

For example, in Shessel and Reiff's (1999) study, participants (aged 26 to 60 years) described how basic processing problems affected their daily functioning. Difficulties were described in filling out forms, reading legal documents, banking, getting lost, retrieving words in conversation, and time management. As one participant explained, "the problem with a disability is, it's not life-threatening, it's life-affecting. And it affects every facet of your life" (p. 309). Half of Hellendoorn and Ruijssenaars' (2000) participants believed their LD impacted their daily routines. Similarly, the 1995 National Adult Literacy Survey (NALS) documented the functional literacy levels of adults with LD (aged 25 to 64 years) in comparison with their nondisabled peers (Vogel and Reder, 1998b). This survey showed that, of the four possible literacy levels derived from performance on daily life tasks, 57% of the participants with LD performed at the lowest level, compared to only 10% of people without LD. Only 21 and 2% of the adults with LD performed in the third and fourth levels, respectively.

Gerber et al. (1990) evaluated how the experience of cognitive processing problems changes between childhood and adulthood. In their study of 133 adults with LD (aged 23 to 71), they asked participants to describe whether the problems they experienced in childhood had become worse, become better, or remained stable. Their survey included questions about skills in listening, speaking, reading, writing, spelling, math, visual perception, auditory perception, coordination, impulsivity, distractability, hyperactivity, and attention span. Their oft-cited results showed that, on many items, and regardless of academic, vocational, and personal attainments, most participants rated basic processing problems as becoming worse as they got older. Gerber et al. concluded that processing problems for adults with LD are "exacerbated by increasing demands in adulthood" (p. 572). Gerber et al.'s (1990) study is often interpreted as showing that processing problems associated with LD may worsen over time. But an alternative explanation is that it is the experience of problems that worsens, rather than the severity of the problems themselves. As the demands in adulthood accelerate, the discrepancy between abilities and setting demands may widen, resulting in a greater impact of the LD on successful functioning. It is also possible that retrospective comparisons of current and past experience are simply not reliable, if adults base judgments on shifting criteria, or rate current negative experiences as worse than similarly negative but poorly remembered experiences from the past. Nonetheless, consistent with other research, Gerber et al.'s findings document the persistence of basic processing problems in adulthood. Their study adds by showing that the experience of LD may shift over time with changes in setting demands.

C. Educational Outcomes

Research suggests that adults with LD are less likely to reach educational levels comparable to those of their nondisabled peers. For example, results from the National Adult Literacy Survey (NALS) compared proportions of non-LD and LD adults on the highest level of education attained (Vogel & Reder, 1998a). Findings were that 27% of adults with self-reported LD (aged 25 to 64) had completed only 0 to 8 years of school, compared to only 4.2% of non-LD participants. Thirty-four percent of nondisabled individuals stopped education with a high school diploma or a GED equivalency, and 22 and 27% had at least some college education or a college degree, respectively. Comparatively, in the sample of adults with self-reported LD, 17% stopped with a high school diploma or equivalent, 12% had attended some college, and only 8.7% received college degrees. Similarly, in the Kauai longitudinal study, Werner (1993) found that LD individuals were more likely to have stopped their education after high school than their nondisabled peers (60 vs 21.4%, respectively). They also were much less likely to have attended technical training programs (10 vs 21.4%) or four-year colleges (10 vs 64.3%) or to be satisfied with their school achievement.

Even though the proportion of adults with LD in postsecondary education increases across time in the first 5 years out of high school, enrollment rates remain lower for adults with LD than they are for nondisabled peers (Adelman and Vogel, 1998). For example, when tracking the postsecondary enrollment of students 0 to 2 and 3 to 5 years after graduation, Blackorby and Wagner (1996) found that only 14% of young adults with LD were enrolled in postsecondary education 0 to 2 years out of high school, compared to 53% of non-LD peers. Three years later, close to 31% of the adults with LD were enrolled, but this rate still lagged behind that in the general population (68%) and that in a matched nondisabled group (47%).

Based on data from the NELS follow-up study, Rojewski (1999) determined that educational attainment was also influenced by gender. In their study, students with LD were less likely to earn a high school diploma or equivalency certificate than were students in the general population. But it was women with LD who were the least likely to have graduated from high school. Similarly, by two years after high school, fewer than $\frac{1}{3}$ of males with LD were pursuing postsecondary studies, compared to $\frac{1}{2}$ of the non-LD male sample. But again, it was the women with LD who were the least likely to be at college or university (only 24.6%). One-quarter of women with LD were neither employed nor enrolled in school.

A few studies have suggested more positive educational outcomes. For example, in Raskind et al.'s (1999) follow-up study of ex-students at the Frostig Centre, by ages 28 to 35, 40 out of 41 students had graduated from high school, 95% had attended at least 2 semesters of college, 24% had attended college for 2 to 7 years without graduating, and 24% had completed degrees at the BA or MA level. Further, although findings typically show that LD students attend postsecondary institutions less than nondisabled peers, the number of students with LD attending colleges and universities is rising. Statistics from the U.S. Department of Education showed an increase in the proportion of full-time college freshmen with self-reported LD from 1985 (1.6%) to 1994 (3.0%). As of 1992, students with LD were the fastest growing group of students receiving services from college and university support centers (Gajar, 1992). By 2002, students with LD constituted over half of the individuals supported by disability services in postsecondary settings (Brinckerhoff *et al.*, 2002).

D. Employment and Career Development

A disturbing finding is that students with LD may have lower career aspirations than peers, even when they have the potential to succeed (Adelman & Vogel, 1998). For example, in his study drawn from the NELS database, Rojewski (1999) found that males with LD selected fewer high-prestige options than did non-LD peers and were twice as likely to seek low-prestige occupations. Further, although a larger proportion of females with LD aspired to high-prestige jobs than did males with LD, proportionally more women with LD had low aspirations than did their nondisabled peers. Similarly, Panagos and DuBois (1999) investigated how self-efficacy beliefs were associated with career aspirations of 96 high school students with LD. They found that students who thought they might not be successful (i.e., had low self-efficacy beliefs) expressed less interest in a given career, even when they actually had aptitudes required in the profession. Implications are that students with LD who hold low perceptions of self-efficacy may not feel confident enough to pursue careers, even when they have the skills, attitudes, and abilities necessary to succeed.

Generally, adults with LD are equally likely to be employed as are peers, but they tend to work in less-skilled occupations and to make less money (Adelman & Vogel, 1998; Gajar, 1992; Panagos & DuBois, 1999). For example, Werner (1993) reported very little unemployment among the participants in the Kauai longitudinal study. But LD adults were more likely to be in semiskilled occupations than were non-LD peers (80 vs 20%, respectively), and were less likely to have jobs that were professional, semiprofessional, or managerial (0 vs 71%, respectively). Similarly, findings from the NLTS database (Blackorby & Wagner, 1996) were that students with LD were equally likely to be employed as nondisabled peers, both 0 to 2 years out of high school (59% for each group) and 3 to 5 years afterward (70% for each group). However, even 3 to 5 years out of high school, only 45% of LD young adults made wages over $6 per hour, and most were employed in clerical, crafts, operative, laborer, or service fields.

Results from some studies have contradicted these general trends. For example, in their longitudinal follow-up study of Frostig students, Raskind *et al.*'s (1999) participants were less successful in finding employment. Only

14% of the young adults with LD held full-time employment at ages 18 to 25, and 47% were unemployed. Ten years later, more participants had full-time employment (47%), but 41% were still unemployed. Individual differences within studies also are large, suggesting the presence of unaccounted for factors that mediate success (Adelman & Vogel, 1998; Gajar, 1992; Gerber, 2001). Success on the job has been related to use of effective compensatory strategies (e.g., taking additional time to finish work, asking for help), participation in transition programs, successful graduation from high school, supportive friendship networks, higher verbal abilities, and gender (with females typically having more trouble obtaining employment than males) (Adelman & Vogel, 1998).

E. Daily Living and Social–Emotional Development

In general, adults with LD are more likely than peers to be dependent on others in their daily lives and to continue living with parents (Adelman & Vogel, 1998; Gajar, 1992). As with educational enrollment, rates of living independently increase with age, but remain lower than those of their nondisabled peers (Blackorby & Wagner, 1996). For example, in Raskind et al.'s (1999) study, 74% of previous Frostig students still lived with parents at ages 18 to 25, and even 10 years later, a substantial proportion (42%) still lived at home. It is possible that, because adults with LD are often employed in lower-status, low-paying jobs, they have difficulty establishing independent households (Adelman & Vogel, 1998). However, some studies have identified more positive outcomes for adults with LD (Adelman & Vogel, 1998). For example, in their follow-up study in Holland, most of Hellendoorn and Ruijssenaars' (2000) participants had successfully transitioned to independent living. Large individual differences in outcomes have also been observed within all of the follow-up studies.

Research has also revealed problems for adults with LD in social perception, responding to verbal cues, social interaction, and social maturity (Adelman & Vogel, 1998). Many adults with LD are unhappy with their social lives, feel dependent on families, have trouble making friends, and have limited social contacts (Adelman & Vogel, 1998; Gajar, 1992; Hellendoorn & Ruijssenaars, 2000). Adults with LD are also less likely to participate in social, community, or recreational activities (see also Raskind et al., 1999). They are at risk for constructing negative self-perceptions (i.e., low self-concept), low self-esteem, and low self-confidence (Adelman & Vogel, 1998; Gajar, 1992; Lerner, 2003; Rojewski, 1999).

Unfortunately, adults with LD often report experiencing high levels of distress, anxiety, depression, and frustration, along with feelings of failure and helplessness (Adelman & Vogel, 1998; Gajar, 1992). An alarming trend is that adults with LD may be at risk for serious emotional health problems.

For example, in Raskind *et al.*'s (1999) follow-up study, 42% of interviewed participants reported experiencing depression, schizophrenia, alcohol abuse, or social phobias. Similarly, in her longitudinal study on the island of Kauai, Werner (1993) traced outcomes for students identified as LD at age 10 in comparison to non-LD peers. She found that at age 18, the LD students were more likely to have problems in school (94.7 vs 20%), mental health concerns (31.8 vs 0%), a delinquency record (27.3 vs 0%), low self-assurance, and little sense of control over outcomes. More positively, by age 32, fewer LD adults reported mental health problems, and differences between LD and non-LD adults were reduced.

Still, Shessel and Reiff's (1999) participants also reported struggling with fears of being exposed as "imposters," social isolation, stress, anxiety, negative self-concepts, shame, depression, and anger. Alarmingly, 10 of the 14 participants had accessed counseling services, half reported struggling with depression, 4 had attempted suicide, and 4 had emotional health concerns serious enough to warrant hospitalization. Similarly, although Hellendoorn and Ruijssenaars' (2000) Dutch participants seemed to do well in many ways (in terms of educational attainments, living independently, and having positive relationships with parents and siblings), only 3 out of the 27 participants were happy with their lives. Half had experienced problems with establishing social relationships, had few friends, or reported being bullied. Ninety-three percent described having emotional problems, and about half had received support in that area. Thus, apparently even relatively successful adults with LD are at risk for social–emotional challenges.

Many researchers have examined whether adults with LD are at greater risk for substance abuse than are their nondisabled peers (e.g., Beitchman *et al.*, 2001; Cosden, 1999; Molina & Pelham, 1999; Rhodes & Jasinski, 1990). In her review, Cosden (1999) describes research in this area as adopting one of two approaches. In the first, groups of individuals with LD are followed to determine how many develop substance abuse problems (e.g., Betichman *et al.*, 2001; Werner, 1993; Raskind *et al.*, 1999). One finding from these studies is that most individuals with LD do not develop problems in this area. For example, Raskind *et al.* (1999) found that only 6 of 41 former Frostig students reported substance abuse problems by the time they were 28 to 35 years old. However, research does suggest that, although adults with and without LD are equally likely to *use* substances like drugs and alcohol, adults with LD are more likely to *abuse* those substances than are nondisabled peers (Cosden, 1999). For example, data from the Ottawa Language Study (Beitchman *et al.*, 2001) showed that adults with LD were at a threefold greater risk for substance-abuse disorders than were nondisabled peers, even after accounting for other predictors of substance abuse (behavior problems and family dynamics).

In the second approach to investigating the linkage between LD and substance abuse, individuals with established substance abuse problems are studied to determine how many have LD (Cosden, 1999). Research conducted from this perspective has shown that a larger proportion of substance abusers than would be expected have LD, given the prevalence of LD in the population. For example, of the volunteers from a detoxification unit who participated in Rhodes and Jasinski's (1990) study, 60% met discrepancy criteria for defining LD as adults; 40% percent of the sample had received special education services in school. Implications are that preventative intervention may be warranted for students with LD at risk for developing substance abuse disorders, and that service providers in drug and alcohol programs should be aware that many participants might have LD.

F. Accounting for Conflicting Findings

Within each of the domains already addressed, (education, employment, daily living/social–emotional development), inconsistencies have been found *among* studies, and several analyses have therefore been done in order to account for conflicting results (e.g., Adelman & Vogel, 1998; Gerber & Reiff, 1991; Levine & Nourse, 1998). Variables that account for some of observed differences include the context within which the study was conducted (e.g., urban or rural; public or private school), the characteristics of participants (age, age at which LD was diagnosed, gender, verbal skills, socioeconomic status), and methodological procedures (e.g., how data were combined across participants; how comparison groups were defined). To assist in reconciling apparently contrasting results, researchers have been called upon to carefully describe their studies with attention to variables that might mediate levels of outcomes observed (Adelman & Vogel, 1998; Levine & Nourse, 1998).

But conflicting results have also been found *within* follow-up studies, in that large individual differences have been observed. For example, while some adults with LD may have dropped out of high school, pursued no postsecondary training, be unemployed, and still live with their parents, other adults with LD have graduated from university with doctoral degrees, established positive relationships with peers, spouses and children, and earned healthy six-figure incomes (Gerber *et al.*, 1992; Gerber & Reiff, 1991). Researchers have become increasingly interested in why some adults with LD are more successful than others (e.g., Cosden, 1999; Diaz-Greenburg *et al.*, 2000; Gerber, 2001; Gerber *et al.*, 1992; Murray, 2003; Raskind *et al.*, 1999; Werner, 1993). How do some individuals adapt to adult life so successfully in spite of the persistence of cognitive processing problems characteristic of LD?

V. ACCOUNTING FOR INDIVIDUAL DIFFERENCES

In this section, I describe studies investigating differential patterns of success for adults with LD. These studies provide important insights regarding how adults with LD might be supported to be more successful.

A. Factors Associated with Success

Several frameworks have been offered to account for more or less successful outcomes of adults with LD. One of these frameworks was developed by Paul Gerber and colleagues (Gerber, 1994, 2001) across a series of studies (Gerber *et al.*, 1990, 1992; Gerber & Reiff, 1991). For example, in their causal-comparative interview study, Gerber *et al.* (1992) constructed two matched groups, one of highly successful and one of moderately successful adults with LD, based on criteria reflecting income level, job classification, educational attainments, prominence, and job satisfaction. Again, as described earlier, the groups were matched on age, gender, race, severity of disability, specific learning problems, parents' occupations, and family SES. Most of the participants had endured many years of failure prior to experiencing success. But at the time of the study, many of the successful individuals had Ph.D.s and 21 of them earned more than $100,000 per year. Moderately successful individuals ($n = 25$) were all high school graduates; their salaries ranged from $10,000 to 100,000+ per year, with half earning in the $40,000 to $50,000 range. Gerber *et al.* found that, for all participants, efforts to gain success could be linked to a "quest to gain control of their lives" (p. 479). Further, the difference between the highly and moderately successful groups was not in the severity of their LD or other demographic variables, but rather could be related to "the amount of control *sought* and *realized*" (p. 479, emphasis in the original) and to "internal decisions" and "external manifestations" underlying participants' pursuit of control. Internal decisions associated with success were a desire to succeed, being goal-oriented, and reframing of the LD experience "into more positive or productive experience" (Gerber *et al.*, 1992, p. 479). External manifestations of adaptability included persistence, use of coping mechanisms, creating a goodness of fit between individual abilities and environments, and creation of supportive "social ecologies" (e.g., personal support networks). Gerber and his colleagues concluded that success by adults with LD can be enhanced by promoting these kinds of internal decisions and external manifestations (Gerber, 1994, 2001).

Among the internal decisions associated with success, Gerber (1994, 2001) has emphasized the importance of reframing. He suggests that four stages are required to positively reframe the experience of having LD: (1) recognizing one's disability, (2) understanding one's own strengths and weaknesses,

(3) acceptance, and (4) setting a plan of action toward reaching goals. Reframing is critical because "the key problem adults with learning disabilities face is not the disability itself but, rather, their inability to confront the various challenges they encounter as they learn to live with and overcome it" (Gerber *et al.*, 1992, p. 481). Gerber (2001) also emphasizes the central importance of self-advocacy to success by adults with LD. He argues "each person with LD has his or her own unique profile in terms of severity, cognitive strengths, intellectual ability, and adaptive behavior" (Gerber, 2001, p. 178). To be successful, individuals must be able to describe their profile to others, explain how they learn, and request supportive strategies and accommodations. Finally, Gerber (2001) also emphasizes the importance of empowerment and self-determination. Self-determination has been defined as "an individual's ability to make autonomous decisions, set goals, independently attempt to accomplish goals, independently attain goals, independently evaluate his or her performance, and make adjustments based on goal progress" (Murray, 2003, p. 23). Gerber and his colleagues suggest that success by adults with LD can be supported by fostering positive reframing, self-awareness and self-understanding, self-advocacy, and self-determination.

Raskind *et al.* (1999) provide another framework for understanding outcomes for adults with LD. In preparation for their follow-up study of ex-Frostig students, they defined "success attributes" based on prior research, including self-awareness, proactivity, perseverance, goal-setting, the presence and use of effective support systems, and emotional stability. They then used multiple methods (e.g., in-depth interviews with participants and their families, review of individual case and public records, a checklist, standardized tests) to collect data on each of these attributes, along with other demographic information (age, gender, ethnicity, IQ, academic achievement, life stressors). Finally, they developed a set of criteria (based on employment, education, independence, and community involvement) for categorizing adults with LD as more ($n = 21$) or less ($n = 20$) successful. They found no differences between the successful and unsuccessful groups on age, gender, family SES, ethnicity, or length of time at the Frostig Centre. They also found that the greatest predictor of success was a composite variable including the 6 success attributes ($R^2 = 0.75$), while IQ and achievement added very little to the prediction of successful outcomes. They concluded, as did Gerber *et al.* (1992), that the most powerful predictors of success by adults with LD in adulthood are not LD severity or academic skills. They recommend interventions focused on developing success attributes and compensatory strategies, not just on remediating basic skills.

Other studies have elaborated understanding regarding factors associated with success by adults with LD. For example, in their interview study of 51 adults (aged 18 to 40 years), Polloway *et al.* (1992) found that successful participants used coping strategies (e.g., using computers to help with writing or memory; strategies for meeting demands at work), which they usually constructed through trial and error rather than being provided with instruction. Success was also associated with positive external influences, such as participating in sports programs, having support of family members, or assistance from a tutor. Similarly, in their interview study of Dutch adults with dyslexia, Hellendoorn and Ruijssenaars (2000) found that 26 out of the 27 participants used positive strategies for coping (e.g., asking for help, using learning strategies). However, they also found that 24 of the participants used negative coping strategies (e.g., avoidance, camouflage, repression of problems). Implications derived from across these two studies are that success by adults with LD can be promoted by supporting development of positive and personalized coping strategies and positive external supports.

Finally, consistent with the frameworks presented above, Weller *et al.* (1994) drew on the concept of adaptivity to explain the success of adults with LD. They explain that "adaptive behavior (or more descriptively, *adaptivity*) is a proactive process through which individuals organize their lives in purposeful, flexible, and advantageous ways to meet the demands of multiple environments" (p. 282, emphasis in the original). Weller *et al.* define requirements for being adaptive, including perceiving, understanding, critical analysis, deciding, metacognitive awareness of one's own strengths and weaknesses, and planfully constructing relationships between oneself and environments to promote more successful outcomes. Adaptive strategies can include modifying personal behaviors to meet environmental demands, shaping environments to meet personal needs, selecting environments strategically, ignoring environmental requirements, delaying responses, and avoiding environments while finding another way to achieve one's objectives. Weller *et al.* conclude by arguing for interventions that promote students' active and mindful adaptation.

B. A Risk and Resilience Framework

Many authors have adopted a "risk and resilience" framework as a conceptual model for examining outcomes for adults with LD (e.g., Cosden, 1999; Hellendoorn & Ruijssenaars, 2000; Murray, 2003; Werner, 1993; Wong, 2003). This perspective frames LD as just one of many factors that place an individual at risk for poorer outcomes. Further, the goal of research from a risk and resilience perspective is to identify protective and buffering factors that might mediate outcomes (Wong, 2003). As Murray (2003) explains, "A risk and resilience model provides a framework for exploring the impact of individual, social, and contextual experiences on the long-term outcomes of youth with high incidence disabilities" (p. 24). This approach suggests directions for intervention so as to reduce modifiable risk and/or bolster protective factors.

For example, Werner (1993) adopted a risk and resilience perspective to frame her findings from the Kauai longitudinal study. Because the Kauai study tracked a birth cohort over time, Werner was able to identify risk and protective factors that could be related to positive outcomes in adulthood. She found that early risk factors for poorer outcomes were low birth weight, perinatal distress, congenital defects, being unaffectionate as a baby, below average intellectual development, and personal characteristics such as awkwardness, distractibility, or restlessness. Factors associated with more positive outcomes were temperamental characteristics that elicited positive reactions from others, positive skills and values (e.g., faith that odds could be overcome, realistic plans or goals), positive parental caregiving, supportive other adults, and timely opportunities during key life transitions. Other key buffers against negative outcomes were positive self-efficacy and self-esteem. Further, self-efficacy was found to be bolstered when individuals' positive temperamental characteristics fostered positive relationships with others (which then all together promoted positive outcomes). Werner described how, even though the odds were against the individuals with LD in her study, most individuals had constructed positive, stable lives for themselves by the time they reached adulthood.

Murray (2003) suggests that having an LD is just one among a number of risk factors that might impact on adult outcomes. Based on a review of research across fields of study, she identifies other risk factors that might also influence success by adults with LD. These include gender, ethnicity, low socioeconomic status, poverty, peer rejection, and poor family relationships. Protective factors identified across studies include characteristics of the individual (temperament, internal locus of control, high self-esteem, a positive outlook on the future, moderate to high IQ), a supportive family and positive parenting styles, access to good schools and a sense of belonging in school, positive peer relationships, social support in the community, and involvement in prosocial activities and organization. Notice that many of the risk and protective factors identified by Murray (2003) mirror findings from research accounting for success by adults with LD (e.g., Adelman & Vogel, 1998; Polloway et al., 1992; Rojewski, 1999; Werner, 1993). Also consistent with others, Murray recommends intervention to enhance individually centered protective factors such as self-determination and agency, self-esteem, social problem-solving skills, and academic competence along with support for the construction of positive peer relationships and participation in extracurricular activities that foster a sense of belonging and self-esteem. Murray also calls for research on risk and resiliency at different ages and within important transitional periods.

C. Implications for Intervention

Research accounting for differential success by adults with LD provides important direction for intervention. Recommendations are to help individuals establish a range of internal and external supports that mediate successful outcomes (Murray, 2003; Polloway *et al.*, 1992; Werner, 1993). A fundamental theme that cuts across studies is that, to be successful, LD adults must gain "control of their lives" (Gerber *et al.*, 1992, p. 479). Thus, it is not surprising that multiple authors stress the importance of promoting personal agency and self-determination (Brinckerhoff *et al.*, 2002; Diaz-Greenberg *et al.*, 2000; Gerber, 2001; Murray, 2003). Indeed, Brinckerhoff *et al.* (2002) suggest that support for individuals' self-determination should be the "prime directive" for intervention (p. 488). Many of the recommendations that can be distilled across studies are required in order to promote self-determination. One of these is to promote self-awareness and self-understanding, which are prerequisite to developing personally adaptive approaches for meeting environmental demands (Gerber, 2001; Polloway *et al.*, 1992; Raskind *et al.*, 1999; Weller *et al.*, 1994). Positive self-perceptions (e.g., self-efficacy, self-concept, self-esteem), realistic goal setting, and an internal locus of control also undergird individuals' ability to tackle life tasks strategically (Bandura, 1993; Gerber, 2001; Panagos & DuBois, 1999; Raskind *et al.*, 1999; Werner, 1993; Zimmerman & Schunk, 2001). Self-advocacy is also enabled by increased self-awareness, self-understanding, and an ability to take control over outcomes.

VI. PROGRAMS AND INTERVENTIONS

Since the mid-1980s, attention has increasingly focused on defining programs and interventions to better meet the needs of adults with LD (Brinckerhoff *et al.*, 2002; Gerber, 2001; Lerner, 2003; Lowry, 1990). This section overviews the state of research on the efficacy of programs and interventions.

A. Transition Planning

Since the advent of U.S. legislation requiring transition planning for adolescence with disabilities, efforts have focused on developing transition programs for students with LD (Brinckerhoff *et al.*, 2002; Evers, 1996). However, formal evaluation studies of transition programs are only just emerging. For example, Gajar (1992) describes how legislation in the United States spurred the creation of a transition initiative and over 180 model programs between 1984 and 1989. However, little data were actually generated to evaluate the success of the programs. In their review, Adelman and Vogel (1998) found little evidence of positive employment outcomes associated with high school education or vocational training. Instead, students were frequently not qualified for fields in which they were trained or failed to find jobs in the trained areas. More recently, however, Evers (1996) summarized findings from seven studies suggesting positive employment outcomes associated with high school transition programs. As one example, using a multiple-baseline design, Clement-Heist *et al.* (1992) found that a combination of simulated and *in situ* support had a positive effect on four high school students' mastery and application of work-related social skills.

Advice is readily available regarding what to address in transition plans and programs (e.g., Brinckerhoff *et al.*, 2002; Lerner, 2003). Lerner (2003) explains that transition plans should include current levels of performance, interests and aptitudes, post-school goals, transition activities, responsible persons, and procedures for reviewing progress toward goals. Consistent with research on factors associated with success for adults with LD, Brinckerhoff *et al.* (2002) recommend that transition programs be student-centered so as to foster self-determination. Students should be assisted to participate in development of their own transition plans, select courses, identify postsecondary and vocational options, recognize and prepare for adult setting demands, describe their disability to others, learn about their legal rights, and evaluate LD support services.

B. College and University Programs

Most postsecondary institutions in the United States and Canada now provide support services for students with LD (Adelman & Vogel, 1998; Brinckerhoff *et al.*, 2002; Gerber, 2001; Wong & Hutchinson, 2001). Some universities and colleges provide nondegree programs designed to promote independence, life skills, budgeting, computer use, or work experience (Lerner, 2003; Roffman *et al.*, 1994). Most two-year and four-year institutions also have support centers offering remedial programming, tutoring, accommodations, instruction in compensatory strategies or survival skills, and/or vocational exploration and training (Lerner, 2003; Lowry, 1990). Follow-up studies are emerging that document outcomes for graduates of postsecondary programs (e.g., Ganschow *et al.*, 1999; Greenbaum *et al.*, 1996; Sitlington *et al.*, 1994; Vogel & Adelman, 2000). However, research is needed to tease apart the effects of program components at a more specific level.

C. Accommodations

In the United States, legislation (ADA, the Vocational Rehabilitation Act of 1973) mandates provision of reasonable accommodations for postsecondary students with LD (Brinckerhoff *et al.*, 2002; Lerner, 2003; Rothstein, 1998;

Scott, 1994). As a result, colleges and universities are currently challenged to develop policies for providing appropriate supports. Accommodations most frequently provided are extended time on exams, course substitutions, allowing part-time rather than full-time study, modified exam procedures or instructional methods, and access to books on tape, note-takers, or assistive technology (Lerner, 2003; Raskind, 1993, 1998; Scott, 2002). But Scott (2002) advises that service providers be aware of shifting environmental demands when defining appropriate accommodations. For example, today's virtual classrooms require access to the Internet and/or interaction among students by E-mail or in chat rooms. These emerging setting demands may require nontraditional types of supportive accommodations.

Providing accommodations to students with LD has generated considerable controversy. For example, questions have been raised about whether waiving program requirements (e.g., in math or in foreign languages) compromises the academic integrity of programs. Similarly, the fairness of providing extended time has been questioned if students without disabilities have to complete the same tests under time constraints. Runyan (1991) conducted a study with college students to investigate this latter question. She compared the performance on a reading comprehension test of 16 students with LD to that of 15 peers matched on ethnicity, gender, age, and SAT scores, under both timed and untimed conditions. She found that, in the timed condition, students with LD read slower, answered fewer questions, and so received a lower overall score. In contrast, under untimed conditions, the students with LD performed as well as peers. Significantly, the average performance of non-LD students did not differ between the timed and untimed conditions. Runyan concluded that providing extended time compensates for the slower processing of students with LD without disadvantaging nondisabled peers. But because students with LD differed in terms of how much extra time they required, Runyan suggested setting support parameters on an individual basis.

Self-determination by adults with LD is fostered when individuals who are aware of their own strengths and weaknesses select, use, or request accommodations strategically to meet environmental demands. Not surprisingly, researchers have described use of accommodations as a positive coping strategy (Gerber, 2001; Hellendoorn & Ruijssenaars, 2000; Polloway et al., 1992). More research is warranted, however, on how accommodations might be helpful for adults with LD within vocational and community settings (e.g., Jacobs & Hendricks, 1992).

D. Assistive Technology

Until recently, applications of technology for LD students focused primarily on remediating basic skill deficits (Raskind, 1998). But Raskind (1998) suggests that the concept of assistive technology provides an alternative to this more "traditional" deficit model (see also Day & Edwards, 1996). Within U.S. legislation, assistive technology is defined as "any item, piece of equipment, or product system...that is used to increase, maintain, or improve the functional capabilities of individuals with disabilities" (Bryant *et al.*, 2002, p. 391). Conceptualized in this way, assistive technology serves a compensatory rather than a remedial function, with the potential to provide positive coping strategies for adults with LD (Polloway *et al.*, 1992). Assistive technology helps individuals with LD "bypass, circumvent, or work around specific learning disabilities" in order to achieve valued goals (Raskind, 1998, p. 255).

Bryant *et al.* (2002) describe three types of benefits associated with use of assistive technology: increases in meaningful inclusion within academic environments (e.g., when instruction is accessible through alternative modes of presentation); increased independence (e.g., when a student can access text independently rather than having to rely on a reader); and increased ability to successfully navigate one's disability (e.g., to understand one's own strengths and weaknesses and ways to compensate for disabilities). Both Raskind (1993) and Bryant *et al.* (2002) provide excellent overviews of assistive devices available to support students' functional abilities. For example, supports for reading include not only books on tape, but also optical character and speech synthesis systems that scan texts and read them aloud. Supports for writing include software that supports idea generation (e.g., outlining or brainstorming), text production (e.g., word prediction or voice recognition software), and editing (spelling and grammar check systems). Examples of math supports are talking calculators and optical scanners that read word problems aloud. Listening supports include personal FM listening devices and tape recorders with variable playback speeds that do not distort sound quality. Personal data managers, databases, and note-taking tools support organization and effective learning.

Raskind (1998) reviewed studies on assistive technology for adults with LD conducted in the mid- to late-1990s. He concluded that use of assistive technology is generally associated with positive outcomes, but that not all LD learners profit equally from the same assistive devices. Therefore, Raskind cautioned that assistive devices should be well-matched to an individual's needs. Scott (2002) concurs, arguing that choosing among assistive alternatives requires considering individual strengths and weaknesses in relation to setting demands.

E. Academic Interventions

Recommendations regarding academic interventions for adults with LD are plentiful in the literature, but few formal studies have evaluated specific approaches to intervention. For example, Sturomski *et al.* (1998) completed a comprehensive review of research on literacy interventions for adults with LD conducted between 1982 and 1995. They concluded that there is a "lack of information regarding what works with adults with learning disabilities" (p. 95), and that there exist "few practices that could be recommended as best practices from published research" (p. 97). Similarly, when searching the literature prior to writing this chapter, only 9 empirical reports were found (see Table II).

An example of intervention research is provided by Wilson (1998), who describes two studies investigating the efficacy of a multisensory approach to instruction (the Wilson Reading System (WRS)) for promoting decoding and spelling skills by adults with LD. In the first study, Wilson evaluated the efficacy of WRS in improving spelling by college students with LD. Thirty students with dyslexia (aged 18 to 32 years) were assigned to one of three groups: a WRS intervention group, a group that received intervention using a non-phonetically based program, and a no-intervention comparison group. Results showed a superiority of the WRS in increasing spelling accuracy when compared to the other two groups. In a second, smaller study that included 9 students, 6 with language-based LD, Wilson also found evidence of improved decoding following WRS instruction. Thus, the WRS appears to provide one effective strategy for promoting foundational reading skills by adults with LD.

Many writers provide recommendations regarding how to structure in-struction effectively to promote concept acquisition by adults with LD (e.g., Brinckerhoff *et al.*, 2002; Westberry, 1994). However, few empirical studies have included samples of LD adults. One exception is the study by Kitz and Thorpe (1995), who compared algebra instruction for college students in a remedial program provided in a traditional format to instruction provided through a videodisk system. Instructional principles embedded in the video-disk program included direct instruction, a focus on mastery, frequent quizzes, feedback, and extensive reinforcement. Results showed superior comprehension for students in the videodisk instructional condition, both at the end of the program and into the next semester.

A consistent recommendation is to provide instruction in learning strat-egies (e.g., Applegate *et al.*, 1994; Brinckerhoff *et al.*, 2002; Gerber, 2001; Grant, 1994; Lerner, 2003; Scott, 2002; Westberry, 1994). For example, a common recommendation is to adapt the Strategy Intervention Model (SIM) developed by Deshler and his colleagues for use with adolescents with LD (see Deshler *et al.*, Ellis, & Lenz, 1996; Ellis, 1993). In SIM, students are taught, using a combination of direct instruction and modeling, about how and why to implement powerful learning strategies for use across a range of important academic tasks. Students' independent application of strategies is promoted by linking strategy and content instruction (Ellis,

1993; Grant, 1994), focusing students' attention on positive outcomes associated with effortful strategy use (Borkowski, 1992) and directly teaching for transfer (Ellis, 1993). A considerable amount of research has validated the efficacy of SIM for supporting adolescents with LD. Clearly, more research is warranted to investigate adaptations of learning strategies interventions within postsecondary and adult education settings.

Lipson (1995) provides an example of research on learning strategies instruction for adults with low reading skills. In her study, Lipson tested whether direct instruction in semantic mapping strategies improved the reading comprehension of college freshmen enrolled in a remedial reading course. Participants were assigned to one of three conditions: direct instruction in semantic mapping ($n = 16$), answering or creating questions based on text, or reading and discussing the content. Students' performance was compared on questions that could be answered from the text (text explicit), inferred from the text (text implicit), or also required prior knowledge (script implicit). Lipson found that group of students who learned to create semantic maps outperformed other students on both the text explicit and implicit (but not script implicit) questions. Although it is not clear whether participants had been formally diagnosed as LD, this study shows that struggling, young adult readers can learn higher order reading skills.

Suritsky and Hughes (1991) recommend instruction for students with LD in note-taking strategies. Compared to nondisabled peers, college students with LD use fewer abbreviations, write more slowly, and record less important information (Hughes & Suritsky, 1994). The most frequent solution to this note-taking difficulty is to provide accommodations in the form of note-takers or tape-recorders. However, given research documenting the advantages to learning and remembering that accrue from actively taking notes, Suritsky and Hughes recommend teaching students with LD to take notes for themselves.

F. Interventions in Vocational, Daily Living, and Social–Emotional Contexts

Little research has been conducted on interventions outside of school contexts. For example, the vast majority of studies located for this review were conducted with college or university students (see Table II). Similarly, when Cronin (1996) reviewed the literature focused on life skills development by high school students with LD, she found ample evidence that students with disabilities struggle after leaving high school, but little data on how to support students' acquisition of life skills so as to support important post-school accomplishments. Research is also needed on interventions that promote social–emotional development. Price (2002) argues for psychosocial support that assists in establishing independence, developing satisfactory relationships, improving self-esteem and confidence, and overcoming depression.

G. Promoting Success Attributes

Reiff, Gerber, & Ginsberg (1994) provide recommendations for instructional strategies with promise to promote the attitudes, values, and skills identified in their research as associated with success (Gerber, 2001; Gerber et al., 1992). For example, they provide concrete suggestions for promoting internal and external processes they defined as essential to manifesting control, including promoting desire/motivation, goal orientation, reframing of LDs in a more positive way, persistence, creating a good fit between their strengths and needs and the demands of environments, and creating positive social ecologies. Similarly, Gerber et al. (1996) provide a description of what is required to promote successful reframing. For example, they suggest that students be supported to learn how to break problems into parts, brainstorm, generate alternatives, choose and take action, and evaluate final products.

Recommendations made by Gerber and his colleagues are grounded in research conducted with children or adolescents. Again, few studies have been conducted with adults with LD. One exception is a recent study by Roffman et al. (1994), who evaluated the efficacy of a course designed to foster self-understanding and self-advocacy of college students with LD. The 15-hour course was offered as part of a comprehensive 2-year program focused on vocational preparation, independent living skills, social skills, and practical academics. Roffman et al. found that, when compared to students in the comparison group, course participants better understood their LD and were better able to describe strengths and needs in a mock interview situation.

H. The Strategic Content Learning Approach

Strategic Content Learning (SCL) is an instructional model designed to promote self-regulated approaches to tasks across ages and across environments (Butler, 1995, 1998a). However, SCL instructional goals and principles are particularly well suited to adults with LD, and a number of studies have been conducted on SCL efficacy with this population (Butler, 1995, 1998c; Butler, Elaschuk, Poole et al., 2000; Butler, Elaschuk, & Poole, 2000) (see Table II). In this section, I briefly define self-regulated learning in relation to success by adults with LD, before introducing the SCL model and overviewing research on SCL efficacy.

Models of self-regulation define cognitive, metacognitive, motivational, and affective beliefs and processes required for successful adaptation across life domains (Corno, 1993, 1994; Zimmerman & Schunk, 2001). As such, self-regulation is central to the adaptivity associated with success for adults with LD (Weller *et al.*, 1994). Further, successful self-regulation requires interpreting setting demands (e.g., demands of a given academic task or work requirement), setting achievable goals, selecting, adapting, or even inventing strategies to accomplish desired goals, monitoring outcomes, and adjusting performance strategically when obstacles are encountered (Butler & Winne, 1995; Zimmerman, 1994). As such, self-regulation and self-determination also are closely related (Diaz-Greenberg *et al.*, 2000). Self-determination requires successful self-regulation, which entails defining and then planfully and strategically managing environments and personal resources so as to achieve meaningful goals.

SCL is a student-centered approach that promotes self-regulation in the context of meaningful work. In SCL, instructors and students work collaboratively to articulate setting demands (e.g., task requirements), co-construct personalized strategies for achieving goals, try out strategies (i.e., learning, coping, compensatory), monitor strategy efficacy, and revise strategies as necessary until success is achieved. Thus, in SCL students are engaged in the process of strategy development. They are empowered to take control over outcomes through planful and strategic self-regulation (see Butler, 1998b, 2002, for more information).

To evaluate the efficacy of SCL in meeting the needs of adults with LD, Butler embedded SCL instructional principles in service delivery models common within postsecondary settings. Four studies evaluated SCL efficacy when used to provide one-on-one tutoring by learning disability specialists or teachers (Butler, 1995, 1998c, 2003); two studies evaluated SCL as a model for providing instruction by peer tutors (Butler, 2003); and one study evaluated SCL principles when adapted to structure small-group instruction on reading (Butler, Elaschuk, Poole *et al.*, 2000). Each study embedded multiple in-depth case studies within a pretest–posttest design. Thus, empirical reports are available, tracing not only descriptions of outcomes for groups of students (e.g., Butler, 2003) but also in-depth case studies for individual students (e.g., Butler, Elaschuk, & Poole, 2000). Butler's studies were conducted in college or university settings, but participants were heterogeneous. They ranged in age from 18 to 55, and were engaged in programs at very different levels (from adult basic education to graduate work) and with a variety of foci (e.g., academic study; training programs for becoming a special education assistant, a diesel mechanic, or a medical lab technician).

Positive outcomes can be associated with SCL instruction (Butler, 1995, 1998c, 2003). Study participants have been found to improve task performance (e.g., in reading, writing, math) and to develop positive self-perceptions, beliefs in personal control over outcomes, and increased metacognitive knowledge about tasks and effective learning processes. Most critically, participants have learned *how to construct* personalized and powerful strategies for accomplishing goals, based on an understanding of their own strengths and needs. Thus, SCL appears to support development of success attributes by adults with LD, such as positive self-perceptions, control over outcomes, increased self-awareness and self-understanding, use of positive learning or compensatory strategies, and self-determination.

VII. REFLECTION: PROGRESS AND FUTURE DIRECTIONS

In the past 20 years, considerable progress has been made in the still young field of adult LD. Solid foundations for the field have been established through legislation and advocacy (LDA, 1994; NJCLD, 1987, 1999). Studies have clearly documented the challenges faced by adults with LD across important life domains (educational, vocational, daily living, social–emotional). At the same time, research on individual differences has revealed alterable "success attributes" (Raskind *et al.*, 1999) and buffering factors that can form the basis for intervention.

Adopting a lifespan development perspective also reminds us that there are multidimensional and pluralistic paths that adults with LD may take toward achieving positive outcomes (Gerber, 1994, 2001), and that the impact of LD is a function not just of individual characteristics, but of the interaction of individual characteristics with demands across environments and at different ages. It follows that, if we can promote success attributes in individuals with LD (e.g., self-awareness, compensatory strategies) and at the same time create an optimal goodness of fit between individuals and environments, we may ultimately circumvent the perception (and experience) of the processing differences associated with LD as a *dis*ability. Consider one highly successful bike mechanic's self-report: "I am only learning disabled on rare occasions since leaving high school" (Gerber, 2001, p. 177).

Progress also has been made in developing programs (high school transition, vocational education, postsecondary programs) and interventions (e.g., accommodations, assistive technology, academic interventions) with promise to foster success of LD adults. For example, strategies that promote self-regulated performance (e.g., SCL) can be applied to build self-confidence, self-understanding, self-determination and adaptivity across important life domains (Butler, 1993, 1995, 1998a, 2003).

But further research is clearly called for in a number of areas. For example, although it is positive that researchers are defining variables that mediate success by adults with LD, rather than just focusing on negative outcomes, methodological procedures must be closely examined to account for differences across studies (e.g., Levine & Nourse, 1998). Further, attention should more systematically focus on how LDs manifest themselves across ages and life domains (Gajar, 1992; Gerber, 1994, 2001; Polloway *et al.*, 1992). Currently, research includes just young adults with LD (particularly college students) or includes adults of varying ages without differentiating results across ages. More intervention research also is clearly required, across a fuller range of educational, vocational, daily living, and community settings (Cosden, 1999; Evers, 1996; Lowry, 1990; Sturomski *et al.*, 1998; Vogel & Reder, 1998a).

In conclusion, research on LD returned to its roots by refocusing on LD in adulthood. And in the past 20 years, research has blossomed in this important field, so that the challenges of adult LD are better recognized. However, the field is still young, and much work is required to understand life for adults with LD in the "other 70 years" (Gerber, 2001). Research in this area has promise, not only to provide important benchmarks for families and practitioners working with children, but also to assist a fuller range of educators, employers, and community members who strive to support the success of adults with LD.

References

Adelman, P. B., & Vogel, S. A. (1998). Adults with learning disabilities. In B. Y. L. Wong (ed.), *Learning about learning disabilities*, 2nd ed. (pp. 657–701). Toronto: Academic Press.

Applegate, M. D., Quinn, K. B., & Applegate, A. J. (1994). Using metacognitive strategies to enhance achievement for at-risk liberal arts college students. *Journal of Reading*, **38,** 32–40.

Apthorp, H. S. (1995). Phonetic coding and reading in college students with and without learning disabilities. *Journal of Learning Disabilities*, **28**(6), 342–352.

Bandura, A. (1993). Perceived self-efficacy in cognitive development and functioning. *Educational Psychologist*, **28,** 117–148.

Beers, S. R., Goldstein, G., & Katz, L. J. (1994). Neuropsychological differences between college students with learning disabilities and those with mild head injury. *Journal of Learning Disabilities*, **27**(5), 315–324.

Beitchman, J. H., Wilson, B., Douglas, L., Young, A., & Adlaf, E. (2001). Substance use disorders in young adults with and without LD: Predictive and concurrent relationships. *Journal of Learning Disabilities*, **34**(4), 317–332.

Blackorby, J., & Wagner, M. (1996). Longitudinal postschool outcomes of youth with disabilities: Findings from the National Longitudinal Transition Study. *Exceptional Children*, **62**(5), 399–414.

Borkowski, J. G. (1992). Metacognitive theory: A framework for teaching literacy, writing, and math skills. *Journal of Learning Disabilities*, **25,** 253–257.

Brinckerhoff, L. C., McGuire, J. M., & Shaw, S. F. (2002). *Postsecondary education and transition for students with learning disabilities* (2nd ed.). Austin, TX: Pro-Ed.

Bruck, M. (1993). Component spelling skills of college students with childhood diagnoses of dyslexia. *Learning Disability Quarterly*, **16**(3), 171–184.

Bryant, B. R., Bryant, D. P., & Rieth, H. J. (2002). Assistive technology. In L. Brinckerhoff, J. M. McGuire, & S. F. Shaw, *Post-secondary education and transition for students with learning disabilities*, 2nd ed. (pp. 389–429). Austin, TX: Pro-Ed.

Butler, D. L. (1995). Promoting strategic learning by post secondary students with learning disabilities. *Journal of Learning Disabilities*, **28**, 170–190.

Butler, D. L. (1998a). A strategic content learning approach to promoting self-regulated learning. In B. J. Zimmerman & D. Schunk (eds.), *Developing self-regulated learning: From teaching to self-reflective practice* (pp. 160–183). New York: Guilford Publications, Inc.

Butler, D. L. (1998b). Metacognition and learning disabilities. In B. Y. L. Wong (ed.), *Learning about learning disabilities* (2nd ed.) (pp. 277–307). Toronto: Academic Press.

Butler, D. L. (1998c). The strategic content learning approach to promoting self-regulated learning: A summary of three studies. *Journal of Educational Psychology*, **90**, 682–697.

Butler, D. L. (2002). Individualizing instruction in self-regulated learning. *Theory into Practice*, **41**, 81–92.

Butler, D. L. (2003). Structuring instruction to promote self-regulated learning by adolescents and adults with learning disabilities. *Exceptionality*, **11**(1), 39–60.

Butler, D. L., Elaschuk, C. L., & Poole, S. (2000). Promoting strategic writing by postsecondary students with learning disabilities: A report of three case studies. *Learning Disability Quarterly*, **23**, 196–213.

Butler, D. L., Elaschuk, C. L., Poole, S. L., Novak, H. J., Jarvis, S., & Beckingham, B. (2000, April). Investigating an application of strategic content learning: Promoting strategy development in group contexts. Presented at the Annual Meetings of the American Educational Research Association. New Orleans, LA.

Butler, D. L., & Winne, P. H. (1995). Feedback and self-regulated learning: A theoretical synthesis. *Review of Educational Research*, **65**, 245–281.

Clement-Heist, K., Siegel, S., & Gaylord-Ross, R. (1992). Simulated and *in situ* vocational social skills training for youths with learning disabilities. *Exceptional Children*, **58**(4), 336–345.

Corno, L. (1993). The best laid plans: Modern conceptions of volition and educational research. *Educational Researcher*, **22**(2), 14–22.

Corno, L. (1994). Student volition and education: Outcomes, influences, and practices. In D. H. Schunk & B. J. Zimmerman (eds.), *Self-regulation of learning and performance: Issues and educational applications* (pp. 229–251). Hillsdale, NJ: Erlbaum.

Cosden, M. (1999). Risk and resilience for substance abuse among adolescents and adults with LD. *Journal of Learning Disabilities*, **34**(4), 352–358.

Cosden, M. A., & McNamara, J. (1997). Self-concept and perceived social support among college students with and without learning disabilities. *Learning Disability Quarterly*, **20**(1), 2–12.

Crawford, R. (1997). Vocational programs and practices. In S. Goldstein (ed.), *Managing attention and learning disorders in late adolescence and adulthood* (pp. 287–314). Toronto: John Wiley & Sons.

Cronin, M. E. (1996). Life skills curricula for students with learning disabilities: A review of the literature. *Journal of Learning Disabilities, 29,* 53–68.

Day, S. L., & Edwards, B. J. (1996). Assistive technology for postsecondary students with learning disabilities. *Journal of Learning Disabilities,* **29**(5), 486–492, 503.

Deshler, D. D., Ellis, E. S., & Lenz, B. K. (1996). *Teaching adolescents with learning disabilities: Strategies and methods* (2nd ed.). Denver, CO: Love Publishing Co.

Diaz-Greenberg, R., Thousand, J., Cardelle-Elawar, M., & Nevin, A. (2000). What teachers need to know about the struggle for self-determination (conscientization) and self-regulation: Adults with disabilities speak about their education experiences. *Teaching and Teacher Education,* **16,** 873–887.

Ellis, E. S. (1993). Integrative strategy instruction: A potential model for teaching content area subjects to adolescents with learning disabilities. *Journal of Learning Disabilities,* **26,** 358–383, 398.

Evers, R. B. (1996). The positive force of vocational education: Transition outcomes for youth with learning disabilities. *Journal of Learning Disabilities,* **29**(1), 69–78.

Gajar, A. (1992). Adults with learning disabilities: Current and future research priorities. *Journal of Learning Disabilities,* **25**(8), 507–519.

Ganschow, L., Coyne, J., Parks, A. W., & Antonoff, S. J. (1999). A 10-year follow-up survey of programs and services for students with learning disabilities in graduate and professional schools. *Journal of Learning Disabilities,* **32**(1), 72–84.

Gerber, P. J. (1994). Researching adults with LD from an adult-developmental perspective. *Journal of Learning Disabilities,* **27,** 6–9.

Gerber, P. J. (2001). Learning disabilities: A life span approach. In D. P. Hallahan & B. K. Keogh (eds.), *Research and global perspectives in learning disabilities* (pp. 167–180). Mahwah, NJ: Erlbaum.

Gerber, P. J., Ginsberg, R., & Reiff, H. B. (1992). Identifying alterable patterns in employment success for highly successful adults with learning disabilities. *Journal of Learning Disabilities,* **25**(8), 475–487.

Gerber, P. J., & Reiff, H. B. (1991). *Speaking for themselves: Ethnographic interviews with adults with learning disabilities.* Ann Arbor, MI: The University of Michigan Press.

Gerber, P. J., Reiff, H. B., & Ginsberg, R. (1996). Reframing the learning disabilities experience. *Journal of Learning Disabilities,* **29**(1), 98–101, 97.

Gerber, P. J., Schnieders, C. A., Paradise, L. V., Reiff, H. B., Ginsberg, R. J., & Popp, P. A. (1990). Persisting problems of adults with learning disabilities: Self-reported comparisons from their school-age and adult years. *Journal of Learning Disabilities,* **23**(9), 570–573.

Gottesman, R. L., Bennett, R. E., Nathan, R. G., & Kelly, M. S. (1996). Inner city adults with severe reading difficulties: A closer look. *Journal of Learning Disabilities,* **29**(6), 589–597.

Grant, R. (1994). Comprehension strategy instruction: Basic considerations for instructing at-risk college students. *Journal of Reading,* **38**(1), 42–48.

Greenbaum, B., Graham, S., & Scales, W. (1996). Adults with learning disabilities: Occupational and social status after college. *Journal of Learning Disabilities*, **29**(2), 167–173.

Gregg, N., & Hoy, C. (1990). Referencing: The cohesive use of pronouns in the written narrative of college underprepared writers, nondisabled writers, and writers with learning disabilities. *Journal of Learning Disabilities*, **23**(9), 557–563.

Hall, C. W., Spruill, K. L., & Webster, R. E. (2002). Motivational and attitudinal factors in college students with and without learning disabilities. *Learning Disability Quarterly*, **25**(2), 79–86.

Hellendoorn, J., & Ruijssenaars, W. (2000). Personal experiences and adjustment of Dutch adults with dyslexia. *Remedial and Special Education*, **21**(4), 227–239.

Hughes, C. A., & Suritsky, S. K. (1994). Note-taking skills of university students with and without learning disabilities. *Journal of Learning Disabilities*, **27**(1), 20–24.

Jacobs, A. E., & Hendricks, D. J. (1992). Job accommodations for adults with learning disabilities: Brilliantly disguised opportunities. *Learning Disability Quarterly*, **15**(4), 274–285.

Johnston, C. L. (1984). The learning disabled adolescent and young adult: An overview and critique of current practices. *Journal of Learning Disabilities*, **17**, 386–391.

Kitz, W. R., & Thorpe, H. W. (1995). A comparison of the effectiveness of videodisc and traditional algebra instruction for college-age students with learning disabilities. *Remedial and Special Education*, **16**(5), 295–306.

Learning Disabilities Association of America (LDA). (1994). Resolution on adult education for persons with learning disabilities. *Journal of Learning Disabilities*, **27**(1), 4.

Leong, C. K. (1999). Phonological and morphological processing in adult students with learning/reading disabilities. *Journal of Learning Disabilities*, **32**(3), 224–238.

Lerner, J. W. (2003). *Learning disabilities: Theories, diagnosis, and teaching strategies.* Boston, MA: Houghton Mifflin Company.

Levine, P., & Nourse, S. W. (1998). What follow-up studies say about postschool life for young men and women with learning disabilities: A critical look at the literature. *Journal of Learning Disabilities*, **31**, 212–233.

Lipson, M. (1995). The effect of semantic mapping instruction on prose comprehension of below-level college readers. *Reading Research and Instruction*, **34**(4), 367–378.

Lowry, C. M. (1990). Teaching adults with learning disabilities. *ERIC Digest*, (**99**), 5 pages.

Madaus, J. W., Foley, T. E., McGuire, J. M., & Ruban, L. M. (2001). A follow-up investigation of university graduates with learning disabilities. *Career Development for Exceptional Individuals*, **24**, 133–146.

Molina, B. S. G., & Pelham, W. E. (1999). Substance use, substance use, substance abuse, and LD among adolescents with a childhood history of ADHD. *Journal of Learning Disabilities*, **34**(4), 333–342.

Mosberg, L., & Johns, D. (1994). Reading and listening comprehension in college students with developmental dyslexia. *Learning Disabilities Research and Practice*, **9**(3), 130–135.

Murray, C. (2003). Risk factors, protective factors, vulnerability, and resilience: A framework for understanding and supporting the adult transitions of youth with high-incidence disabilities. *Remedial and Special Education*, **24**(1), 16–26.

National Joint Committee on Learning Disabilities (NJCLD). (1987). Adults with learning disabilities: A call to action. *Learning Disability Quarterly*, **9**, 164–167.

National Joint Committee on Learning Disabilities (NJCLD). (1999). Learning disabilities: Issues in higher education. *Learning Disability Quarterly*, **22**(4), 263–266.

Panagos, R. J., & DuBois, D. L. (1999). Career self-efficacy development and students with learning disabilities. *Learning Disabilities Research and Practice*, **14**(1), 25–34.

Polloway, E. A., Schewel, R., & Patton, J. R. (1992). Learning disabilities in adulthood: Personal perspectives. *Journal of Learning Disabilities*, **25**(8), 520–522.

Price, L. (2002). The connections among psychosocial issues, adult development, and self-determination. In L. C. Brinckerhoff, J. M. McGuire, & S. F. Shaw (2002). *Postsecondary education and transition for students with learning disabilities* (2nd ed) (pp. 131–156). Austin, TX: Pro-Ed.

Raskind, M. H. (1993). Assistive technology and adults with learning disabilities: A blueprint for exploration and advancement. *Learning Disability Quarterly*, **16**(3), 185–196.

Raskind, M. H. (1998). Literacy for adults with learning disabilities through assistive technology. In S. A. Vogel & S. Reder (eds.), *Learning disabilities, literacy, and adult education* (pp. 253–270). Toronto: Paul H. Brookes.

Raskind, M. H., Goldberg, R. J., Higgins, E. L., & Herman, K. L. (2002). Teaching "life success" to students with LD: Lessons learned from a 20-year study. *Intervention in School and Clinic*, **37**, 201–209.

Raskind, M. H., Goldberg, R. J., Higgins, E. L., & Herman, K. L. (1999). Patterns of change and predictors of success in individuals with learning disabilities: Results from a twenty-year longitudinal study. *Learning Disabilities Research and Practice*, **14**(1), 35–49.

Reder, S. (1998). Reflections on theory, practice, and research: What we have learned and what we still need to know. In S. A. Vogel & S. Reder (eds.), *Learning disabilities, literacy, and adult education* (pp. 333–343). Toronto: Paul H. Brookes.

Reder, S., & Vogel, S. A. (1997). Lifespan employment and economic outcomes for adults with self-reported learning disabilities. In P. J. Gerber & D. S. Brown (eds.), *Learning disabilities and employment* (pp. 371–394). Austin: Pro-Ed.

Reiff, H. B., Gerber, P. J., & Ginsberg, R. (1994). Instructional strategies for long-term success. *Annals of Dyslexia*, **44**, 270–288.

Reiff, H. B., Hatzes, N. M., Bramel, M. H., & Gibbon, T. (2001). The relation of LD and gender with emotional intelligence in college students. *Journal of Learning Disabilities*, **34**(1), 66–78.

Rhodes, S. S., & Jasinski, D. R. (1990). Learning disabilities in alcohol-dependent adults: A preliminary study. *Journal of Learning Disabilities*, **23**, 551–557.

Roffman, A. J., Herzog, J. E., & Wershba-Gershon, P. M. (1994). Helping young adults understand their learning disabilities. *Journal of Learning Disabilities*, **27**(7), 413–419.

Rojewski, J. W. (1999). Occupational and educational aspirations and attainment of young adults with and without LD 2 years after high school completion. *Journal of Learning Disabilities*, **32**(6), 533–552.

Rothstein, L. F. (1998). The Americans with Disabilities Act, Section 504, and adults with learning disabilities in adult education and transition to employment. In S. A. Vogel & S. Reder (eds.), *Learning disabilities, literacy, and adult education* (pp. 29–41). Toronto: Paul H. Brookes.

Rubin, S. S., & Johnson, C. M. (2002). Lexical access in college students with learning disabilities: An electrophysiological and performance-based investigation. *Journal of Learning Disabilities*, **35**(3), 257–267.

Runyan, M. K. (1991). The effect of extra time on reading comprehension scores for university students with and without learning disabilities. *Journal of Learning Disabilities*, **24**(2), 104–108.

Scott, S. S. (1992). The dynamic process of providing accommodations. In L. Brinckerhoff, J. M. McGuire, & S. F. Shaw, *Post-secondary education and transition for students with learning disabilities*, 2nd ed. (pp. 295–332). Austin, TX: Pro-Ed.

Scott, S. S. (1994). Determining reasonable academic adjustments for college students with learning disabilities. *Journal of Learning Disabilities*, **27**(7), 403–412.

Scott, S. S. (2002). The dynamic process of providing accomodations. In L. C. Brinckerhoff, J. M. McGuire, & S. F. Shaw (eds.), *Post Secondary Education and Transition for Students with Learning Disabilities, 2nd ed.* (pp. 295–332). Austin, TX: Pro-Ed.

Shessel, I., & Reiff, H. B. (1999). Experiences of adults with learning disabilities: Positive and negative impacts and outcomes. *Learning Disability Quarterly*, **22**(4), 305–316.

Sitlington, P. L., Frank, A. R., & Carson, R. R. (1994). Postsecondary vocational education—Does it really make a difference? *Issues in Special Education & Rehabilitation*, **9**(1), 89–100.

Sturomski, N., Lenz, K., Scanlon, D., & Catts, H. (1998). The national adult literacy and learning disabilities centre: Standards, criteria, procedures, and strategies for screening and teaching adults with learning disabilities. In S. A. Vogel & S. Reder (eds.), *Learning disabilities, literacy, and adult education* (pp. 93–105). Toronto: Paul H. Brookes.

Suritsky, S. K., & Hughes, C. A. (1991). Benefits of notetaking: Implications for secondary and postsecondary students with learning disabilities. *Learning Disability Quarterly*, **14**(1), 7–18.

Swanson, H. L. (1994). Short-term memory and working memory: Do both contribute to our understanding of academic achievement in children and adults with learning disabilities? *Journal of Learning Disabilities*, **27**(1), 34–50.

Vogel, S. A., & Adelman, P. B. (2000). Adults with learning disabilities 8–15 years after college. *Learning Disabilities: A Multidisciplinary Journal*, **10**(3), 165–182.

Vogel, S. A., & Reder, S. (1998a). Educational attainment of adults with learning disabilities. In S. A. Vogel & S. Reder (eds.), *Learning disabilities, literacy, and adult education* (pp. 43–68). Toronto: Paul H. Brookes.

Vogel, S. A., & Reder, S. (1998b). Literacy proficiency among adults with self-reported learning disabilities. In C. E. Smith (ed.), *Literacy for the twenty-first century: Research, policy, practices, and the National Adult Literacy Survey* (pp. 159–171). Westport, CT: Praeger.

Weller, C., Watteyne, L., Herbert, M., & Crelly, C. (1994). Adaptive behavior of adults and young adults with learning disabilities. *Learning Disability Quarterly,* **17**(4), 282–295.

Werner, E. E. (1993). Risk and resilience in individuals with learning disabilities. *Learning Disabilities Research and Practice,* **8**(1), 28–34.

Westberry, S. J. (1994). A review of learning strategies for adults with learning disabilities preparing for the GED exam. *Journal of Learning Disabilities,* **27**(4), 202–209.

Wilson, A. M. & Lesaux, N. K. (2001). Persistence of phonological processing deficits in college students with dyslexia who have age-appropriate reading skills. *Journal of Learning Disabilities,* **34**(5), 394–400.

Wilson, B. A. (1998). Matching student needs to instruction: Teaching reading and spelling using the Wilson reading system. In S. A. Vogel & S. Reder (eds.), *Learning disabilities, literacy, and adult education* (pp. 213–235). Toronto: Paul H. Brookes.

Wong, B. Y. L. (2003). General and specific issues for researchers' consideration in applying the risk and resilience framework to the social domain of learning disabilities. *Learning Disability Research and Practice,* **18,** 68–76.

Wong, B. Y. L., & Hutchinson, N. (2001). Learning disabilities in Canada. In D. P. Hallahan & B. K. Keogh (eds.), *Research and global perspectives in learning disabilities* (pp. 197–215). Mahwah, NJ: Erlbaum.

Zimmerman, B. J. (1994). Dimensions of academic self-regulation: A conceptual framework for education. In D. H. Schunk & B. J. Zimmerman (eds.), *Self-regulation of learning and performance: Issues and educational applications* (pp. 3–21). Hillsdale, NJ: Erlbaum.

Zimmerman, B., & Schunk, D. (2001). Reflections on theories of self-regulated learning and academic achievement. In B. Zimmerman & D. Schunk (eds.), *Self-regulated learning and academic achievement: Theoretical perspectives* (2nd ed.) (pp. 289–307). Mahwah, NJ: Erlbaum.

CHAPTER 18

Understanding Learning Disabilities through a Father's Perspective

J. D. Mashburn
Silver Springs, Maryland

CHRISTINE GREENHAW MASHBURN INSTITUTE, 2000

When my wife, Mary Lou, and I make our annual pilgrimage to this verdant campus and these hallowed halls to participate in the Christine Greenhaw Mashburn Institute, our presence often stimulates the curiosity of the teachers in training. How did it happen that a physician and his wife developed such an interest in the field of special education, and specifically in the area of minimal learning disorders? Through the years, our answer has been brief and general. After two of our four children endured the burden of this dysfunction, we dedicated our modest means and talents to the assistance of children in the schools of Arkansas who also share this heavy load.

Today, now that we have had over 30 years of experience, I will give to this group a detailed natural history of this disorder and how it impacted one of our sons and his parents. It is my hope it will be of benefit to you as you work with the affected child in your classroom and help you to understand how this mission evolved in our lives.

Learning about Learning Disabilities, Third Edition

The apostle Paul wrote these words in his letter to the church at Rome, "Tribulations bring about perseverance; and perseverance, proven character; and proven character, hope."[1]

With that thought, we begin our story.

Following a normal gestation and delivery, our third son was born on September 12, 1961, in the Methodist Hospital in Memphis, Tennessee. They said he looked just like his daddy. He was named Zack, after his paternal grandfather.

There were no problems during the neonatal period, and he progressed well in the next 12 months into a healthy infancy. In fact, there were a few indications of precocity, walking at 8 months and saying his first words at 11 months.

The early childhood years were happy and active. He was our only child who awakened every morning with a smile on his face. He had the usual curiosity and "business" of a 2- to 3-year-old, helping his dad by dropping grass clippings into the gas tank of the lawn mower, and assisting his mother by marking the couch with brown shoe polish.

When Zack reached his 5th birthday, there was every indication he was ready for limited, organized learning, and he was enrolled in a small, private kindergarten. Zack enjoyed these activities and completed the 9-month course without any major difficulties. At the year-end parent–teacher conference, we were told he had some difficulty in letter recognition, but the teacher felt confident this would correct with age, and she recommended that he proceed into first grade.

The following fall we enrolled Zack in the first grade with all of the happy excitement and expectations that accompany the introduction of your 6-year-old to the educational system. Little did we know that he was entering a door to a long, dark, lonely passage filled with frustration, fear, and heartache.

The first-grade year confirmed the kindergarten teacher's concern about letter recognition, but did not fulfill her optimistic prediction of correction with time and older age. The first grade is usually not the bull pit of competition which some instructors make of higher grades. However, even at this early, gentler level of learning, Zack's teacher was worried about his progress when compared to other students. There were no alarm bells going off yet, but there was some discussion about possibly repeating the first year; you know, letting more maturity and time correct the problem.

Even at this stage, we were sensitive to the stigma repeating a grade might place on a six- to seven-year-old. However, we were facing a move from Memphis that summer. We reasoned that Zack would be in new surroundings and among new students. No one would have to know except him. And,

---

[1]Romans 5:3,4.

besides, it was not unusual for parents to hold their child until the age of 7 before beginning school. So, after our move, we enrolled Zack in the first grade again, in the new school.

Do you think this was a "non-event" in his eyes? Let me tell you, each year for the next 10 years, Zack would remind us that actually he should be one grade ahead of where he was.

Lesson Number One. Never underestimate the impact of failure on the psyche of a 6-year-old.

In spite of the continued difficulties, Zack was promoted to the second grade. In retrospect, I think several factors were at work here. First, he was a very intelligent child. This is the paradox which defines the condition of word assimilation defect (dyslexia, minimal learning disability, etc.) This intelligence is a two-edged sword for the student. One edge of the sword creates an intolerable dilemma for this intelligent student, who is forever trying to understand why he/she cannot learn. The other edge convinces the instructor that this obviously intelligent student could do the work if they would only try. Clearly, they are indolent, indifferent, and have priorities other than learning. The teacher becomes just as confused and distraught as the student, a perfect formula for disrupting the teacher's hard-earned lesson plans and earnest patience.

And so the student is promoted in spite of the obvious deficiencies in the mechanics of reading and writing. First, because he/she is intelligent. Second, because it is time for some relief for the long-suffering teacher. Time to let the next teacher have their turn trying to solve this unsolvable problem.

Of course, this "social" promotion is the only way to handle the non-learning child in a school system unequipped for special needs students. You cannot keep a child in the first or second grade forever. At least they will benefit from the social interaction of their peers. Or will they? But, I am moving ahead of my story.

The second grade was a seminal year for all of us. It was very clear now that Zack was not learning to read or write. There was a problem. It was as much of a mystery to us, or more so, as it was to his teacher. Why could this son, who was as intelligent as his two older, high-achieving brothers, not learn? Of all the many theories we have worked our way through over the years to explain this perplexity, not once did we, his parents, ever blame indolence, indifference, or lack of motivation. We knew our son.

As he faced this accusation of not trying each year at school, he did find some relief at home. I take comfort in this fact. But my heart aches for the minimal learning disabled student who must return at the end of the day to a home where he or she will face the misguided accusations.

This is not to say that Zack's evenings at home were all peaches and cream. Although we recognized that he really was trying, our own ill-advised efforts to force the learning process often transformed the tranquil home scene into one of tension, frustration, and mortification—sadly, a continuation of the same emotions he was experiencing during the day at school.

As Zack passed listlessly into the third grade, we all moved vigorously into a period of testing and alternative treatments. After all, we were only human. Like everyone faced with an illness, we wanted a shot, pill or operation to solve the ailment immediately and completely. Unfortunately, and as a physician I knew, that life, in most cases, simply is not that easy.

First, we went to the ophthalmologist to make sure his eyesight was adequate; next to the otolaryngologist to confirm normal hearing. Over the following two years, we contributed to the coffers of numerous child psychologists and psychiatrists. I remember Zack spending literally hours in the testing room. He would come out with a glazed look in his eyes, totally exhausted. If he had any doubt from his school experiences, this period of extensive testing confirmed in his mind that he was damaged goods.

We were told that he had a learning disability. Surprise! Mention was made of a condition known as dyslexia, a term becoming fashionable in the 1970s, in which the child reverses the letters. All right, but what do we do about it? Vague, generalized comments were made about finding teachers who understood the problem. One consultant, a neurosurgeon who had developed an interest in learning disorders, did give us one bit of good, solid advice. He told us to stop the lesson assignment studies at home. It was much more important for the family to provide a haven of peace and love as a refuge from the turmoil he was experiencing at school. We followed this wise recommendation, to the great relief of us all.

In the early 1970s, we were unsuccessful in finding a local teacher or system familiar with or sympathetic to the problem of dyslexia. It was still the consensus, even in the so-called enlightened Washington, DC, area, that a child who was not learning was simply either dumb or lazy or both. So I launched into the audacious plan of teaching the teachers. At the beginning of each grade school year, I would sit down with Zack's new teacher and give a brief course on dyslexia, as if that would take care of the problem for that year! Of course, nothing changed, except that my name became anathema among the staff of our school.

By the fifth grade, we entered the phase of alternative methods of teaching, learning, and correction. These were the times of after-school trips to tutors and fringe clinicians, such as the clinic that offered improvement to dyslexics through eye exercises. The latter endeavor did accomplish one thing. It gave him dull headaches after each exercise in the afternoons while his peers were refreshing themselves with after-school recreation.

In the seventh grade, he was still trying mightily to make a passing score. This is the beginning of relatively complicated math problems and literature assignments. I remember reviewing one science paper he brought home.

It consisted of multiple questions requiring interpretation of the discussion-type question and application of mathematics to arrive at the correct solution. He had filled three handwritten pages in a herculean effort to achieve success. And what did his instructor give him in return? A large red X over each of his exercises and hard-earned answers, and a large red zero at the top of the front page for his grade.

I thought that I understood what my son was experiencing until I sat down and had a memory session of my own experiences in the educational system. I had always been a high achiever, based on a little talent and a lot of work. I remembered how one red X could put a pretty bad taste in my mouth. But I had never failed a complete test, never. The emotional response to such an experience never imprinted on the electrical circuits of my brain. Until I entered medical school. Then one time I received a test paper with a large red F at the top. The shock of failure and futility was so overwhelming that it is very clear in my memory (and recurring dreams) to this day. Then the thought hit me. This is what my son is experiencing every day at school, and there is nothing I can do to help him.

Another description to help understand what Zack endured was described to me by another person with word assimilation defect. He likened the typical classroom with its blackboard figures, pages filled with words, and verbal cacophony between teacher and students to someone trying to make sense out of watching the visual part of one television program while listening to the sound track of a different program.

But still he kept trying. It was our custom to read a bed time story to Zack before going to sleep. One evening as he sat by me on the bed, he began to follow the words as I read them aloud. As long as I was reading to him he could follow the words very well and was emboldened to say, "Now, Dad, let me read." He began with confidence, but as he continued down the sentence the words came slower and slower until finally he fell back, burying his face in his pillow, crying softly, "I just can't do it."

The eighth grade was another landmark in Zack's dark passage. This was the year he did stop trying, confirming the self-fulfilling prophecy of his many teachers. You see, it is really very simple. If you do not try, you cannot fail. And Zack had had all the failure his sanity could handle. One day, his mother picked up his shoes with intricate patterns on the rubber soles. She noticed how he had outlined the patterns and filled in the dozens of spaces with his ballpoint pen. This is what he was doing to fill the empty, meaning-less hours of his classes.

But he was still struggling with this monkey on his back. An intelligent person who cannot learn. A reasoning mind locked in a dark room without doors or windows.

Zack changed in other ways as well. He no longer smiled when he awakened in the morning. It was a real struggle to roll him out of bed in time for school. He was discovering the sweet narcosis of sleep as an escape from his tribulations.

By the ninth grade, natural sleep was not enough. We could tell from his blood shot eyes, hacking cough, and musty body odor that he also had discovered marijuana. He was drifting inexorably into the rock culture of the 1970s.

Zack had demonstrated a real talent in drawing. What a contradiction. He could not connect what he was seeing with the word association areas of his brain, but he had excellent eye–hand coordination. Accordingly, we engaged a tutor for drawing and enrolled him in a school of art. But nothing took. This was not manly enough. Athletics was out because he had inherited the incoordination of his dad. Even the playground gave him no relief from the classroom failure, as he was always the one picked last for the ball team.

By now, the testosterone was rising and he was seeking a better way to demonstrate his manhood among his peers of long hair, loud music, and mind-altering drugs.

At the end of the tenth grade, Zack requested permission to drop out of school and begin work as a front man in a service station (the days of self-serve had not yet arrived). This may come as a surprise, but there was an element of relief for us all at this moment, knowing that it would bring an end to this charade of formal education. Of course, deeper in our hearts, we cried bitter tears of sorrow and anxiety, knowing what awaited anyone without an education at the end of the twentieth century—a life on the fringes economically, culturally, and legally.

Lesson Number Two. Never underestimate the impact of failure on the psyche of a 16-year-old.

For the next one and a half years, Zack had his introduction to the world of manual labor. To be sure, it was different from the heartache and frustration of the cerebral classroom. But the service stations and body shops had their own brand of demeaning environment for the unskilled, topped off with long hours and low pay. He found the grass outside of school considerably more brown and dry than he had thought.

Then Zack did something so typically human. If he could just change the scenery, everything would fall in place. So he packed his things and joined his older brother in a move to California in the fall of 1979. His brother was going out to medical school, and Zack would go out to seek his fortune.

Our reaction to his departure again was bittersweet. We feared for what awaited him in a far and distant land. And yet, at least the disconsonance of his lifestyle would be removed from our home. So we gave him a big hug, wished him well, and then went into our house to begin a vigil of prayer and hope which would continue for the next 10 years.

Very soon, Zack tasted the withering life of poverty produced by the low income of unskilled labor. His jobs drifted from service stations, to door factory, to paper carrier, to fast food joints. He lived in slum rentals and an abandoned house. He knew what it was to be hungry and thankful for a handout baked potato at the back of a restaurant where a friend worked. But he never once asked for financial help from us. He was so desperate to prove that he could succeed.

After three to four years of wandering in the low-level job market, Zack settled into a position of courier at the same large teaching hospital where his brother was training. Although he demonstrated a degree of regularity and persistence in this post, he could never make his peace with the fact that it was at the bottom of the pile in a building filled with high achievers. There are a thousand and one ways society has of reminding the intelligent observer of his position in life. A pretty, young student nurse was attracted to Zack as he came and went on the different wards (he always was a handsome young man, if I do say so). After the initial bilateral flirtations, casual conversations followed. As soon as she learned that he was a full-time courier, she lost all interest in continuing the friendship, even on a platonic level. This made such an impression on Zack that he shared this with us in one of our many telephone visits.

So, Zack continued to search for ways to prove his worth and abilities. He became convinced of the opportunities offered in the rug-cleaning business, if only he had a vehicle. In 1983, we decided to use the money I had inherited from my mother to help him purchase an Isuzu Trooper so he could try his hand at cleaning carpets. The rug cleaning venture was not successful, but placing a vehicle in his hands certainly had unforeseen results.

One night, Zack took a friend to a 7–11 store to purchase some milk. He waited in the Isuzu while the friend went in to make the purchase. There were four young men milling around outside the entrance to the establishment. As Zack's friend passed by, eye contact was made, words were exchanged, and, since the testosterone was running high on both sides, a physical alteraction developed. Zack was desperate to help his friend but realized they were no match for the four hoodlums. Using poor judgment, he started the Isuzu and ran it up on the sidewalk toward the scuffling group, hoping to disperse the assailants. At that point, the aggressors pulled out handguns and proceeded to arrest Zack and his friend. It turns out the four young hoodlums were undercover police, there to protect the community! His friend was released, but Zack was charged for assault with a deadly weapon, to wit, an automobile, and incarcerated in the county jail. The police were able to report a successful night "protecting" the community. But it certainly ruined ours when Zack's friend called to give us the news.

The next week was consumed with multiple calls to California to find a criminal lawyer, arrange for bail, and agree to a recommended plea bargain, which would bring this rueful and, we felt, unfair, episode to an end.

Zack returned to the hospital as a courier and his struggle for self-esteem. Mind-altering chemicals continued to play a role in this struggle, but not in the way our friends and professional therapists thought. We knew he was not heavily into the so-called hard drugs. We knew that drugs were not the primary problem; and so, to the surprise and consternation of some observers, we never pursued a course of drug rehabilitation. We knew our son.

The drug which began to play a large role in his life was dextroamphetamine (Dexedrine, speed). Zack obtained this easily on the street and found that it had a surprising effect compared to the other chemicals he had tried. As all college students and long-distance travelers know, this drug clears the mind in preparing for finals or night driving. Some pediatricians use it in certain minimal learning disabilities. Is it any surprise that Zack became a regular customer of the Dexedrine street vendor? Here was a chemical which cleared his mind, lifted his spirits, and even improved his reading and spelling! And so, as a pediatrician might, Zack began to treat himself.

Of course, without the supervision of a professional, this led to abuse of the drug. Withdrawal after high doses results in excessive lethargy and depression. Prolonged high doses may produce mental dysfunction. One of Zack's friends told me that Zack's life became a seesaw between highs of exhilaration and lows of severe depression. His friend said he had never before seen such severe depression.

One night, while driving the Isuzu, Zack began to hallucinate. He thought the light of an oncoming car was Christ returning to earth. He drove toward the lights, hoping to be embraced in the arms of Jesus. The resulting crash opened another chapter in his life.

Fortunately for everyone involved, each vehicle was traveling approximately 10 miles per hour, so no one was injured physically. According to the police report, when they arrived, Zack was still sitting in the Isuzu holding on to the steering wheel and praying incoherently. They pried his hands from the steering wheel, pulled him out of the car, and forced him onto the ground, where he was handcuffed and arrested.

This episode would prove to be much more serious than the previous encounter with the law. Zack was transferred from the county jail to a large regional prison. He requested a public attorney, not wanting us to spend any more money on his difficulties. This proved to be a major mistake. He could see from the start the lawyer assigned to his case was totally incompetent, disinterested in his plight, and actually hostile toward him. Can you imagine the dismal outlook of someone charged with a much more serious crime, such as murder, forced by poverty to accept such a person to prepare for his or her defense? Zack was lucky. His crime did not come under a category as serious as murder, and he had a family who would remove him from the ominous shadow of the public attorney.

Now followed another round of telephone conferences with the same criminal lawyer we had used before. We were becoming well acquainted with each other! He recommended obtaining a statement from the psychiatrist who had counseled Zack in his teenage years, confirming that he had a learning disorder. Hopefully, this might have a positive bearing on the outcome. When I called the doctor, he refused to give us a statement. Instead, he lectured me on the necessity of letting go, ending the enabling, and applying tough love. He told me of his own nephew who refused to stop taking drugs and eventually was killed in an automobile accident. Some things we just have to accept.

The wheels of justice do indeed grind slowly. For some trapped in the maze of our current court systems, it stops altogether. The days turned into weeks, and the weeks into months, as Zack went through several hearings and postponements. In the meantime, he was experiencing life in a large prison. The atmosphere is that of punishment rather than rehabilitation. Keep in mind, he had not yet been legally convicted! Physical and emotional abuse from guards is ever present. The prisoner has only five minutes to consume his plate of food at each meal. This turns each mealtime into a scene similar to pigs at a slop trough. If there is any humanity in a person before entering these places, it is dehumanized out of him as he passes through. And this is in the enlightened state of California. I am severely depressed when I think of the inhumanity in a Cummins Farm of Arkansas, where headless corpses have been unearthed, or a Texas Plantation Prison, where an inmate has had the fingers of a hand axed off by a fellow prisoner in order to be removed from the control of a sadistic guard. These institutions are a reflection of you and me, of us all, of the society in which they exist.

Finally, after one year, Zack was released on probation with a felony conviction on his record. His supervisor of couriers at the hospital (a man whose life truly exemplified the character of Christ) was willing to re-employ him. We flew out to help him try to put his life back together. We sold the Isuzu for junk. We found a small condominium within walking distance of his work and paid the rent each month until Zack could get back on his feet.

Things settled down somewhat, no doubt in part to the fact that Zack did not have an automobile to complicate his life. He was still using Dexedrine to get through the day, but fantasy also began to play a larger role in his coping with life. He had tinkered with a guitar and rock music for many years, but now he began to believe that he actually was destined to become a rock star. He savored the scenes of his fame. He assured us when he reached the top he would build a beautiful home for his mom and me in Beverly Hills. He practiced with several groups, and even appeared in a few local "gigs," as they call the programs.

But Zack was just setting himself up to taste failure one more time. You see, he had inherited his dad's harmony genes as well, which was bad news for his dreams of stardom in the musical world. When the cold, hard fact of dissonant chords finally broke through his fantasies, it was the last straw. After 10 years of seeking his fortune in California, we received his call. He said, "Dad, I give up. I can't make it. Will you come and get me?"

The advice of the psychiatrist kept racing through our heads. As enablers, were we actually contributing to his dilemma? Would bringing him into our home really solve the problem? The next day, I sought the counsel of another psychiatrist, a personal friend whom I knew on our hospital medical staff and in whom I had much confidence. I explained to him the history and situation. His response was, "This story most likely will end tragically. You must accept it, and let him sink or swim on his own." In other words, stop enabling. It seems we had heard that somewhere before.

And so—we packed our bags, again, and flew out to help him move back home.

When we walked into his condominium, we were not prepared for the scene. In his world of fantasy, he had created a recording studio and sound system throughout the residence. There were wires everywhere. The drawers were filled with well-organized fuses and transistors. The walls were covered with foam material to prevent the loud rock music from disturbing the neighbors. It took his mother and me three days to dismantle the material and make the residence acceptable to the landlord.

All during this time, Zack was in a state of withdrawal from Dexedrine, lying on the floor asleep. We stepped over his body coming and going as we carried things out to the rental car or the dumpster. In one of his wakeful moments, we were driving to a local music store to sell the valuable sound system, a very painful experience for him. He said, "Dad, do you know what verbal abuse is?" I replied that I understood what he meant, but I was sure I had not had the experiences he had had with such authority figures as police, prison guards, employers, supervisors—and teachers. He said, "I am so confused. I have positive feelings toward you for the help you have given me, and yet I have such anger toward you in all of this." I said, "I know, son. I understand. To you, I am one of the authority figures."

Finally, we severed all of his ties with California and, at the age of 28 years, Zack returned with us to his home in Maryland, and a very uncertain future for us all.

Lesson Number Three. Never underestimate the impact of failure on the psyche of an adult.

We found a clinic specializing in training and finding employment for young people unable to function successfully in the standard educational setting. During the evaluation interview, Zack sat tensely with his toes turned inward. The psychologist remarked that it was obvious his self-esteem was in the cellar. The clinic felt it had something to offer and agreed to enroll him immediately.

All three of us arose the next morning with hope in the air. His mother prepared a sack lunch and I dropped Zack off at the clinic at 8 A.M. At 11 A.M., I received a call from Mom with distress in her voice. She said Zack had walked out of the clinic and was somewhere on Wisconsin Avenue. She was preparing to find him and bring him home. I was stunned. My mind filled with doubt and despair. Were the psychiatrists right? Were all of our efforts just prolonging the misery, set-ups for false hopes followed by continued failures? For the first time, I also experienced another emotion for my son—anger. Why could not he just give this clinic a try, just show up? That is all we were asking.

When I arrived home that evening, all of these emotions were very visible in my voice and body language. Zack told us they had placed him in a group of young, troubled teenagers. Their first assignment was to draw a picture and then explain its meaning to the group. The whole scene came crushing down on him as confirming the opinion that he really was abnormal. He could not handle the thought that he was one of these silly, babbling teenagers. So he walked out.

It was not long before our conversation degenerated into a useless verbal battle. I was the authority figure once again and he was the victim, a scenario with which he was all too familiar. Zack challenged me to a physical settlement in the backyard. At this point, his mother walked over, enveloped him in her arms, and said, "No one knows all of the abuse you have had through the years. We understand, and we love you very much." We all had a good cry, and then made a stab at eating our supper. I do not know how a family handles their crises without a mother's love.

While in California, Zack had obtained a sixth-grade English workbook which he had studied on his own, without much success. He just happened to have brought this back with him to Maryland. After looking it over, we all agreed that this might be a good springboard for some home schooling in place of a structured program like the clinic. Zack would be given an assignment for the day. Each evening, I would go over his work with him and write a grade in red at the top of the page. I always gave some form of A such as A+, A, or, if he missed an answer, A−, which he actually began to earn after a few days of one-on-one guidance and encouragement. If the work was perfect, he received an A+, with much hoopla and celebration. He enjoyed these exercises and looked forward to each day's assignment. These became happy times over a 3-month period.

When we completed the workbook, Zack felt so encouraged that he bought a set of GED books and ordered material from the State Department of Education to obtain his high school degree. This material contained sample tests similar to those given at the time of the GED examination. A few days later, Mom met me at the door as I arrived home from the hospital. She said, "There is a problem. Zack is in the garage. He attempted the sample essay test and did not do very well with the spelling and sentence structure." I walked out to the garage and found this grown man pacing in a circle like a caged tiger. When he saw me, he said, "Dad, it's no use. It's just like forcing myself to be a rock star. I cannot learn to read and write any more than I can play a guitar. I might as well face it. I've got to find something I can do without it." To my dismay, I realized that, once more, we had set him up for failure. How much more could this man take?

We went into the house, sat down, and began to discuss his options. His mother had noticed an ad for a truck driver's school in Baltimore. He liked that idea, and we agreed to pay the tuition and provide the transportation so he could enroll the next day. That evening, we had another one of those quiet, flavorless suppers. Our hearts were heavy with thoughts of a hard, lonely life on the interstates of America.

Then the telephone rang. There is something about a ringing telephone that is intriguing to the imagination. The challenge of the unknown. You really do not know for sure how your life will change when you answer that ring. It may be, and usually is, something as mundane as a confirmation of your next dental appointment. But it could be, as it has been before, the tragedy of a death in the family. Or even, as it has never been before, that you have won the million-dollar jackpot!

The voice on the other end asked for Zack. He explained that he was a friend of a friend who told him Zack might be interested in a job. There was an opening as an assistant lineman in the communication company where the caller worked. Would he be interested? Would he! Zack asked, "When do I start?" Well, first he has to be interviewed. (Dear God, please do not let this be another set-up for failure.) The clothing required on the job was blue cotton shirt with collar and clean blue jeans. He should report to the office for the interview at 7 A.M.

We went over to Sears that night and purchased the shirt and pants. Zack arose at 5:30 A.M. the next morning without any urging. He was on his way before sun-up in our old pickup truck, a holdover from our daughter's horse days. He returned in 2 hours and told his mother he had been hired to begin work the following Monday. There was a cautious, subdued celebration that evening.

From the beginning, Zack arose at 5 A.M. and was leaving our driveway at 6 every day with no help from us. One day, I was up as he was going to the truck. I watched him walk across the driveway and saw that he had a smile on his face—and this is when going to work! What is going on here?

Of course, as parents, our curiosity about his work and activities had risen to a fever pitch. We peppered Zack with questions at the supper table. He created a rule which became a family joke. He said we were limited to three questions per day. When we asked a question at the beginning of supper, he would say, "That's number one!" and we would all have a good laugh.

We learned that the work consisted of installing telephone, computer, and fiberglass lines in intricate patterns from elaborate, complicated control boards to telephones and computers throughout large office buildings. The lines had to be concealed to prevent disruption of the interior decoration and, at the same time, not disrupt the basic structure of the building. One time, the decision was made to use an old, tall, abandoned chimney as a conduit for the cables. Zack took the cables and "walked" down the long chimney by bracing his feet on one side and his back on the other. This is called commitment to your work! It seemed that wiring control boards and buildings came natural to him. Remember the condominium converted to a recording studio in California? This time, he was paid a salary to do it, plus gaining a sense of accomplishment.

And what does a little success do for a person? I'll tell you what it does. In 6 months, he was named employee of the month. At the year-end Christmas dinner, he was awarded the Golden Reel as the employee of the year. A few days later, Zack was called into the office of the CEO. The chief told him he was being promoted to foreman, the first time in the history of the company this had happened to an employee with only one year's experience.

And the rest, as they say, is history. Zack has been in charge of jobs in Alaska, Seattle, Hawaii, New York, and Little Rock, resulting in letters of commendation from these places back to the home office. His latest assignment was the huge headquarters of Nortel Corporation in a suburb of Washington, DC. He was responsible for the team that installed 53 miles of communication lines in that facility.

Zack has established solid credit, first with a bank account, then a credit card, then an automobile purchased with a loan. He has married a wonderful lady, whom he met while installing lines to her office. Together, they are buying a nice home with a swimming pool in the backyard (his pride and joy—he is still a kid at heart).

This year, they presented us with a beautiful baby girl. When the CEO of his company called to see how things were going shortly after her birth, Zack's wife told him Zack was making a very good father. The chief replied, "Well, Zack is cut out of a different piece of cloth from the rest of my workers. If he is just half as good at being a parent as he is at his job, he will be a great dad!"

Lesson Number Four. Never underestimate the impact of success on the psyche of anyone, regardless of their age.

And, you know, Zack still cannot read or spell. Well, not fluently. It just isn't in the genes. But does that, somehow, make him not a whole person? He can read the technical instructions of his job with their basic sentence structure. And he can write out reports for his company. And, you know what? The company doesn't make red marks over his misspelled words.

They know what he is saying, and they know they can depend on it. And that, my friend, makes all the difference.

Let me ask you, which teacher was most successful; the one who taught Zack, or the professor who taught the brilliant Michael Milken, the famous convicted thief of Wall Street? You see, you are dealing with more than numbers and letters each day in your classroom.

There are 6 billion people in the world today, and no two are exactly alike in mind or body. There is no common formula for handling the problem student in your classroom. But I can tell you this, each and every one of the six billion on this planet, including those problem students in your class-room, have a common need, that for success and approval.

Pastor Mel Rees had taught in a small church school in his early years. One day, a man called the church office to make an appointment with him, explaining that he had been one of his students years ago. Pastor Rees said, "Of course, I remember you. Please come over. I will be happy to see you again."

When the man arrived, they exchanged warm greetings. After taking a seat in the office, the visitor said, "Pastor, I have been carrying the burden of a guilty conscience for a long time. I want to get rid of it.

"Years ago, you gave our class a final examination in mathematics." "Yes," the Pastor replied. "I remember that time." The former student then said, "Well, I want to tell you that I cheated on that examination, and I am sorry."

There was a pause, then the pastor said, "I know you did."

The man looked up with surprise and exclaimed, "You did!?"

The pastor explained, "Yes, but I knew you were not a cheater."[2]

The classes you have attended these past two weeks are designed to give you additional tools for affirming to the learning-challenged student that they are not sediment at the bottom of the class and for helping them find this success and approval they need so desperately.

And now you know why there is a Christine Greenhaw Mashburn Institute.

Thank you,

J. D. Mashburn, M.D.

---

[2]Sermon, WGTS Radio Station, Takoma Park, Maryland, circa 1988.

Index